The Untouchables
In Contemporary India

The Untouchables in

CONTRIBUTORS

S. Chandrasekhar
Morris E. Opler
J. Michael Mahar
Joan P. Mencher
Walter C. Neale
Eleanor Zelliot
Owen Lynch
Adele Fiske
Lawrence A. Babb
K. C. Alexander
Lelah Dushkin
Marc Galanter
Robert J. Miller
Pramodh Kale
Beatrice Miller
Harold R. Isaacs
André Béteille

Contemporary India

J. MICHAEL MAHAR
Editor

THE UNIVERSITY OF ARIZONA PRESS
Tucson, Arizona

About the Authors...

K. C. ALEXANDER, author of the "Neo-Christians of Kerala," is an Indian sociologist, in 1970 named deputy director of the National Institute of Community Development at Hyderabad. His research into the application of Merton's reference group theory to the analysis of human behavior has resulted in several articles for scholarly journals. Alexander is the author also of *Social Mobility in Kerala, Participative Management in India: Two Case Studies,* and *Employers' Organizations in India* (with P. W. D. Matthews).

LAWRENCE A. BABB, author of "The Satnamis: Political Involvement of a Religious Movement," studied the Satnami religious sect and its relation to Untouchability during a year of field work in Madhya Pradesh, returning to the United States in 1968 to teach in the Indian Civilization program at the University of Chicago. In 1969, he joined the faculty of the Department of Anthropology at Amherst. He has since published numerous articles on Hindu religion and ritual from the Chhattisgarh region of eastern Madyha Pradesh.

ANDRÉ BÉTEILLE'S view of "Pollution and Poverty" evolves from his research and writing in the field of political sociology, emphasizing social stratification and agrarian class relations in India. A native of Channagar, India, Béteille joined the sociology faculty at the University of Delhi in 1959 and has been a Simon Fellow at the University of Manchester and a Jawaharlal Nehru Fellow during the development of this study. His books include *Caste, Class and Power: Changing Patterns of Stratification in a Tanjore Village, Castes Old & New,* and, as editor, *Social Inequality: Selected Readings.*

SRIPATI CHANDRASEKHAR, who adds to this volume his "Personal Perspectives on Untouchability," in 1967 was named Minister of Health and Family Planning in the Cabinet of Prime Minister Indira Gandhi. One of the world's leading demographers, Chandrasekhar has written hundreds of articles and a score of books and monographs on family planning as it relates to the living standard of over-populated, under-developed nations. Former director of the Indian Institute for Population Studies at Madras, Chandrasekhar has lectured in Europe, Asia, Africa, and the United States; has taught at the University of Pittsburgh and the University of California at Riverside; and has been associated with the Battelle Research Institute in Seattle. Before entering the Central Cabinet, he was elected in 1964 to the Rajya Sabha or upper house of the Indian Parliament, representing the Indian National Congress Party for the state of Madras.

LEHAH DUSHKIN has published several articles on the Scheduled Castes, a main theme in her study of "Scheduled Caste Politics" in this volume. She spent three years doing field work in India, concentrating her investigations on twentieth-century political movements and social change in the state of Mysore. A graduate of Smith College, with a Ph.D. in South Asian Regional Studies from the University of Pennsylvania, Professor Dushkin joined the faculty at Kansas State University in the Department of Sociology.

ADELE M. FISKE, author of "Scheduled Caste Buddhist Organizations," went to India in 1966-67 and again in 1970, observing the religious aspects of the reform movement initiated by Dr. B. R. Ambedkar, especially the Neo-Buddhist organizations. This research grew out of her post-doctoral studies in the history of religion at Columbia University. Professor Fiske is director of the East Asian Center at Manhattanville College, and in 1971 was a visiting lecturer in the Department of Religion at Yale.

MARC GALANTER, author of "The Abolition of Disabilities; Untouchability & the Law," has been studying the role of law in the development of modern India since his first visit to India as a Fulbright scholar in 1957-58. The present study represents a convergence of his interests in the relation of law to primordial groupings and in problems of effective implementation of legal policies. A lawyer and a member of the University of Chicago faculty in Social Sciences, Galanter has been co-director of a workshop in empirical research for Indian law teachers. He was also named Senior Fellow in the Law and Modernization Program at Yale Law School.

HAROLD R. ISAACS, author of "The Ex-Untouchables," has been writing about international affairs for nearly 40 years, first as reporter and correspondent, and, since 1953, as a senior research associate at the Center for International Studies at the Massachusetts Institute of Technology where he has also served, since 1965, as a professor of political science. Long a student of war and politics in Asia (*No Peace For Asia, The Tragedy of the Chinese Revolution*) and of the problems of the nationalist emergence (*Africa: New Crises in the Making, Two-Thirds of the World*), he began, after joining the M.I.T. Center, to examine the impact of world affairs on the images and self-images of people affected by major political change (*Scratches On Our Minds: American Images of China and India, Emergent Americans: A Report on Crossroads Africa*).

More particularly during the 1960s, he explored the interaction of political change and group identity in a number of widely varied settings (*The New World of Negro Americans, India's Ex-Untouchables, American Jews in Israel*).

PRAMODH KALE was born and brought up in the locale of the stories he translated for this volume — Maharashtra in western India. Member of a pioneer family in India's cinema enterprise, Kale's interest in films, the theater, and literature led to doctoral research into ancient Indian dramaturgy. As a teacher of the cinema and literature of India at the University of Minnesota, Kale has translated many other short stories, a novel, and film scripts from India.

OWEN M. LYNCH, author of *The Politics of Untouchability* and other works about India, did field work during the 1960s with the Jatavs of Agra City, drawing from this experience the material for his article "Dr. B. R. Ambedkar: Myth & Charisma." After receiving the doctoral degree in anthropology from Columbia University in 1966, Lynch joined the faculty of the State University of New York at Binghamton. He also did linguistic field work with the University of Chicago Munda Languages Project. In 1970-71, he returned to India to research the problems of squatters in the city of Bombay.

J. MICHAEL MAHAR in the article "Agents of Dharma in a North Indian Village," taps experience gained in the early fifties in a North Indian community where he pursued his doctoral studies as a member of a Cornell University research team. He returned to the same village in 1968-69 for assessment of changes that had occurred during the intervening years. As editor of the present volume he has sought to integrate the cumulative insights of a variety of scholars within the disciplines of anthropology, economics, history, law, political science, and sociology. In 1958 Mahar joined the University of Arizona faculty as professor of Oriental Studies. He is the author of *India: A Critical Bibliography*.

JOAN P. MENCHER'S interest in social structure and ecology and her inquiries into economic inequalities in rural India served as the basis for her article on "Continuity & Change in an Ex-Untouchable Community." In 1969, Professor Mencher began a two-year study of the relationship between social structure and modernization in Madras and Kerala, collaborating with Conrad Arensberg of Columbia University and K. Raman Unni of the School of Architecture and Planning in New Delhi. These studies took her to India on leave from her associate professorship at Lehmann College, City University of New York, and research associate in anthropology, Columbia University.

ROBERT J. AND BEATRICE D. MILLER, authors of "The Burden on the Head Is Always There," and "The Man Inside," in the early 1970s were living in New Delhi where Robert was resident director of the American Institute of Indian Studies and Beatrice continued research into new ways of studying cultural perceptions. The Millers have been an anthropological team since undergraduate days at the University of Michigan, going to India for their first field work in 1953. Both hold doctorates from the University of Washington, and later taught at the University of Wisconsin in Madison where Robert was chairman of the Department of Anthropology.

WALTER C. NEALE's years of research into Indian village economy and his field work in India have focused on economics of the rural community culminating in accounts such as "The Marginal Laborer and the Harijan in Rural India," in this volume. He is author also of *Economic Change in Rural India,* and *India: The Search for Unity, Democracy, and Progress.* Neale's doctoral research at the University of London was on land tenure and reform. He was later research associate in agricultural economics for the India project of the Massachusetts Institute of Technology, a lecturer at Punjab University, and a research Fellow at Lucknow. In 1968 he joined the economics faculty at the University of Tennessee.

MORRIS E. OPLER, who wrote the Introduction to this volume, was director of Cornell University's work on South Asia from 1948 to 1966, heading a program of instruction and field work which introduced a number of American scholars to serious research in India and South Asia. An outstanding authority on Apache Indian tribes of the American Southwest, Opler in 1947 began his study of the culture and thought of India. Following retirement from Cornell in 1969, he joined the faculty at the University of Oklahoma as professor of anthropology and a member of the Institute of Asian Studies. He is a former president of the American Anthropological Association.

ELEANOR ZELLIOT is author of "Gandhi & Ambedkar: A Study in Leadership" as well as compiler of the bibliography for this volume. Professor of Indian history at Carleton College and holding her doctorate from the University of Pennsylvania, she undertook research on Ambedkar and the Mahar movement in India from 1963 to 1965 as a Fellow of the American Institute of Indian Studies. Professor Zelliot credits the success of her research to the "openness and hospitality of Ambedar's people" and adds that her study of Gandhi was inspired by "a life-long attachment to Gandhian ideals."

Contents

MAPS AND CHARTS

Foreword – Personal Perspectives on Untouchability

S. CHANDRASEKHAR

ON A VERY WARM SUMMER DAY in May some forty years ago, when I was about ten years old, I was traveling in a horse carriage with my father from Vellore, a town in Madras Presidency, to Katpadi Railway Junction four miles away to meet a relative arriving there by train. As we were crossing the broad waterless river Palar, the sand shimmering in the midday sun, we saw an unruly crowd of about fifty or sixty people. My father had the driver of the carriage stop and we saw to our horror a thin, middle-aged man being beaten and chased by the crowd from a Hindu temple on the river bank below. A little inquiry revealed that the man was an Untouchable who had committed the unforgivable crime of drawing water from the temple well to quench his thirst on that hot day. He was "caught in the act" by the temple priest who raised an alarm, attracting the crowd that was belabouring the man. We got down from the carriage and my father shouted to the people below on the sands to leave the man alone, which — because my father, who was a civil servant in the Madras Government, and looked like an obviously important citizen — they did, at least for the time that we stopped.

This was my first unhappy experience of untouchability as practiced in South India. I can still recall my father, as we drove on, explaining and condemning the system in no uncertain terms. Although he was a practicing Vaishnavite and a caste Hindu, he felt that all thoughtful Hindus must do something to outlaw the system; and even then he believed that untouchability could not be outlawed unless the caste system itself was abolished. During the next four decades I was to become intimately

xi

involved in carrying forward many of the social concerns of my father. This period, which corresponds to the temporal setting of the present volume, is of particular interest to my generation as we have known at firsthand most of the men and events described and analyzed in this book.

There was a kind of dichotomy in the attitudes toward caste and kindred problems in our comfortable upper middle-class home. Though both my parents were caste Hindus, their marriage was an inter-subcaste one — rare in those days. My father was at heart as well as by education and training a social reformer who had joined the Brahmo Samaj movement at an early age. He found no conflict between his Brahmo Samajism and his Vaishnavism, for after all the great Ramanuja, the founder of Vaishnavism, was a champion of the Untouchables. A picture of Raja Rammohan Roy, the great nineteenth century Bengali social reformer, hung in front of my father's desk in his book-lined study. My mother, on the other hand, was a traditional Hindu wife. Though she had come under the influence of the great Andhra scholar and pioneer social reformer, Kandukuri Veeresalingam Pantulu in Rajahmundry, she was inclined to follow the path of least resistance in matters that involved breaking with tradition. But being a good wife she accepted her husband's views, though not without occasional protest, and did his bidding, however hard it must often have been for her.

The mores of a small town in the thirties on the eve of Mahatma Gandhi's Satyagraha and Salt March were nothing if not conventional and traditional in the extreme.

It is difficult to say how much physical violence accompanied the transgression of caste mores in the Hindu communities across the country through the centuries. While caste ex-communication by village Panchayats for the breaking of caste rules was common, communal riots between various Hindu castes and Harijan groups (as well as between Hindus and Muslims) were not wanting. And in recent years while the relations between the caste Hindus and the Untouchables have been peaceful there still takes place an occasional instance of brutal violence as in the case of the burning of a Harijan boy for stealing brass vessels in an Andhra Pradesh village in 1969.

In the 1930s a major step in breaking down caste barriers was the creation of inter-dining associations in many cities and towns. Orthodox and caste-conscious Hindus seldom ate out and restaurants were few; those who went out to work either took their lunches with them or had a servant bring them. When traveling, in addition to luggage and bedding, a "tiffin-carrier" containing sufficient food for the journey was taken along. Life was slow and complicated for those with caste scruples, but any amount of effort was considered more than worthwhile to avoid the "pollution or contamination" of food cooked by the wrong hands.

It was considered nothing short of revolutionary when educated and reform-minded caste Hindus, usually from well-to-do families, began to break the commensal barriers. I remember accompanying my father and my older brother to dinners of the Inter-dining Association in our town. Leading citizens took turns as hosts and there was an excitement about these evenings which only a Cause can engender. Sometimes a foreigner who had a sufficient number of Indian friends of various castes and persuasions played host. These were either British officials who loved India and had genuine concern for her welfare or American missionaries — usually medical doctors or educationists. Invariably vegetarian food was served and Hindus of different castes, including Harijans and occasionally a Muslim or a Christian, would all dine together in an atmosphere of somewhat self-conscious, ostentatious good-will. The nation's social problems were discussed. There were as many solutions to caste and other social problems as there were diners, running the gamut from veiled orthodoxy to do-it-now radicalism. The dinners and discussions were important enough to rate a small story in the newspapers. At that period, in our community at any rate, no ladies attended the dinners. That would come later. There were a few teenage children, like myself, but again these were only boys. Although sometimes the arguments at the table were boring and above my head, I greatly enjoyed these dinners for I felt part of the adult world. It gave me an important feeling to be with my father and bask in the great respect in which he was held in the community. In addition there was a special sense of doing something outside the purview of the average Hindu.

Although from this distance the whole business appears somewhat pathetic, those dinners served a purpose in helping the orthodox realise that food well-prepared was good no matter what the caste or community of the person with whom one ate it. And whatever the horror of the womenfolk who looked askance at such goings-on (it has always been convenient for men to blame women for slow or no progress), everyone soon realised that the heavens did not fall after all.

The food, incidentally, was prepared by Brahman and other high caste Hindu cooks. It was another, far bolder step for upper caste Hindus to eat food prepared by so-called low caste servants.

After taking the Economics Honours degree from the Madras Presidency College in 1938 I was awarded a research fellowship to work for the M. Litt. research degree at the University of Madras. I wanted to work on India's population problems but unfortunately it was a subject vetoed by the University Professor, Dr. P. J. Thomas, an Oxford-educated Indian Catholic from Kerala. Perhaps he was afraid it might lead to some discussion of birth control, which was more than taboo with him. He suggested as an alternative that I enquire into the economy of the hides and skins industry, a major industry in the Madras Presidency and a subject on which no research had been done. Although at first the suggestion did not appeal to me, I was later to appreciate it, for my work brought me into touch with the Muslims and Harijans involved in the industry, people who were not among my usual circle of friends. The entrepreneurs were largely Muslims and the laborers, Harijans — skilled and unskilled — who skinned the dead animals and tanned the skins and hides before they were shipped to England. No caste Hindus would enter such a menial occupation. Direct contact with these workers gave me my first adult experience of the life of the Harijans and its poverty and squalor.

Unexpectedly, the completion of my monograph won me a fellow-ship from Madras University to go for my doctorate to Columbia University. This was September, 1940, and the British Empire was at war. Although the academic year had already started, I didn't want to wait for a whole year before entering Columbia, and a frantic exchange of letters and cables brought me admission to the February, 1941, semester.

Then my father suggested that I should meet Mahatma Gandhi and obtain his *ashirvads* (blessings) in traditional Hindu fashion before leaving India. There wasn't much time to write to the Mahatma and request a meeting. I was anxious to catch the only ship available for the next few months — a Japanese liner leaving Bombay for San Francisco via Japan.

When I learned that the Mahatma was in his ashram in Sevagram, a village near Wardha in the Central Provinces (now Maharashtra) I promptly left for Wardha, armed with two letters of introduction to the Mahatma, one from my father and the other from Kasturi Srinivasan, the well-known publisher and editor of *The Hindu,* India's prestigious nationalist English daily in Madras.

After a whole day and a sleepless night on the Grand Trunk Express, which had nothing "grand" or "express" about it, I got off at Wardha on a chilly, drizzling early October morning. I shaved and bathed at the local travellers' bungalow and then took a tonga to Sevagram, an hour's rattling ride over a slushy apology for a road.

It was about 8:30 in the morning when I got to the ashram and the day's activities were well under way since the ashram day began at 4:30 A.M. Needless to say, I was very excited at the prospect of talking with the Mahatma. (My full account of the interview, "I Meet the

Mahatma," appeared in *Crisis,* Journal of the NAACP, New York, October, 1942.)

After scanning the letters of introduction, particularly the one from K. Srinivasan in which the newspaper magnate requested Gandhi not to put me off since I was in some haste to catch my steamer at Bombay, Gandhiji began the interview abruptly:

"Do you think you stand a chance?" he asked, looking at me with one of those mischievous toothless smiles of his.

"Chance of what, Gandhiji?" I queried, confessing that I didn't understand the question.

"Against Roosevelt and Willkie, of course, at the polls," he added, and seeing me look first puzzled and then break into laughter at his delightful humour, he added, "Since you are in such great haste to go to America I thought you were anxious to contest for the Presidency."

Then the joke over — the serious, tense young student set at ease — Gandhi became serious. "Why exactly to America?" I explained the why of my trip and in the talk that followed Gandhiji seemed particularly concerned to bring home to me two problems.

One was that American democracy not only excluded the Negro but positively persecuted him — the days of lynching were not yet over. He felt strongly that everyone should at some time experience from the receiving end some prejudice and discrimination, for otherwise one could never know what it was to be an underdog. (The great Mahatma had experienced color prejudice and discrimination in South Africa.) He warned me against unconsciously imbibing the American superiority complex about Negroes and said that on returning to India I should unlearn many things American. Though he had never visited America he knew only too well American, particularly Southern American, racial mores. But although he condemned American practices that fell far short of the American ideals of democracy and racial equality, he had great admiration for those who were working toward such ideals.

He talked to me about the plight of the Harijans. He was happy that I had written a monograph on India's leather industry which meant that I was familiar with the problem of the downtrodden Harijan labour in that industry. In the midst of all the national political upheaval that the Mahatma was managing, he found time to interest himself with the problems of the tanning industry. He told me about the modern sanitary tannery which his ashram had set up for the villagers in the neighbouring rural areas. Gandhi suggested that I should see what they had been doing and offer any suggestions that I might have! And I was barely twenty-one.

We also talked about the question of public sanitation and hygiene.

Tradition had classed the work of sweepers and scavengers as unclean, and the Harijans had to do it. The first test of anyone desiring to become a part of the ashram and a follower of Gandhi was to do some scavenging work. The difficulties of the Harijan *Bhangi* (scavenger) engaged his attention to such an extent that he would write about their problems in almost every issue of his newspaper, *The Harijan.*

In the presence of the Mahatma I could feel his deep concern — a kind of mystic passion — to identify himself with the poorest, the most depressed and downtrodden of his fellow human beings in India, if not the world, and his determination to do everything in his power to make man's inhumanity to man an ugly memory of the past. It is needless to add what the world knows, that Mahatma Gandhi, despite his anachronistic and quaint belief in *varnashrama dharma,* pioneered in a myriad ways, more than anyone else since the Buddha, to awaken the conscience of Hindu India to ameliorate the lot of the Harijans.

In 1947, when after seven years in the United States I returned to India on the eve of her freedom, I visited New Delhi to meet some friends. New Delhi in 1947 was very different from New Delhi in 1971. The earlier Delhi was more like a sleepy provincial town than the capital of an important and populous nation. The most striking difficulty for a visitor from abroad, albeit an Indian, was lack of hotel space. The partition of the nation and its attendant refugee influx had increased the capital's population enormously. My wife and I, after some difficulty, obtained a room for a few days in Western Court, a government-run hostelry where officials stayed on brief visits to the capital. At that time many prominent political leaders were staying there during the exciting days before the transfer of political power and the setting-up of the new interim government.

I had several letters of introduction from Indian and American friends abroad to Indians both famous and unknown. One such letter was to Dr. B. R. Ambedkar from a distinguished professor emeritus from Columbia University Law School who had befriended young, lonely Ambedkar when the latter was a student at Columbia during World War I. He had followed Ambedkar's career in India and his rise to the leadership of his people and political fame. (The same American professor, older and retired, befriended me as well during my student days at Columbia and New York University during World War II years.)

Ambedkar was occupying a suite of rooms on the same floor that we were, and one evening I called on him with the letter. He was then Member of India's Constituent Assembly and Chairman of the Drafting Committee to draft the Constitution of Free India. He was surrounded by a crowd of admirers and hangers-on. He was delighted to hear from his old American professor. We had a long chat and he was pleased that I had received some of my education in the United States. He said that while America had its own "untouchability" problem, his student years had been happy and satisfying. What he remembered particularly about his day was the profound ignorance even of educated Americans about India and things Indian. He asked me whether things had changed and whether the American press was enlightening its readers about India. We then discussed various features of American life, and he asked me at the end what aspect of America most impressed me as something that could be emulated in India. There were many things about America that I liked and admired and several which I wished India could adapt to her needs. I said that the melting pot phenomenon in the making of the American nation appealed to me most, and I added that intercaste marriage was perhaps the best and the only abiding solution to the problem of caste and untouchability. His eyes lighted up, and he was delighted. But he was quick to point out that the American melting pot did not include the Negroes. He went into a learned discourse on how intercaste marriage could be promoted and the countless difficulties that would have to be overcome. He looked at my American wife and said, "I see your husband practices what he believes, and I hope he will preach this. Your husband is what we call a 'caste Hindu' and I am glad he really believes in intercaste marriages." He rang a bell and when a servant appeared inquired whether Mrs. Ambedkar was free to say hello to some friends who had just come from America. Mrs. Ambedkar came in after a few minutes, and now the conversation was directed more toward my wife. Later I learned that Mrs. Ambedkar was a Maharashtrian Brahman, a medical doctor, whom Ambedkar had recently married.

We kept in touch, and I met him once again in Delhi, in his spacious ministerial residence after he had become Law Minister in Jawaharlal Nehru's first Cabinet. This time, as I recall, he was in somewhat indifferent health and a masseur was massaging his legs. An admiring crowd, larger now, was still there, many of them waiting in the portico of the bungalow. I recall his telling me that the institution of untouchability was an integral part of Hinduism since caste was a major tenet of Hindu religious belief. Hence untouchability was not merely a social or economic problem but a "religious problem." The only lasting solution was mass conversion to another and more democratic religion such as Buddhism.

In October, 1956, true to his long-cherished belief, Dr. Ambedkar took what he called the "most important step" of his life when he, with some 500,000 followers belonging to his own Mahars — a Maharashtrian Harijan group, left Hinduism and embraced Buddhism. After the conversion ceremony, addressing a large meeting he pointed out, "The Hindu religion offered no opportunity for the Untouchables to improve their lot, for it is based on inequality . . . on the other hand, Buddhism . . . is based on equality and justice . . . I would like to see all India become Buddhist."

The implementation of this wish to bring Buddhism with all its beauty and compassion, greatness, and gentleness to all of his people would have been a challenging task, and Dr. Ambedkar, with his great abilities and enthusiasm, could have done it. Tragically enough he passed away two months after his conversion, in his sixty-fifth year, at the end of 1956. And with the loss of this distinguished and undisputed leader, the untouchable movement broke into numerous quarreling groups.

Fifteen fateful years have elapsed since Ambedkar's death but no Harijan leader of his ability or integrity has yet come forth to lead these downtrodden millions into the promised land of freedom and equality. Although until March, 1971, there were two Harijan leaders — D. Sanjiviah, the affable former Andhra chief minister and Congress president, and Jagjivan Ram — representing the south and north respectively in the Central Cabinet, neither of them had any mass following comparable to that of the late Ambedkar.

In 1948 when I was a professor at the Annamalai University in South India I was invited to preside over the Madras Presidency Students Conference. A principal speaker at the conference was C. N. Annadurai, the dynamic leader of the DMK (Dravida Munnetra Kazhagam) party in Madras. This party which was in opposition to the ruling Congress Party had seceded from the parent DK (Dravida Kazhagam) party, founded and led for half a century, by the remarkable veteran freethinker, Periyar E. V. Ramaswamy. (Though he is ninety-three years old, he continues to lead the party today with his wonted iconoclastic vigor.) Annadurai at that time was for the secession of the four southern states (Madras, Andhra, Kerala and Mysore) from the Indian union on the grounds of the unjust imposition of the Hindi language by the North. He spoke at length on the need for the abolition of the caste system. And his main thesis was the promotion of intercaste marriages. Since my own presidential address to the conference had devoted considerable thought to the same subject, and we were in agreement on many things, we became friends from that day.

In pursuance of one of the major resolutions of the conference, we set up the All-India Intercaste Marriages Association with Annadurai as the President and myself as General Secretary. This association was intended to educate and encourage the country's youth on the need for such marriages and to provide monetary incentives for them. But, unfortunately, for want of funds and full-time workers, the organization remained largely a paper one, though Annadurai (and I) continued to speak on the subject at every possible opportunity.

We continued to meet on many occasions, both public and private, and I always found him dedicated, scholarly and reasonable — rather a rare combination in Indian political life. During the sixties we were both elected from Madras to the Upper House (the Rajya Sabha) of the Indian Parliament and we met in the House and every day at the Parliament Library. In 1967, after the general elections, we both became Ministers, Annadurai Chief Minister of Madras State and I Union Minister for Health and Family Planning at the Center.

As the head of the Madras Government, Annadurai did excellent work in trying to ameliorate the lot of the common man. And in the midst of all his other heavy responsibilities, he did not forget his belief in inter-caste marriages. He instituted official medals and monetary incentives to encourage such marriages — (the first official step in this direction in Madras State) and continued to stress their importance in overcoming caste barriers and prejudices at every opportunity.

Most unfortunately he passed away unexpectedly in 1969 when he was only sixty years old, leaving a void which has not been filled so far in Tamil Nad.

Another, albeit slender, source of intellectual attack against the caste system was from the Indian Rationalist Association which was founded in Madras in the thirties by Periyar E. V. Ramaswamy, previously mentioned as founder of the Dravida Kazhagam in the South. While E. V. Ramaswamy, through a variety of vitriolic Tamil periodicals, took the message of anti-caste equality to the masses, Mr. S. Ramanathan, a friendly, dedicated soul and a Congress Party politician, provided, as president of the association, able and broad intellectual support to the movement through his English monthly, *The Indian Rationalist*. The association later received some support from Maharashtra and the Punjab, but despite such patrons as Bertrand Russell, Hector Hawton, and Charles Bradlaugh Bonner, it languished for want of financial support. At no time did the periodical reach more than 5,000 readers. Mr. Ramanathan, a business man in private life, paid the printer's bill from his own pocket.

I learnt from Mr. Ramanathan that he and Periyar E. V. Ramaswamy became fast friends from the rationalist ideological point of view during their tour of the Soviet Union in 1942. They had been nurtured in earlier years on both the *Nyaya Vaiseshika* and *Sankhya* schools of Hindu rationalist thought and on the writings of humanists ranging from Ingersoll to Bertrand Russell. The Russian trip seemed to convince them that one of the major problems of India was excessive religion; they were apparently drawn more to Soviet official atheism than to communist economic ideology.

While E. V. Ramaswamy and S. Ramanathan agreed on the pressing need for a rationalist attitude in the Hindu way of life, they followed different political ideologies. As pointed out earlier, E. V. Ramaswamy was opposed to the Congress Party while Ramanathan was an active member of it, courted imprisonment more than once for doing *Satyagraha*, and served a term as minister in C. Rajagopalachari's cabinet in Madras.

Ramanathan, who died in 1969 at the age of 70, was kind enough to invite me to preside over the Second All-India Rationalist Conference held in 1952 at Tenali, Madras State (now Andhra Pradesh), when I was a professor at the University of Baroda. The first conference held in Madras two years earlier was presided over by the distinguished Maharashtrian scholar, diplomatist and administrator, Sir Raghunath Paranjype of Poona, Senior Wrangler from the University of Cambridge who had held many responsible positions in both the British Indian administration and in free India. He was neither a politician nor a mass leader, but an outspoken publicist and the author of a trenchant book on the need for a rationalist outlook, *The Crux of the Indian Problem* (Poona, 1932). He wrote, urging me to accept the invitation, and kindly suggested topics for my address.

Another moving rationalist spirit at the conference was Professor Gora (not his exact name but the name by which he is known in India, given to him by Gandhi) who was then (and for some time after) running an Atheistic Ashram at Vijayawada. (In the early thirties Gora was to debate with the Mahatma on India's need for atheism or at least agnosticism and Gandhi's famous reply was that Gora's *a-deva* (non-God or anti-God) was more spiritual than many a man's *deva* (God). Gora is one of the undeservedly unrecognised saints of India. Though a Brahman, he was one of the few in caste-ridden Andhra Pradesh to permit his daughter to marry a Harijan. In fact, all his children were encouraged to marry outside their caste.

The conference itself was a success, judged by the audience it attracted and the number of editorials it provoked in the nation's newspapers. Beyond that, it is difficult to say whether the Indian Rationalist Association or its periodic conferences, anymore than the British Rationalist or the American Humanist associations have exerted any lasting impact on peoples' minds or their attitudes toward basic social questions.

That these questions are in general the same ones that are confronting India some twenty years later is demonstrated by the following extract from my presidential address at the 1952 conference:

RACE AND THE COLOUR PROBLEM

A major international superstition is racism and its corollary of colour prejudice. Though the world today has shrunk from immense geographical dimensions to an interdependent and accessible unit, the peoples of the world continue to live in different hostile and exclusive compartments based on political ideologies, racial identities, national loyalties, religious affiliations and other narrow allegiances. And racism, more than any other loyalty, has played havoc with the progress of mankind.

It is now admitted that there are no pure races. Commerce, colonization, conquest — or whatever the cause of race-mixture — have led to the hybridization of mankind. The possibility of ultimate assimilation of all ethnic groups is beyond doubt. Once the cultural barriers against inter-"racial" marriages are removed, the assimilation of these groups can be hastened and "superior" and "inferior" races will vanish forever. Race-mixture itself might be the most effective solution to our racial problems.

CASTE SYSTEM AND PROVINCIALISM

The most formidable social and to some extent economic and political problem in India is that of the caste system. Much has been written on the genesis, growth and the present position of this pernicious system. To me, the gravest evil of the caste system is that it has rendered our society undemocratic and a sociological myth. It has so cut and recut our society into myriad bits that our people exist not as a homogeneous society but as congeries of mutually exclusive and often hostile social-tight groups. Half a century ago, everyone, by and large, defended the system in the face of certain Western intellectual onslaughts. In the recent past, we have not heard so much a defence of the system as a description of it, and how it once served a useful purpose in the evolution of our polity. Today, I daresay, every serious student of this question concedes that it has outlived its utility and has become now a painful, undemocratic, and anti-national anachronism. The question, therefore, is not whether the system is desirable but how best to abolish it in the shortest possible time.

The Government of India should be launching an active nationwide campaign against caste, particularly in our schools and colleges, where young and impressionable minds can be taught democratic attitudes to counteract the undesirable influence of the home in this matter. Since the only effective solution to the caste problem is intercaste marriage on the widest scale, the education of our youth in democratic attitudes and ideals is a prerequisite.

Allied to the problem of communalism is that of provincialism, or "linguism" or, in a word, lack of assimilation and Indianization. Despite diversities of geographical layout, climate, language, religion and mores, India is blessed with a fundamental cultural unity and continuity. This unity must be developed if India is not to grow up as a country of mutually exclusive and antagonistic blocs, languages, creeds and pools of unassimilated minority cultures. Ours is not a unified culture like the German, French or British cultures. It is of a composite type and the component parts stand out in bold relief. Our regional and cultural linguistic blocs such as Andhra, Bengali, Gujarati, Kerala, Maharashtra, Tamil are fissiparous and centripetal in effect and there is no strong, central or cementing unity. Lack of assimilation between these segmentary culture patterns constitutes a serious problem and raises acute political and cultural issues. If these continue to grow independent of each other, they may, with the further growth of provincialism in the narrow sense, become totally exclusive and endanger our national unity.

Political leaders, whether they are rationalists or not, must give some serious thought to this question. We have two outstanding examples of somewhat similar problems and the way they were tackled. They are the Soviet Union and the United States. While the Soviet example of the grant of cultural autonomy to its many nationalities within the framework of Soviet politics is admirable, the unequal development of these various cultures is unenviable. On the other hand, we have the experience of the United States, where every immigrant group has brought with it its own culture-pattern and has blended it into the melting pot of the American way of life. It is essential that we study these two different approaches and adopt what is most suitable for us. I believe, however, that an effort in the right direction would be to promote interprovincial and inter-religious exchanges and marriages.

In May, 1969, Mr. Jagjivan Ram, the well-known Bihari Harijan leader and Minister of Food and Agriculture in the Central Cabinet, and I were invited to address a large meeting at Quilon (not far from Trivandrum) to felicitate Mr. R. Shankar, the Kerala Ezhava (Harijan) leader and former Chief Minister of that state on his sixty-first birthday.

Kerala, in the past, was the southern state where untouchability was practised in some of its worst forms, including unapproachability. It has become the state where the Harijans (the Ezhavas) have registered great progress in terms of literacy, general and professional education, ordinary and prestigious jobs, and per capita income compared to Harijans elsewhere in India, particularly in the backward Hindi belt. Of the three "communal" groups in Kerala, the Hindu Nayars, the Christians, and the Ezhavas, the Ezhavas have attained sufficient social and economic status to be reckoned with as a major political force. In fact, they have technically ceased to be members of the scheduled castes.

We both addressed the overflowing audience in a specially erected *pandal* (hall), paying tribute to the good work Mr. Shankar had done, particularly in organising and building several colleges. We pleaded for the eradication of untouchability and the caste system itself. When I expressed the hope that if every young man and woman could marry someone from any other caste or sub-caste, half the battle would be won in a generation, Jagjivan Ram agreed. The meeting over, we drove back to the Trivandrum Raj Bhavan — the Governor's mansion — where we were staying. While at lunch, we received the shocking news of the death of Dr. Zakir Husain, the saintly and beloved Muslim President of India. Prolonged mourning had been declared and we were summoned immediately to New Delhi.

We caught the only available plane the next morning. The papers, full of mourning, were already speculating on who was likely to be the next president. Mr. Jagjivan Ram's name was prominent among those being discussed. The press gave various reasons for wanting to elevate the Harijan Minister to the Presidency. First, it would show orthodox Hindus at home as well as skeptics outside that modern India did not believe in untouchability. What is more, it would be known that in the egalitarian democracy that India was building, an ex-Untouchable could occupy the highest office. Finally, because he was a senior Congress Party leader and an astute politician whose place in the Central Cabinet appeared to be quasi-permanent, Jagjivan Ram, the papers agreed, would make a good president.

Sitting next to him on the plane, I asked Jagjivan Ram whether he was interested in becoming India's next president. He said that the ornamental office did not attract him; he considered himself young (he was then only sixty), and he still wanted to be in active politics. I am sure he could have become the president had he wanted it. In a way I wish he had, for it would have prevented the fateful presidential election that led to the unfortunate split of the Congress party.

As for a balance sheet of progress: of today's total world population of some 3.6 billion, about every seventh person is a citizen of India, 547 millions according to the 1971 census. And every seventh Indian is a Harijan or member of the Scheduled Castes — more than 85 million people whose cultural, economic and social progress and their overall welfare is of paramount importance to the country as a whole.

In the twenty-four years that have elapsed since India regained her political freedom (1947-1971) the nation has registered considerable progress in democratic consciousness, educational development, economic growth, and social advancement. This progress is reflected in the strides taken by the Harijan community. But if, despite this progress, India continues among the poorest countries of the world, it is because in 1947 she was utterly undeveloped. She is now in the process of development and one may hope that within another generation she will join the ranks of the advanced and developed nations.

While the present volume describes the progress of the Harijans in greater detail, it may be of interest to note here that the first and major step towards the amelioration of the lot of the Harijans, tribals, and other minorities must be traced to the universal franchise embodied in the constitution of free India, which has enfranchised millions of adults despite their illiteracy and grinding poverty. Naturally this has conferred on the Harijans considerable political power which, wisely exercised, can put their friends in power. Since numbers matter in a democracy, Harijan demographic strength has become a force to be reckoned with in the national elections.

Secondly, by and large, interdining between caste Hindus and Harijans and the integration of all groups in schools and colleges have come to be accepted. There is little dissent or protest. In urban areas such questions rarely arise, but even in rural areas where progress has been slow, untouchability as a social problem is diminishing.

Thirdly, residential segregation, a recognizable feature through the centuries, is no longer a caste problem per se but virtually an economic problem. This is progress because housing today in urban areas and in most villages depends on what a citizen can afford, either in rent or in ownership. Of course, most rich people who live in fashionable suburbs or attractive housing colonies are caste Hindus, but Harijans who can afford to live in these areas are gaining access. There is a tremendous housing shortage in India but once the economic status of the average Harijan family is raised, their housing need will take care of itself.

Finally, there has been a welcome shift in the occupational distribution of the population. Once almost all the high-paying and prestigious jobs were held by caste Hindus. The fourfold classification of castes on a broad occupational basis, however, has been at best a notional one and did not correspond with reality through the ages. We have indisputable evidence to show that many royal houses in southern and western India belonged and continue to belong to the fourth caste: the Maratha ruling houses including the Maharastrian Nayaks as well as the Nayak rulers of Madurai (the precursors of present-day Naidus), the Nayars of Kerala and the Reddys of Andhra — all have held high positions as rulers or petty chieftains. And, in fact, almost all the large Zamindars and Talukdars south of the Vindhyas belong to the fourth caste. (Incidentally, workaday Hinduism has even elevated Harijans to sainthood — Nandanar, for instance, to quasi-divinity fit to be worshipped.)

Today no citizen is denied any job on the basis of caste, religion or sex, so long as he or she has the necessary academic credentials, skills, or training. There are, of course, exceptions. For instance, there has long been a serious complaint in Andhra Pradesh that as the Government is dominated by Reddys (an agriculturist caste), not only Harijans but members of all non-Reddy castes find it difficult to get jobs (beyond token representation). In Madras State a major grievance against the state government is that members of the Brahman community have been discriminated against in the matter of government employment and, particularly, in admission to professional colleges. Such regional caste discrimination exists in a few other states as well.

But, in general, almost every sub-caste is represented in all the professional groups — teachers, physicians, lawyers, engineers, civil servants, etc. What is more interesting, there are Brahmans (who have about 2,000 superior and inferior sub-castes) in the hides and skins business (once the monopoly of the Muslims and the Harijans) and non-Brahmans performing priestly chores. (Priests, by the way, have always been very poorly paid, no matter what their caste, for in Hinduism there is no paid priesthood.)

Such progress as has been achieved is largely due to legislation and government directive. The enactment of the Untouchability Offences Act (which came into force on June 1, 1955) made it possible for the Harijans to enter any Hindu temple or religious institution, draw water from any tap or tank, stream, or well, use any public restaurant, hotel, place of entertainment, and other facilities. A certain number of seats have been reserved for Harijans in schools, colleges and professional institutions, municipal councils, city corporations, state legislatures and the Parliament. A certain quota of jobs in government has also been reserved for Harijans.

India is perhaps the only major country where an enlightened national government is trying to change the traditional obscurantist mores of an ancient society (hitherto predicated upon inequality in the name of religion) into a modern democratic and secular society and nation. Viewed against the tremendous barriers confronting those endeavoring to engineer such social change, history's verdict will probably be that the Government of India and the constitution-makers (Ambedkar, et. al.) laid the firm foundations on which a new India could be built. Much remains to be done, but it requires as much a change of heart on the part of caste Hindus as legal protection and promotion of the interests of the Harijans.

What of the future?

To ensure faster and more abiding progress, not only in promoting the welfare of Harijans but in abolishing the caste system itself, two important areas need to be explored afresh. One area is the role of science and technology in abolishing a primitive system, the other the role of education in freeing the minds of India's youth from the fetters of casteism.

In this atomic age and the year of 1971, India has a caste of scavengers! Incredibly a large group of people are still confined to the traditional task of removing night soil, cleaning latrines, and washing bathrooms. Again, the reason is not so much that caste Hindus are a particularly cussed community as that modern technology has not been brought to the people of India. In a word, the introduction of modern bathrooms with flush toilets and, of course, running water, would help to eliminate the scavenging caste. The point I am trying to make was forcibly brought out years ago by the well-known Indian writer, Mulk Raj Anand in his moving novel, *The Untouchable*. Science indeed has an effective answer to untouchability but unfortunately, because of her poverty, India is still years behind the advanced countries in the matter of the application of science to the needs of daily living.

The second approach is to be found in education that will lead to intercaste (and eventually interlinguistic and interreligious) marriages. Sooner or later India must become an emotionally integrated society. Intercaste marriages have remained an intractable problem complicated by two major difficulties: the reactionary Hindu law on the subject and the tradition of arranged marriages.

Through the centuries intercaste marriages among the Hindus, or marriages across such religious lines as Hindu-Muslim, were not permitted by the personal laws of both religions. An intercaste marriage could take place under the Special Marriage Act of 1872, however, if both the partners of differing castes declared that they did not profess Hinduism, which was a difficult thing to do. Now the Special Marriage Act of 1954 has solved the problem by permitting intercaste marriages without requiring either partner to deny his or her faith. Since a major reactionary prop of the traditional caste system was its inherent ban on intercaste marriages, this legislation gave a serious blow to the caste system.

The other difficulty is attitudinal and cultural. If today intercaste marriages are more an exception than the rule, it is because young people are herded into the married state by their parents and guardians. The young bride and groom have, by and large, no say in choice of partners. The elders, normally conservative, choose to unite persons who are generally related to each other or who belong to the same caste or sub-caste and linguistic group. Once young people are permitted to choose or at least have a say in the choice of partners, the area of choice might conceivably go beyond caste, language and eventually even religious boundaries.

Despite these barriers intercaste marriages have been on the increase in the post-freedom years. Even before India's freedom, India's politically prominent families — Gandhi, Jinnah, Sorojini Naidu, Nehru, Rajaji, Radhakrishnan, Ambedkar, Masani, E. V. Ramaswamy, to name only a few — have encompassed intercaste marriages. A thousand other instances among families well known in other spheres can be cited. In major cities such as

New Delhi, Bombay, Calcutta, Hyderabad, and Madras, it is not unusual to find several castes represented in certain families through marriage. Among the members of the extended or joint family of the present writer are included at least half a dozen sub-castes of Raos, Iyengars, Naidus, Kammas, Reddys, besides Christians and Parsees. And what is more, these relatives belong to three linguistic groups — Andhras, Tamils, and Malayalees.

True, a majority of such intercaste marriages as these are confined to the highly educated, affluent, modernized and reform-minded families, and consequently are not a statistically representative sample of the Indian population. The trend of reform is visible, however, and some day the trickle of such marriages may become a flood. When it does, no one in the course of time will be able to claim that he or she belongs to any particular caste or sub-caste, and caste affiliation will cease to have any value or validity.

The future shows the people of India confronted with many problems relating to caste. The first is to guard democracy in India against the inroads of caste. While caste as a social problem and an economic restriction is slowly being resolved, it is assuming in modern India a new and undesirable form. While India is the world's largest democracy, the influence of caste on the choice of candidates to contest elections is negating the democratic ideal. The political parties, without exception, set up candidates belonging to the caste of the majority of the constituency concerned.

No less a person than Dr. S. Radhakrishnan, the distinguished Indian philosopher, pointed out when he was President of India: "Caste has ceased to be a social evil but has become a political and administrative evil. We want to get out votes and we set up candidates suited to the people who have to vote. If it is a Nadar constituency we set up a Nadar. If it is a Harijan constituency we set up a Harijan. If it is a Kamma constituency we set up a Kamma. This is what we have been doing. It is therefore essential that politics should be as far as possible lifted out of this kind of morass" (*Bhavan's Journal,* Bombay, May 13, 1962).

On the eve of general elections in March, 1971, I sat at the headquarters of the ruling Congress Party in one of the states, watching for several days the way the leaders selected candidates for various constituencies. (The leaders were semi-literate politicians practicing the politics of poverty.) The first question invariably put to the prospective candidate aspiring to contest a particular state or parliamentary constituency was about his caste. The second question concerned the amount of money he could raise or spend to finance his election, apart from a donation to the party. Besides this, the leader made every effort to choose as many candidates belonging to his *own* caste as possible. Once the day's labours were over, everyone rushed off in the evening to address various audiences on the resolve to build "a casteless and classless democracy."

Another problem is that numerous sub-castes located on the periphery, who could be considered caste Hindus, are clamouring to be classed as "backward." The reason is simple: these groups do not care what their labels are so long as they have certain subsidies and scholarships, an assurance of quotas in government jobs, and certain reserved representation in the legislature. At an all-India conference of all the state ministers and officials in charge of Backward Classes Welfare held in New Delhi in May, 1971, Prime Minister Indira Gandhi spoke out courageously: "We should be against making backwardness a vested interest. We thought the word 'backwardness' would gradually go out of our vocabulary but we find more and more people seeking to get listed as backward. It is being joked that at this rate the whole population would be listed as backward. This is a backward-looking approach" (*The Hindu,* Madras, May 22, 1971).

While helping in all possible ways the disadvantaged elements of our population, we must resist the temptation to identify backwardness with a particular caste or sub-caste. A new definition of backwardness is needed. Poverty, illiteracy, and ill-health are to be found in every group irrespective of caste or religious affiliation. It is the responsibility of the government to raise the living standards of every citizen and community, not to tacitly assume that a man is comfortable because he belongs to a particular community or that another is deprived because he belongs to a community which at some point in our history was classified as backward. There are today well-to-do Harijans and scheduled castes, and poverty-stricken Brahmans and other caste Hindus. In fact, in some parts of the country, the Brahmans are discriminated against because they are considered solely responsible for the centuries-old discrimination against the Harijans and other castes.

While we strive to remove caste prejudice and abolish caste discrimination, we must guard against the temptation to bigotry directed against those who were in the past responsible for discrimination.

S. CHANDRASEKHAR

Editor's Preface   J. MICHAEL MAHAR

SINCE THE ATTAINMENT of independence in 1947 the Republic of India has undertaken one of the most profound reorderings of society ventured by a democratic nation in modern times. A major break with tradition is expressed in Article 17 of the Constitution adopted in 1950 which abolished "untouchability," a practice rooted in the social and religious life of India for more than 2,000 years. Estimates of the number of people affected by this change range from 15 to 25 percent of a population rapidly approaching the 600 million mark. Disparities in the enumeration of "Untouchables," or more appropriately "Ex-Untouchables," are due in part to a variety of terms coined over the years to describe this segment of Indian society. British census commissioners devised the category of Scheduled Castes for census use, while programs developed to ameliorate the Untouchables' lot in life often referred to them as Depressed Castes. Viewed in terms of the orthodox Hindu fourfold division of society, initially stated in a Rig-Vedic hymn of the first millennium B.C., the Untouchables are seen as beyond the pale — a fifth order, or Exterior Caste grouping. Gandhi introduced a new term, "Harijan" (children of God) in an attempt to avoid the disparaging connotation of such vernacular terms as pariah, widely used in daily life.

The same variety of terms used to designate this segment of Indian society reflects the variegated nature of untouchability as a social and cultural phenomenon, and the diversity of groups subsumed under such labels. There is no single measure or uniform criterion for identifying an Untouchable. Definitions of "untouchability" are manifold, depending upon context, but there is a common premise that untouchability is a stigma attached to certain people because of their polluted state.

The stigma, congenital according to one's caste, lasts a lifetime and cannot be eliminated by rite or deed. Defined in relation to behavior, untouchability refers to the set of practices followed by the rest of society to protect itself from the pollution conveyed by the Untouchable. This concern with "ritual" pollution is not limited to the role of the Untouchables, however; rather, it is part of a configuration of "themes" whose ramifications throughout Indian society are traced in the introduction to this book. The author of the introduction, Morris E. Opler, further indicates that concern with pollution also served to keep the Untouchables in an inferior economic and political position through enforcement of sumptuary laws and physical separation.

Although foreign observers, from Megasthenes (fourth century, B.C.) to the present, have reported the residential segregation of Untouchables and the various other disabilities imposed on them, scholarly accounts of untouchability have been few in number and limited to one aspect of the subject, or to observations in a single village or region.

The present account, while it does not attempt to provide a comprehensive view of the role of the Untouchable in modern India, does offer a greater variety of scholarly perspectives and a broader range of observations on that subject than any previous publication.

Unity among the perspectives stems from the fortuitous convergence of independently conceived and executed research, undertaken in the past decade by a dozen specialists on South Asia. Realization of this common interest during casual encounters at professional meetings led to arrangements for a conference at the University of Arizona, sponsored by the Association for Asian Studies in November, 1967. In revised form, the papers presented at that conference serve as the nucleus of this volume to which other pertinent writings have been added. The disciplinary perspectives represented include law, anthropology, history, economics, sociology, political science, and religion.

Translation of the Indian Constitution's Article 17 into legal statutes in 1955, and the role of the courts in the implementation of these laws, are reviewed and assessed by Marc Galanter. Galanter not only examines the disposition of court cases treating untouchability in independent India, but he also traces judicial decisions back to precedents established during the period of British rule. Lelah Dushkin provides a comparable review and assessment of the evolution of the policy of protective discrimination and its post-Independence development, with particular attention to guaranteed political representation and preferential treatment in education and government employment.

As evinced throughout history, particularly in similar efforts to alleviate the lot of the black people in the United States in recent years, human behavior is not readily affected by judicial and legislative precept. Changes in response to such external stimuli, however, cannot be denied, despite the nebulous or doubtful nature of change occurring in the mind, heart, and habits of man. Although information regarding such change is not subject to ready measurement, it can be assessed in part by direct participation in the lives of those affected. Here the contribution to this volume of the anthropologists — especially of Joan Mencher and Michael Mahar — points to some of the consequences of innovation whose full import will not likely be known for several generations. The anthropologists' studies also afford some understanding of the place of the Untouchable in the matrix of community life where social, economic, and political forces have served to keep him at the bottom of one of mankind's most clearly articulated systems of social stratification. While village studies reveal marked regional differences in the position and prospects of the Untouchable in rural communities, a subtle ground swell of changing attitudes and aspirations attributable to government policy can be detected.

The high proportion of Untouchables among the ranks of the landless agricultural worker links their common fate to the economic forces generated by overpopulation and the increasing pressure on the land. Walter C. Neale and André Béteille examine the broad implications of these forces in the light of economic theory and its prognosis regarding the role of Untouchables in the labor force of Indian rural communities.

In addition to changes emanating from government policies and programs, a major effort to ameliorate the lot of the Untouchables has originated from these people themselves. In keeping with earlier efforts at social reform in India exemplified by Sikhism and the Kabir Panthi Sect, religion has served in recent years as a major vehicle for the dissemination of revolutionary ideas among the Untouchables, and has provided also a model for the organization and support of such change. The most widespread and influential movement of this kind is the conversion of Untouchables to Buddhism, a phenomenon whose proportions are reflected in the Census of India which recorded 181,000 Buddhists in 1951 and 3,260,000 in 1961.

The rapidity and wide spatial distribution of the Buddhist conversion movement since 1956 is considerably elucidated in Adele Fiske's account based on her tour of several regions of India in 1967. Her account of the leaders, their local organizations, and the linkages between such organizations provides one of the few detailed descriptions of recent developments at the grass-roots level, stemming from the charismatic leadership of Dr. B. R. Ambedkar. Ambedkar's role as the major spokesman for the Untouchable community, from the 1930s until his death in 1958, is reviewed by Eleanor Zelliot in a comparative study that also treats the often conflicting views of Ambedkar and Mohandas K. Gandhi. The direct impact of Ambedkar's ideas and personality on a single Untouchable community, the Jatavs of Agra, is examined by Owen Lynch.

Although the Buddhist conversion movement initiated by Ambedkar is most extensively treated in this volume, earlier movements of a similar nature, many of which still exist, also sought to slake the thirst of the Untouchable for religious validation of his aspirations toward higher status within the Hindu tradition. The Neo-Christians of Kerala, described by K. C. Alexander, exemplify the Christian missionary movement, revealing as well some of the ways in which the stigma of untouchability is manifest within the Christian community. Lawrence Babb's account of the Satnamis of Madhya Pradesh provides another example from numerous little-known movements of this kind. A locally based movement originating in the nineteenth century, the Satnamis have in recent years become articulated with the national political structure of the Congress Party. The broader social, economic, and political integration of the Satnamis fostered by this alliance points to one of many directions that might be followed by the far more numerous and more widely dispersed Buddhists.

Some of the social and emotional consequences of Untouchable status and the Untouchables' conversion to Buddhism are explored by Robert and Beatrice Miller. Their analyses of several short stories written in Marathi, by an author of Untouchable origin, convey the personal dimension of institutions and social changes described in more general terms in the other accounts. The Millers' literary sources also depict the problems of group identity and self-image that often ride with the psychological release accompanying conversion to Buddhism or the attainment of nontraditional roles. The emotional ambivalence and social dislocation stemming from such changes are also examined in Harold Isaacs' insightful study of the Ex-Untouchable in an urban setting.

A number of common topics are treated from various perspectives throughout the collection: the repercussions of government policy within village communities, the administrative and legal problems posed by such changes, and the plight of the individual caught up in a period of rapid transition from one of the world's most ancient ways of life to an uncertain future. A recurrent concern is to assess the consequences stemming from one of the boldest attempts ever ventured to improve the lot of an economically and socially depressed minority through government action.

J. MICHAEL MAHAR

Introduction

The Village Drummers — a traditional Untouchable occupation

Joan P. Mencher

MORRIS E. OPLER

North Indian Themes –
Caste and Untouchability

MY IMMEDIATE PURPOSE is to see whether a very rich and complex traditional culture, that of North India, can be analyzed in terms of themes. A further aim, of course, is to indicate the relation between the North Indian themes which are recognized and such institutions as caste and untouchability. Some explanation for the choice of the term "themes" may be useful. I sense the necessity of identifying organizing forces in cultures, but, because I suspect that the term "values" impels us (often unconsciously) to probe for what we have come to feel is ethical or edifying, I prefer to use the more neutral term "themes." After all, some incentive that we do not particularly admire may exist or may become a powerful force in a specific culture. Its moral merits may be debatable; its *importance,* however, may be undeniable. The criteria for determining themes (cultural pervasiveness, repetition, importance, etc.) have been set forth and discussed in some detail in previous papers.[1] Because of the number of themes of North India to which I would like to call attention — eleven, as I see it — all that can be offered in a paper is a suggestive outline; more complete justification and analysis have to be reserved for a later book.[2]

This is an amplification of a paper which appeared in the *Southwestern Journal of Anthropology,* Vol. 24, No. 3 (Autumn, 1968), under the title, "The Themal Approach in Cultural Anthropology and Its Application to North Indian Data."

[3]

Cultural Fission

In my view, the themes of a culture constitute an interpenetrating set of postulates or affirmations which encourage practices along certain lines, and the point at which one begins descriptively is a matter of convenience. Perhaps the tendency toward fission or cleavage in traditional North Indian culture is as good a theme as any with which to begin our survey. There is no need to strain for evidence, in the Indian context, of this inclination for the whole to break into smaller units. The existence of the four varna (or broad social divisions of the society), the presence of the numerous castes, and the further separation of the castes into subcastes are examples of the tendency. In North India, descent lines frequently divide into parallel or rival lineages, villages of a region often break off into competing clusters, and the inhabitants of a community may separate into contending factions. Such partitions of the whole are not characteristic of social groupings alone. Nowhere else has the partition of land proceeded as relentlessly as in India. Divisiveness is a constant threat even to the strong family organization and to what I shall call "familism," for it is anything but easy, in spite of sentiment and economic advantages, to prevent brothers of a joint family from separating after the death of their father. Religion is not untouched by this theme: knowledge, devotion, and good works are each possible and separate paths to salvation. The segments that result from Indian fission are differentiated but are not alienated from one another. Additively they comprise a recognized whole even though they are no longer an organic unity. Thus the Brahmans, Kshatriyas, Vaishyas, and Sudras form a varna system that is thought of as logically complete, and the clans into which the Kshatriyas have divided, in spite of their rivalries, constitute the Kshatriya varna. This ability to maintain common characteristics in spite of separation and to represent related goals in spite of differentiation is probably what Indians mean when they speak, as they often do, of "unity in diversity."

The Themes of Hierarchy and Dharma

The second theme to which I call attention has to do with hierarchy. The varna, castes, and subcastes are not only distinct — they are graded. In fact, there is very little in Indian life and thought which is not placed in some hierarchical series. The great divisions of time decline in merit throughout their progression. The holy men, or sadhus, who are supposed to be casteless and unworldly, nevertheless belong to ranked groups jealous of their prerogatives and sensitive concerning their rightful place in the religious processions. Interpretations pertaining to age, sex, food, work, and even the parts of the human body are all colored by the theme of hierarchy. The very supernaturals are arranged in a progression from high gods to the humblest of local spirits.

A third theme that I discern in Indian thought and behavior is a strong concern for duty or right action (dharma). It involves one's duties as a Hindu and is therefore often defined as the very essence of religion. Yet it encompasses one's duty to family, caste, and even to one's self-image just as much as it does one's religious obligations. It is closely related to the theme of hierarchy, for it emphasizes duty according to caste, station, age, and sex. In some respects it might be considered to be the moral counterpart of the theme of hierarchy. Consequently, in the main, it has been a conservative force and a bulwark of tradition.

Concern Over Ritual Purity

A fourth theme, one that influences a great range of behavior, is the concern over ritual purity. The other face of this coin is, of course, the fear of pollution. Indian purity and pollution are often discussed mainly in the context of untouchability, of the polluting influence of the touch or presence of the low caste person on the highborn. The extensions of the theme go far beyond this, however. Certain acts, such as the killing of a cow or the killing or mistreatment of a Brahman, are in themselves defiling and can be expiated only by ritual and purification. Certain periods and situations are polluting — a period after death for the chief mourner, a period after delivery for the mother, the period of menstruation for a woman. The kitchen of an orthodox household is considered polluted and the food being prepared in it unfit for household consumption if a child of the family, dirty from play, runs into it by mischance or if a woman of the family begins to cook in it without bathing and putting on fresh garments. Food and water are easily defiled; food boiled in water rather than fried in butter is particularly vulnerable in this respect. Food cooked outside the home by men of the family is less likely to be polluted than the same food cooked inside the home by women of the household. Contact with human or animal filth can pollute; so can the resumption of normal activities after the sacred thread one wears has broken and before it is replaced. Every place of worship, whether it be a family shrine or a temple, must be purified before ritual can begin. There is incessant use of fire and bathing for ritual purification. The number of ideas and practices which have grown up around this theme is enormous, and their subtleties and refinements are exceedingly intricate.

Primacy of the Male Principle

A theme that few students of traditional Indian culture would have much difficulty in identifying is one that affirms the ascendancy of the male principle. There is, as we shall see, a negative side to this, namely, some fear and suspicion of the female principle. In Indian philosophical thought, the highest manifestation of spirituality — perfect serenity and absence of desire — is considered to be a male attribute. The striving and activity that result in creation and change are attributed to female energy, or *shakti*. This insures life and mobility; by the same token it initiates a lapse from perfection and therefore ultimate sorrow. The female principle is always disturbing; the godlings of disease are invariably goddesses. Indian ritual observances are a good index to the differential estimation of the sexes. There is a rite to insure male offspring; the rituals of the sixth and twelfth days after birth are more elaborate if the newborn infant is a boy; the sacred thread ceremony, which formally inaugurates education, is limited to males; there are a number of ceremonies (for which girls and women take responsibility) to promote the health and longevity of males; and in the rituals to honor ancestors, the emphasis is upon aiding the spirits of departed males. At the time of a birth in a family, women of the neighborhood gather to sing songs of rejoicing only if the new family member is a boy. In fact, among the Kshatriyas, female infanticide formerly occurred. Until very recently, formal education for girls was rare, and inheritance laws and practices greatly favored the male. Even now there are marked differences in the amounts of education a typical family is willing to sponsor for boys and girls, and there is a decided differential in the sums a family will spend on medical services for males and females. In marriage the groom is expected to belong to a section or subsection of the caste that is higher in rank than that of his bride. Women are considered morally frail and in need of constant supervision; family difficulties are usually attributed to their pettiness and penchant for quarreling. In many areas of North India the high castes practice seclusion of women and prohibit the remarriage of widows; no such restrictions are placed on high caste men. A woman's status and acceptance in her husband's family are closely related to her ability to provide healthy sons to perpetuate the line.

The Theme of Familism

Another theme which is easily discernible in Indian culture I have called "familism," the conviction regarding the right of precedence of the close kin group over the individual. Among the expressions or projections of this theme are the strong positive feelings for the joint family, the willingness to pool family property, and the opposition to the separation of the smaller units from the joint family. It must be remembered that debts have traditionally been considered family responsibilities, no matter by whom incurred, and that persons who leave the family seat for outside employment are expected to remit as large a share of their earnings as possible to the family. Even punishment is visited upon the family rather than upon the individual; unless it abandons him, a family suffers outcasting along with a member who has outraged the community. An examination of marriage arrangements indicates the paramount interest of the family in the event. Various kin help make the decision, and they have important roles in the ritual and practical aspects of the occasion. Ancestor worship is the ritual cement of the family. In more mundane matters there are vigorous attempts to take care of one's own kin, too; in spite of legal penalties, nepotism is hard to suppress. Even in the modern context and against the backdrop of community development project efforts, the influence of familism is quite evident. Family loyalties and feuds are often at the root of difficulties encountered in stimulating concerted community action.

Harmony and Nonviolence

I have been impressed by the effects on Indian culture of the theme which urges and encourages harmony. For some contexts perhaps "balance," "consensus," or "compromise" are better terms for what is involved. It is the duty of the *malik,* or male head of the family, to deal justly and equitably with all family members and to prevent friction. The *panch,* or arbitrators in local and caste disputes, arrive at compromises rather than at clear-cut decisions which might fan grievance and set the stage for future conflict. The classical Hindu view of sickness (the *tridosh* theory) considers illness to be an imbalance, due to faulty diet or improper behavior, in the forces within the body which regulate health. Even at the highest level of philosophical and religious abstraction, serenity and calm are the goals, rather than a fighting faith or a restless quest for more vivid religious experience.

Somewhat similar in spirit to the theme of harmony, but exerting its own individual influence, is the theme of nonviolence, or *ahimsa.* This encompasses, among other things, the refusal to take life, the strong sanctions against "cow slaughter," and the vegetarianism that so many Hindus practice. I consider outcasting an expression or product of this theme: a person who violates caste rules or offends caste sensibilities is excluded and ignored rather than physically assaulted or executed. A family elder who is unhappy over the behavior of younger kin will fast and observe silence until his worried relatives promise to mend their ways. The religious teacher, or guru, of a family in which there is conflict will demonstrate his dissatisfaction by fasting until his abashed charges effect a reconciliation. A mistreated wife arouses sympathy by a quiet protest of this order. An offended Brahman will sit before the door of the one who has ill-used him, fasting and allowing his hair and nails to grow long. If any passerby inquires about his grievance, he does not hesitate to give full details. Public resentment rises against the one who has so upset a holy man. Should the Brahman die in a state of protest, the one responsible for his self-mortification would be considered guilty of a very grave sin. This type of behavior is the weapon which Gandhi and the Congress Party leaders used so dramatically against the British. Part of its effectiveness stemmed from the fact that the Indians so well understood and responded to its themal nature.

The Rational and the Transcendental

I well remember a visit I made to a Hindu religious center near Allahabad in North India. There at a shrine was a depiction of the important centers of the human body according to yogic doctrine. The image was mostly head and upper torso; it dwindled and atrophied as the lower part of the body was approached. All the centers important to knowledge and religion were pictured at the head. Everything possible was done graphically to magnify the importance of the mind, brain, and head and to minimize the role—and even the consciousness of the existence — of the rest of the body. It was clear that, as far as this branch of yoga was concerned, the lower part of the body and the loins had best be forgotten. What was being presented here was an aspect of the theme of intellectualism or rationalism, the affirmation that mind, or the intellect, is the prime reality and that the physical body is a poor and ephemeral thing. We can introduce here only a few of the expressions of this theme. The great seers, or Rishis, from whom sacred knowledge was passed to man, were born from the mind of God. By sheer knowledge these great seers grew to rival the gods in power. The respect in which the teacher, the guru, is held by Indians is well known. In the code of classical education, the mind was to be constantly exercised and the urges of the body suppressed. A student was pledged to Brahmacharya, or chastity. To him, as to others, the body was represented as a temporary cage and unimportant; its urges were to be mastered and were not to be allowed to become a distraction from study.

A companion theme to rationalism can be characterized by the term "transcendentalism." This theme not only supports the glorification of mind and the de-emphasis of the body, but it argues that reality is not to be found in the things of this earth. Its essential message is that the soul, rather than anything else, should be the object of our concern and that salvation, or final liberation of the soul from rebirth in determinate forms, should be the goal. All else is beguiling appearance, or *maya,* which will pass only to make way for other insubstantial and fleeting apparitions. Consequently, according to this theme, it is just an invitation to pain and regret to become too much attached to objects that are bound to slip from one's grasp or to cling to intimates whose coexistence with one is an accidental and temporary matter. Before we have the intelligence to grasp this, continues the argument, we are ordinarily deep in the toils of *maya;* the remainder of our life should be a withdrawal, through determinate stages, or *ashrama,* from the tempting distractions of the world in favor of a turning to religion. Actions should be directed toward accumulating merit in order to hasten final spiritual liberation. Consequently there is great emphasis in Hindu thought and religion on vows, fasts, and especially on sacrifice for spiritual ends. Renunciation is a common motif of Indian literature and art. Elaborate funeral rites are conducted to aid in the soul's journey.

Existence as Cyclical

The eleventh and last constituent of the North Indian themal system that I have been able to distinguish has to do with the conception of the rhythm of existence. We of the West tend to assume the inevitability of progress and of an upward evolutionary spiral. We are fond of assuring one another that history does not repeat itself and that each successive day is pregnant with new possibilities. The Indian theme which contrasts with this anticipates recurrence where we look for novelty; it asserts that existence proceeds in a cyclical manner. Thus, until final salvation intervenes, the soul is subject to endless cycles of rebirth. The world is regularly destroyed and rejuvenated. Time is divided into four great Yugas, or epochs, which succeed one another in fixed order. Not only is the sequence predetermined, but the characteristics of a period are always the same. I get the impression that, because of the influence of this theme, many Indians expect prominent families to rise and fall and rise again over time in the local context, that they expect governments to come and go, and that they are skeptical of the endless utopias pictured by planners and developers. Perhaps what I have expressed here in themal terms is more popularly referred to as the "fatalism of the East."

The Interaction of Themes

Although they are individually distinguishable, the themes of a system such as I have sketched have important reference for one another. Some obviously support others. The theme of male ascendancy is undoubtedly strengthened by the existence of a strong feeling for hierarchy. Some themes act as limitations or restraints on others. The emphasis on hierarchy encourages a strong sense of self-esteem and stimulates feelings of outrage when the position or prestige of a person or group is challenged. The themes of harmony and nonviolence provide some curbs on the vehemence with which the aggrieved strike out in such instances. Of course, the themes of harmony and nonviolence are themselves prevented from fullest expression by any fresh scars of social fission, by sensitivities jarred by considerations of hierarchy, or by resentments stimulated by familism. We have already noted that the theme of fission is likely to clash with that of familism when brothers ponder whether to continue a joint family arrangement. As this indicates, the bare identification of themes is merely a prelude to the study of the relation of themes to one another and of the adjustments and compromises in human activity which they dictate.

The material presented here, though it deals with but one culture, is meant to suggest that behind human behavior and the institutions into which it crystallizes lies a network of broad affirmation and assumptions — a themal system. This themal system changes over time, but ordinarily, slowly enough so that it can be described for a given period. Themes, and therefore themal systems, are conceptually manageable because they are condensed and abstract, but they are also solid and demonstrable because they are based on empirical fact, on the concrete data pertaining to the culture in question. In turning to a study of themes, we do not have to shuffle speculations or ignore the actual materials relating to human behavior which we have so laboriously accumulated. Rather, we follow the acts of man to their stimuli, to the themes they patently express and symbolize. As a result, we obtain some sense of cultural convergence. We see relations, consolidations, and purposes instead of scattered data. We understand at length that human behavior and its localizations, or cultures, are the elaboration of the fundamental and the simple by the infusion of subtlety, variation, and symbolism.

Finally, I would suggest that the study of institutions can be referred with profit to themal analysis. Since this book deals essentially with caste, and particularly with that extension of caste, untouchability (by which I mean here all the practical and psychological handicaps suffered by a Hindu of very low caste), it may be useful to determine what light a consideration of themes can throw on the present state and probable future of these institutions. Indian caste has hitherto most often been discussed largely as a reflection of social stratification; attempts to challenge or to modify it are said to be difficult because India has such a rigidly stratified social system. Yet what accounts for the "rigidity" and the resistance? In what does the inflexibility consist? To what traditions and rationalizations can the defenses of caste thinking and acting be traced? If analysis probes no deeper than to refer the matter to "social stratification," it amounts to little more than an exercise in circular reasoning. Meanwhile, Hindus continue to marry within caste almost without exception, and the successive reports on the progress of the abolition of untouchability continue to be gloomy.

How Themes Persist

Even a cursory examination of caste and untouchability in terms of themal analysis gives some indication of the reasons for the persistence of the features in which we are interested. The tendency to fission or cleavage that marks the culture makes reasonable and acceptable to its carriers the many castes, their subdivisions, and their requirements. This tendency to fission in the culture has not been reversed by recent political developments; if anything, it has been stimulated. The rivalries between north and south, the creation of linguistic states, and the proliferation of political parties point to the vitality of the theme in spite of all the straining to achieve national unity. Nor has the theme of hierarchy, another bulwark of casteism, lost too much ground in the last two decades. The princes and their retainers are gone, but a political and administrative hierarchy has arisen that more than fills their vacated niches. As a result of all this, to the surprise of many naive observers, caste rather than class has become a rallying point in many political campaigns, and even the extreme left chooses its candidates with an eye to the caste composition of the constituency.

Other strong affirmations that we have encountered in our review of themes also encourage rather than challenge caste and untouchability. The theme of duty, which includes caste duties as an important element, perpetuates distinctive caste practices and identifications. The concern for ritual purity and the fear of pollution, so central to Hinduism, sharply reduces the kind of interpersonal experience, intellectual exchange, and meaningful contact that could blur caste lines. Until this theme undergoes major relaxation or modification, there is little reason to think that the psychological props of untouchability will be seriously weakened or abandoned. Even the theme of familism contributes to the perpetuation of casteism, for it inhibits individual family members from striking out for themselves across caste lines. At least until the present time, the theme of the ascendancy of the male principle has been an indirect support of caste distinctions, for among other things it has guaranteed that the woman be a member of a subordinate division of her husband's caste, and it has thus prevented competition between the principles of caste and sex. Its consonance with a hierarchical order is also obvious. In short, we find that caste is entrenched and resistant not simply because we can say that the Indian social order is marked by stratification, but because a majority of the themes of the culture sanction some important aspect of caste practice.

Moreover, and this is most important, no part of the traditional themal system poses a serious threat to caste and untouchability; limiting themes which would contain the boundaries of caste are conspicuous by their absence. Thus, there is little in the traditional system to be cultivated and strengthened to the detriment of caste ideas. The Hindu theme of rationalism or intellectualism is too imbedded in antimaterialism to offer a solid point of departure against caste injustice. Rather than calling for firm rejection of present hardships, Indian transcendentalism promises ultimate escape from caste rigors. Nor does the cyclical view of existence encourage a critical attitude toward institutions, for by this guide they are considered at once too ephemeral and too inevitable for that. Even the theme of harmony, which should be difficult to reconcile with stark social inequality, has not been too serious a threat to caste, for its traditional thrust is to spur a search for some adjustment within the system rather than to challenge the system. Its influence is more likely to be mildly ameliorative than revolutionary.

Thus it seems fairly certain that caste and one of its polar expressions, untouchability, will not soon be swept away by a frontal attack. Caste will weaken noticeably only when the themes which lend it dignity and meaning lose momentum and general acceptance. Several of them are undergoing some slow erosion, and the sharpest edges of caste contrast can be expected to undergo continual blunting. Still, the total edifice shows no signs of crumbling yet, and what many beholders consider to be an anomaly in a modern state — caste and untouchability in India — are quite sure to persist for some time to come to perplex those scholars who have been impatiently waiting for class or national consciousness to erase them from the scene.

NOTES

[1] The bibliographic entries below will guide the reader to the author's previous work on themes:

OPLER, MORRIS E.

1945   Themes as Dynamic Forces in Culture, *American Journal of Sociology* 51:198–206 (No. 3).

1946a   An Application of the Theory of Themes in Culture, *Journal of the Washington Academy of Sciences* 36:137–66 (No. 5).

1946b   Rejoinder, *American Journal of Sociology* 52:43–44 (No. 1).

1948   Some Recently Developed Concepts Relating to Culture, *Southwestern Journal of Anthropology* 4:107–22.

1949   The Context of Themes, *American Anthropologist* 51:323–25.

1959   Component, Assemblage, and Theme in Cultural Integration and Differentiation, *American Anthropologist* 61:955–64.

1960   Myth and Practice in Jicarilla Apache Eschatology, *Journal of American Folklore* 73:133–53.

1962   Cultural Anthropology and the Training of Teachers of Foreign Languages, in *Seminar in Language and Language Learning: Final Report* by Dwight L. Bolinger and others. Seattle: University of Washington, 90–96.

1967   Article on "Themes of Culture," in *Wörterbuch der Soziologie*, Wilhelm Bernsdorf and Friedrich Bülow, eds. Stuttgart: Ferdinand Enke.

[2] Instances of nonconformity to a theme of a culture can be found, of course. It must not be thought that the behavior of every individual or all the behavior of any individual conforms neatly and completely to the themes of a culture. Themes account for a good deal of behavior, they prevent still other behavior from departing too far from their prescriptions, and they carry the threat of punishment from external sources or compunctions of conscience for those who do not heed them. Themes set the course and current of thought and action, but they do not eliminate the ripples and agitations of the waters. Nor do they guarantee that the river will not change its course sometime in the future.

There may be some differences in emphasis in the themal systems of North and South India; for instance, the theme of male ascendancy may be less strongly developed in the south. For this reason and because the writer's own research opportunities have been mainly in North India, the application of the themal approach is confined in this paper to North Indian data.

The themal system described has greatly influenced Muslims of the South Asian subcontinent; graded, caste-like social units, for example, are found among the Muslims. Yet many of the themes have special ties to religious and philosophical tenets of Hinduism and have their strongest influence upon the behavior of the Hindus of North India.

In the post-Independence period there has been a determined attempt by the Indian central and state governments, through legislation and educational programs, to challenge such themes as hierarchy and male ascendancy. Yet most of the population, especially in the rural regions, still responds positively to the themes identified.

PART I

The Untouchable's Role In Rural Communities

A sweeper-girl preparing dung cakes for her employer

J. M. Mahar

1.

J. MICHAEL MAHAR

Agents of Dharma in a
North Indian Village

THE ROLE OF THE UNTOUCHABLE in contemporary Indian society may be viewed as subject to two disparate and often conflicting sets of beliefs and values, here characterized as the "old" and the "new" dharmas — an ancient Indian concept often translated as "universal moral order." The "old" dharma, rooted in Hindu religious thought, provides ideological support for the caste system and the Untouchable's inferior position within that system. The "new" dharma, espoused in the Constitution adopted by the Republic of India in 1950, advocates principles of social and political equality for all and the abolition of untouchability. The following account examines the confrontation of these "dharmas" in the context of a North Indian village with particular attention being given to the "agents" of dharma and the effect of their actions on the lives of Untouchables residing in the village.

The setting of this study is the village of Khalapur, located ninety miles north of Delhi in the district of Saharanpur, Uttar Pradesh. Agriculture, with wheat and sugar cane as the principal crops, is the mainstay of the village economy. In 1954 Khalapur's population of 5,117

This account draws on material gathered in Khalapur as a member of a Cornell University research team from October, 1954, to June, 1956, and again under a Fulbright-Hays grant, from July, 1968, to June, 1969. Acknowledgement also is expressed here to Penelope Addiss for her many useful comments on this study; Gerald D. Berreman for his intellectual stimulation and observations during the latter phase of fieldwork; and Pauline M. Kolenda, whose publications on the Untouchables of Khalapur greatly enriched the perspective underlying this analysis.

included representatives of thirty castes including four groups considered
to be Untouchables and a full complement of the artisan and service
castes commonly found in the northern Gangetic plain. Rajputs are the
"dominant" caste of Khalapur as they own 90 percent of the land and
constitute 42 percent of the population. The second largest caste in
Khalapur, constituting 12 percent of the population, are known as
Chamars. These Untouchable agricultural laborers provide much of the
manpower for landowners in Khalapur and elsewhere in the region.
The traditional occupations of the other three Untouchable castes of
Khalapur are Sweeper, Shoemaker, and Weaver. Respectively they constitute 4, 2, and 1 percent of the village population. All told, one out of
every five residents of Khalapur is an Untouchable.

The Old Dharma

A legacy of the past still evident in Khalapur is the spatial isolation
of the Untouchables' residential quarters which are scattered about the
periphery of the village settlement. Prior to 1947, upper caste control
of the Untouchables was manifest in the right of eviction vested in the
landowner upon whose land an Untouchable was permitted to build his
house. The Untouchables' spatial isolation from the rest of the community may be viewed as the physical expression of more subtle social
barriers based on the avoidance of ritual pollution and other beliefs
rooted in Hindu tradition. Although physical contact with Untouchables
appears not to have inhibited many aspects of daily life, the Untouchable's touch was held to defile such things as cooked food, water, and
sacred places. Consequently, Untouchables were not allowed near upper
caste hearths or wells, and they were prohibited from entering the
village temple. Even in death, restrictions of this kind were applied to
Untouchables as they had to burn their dead in separate cremation
grounds. The observance of such distinctions, however, did not prevent
the development of lifelong associations in which Untouchables were
privy to the most intimate aspects of their employers' lives, and routine
interaction within the confines of tradition was usually free of tension
and conflict. The compartmentalization of attitudes relating to Untouchables was expressed by an elderly Rajput who had kept a Chamar
mistress for more than twenty years. When asked to explain how he
reconciled this liaison with his quite orthodox views on polluting powers
of Untouchables, the gentleman replied that he felt no qualms as he
had never accepted so much as a glass of water from her hands.

Untouchables were also called upon to perform *begar,* tasks outside the daily round for which no immediate compensation was paid. Such tasks included the women's plastering of their employers' houses prior to the monsoon and grinding of flour with stone querns, and similar manual labor by men and women on occasion. On the other hand, upper caste employers were expected to contribute to the payment of their employees' wedding expenses, and to aid them in sickness and old age. Upper caste employers were also expected to protect their Untouchable servants in conflicts with others and to arbitrate disputes that could not be reconciled within the Untouchable community. This paternalistic relationship, frequently reaffirmed by the distribution of food and clothing to servants on religious holidays and other occasions, elicited feelings of loyalty and dependence from the Untouchables.

While sharing many disabilities in common, the four Untouchable castes of Khalapur had no occasion to act in concert in the past. Nor did they conceive of themselves as sharing a common group identity. While all four castes advance claims to higher caste status based on origin myths, their myths are different, and they express little interest in or support for each other's claims. Each caste maintains its own well from which the other Untouchables may not draw water. Restrictions on commensality observed by the upper castes also govern the interaction of the Untouchables. These include restricting the smoking of hukka to members of one's own caste, and the prohibition against accepting cooked food prepared by a caste of lower rank. The economic relationships and ancillary ties between the four Untouchable castes and the upper castes, especially landowners, also differ in many respects. Only the Sweepers and Shoemakers pursue their traditional occupations within the system of reciprocal rights and obligations known as the *jajmani* system. In addition to receiving a fixed share of their employer's harvest, these castes were entitled to collect fuel and fodder from their patron's fields, and other "fringe benefits." The defiling nature of their work, including the Sweepers' handling of human excrement and the Shoemakers' removal of dead animals, provided them with bargaining power not available to the Weaver or Chamar whose goods and services could be provided by others. The *jajmani* system also fostered corporate action in such matters as the allocation of patrons, thereby limiting competition for traditional jobs, and the group's refusal to serve patrons who fail to honor their obligations. The Weavers and Chamars, on the other hand, were more subject to the vagaries of the marketplace due to competition from machine-made cloth and the willingness of many castes to work as agricultural laborers.

The numerical preponderance of Chamars among those skilled in cultivation set them apart from the other Untouchables in matters of employment. Compared to the strong ties fostered by the *jajmani* system, the link between tenant and landlord was relatively unstable. This instability may be attributed in part to the individual rather than group basis of landlord-tenant relations. There also appears to have been an element of competition between landlords for the Chamar's service. Prior to 1900, when, according to local accounts, there was no shortage of land in Khalapur, the prestige and economic return to be derived from the control of large landholdings was dependent upon the acquisition and retention of tenants, most of whom were Chamars. Debt often served as a means of retaining tenants, although it also fostered conflict and tension. According to both landlords and tenants, a common practice in the past was for a landlord to provide a Chamar with seed, equipment, and an advance in cash or grain for which the Chamar promised to cultivate the landlord's fields for one-fourth of the crop. Frequently the Chamar would turn to his employer for additional loans to meet wedding or other expenses. Not uncommonly, the initial loan plus interest, ranging around 25 percent per annum, and the exigencies of daily life would increase the Chamar's debt to his employer to the extent that he could not expect to pay it in his lifetime. Since loans were often held to be the responsibility of a man's sons, an entire family might become bound to a landlord. In many instances while this arrangement appeared not to have troubled either party, especially if the Chamar's daily needs were reasonably well met, nevertheless the existence of the debt limited the Chamar's choice of employer.

Another restriction on the Chamar's freedom of choice in matters of employment is described in a British settlement report prepared in 1839 for the district in which Khalapur is situated. According to this account Chamars were bound to work for those upon whose land their house was located. In Khalapur, the "Puttee" divisions of the village site referred to below were dominated by Rajput lineages.

The disputed rights requiring adjustment at the time of settlement, have been very few, and the ground of dispute is so easily ascertained from the parties themselves, that the cases are very simple. The most frequent cause of dispute has been a claim to an equal division of the Village site. I notice this, because for some time I did not learn the real nature of these claims, the land now forming the village site, had been common property; *one Puttee has located Chummars*, or rent-paying cultivators, another has not. *These non-proprietary residents work in the Puttee which located them*, and the manure formed in their bullock sheds and yards, goes to its land. The other Puttee then advances a claim, that the land forming the village site, should be divided, according to the acknowledged shares, and possession in the cultivation of the two Puttees. They have frequently obtained it, although a great outcry is always raised by the other party against such a claim. *They then threaten such portion of the Chummars and cultivators as live in the portion of the village site they have acquired with ejectment from their tenements, unless they work for them, exclusively;* but indeed few threats are necessary, for the people understand the previous process thoroughly, as a division of cultivators and laborers, and *the persons transferred, look upon it as an understood thing that they become the ryuts, as they call themselves of the other party.**[Italics added] [1839:52].

Another implication of this account, that Chamars were pawns in the rivalry between landlords, indicates considerable antiquity in the political role of Chamars, a fact that emerged in post-Independence village politics.

A comparison of Chamar genealogies with those of other castes reveals other reasons for their subordination — their lack of numerically strong and residentially stable kin groups. The small size of Chamar kin groups was attributed in part to the fact that they rarely owned land. In contrast to the land-owning Rajputs, who readily trace their descent back seven or more generations, very few Chamars could recall the names of their great grandfathers. The shallow depth of Chamar lineages appears to be a correlate of their high degree of residential mobility in comparison to other castes represented in Khalapur. A common reason advanced to account for Chamar change of residence was escape from debt. While both landlord and Chamar informants agreed that Chamars frequently resolved debtor-creditor conflicts by clandestine departure for another village, the landlords viewed such behavior as absconding without paying a just debt, while the Chamars regarded the same act as the only alternative to a lifetime of slavery. Creditors appear to have made little effort to extradite debtors or to enforce debt claims even though debtors rarely fled more than twenty miles. This may be due to the poverty of the debtors from whom little could be obtained and the wide variety of landowning castes in the area whose rivalry offset their common interest as landlords.

Another aspect of kinship organization, that of affinal alliance, also appears to affect the Untouchables' role in society. In contrast to the Rajputs, whose marriage ties extend on the average more than thirty miles from Khalapur, the average distance of Untouchable marriages is less than fifteen miles. The occupation of those with whom Untouch-

---

*Edward Thornton, *Report on the Settlement of the district of Seharunpore* completed 1st February, 1839. Submitted to Government by the Sudder Board of Revenue, N.W.P. 18th October, 1840.

ables establish marriages also stands in marked contrast to those of the Rajputs and other upper caste landowners. While the affinal ties of the landowning castes intimately link them to families possessing wealth and authority in the economic and governmental structure of the region, the Untouchables marry menial laborers and, on rare occasions, minor clerks in the government bureaucracy. Since employment opportunities outside the village and access to political power and government authority are strongly influenced by considerations of kinship, the disparity in economic and political power found between Untouchable and landlord in Khalapur also prevails in their relations with the world beyond the village.

Social Disabilities

One disability shared in common by all four Untouchable castes has been the refusal of the village Brahmans, Barbers, and Washermen to serve them. Consequently, marriage rites and other ceremonies, performed by Brahman priests for the other castes, have been performed by caste elders within each Untouchable group. A member of each group has performed the role of barber as a part-time occupation, and the services of a Muslim washerman in a nearby village have been used on the rare occasion when the Untouchables have not washed their own clothes. Thus, the denial of services to Untouchables has served to define their lowly place in the caste hierarchy.

It is, however, the members of the "dominant" Rajput caste who have acted as the enforcement agents of the "old dharma." They have actively kept the Untouchables in their place and policed any threat to the status quo, as exemplified in an episode observed in 1955:

A man of the Shoemaker caste was observed as he was about to enter Khalapur with a load of tanned cow hides on his head. An elderly Rajput rose from his porch, brandished a stick, and threatened to thrash the shoemaker if he did not reverse his course and proceed around the outskirts of the village.

Although the "voice of dharma" was rarely raised in such an explicit manner, other lessons imparted by Rajputs regarding the niceties of behavior based on caste status were observed, including the beating of Untouchables caught drawing water from upper caste wells located in the jungle.

Spatial expression of status has also been observed in situations where men of various castes gather to discuss affairs of the day. Although Untouchables occasionally join in such discussions, and the tenor and content of the conversation is that of men born and raised within a hundred yards of one another, the Untouchable inevitably squats a few yards from the group and never sits on a cot in the presence of social superiors.

On one occasion, for example, an elderly Chamar was invited into the anthropologist's room and asked to be seated on a chair. At first the Chamar declined, but after much urging, he sat down. Shortly thereafter a middle-aged Rajput happened to glance into the room. He immediately cursed the Chamar and told him to remove himself from the chair or he would be beaten for his impertinence.

Clothing also serves to distinguish the Chamar women, whose distinctive blouse and skirt stand in sharp contrast to the saris worn by other women of the village. Policing of sumptuary "laws" was rare, but incidents of the following kind no doubt serve to reinforce this custom:

In 1954 the young wife of a shoemaker, a woman of city origin, appeared in the village wearing a necklace made of gold. While silver ornaments are worn in abundance by Untouchable women, the use of gold was "known by all" to be forbidden to Untouchables. Accordingly, the shoemaker's wife was called to account by Rajput women who told her to remove the necklace or she would be beaten. She complied.

While the costume worn by Chamar women readily sets them apart from other castes, clothing worn by men of the Untouchable castes is as varied as that worn by other men of the village. Other aspects of physical appearance, including skin pigmentation and stature, appear to vary within the Untouchable population to the same extent as they do in other castes. However, while no difference in physical traits distinguishes Untouchables from the upper castes, their mode of behavior in social situations is markedly different.

The inculcation of attitudes of inferiority may be seen in the every-day experience of the very young. It does not require much time for the Sweeper child accompanying his mother on her daily rounds to realize his position in society. The nature of the tasks performed by an Untouchable's parents, the mode of address and the tone of voice used by upper castes in issuing instructions, are readily apparent to children. The sending of Sweeper children to collect food left over from upper caste feasts, their receipt of "gifts" on inauspicious occasions such as the eclipse of the sun, and their "right" to the clothing of the dead — all serve to reaffirm their association with pollution and inferior status. The aversion to Chamars of the agricultural laborers' caste, on the other hand, is not founded on their present occupation or habits, which differ little from those of upper caste farmers. Rather, their stigma is attributed to their association with leatherwork in which none of the Khalapur Chamars have engaged for more than a century. The link with polluting activities is even more tenuous for members of the Weaver caste, who participate more freely than the other three Untouchable castes in the social life of their upper caste neighbors.

Upper caste children readily learn their superior station in life by observing their parents issuing orders to the family Sweeper or Chamar laborer (Mintern and Hitchcock 1966:10). The inculcation of upper caste attitudes and manners are furthered by a variety of means including the telling of religious stories praising the heroic exploits of their Rajput ancestors in struggles for temporal power. On the other hand, the achievements of the Untouchables' mythical ancestors, such as Valmiki and Rai Das, are in the other-worldly realm of religion. The strong imprint of caste identity imparted by the family is exemplified in a story told by an elderly Rajput whose childless wife "adopted" the orphaned daughter of one of his Chamar employees in 1945. Although bringing an Untouchable child into a Rajput home was viewed as very deviant by the community, the spatial isolation of this Rajput household on the periphery of the village, adjacent to the Chamar quarters, and the absence of other children in the home of a woman beyond childbearing age, appear to have contributed to the general acceptance of this arrangement.

From the age of five, the Chamar girl lived with her Rajput foster parents. However, when she reached puberty her foster father summoned the elders from the Chamar quarters and told them to find a husband for the girl. Arrangements were duly made through the usual channels of kin ties and members of the Chamar community carried out the customary wedding ceremony in the Chamar quarters. Although the Rajput foster parents did not attend the wedding, they contributed substantially to the girl's dowry and paid the wedding costs.

A few days later while the Rajput was passing through his mango orchard he heard someone sobbing. Looking into a tree he saw his foster daughter hidden in the foliage. After calming the girl he took her to his home where she told of the abuse and mistreatment which she had received from her in-laws. She said they had beaten her and locked her in a room from which she escaped at night and then followed the canal back to her parental village. She did not come directly to her foster parents as she was too ashamed to face them. The Rajput, infuriated by the girl's tale, went to the other village and soundly thrashed the girl's husband and father-in-law. He in turn was set upon by the Rajputs of that village who told him that no outsider could beat their servants. An inter-village panchayat (council) was held to review the issue which was finally resolved by the return of the girl's jewelry, given to her by her foster father, and the dissolution of the marriage.

Elder members of the Chamar community confirmed this story as told by the Rajput, but they added a few critical details. According to them, the girl was beaten because she refused to perform menial chores assigned by her mother-in-law. This challenge of adult authority was compounded by the girl's attitude toward her in-laws and their neighbors. She apparently let it be known by word and gesture that she considered them to be uncouth Untouchables unworthy to command the "daughter" of a Rajput. As one Chamar expressed it, "she stunk like a Rajput." Although there exists considerable variation in the behavior of individuals, caste differences in manner and speech often serve to distinguish the Untouchables from others (Gumperz 1958).

Caste disparities in self-image and social skills engendered by childhood training also influenced the ability of adults to contend with the world beyond the village. An example of this appears in the case of a Chamar who went to Delhi to obtain treatment for tuberculosis.

Three days after leaving for Delhi the Chamar returned to the village in tears. When asked why he was not admitted to the government hospital the Chamar related a tale reflecting his ignorance of hospital procedure and his fear of the orderlies and clerks. He apparently had sat in the entrance to the hospital for two days. When no one offered to help him he came home. His Rajput employer, upon hearing this tale, let loose a string of abuse aimed at the callous city-dwellers and the Chamar's stupidity. Then, as he was planning to visit relatives in Delhi the following day, he offered to take the Chamar to the hospital.

Upon arrival at the hospital, the Rajput marched up to the admissions desk and demanded in a loud voice that someone attend to the needs of his companion. He guided the Chamar through the maze of hospital procedure, and then sallied forth to see the sights of the city.

Differences of this kind and the Untouchable's dependence upon upper caste intermediaries in dealing with extra-village institutions and authorities, appear in many other aspects of village life.

In summary, agents of the old dharma affecting the lives of the Untouchables in Khalapur include the Brahmans and other serving castes whose denial of services set the Untouchables apart from the other castes in the community. The Rajputs, through their exercise of economic and political power, punished individual deviance from the role prescribed for Untouchables. Members of one's family and caste fellows also inculcated modes of behavior in keeping with one's caste identity. Ancient traditions including the transmission of craft skills within the caste, and restrictions on the use of wells and temples, also served to keep the Untouchables in their place. The government, mainly administered at the local level by members of the upper castes, did little to offset the dominance of the agents of the old dharma in village affairs prior to India's Independence.

The New Dharma

During the years immediately following India's Independence in 1947, the villagers of Khalapur were deeply affected by the spirit of reform that pervaded the nation. Agents of the new dharma, enunciated in the Congress party platform and the Constitution of 1950, came to the village on a number of occasions. Meetings were held in which prominent Congress party leaders, including the Chief Minister of Uttar Pradesh, told the Untouchables of their new rights and the abolition of untouchability. The governor substantiated his views by drinking a glass of water provided by a village sweeper in full sight of the crowd. He asked the upper castes to adopt Gandhi's use of the term "Harijan" instead of traditional terms for Untouchables. One meeting, attended by members of all the castes, was held in front of the village temple. The outside authorities told those assembled that Untouchables were now free to enter the temple and their children could attend the local schools. They were also told that the Untouchables had title to their home sites. The practice of *begar,* forced labor, was also declared illegal. On other occasions, Congress party members of Untouchable origin visited the Chamar quarters and reiterated the message.

These new ideas were enthusiastically welcomed by the Untouchables, and openly acknowledged by a few upper caste leaders, mainly members of the Congress Party. Overt opposition to these reforms did not appear during the initial year or two following the meetings. However, after the first wave of enthusiasm had passed, life fell back into the old routine, including reversion to calling Untouchables by common terms such as "Bhangi" and "Chamar," instead of the term "Harijan." While none of the landlords disputed the Untouchables' claim to their house sites, and the admission of Untouchables to the village school was substantially increased without incident, Untouchables were actively discouraged from using the village temple and public wells. Although two instances were noted in which Untouchable men were beaten for their surreptitious use of upper caste wells, a government program to improve village water facilities served to mute this issue as the Untouchables were given funds to renovate wells in their neighborhoods.

Education

Although the Untouchable gained very little material benefit from other government programs, and refrained from testing his new rights of temple entry, the new dharma's dispensation regarding education was implemented in both the elementary and secondary schools located in the village. Prior to Independence few men of the Untouchable castes had attained literacy and most of them were educated outside Khalapur or by informal study with a literate member of their own caste.

While less than a dozen Untouchable boys were enrolled in the village primary school in 1947, by 1954, three Sweeper and two Chamar boys had progressed to the eighth grade of the "Inter-College" established in Khalapur in 1950. These Untouchables sat in the classrooms with upper caste students and participated in the full curriculum, but they kept to themselves in most social situations, and they were not allowed to use the school dining facility. Untouchables from other villages resided in the Untouchable quarters of Khalapur rather than in the school hostel.

Although social barriers to education were removed for the Untouchables, economic restraints kept most of the boys in their traditional occupations as cowherders or field hands. Government financial assistance amounting to Rs. 5 a month was provided only for Harijan students in the first grade of the elementary school. The Inter-College Harijan fund, administered by the principal, could support only two scholarships. Students in the seventh to the tenth grades receive Rs. 10 to Rs. 12 a month, and those in the eleventh and twelfth receive Rs. 15 per month, a sum equalling about half the current wage paid an adult male field hand. In one instance, that of a Chamar who managed to obtain a B.A. degree in a town nearby, the government scholarship was not paid until the completion of the college year. This delay in payment forced his family to borrow funds for his education at a rate of interest that reduced the value of the scholarship by a third.

Education at the Inter-College level engendered new aspirations among the Untouchable students. Their knowledge of Sanskrit provided the Untouchable community with access to sacred texts previously denied them. This was most apparent among the Sweepers who elevated a fifteen-year old student to a position of prominence in their ritual life. This youth's recitations from the Veda became a major feature of their life cycle and calendrical rites. Several of the educated Sweeper youths established classes to teach their elders how to read and write, acting in response to an Independence Day speech given at the Inter-College by an Indian social scientist who called upon the students to improve their nation by improving their community. They also sought to introduce higher standards of sanitation in their living quarters and launched a plan to encourage the daily sweeping of the village lanes. Although both schemes fell into abeyance after a month or two, due to the indifference of the elders, the alliance of nationalist sentiment with group aspirations elicited a dramatic response among Untouchables that might well have been sustained with support and leadership based outside the village.

Although several organizations for the improvement and "uplift" of Untouchables existed in the region, including one headquartered at Hardwar forty miles from Khalapur, they seemed to have exerted little discernible influence in the village. Apart from one elder of the Sweeper community none of the village Untouchables mentioned participating in such organizations although a few had attended meetings for Harijan "uplift" in the bazaar town located six miles from Khalapur. This one exception, the only literate sweeper of his generation in the village, maintained contact with the leaders of the Valmiki Improvement Society situated in the district headquarters forty miles distant. Support for the society was drawn mainly from the Sweeper enclave of the local railroad cantonment, where a shrine to Valmiki was built. This shrine served as a meeting place for religious ceremonies and organization of an annual parade held on Valmiki's birthday. Leaders of the society expressed little interest in linking their organization to other caste-based groups seeking to ameliorate the lot of Untouchables in general. The society apparently made no effort to recruit members from among caste fellows residing in the surrounding villages. The few links that existed, as exemplified by the Sweeper from Khalapur, were forged by individuals interested in the religious activities of the society or those who had exchanged women in marriage with families residing in the railroad cantonment.

Voluntary organizations for the purpose of uplifting the Untouchable population do not appear to mesh with the traditional intervillage networks based on marriage and kinship, although the opinions and support of caste elders and kinsmen are still sought for the arbitration of disputes between caste members, the codification of customs pertaining to marriage, and other caste matters. This failure to tap traditional channels of communication and authority may well be due to the urban origin of many of those seeking to organize their village brethren, and the reliance of such organizations on pamphlets and mass meetings as the primary means for enlisting interest and support. The goals of these organizations, as set forth in their pamphlets, offer little to interest the villager as they are couched in sweeping generalities often rooted in the premise that the Untouchables must improve themselves in order to gain their rightful place in society.

On the other hand, political parties and the introduction of elections provided the Untouchables with an appreciation for the power of the vote. Their mentors in Khalapur were the Rajputs, who, in the initial election of 1949 advanced competing candidates for the office of village *pradhan,* chairman of the village council. Although such traditional ties as those binding landlord and tenant, employer and employee, ultimately decided this contest — the fact that Rajputs considered it necessary to solicit support from Untouchables, even though by intimidation in many instances, set many Untouchables to considering the potential of their vote in future elections (Retzlaff 1962). For instance, in 1955, members of the Shoemaker caste stated they would support a candidate for village *pradhan* only if he promised to remove the yard used for the disposal of dead animals from their compound to a site outside the village settlement. Other Untouchables voiced their desire to acquire more land for housing from an area contingent to their compound that was under the jurisdiction of the village council. Despite this interest in local elections, candidates for state and national office and related political issues held little interest for the Untouchables during the decade following Independence. The Congress ticket received most of the Untouchables' votes as the Congress-controlled government was credited with introducing the reforms that touched upon the Untouchables' lives.

One of the most ambitious reforms was the Zamindari Abolition Act passed by the Congress-controlled Uttar Pradesh legislature in 1953. The intent of this legislation was to abolish large estates consisting of land tilled by tenants and to vest ownership of this land in the hands of the cultivator. This law provided that tenants who had tilled the same parcel of land during the preceding five years might file claim to the land. If a tenant's claim was validated, he could then obtain a clear title by paying the government ten times the annual tax due on the parcel of land. The Zamindar whose previous rights to this land were thus superceded received government bonds as compensation.

Although the Zamindars of Khalapur lost all their rights to land outside the village, only four of the 6,000 acres of Khalapur land passed into the hands of the Untouchables, even though many of them, especially the Chamars, were tenant farmers. Several factors impeded the implementation of Zamindari Abolition in Khalapur. For one, the Zamindars were aware of the major provisions of the law prior to its enactment. By transferring excessive land to their relatives and by shifting tenants from one parcel of land to another each year, they managed to retain much of the land within the traditional land-owning castes. In the few instances where Untouchables could claim continuous cultivation of a plot of land for five years, the procedures for filing a claim required coping with bureaucratic complexities which few could comprehend. The problem of raising the capital needed to pay the government, and the reluctance to entrust such a sum to government officials, also served to deter Untouchables from pressing their claims. Only two Untouchables, one a Shoemaker, the other a Chamar, managed to gain title to land under this law and the Chamar was forced to sell his holding two years after its acquisition. This sale was brought about by various harassments that culminated in the destruction of his crop by "unknown" marauders shortly before harvest. Coercion of this kind and "hints" from powerful landlords finally forced him to sell his land to a Rajput neighbor. In this manner, agents of the old dharma effectively stifled one effort to enhance the economic position of the Untouchables. While some Untouchables voiced their resentment of the Rajput's thwarting of the law, others felt that the land rightfully belonged to the Rajputs. All of the Untouchables viewed the situation as being one in which they could not challenge the Rajputs and expect to remain in the village.

The abolition of Zamindari holdings in other villages forced many Zamindars to turn to the direct cultivation of land previously tilled by tenants. Land consolidation, carried out in 1955, furthered this trend by providing each owner with a few large plots of land instead of many fragmented holdings. In contrast to the past, when a landlord felt obliged to provide economic assistance to sick or elderly employees, or to loan large sums for an employee's wedding, the growing reliance on wage labor paid in cash led to the transformation of employer-employee relations. This change was furthered by a substantial increase in the volume of cash in the village, generated by a greater demand for sugar cane after Independence. However, the Untouchables' loss of economic security based on landlord paternalism was offset in large part by an increase in the demand for their labor brought about by the introduction of improved methods of cultivation in the 1950s.

The major impetus to change in agriculture came from the nation-wide community development program started in Khalapur in 1954. This government program introduced improved varieties of crops, chemical fertilizer, and new techniques of cultivation. Most of these innovations were labor-intensive and increased the demand for agricultural laborers. This, coupled with an increasing flow of cash from the sale of sugar cane, led the Chamars to strike for higher wages. After a week-long series of negotiations between elders of the Chamar and Rajput castes, a wage increase from 25 to 30 rupees a month was established. During the following decade, similar negotiations led to a doubling of the 1954 wage scale. Inflation offset much of this gain in wages as the cost of living increased at approximately the same rate.

Apart from sharing in the general prosperity that accompanied the transformation of agriculture, the Untouchables derived few material benefits from the community development program. The one concrete contribution to their welfare was the construction of improved wells in the living quarters. This was done in a joint effort, with the government providing materials and the Untouchables contributing their labor. The Shoemakers also obtained a Rs. 1500 loan from the government to aid them in the manufacture of shoes for sale outside the village. This loan was used to help pay for the construction of a brick building used as a workshop and men's quarters. The loan did not, however, appear to have substantially increased production as the Shoemakers claimed they were unable to repay the loan a decade after its receipt. A community development program to improve the production of handmade cloth failed to aid the Untouchable Weavers as the trainee-stipends were allotted to several destitute Rajput youths, who made no use of the training.

Since the main thrust of the community development program went to the improvement of agricultural productivity, many of the benefits from such nation-building activity accrued to those who owned the land. Much the same conclusion can be drawn from the Shramdan (voluntary contribution of labor) road-building program. Improved roads were of most benefit to those who wished to transport sugar cane to the mills located several miles from the village, as exemplified in the acquisition of rubber-tired bullock carts by landowners. Although this was defined as a "voluntary" program, the Chamars were ordered by Rajput members of the village council to provide one able-bodied man per family each day of the Shramdan program. Rajput participants in Shramdan most often contributed their "supervisory" skills to the task at hand while the lower castes wielded pick and shovel (Dube 1958).

A Decade Later

An investigation conducted in Khalapur during 1968-1969, revealed some improvement in the economic conditions of the Untouchables, but little overt change in their social and political status in the village. Although many features of the "new dharma" remained viable, much of the village life was still regulated by the "old dharma" in muted form. The most readily apparent change during the previous decade was the marked increase in prosperity created by improvements in agriculture. Greater profits from the sale of sugar cane during the preceding three years, due to a loosening of government controls, placed substantial sums of cash in the hands of landowners. Much of this money was invested in new housing built of fired brick, a traditional expression of affluence, and a response to the substantial increase in population. The introduction of electricity into the village also provided wealthy families with an opportunity to invest in home lighting, radios, and minor appliances. On the side of productive investment, several landowners had acquired electric-powered chaff-cutters and tubewells. The number of tractors had increased from one to six and a wide variety of tractor-powered farm implements was to be seen.

The obvious affluence shown by the land-owning upper caste villagers was not as readily apparent among the Untouchables. Although one Chamar compound had constructed a small cement shrine for Rai Das, their patron deity, only one Chamar family had built a house of fired brick. For most Untouchables, the living space available for their use was considerably reduced due to increased population. None of the Untouchables made use of electricity and only three of them owned transistor radios. Four youths, employed outside the village, had acquired bicycles, and a dozen men wore wristwatches for the first time in their lives. Little change was noted in attire other than a greater incidence of a "pajama" (shalwar-kamiz) style of women's wear introduced from the Punjab. This adoption of a different mode of dress avoided a possible confrontation on the issue of Untouchable women wearing saris. Prohibitions against the Untouchable's use of the village temple and upper caste wells were still observed, and no one had ventured to challenge such restrictions in the courts even though the illegality of these practices was known.

On the positive side, Untouchable children appeared to be much better fed and clothed than a decade earlier and most families could afford medical care and medicine previously beyond their means. Such changes may be attributed in large part to full employment. Both upper and lower castes agreed there was a shortage of field hands in the village, although the purchasing power of their wages, Rs. 55 to 60 a month, remained about the same due to inflation.

In 1968, the number of Untouchable male children in school had increased substantially over those enrolled in the 1950s, but the percentage of those in school was far below that of the landowning castes. Although no Untouchable girls were attending school, their parents said this was due to the need for the girls' assistance at home rather than any restrictions imposed by others. Little concern was expressed for the need to provide educated wives for educated men. One group of pre-school children was observed "playing school" with a first-grader acting as teacher. The participation of girls in this form of play points to the possibility that such anticipatory training might lead to the education of girls in the not-too-distant future. The major barrier to the education of Untouchables was held to be economic. Untouchable parents said that government scholarships did not meet all school expenses and most families did not want to lose the income earned by their children as cowherders and field hands.

The eight Untouchable graduates of the local Inter-College had obtained "white-collar" jobs, six of them as primary school teachers in villages within the district. The other two had gone on to college and later acquired technical positions in the lower echelons of the civil service. They resided in towns more than a hundred miles from the village. One of these men reported that he had experienced very little discrimination in his place of work and residence, but he missed the association with friends and relatives. Apparently the other suffered a mental breakdown, as he killed himself and his wife after they had a series of violent quarrels. A similar case of domestic strife, ending in the death of the wife, was reported for another Untouchable graduate of the Inter-College, who taught in a distant village. Since extreme behavior of this kind is relatively rare among Untouchables, who, in contrast to the upper castes, allow divorce, the possibility arises that the "freedom" imparted by education and residence outside the parental village may take considerable emotional toll through social isolation and greater dependence upon the immediate family.

One Chamar obtained a teaching position in one of the three Khala-pur primary schools. Although the presence of this Untouchable "master" in the classroom, composed mainly of upper caste pupils, was readily accepted by the villagers, this young man and his family continued to reside in the Untouchable quarters. While treated as a colleague in the school setting, and an active participant in the teachers' union, this Untouchable teacher avoided situations involving interaction with upper caste villagers outside the classroom. On the few occasions where interaction of this kind was observed, both parties were embarrassed by the problem of seating which was resolved by placing the Untouchable teacher on a separate cot. After one situation of this kind, the Rajput housewife insisted that the men of her family who had sat with the Chamar bathe before she would serve them food.

Outside the village, however, the Chamar teacher maintained numerous contacts with government officials and the leaders of the teachers' union. During the successful statewide strike for higher wages sponsored by the teachers' union in the fall of 1968, this young man marched with his upper caste colleagues in a protest staged at the district headquarters. His class also won an award in a district tournament, an achievement in which he took much pride. Although this young man had not ventured into politics, nor was he affiliated with any Harijan improvement organization, his contacts with officialdom outside the village and the organizational skills learned in the teachers' union provide him with a basis not known by his father and most of his peers, for future action on his caste's behalf.

While the term "Harijan" was commonly used by the upper castes when referring to Untouchables, the old patterns of interaction prevailed in the daily round of activities within the village. Outside the village setting, however, traditional patterns of this kind were rarely observed.

For example, individuals whose caste identity was well known to one another, and who would never sit together on a cot in the village, felt no qualms about squatting shoulder to shoulder in the narrow confines of the horse carts that provided regular taxi service between Khalapur and the nearest town, a service developed after the construction of an all-weather road in 1957. In this highly "touchable" setting, Sweeper and Rajput, Chamar and Brahman, were observed casually conversing with one another about village affairs.

Accommodation to the new dharma was also noted in situations involving officials of Untouchable origin who were generally treated with the respect due an educated man of authority. One case was observed in which a touring minor official, a Chamar, was invited to spend the night in a Rajput's *chopal,* or men's quarters. He was provided a bed and bedding, and served his evening meal with other men of the family. This Chamar entered freely into the Rajputs' conversation and even ventured contradictory opinion on matters of puranic lore. The Rajputs' ready acceptance of this official stood in marked contrast to the host's treatment of his Chamar employee and other Untouchable residents of the village who were never allowed to sit on his cots.

The importance of the village panchayat also appears to have diminished during the preceding decade. This may have been due to a reduction in the village land subject to the panchayat's control, a factor of major importance in the early 1950s when village land was subject to sale. The penetration of outside government agencies, such as the community development program, into the lives of the villagers, may also have divested the council of some authority. The president of the panchayat, a member of the Vaish (merchant) caste, seemed to be playing a rather passive role dedicated to maintaining the status quo. The Untouchable members of the panchayat continued to occupy a nominal position with little power. Their presence on the village council, however, was still a physical affirmation of the Untouchables' right to hold public office even though this right was based on authority located outside the village.

In contrast to previous elections, the 1964 election of a representative to the national legislature included a candidate of Untouchable origin. This young man, a resident of Lucknow, the state capital, contested the election on the Republican Party ticket. Although only two of the 1600 Untouchables of Khalapur were active members of the Republican Party, many others attended an election rally held in a nearby town in order to hear a speech by the son of Dr. Ambedkar. When the time came to vote, however, the Untouchables of Khalapur and other villages in the area gave little support to the Republican candidate. A common reason given for this electoral behavior was that the Republican candidate had little prospect of winning — a vote cast for him was a vote lost. Even those who favored the goals of the Republican Party contended that it was not sufficiently strong to win public office, and therefore their vote would be most effective if given to the Congress Party which held power and was sympathetic to their interests. This assessment of the Republicans' strength was well founded if judged in terms of previous elections and the one held in February, 1969, when only one of 341 seats in the state legislature was won by that party. Another common reason given in 1969 for supporting Congress was that votes diverted to the Republican Party might enable the Jana Sangh, a militant Hindu party, to win the election. This prospect was looked upon with disfavor by all the Untouchables with whom the matter was discussed.

The absence of a leader was the most common reason advanced to account for the weakness of the Republican Party and the reluctance of Khalapur Untouchables to become actively involved in politics. In the absence of leadership and a strong organization based on resources outside the village, the consensus was that little could be achieved by active participation in party politics. Concern was also voiced regarding the Rajputs' reactions and likely punishment of anyone who might seek to promote a militant political program on the Untouchables' behalf.

The Buddhist movement that had gained widespread acceptance in the Untouchable communities of Agra and Maharashtra in the 1950s and 1960s had no adherents in Khalapur. The few who knew of the movement expressed their unwillingness to participate in it, as they felt conversion to Buddhism would not improve their position in the village — a Chamar by any other name would still be treated as a Chamar. Several men also voiced the view that they were Hindus, and they did not want to foresake their own religion despite the denial to them of Brahman services and access to the village temple. In this sense, further diminution of the old dharma appears to depend upon more profound changes outside the province of the village community.

2.

JOAN P. MENCHER

Continuity and Change in an Ex-Untouchable Community of South India

ANTHROPOLOGICAL STUDIES in South India have focused largely on the higher castes, or on the lower castes from the vantage point of the higher, even though the traditional system and ongoing changes often appear very different when seen from below. A few notable exceptions include Aiyappan's work among the Nayadis and Tiyyars (1937, 1944, 1948, and 1965). The present study concentrates on those aspects of the past and present that affect the role of the Paraiyans, a caste whose name has become synonymous with "Untouchable" in the English variant "pariah." The spelling of Paraiyan adopted here follows that used in the 1961 Census of India, although many variants appear in earlier accounts. During the past few decades, members of this caste have stopped using their traditional name, due to its derogatory associations, and prefer to call themselves Harijan, or Adi-Dravidas — which means original Dravidians. The latter term is based on the belief that the Paraiyans were the original settlers of the land, later displaced by those who imposed the caste system upon them. Although Thurston (1909) speaks of many subcastes among the Paraiyans, most of the names that he cites are probably regional variants rather than an indication of distinctive divisions.

This paper is based on research conducted in Madras State in 1963 as a post-doctoral fellow of the National Science Foundation. The collection of additional data and the writing of this paper were done while the author was the co-director of a project dealing with aspects of continuity and change in India sponsored by the National Institute of Mental Health and Columbia University. The author would like to express her gratitude to the people residing in the Untouchable quarter of the sample villages, and to Professor F. C. Southworth for his many useful comments.

In the area where this research was conducted only two small subcastes were found apart from the major grouping. These subcastes were the Paraiyan washermen and a type of priest, or *pujari,* who served the Paraiyan community.

In 1961, the Paraiyans constituted 58.65 percent of the Scheduled Caste population in Madras State, with the highest incidence of Paraiyans to be found in Chingleput District, the site of this study. In Chingleput, where Paraiyans constitute almost one-third of the population, and in other rice-producing areas in the broader region of Tamilnad, the Paraiyans and other Scheduled Castes provide most of the agricultural labor. Since few Paraiyans follow any other occupation, this study will examine their role in rural communities based on a detailed investigation of one village, supplemented with material from a second village, census data for the entire district, and incidental information from student investigators conducting an independent survey of ninety-six other villages.

Although much has been said about the "security" afforded by the caste system to the lower groups (see especially Ishwaran 1966), interpretations of this kind tend to express the viewpoint of the man at the top, or in the middle ranges of the caste hierarchy. While it is true that the Paraiyans have always had a secure place within the traditional social structure, such "security" does not mean that they *liked* their role, or even that they accepted it. In modern times many question the not uncommon high caste belief that the lower castes are resigned to their lowly status. Although such expressions as "God has put me here, I must have done something bad in my past life, maybe next time I will be born higher," undoubtedly occur, one suspects there has always been considerable hostility and resentment toward those higher in the social structure.

Contemporary changes to be considered in this analysis of the social forces impinging upon the Paraiyans include the commercialization of traditionally caste-linked occupations, the decrease in the number of castes represented in village communities, and the slow breakdown of caste prerogatives. Also examined are the effects of the introduction of western political institutions, especially political parties and an electoral system based on universal franchise, and the success or failure of government programs to assist Harijans.

Among the many problems to be explored in this study is the vital one of modern legislation, particularly laws affecting land tenancy and the abolition of untouchability, which has begun to have an effect on conditions throughout the area, though slowly and often indirectly. The effect on village Paraiyans perhaps has not been as great as the legislators' idealistic expectations. There exist various ways of circumventing the laws and the Paraiyans' condition is subject to many forces outside the province of the law.

As will be seen below, in spite of all the changes currently being attempted, and in spite of the Harijans' slowly developing awareness of their new powers and opportunities, actual change to the early seventies has been very limited.

Background

The Paraiyans, with the Pallans and Chakkilis, form the bulk of the Untouchable population of Madras State. The Pallans are found only in the southernmost districts, and the Chakkilis largely in Coimbatore District. Consequently, in the region of northern Madras under discussion, the Paraiyans are the main Untouchable group. Despite considerable controversy about their position in earlier times, when the British took over in the nineteenth century, the Paraiyans' status as categorized by Ellis and others (e.g. Bayley and Hudleston 1892) was that of agrestic slaves bound to the soil. Treated as Untouchable by all caste Hindus, and even by many other semi-untouchable castes such as Ambattan (barbers) and Wannan (washermen), the Paraiyans lived outside the main village in separate *cheris* or Harijan hamlets. The *cheris* were generally located on the least desirable lands, such as areas subject to flooding by the monsoon. Often overcrowded, they rarely possessed such rudimentary sanitary facilities as a clean source of drinking water. As late as 1970, when the Paraiyans spoke of the *ur* or village they still excluded themselves and their own residential area.

In the past, some Paraiyans were owned by individual landlords, some by a village community, and others were "free." Records tell of Paraiyans who, in times of severe scarcity, sold their brothers, sisters, and even themselves into slavery. According to Place, writing in 1795:

> The labouring servants are for the most part *pariars*, who can by no means acquire property in land; and I have not met with an instance of their having done so. They receive wages, partly in money and partly in those fees . . . called *callovassum*, and if not the slaves of the *meerassadars*, renew their service every year. [153]

Dharma Kumar's recent study of agrestic servitude in Tamilnad contains one or two observations relevant here. She notes:

> . . . it is clear that at the beginning of the nineteenth century the *pannaiyals* [unfree laborers] in some Tamil areas were in a condition of servitude. They were born into servitude, and they died in it. . . . They could not leave their

master's land; this was so generally recognized that in the early years the Collectors would help to catch runaway labourers. . . . Whether or not a *pannaiyal* might be sold independently of the land he tilled was a convention which varied from district to district in the early decades of the nineteenth century. In South Arcot the "slaves" could be sold to anyone and to an "alien village," but this was rare. . . . Pallans and Paraiyans did enter into a contract of slavery, in return for maintenance throughout their lives; they could be sold, though not to distant parts of the country but actual sales were rare. . . . In Chingleput in 1819 "these persons are not in any way attached to the land but are the property of the individual and may by him be called away. . . . " [1965: 42-44]

This was not part of the caste system, nor was it simply indentured servitude, though many instances of the latter also occurred among Paraiyans.

Kumar notes further that "unfree labourers were frequently concentrated in the irrigated areas," and correlates this with the greater demand for labor in these areas (1965: 60-61). Economic factors of this kind probably accounted in part for the high concentration of Paraiyans and Pallans in wet rice areas where their role in the economy was analogous to that of field slaves in the American South before the Civil War, though the masters did not have any control over Paraiyan mating. Furthermore, not all of the Paraiyans were linked to the land in the same way.

Kumar's study also helps clarify a question commonly asked regarding those Paraiyans who were tied to specific land: Did "serfs" of this kind have any rights to cultivate the land or to share in the crop? Indeed some anthropologists (Leach 1960: 6) assume the existence of such rights, and others have suggested that these "serfs" were not subject to the insecurity of employment of today's wage laborer. Kumar, however, points out that:

. . . these rights were not invariably granted. . . . The tied agricultural laborer did not always have the right to work and earn; if his master could not employ him, he need not always pay him but could let him try to get some employment as a casual laborer. The issue would be raised presumably at times like these when his rights were most needed, that they were most insecure. [1965: 191]

There is also evidence that before the twentieth century some Paraiyans were "attached" or belonged to certain villages where they held low status village offices. Such offices included that of the *vettiyan* who was in charge of regulating the use of irrigation water in the fields; the *taliary,* a local policeman who had jurisdiction over certain minor offences, and escorted travellers from one village to another; and the boundary man, who kept track of village boundary markers and gave evidence in land disputes. These offices required the use of brute force, or subjected the individual to harsh conditions (the *vettiyan* often spent the night in the fields, catching whatever sleep he could). They were also jobs which could be done without coming close to caste Hindus. Circumstantial evidence as well as latter-day practice suggests that the Paraiyans' traditional role as "village policemen" did not bring them directly into contact with high castes. Even with intermediate castes they came into contact only rarely in this capacity, and mostly with outsiders. The Paraiyans who did this sort of work were usually attached to the village, not to any one family. They were either paid from a common grain heap, or else received small contributions from all the landowners in the village. Occasionally they were given the temporary use of land, usually non-irrigated, which belonged utimately to the village. The Paraiyans were also responsible for the removal of dead cattle.

Paraiyans were called to assist at non-Brahman funerals by drumming and performing other services, and to beat the drums at certain non-Brahman temple festivals. The performance of such tasks required little in the way of special skills. The jobs ran in certain families, though often one son in a family might have had the exclusive right to this work. It is uncertain whether the Paraiyans who held these jobs were also agrestic slaves, or had a slightly higher status.

Slowly, during the nineteenth and early twentieth centuries, the agrestic slave status gave way to that of casual laborer, a change that might or might not have resulted in insecurity of employment and economic loss. During the same period, a few Paraiyans managed to acquire a little land, since it was no longer possible to prohibit such ownership. It is not clear just how this land was obtained. Possibly, some Paraiyans took up uncultivated land, abandoned after the terrible depredations of Hyder Ali and several years of drought — land that the British wanted to push back into cultivation. In some instances, land allotted to a Paraiyan working as *vettiyan* might have become his freehold when *ryotwari* tenancy was introduced in the mid-nineteenth century.

Paraiyans After Independence

Before looking at the Paraiyans' situation in the context of specific villages, it may be useful to look briefly at their position and that of other Scheduled Castes as reported in the Madras census. Returns from as early as 1931 reveal that the percentage of Scheduled Castes in the Madras population has been consistently higher than in India as a whole. In 1951, while the all-India percentage of Scheduled Castes was 14.69 percent, the Madras figure was 18.01 percent — only three states ranked higher than Madras. In the rural areas of Madras, according to the 1961 census, about 21 percent of the population consisted of Scheduled Castes. In Chingleput District, where this study was conducted, the figure was close to 32 percent. While Chingleput ranked highest in the state in the percentage of Scheduled Castes in its population, there exists a larger number of Harijans in the neighboring districts of Tanjore and South Arcot due to the greater size of their total populations.

The rural Harijans' dependence on agriculture as their major source of employment, and the modest size of their landholdings, may be seen in Tables 2.1 and 2.2.

Table 2.1

Distribution of Employment per 10,000 in Madras Rural Population — 1961

	Scheduled Castes	General Population
Landholder	1,786	2,530
Agricultural Laborer	2,452	1,082
Non-worker (mostly women, children, and the aged)	1,301	1,351
Other		

Table 2.2

Size of Landholdings per 10,000 Cultivating Households — Madras State, 1961

	Scheduled Castes	General Population
Less than 1 acre	2,442	1,461
1.0 - 2.4	4,190	3,311
2.5 - 4.9	2,248	2,551
5 - 9.9	874	1,685
10 - 29.9	201	861
Over 30	10	110
Unspecified	35	21

SOURCE: Derived from tables appearing in Census of India, 1961, Vol. IX, Madras Part V-A (i) Scheduled Castes and Tribes (Report & Tables), 1964. Madras Government Press.

This dependence is reflected in the concentration of Scheduled Castes in the Palar — South Penner and Cauvery divisions, major rice-producing areas, where many field hands are required to tend the paddy lands. Most of this labor is provided by the Scheduled Castes. The 1961 distribution of Paraiyans, who constitute 58.65 percent of the Madras Scheduled Caste population, reflects their primary reliance on this kind of employment, in that 6,551 of every 10,000 Paraiyans live in the rice-producing districts of this region: Chingleput, South Arcot, North Arcot, and Tanjore.

Throughout the region, most villages have a *cheri* or Harijan ham-

let within a mile of the village site. Occasionally a *cheri* might serve
two or more small villages, but in any case there usually is a *cheri* nearby.
The caste composition of villages in this area is quite varied as is the ratio
of Scheduled Castes to other castes represented in the population of the
region. Variations of the latter kind may be seen in Table 2.3 in which the
primary site of this study is designated as Village MM.

Table 2.3

1961 Population of Village MM and Surrounding Villages

Village*	Area in Square Miles	Number of households	Population	Scheduled Caste population	Scheduled Caste Percentage of Total Population
1.	2.25	245	1094	308	28 %
2.	1.83	141	627	221	35 %
3.	.99	114	521	—	—
4.	2.01	205	939	531	56 %
5.	2.21	180	774	121	15 %
6.	1.80	121	536	150	25 %
7.	1.30	173	719	63	8.7%
8.	1.94	344	1432	283	19 %
MM	3.52	354	1327	131	9 %

SOURCE: Census of India, 1961, Vol. IX, Madras, Part X-VI, District Census Handbook
Chingleput Vol. 11, 1965.

*Villages adjacent to MM are designated here and in the text simply by number.

While the ratio of Paraiyan to upper castes (shown in Table 2.3)
is an important variable in the determination of the Paraiyan's position
in any given community, other factors influence the allocation and exercise of power, and related matters. For example, the degree of unity among
Paraiyans in a *cheri,* and the degree of unity among the dominant castes
in the village that they serve, may be more important than sheer numbers
in determining the nature of inter-caste relations. In some cases the attitudes of leading caste Hindu landlords are a critical factor. The amount
of land owned by Paraiyans may also affect such relations.

Analysis of the Paraiyan Position

The major directions of change in the 1960s and the principal
forces affecting Paraiyans in rural areas can be described despite the
complexity of a system undergoing transition at uneven rates, and the
welter of data available on the subject. The analysis here will concentrate
on changes in the relationships between Paraiyans and the higher castes,
as well as on the economic status of the Paraiyans themselves.

Since most of the Paraiyans reside and work in rural communities, the analysis focuses on two villages in particular, situated in the Chingleput district, designated henceforth as MM and MG, which have not yet felt the direct impact of industrialization. MM is about forty miles from Madras City and thirteen miles from the temple city of Kanchipuram. MG is eight miles on the other side of Kanchipuram and fifty-five miles from Madras City. Neither MM or MG is on the main road, though both are intersected by bus routes. An important contrast between the two villages was that Brahmans constituted about 10 percent of MM's population, while there were no Brahmans in MG.

It is important to distinguish between Brahman and non-Brahman villages in Tamilnad. Brahmans, for the most part, tend to live in villages where they are in sufficient number to form a real community. In such villages, which have a Brahman street or *agraharam,* the Naickers (or their counterparts, the Padiyachis in South Arcot, and in North Arcot, the Gounders) have been the link between Paraiyans and Brahmans. Indeed, in the past, Paraiyans never worked directly for Brahmans. A Naicker, on the other hand, might employ a Paraiyan as a field laborer, or under certain circumstances might have given land to a Paraiyan on a sharecropping basis. On occasion, a Naicker sharecropping with a Brahman might employ a Paraiyan day-laborer, this being as close as the Untouchable ever came to the Brahman. The force of this tradition continued to be felt in 1967 by many Paraiyans including one informant of village MM who described the situation in the following words:

We can't go on that street [the Brahman street]. One has to get bullock and all, if he is doing *varam* [working as a share cropper] for a man, also even if working as a coolie [day-laborer]. Now sometimes we go on that street, but they don't like it, and Iyers won't hire us. [The term Iyer, more properly Shaivite Brahman, is used by the local Paraiyans for all Brahmans.]

At the same time, however, one Paraiyan in the same village was holding a half-acre on *varam* from a Brahman, and more significantly, several of the younger Brahmans were saying that they would employ Paraiyans after the death of their elders.

Traditionally, the Paraiyans were not supposed to sit on top of a bullock cart when carrying paddy through a village street. By 1967 many Paraiyans did this in MM, though older men often dismounted when nearing the Brahman street or the houses of prestigious Naickers. Similarly, although Paraiyans were not allowed to walk down the main Brahman street in the past, by the 1960s, younger men would walk on this street but the older men and women still avoided it.

The gap between the Paraiyans and other villagers can in part be

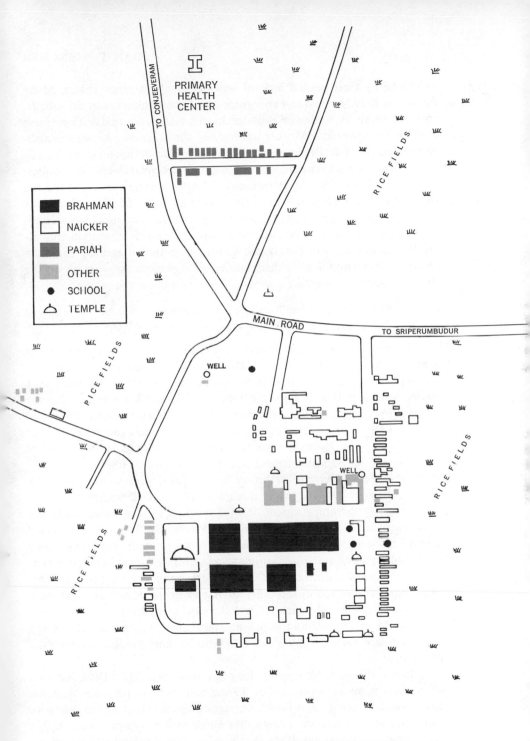

Fig. 2.1 Village M M — Chingleput District, Madras State, 1963

measured by their mutual lack of knowledge about other castes. Many Paraiyans in MM could not recognize all of the Brahmans in the village, and vice versa. A Brahman assistant in this research noted with surprise that the Paraiyans in MM were unaware of the difference between Vaishnavite and Shaivite Brahmans in Tamilnad. The division of the Vaishnavite Brahmans into two major sub-groups, the Tengalais and Vadagalais, was also unknown by the Paraiyans — despite the fact that in MM the Brahman residential area was clearly divided, one-half being Tengalais and the other Vadagalais. Considerable ignorance prevailed also on both sides regarding caste-linked customs and world view. Rather than emulating the Brahmans, the Paraiyans would make fun of special Brahman customs, as exemplified by their teasing of a project assistant about the Brahman custom of giving a dowry. They would say:

We buy the cow [i.e., we pay for the girl]. We have self-respect, but with you people, the cow itself [meaning the girl's father] gives money.

In the village of MM's total population of 1,362 people in 1963 (author's census), there were 127 Brahmans, 912 Naickers (numerically the largest caste in Chingleput district), and 139 Paraiyans. The Paraiyans owned less than 1 percent of the total agricultural land, the Brahmans about 25 percent, and Naickers most of the rest. The largest portion of Brahman land was sharecropped by Naickers, or cultivated by Naicker day-laborers. The Paraiyans for the most part worked as day laborers for Naickers, or as sharecroppers on a 50-50 basis. However, only 16 acres, less than 1 percent of the cultivated land, were sharecropped by Paraiyans. None of the MM Paraiyans worked outside the village.

One young Paraiyan man of MM worked as a permanent servant on a yearly salary for a fairly affluent Naicker family. Two others received a small amount of paddy from the cultivators for their work regulating irrigation water as *vettiyans,* another worked as a *taliary,* village watchman, for a government salary of about forty-seven rupees a month. One man, who had served in the army in Assam, was retired in 1967 on a very small pension. Although a few Paraiyans owned small plots of land, none could subsist without supplementary employment. In the village of MG, a few Paraiyan families held sufficient land holdings to be independent.

In the village of MG, in a total population of 1,582 (1961 census), 47 percent were Paraiyan, about 35 percent belonged to the Mudaliar caste (high-ranking, non-Brahman agriculturalists), 10 percent were Naickers, and there were a few other small castes. Despite their higher percentage of population, Paraiyans in MG owned only 6 percent of the total agricultural land, including 4 percent of the total irrigated land, in the village. About 1960, after a visit to the village by Vinoba Bhave, an additional 82.58 acres, constituting 5.6 percent of the total cultivable land, were donated by the village to the Bhoodan Board for distribution to the poor. Characteristic of such situations, this land was dry, non-irrigated, about one-and-a-half miles from the village site, that had been set aside for use by the entire village as grazing land. As of 1963, some of the land had been given in usufruct, under the board's ownership, to Harijans and other poor people. This arrangement was a source of controversy as the Harijans felt they should have received papers giving them clear title to the land. In addition to this common grazing area, there was some government land in the village that was not cultivated by anyone. The Harijans were trying to get it; indeed a few were surreptitiously cultivating about twenty acres of it, but the caste Hindus were seeking to retain its use as a grazing area for their cattle. In October 1970, close to 100 acres of this land were given to landless Harijans, under an order from the Collector of the District. The village Mudaliars were prepared for this, however. There was already talk that the Harijans would have to get credit to farm the land. It was anticipated that they would get into debt, and the land would go to some Mudaliar. The only way to avoid this would be through long-term government loans in kind, or possibly a government-built tube well to irrigate the land. These were under consideration in the early 1970s.

In the village MG, 3 or 4 percent of the land owned by Mudaliars was cultivated by Harijans as sharecroppers. The remainder of the share-cropping was done with Naickers and other caste Hindus. On the other hand, nearly 50 percent of the Mudaliars hired Harijans on *al-varam* (literally *man-varam*). Under this arrangement, a man is hired for a year at a time. He takes complete charge of the landlord's land. He is responsible for irrigating the field on time and similar activities. The landlord supplies the bullocks, the seeds, and whatever fertilizer is used. This type of work is done mainly by Harijans, since it is considered somewhat demeaning for a Naicker. Under *al-varam* the man who does the work gets one-sixth or less of the crop. Some men work long intervals on *al-varam* for a particular landlord; other landlords prefer to switch the men around from time to time, using the threat of firing as a means of control. The *al-varam* method of sharecropping is not practiced in MM.

Until a decade ago, the village of MG had only one *cheri,* which became crowded. Around 1960, heavy pressure from the local Harijans and officials of the community development block forced the Mudaliars to allow the Harijans to build another hamlet on a dry area across some paddy fields from the traditional site. Because block development officials administered this project, the houses were not built too close together. While a Harijan family might be entitled to a house site in the *cheri,* the expense of building a house had to be borne by the family. According to one man who had recently built a simple mud house with thatch roof, it cost about Rs. 300 ($40) for all of the materials. This is a considerable expense for a poor man, and often involves getting deeply into debt. This debt in turn might delay a son's marriage for several years. Partly for this reason, as of 1967, not all of the men allotted space in the new *cheri* had built their houses. Those who had settled in the new site included a majority of the men with non-agricultural jobs and those employed outside the village. The latter group included a number of men employed in the town of Kanchipuram: for example, two who worked for a large landowner there, two others who worked in factories and another who worked as a helper on a truck. It seemed that several of the non-agriculturists worked in a local brick factory owned by one of the village Mudaliars. Since these men were paid in cash, they may have possessed the money needed to build a new house, whereas many of those without such employment were forced to remain in the old *cheri* for lack of funds.

Although the Mudaliars of MG are a high-ranking, non-Brahman caste, in the past they dealt directly with the Paraiyans, unlike Paraiyan-Brahman relations in MM. The Paraiyans, however, were expected to observe various proprieties and to maintain an obsequious manner in the presence of Mudaliars. For example, Paraiyans did not venture beyond the verandah of a Mudaliar house, nor did they wear sandals or a shirt in the presence of a Mudaliar. In the 1960s, such restrictions were relaxed to a much greater degree in MG than in interaction between Paraiyans and Brahmans in MM. In MG, the Paraiyans, especially the younger ones, almost seemed to be proud of annoying the Mudaliar landowners. The marked contrast between these two villages in Paraiyan and upper caste relations may be due in part to the tradition of direct contact between Paraiyan and Mudaliar, and the fact that Paraiyans constitute the largest caste group in MG.

In MM, if one compares the generation of Paraiyan men over forty-five with those now in their twenties, the difference in attitudes is striking. Despite individual variations, one can see among the younger men a desire to ignore traditional attitudes, to "go wherever we want to," and to "talk up" to the Naickers. In one instance, a young Paraiyan from the MM *cheri* was threatened with a beating by Naickers in a nearby village, when he rode down one of their main streets on a bicycle. A month later, his mother's elder brother's son, who was a relative traditionally expected to "protect" him, threatened to beat up one of the offending Naickers at a temple festival held in MM. While aggression in this episode was limited to verbal abuse of the Naicker, this incident shows that a Paraiyan is able to censure publicly a member of a higher caste — and occasionally get away with it. In the past, though there may have been more than one unsuccessful or semi-successful attempt at revolt by an entire colony, it was harder for Paraiyans openly to express resentment about the way they were treated. Rebellion was dangerous for an individual man, who was more likely to get drunk, maybe to beat his wife, fight with his friends, or just act "lazy." The Paraiyans did exercise a minimal type of control over the excesses of landlords and higher caste people through the latter's fear of the Paraiyan's knowledge of "black magic." This was more prevalent in Kerala where higher caste Nayars literally could kill a Paraiyan for "polluting" a Nayar. (For an example of partial social control through fear of magic, see Mencher 1964).

In many ways the younger men have resented the attitude of their elders, who have tended to be more afraid of the higher caste people and reluctant to risk offending them. The older men have taken the attitude: "Why go where we are not wanted, why give them any reason to talk badly about us?" The younger men have not accepted this attitude, and to some extent, they have been supported by some of the younger Naicker men. For example, in 1967, a Paraiyan man was playing cards with a Naicker man on a Naicker street, something that would not have occurred fifteen years ago. A quarrel broke out between them, and the two began throwing objects at each other. While other Naickers tried to break up the fight, they did not take sides in the issue, preferring to consider it an argument between two individuals, who were both wrong.

Today, a young man from the MM *cheri* might feel far freer to answer back in kind to a Naicker. One Paraiyan youth told this story:

I work for M. Naicker. I am responsible and take care of his lands [on *varam*]. I take my own water. One night I went to run water on my land. I opened [the sluice] and went to sleep. Then some Naicker came out and took the water. Then, I disconnected his line and took. He started to call me some language and to fight. Again he connected and I disconnected. Then other Naickers came. They started saying, "Oh, he is a. . . . Previously they didn't even have drinking water, now they are so proud." Then one of them said, "Oh, he has the support of some Naickers, that is why he can talk so boldly." Then they left.

According to informants of both castes, such fights simply could not have happened in the past. The occurrence of conflicts of this kind in recent years is indicative of other changes in inter-caste relations. Previously, Paraiyan boys were afraid to go about wearing decent clothes, even if they could afford them. As of 1970 they would do so, even though behind their backs some people would talk about their being unduly proud.

Whether changes of this kind might eventually result in extensive change is hard to say. In MM, a Paraiyan Panchayat member from a neighboring village (identified as village No. 4 in Table 2.3) was heard to say, "In our village, we are in a majority, and some of us have property, so we can be more bold. Money and strength count for much as do people's attitude. But in the village of MM people like this [pointing to one of the elders] are holding others up." Inter-village variations of this kind were frequently noted by other villagers. Mudaliars of MG often contrasted the Paraiyans of their village with those of an adjacent village that had almost the same caste composition, and with whom MG villagers often married. According to the Mudaliars, the Paraiyans in the adjacent village were not insolent and their general behavior was better than that of the MG Paraiyans. On the other hand, the Paraiyans of MG viewed the Mudaliars of the adjacent village as being better in their treatment of Paraiyans. They also claimed that the Paraiyans in the other village were able to earn more, and the number of well-to-do Paraiyans there was greater than in MG. Both points of view turned out to be true. The superior position of the Paraiyans in the adjacent village, and the more relaxed state of Mudaliar-Paraiyan relations there, appears to be due in part to the presence of several well-to-do and able Paraiyans who act as spokesmen for their caste fellows. These Paraiyans were also more united than the ones in MG, an important variable discussed at greater length below.

To some extent, the caste structure itself is changing. While some traditional roles have not changed, an example of the process of transformation and the tenacity of tradition may be seen in the case of a leading Naicker family in MM, whose head died a few years ago. This family was formerly considered to be the most important in the village, and during all non-Brahman festivals and other special occasions, the lower castes were expected to come first to their house to pay homage. In the early 50s, however, this custom began to be discontinued by Paraiyan drummers, as well as barbers and washermen. Some years later, the head of this Naicker family decided not to patronize these people. He hired someone else to irrigate his fields. He took his laundry to a nearby town, and had his hair cut there. When he died these service castes exercised their traditional prerogatives by refusing to bury him until his widow paid a "fine" to the Paraiyan in charge of irrigation, and to the washerman and the barber.

Another case in point: Traditionally in MM there were four Paraiyan men in charge of the irrigation tank, at one juncture, two of the men who held this post decided not to work, since they were too old. The other two tried to carry on alone, but they could not cope with all the work; there was nothing the village people could do about it, except to steal irrigation water at night when they needed it. In earlier times, the villagers would have had more control over the Paraiyans: either the first two men would not have been allowed to retire, or others would have been forced to help with the work. The older Paraiyans say that no one really wants to do this kind of work, since it involves the *vettiyan* in fights between various landowners, and the pay is not enough for the labor involved.

In the first case the commercialization of traditional occupations enabled the family to manage without the services of the village barber or washerman for twelve years. When the need arose for a burial, tradition prevailed. However, it is conceivable that even in life crisis ceremonies, dependence on other castes will diminish. For instance, the barber woman's role of midwife is being supplanted by a trained government midwife, from the recently created health center in MM, who serves all castes, including the Paraiyans.

Some lessening of the dependence on traditional reciprocal relationships, though varying from village to village, has fostered a tendency in this region for members of service castes to go to larger towns. In the city of Kanchipuram, washermen, blacksmiths, and carpenters of village origin have undertaken commercial ventures based on their traditional skills. This change had a profound effect on the Paraiyans. In town, the Paraiyans and the caste Hindus patronize the same shop, and deal with the same people on a cash basis. It also has profound implications for

Table 2.4

Proportionate increase in Scheduled Caste Population
Between 1931-1961 in Some of the Villages Surrounding MM

Village	1961			1931		
	Total Population	Scheduled Castes %		Total Population	Scheduled Castes %	
1.	771	169	21.0	1094	308	28
3.	331	2	.6	521	—	—
4.	491	252	51.0	939	531	56
6.	417	68	16.0	536	150	25
8.	1230	111	9.0	1432	283	19
MM	1070	103	9.6	1327	131	9

SOURCE: 1931 data from the Census of India, 1931. 1961 data from the Census of India, 1961, Vol. IX, Madras, Part X-VI, District Census Handbook Chingleput Vol. 11, 1965. Madras Government Press.

village social structure in that it indicates a tendency in the direction of reducing the rural population to two major groups — landlords (both large and small) and landless agricultural laborers (see Mencher 1964b). Table 2.4 indicates a somewhat disproportionate increase in the Paraiyan population in a few of the villages around MM, but not in all.

In the 70s, there had been no change in attitudes toward inter-marriage, although extra-marital affairs do occur across caste lines. According to elderly informants, liaisons of this kind also existed in the past. Then, as today, everyone criticized such relationships, but they were tolerated as long as violence did not erupt. These affairs were not viewed as a threat to caste endogamy as the relationships were considered to be transitory and illegal. The women involved need not be of a lower caste. Indeed, the majority of instances noted in MM involved Paraiyan men with Naicker women.

Traditional attitudes regarding inter-dining continued to prevail in most situations with occasional exceptions in public tearooms or during political campaigns. Although minor changes in inter-personal relations indicated that the former pollution complex was weakening, a clear distinction remained between eradicating untouchability as such, and the retention of caste distinctions. Even though an individual Paraiyan might have more money than an individual Naicker, the Naicker, like the white in the American South, was still clinging to the superiority of his caste. In both MG and MM, the Paraiyans in the 1960s did not exercise their legal right to enter the main village temples dedicated to Perumal or Ishwaraswami. However, during the February, 1967, election campaign, several MG Paraiyans reported being invited into the Ishwaraswami temple by the Congress candidate to hear a campaign speech by a former member of Parliament. This was told with a humorous air, concluded with the remark, "Well, we won't get in there again until the next election." (In

Table 2.5

Distribution of Literates by Age in Madras State — 1961 Census

Age	General Population	Adi-Dravida	Paraiyan
5 - 9	34.6%	23%	22%
10 - 14	51%	31%	29%
15 - 19	44%	26%	21%
20 - 29	38%	20%	17%
30 - 44	34%	16%	14%

SOURCE: Derived from tables appearing in Census of India, 1961, Vol. IX, Madras Part V-A (i) Scheduled Castes and Tribes (Report & Tables), 1964. Madras Government Press.

1971 they were not invited in, since it was assumed to be a foregone conclusion that they would vote against the Mudaliars anyhow.)

Education is one of the major forces affecting inter-caste relations and many other aspects of the Paraiyan's life. One measure of the substantial increase in education in Madras since Independence appears in Table 2.5.

While the 1961 census material presented above indicates that the percentage of literate Adi-Dravida, or Scheduled Castes, has almost doubled in the past generation, their literacy rate remains far below that of the general population at all age levels. The discrepancy between the literacy rates given for Paraiyans and Adi-Dravidas may be due to the common practice of many semi-educated Paraiyans identifying themselves as Adi-Dravidas.

An examination of the educational level of literates reported in the 1961 Madras census reveals that at the primary level the Paraiyans compare favorably with the general population at both the state and district levels.

Table 2.6

Educational Level of Literates in Madras State — 1961

| | Urban | | Rural | | |
	General Population %	Paraiyan %	General Population %	Paraiyan %	Chingleput District %
Primary	33	37	18	16	16
Matriculate and above	13	4	3	1	1
Literate*	54	59	79	83	83

*Educational level, other than literate, not specified.

SOURCE: Derived from tables appearing in Census of India, 1961, Vol. IX, Madras Part V-A (i) Scheduled Castes and Tribes (Report & Tables), 1964. Madras Government Press.

Beyond the primary level, however, the educational attainments of the Paraiyans are way below that of the general population, especially in urban areas where a very high percentage of the population consists of Brahmans. The almost identical figures given in Table 2.6 for the Paraiyans and the general population of Chingleput District, reflect the fact that Paraiyans constitute almost one-third of the district population. This close correspondence may also be due in part to the widespread acceptance by Paraiyans of education as a way out of their traditional position, in contrast to the Naickers, the largest caste in Chingleput, who tend to place little value on education beyond mere literacy. The latter view is most prevalent among Naickers with small landholdings.

In the village of MM the percentage of Paraiyan children in primary school is at least as high as that of the Naickers and there is little to distinguish the Paraiyans from the other castes in the school setting. As a direct result of government policy, initiated in 1948, Paraiyan children are no longer expected to sit separately in school. However, as late as the 1960s, it was rare for a Paraiyan child to play with a Naicker child away from school. In contrast to MM, where Naicker children were occasionally seen in the Paraiyan *cheri,* children from other castes were never found in the *cheri* of MG.

In the village of MG, while the percentage of educated Paraiyans was far smaller than in MM, the MG group included several high school graduates and a few advanced students who were likely to graduate in the late 1960s. Although Paraiyan parents in MG also viewed education as a way out of the system, they were reluctant to send their children to a school dominated by Mudaliar children whose superior status was reflected in the markedly better quality of their clothing. Another inhibiting factor was that Paraiyan students had to walk through the upper caste section of the village in order to reach the school. Although Paraiyans and other villagers had begun sitting together at school festivals in some villages, this was not common to all villages. Even though they might sit among the caste Hindu women, the older Paraiyan women tend to be somewhat afraid of them. This is related to their economic dependency, and is not seen as much among younger women.

Table 2.7

Male and Female Literacy Rates, Madras State — 1961

	General Population		Scheduled Castes	
	Male	Female	Male	Female
Chingleput District	46.6%	17.6%	25.5%	6.5%
State	51.6%	21.1%	27.5%	6.7%

SOURCE: Derived from tables appearing in Census of India, 1961, Vol. IX, Madras Part V-A (ii, p. 37), Scheduled Castes and Tribes (Report & Tables), 1964. Madras Government Press.

Among the boys, the question remains: education for what? Though some are completing their education through high school, the problem is what comes next. In many cases, they do not have the necessary information about government grants for Harijans, or even if they do, they cannot afford the clothes, books, and food which are involved in schooling away from the village. Teacher training, which lasts only two years, is the only practical step for the majority of Paraiyan boys who by some miracle manage to complete high school.

The loosening of caste-based restrictions on the Paraiyans is one of the many consequences of the modern political system. On the other hand, the increased awareness of one's own group as a political entity, and the importance of group solidarity, have served to strengthen other aspects of the caste system. While Paraiyans recognize that only in rare instances are they likely to control village panchayats, or councils, they have become aware of the influence that can be exerted through caste-based bloc voting. As one Paraiyan youth of MM said:

All *cheri* people are going to vote for X this time. Last time we voted for Y, but it didn't do any good. Only one well has been built in the past ten years, and occasionally they give some house-site. Once government sent books to the *cheri* people and other poor people, but the panchayat president didn't give. He put them in a waste basket in his house. Once, the government offered cows to poor *cheri* people, but asked panchayat for details and they said no one needs. In this way, they stop any help to us. So this time, we are not going to vote the same party. If any Harijan or poor Naicker on panchayat tries to help us, they are made to keep quiet. But, we will get rid of the president by vote.

This attitude — that the vote can be used to further Paraiyan interests — may bring about profound changes in the long run, though in 1970, the same Panchayat President, "Y," was again elected in MM by a considerable margin which included a large number of *cheri* votes from people economically dependent on him. In MM, the Naickers are split between two major political parties, Old Congress and the Dravida Munnetra Kazhagam (DMK). Most of the more orthodox Naickers belong to Old Congress, whereas the younger, more radical ones belong to the DMK, which gained control of the Madras State government in 1967. Although most of the older Paraiyans supported Old Congress earlier, since 1967, at least in MM, more and more have been siding with the DMK. The competition for Paraiyan votes between Naicker supporters of these opposing parties provided the Paraiyans of MM with greater political leverage than their caste fellows in villages where the upper castes belong to only one party.

In a village like MG, with its large Paraiyan population, the village council has been composed of three Mudaliars, two Naickers, one carpenter, and four Paraiyans. In this situation the Mudaliars have had to remain united, and maintain a coalition with the Naickers and/or carpenter, in order to keep the Paraiyans from gaining the majority. The Mudaliars have also aided the Paraiyans in an effort to convince them that they have more to gain by keeping the Mudaliars in power than by direct exercise of political authority. As in MM, most of the older Paraiyans belong to Old Congress, the party of the Mudaliars in this region, whereas some of the younger ones support DMK. Such cleavages and the absence of unity among the Paraiyan leaders of MG, are also used to advantage by the Mudaliars.

There is a growing tendency for people with common economic interest to join forces politically. For example, the poor, landless Naicker may have more in common with the Paraiyan than with the wealthy members of his own caste. While some of the poorer Naickers resent government concessions to Paraiyans, their resentment is often not as strong as that of wealthier Naickers who also possess the power to thwart government programs aimed at improving the lot of the Harijan.

The ultimate resolution of the many problems confronting the Paraiyans, and other Untouchable castes, is dependent in large measure upon the overall economic development of the region. To the poor villager, regardless of caste, the need to acquire land to cultivate is of primary importance — there is not enough land to satisfy the needs of the low caste Hindus, let alone the Paraiyans. In this sense, the Paraiyan's problem in the village is the problem of the rural proletariat everywhere, with the added stigma of untouchability.

3.

WALTER C. NEALE

The Marginal Laborer and the Harijan in Rural India

HARIJANS are a "marginal" group in rural India: marginal in the economic sense and marginal in the view of non-Harijan members of Hindu society. This essay considers three questions which stem from the marginal character of the Harijan in economic and social life:

1. As Indian rural structures and activities change, how would a standard economist expect the economic condition of the Harijans to change?
2. How would these expectations differ from those of Georgescu-Roegen (1960) and Chayanov (1966), the two "peasant theorists" who recently have most influenced debates among economists?
3. How may what actually happens in India diverge from expectations derived from either of these models?

At the outset, two assumptions about Indian reality appear to be supported by the literature, by observation, and by the landholding census: (1) that most Harijans do not own land, or enjoy the benefits of a "protected tenancy"; and (2) that most Harijans "earn" an important part of their incomes by working on the land of others and/or attaching themselves to landholding cultivators. These assumptions allow Harijans to be regarded as "labor" for the purposes of economic analysis.

The Standard Model and the Harijan

The standard economic model postulates that as increasing quantities of labor are used in conjunction with fixed amounts of other inputs — in India, let us say, land, irrigation water, livestock, tools, seeds, fertilizers,

[57]

and pesticides — there is a decrease in the resulting additions to product,[1] possibly to zero and conceivably below, actually reducing the total output.[2]

The standard model also postulates that the employer "maximizes profits." From this it follows that the employer will pay a worker no more than the value that the worker adds to the total product. If another worker hired would add nothing (i.e., if his marginal product would be zero) or add even less than the current going wage (i.e., the cost to the employer of hiring him), then the employer will not hire. By the same logic, the employer will reduce his work force if his resulting saving in wages (and other perquisites) exceeds the loss consequent upon a (relatively small) decline in total output.

A goodly number of economists (e.g., Nurkse [1953], Georgescu-Roegen [1960], Dobb [1951]) believe that in such heavily populated countries as India the additions to total product (the "marginal product of labor") have already fallen to zero. In this case an absolute reduction in the number of people working in agriculture would leave the total agricultural product unchanged. Other economists think that the marginal product of labor is positive. They point to the facts that wages *are* paid and that there *are* labor shortages during harvest. It is possible to account for this evidence by arguing that for much of the year labor's marginal product is zero, rising to a level at or above the going daily wage only for short periods.[3] Another and increasingly common postulate to account for the evidence is that a rural "institutional wage" above the (possibly zero) marginal product of labor continues to be paid because there is a system for spreading the product among all rural dwellers. This view seems to be shared by economists as diverse in other opinions as Chayanov (1966), Georgescu-Roegen (1960), W. Arthur Lewis (1954), and Ranis and Fei (1961).[4]

To return to the standard model and its implications: *if* there is a continuing increase in India's rural labor force (a certainty), *if* there is no increase in her arable acreage (certain within a very small percentage error), *and if* there is little or no increase in irrigation facilities and other fixed and working capital inputs (almost certainly untrue), *then* the marginal productivity of the additional labor will be less than that of currently used labor, and no new laborers will be hired. But even allowing for an increase in irrigation, fertilizers, and so on, there will be a rising proportion of rural unemployed, not only in the same but in greater proportions as the supply of rural labor increases, unless farmers use much larger amounts of these capital inputs to "make up for" the fixity of the input of arable land.

How much the increased use of capital will raise the marginal productivity of labor will depend upon the kinds of new capital used. Irrigation considerably raises the demand for labor; pesticides, better seed drills and harrows, or more fertilizers on already irrigated land raise the demand much less. Tractors increase the demand for skilled (and machinery-respecting) laborers but decrease the number of bodies needed. Fortunately for the Indian agricultural laborer, many present programs are increasing the kinds of capital which require more labor,[5] but some of the programs directed at spreading better practices (e.g., use of higher-yielding seeds) increase the *productivity* of a farm's labor without increasing the *number* of men needed. The adoption of a mixed crop of wheat and potatoes such as can be seen occasionally now in Etawah District greatly increases (and spreads over the season) the demand for laborers, but the practice of green manuring between grain crops requires more work from laborers already employed without requiring an increase in the number of men. Thus any specific predictions about the effect of new capital must be made case by case and crop by crop. There is no way to be sure, for India in general or even for a specific region of India, whether the increased demand for labor will be large or small relative to the increased use of capital inputs measured in money values, nor is it certain how the increased demand for labor will be divided between demand for more laborers and demand for more laboring.

What can be said about the effect of fixity of land supply, of increasing population, and of increasing use of capital upon the position of the Harijans? In the standard model an employer would be indifferent about which of two workers of equal skill and devotion to duty he hired. Thus while we would expect there to be more unemployed Harijans, we would also expect some increase in the total number of Harijans employed. But India's rural labor supply is not homogeneous, as is the postulated labor supply of the standard model: that is, some Indian labor is "better" than other labor — not because it is more skilled or harder working, but rather because it has the virtuous, ascriptive character of kinship or caste brotherhood. The rural labor supply will increase in each of two distinct categories — (1) the supply available from the kin of the landholding peasants; and (2) the supply of Harijans. From the point of view of an Indian peasant family, sentiment gives a higher priority to employing a brother or cousin than to hiring a Harijan; and sentiment is reinforced by the moral obligation to provide for one's kin. Not only is it to be expected that all fresh employment opportunities will be reserved for the new members of the landholding castes, but also that peasant farmers will discharge Harijan laborers in order to replace them with the additional family laborers as these become available.

The standard model's prognosis for Harijan labor is indeed bleak — and it is for this reason that the title refers to the Harijan as "marginal" in a double sense; because he is classified as socially "marginal" by Hindu society, he will also become the economically marginal man — to be let go as the marginal productivity of labor falls with the expanding population.

Chayanov and the Harijan

Chayanov and Georgescu-Roegen both deny that the marginal, profit-maximizing model can be used to explain the behavior of peasant farmers. Chayanov says that the Russian peasant "labor farm" cannot maximize profits since the head of the household cannot compute profits where there are no wage payments. Without wage payments one must deduct from the gross product the expenditures required by the farm during the year to arrive at the family's "labor product."

This family labor product is the only possible category of income for a peasant or artisan family unit, for there is no way of decomposing it analytically or objectively. Since there is no social phenomenon of wages, the social phenomenon of net profits is also absent. Thus, it is impossible to apply the capitalist profit calculation. [Chayanov 1966: 5]

Whereas the inability of the peasant (or an observer-accountant) to compute profits is not logically decisive,[6] Chayanov's evidence strongly indicates that a combination of family size and an accepted "decent" standard of living determines farm size and the intensity with which the family labor is employed. The family will expand its farm, if it can rent or buy more land, until every member of the family who can work on the land is fully employed at the peak season. As the children grow into laboring adults the farm expands; as the adult offspring leave home to set up new households the farm area contracts (Chayanov 1966: 56-64). Since "there is always a proportion between . . . [the farm's] parts and a certain conformity in their relation peculiar to each farming system . . . , determined by technical expediency and necessity," any "violation" of which "leads to . . . [a] reduction in the productivity of labor and capital expenditure, . . . the farm can, in fact, be organized in the most varied sizes" (Chayanov 1966: 91). Since "it is natural that the production element, the availability of which is less than the norm demanded by technical harmony, becomes to a considerable extent a determining factor for the agricultural undertaking" (Chayanov 1966: 93), it follows that farm size can be limited by the availability of labor, which "is fixed by being present in the composition of the family," and by an inability to acquire more land (Chayanov 1966: 92). Where more land can be obtained, it will be, up to the level of the family's "willingness to work." Where it cannot be obtained, or not easily obtained, the family will work the land it has more intensively despite the reduction in the "labor product" per unit of labor time.

The next question Chayanov answers is: what limits the family's willingness to work? Or, as he puts it, what limits the "intensity of self-exploitation"?

Two categories are of the greatest interest. On the one hand are factors that lie in the internal structure of the family itself; chiefly significant is the pressure of family consumer demands on the workers. . . . [In some areas the] measure of self-exploitation depends . . . entirely on the number of consumers and not at all on the number of workers. . . . However, such an exceptional determining influence of the demands of consumption takes place only when *other things are equal.* Moreover, it is exceedingly significant and entirely of a pattern that an increase in workers' output caused by an increment in numbers of consumers does not cause a parallel increase in well-being, and in some budget inquiries (Novgorod) *even leads to a reduction in it.* . . . [As family consumer demands increase] the rate of self-exploitation of peasant labor is forced up. On the other hand, energy expenditure is inhibited by the drudgery of the labor itself. The harder the labor is, compared with its pay, the lower the level of well-being at which the peasant family ceases to work, although frequently to achieve even this reduced level it has to make great exertions. [Chayanov 1966: 76, 78, 79; italics in original]

The willingness to exert oneself in laboring

is determined by a peculiar equilibrium between the family demand for satisfaction and the drudgery of labor itself. . . . It is obvious that with the increase of produce obtained by hard work the subjective evaluation of each newly gained ruble's significance for consumption decreases; but the drudgery of working for it, which will demand an ever greater amount of self-exploitation, will increase. As long as the equilibrium is not reached between the two elements . . . , the family . . . has every cause to continue its economic activity. As soon as this equilibrium point is reached, however, continuing to work becomes pointless. . . . [Chayanov 1966: 5,6]

When this equilibrium level of willingness to work is high and there is a limited area of land, the peasants' behavior also varies from that of a wage-paying business firm, for

. . . a capitalist business can only increase its intensity above the limit of its optimum capacity if the changed market situation itself pushes the optimum in the direction of greater intensity. In the labor family unit, intensification can also take place without this change in the market situation, simply from pressure of the units' internal forces, mostly as a consequence of family size being in an unfavorable position to the cultivated land area. . . . In a monetary

land market properties do not change hands unpaid for. . . . What determines
the land price? . . . Peasant farms that have a considerable amount of land
and are, therefore, able to utilize the family's whole labor power at an optimum
degree of cultivation intensity need not lease or buy land. . . . If a family can
dispose of only a small plot which allows them to use only part of the given
labor power, acquiring a new item with a view to using unemployed labor
power is extremely significant, for this allows them to bring the unit's intensity
near the optimum and to utilize working hours previously lost in enforced
inactivity. . . . We can even maintain . . . that the more the peasant farm
will be ready to pay for land, the less it owns already, and, therefore, the
poorer it is. [Chayanov 1966: 8,9]

A sort of floor — an elastic-in-the-face-of-necessity floor — is placed
under leisure by the peasant's desire for a minimum acceptable standard
of living; a sort of ceiling — somewhat elastic upward — is placed above
the peasant's desire for income in excess of the minimum standard of living.
It seems that Chayanov's model peasant maximizes the sum of the analytical categories, "profits" plus "utility of leisure."[7]

But note that Chayanov's model diverges in one vital respect from
the situation in India. Chayanov's peasant family does not hire labor[8]
while many Indian cultivators certainly do. The model appears, at
best, to throw light on two phenomena noted in India: (1) the "intensity
of self-exploitation" with which small ryots work their land; and (2)
the apparently grossly high prices which Indian cultivators are willing
to pay for land.[9] It does not tell us about the position and prospects of
the Harijan unless we are willing to draw a parallel (perhaps unwarranted) between the Russian peasant family and the Indian agglomeration
of dominant caste cultivator and his hangers-on. If we assert this parallel,
for argument's sake, then the Indian equivalent is the *jajman-kamin* or
faction group. What would Chayanov say of this group? Would it try
to acquire land as it grew in size? Failing to acquire more land, would
it work the land it has more intensively?[10] The statistical evidence from
India is too scanty to test the correlation,[11] and it is difficult not to believe
that in India the causation runs the other way: large holdings create large
groups, a point frequently found in the literature and strongly implied
in the assertions that the continual splitting up of holdings has been a
significant cause of the decline of the jajmani system.[12] But even if Chayanov's model does not fit India past and present, if it does fit the small-
holding peasant family situated in a commercial environment, then again
the outlook for the Harijan is drear. The jajmani groups are breaking up;
land reforms have created a class of middle-caste peasant proprietors;
and the setting of Indian agriculture is becoming increasingly commer-
cialized. The Harijan laborer will [on Chayanov's assumptions about the

closed nature of peasant farm families] find himself unemployed and without access to land. If the Indian cultivator continues to hire labor he will do so only at the peak season, for at other seasons the "drudgery" at the margin of his own *under*-employed labor will be less than the wage he must pay the Harijan, unless that wage is very low indeed.

Georgescu-Roegen and the Harijan

Georgescu-Roegen (1960) denies that one should use the standard marginal analysis for poor, overpopulated countries because:

1. the marginal productivity of labor in these countries is zero, or at least less than the "historically determined *minimum* standard of living." Therefore, "unless we know that the 'equilibrium' price of labor is at least equal to the minimum biological subsistence, the [marginal productivity] theorem has only meagre economic relevance."
2. if only that amount of labor were employed which would keep the marginal productivity of labor at this minimum, there would be unwanted leisure and starvation eliminating the excess labor, or there would be social turmoil.
3. if leisure is unwanted and therefore valueless, as he says it is in these countries, then these countries would be worse off if they followed the marginal rule because they would lose that wanted, "extra" product of additional labor which is less than the minimum wage and acceptable standard of living but still greater than zero.

These countries "solve" the problem of distributing the product when some workers — the sub-marginal ones — produce less than their incomes "only because the group follows some institutional patterns grown out of its particular historical conditions" (Georgescu-Roegen 1960: 27).[13] To account for what might be called this "non-economic" behavior Georgescu-Roegen argues that in small communities a person looks upon his total well-being as a function of others' incomes as well as of his own (Georgescu-Roegen 1960: 27).[14] Thus one finds men "ploughing the land of the widow" (Georgescu-Roegen 1960: 28) and "the gleaners, who received a share greater than the quantity of corn gleaned" (Georgescu-Roegen 1960: 25). He also presents a case which says less for man's sympathy for man: where in late feudalism the landlord took his share in corvée and crop-sharing, it was to his interest to share in the largest possible (i.e., marginal product = zero) product (1960: 23-26).

The point of his argument then becomes that "to regulate production by profit maximization is probably the worst thing that can happen to an overpopulated economy, for that would increase unwanted leisure while diminishing the national product." And this accounts for "the fact often commented upon that in Eastern Europe capitalism worsened the lot of the peasant" (Georgescu-Roegen 1960: 34).

In Georgescu-Roegen's model the Harijan, as the "first to go" when the marginal product of labor falls (or has fallen) below the wage rate, will suffer from the commercialization of Indian agriculture combined with the decline in *jajman-kamin,* patron-client ties — which correspond to Georgescu-Roegen's restraints of the East European "feudal *contrat social"* on the landlord [1960: 33]. Again, the Harijan as the marginal man in India's social structure becomes the sub-marginal man in her economy.

In Conclusion: Born Losers

Now for the third question: should one expect what happens in India to diverge from these models? "Yes," or "Maybe," and for two reasons. First, as the economic models treat the problem, there is a marked absence of a political variable,[15] but the Harijan is a voter in India — in local elections as well as national. If currently very poorly organized, if largely ignorant of how to manipulate the parliamentary and *panchayati raj* systems, the Harijans are too many to be relegated to a permanent army of the unemployed in a country without unemployment compensation or rural breadlines. At present the system, however meagrely, still provides them some wherewithal. Even where there have been land reforms which prohibit tenancies, field labor has continued to be organized, in fact, even if in contravention of the law, on crop-sharing contracts which permit the Harijans to work at the margin of their efforts for less than the going wage in the area. If today Harijans live in fear, if they depend upon the cultivating castes for their meagre wherewithals, then this very dependence indicates that the rules of marginalism combined with increasing population have not yet been rigorously applied to them. Were the "institutional" support which they now receive to disappear, one doubts that they would continue to remain politically quiescent — although, of course, their first or even their ultimate response may not fit within the constitutional framework.

A second reason for doubting that economic "rationality" will relegate the Harijans to oblivion is the growth of the capital stock of India. The marginal product of labor on the farm will rise as investment in agriculture increases, and the demand for hired labor should rise in turn. Although, as pointed out earlier, the additions to agricultural capital must be disproportionately large compared to the rate of increase in population, they may well be. The spread of irrigation alone greatly increases the need for field labor.[16] And then there is the off-take of labor into urban industrial pursuits. But these points raise questions about whether in fact India will invest enough fast enough; and the optimism on this score which a few of us feel is not widespread among economists.

Whatever the validity of hopes for improvement, whatever the merits of the economists' arguments, and however unclear the lessons some of these arguments offer for public policy — at the level of the individual the moral of the economic models coincides with the lesson of lay and ethnographic observation: "If given a choice, do not beget yourself of Harijan parentage."

NOTES

[1] This is the "Law of Diminishing Returns." I have said "postulates" although many would say that the statement has been verified empirically. I would be inclined to agree in this particular case, but the schema of neo-classical and post-neo-classical economics depends on a number of untestable postulates, so that the tested truth of some "postulates" or "statements about matters of fact" do not save the system as a whole from the difficulties of postulating the untestable.

[2] This last is "The Law of Absolutely Diminishing [or Negative] Returns."

[3] That is, in October-November and March the daily productivity of additional labor is greater than, say, Rs. 1; but its annual productivity is no more than, say, Rs. 100.

[4] There are difficulties in reaching firm conclusions about what "the wage" actually is, and about how the "institutional wage" is maintained because economists and ethnographers slice up the world somewhat differently than do the circumstances in an Indian village. Thus some of the Harijans' "sources of wherewithal" — which are *tied* to the fact that they work as field laborers — are either not counted (often the case in economic surveys), or "buried" in other classifications by the ethnographers. In addition to the cash and kind payments and the associated meals supplied in the fields "for work performed," Harijans often enjoy
  (1) "hand-outs" of various sorts
  (2) "hand-outs" of various sorts to their wives
  (3) borrowing rights, in which full, let alone prompt, repayment is
       neither expected nor fulfilled
  (4) rights to collect edibles, fuel, and fodder in the waste
  (5) *de facto* "rights" to do some pilfering and stealing
  (6) earnings from other intra-village employments, which they would not
       get if they did not live in the village and work as field laborers.
It would be nice — in fact necessary if one is to compute "the relevant wage" — if these data were collected and collated. Even so there would be many difficulties in evaluating such "sources" in order to gross up to the proper wage; but it would be a long step forward.

Helpful also would be more detailed descriptions of how these other "sources of wherewithal" are tied to living-and-working in the village, and how closely they are tied.

[5] What the literature now calls "investment in human capital."

[6] Professor James R. Millar, of the University of Illinois, has pointed out to me that if the inputs of land and labor are fixed — as they are in Chayanov's descriptions of Russian peasant farming — then the value of the analytical category "profits" would be maximized *if* each separate choice of the peasant whether to buy or not to buy an input was made so as to give the farmer the largest possible increased net return on the purchase price of the input. This would be true even though neither the peasant family nor an accountant could compute the profits.

The logical consequence of the "economically rational" choices must be a maximum value for the (numerically unascertained and unascertainable) profits.

[7] Since the balancing, which equates the utility of leisure with the utility of income minus the disutility of work at the margin, is an act occurring within the mind [soul, heart, *id*, guts; "the internal economic confrontation of subjective evaluations" (Chayanov 1966: 7)] of each decision-making peasant, it is as hard to deny this proposition as it is to believe that it means anything. Chayanov's solution to the problem of how the peasant decides to work more or less is no happier than any solution which relies upon untestable postulated processes.

[8] Why Chayanov's peasant family does not hire labor is not clear. He asserts the fact, but does not tell us whether the family "will not," for instance, hire "outsiders" or whether there are no "outsiders" willing to be hired. When he speaks of peasants' earnings off the farm, the reference is to "trades and crafts."

[9] I do not mean to assert that Chayanov's model is the explanation of these Indian phenomena; only that it is "at best" consistent with them.

[10] To the point of "subjective equilibrium." And here one cannot avoid the wry thought that it is the dominant casteman who judges the suitability of the equilibrium and the Harijan who undertakes the "drudgery."

[11] The Russian evidence, however, supports Chayanov's model quite persuasively.

[12] See Beidelman (1959: 53-6) and Woltemade (1967: 136-51) for citations.

[13] Georgescu-Roegen (1966: 28) argues that this "is why a mechanistic schema of peasant behavior, like the schema of Standard Theory, proved to be an impossible project for all who thought of it," and cites Chayanov as an example.

[14] And "even *homo capitalisticus* — which standard theory is deemed to describe — often varies his tips according to his impression of the attendant's neediness, or patronizes a shop only because its owner is hard-pressed."

[15] I should say at once, and emphatically, that Georgescu-Roegen's article does not ignore politics, but deals with them only tangentially, as when he points out that East European jacqueries were a consequence of making feudalism capitalistic (marginalistic) too quickly. What he does not do is discuss the converse, feed-back effect of political action upon the economic variables, although some asides in the text make it clear that he could do so, and doubtless would like to do so.

[16] Cf. the account of Wangala village in Epstein (1962: chs. 2 & 8).

PART II

Religion and Reform

The Ambedkar memorial — Bombay

Owen Lynch

4.

ELEANOR ZELLIOT

Gandhi and Ambedkar –
A Study in Leadership

THE CONSTITUENT ASSEMBLY of independent India passed a provision legally abolishing untouchability on November 29, 1948, nine months after the death of Mahatma Gandhi. As the measure was approved, the house resounded with cries of "Mahatma Gandhi ki Jai" — victory to Mahatma Gandhi — a tribute to Gandhi's thirty-year effort to remove the practice of untouchability from the Indian scene. Present at that session of the Constituent Assembly as chairman of the drafting committee for the constitution was Dr. B. R. Ambedkar, an Untouchable. Three years before, he had ended his book *What Congress and Gandhi Have Done to the Untouchables* with the bitter words, "The Untouchables . . . have ground to say: 'Good God! Is this man Gandhi our Saviour?' "

The irony of the moment was lost on those present — a legalistic measure was taken in the name of Gandhi who had no use for legalism, coupled with lack of recognition for Ambedkar, the Untouchable who had drafted the measure and who had bitterly fought Gandhi to secure legalistic solutions to the problem of untouchability. The amalgamation of the two approaches to the problem in that moment, however, does symbolize India's continuing attempt to synthesize the ways of Gandhi and Ambedkar in efforts to remove the stigma of untouchability from democratic national life.

Both Mohandas K. Gandhi and Bhimrao Ramji Ambedkar are known, to different groups, as the "savior of the Untouchables." Gandhi was a caste Hindu, the "Father of Independence" who is said to have spoken and written more on untouchability than on any other subject.

[69]

Gandhi publicly put the abolition of untouchability along with Hindu-Muslim unity, as the essential prerequisite for India's true independence. He also made popular the term "Harijan" (children of God) for the Untouchables. Ambedkar was the most highly educated Untouchable in India, recognized by many as the Untouchables' chief spokesman, the founder of a political party for Untouchables, and the moving spirit behind organizations, schools, and colleges established for their uplift. One of Ambedkar's final acts was the initiation of a Buddhist conversion movement that ultimately attracted more than 3 million Untouchable adherents. On the day after Ambedkar's death, Nehru described him as "a symbol of the revolt against all the oppressive features of Hindu Society" (*New York Times,* Dec. 6, 1956).

Despite their common concern, Ambedkar and Gandhi were often at odds in their programs for the abolition of untouchability. In 1932 Gandhi thwarted Ambedkar's attempt to gain political concessions from the British, concessions that Ambedkar believed to be essential for the Untouchables' progress. Ambedkar retaliated by criticizing Gandhi more harshly than he did the orthodox Hindus who upheld untouchability as a religious essential. The conflict between these leaders is examined below in terms of their ideological differences and the different solutions which they advocated for the resolution of one of India's major social problems.

Gandhi may be described as a dominant group leader working for a national goal, who was concerned, both from a moral standpoint and from a realization of the need for unity, about injustices to a low status group within the nation. Ambedkar's correlative role was that of the militant leader of a politically conscious segment of the same depressed group. Seen in this light, the conflict between these two men has some parallels with certain aspects of the Black Power movement versus "White Liberals" in America of the 1960s.

The Indian situation, however, included several unique elements in that the leadership of the majority and minority groups represented, in simplistic terms, idealistic Hindu traditionalism and Western-influenced modernism. The Indian scene was also marked by a society-wide hierarchical system of social groups justified by religion; by the presence of other vocal minorities, especially that of the Muslims; and by the administrative power of still another group, the British government in India.

This study is concerned with the interaction of Gandhi and Ambedkar in the Indian milieu, more specifically with Ambedkar's reaction to Gandhi's policies and actions. Although a view from Ambedkar's standpoint of Gandhi's efforts to eradicate untouchability distorts the Mahatma's role in Indian history, this perspective, taken together with the abundance of literature on Gandhi, reveals a lesser known aspect of the Untouchables' role in contemporary India.

Before discussing Gandhi's actions and Ambedkar's reactions to them, it would be well to look at the background and ideology of each man. Gandhi's statements on untouchability have been collected in several small volumes: *Caste Must Go; All are Equal in the Eyes of God; None High: None Low; The Bleeding Wound!; My Soul's Agony; My Varnashrama Dharma; The Removal of Untouchability,* and others, which draw chiefly from his two newspapers, *Young India* and *Harijan.* Descriptions of his work, which sometimes include private asides as well as public pronouncements, have been written by his close associates about the Vaikam Satyagraha (Desai, 1937), his experiences at the Round Table Conference in London (Desai, in Gandhi, 1947), his Communal Award fast (Pyarelal, 1932) and the 1930s anti-untouchability campaigns (R. Nehru, 1950). Material on Gandhi has been taken from these works and two other sympathetic but frank accounts of Tendulkar (1952), and Desai (1953).

Ambedkar's underlying beliefs and aims have been derived from his writings on caste (1917, 1936, 1945, 1946, 1947, 1948), his testimony to various British commissions, biographies in English (Keer, 1962) and Marathi (Khairmode, 1952, 1958, 1964, 1966), and my own study of his life.

Mohandas Karamchand Gandhi (1869–1948)

At the beginning of his autobiography Gandhi identifies his caste as Bania (merchant) and states that for three generations his forefathers had not practiced the caste occupation, but had served as prime ministers in several princely states of the Kathiawad peninsula (now Gujarat). This was, and is, an essentially conservative region in its adherence to traditional patterns of social relations. Hindu and Jain merchant groups constitute an influential segment of the population. Vaishya, or Bania, castes are third in the traditional four-fold division of Hindu society, included with Brahman and Kshatriya among the twice-born. However, in Gujarat, probably more than in any other part of India, Banias are without peer in wealth, influence, and piety. They tend toward orthodoxy. Gandhi's *jati,* the Modh Banias, outcasted him in 1888 upon hearing of his proposed trip to London for study, and evidently never rescinded the proscription.

Gandhi's autobiography, which covers his life up to 1921, when he

was fifty-two, contains only a few references to Untouchables or untouchability. The most striking reference is the story of his insistence on the
admission of an Untouchable family to the ashram he had established
near Ahmedabad in 1915. At the time of his assumption of leadership
of the Indian National Congress in 1920, Gandhi made what seem to
be his first strong public statements on untouchability. They reflect his
dual role as Mahatma and politician in Indian life, already apparent at
that time. As politician, Gandhi said: "Swaraj is as unattainable without
the removal of the sin of untouchability as it is without Hindu-Muslim
unity" (*Young India,* December 29, 1920). As Mahatma, Gandhi said:
"I do not want to be reborn. But if I have to be reborn, I should be born
an Untouchable. . . . (*Young India,* April 27, 1921). As both Mahatma
and politician, Gandhi sought to weave the divergent interests in India
into a unified opposition to the British, at the same time trying to pursue
a course of reform without rending the social fabric of Indian society.
In Dalton's words, "Indian society saw Gandhi, and Gandhi regarded
himself, as occupying the peculiar position of a figure above the discord
around him, and uniquely capable of harmonizing it" (Dalton, 1967: 170).

Gandhi inherited the Congress position on untouchability first
recorded in a resolution in 1917 which urged "upon the people of India
the necessity, justice, and righteousness of removing all disabilities imposed upon the Depressed Classes" (Quoted in Ambedkar, 1946: 1).
The Congress resolution seems to have been made in response to a
meeting of the Depressed Classes in Bombay earlier in 1917 which asked
for such a resolution, in almost the same wording, in exchange for
support of the 1916 Congress-Muslim League constitutional scheme
(Natarajan, 1962: 148). Gandhi's contribution to the position was to
personalize it. Volunteers for the Non-cooperation Campaign in 1921
signed a pledge which placed responsibility on the individual: "As a
Hindu I believe in the justice and necessity of removing the evil of untouchability and shall on all possible occasions seek personal contact
with and endeavor to render service to the submerged classes" (Sitaramayya, 1946: 226). This emphasis on the caste Hindu's obligations to
the Untouchables remained a major tenet of Gandhi's teaching.

Gandhi's statements on the evil of untouchability were unequivocal
from the first, although his views regarding other caste-based practices
changed and grew less orthodox with the years. In 1920 he voiced
moderate opposition to social intercourse between castes which some
reformers advocated: "Interdrinking, interdining, intermarrying . . . are
not essential for the promotion of the spirit of democracy" (*Young India,*
December 8, 1920). Twenty-six years later, he said, "If I had my way

I would persuade all caste Hindu girls coming under my influence to select Harijan husbands" (*Harijan,* July 7, 1946). Underlying Gandhi's change in attitude toward social practices was an unchanging belief in *varnashramadharma,* the divinely ordained division of society into four groups defined according to duty: Brahman, Kshatriya, Vaishya, Shudra. Although Gandhi castigated the Indian caste system of his day with its superior and inferior divisions, he held to the end a belief in the traditional ordering of society for the preservation of harmony and the growth of the soul, and with it, traditional duties. "The Law of Varna prescribes that a person should, for his living, follow the lawful occupation of his forefathers," but with the understanding that all occupations are equally honorable: "A scavenger has the same status as a *Brahmin*" (*Young India,* November 17, 1927).

According to Gandhi, untouchability had no part in this divine ordering — the treatment of castes below the Shudra level as unclean was not only inhumane, but harmful to Hinduism. Gandhi described it at various times as a curse, an excrescence on Hinduism, a poison, a snake, a canker, a hydra-headed monster, a great blot, a device of Satan, a hideous untruth, Dyerism and O'Dwyerism, and the bar sinister. An Untouchable, wrote Gandhi, "should be regarded as a *Shudra* because there is no warrant for belief in a fifth caste" (*Young India,* April 23, 1925). While Shudras were created to serve the other three castes, their work was honorable. All varnas possess equality of status, but not equality of opportunity. "One born a scavenger must earn his livelihood by being a scavenger, and then do whatever else he likes. For a scavenger is as worthy of his hire as a lawyer or your President. That, according to me, is Hinduism" (*Harijan,* March 6, 1937).

Other early reformers, including Vivekananda and Dayanand Saraswati, espoused a similar conception of the ideal society as one composed of equal, harmoniously integrated varnas. The belief that untouchability was a perversion of true Hinduism, and a view of the Untouchable as one deserving of Shudra status, was acceptable even to such an orthodox Hindu leader as B.G.Tilak. Shortly before Gandhi's assumption of leadership in Congress, Tilak wrote, "It is a sin against God to say that a person is untouchable, who is not so to God Himself. . . . Hinduism absorbed the Shudras, can it not also absorb the untouchables?" (Tilak, 1918).

With his gift for symbolism, Gandhi selected the Bhangi, a scavenger caste of North India, to represent the problem of untouchability. Gandhi's abhorrence of untouchability, and his association of such practices with the Sweeper caste, appear rooted in childhood experience. Although not mentioned in his autobiography, Gandhi's reactions to his family's sweeper at the age of twelve are recorded in an article that he wrote in *Young India* (April 27, 1921).

A Scavenger named Uka, an "untouchable," used to attend our house for cleaning latrines. Often I would ask my mother why it was wrong to touch him. If I accidentally touched Uka, I was asked to perform ablutions, and though I naturally obeyed, it was not without smilingly protesting that it should be so. I was a very dutiful and obedient child, and so far as it was consistent with respect for parents, I often had tussles with them on this matter. I told my mother that she was entirely wrong in considering contact with Uka as sinful.

Uka remained the symbol for Untouchables in Gandhi's mind. Scavenging and the Bhangi figure prominently in many of Gandhi's pronouncements and actions. He himself cleaned a dirty latrine at the Calcutta Congress of 1901 and records it in his autobiography. He often used the metaphor of the mother's cleansing work for her child as a counterpart to the Bhangi's work for society. Sanitation work at Gandhi's ashrams was done by all members as a means for demonstrating the honorable nature of these essential duties. In later years Gandhi stayed sometimes in suitably cleaned Bhangi colonies. During the last days of his life, Gandhi even declared: "I would rejoice to think that we had a sweeper girl of a stout heart, incorruptible and of crystal purity to be our first President . . . assisted in the discharge of her duties by a person like Pandit Nehru" (Pyarelal, 1958: 228).

Although Gandhi was not the first to cry out against untouchability, he was the most prominent caste Hindu to proclaim that it was harmful to Hinduism, to make its removal a personal responsibility of the caste Hindu, to keep it before the public eye with passionate oratory and vivid imagery, and to found an organization for service to Untouchables. Perhaps as important as his ideology and his pronouncements was his personal example, from the beginning, of touching the Untouchable.

Bhimrao Ramji Ambedkar (1892–1956)

Ambedkar came from Western India, as did Gandhi, and was a London-trained barrister, as was Gandhi, but his caste, social background, and intellectual environment were very different. He was a Mahar, the largest Untouchable caste in the area now called Maharashtra, where this group constitutes about 10 percent of the population. The Mahars were, in British administrative parlance, "inferior village servants," whose traditional duties involved the maintenance of streets, walls, and cremation grounds, carrying messages, hauling away dead cattle, and similar menial and polluting tasks. However, the Mahars were not responsible for the cleaning of latrines or the removal of night soil. This work was and is done by Bhangis imported from the north and by Gujarati Untouchable migrants. During the 19th and early 20th centuries, a substantial number of Mahars removed themselves from their traditional village servant role. The establishment of British rule in Bombay Presidency provided Mahars with the opportunity for service in the army, employment in cotton mills, ammunition factories, railroads, dockyards, construction work, and as servants in British homes. The 1921 Census records that only 13.5 percent of the Mahar working force of nearly 300,000 were employed in their traditional occupation even though most Mahars maintained strong ties with their ancestral village.

The emergence of Mahar leaders and a new spirit of militancy in the 19th century was due in large measure to the influence of education acquired in the army (Ambedkar, 1946: 189) and in domestic service. In the twentieth century, leaders also emerged from the ranks of primary school teachers. Early efforts to legitimize Mahar claims to higher status were based on the assertion that their ancestors were of the Kshatriya varna (warrior class), a claim not uncommon among Untouchables elsewhere in India (Chapter 5, this volume). This claim was advanced in petitions submitted to the British in the 1890s to protest the closing of Mahar enlistment in the army. Although army recruitment of Mahars was stopped at about the time of Ambedkar's birth in 1892, his father and grandfather served in the army, and his early education and environment were those of a child in army cantonment schools and pensioned soldiers' colonies. Despite this background, Ambedkar differed from previous Mahar leaders in that he never claimed high caste status for Untouchables, since such claims implied an acceptance of upper caste superiority, nor did he invoke another common claim — that Untouchables were pre-Aryan, the original settlers of the land. While Untouchables in Madras and the Punjab were to base their demands for separate political status on a claim to pre-Aryan origin, Ambedkar argued that the Untouchables' position in Indian society was of social, not racial, origin and therefore subject to change.

Ambedkar's views as to the origin of untouchability are presented in *The Untouchables* published in 1948, late in his political career. According to this account, untouchability originated in the practices of separation and denigration imposed on those who remained Buddhists during an earlier period of renascent Hinduism. Despite the repressive role attributed to Hindus, Ambedkar's attitude toward Hinduism

remained ambivalent for much of his life. In the early 1920s he participated in efforts at "Sanskritization" in which Untouchables imitated
high caste religious ritual. But he soon found that the performance of
Vedic style weddings, the donning of the sacred thread, and similar
efforts to emulate upper caste ritual practice had little effect on the
attitudes of others. Such innovations were dropped in the 1930s. However,
from 1927 to 1935 Ambedkar helped organize campaigns to force
the opening of Hindu temples to Untouchables. This also proved to be
ineffective and in 1935 Ambedkar decided to reject all claims to Hinduism
by converting to another religion. At about this time, he presented in
The Annihilation of Caste a list of reforms for Hinduism that appear
naive and legalistic, based on abstractions rather than possibilities. The
cardinal reforms listed were: there should be one standard book of the
Hindu religion, acceptable to all Hindus; priests should receive their
office not by heredity, but by state examination; priests should be
limited in number by law and should be subject to disciplinary action
by the state (Ambedkar, 1936a). Ambedkar's final resolution of the
Untouchables' religious dilemma was adopted in 1956 when he converted
to Buddhism in an attempt to link the Untouchables to the greatness of
India's past while denying the contemporary concept of caste. This
solution was in keeping with Ambedkar's pride in India's culture, a theme
that appears intermittently throughout his writings, and his admiration of
such religious reformers as the Buddha, Kabir, and Mahatma Phule.

Although Ambedkar experienced discrimination and humiliation
during his youth, the Maharashtrian atmosphere of reform allowed him
exceptional opportunities for education and later for leadership. As a
bright Untouchable boy, and later as an educated, militant Untouchable
leader, he was aided by caste Hindu reformers. The Gaikwad of Baroda,
whose financial contributions to reformers and educators in Bombay
Presidency were of considerable consequence, gave Ambedkar a stipend
during his college days as part of the Baroda policy of educating Untouchables. Later the Gaikwad helped Ambedkar to go abroad for further
education where he obtained an M.A. and a Ph.D. from Columbia
University in New York, a D.Sc. from London University, and entrance
to the Bar from Grey's Inn, London. Ambedkar returned to Bombay in
1923 to begin his organizational work among Untouchables, and soon
came into close association with caste Hindus who encouraged his leadership. Many of his closest associates were high caste Hindus who formed
his intellectual circle in a day when no other Mahar shared his intellectual
interests. Caste Hindus also worked on the staff of Ambedkar's newspapers and labor unions, formed an inter-dining group of which he was
president, taught in his educational establishments, and in 1936 they

helped form his first political party, the Independent Labour Party. It was a Brahman, G. N. Sahasrabudde, who backed Ambedkar in one of his most dramatic rejections of Hindu orthodoxy, the burning of the ancient law book *Manusmriti* in 1927 as a protest against traditional caste restrictions.

Ambedkar, therefore, did not find Gandhi's condemnation of untouchability radical; he was in close touch with reformers who not only condemned untouchability, but the varna concept of caste as well, and who accepted his leadership in determining solutions to the problem. Not only as a highly educated Untouchable to whom pity was anathema, but also as a Maharashtrian reformer, Ambedkar found Gandhi's general ideology unappealing. Ram Joshi's latter-day evaluation of the Maharashtrian urban intelligensia's attitude toward Gandhian reform describes the milieu in which Ambedkar worked: "They disdained Gandhi's traditional outlook and modes of behavior.... They considered his philosophy outdated and rejected his program, which was based primarily on a concern for the rural masses. . . . In any case, they had no interest in a . . . drab reform program which could neither stimulate their intellect nor excite them to revolutionary action" (Joshi, 1968: 194-5).

Ambedkar's programs were intended to integrate the Untouchable into Indian society in modern, not traditional ways, and on as high a level as possible. This goal stood in marked contrast to Gandhi's "Ideal Bhangi" (*Harijan*, November 28, 1936) who would continue to do sanitation work even though his status would equal that of a Brahman. Ambedkar's ideal for the depressed was "to raise their educational standard so that they may know their own conditions, have aspirations to rise to the level of the highest Hindu and be in a position to use political power as a means to that end" (Thakkar, 1945: 7). Both reformers had a vision of equality, but for Ambedkar equality meant not equal status of the varnas, but equal social, political, and economic opportunity for all. Ambedkar planned his programs to bring the Untouchable from a state of "dehumanization" and "slavery" into one of equality through the use of modern methods based on education and the exercise of legal and political rights. At the same time, Ambedkar's modernizing ideology was tempered in practice by a clear perception of the tenacity of caste and tradition. He sought to awaken in the Untouchables an awareness of their debased condition and common interests that would promote the unity needed for the development of effective organizations and mass action. For such reasons, Ambedkar advocated a separatist policy accentuating caste distinctions as an initial stage in creating a society in which identities would be unimportant.

Ambedkar's commitment to education as a major means for

Untouchable advancement led him to initiate in the 1920s a program for the creation of hostels for Untouchable students. This effort resulted in the development of a system of colleges organized by the People's Education Society, founded by Ambedkar in 1945. While Ambedkar exhorted numerous conferences of Untouchables to expand their educational opportunities at every level, much of his own effort was aimed at producing highly educated men, capable of raising the image of the Untouchable through their ability to function at the highest level of Indian urban society. He also advocated the abandonment of customs and practices associated with the stereotype of the Untouchable, including the consumption of alcoholic beverages and carrion beef. Such pronouncements on the need to live clean and moral lives sound very much like Gandhi's. However, Ambedkar's vision of the Untouchable's future role went far beyond that of Gandhi, or indeed that of any other Untouchable leader.

Ambedkar's political policies were developed in the light of India's democratizing political reforms. During his lifetime Ambedkar saw the representation of Untouchables in the Bombay Provincial Legislative Council grow from one appointed member (granted in 1921 by the Montagu-Chelmsford Reforms) to full-fledged elected representation based on the system of reserved seats. Achievements of this kind, founded on "protective discrimination" and western forms of government, supported Ambedkar's contention that political power must be assured the Untouchable minority even if separatism was fostered by the granting of such power. This view, coupled with Ambedkar's firm belief in the power of representative political bodies to correct social and economic injustice, underlies many of the issues that arose between Ambedkar and Gandhi. Ambedkar's adaptation of western concepts to the Indian scene is also reflected in the terms he used to justify Untouchable political rights: democracy, fraternity, and liberty. In his Marathi speeches, Ambedkar conveyed the implication of these concepts in a single word, *manuski,* that was readily understood by the most illiterate Mahar villager. Although *manuski's* literal meaning is "human-ness," it serves to evoke feelings of self-respect and humane attitudes towards one's fellow man.

In 1946, Gandhi said, "I myself have become a Harijan by choice" (*Harijan,* June 9, 1946). Ambedkar had no choice. His actions were molded not only by his own personal background and achievements, and the Maharashtrian thought of his day, but also by his status as an Untouchable. The Untouchable caste he came from had begun social and political movements before he assumed a position of leadership.

His contribution was to raise these attempts to a level of effectiveness such that the caste could achieve en masse a religious conversion, build a political party, and greatly increase its participation in education at all levels. Beyond his own caste, Ambedkar helped to shape the vast program of legal rights and safeguards for Untouchables which India developed. He directly influenced some other Untouchable castes through the conversion movement and his political parties, and indirectly affected many more. In his own person, as lawyer, writer, statesman, constitutionalist, he was an example to all India of what an Untouchable could become.

Ambedkar's Reaction to Gandhi

The Vaikam satyagraha of 1924-25 in Travancore state offered Gandhi his first opportunity to act publicly on behalf of Untouchables and produced Ambedkar's first public comment on Gandhian methods. Gandhi was not the initiator of the campaign to remove the prohibition against Untouchables' use of the roadway passing the temple at Vaikam, but he was in contact with campaign leadership and visited the area during the second year of the satyagraha to negotiate with temple and state officials (Bondurant, 1958: 46-52). The satyagraha for the use of the road was begun by several South Indian caste Hindus, a Syrian Orthodox Christian, and some followers of Sri Narayana Guru, the spiritual leader of a populous and comparatively well-to-do Depressed Caste, the Ilavas.* Although undoubtedly patterned after the Gandhian satyagraha method and supported by many Gandhians, the satyagraha was also an outgrowth of the Ilavas' own movement to gain political and religious rights. It came in the wake of the Ilavas' 1918 appeal to the Travancore government for the opening of state temples to all Hindus and their 1921 threat to convert in a body to Christianity.

Gandhi's negotiation with a Nambudiri Brahman trustee of the Vaikam temple at the time of the satyagraha, faithfully recorded by his secretary Mahadev Desai (Desai, 1937: 17-21) shows something of the temper of the orthodox at the time as well as Gandhi's method of persuasion:

Gandhiji: Is it fair to exclude a whole section of Hindus, because of their supposed lower birth, from public roads which can be used by non-Hindus, by criminals and bad characters, and even by dogs and cattle?

---

* The Ilavas, also spelled Ezhavas or Iravas, were counted as a Depressed Class in the 1931 census, but are not now considered a Scheduled Caste.

Nambudiri Trustee: But how can it be helped? They are reaping the reward of their *karma.*

Gandhiji: No doubt they are suffering for their *karma* by being born as untouchables. But why must you add to the punishment? Are they worse than even criminals and beasts?

Nambudiri Trustee: They must be so, for otherwise God would not condemn them to be born untouchables.

G: But God may punish them. Who are we human beings to take the place of God and add to their punishment?

N: We are instruments. God uses us as His instruments in order to impose on them the punishment that their *karma* has earned for them.

G: But supposing the Avarnas outside *varna,* i.e., untouchables, said that they were instruments in the hands of God in order to impose afflictions on you? What would you do?

N: Then the Government would stand between them and us and prevent them from doing. Good men would do so. Mahatmaji, we beseech you to prevent Avarnas from depriving us of our old privileges.

After a thorough discussion of the religious authority behind the prohibition against the Untouchables' use of the road, Gandhi made a last proposal: "Would you accept arbitration? You appoint a Pandit on behalf of the Satyagrahis, and the Dewan acts as Umpire. What do you say to that?" No reply was recorded. Although the temple authorities finally capitulated and the road past the temple was open to all (or moved farther away from the temple — the denouement of the satyagraha is not clear), Untouchables were not allowed to enter the temple until 1936. At that time, coincident with another Ilava threat to convert to Christianity, Travancore became one of the first states to enact a law opening its state temples to Untouchables.

Although the Vaikam satyagraha represents the only time Gandhi used non-violent direct action on behalf of Untouchables' rights, it fore-shadowed many aspects of subsequent Gandhian activity: stress on the orthodox Hindus' inhumane treatment of Untouchables, attempts to secure voluntary lifting of the ban by changing the hearts of the caste Hindus, and working within a Hindu framework of ideas. The temple trustees' negative response was also typical of later reactions to Gandhi's policies which often elicited bitter criticism from orthodox Hindus.

Ambedkar referred briefly to the Vaikam satyagraha in a speech that he delivered in 1924 to a provincial conference of the Depressed Classes. It was his first large public meeting after the completion of the London phase of his education, and also the founding meeting of his first organization, the Bahishkrit Hitakarini Sabha (Organization For the Welfare of the Excluded). At this time, Ambedkar spoke against conversion to another religion as a means of removing disabilities, and he stressed self-improvement, unity, and organization as the paths to a better life for Untouchables. He used the Vaikam satyagraha with its high caste participants as an example, not of caste Hindu-sympathies, but of the political importance of the Untouchable:

If we remain Hindus as we are, then the Aryan religion will persevere in this country. On the other hand if we become Muslim, then there will be a predominance of that foreign culture in India. If this were not so, the Brahmans would not have been ready to offer satyagraha for the untouchable class at Vaikam. [Ambedkar, 1924]

The following year the Bombay Province Depressed Classes Conference, again with Ambedkar as president, heard Ambedkar present a more detailed analysis of the Vaikam satyagraha, which Gandhi had then joined. The address as a whole was still conciliatory in tone and more emphatic on internal reform than on changing Indian society, but there was no wholehearted support for Gandhi. Although Ambedkar stated that for Untouchables "the most important event in the country today is the satyagraha at Vaikam," he pointed out that after a whole year of protest there had been no result. He next spoke of Gandhi:

Before Mahatma Gandhi, no politician in this country maintained that it is necessary to remove social injustice here in order to do away with tension and conflict, and that every Indian should consider it his sacred duty to do so. . . . However, if one looks more closely one finds that there is a slight disharmony . . . for he does not insist on the removal of untouchability as much as he insists on the propagation of Khaddar [home-spun cloth] or Hindu-Muslim unity. If he had he would have made the removal of untouchability a precondition of voting in the party. Well, be that as it may, when one is spurned by everyone, even the sympathy shown by Mahatma Gandhi is of no little importance.

Ambedkar went on to note that the orthodox Brahmans at Vaikam had used scripture to justify their position to Gandhi:

This clearly indicates that either we should burn all these scriptures or verify and examine the validity of their rules regarding untouchability . . . and if we are unable to prove their falseness or invalidity, we are to suffer untouchability till the end of time! . . . Truly these scriptures are an insult to people. The government should have confiscated them long ago. [Khairmode, 1958: 117-118]

Although Ambedkar did not completely reject Gandhi's support until their political battle over Depressed Class political rights in 1931, two remarks in the 1925 address portend his later actions. His scathing comment on Hindu scripture culminated in a public burning of *Manusmriti* in 1927, and in 1935 Ambedkar announced his vow to leave Hinduism entirely and to convert to some other religion. Ambedkar's complaint that Gandhi had not required an oath of disbelief in untouchability as a precondition for membership in Congress later turned to a wholesale condemnation of Congress resolutions on the subject as hypocrisy.

Before Ambedkar's rejection of Hinduism in 1935, the Mahars made several attempts to gain religious and social rights by using the Gandhian technique of satyagraha, mass action without violence. A Depressed Classes conference was held in Mahad, a small town south of Bombay, in 1927. During the course of that conference, a group of several thousand moved en masse to a tank in the Brahman section of the town, where the leaders of the procession stooped and drank water. After the conference, the tank was ritually purified by the townspeople. Later in the year Ambedkar called another conference in Mahad to reiterate the Untouchables' right to use the public water supply. It was at this second conference that the *Manusmriti* was publicly burned. This radical gesture was balanced by Ambedkar's decision to comply with a court injunction prohibiting further satyagraha for water rights. He preferred to fight a ten-year court case, which he won, rather than take to the streets again. In spite of the long delay in the resolution of this issue, the Mahars look upon the Mahad satyagraha as the beginning of their political awakening. The spirit and unity demonstrated in that first mass action became a Mahar legend. Some caste Hindus attended the conferences, but the burning of *Manusmriti* cost Ambedkar the approval of all but the most radical of his caste Hindu supporters.

The second Mahar satyagraha was initiated in 1929 in an attempt to gain entry to the Parvati temple in Poona. This effort was also conducted in the Gandhian style, but it was not approved by Gandhi or Congress. Untouchables from several castes led by a Mahar from Poona named Shivram Janba Kamble, together with some Maratha and Brahman sympathizers, joined in a four-month attempt to enter the gates of the temple complex on Parvati Hill. A song written by a Mahar for the satyagraha related that the marchers climbed the steps to the temple gates shouting the names of Lord Shankar, Shivaji Maharaj, Cokhamela (a Mahar saint-poet of the fourteenth century), and Dr. Ambedkar (Jamgekar, 1930).* Gandhi's name was not mentioned, but the technique and inspiration for the satyagraha undoubtedly were drawn from Gandhi's teachings. Although Ambedkar's name was shouted by the marchers, he was not present.

---

*This poem by Tulshiram Lakshman Jamgekar was published in 1930 in Poona by Anant Vinayak Patwardhan and T. L. Jamgekar under the Marathi title, *Parvativaril Satyagrahaca Powada.*

The Anti-Untouchability Sub-Committee created by Congress in March of 1929 investigated the satyagraha. The committee, which included the Hindu Mahasabha leader Pandit M. M. Malaviya and Jamnalal Bajaj, a Marwari businessman from Wardha who had built a Temple for Untouchables in his own home district, expressed their disapproval of the satyagraha and recommended that Congress not support it. According to their report (Indian National Congress 1929), half a dozen temples had already been opened; negotiations with the temple trustees were being upset by the "atmosphere of bitterness and distrust" created by the satyagraha; and the "Bombay untouchable leaders . . . did not make too much of a fetish of non-violence." The latter criticism is inconsistent with another statement in the report that the Poona satyagraha observed "exemplary non-violence" in the face of attack.

Although there was no direct confrontation between Ambedkar and Gandhi on this issue, the failure of the satyagraha (Parvati was not open to Untouchables until India's independence in 1947) and the lack of Congress support in an action performed according to Gandhian principles increased distrust on the part of Ambedkar and his followers for Congress and Gandhi. The last of the Mahar satyagrahas, held from 1930 to 1935 at Nasik, widened the breach.

This largest and longest satyagraha effort took place at the Kalaram temple in the important pilgrimage center of Nasik. Organized by Ambedkar and local Mahar leaders, the Kalaram satyagraha involved thousands of Untouchables in intermittent efforts to enter the temple and to participate in the annual temple procession. As in the case of the Parvati satyagraha in Poona, the attempt was unsuccessful. Here, too, opposition came not only from the orthodox Hindus but also from some local Congressmen. The outcome of the Kalaram satyagraha, however, was not only further disillusionment with the satyagraha method and the attitude of Congress, but also a rejection of Hinduism and a strengthening of the separatist political stance then developing among Untouchables.

In 1930, the first year of the Kalaram satyagraha, Ambedkar appeared before a large conference of the Depressed Classes at Nagpur. Although he had helped plan and encouraged the Nasik satyagraha, he barely mentioned the Untouchables' attempt to enter the Kalaram temple in his presidential address to the conference. Instead, he dwelt on political matters. Ambedkar had just been designated as one of two Depressed Class representatives at the Round Table Conference to be held in London, and he stated the position he would present to that august body in its deliberations on the future constitution of India. He held that only *swaraji* (independence) would bring the possibility of equality to the

Depressed Classes, a position not before stated by an Untouchable leader. Ambedkar's option for independence, however, contained a proviso. He told his audience that while he agreed with Congressmen who said that no country was good enough to rule over another, he intended to tell Congress "point blank that the proposition does not end there and that it is equally true that no class is good enough to rule over another class" (*Indian Annual Register* 1930: II, 369).

In his Nagpur speech, Ambedkar also indicated that he did not intend to press for a separate electorate for Untouchables, one in which they could vote for their candidates independently of the caste Hindu vote. This position differed from the plea for a separate electorate, similar to that won by the Muslims, advocated in 1928–29 by most of the Depressed Class groups in their testimony to the Simon Commission. Ambedkar, however, did ask for guaranteed rights, including "adequate" representation on all elected political bodies. This more moderate stance was still out of line with the Congress position. In 1928, the Nehru plan for government had rejected the idea of specific guaranteed rights for Untouchables at the same time that it abrogated the 1916 Congress-Muslim League agreement assuring communal representation for Muslims.

At the first Round Table Conference, held in 1930, which no Congressman attended because of the Non-Cooperation movement of that year, Ambedkar altered his moderate goal. Since his plea for adult suffrage had been rejected by the British, and the Muslim demand for separate electorates appeared unalterable, Ambedkar shifted his position and argued for separate electorates for the Depressed Classes during a ten-year period. Consequently, Ambedkar's political stance in regard to Congress was stiffened considerably prior to his encounter with Gandhi at the second Round Table Conference held in London in 1931.

At the second Round Table, Ambedkar confronted Gandhi, who not only refused to consider separate electorates for the Depressed Classes but also opposed any form of special representation involving reserved seats. The two men had met for the first time in Bombay just before the second Round Table Conference. Ambedkar's caste Hindu friends had arranged the meeting, but it did not lead to understanding. Ambedkar felt that he had been treated rudely, and Gandhi said later that he had not known Ambedkar was an Untouchable until the London Conference (Desai, 1953: 52), which implies that he knew little of Ambedkar's work in Bombay. This unsatisfactory meeting, and the basic disagreement between these leaders on the issue of special representation for Untouchables, made negotiation during the Round Table conference sessions difficult. The situation was exacerbated by Gandhi's questioning of Ambedkar's bona fides: "I say that it is not a proper claim which is registered by Dr. Ambedkar when he seeks to speak for the whole of the Untouchables of India. . . . I myself in my own person claim to represent the vast mass of the Untouchables" (Indian Round Table Conference, 2nd, 1932, p. 544).

After the third Round Table Conference, during which Gandhi was in jail, the British government announced a decision regarding representation which it was hoped would effect compromise between Congress and Ambedkar. This communal award of 1932 gave the Depressed Classes a double vote, one in a special constituency for a modest number of reserved seats, and one in the general electorate. Gandhi's response to the communal award was to enter a "fast unto death" on September 20, 1932. On the first day of the fast, he wrote in a letter to P. N. Rajbhoj, a Chambhar Untouchable from Poona:

My fast was reference only to separate electorates. . . . I must say that I am not in love with the idea of Statutory reservation. Whilst it is not open to the same objection that separate electorate is, I have not a shadow of doubt that it will prevent the natural growth for the suppressed classes and will remove the incentive to honourable amends from the suppressors. What I am aiming at is a heart understanding between the two, the greatest opportunity of repentance and reparation on the part of the suppressors. I am certain that the movement is ripe for the change of heart among them. I would therefore favour widest possible franchise for the suppressed and establish a convention between the two sections for securing proper election of representatives of the suppressed. [Letter to P. N. Rajbhoj]

This seems to be the voice of Gandhi speaking as Mahatma. A somewhat more political motive for Gandhi's protest is indicated in the report of a conversation between Gandhi and Sardar Patel a day after the fast began. Gandhi's secretary, Mahadev Desai, recorded Gandhi's comments:

The possible consequences of separate electorates for Harijans [this must be Desai's editing — the word Harijan was not yet used by Gandhi] fill me with horror. Separate electorates for all other communities will still leave room for me to deal with them, but I have no other means to deal with "untouchables." These poor fellows will ask why I who claim to be their friend should offer Satyagraha simply because they were granted some privileges; they would vote separately but vote with me. They do not realise that the separate electorate will create division among Hindus so much that it will lead to blood-shed. "Untouchable" hooligans will make common cause with Muslim hooligans and kill caste-Hindus. Has the British Government no idea of all this? I do not think so. [Desai, 1953: 301]

The British Government's response to Gandhi's fast was to declare that a solution to the representation of the Depressed Classes had to be settled within the Hindu community. Consequently, the man whose leadership of the Depressed Classes was challenged by Gandhi in London, became the arbiter of Gandhi's fate. Ambedkar met with various Hindu leaders under ever-increasing tension as Gandhi's condition worsened. Since reserved seats had been unenthusiastically accepted by Gandhi in the period following his confrontation with Ambedkar in London, the issue was a separate electorate, a cause Ambedkar had adopted only the year before. Ambedkar drove a hard bargain, trading a separate electorate for a separate primary election plus a large increase in the number of seats reserved for Untouchables — from the seventy-eight given in the communal award to 148 seats.

In the ensuing years, neither caste Hindus nor Depressed Class politicians were happy about this agreement, called the Yeravda or Poona Pact. Caste Hindus, particularly in Bengal, felt that reserved seats for the Depressed Classes unduly diminished the number of legislative seats available to Hindus in areas with a large Muslim population. Depressed Class leaders found the primary system to be expensive and unwieldy, and Ambedkar made at least one futile attempt to change it. Some Depressed Class leaders felt that Congress did not nominate able and truly representative Depressed Class members for reserved seats. Although Congress never formally approved the Poona Pact, it became, after the provision for a primary election was abandoned, the basis for all future elections.

The Poona Pact in itself accomplished little more than might have emerged from an earlier compromise, but the dramatic circumstances in which it was forged gave a great deal of publicity to Gandhi's concern for the Untouchable and to Ambedkar's leadership. Both men intensified their efforts to eliminate untouchability during the next two decades, each continuing to follow the line of action already established. Gandhi sought to change the heart of the caste Hindu by moral pressure within the framework of Hindu tradition. Ambedkar continued to work in the fields of education and politics in an attempt to gain legal rights for the Untouchable in the secular world.

Among Gandhi's activities was the organization of a group devoted to the removal of untouchability. Formed in Bombay on September 30, 1932, it was first called the All India Anti-Untouchability League. Pandit Madan Mohan Malaviya of the Hindu Mahasabha presided at the first meeting; the industrialist Ghanshyamdas Birla was named president, and the secretary was Amritlal V. Thakkar, a social worker among the tribes. Several Untouchables were on the central board, including M. C. Rajah of Madras, named in 1927 as the first Untouchable to serve in the central legislative assembly, Ambedkar, and Rao Bahdur Srinivasan of Madras, Ambedkar's fellow delegate to the Round Table conferences. The name of Gandhi's organization was soon changed to the Servants of Untouchables Society. This title was then translated into Hindi as the

Harijan Sevak Sangh, using the term Harijan (children of God) adopted by Gandhi as a new appellation for the Untouchable. The purpose of the society was to use peaceful persuasion to secure access for the Depressed Classes to all public wells, roads, schools, temples, and cremation grounds. Social reforms such as inter-dining and other caste-based practices were admittedly outside the scope of the new organization. Gandhi toured 12,500 miles over India from November, 1933, to the end of July, 1934, to preach against untouchability and to collect funds for the organization.

Although Ambedkar was a member of the first central board, his connection with Gandhi's organization lasted only a few months. While enroute to the Third Round Table Conference in 1932, Ambedkar wrote a long letter to the organization's secretary A. V. Thakkar (a letter that Ambedkar claimed went unanswered) stating that he wanted the Anti-Untouchability League to be concerned primarily with civic rights and equal opportunity in economic matters and social intercourse (Ambedkar, 1946: 134-141). Ambedkar's view of the proposed goals of the League proved to be quite different from that of its founders. Ambedkar soon resigned and other Untouchable members on the board seem to have disappeared quietly from the scene. In its form as the Harijan Sevak Sangh, the new organization was closed to Untouchable leadership. Gandhi defended this policy in response to criticism by explaining that it was an organization for penitents, for the expiation of the guilt of the caste Hindus. For this reason, Untouchables should advise but were not to be the doers (See Ambedkar, 1946: 142, 279-290; Pyarelal, 1958: 667-8).

The years immediately after the Poona Pact were Gandhi's most intense period of work for anti-untouchability, but he failed not only to win the support of Ambedkar, but also to conciliate the orthodox Hindus. They took exception to his program and to his personal actions as well. An article vehemently critical of Gandhi for his temple entry campaign and also for his allowing the marriage of his son to the daughter of C. Rajagopalacharia, a Madrasi Brahman, appeared in a Bombay journal, *The Indian Mirror* on August 5, 1933. This article included the accusation, expressed in a poem by Professor J. Mangiah, that Gandhi turned "good" Untouchables into malcontents:

> Untouchables our folks are good,
> Till Gandhi told them they were Gods
> Content they were to faith they stood
> To Congress lessons now each nods.

Sardar Patel, always the pragmatic advisor, told Gandhi during the Harijan campaign, "Why have you placed yourself between two stones? I keep telling you not to do so. Let the two stones grind each other. Why must you come in between?" (Panjabi, 1962: 79).

While the orthodox resented Gandhi's use of the word Harijan for Untouchables and rejected Gandhi's attempts at persuasion regarding the temple entry issue, educated Untouchables found the word Harijan patronizing and the results of the temple campaign insignificant. Jagjivan Ram, a rising young Untouchable politician in the Congress organization of Bihar State, described the Harijan Sevak Sangh as being erroneous in conception, faulty in emphasis, and halting in execution (Sharma, 1957: 107). He addressed a spirited protest to Gandhi when Gandhi asked a Christian missionary to pray for the Harijans but not to try to convert them as they did not have "the mind and intelligence to understand what you talked. . . . Would you preach the Gospel to a cow?" (*Harijan,* December 19, 1936). Gandhi replied that no ill will was intended; for him the cow was a symbol of gentleness and patient suffering (Sharma, 1957: 83). It was clear, though, that in Gandhi's concept of service to the suffering Untouchables, there was little room for the educated, politically conscious Untouchables pressing for civil rights.

Through the mid-1930s Gandhi continued his labors to exorcize the evil of untouchability by an arduous nine-month Harijan tour, a lengthy fast to purify his soul and to call attention to the existence of the blight of untouchability, and attempts to secure temple entry. During the same period Ambedkar moved farther and farther away from the possibility of cooperating with Gandhi's program based on religious reform or with Congress' political measures. In 1935, Ambedkar announced at Yeola, a town in Maharashtra near the site of the earlier struggle for temple entry at Nasik, that although born a Hindu, he would not die a Hindu. The following year, a conference of Mahars held in Bombay City passed a resolution to disassociate themselves from Hinduism by converting to some other religion. Ambedkar's plan provided that each Untouchable caste was to make its own decision. Although the idea was widely discussed among Untouchables in north India and in Travancore in the south, no caste other than the Mahars committed itself to leaving Hinduism en masse. The Mahars, however, did not implement their decision even though Christian, Muslim, and Sikh religious leaders announced themselves ready to receive Untouchable converts. Ambedkar's 1935 conversion speech and the Mahar response to it bore every evidence of sincerity, but none of the existing religions satisfied Ambedkar's criteria. Islam and Christianity were evidently disqualified because they were foreign and not Indian in origin. Sikhism was seriously considered, but there was no guarantee that the hard-won political rights of the Untouchables would be continued if they became Sikhs. Although Ambedkar was already attracted to the Buddhist past, there were no effective Buddhist organizations in India and little of the interest in Buddhism that was to appear in post-Independence India (See Fiske, this volume, Ch. 6).

The decision to convert may also have been postponed because of Ambedkar's intense political and administrative activity during the following decade. In 1937, his newly formed Independent Labour Party backed fourteen Scheduled Caste candidates for reserved seats and four caste Hindus for general seats in the Bombay Legislative Assembly. The party won eleven reserved and three general seats. (Two of the defeated candidates had contested seats in the area where the Mahad satyagraha had taken place ten years before.)

Although Ambedkar's party was successful in the election, its position as a small minority in a Congress-dominated assembly was very weak (See Isaacs, Chapter 13, this volume). The party was rarely successful in its areas of concern, chiefly labor and agricultural policies. In 1942, Ambedkar reformulated his political plans. He formed a new party, the Scheduled Castes Federation, and limited it to Untouchables in the hope of uniting all Untouchables in a new battle for political power. Ambedkar had been selected the same year to serve as the member for Labour on the Viceroy's Executive Council, a post which gave him considerable power in formulating policy and granting patronage, but kept him from spending much time on party organization. His energies were devoted to administration on the highest governmental level and to writing a series of books on national problems and the situation of the Untouchable.

It was during this period of the mid-1940s that Ambedkar launched his most vitriolic attacks against Gandhi. Ambedkar's personal political success, and the recognition accorded him as an able administrator, did little to assuage his anger. Although he recognized that the prospects for the Depressed Classes had been improved through the extension of educational opportunities and the reservation of government jobs, he was acutely conscious of the continuing disabilities that affected most Untouchables. Ambedkar's criticism was not of the orthodox Hindu, whom he had given up years before as hopeless, but of Gandhi and the Congress — those who would inherit political power in the impending withdrawal of British rule.

What Congress and Gandhi Have Done to Untouchables, first published in 1945, contains Ambedkar's most impassioned criticism. It is basically a plea for a separate electorate for the Untouchable. Public statements, voting records, and numerous incidents showing the isolation and mistreatment of Untouchables are presented to support the contention that political separation from the Hindus in the electoral system is necessary for the attainment of Untouchable political rights. An indictment of Gandhian philosophy and action is a major theme of the book. The Harijan Sevak Sangh is held to be a political charity, intended to bring Untouchables into the Congress camp. The Temple Entry campaign is criticized for its lack of success and the turning off and on of this issue to further Congress political interests. The *varnashramadharma* scheme is described as an unnatural ordering of society, impracticable and inhumane in its allocation of occupations by heredity. Gandhi's idea of ennobling the scavenging profession is viewed as "an outrage and a cruel joke." In many ways Ambedkar's reactions parallel current Black criticism of Lincoln's resolution of the problem of balancing the interests of a depressed minority against the need to foster national unity. According to Ambedkar, "Mr. Gandhi's attitude is that let Swaraj perish if the cost of it is political freedom of the Untouchables" (Ambedkar, 1946: 283).

Ambedkar's words appear to have exerted little influence on the British. The Cripps Cabinet Mission, sent to India in 1946 to arrange the transfer of power to Indian hands, was more influenced by the failure of the Scheduled Castes Federation in the 1946 elections. Consequently, the British provided no special political rights for the Untouchables beyond reserved seats in the legislatures. Ambedkar's response to the Cripps proposal was to launch huge satyagraha demonstrations before the state legislatures at Poona, Nagpur, Lucknow, and in the industrial city of Kanpur from July to October of 1946. This effort failed to move the planners of India's future.

After 1947

The creation of Pakistan in 1947 stilled the Muslims' demand for a separate electorate and eliminated the possibility that Scheduled Castes might obtain such an award. Although Ambedkar's major effort on behalf of his community failed, his role as a national leader was recognized and enhanced by his election to the Constituent Assembly. Initially elected to this body in 1946 through the cooperative efforts of the Scheduled Castes and Muslim League in Bengal, after the partition of Bengal in 1947 he was continued in the same position by the Congress of Bombay — evidently as a gesture of good will. In August of 1947, Ambedkar was named Law Minister in the first cabinet of independent India, while retaining his position as chairman of the committee responsible for drafting a constitution for the new nation.

The first years following Independence were a period of cooperation between politically conscious Untouchables and Congress Hindus. Ambedkar skillfully piloted the constitution through the Constituent Assembly.

In doing so, he relinquished some of his radical ideas, such as the nationalization of agriculture, in order to create a constitution based on consensus. However, the refusal of Congress leaders to support Ambedkar's Hindu Code Bill led him to resign from the cabinet in 1951. His resignation statement indicated frustration over Nehru's domineering leadership as well as India's treatment of Untouchables.

In the last years of his life Ambedkar devoted himself chiefly to his interest in Buddhism. In the months before his death in 1956 he took two actions based on his belief that separatist action on the part of Untouchables and other dispossessed groups was necessary for their eventual integration. He became a Buddhist on October 14, 1956, setting in motion a conversion movement that was to encompass three million people.* He also announced the establishment of the Republican Party, which was to be an instrument of political power for all the dispossessed, including the Scheduled Tribes, as well as the Scheduled Castes. His death left both new movements in the hands of those Untouchables most thoroughly organized by his work — the Mahars of Maharashtra.

Legacies of Leadership

Despite Ambedkar's criticism of Gandhi, and Gandhi's unwillingness to include such men as Ambedkar in the structure of his reform schemes, there were indications that each was conscious of the other's necessary place in any final solution of the problem of untouchability. Ambedkar recounted to reporters on the evening before his conversion to Buddhism that years before he had told Mahatma Gandhi, "I will choose only the least harmful way for the country" (*Nagpur Times,* October 14, 1956). On the other side, there is widespread belief on the part of many Mahars that Gandhi wanted Ambedkar to be prime minister. This is supported by a note in the *Illustrated Weekly of India* to the effect that if Gandhi had had his way, "B. R. Ambedkar, lifelong opponent of Gandhism, would have been even at the head of the state" (January 22, 1950).

The paths of Gandhi and Ambedkar, while they often diverged, ultimately converged, forcing on the Indian conscience the problem of untouchability as an issue of national concern. Nurullah and Naik reinforce this view in their analysis of the influence exerted by these two men.

---

*For a fuller discussion of the Buddhist movement and Ambedkarian politics see my article "Buddhism and Politics in Maharashtra," in *South Asian Politics and Religion,* Donald E. Smith, ed. Princeton University Press, 1966, and Fiske's discussion in Ch. 6, this volume.

Gandhiji's main work lay among the caste Hindus, and its greatness is to be measured by the extent of change brought about in the minds of the caste Hindus. But however painful, it is a fact of history that he did not have a very large following among the Harijans themselves. On the other hand, Dr. Ambedkar was a Harijan by birth . . . and therefore was destined to be the leader of these people by virtue of his birth, complete identification with their cause and unequalled capacity. . . . In a way, his work was complementary to that of Mahatma Gandhi, although owing to differences of approach, he often came in conflict with Gandhiji and the Congress.

The great service of Dr. Ambedkar to the cause is the awakening that he created among the Harijans. He gave them a leadership which they sadly lacked and which was very badly needed. He put the problem of the Harijans before the country in its true perspective — political, social and economic. [Nurullah and Naik, 1951: 723-33]

There are no equivalents of either Gandhi or Ambedkar in India today, no famous Mahatma preaching that Untouchability is a sin, no statesman-cum-partisan leader serving as an outspoken champion of Untouchables. Although Jagjivan Ram comes nearest to filling this latter role, he is primarily known as an astute politician. In a sense, the viewpoints of Gandhi and Ambedkar were amalgamated in such a way that political and social measures which Ambedkar would have approved are taken in the name of Gandhi. The scene described earlier in the Constituent Assembly illustrates this. Although the measure legally abolishing untouchability was adopted with cries of "Victory to Mahatma Gandhi!", Gandhi never advocated legal measures, feeling as he did that all change must come voluntarily from the heart. Yet such was his effect on the Hindu mind that the practice of untouchability is now considered, at least by the educated, as wrong, and the uplift of the Untouchable to the level of others as a good. In a recent speech to the Rajya Sabha, Prime Minister Indira Gandhi called for bringing "one of [Gandhi's] near dreams to reality" by giving education, employment, and land ownership to Harijans and ensuring "that people belonging to the Scheduled Castes and Tribes are put in positions of Authority where they can solve their own and others' problems" (*Times of India,* August 13, 1967).

The vast machinery of protective discrimination for the Scheduled Castes was developed chiefly in the 1930s and 1940s under the British, and legitimized psychologically by the Gandhian campaigns of the period. The post-Independence government adopted most of these measures and further refined and extended them (See Dushkin, Chapter 9, this volume). Benefits since accorded to Untouchables have included reserved seats in all legislative bodies, the reservation of government jobs, aid to students through the college level, prizes to villages demonstrating equality, gifts of money for marriages in which one partner is an Untouchable, support for housing projects, and legal machinery for suits against discriminative practices. (See Galanter, Chapter 10, this volume). Such measures reflect the attitudes and policies developed by the leaders and events of the past. They have also inhibited the emergence of a new Mahatma decrying passionately against remaining injustices, or the development of a separatist Untouchable leader capable of building a movement outside the walls of government privilege and patronage. These privileges have also walled off the continuing problems of the Untouchable from the Indian consciousness. Untouchability is news only when a government commission is appointed to investigate some aspect of the problem, or when a particularly dramatic event occurs, such as the burning of forty-two Untouchables in a hut in an east Tanjore district village during landlord-tenant conflicts (*Blitz,* January 4, 1969). Even public expressions of orthodox views are relatively rare as evidenced by the sensational news coverage given in 1969 to the Shankaracharya of Puri's public pronouncements in defense of untouchability.

While Gandhi may be credited with the general atmosphere of concern for the Untouchable expressed in India's official policies, efforts of the kind he most favored have diminished since his death. A continuation of the Gandhian tradition may be found in several voluntary agencies that maintain hostels and child-care centers for the Depressed Classes and seek to alter attitudes through propaganda. Vinoba Bhave, Gandhi's spiritual heir, initiated a voluntary land redistribution program that benefits some Untouchables through gifts of land to the landless.

Men like N. R. Malkani, a long-time Gandhian worker, have continued to labor for the Bhangi by working on the modernization as well as the humanization of scavenging (Malkani 1965). However, such efforts have not received widespread financial support from private citizens. "With the advent of freedom, the public response became somewhat cold and the people began to argue (rightly or wrongly) that in a welfare state it was the State which should provide all the aid needed by such institutions" (Dave 1966: 159).

A continuing undercurrent of faith in the varna system appears to guide many social workers and reformers. K. K. Thakkar, in the *Indian Journal of Social Work* (Vol. 17, No. 2: 44–49) suggests that the Shudras should assist the three upper varnas who are credited with doing "constructive work." He tempers this view by advocating that varnas should be assigned on the basis of ability rather than birth. Dr. Pandharinath Prabhu of the Tata Institute of Social Sciences, in discussing caste and class at the seminar on "Casteism and the Removal of Untouchability"

in Bombay in 1955, reflected the views of Gandhi and other Hindu religious reformers in his conception of varna: "In fact, the entire Varna
System is devised to co-ordinate and assemble the best and the utmost
of group welfare, by yoking each section of the group to duties and
responsibilities in terms of the efficiency of the specific work and service
each of the sections is able to render unto the community life" (*Seminar
on Casteism,* 1955: 116). As in Gandhi's day, this approach has been
more concerned with duties than with rights, it has not produced leaders
from the ranks of the Untouchables, it has not offset the subtle discrimination felt by the educated Untouchable (Isaacs, Chapter 13 this volume) —
it has little influence in most Indian villages where Untouchable living
quarters, wells, and temples are still separate from those of caste Hindus.

Ambedkar's influence has also persisted. His ideas on political rights
and privileges have been generally accepted by Untouchables. He himself
still stands as an example of what an Untouchable can become. As late
as the 1960s, Scheduled Castes were still seeking self-respect by attempting to secure national recognition of his achievements. A "Charter of
Demands" presented by the Republican Party to the government in
1965 and backed by a satyagraha involving a third of a million people,
headed its program with the demand that a portrait of Dr. Ambedkar
be placed in the Parliament Building. (A statue of him has now been
erected on that site.) In 1969, three Swatantra Party Harijans not actually
allied with Ambedkar's political movement undertook a fast in Ahmedabad to protest the absence of Dr. Ambedkar's portrait from the Gujarat
Legislative Assembly.

In addition to the vital element of self-respect which Ambedkar
engendered among Untouchables, his vision of progress through education
and politics, rather than the Gandhian vision of a change of heart among
caste Hindus, has come to inspire most Scheduled Caste leaders. However, these leaders and their followers are rarely united beyond their own
regions. In general, they support the dominant party of the area — the
Communist Party in Kerala, the DMK in Madras, Congress in many
provinces. Only in Maharashtra and portions of Uttar Pradesh has
Ambedkar's Republican Party commanded any significant number of
votes in recent elections. Excepting the 1957 elections in Bombay State,
where the demand for a united Maharashtra temporarily obliterated party
and caste differences, Republican Party candidates have held only a few
legislative seats. However, the political awakening fostered by Ambedkar
has come about in many areas, and, with the lessening of the Congress
Party's monolithic hold since 1967, the possibility that the Untouchables
may hold influence as a balance between two blocs of political power

has come somewhat nearer reality (Dushkin, Chapter 9 this volume).

Ambedkar's view that the problem of the Untouchable is economic, social, and political, as well as religious, widely prevails in India. The Untouchable who enters the modern sector of Indian society as school-teacher, factory worker, or government servant, is comparatively free from earlier social disabilities. Even though there may be subtle discrimination in some areas, and a closed door in others, the educated Untouchable functions in a world where a concern with pollution is mitigated by other considerations. However, for the majority of Untouchables, who are landless villagers, the only open road to a higher economic and social status entails leaving the security of their village and somehow obtaining education. Gandhi may have softened the Hindu heart, Ambedkar may have awakened self-respect and an interest in politics among Untouchables, but economic dependence upon others continues to restrict the upward movement of the Untouchable.

A Jatav shoemaker of Agra

Owen Lynch

5.

OWEN LYNCH

Dr. B. R. Ambedkar – Myth and Charisma

ON MARCH 18, 1956, an unusual event took place in the city of Agra, India. With defiant solemnity more than 2,000 members of an Untouchable caste known as Jatav converted to Buddhism under the aegis of the Neo-Buddhist prophet, Dr. B. R. Ambedkar. This event was unusual in that Buddhism, for all practical purposes, had died out in India by the tenth century A.D. In Agra in the late 1960s there were more than 2,200 publicly practicing Buddhists and many more that number secretly believing Buddhists.[1] Conversions to Neo-Buddhism have not been confined to Agra, since during the decade 1951-61 there was a 300 percent rise in the Buddhist population of the state of Uttar Pradesh alone.[*]

I shall discuss some of the elements and factors involved in the Jatavs' conversion to Buddhism, as I had come to know it as of June, 1964.[2] I will pay particular attention to two elements, namely the prophet of the movement, B. R. Ambedkar, and the message or myth he revealed. More specifically I will ask what was it that led the Jatavs to accept and embrace the prophet's teaching and myth so wholeheartedly. I also will ask what was it about the prophet of Neo-Buddhism, Dr. B. R. Ambedkar,

The fifteen months of field work upon which this study is based was supported in part by a National Defense Language Fellowship and in part by project number MH 06227 of the National Institute of Mental Health.
[*]India Census Commission. *Census of India, 1961*. Religion. Paper No. 1 of 1963. New Delhi: Manager of Publications, 1963, viii.

[97]

that led the Jatavs to follow him. Why has he become a Jatav "culture hero" whose name, Bhimrao, is used as a form of address, *"Jai Bhim"* ("Hail Bhim"); whose deeds and virtues are constantly celebrated in verse and song; and whose picture, as a haloed Bodhisattva, is found in almost every Jatav home?

The Agra Jatavs

The city of Agra is about 120 miles south of New Delhi. Once a capital of the Moghul empire, it is now but a district headquarters renowned as the home of the majestic Taj Mahal and as the source of sturdy footwear fashioned, for the most part, by Jatav hands. The city itself is not a modern, westernized metropolis, such as Bombay, Calcutta, and Madras. In it one can still find winding, narrow streets, dusty, crowded markets, mud huts, and herds of water buffalo and cows, all part of a more traditional way of life. Even industry is largely confined to cottage shoe factories, pulse and oil mills, and a small iron foundry. The city is broken up into a number of residential areas which are often segregated by caste. In such neighborhoods composed largely or exclusively of their own caste brothers live the Jatavs.

The Jatavs are part (*jati*) of a caste group known as Chamars, whose traditional occupation is the curing and working of leather and the making of shoes. Since the curing of leather (along with eating of carrion) is traditionally considered polluting in India, the Jatavs have been considered highly polluted; they are Untouchables. In modern India the Jatavs are also known as Scheduled Castes. The Scheduled Castes are those Untouchable communities to whom the government of India has granted special concessions and privileges, such as government jobs, scholarships, and reserved seats in local, state, and national legislatures. In the state of Uttar Pradesh a Scheduled Caste person must be by definition a Hindu. For this reason many Jatavs conceal their Buddhist identity. Public declaration of a conversion from Hinduism to Buddhism would lead to a loss of their Scheduled Caste privileges and status.

According to the 1961 census, the population of Agra City was 462,020 (India. Census Commission 1964: 206), while the number of Jatavs was about 71,404 or one-sixth of the city's total population.* This large number of Jatavs was due mainly to the fact that Agra is one of the major shoe-producing centers in India. The shoe industry began to grow in Agra at the turn of the century and prospered under

---

Uttar Pradesh General Population Tables, Vol. XV (Pt. II A).

the impetus of the two world wars. Since shoemaking was their traditional occupation, and since it was also polluting to other castes, the Jatavs have had a virtual monopoly on the production side of the shoe industry. Shoemaking has brought with it moderate prosperity for some Jatavs. Such prosperity has opened the way to formal education and to new opportunities in politics. Against this background of an urban cottage industry linked to national and international markets and an increased political awareness, Dr. Ambedkar stepped into the Jatavs' lives, led them into Buddhism, and became their "culture hero" par excellence. To understand how this came to be, we must first examine Ambedkar's myth and its message, while keeping in mind Jatav low-caste status and their changing economic, educational, and political opportunities. In this study, I will take myth in an extended sense to mean not just a particular legend about a certain hero, event, or idea; but rather a set of traditional or legendary beliefs about a particular subject of social and cultural concern. I will also look at myth from a situational point of view in which "myth . . . is a language of signs in terms of which claims to rights and status are expressed, but it is a language of argument, not a chorus of harmony" (Leach 1965: 278).[3] I am concerned, therefore, with how myths relate to the definition of the situation in actual interactions rather than how they relate to or symbolize the social structure.

The Myth of the Prophet

The basic teaching of Ambedkar was that Buddhism is an indigenous Indian religion of equality; a religion which was anti-caste and anti-Brahman. In ancient Buddhist India, according to the myth, there were no oppressing, upper caste Brahmans and there were no oppressed lower caste Untouchables; all men were equal Buddhists. The root cause of untouchability and the miserable condition of the Untouchables lay in the Brahmanical teaching of Hinduism and the superior position it legitimized for the oppressing Brahmans. Ambedkar once wrote:

If you wish to bring about a breach in the [caste] system, then you have got to apply the dynamite to the Vedas and the Shastras, which deny any part to reason, to Vedas and Shastras, which deny any part to morality. You must destroy the Religion of the Smritis. [Ambedkar 1945a: 70]

How was it that the Brahmans came to oppress and dominate the Untouchables? The answer lies in the myth of the origin of the Neo-Buddhists who, Ambedkar felt, were descendants of the original ancient Buddhists. In ancient times, the myth says, there existed in India "broken men" — stray individuals, survivors of the tribes conquered by invading sedentary agriculturists, who were Brahmans. The "broken men" were Buddhists or converts to Buddhism, and as good Buddhists refused to kill cows for meat, though they would eat the flesh of dead cows. The Brahmans at that time, however, not only ate beef but also sacrificed living cows. Recognizing the superiority of the Buddhist religion, which did not kill or sacrifice cows, many people began to desert the Brahmans and Brahmanism for Buddhism. The Brahmans thereupon became frightened and resorted to one-upmanship. Not only did they forbid the slaughter and sacrifice of cows, but also they forbade the eating of beef. Those who ate beef were penalized with the stigma of pollution and thereby became Untouchables. Thus, the beef-eating Buddhists became Untouchables and so they have remained to this day: broken, polluted, deprived of their land, and relegated beyond the periphery of respectable society.

What is it about Ambedkar's Neo-Buddhist teachings that brought forth such an enthusiastic response among the Jatavs? In the first place, the Buddhist myth was in many ways consistent with a previous myth used by the Jatavs to justify and legitimize their attempts to move up in the caste hierarchy through Sanskritization.[4] According to this earlier myth, the Jatavs were really Kshatriyas[5] who had gone into hiding in Epic times. They had disguised themselves as Chamars in order to escape the wrath of the mythical Brahman Parashuram, who circled the world twenty-one times seeking out and slaying his sworn enemies, the Kshatriyas (cf. Dowson 1961: 230-31). The Jatavs supported the contention that they were really Kshatriyas and not Untouchables by equating the name Jatav with Yadav, the lineage name of Lord Krishna. A Jatav historian writes, "Jatav is an occupational branch of Yadav lineage in which Shri Krishna was born" (Yaadvendu 1942: 96).*

The Buddhist and Jatav-Kshatriya myths are alike and consistent in that both assert a claim to higher status from which they have fallen or been forcibly degraded. Both myths are also attempts to legitimize claims to a better or higher status. Moreover, both myths provide a logical model enabling the Jatavs to overcome a contradiction which they feel has existed in their life situation.[6] These myths give an explanation of how the Jatavs can be men equal to other men and at the same time unequal to other men. Jatavs specifically believe that all men are *insan* (equal members of the human race), yet they know that for ages they have been treated otherwise, as unequal, untouchable, and polluting to upper castes. The mythical resolution of this contradiction is found in

---

*Raamnaaraayan Yaadvendu. *Yaaduvansh Kaa Itihaas*. Aagra: Navyug Saahitaya Niketan, 1942.

the ancient historical circumstances which have led to today's mistaken identity. The myths contend that Jatavs are not Untouchables; they are really upper caste Kshatriyas, or equal Buddhists, as the case may be. Thus, both myths attempt to overcome and explain the living contradiction in which Jatavs believe themselves equal to other men, yet find themselves treated unequally with other men.[7]

Insofar as the two myths were consistent and alike, it was easy to switch from one to the other. Yet there remains the problem of why, in fact, the Jatavs did switch from the Jatav-Kshatriya myth to the Jatav-Buddhist one. There are two basic differences which brought about the switch: the first is one of content, and the second I shall refer to as a logistic condition.

The difference in the content of the myths is that each provides a charter for different social situations,[8] and therefore for different behavior within such situations. In the Jatav-Kshatriya myth the situation, in which the Jatavs interact as Untouchables with other castes, is one of mistaken identity and, therefore, of erroneous definition of how Jatavs ought to interact with and be accepted by other castes. This definition of the situation was consistent and congruent with the caste system and with attempts to change position within it through Sanskritization.

In the Buddhist myth, the situation in which the Jatavs interact is defined as one of enforced deprivation and degradation. This myth sees the Jatavs as conquered by outsiders, deprived of their patrimony, and subjected to the heel of Brahmanical oppression. It also involves the ideology that all men are equal, and, therefore, that the inequalities of the caste system are wrong. Such a definition of the situation is consistent with the post-Independence political system of parliamentary democracy in which the Jatavs now find themselves. It is, moreover, congruent with Jatav political attempts to get rid of casteism and to actualize the ideals of equality set forth in the Indian Constitution.

It is this mythical encoding of actual situations which leads to an understanding of why these myths (and myths in general) can have an oretic or conative function.[9] This function is conative because these myths contain both motivation and strategy. The motivating factor in the Jatav-Kshatriya myth which impelled the Jatavs to Sanskritizing activity was the definition of their social situation as a mistake. They, therefore, felt others were wrong to treat them as Untouchables and they themselves were wrong to acquiesce in such treatment. It was also wrong for them to do things that Untouchables did, such as beef-eating, and they promptly eschewed such customs in following the Sanskritic path.

The motivating factor in the Buddhist myth is its definition of the present Jatav situation as an injustice, a usurpation by alien Brahmans of their legitimate heritage and rights. Therefore, the myth not only legitimizes anti-caste, anti-Brahman, and anti-Hindu sentiments and activities, but actually denies the legitimacy of the caste system itself. Buddhist teaching is now referred to as "Baba Saheb [Ambedkar's] Mission." The Jatavs are so convinced of its truth and validity that they feel it is almost a duty to convert others to the same message. For the Buddhist Jatav the hope of India's future and of its people lies in Buddhism. Zealous feeling for Baba Saheb's Mission is vividly expressed in the few selected lines of a Hindi poem about Ambedkar which I translate below. This poem was written for the first All-India Conference of Neo-Buddhists held in Agra in 1963.

One way out of oppression is there
Brother there is one way to free us from oppression
We must all become united as one.
The Bhim[10] said "If you martyr yourselves (for freedom) then I will know."
Baba Saheb has changed your lives.
The wealth of the religion of the Buddha
Has been given to you as a great treasure.
Keep no Buddhist thing hidden.
Such is the advice given to you.
The wealth of the religion of the Buddha
Has been given to you as a great treasure.
Adopt the Pancha Shil
And make India glorious.
One who bears the seal of India[11]
He is a disciple of the Buddha.
Today there is this Buddhist Conference
To make India Buddhist.

I am of the opinion that the Buddhist myth not only expressed experience already known to the Jatavs, such as their place in and feelings about the caste system, but in addition it formulated a *new* experience and a new perception of social reality. Myth, like ritual, "does not merely externalize experience, bringing it out into the light of day, but it modifies experience in so expressing it" (Douglas 1966: 64). The Buddhist myth and the earlier Jatav-Kshatriya myth appear to have been genuinely creative of a new social experience for the Jatavs. Both myths redefined their social situation in such a way as to encourage attempts to change it accordingly. It is specifically this recreation and reformulation of experience which underlies the motivating power of myths and the conative function or power of mythical symbols.

In addition to motivation, the conative function of myths also involves strategy. Situational myths, like military strategy, are plans or maps of social space in mythical form or code. To paraphrase Clifford Geertz (1966: 29), myths provide not just models *of* reality, but also models *for* reality. Both Jatav myths clearly define the Jatavs as the vanquished underdog and the Brahmans as the victorious enemy. There-fore, Jatav action ought to take account of or be directed against that enemy.

In the Jatav-Kshatriya myth, the logical conclusion was that the enemy Brahman had to be forced to recognize the Jatav's real Kshatriya identity; this could be done by pressing Sanskritic claims and activities. Indeed, the Brahman himself was needed to validate the Jatav claim to a higher status within the caste system; there was no rejection of the system as such.

In the Buddhist myth, the enemy is an *outsider* who has usurped Jatav rights and enslaved them through the tool of Brahmanical oppression, the caste system. The strategic conclusion pointed out by the myth is that the caste system must be attacked and destroyed, Brahmanical Hinduism as a religion foreign to India must be driven out, and Brahmans must return to the Untouchables their rights to land and to equal treatment with all men. The Jatavs see these Buddhist goals reflected in the Indian Constitution, and this adds secular support to their aspirations.

Part of the Buddhist myth as given by Ambedkar contains an explicit strategy. He described the caste system as a four-tiered wall with the Brahmans at the top and the Untouchables at the bottom. If the bottom tier were pulled out, the whole structure would tumble down. This is exactly the strategy followed by the political arm of the Buddhist movement, the Republican Party. The Republican Party, and almost all Agra Jatavs are members, has been opposed to the nationally dominant Congress Party because Republicans feel that the Congress is controlled by a "bunch of Brahman boys."[12]

Max Weber alluded to the necessity of what I have labeled the strategic factor before group or communal action can be taken. Allow me to paraphrase him in the following quotation by substituting the word *caste* for *class*.

The degree in which "communal action" and possibly "societal action," emerges from the "mass actions" of the members of a [caste] is linked to general cultural conditions, especially those of an intellectual sort. It is also linked to the extent of the contrasts that have already evolved, and is especially linked to the *transparency* of the connections between the causes and the con-sequences of the "[caste] situation." For however different life chances may be, this fact in itself, according to all experience, by no means gives birth to "[caste] action" . . . the fact of being conditioned and the results of the [caste] situation must be distinctly recognizable. [Weber 1958: 184]

Both the Jatav-Kshatriya and the Buddhist myths clearly map out the difference of life chances and the *contrast* between low Jatav status and high Brahman status. Yet neither myth makes completely *transparent* the link between the causes of the caste situation and its consequences. In the Jatav-Kshatriya myth the cause is mistaken identity based on the belief in inherited differences of purity and pollution among different castes. In reality the Jatavs were not ritually impure, since when the veneer of time was washed off, their true Kshatriya identity was revealed underneath. Thus, the ultimate cause of the Jatavs' caste situation in this earlier myth was seen as due to mistaken differences in purity and pollution.

In the Buddhist myth the ultimate cause is again seen to be of an ideological sort. The alien Hindu religion of the Brahmans has been imposed upon the Buddhists and has caused differences of status among men. But in this myth there is also a hint at economic and political causes underlying the caste situation. It states· that the Brahmans have usurped the land of the indigenous Buddhists who recognized no differences among men. Implied in this is the suggestion that ownership of land puts the Brahmans on top and non-ownership of land puts the Buddhists on the bottom of society. In effect, the Buddhist myth states that the causes of the Jatav caste situation lie in the foundations of the caste system itself and not just in the Jatav's position within the system.

While such myths do not provide a clear-cut, objective analysis of the caste situation, they do show how it is perceived and understood. They also indicate in what direction attempts to alleviate the situation ought to go. In this sense, myths, by encoding or mapping an interpretation of specific social situations, also contain a strategy for action in that situation.

Indeed, mythical definition of the Jatav situation, more than sociological or economic, increased both the possibility and the probability of communal action. The mass of illiterate Jatavs were and are familiar with mythological symbols and thought; they understand myth much more readily than dry, logical, and scientific analyses of their present social situation. Once they can understand a situation, albeit in mythical form, they are intellectually prepared and affectively motivated to engage in communal action for specific social goals.

There is a major problem in the interpretation of myth and its conative function which I have thus far outlined. Many groups and many low castes have myths about themselves which tell how through treachery, deceit, conquest, and the like, they fell upon hard times and were reduced to low social status.[13] Yet few of them rebel or take concerted, communal action on the basis of the strategy and motivation implied in their myths. While the reasons for this may vary, there is one good reason why the Jatavs — and probably other groups like them —*did* take an active path and did not remain immobile. This reason lies in the objective conditions of their social situation, and I shall refer to it as a logistic condition. By this I mean that there was some concrete means, and therefore real hope, of achieving their goals.

During the pre-Independence era, when the Jatavs held to the Jatav-Kshatriya myth, they had, as previously mentioned, achieved a fair measure of economic, educational, and political awareness. To some extent they had come to understand the courts, British justice and politics, as well as some of the more sophisticated aspects of the Hindu Great Tradition.[14] When the time for action to rectify the wrongs recounted in their myth came, the Jatavs had among them leaders who could provide the financial backing, political skills, and literate understanding necessary to iterate Jatav claims and work them through the appropriate governmental and caste channels.[15]

In the post-Independence period the logistic condition which defined the context for the Jatavs' action has been further expanded. Independent India has adopted the parliamentary system of government, the universal franchise, and the equality of citizens before the law. It has also outlawed the practice of untouchability by upper castes against the Untouchables. Of the new rights acquired by the Jatavs the right to vote is most important. Because they form about one-sixth of the city's population and reside in segregated neighborhoods in densities great enough to dominate certain electoral wards, the Jatavs exercise significant political power in Agra City. To this end, they have even organized their own political party — the Republican Party.

These new factors have added to the Jatav sense of power and worth and hence to their more revolutionary stance. Just as the Constitution defines all men as equal citizens, so, too, does Buddhism define all men as equal. Just as the law makes it a crime for upper castes to practice untouchability, so, too, does Buddhism consider it wrong for them to oppress Buddhists. In following the strategy and motivation of their myth, the Jatav Buddhists feel they are acting in accordance with the law of the land.

The earlier Jatav-Kshatriya myth is not in accord with the Jatavs' post-Independence revolutionary stance because it implies an acceptance of caste, the caste system, and Sanskritization as a means to rise within the system. The Buddhist myth, on the other hand, implies a rejection of all these things and an acceptance of at least the ideal of democratic equality. The logistic condition provided by the vote, citizenship, and parliamentary politics, as the Jatavs accept and use them, requires a strategy, a tactic and a definition of the situation which is congruent with it. This requirement of congruity is best met by the Buddhist myth.

The logistic condition also provided the Jatavs with the concrete means for action based upon their myths. Without such toeholds of power anchored in social reality, there would have been little hope for success in changing their position; their reaction in all likelihood would have been one of passive but resentful acceptance of the status quo (cf. Berreman 1960).

Ambedkar, the Prophet, and His Charisma

Along with the foregoing explanation of the Buddhist myth, its content, its function for the Jatavs, and their motivation for acceptance, the question remains as to why the Jatavs not only accepted, but deified, the myth's central figure, B. R. Ambedkar. Considering the importance of caste, linguistic, and regional loyalties in India, the Jatav deification of B. R. Ambedkar poses several questions. Although of Untouchable origin, Ambedkar was a member of the Mahar, rather than the Jatav caste; his mother tongue was Marathi, not Hindi; and he was a native of Maharashtra far removed from Agra. After Ambedkar's death in 1956, he became a major culture hero of the Agra Jatavs. Known affectionately as Baba Saheb, Ambedkar was elevated to the ranks of the Buddhist pantheon as a Bodhisattva. How did this man, a "foreigner" in Jatav terms, gain such hold over the minds and hearts of the Jatavs? One might attribute this phenomenon to Ambedkar's charisma[16] and to the force of his charismatic personality.[17] Yet, an appeal to charisma as explanatory in itself is unsatisfying; therefore I take it as problematic, and in need of further specification. While I cannot answer for the underlying psychological mechanisms involved in charisma, I do think that some of its empirical socio-cultural components can be identified. There are four components which seem important; they are (a) the cultural, (b) the historical, (c) the structural, and (d) the symbolic. An analysis of Ambedkar in terms of these components can lead not only to a better understanding of how Ambedkar came to be accepted by the Jatavs, but also to what might be called a socio-cultural definition of a culture hero. I believe it can also contribute to the understanding of charisma as a sociological concept.

By *cultural component* I mean a heritage of literature, myths, art, symbols, and values particular to a society or group. There are two north Indian traditions which have had especial importance and impact upon the Jatavs; these are a religious and a heroic tradition.

In the religious tradition the Jatavs were and to some extent still are followers of the sixteenth-century saint, Kabir. Even today Jatav men gather in the evening to sing the beautiful devotional hymns composed by Kabir who tried to reconcile both Hinduism and Islam, and taught that all men were brothers. He rejected caste distinctions and preached that salvation was to be reached through faith and devotion (*bhakti*) to God. Rai Das, who was a Chamar or leatherworker like the Jatavs, is also in the same tradition.

Ambedkar's message, then, was not something completely new to the Jatavs for it struck sympathetic vibrations with Kabir's teachings. Ambedkar claimed that his was a religious message and must be accepted as a religious belief. Thus, as a religious reformer, like Kabir, he was easily accepted by the Jatavs. They readily found a place for him in their tradition as a mahatma and on this basis even the uneducated and unsophisticated among them could relate to and accept him. As one informant told me: "My feeling about Baba Saheb is that he came to us having assumed the body of a messiah, and those things he told us are as true as they are eternal. Baba Saheb was a great man and by his way all ought to become great."

In addition to this religious tradition the Jatavs also have a heroic tradition. Often during the rainy season when work is slack, one can enter a Jatav neighborhood and hear somebody chanting the Epic of Alha and Udal. Alha and Udal were two brothers who by heroic deeds helped the King Parmal in his war against Prithiraj, the twelfth-century Chauhan ruler of Delhi. Although the exact caste origin of these two brothers is not known, the Agra Jatavs say they were Untouchables. For the Jatavs, Alha and Udal have proven that Untouchables are great warriors in heart, word, and deed. Ambedkar, too, has taken a place in this tradition because now there are many ballads sung about him along with the Epic of Alha and Udal. These ballads recount Ambedkar's struggles against untouchability, his fight for an education, and his role as one of the fathers of the Constitution of India. He, too, has shown that an Untouchable can be a great leader, a warrior, and a hero who can take his place among the country's leaders with pride and respect.

The *historical component* of Ambedkar's charisma in Agra consists of the actual relations he had in deed and in word with the Jatavs. The initial contacts occurred during 1930-31 when the Round Table Conferences between the British and the Indian Nationalists were being held in London. During that time, a bitter dispute arose between Gandhi and Ambedkar over who was the real representative of the Untouchables and Scheduled Castes, and over what kinds of political concessions should be given to them. The Agra Jatavs felt that Ambedkar's position was the correct one, and they sent a telegram to London supporting him over Gandhi. This support broadened to such an extent that a unit of Ambedkar's Scheduled Castes Federation was founded at Agra in 1942.

In 1946 Ambedkar came to Agra and spoke to the Jatavs. He had further endeared himself to them during World War II, when he used his power as a member for labor in the Central Cabinet to get a high priority rating for the railroad shipping of Agra shoes. When Ambedkar once again came to Agra in 1956, his reputation as a leader had greatly increased because for some time he had been a member of Nehru's first cabinet, though he later resigned. For the Jatavs he returned to Agra as a conquering hero, and thousands of them flocked to see him and gain his *darshana* (charismatic view). An Agra newspaper reported the event.

The awakening of the Jatavs will not be stopped by the purchase of selfish and self-interested leaders. If the Scheduled Castes don't get their full rights, then there will be a revolution. The eyes of all people ought to be opened to the awakening of the Scheduled Castes, especially the Jatavs who were waiting for hours in a great crowd on the Ram Lila grounds for Dr. Ambedkar. It is a fact that such a crowd was not present when Prime Minister Nehru came, since the crowd was sitting packed close together. In such a condition it could not have been less than a *lakh* of people.

The Jatavs are the natural harbingers or leaders of the Scheduled Castes. Dissatisfaction cannot be eliminated by blinding one's eyes to it or by buying with a little money those selfish and self-interested leaders who for their self-interest would sell their own caste. It can be eliminated when their true leader and the youthful Jatavs will become united to fight for their rights and will make the government believe that their unity is for fulfilling their duty to the Scheduled Castes. [*Sainik,* March 20, 1956]

These historical events and Jatav traditions were buttressed by Ambedkar's actual *structural* positions within Indian society. First of all, he was an Untouchable, and occupied this status in common with the Jatavs. He was felt to be "one of our men," one who could really understand as an insider their problems and feelings. Second, Ambedkar attained statuses of great prestige, power, and responsibility in India. He was a barrister, educated in England, and had also acquired a Ph.D. in economics from Columbia University in New York City. He had been recognized by the British as a leader during the Round Table Conferences, and Nehru had chosen him to be the first law minister in the Central Cabinet of the Government of India. As law minister, Ambedkar had the major responsibility for writing the Indian Constitution and piloting it through the Parliament to become the law of the land. Jatavs today believe that Ambedkar is the Father of the Constitution under which untouchability was abolished and the franchise was given to all. In a structural sense, then, Ambedkar was an Untouchable leader and a person to whom the Jatavs could and did turn, when "a man at the top" was needed.

The third of Ambedkar's structural positions was his status as a revolutionary. As Pandit Nehru himself once said, "[Ambedkar was] a symbol of revolt against all oppressive features in Hindu society" *(New York Times,* December 6, 1956: quoted in Dushkin 1967: 45). Ambedkar was constantly lashing out at what he felt were the injustices of the caste system and the immoralities of Hinduism. His final act of defiance was to leave Hinduism and embrace Buddhism, a religion which, as he saw it, was anti-Hindu and anti-caste. The Jatavs, too, have been considered revolutionary trouble-makers and upstarts in Agra; in this they have felt they are following in Ambedkar's hallowed footsteps.

The *symbolic* component of Ambedkar's charisma lies in the fact that Jatavs have been able to identify with him and take vicarious satisfaction from his deeds and accomplishments. He felt the pangs of untouchability as much as they and understood what it meant to be an Untouchable. One little pamphlet, in Hindi, discussing the discrimination Ambedkar had to undergo as a student, says:

Such fearful experience [of childhood] is terrible enough for a single individual; yet whose life could have been more frightening than that of Dr. Bhimrao Ambedkar who felt as his own the similar terrible experiences of scores of other people. [Kausalyaayan n.d.: 3]*

Despite his untouchability, Ambedkar had traveled abroad and attained high educational and political status. Jatavs take great satisfaction in telling of his deeds and how he, a fellow Untouchable, walked the same halls as the great of the nation. One college student told me, "Parents hold up Dr. Ambedkar as a model to children and tell them how he became educated by his own efforts and worked hard. He is worshipped as a god." This model is continually reinforced in the many songs and poems which have been composed about Ambedkar and his deeds. In these poems, Ambedkar has become for the Jatavs a culture hero par excellence. Just as the Buddhist myth resolves certain contradictions between Jatav belief about themselves and the realities of their social situation, so, too, the figure of Ambedkar has become a mediator between two oppositions (cf. Levi-Strauss 1963:224). He has combined in himself high political and educational status with low ritual and social

---

*Kausalyaayan, Bhadant Aanand. *Baabaa Saahab*. Vardhaa: Sugat Prakaashan Griha, n.d.

status. He is a Bodhisattva who was at one and the same time a lowly Untouchable and a Father of the Constitution of India. Thus, Ambedkar is a symbol of identification and vicarious satisfaction for the Jatavs. The following is a small example of the many poems and ballads which Jatavs now sing about Ambedkar and which expresses their feeling for and about him:

Oh the beautiful little baby Bhim was born.
Oh let the land be given in charity; your people have become immortal,
Oh he taught us the art of politics and raised on high the blue flag.[18]
Oh our Bhim steeped in knowledge, made to shine like the stars his
         oppressed people.
Yes, "Victory to Bhim" is sweet to hear.
Oh Bhimrao has awakened his people.
Yes, writer of the Constitution, he has changed our government.
Yes, he it was who drafted the Hindu Code Bill.

In summary, then, Ambedkar has become a legend in himself. He has become an integral part of and chief hero in the Neo-Buddhist myth whose first prophet he was.

Conclusions

This study has led to conclusions of two types, those of substance and those of theory. My substantive conclusions are as follows:

The Jatavs easily accepted the Buddhist myth because it redefined their social situation in a manner more in accord with the new powers given to them in independent India, and more in tune with the new definition of the social situation outlined in the Constitution of post-Independence India. This myth provided a charter of legitimacy and a religious sanction for their goals and tactics, as well as a motive and strategy for pursuing them.

The Jatavs easily accepted Dr. Ambedkar himself and made him into a culture hero because of their many-stranded and important relations with him. He was one in a long line of saints who abjured the caste system, and he was for them an Untouchable hero like those in their folk ballads. He provided a focus of identification and a sense of vicarious satisfaction for many Jatav longings. Ambedkar was also a leader within the political structure of Indian society and was therefore a real source of help and leadership. Finally, he was a leader who was in fact an Untouchable and a revolutionary, just as the Jatavs; hence, they felt he could understand them better than a non-Untouchable leader, such as Gandhi.

In addition to the substantive conclusions above, I would like to present three theoretical ones about myth and charisma.

In analyzing the appeal of Ambedkar to the Jatavs, I have been led to identify some of the concrete socio-cultural components of his charisma. It seems to me that these cultural, historical, structural, and symbolic components might be present in many or most cases of charismatic leadership, over and above the specific contents of the prophet's message. If this is so, charisma need not remain a wholly nebulous and intangible concept within sociology. An analysis of a prophet such as Ambedkar in terms of these components reveals some of the socio-cultural reasons for defining him as a culture hero.

The consideration of myths in situational rather than social-structural terms leads to an analysis of how and why myths can have dynamic and motivational power for social change. Myths provide not just models *of* reality but also models *for* reality. They have a conative function because of motivation they can engender and because of the strategic analysis of social situations which they can provide to those who believe in them. They encode in culturally familiar and readily understood symbols a map of a social situation in such a way that goal-directed action can be taken. Without such an understanding, communal action is not possible. It is the presence or absence of a logistic condition which accounts for action or inaction upon the definition of the social situation contained in the myth.

One might also make a slight addition to the theory of myth which has guided this analysis, i.e., the theory developed by Leach (1965). In the presentation of his theory Leach considers myth as a language of argument over social status and social rights. However, he concentrates his analysis on how different groups can use different versions of the *same* myth to assert their varying claims. It would seem from the case of the Jatavs that when there exists, as in India, a cultural heritage of many myths, the argument may proceed by using *different* myths which are appropriate to different interpretations of the changing social situation.

NOTES

[1] The reasons for this secrecy will be discussed later on in this essay.

[2] A more complete treatment of this subject may be found in Lynch (1969).

[3] Leach's interpretation of Malinowski seems to be somewhat unfair. While Malinowski did not emphasize myth in the context of change as does Leach and while he emphasized myth's integrative function, he also saw it in the context of conflict and possible change (cf. Malinowski 1948: 117).

[4] "Sanskritization is the process by which a 'low' Hindu caste, or tribal or other group, changes its customs, ritual, ideology, and way of life in the direction of a high, and frequently, 'twice-born' caste" (Srinivas 1966: 6).

[5] The Kshatriyas, or warriors, are the second highest group in the traditional caste (*varna*) hierarchy of India.

⁶"The purpose of myth is to provide a logical model capable of overcoming a contradiction. . . ." (Levi-Strauss 1963: 229). Malinowski (1948: 117), too, seems to have seen this, at least implicitly, long before Levi-Strauss. He says, "The result is that there come into existence a special class of mythological stories which justify and account for the anomalous state of affairs."

⁷In another frame of reference, it can be said that these myths resolve the state of "cognitive dissonance" in which the Jatavs exist (cf. Festinger 1957).

⁸Malinowski (1948: 100) seems to have hinted at myths as situational though never quite explicitly. He says, "In this live context [of ongoing daily life] there is as much to be learned about the myth as in the narrative itself." He also refers to the use of myth to justify conflicting claims of various groups (1948: 117).

⁹The orectic or conative function of a symbol refers to its power to impel or stimulate to action rather than to its cognitive, expressive, or instrumental functions. I am indebted to the stimulating 1966 lectures of Victor Turner at S.U.N.Y. – Binghamton, for this idea.

¹⁰Bhimrao, Ambedkar's first name, means "The Strong One."

¹¹The seal of India was taken from a capital of a column erected by the Emporer Ashoka, reputedly a Buddhist and one of India's greatest ancient rulers. The Jatavs feel that India was great when it was under Buddhist rule and it will become great again under Buddhism.

¹²If all Indian Untouchables could unite against the Congress Party, then they would in fact pose a serious threat to it.

¹³See Berreman (1960) for an interesting cross-cultural account of such myths.

¹⁴In this respect the Arya Samaj was very important. It made a significant impact on the Jatavs and imparted to them a knowledge of Sanskritic rite and belief, as well as a basic set of reading and writing skills, all of which had been previously denied to them.

¹⁵For a more complete account of these events, see Lynch (1969).

¹⁶Weber defined charisma in the following way: "The term "charisma" will be applied to a certain quality of an individual personality by virtue of which he is set apart from ordinary men and treated as endowed with supernatural, super-human, or at least specifically exceptional powers or qualities. These are . . . not accessible to the ordinary person, but are regarded as of divine origin or as exemplary, and on the basis of them the individual concerned is treated as a leader" (quoted in Bendix 1962: 88, footnote 2).

¹⁷The Jatavs often refer to Ambedkar as *mahan* (great, eminent) or mahatma (great-souled one).

¹⁸The flag of the Republican Party which Ambedkar founded is blue. Almost all Jatavs are Republicans (*cf.* Lynch 1969).

6.

ADELE FISKE

Scheduled Caste Buddhist Organizations

THIS ACCOUNT is based in large part on interviews and observations conducted in India in 1966–67. Its purpose is to describe the rather nebulous network of groups and individuals sustaining the movement leading to conversion to Buddhism during the previous decade of an estimated 3½ million of India's former Untouchables. This remarkable phenomenon was initiated by Dr. B. R. Ambedkar's public adoption of Buddhism at a *diksha* (conversion) ceremony held in Nagpur on October 14, 1956. Ambedkar's conversion was motivated by his belief that only in leaving Hinduism could his people free themselves from the burden of pollution and untouchability. The impact of Ambedkar's decision may be attributed to his national prominence as a leader of the Indian Scheduled Castes, a Western-educated barrister of distinction, and a major political figure opposed to Gandhi on the issue of untouchability. In spite of Ambedkar's death on December 6, 1956, retarding the early organization of the movement, his example was soon emulated by several million Mahars, the caste to which Ambedkar belonged, and a few of the other Untouchable communities in his native state of Maharashtra. Efforts to expand the movement beyond this region were initiated by a variety of organizations and leaders about which little is known at this writing.

Particular attention is given here to one of the three organizations founded by B. R. Ambedkar — the Bharatiya Bauddha Mahasabha, or Buddhist Society of India organized in May, 1955. Information is provided in passing regarding the Republican Party, established for political action by Dr. Ambedkar on the day of his conversion, replacing the Scheduled Castes Federation established in 1942, and the People's Education Society, which he founded in July, 1945, to promote secondary and college education for Untouchables.[1] As an introduction, a brief sketch is also provided of Buddhist organizations of similar intent that antedate the Ambedkar-inspired movement.

Buddhist Organizations Founded Prior to 1956

In Calcutta there exists an Indian Buddhist Society loosely affiliated with the Buddhist Society of India. It derives from an earlier attempt to re-establish Buddhism in India and was founded by an "original" Buddhist from Chittagong, Venerable Kripasaran Mahasthavir (1865–1926). At the age of sixteen he became a monk, possessed with the idea of restoring Buddhism in India. In 1886 he went to Calcutta where there was a community of three or four hundred Bengali Buddhists, and in 1892 founded the Bauddha Dharmankur Sabha. Later he established branches with shrines and rest houses in Lucknow, Darjeeling, Shillong, Jamshedpur, and Chittagong, all in northeast India. He made many missionary journeys, founded a library in Calcutta, and published a Bengali language journal, *Jagajyoti*. A commemorative publication issued in 1965 as part of a Mahasthavir Centenary Celebration contains no explicit reference to work among the Untouchables by this society and its founder in its early days, nor is there in the text any indication of collaboration between this society and the followers of Dr. Ambedkar. However, an editorial published in *Buddhist India* in 1927, the year after Mahasthavir's death, speaks of his activities and points to the potential use of Buddhism for social reform: "It has, therefore, become necessary to educate the Indian citizens again in the highly developed, uniform, and spiritually democratic systems of the Buddhist bhikshus and bhikshunis."[2]

The Maha Bodhi Society of India was founded by Anagarika Dharmapala (David Hewarvitarne, d. 1933) of Ceylon on May 31, 1891. The headquarters of the society have been in Calcutta since 1904; other centers are in Bodh Gaya, Delhi, Sanchi, Bombay, Madras, Lucknow, Ajmer, Nowgarh, Kalimpong, and Bangalore. The society's initial purpose was restoration of the Maha Bodhi temple at Bodh Gaya and other Buddhist shrines. In 1892, it began publishing the *Maha Bodhi Journal,* and later the Pali and Sanskrit Buddhist texts, translations of the scriptures into Hindi vernaculars and English, and popular books and pamphlets in many languages. Centers engage in educational and social activities, provide libraries, and reading rooms, weekly lectures and

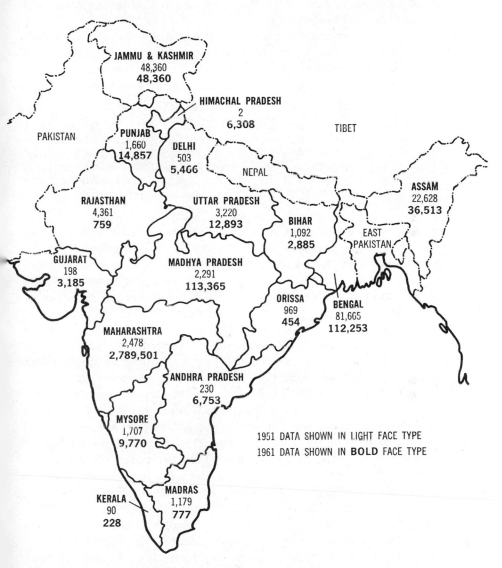

Fig. 6.1 Buddhist Population Centers of India

sermons, and accommodations for pilgrims. Until Independence, the society was closely connected with Ceylon, and most of the centers are still directed by Ceylonese monks.

In South India, the conversion of Scheduled Caste people to Buddhism antedates the Ambedkar movement. The major organization in this area, the South India Buddhist Association, was founded by an Untouchable leader, Pandit Ayoti Das, in the 1890s. To summarize a booklet published in Tamil:

Pandit K. Jyothithasar (Ayoti Das) was born in 1850. At first he was a Vaishnavite, but later he decided to learn the truth contained in other religions as well. From 1875 to 1897 he devoted his time to the study of Christianity, Jainism, and Buddhism. In 1897 he became a Buddhist and did his utmost for the spread of Buddhism. He was also a physician for the poor and a social worker. From 1907 to 1914 he was the editor of the magazine *Yamilan*. He died May 5, 1914.

This account omits certain facts stressed by such southern Buddhists as Mr. Aryashankar, head of the Cycle Rickshaw Drivers and Transport Coolies Union in Madras city, who said that the Pandit was an Untouchable, devoted to the cause of his people for whom he wrote a book on Buddhism in Tamil. Very few copies of this are extant. Mr. Aryashankar has one; according to him most copies were deliberately destroyed by the Brahmans in order to prevent the spread of Buddhism among the people. Another early leader mentioned by South Indian Buddhists was Pandit G. Appaduraya. Although his picture is hung in the Coxtown vihara of Bangalore founded in 1907, and other temples, those interviewed knew only that he was a holy man like Pandit Ayoti Das.

There is evidence in the *Maha Bodhi Journal* that the South India Buddhist Association was primarily concerned with the betterment of its Untouchable members. On November 21, 1920, P. Lakshmi Narasu presided at a conference held in Mayo Hall, Bangalore.[3] The resolutions passed by the conferees requested the Government of India to initiate for all the poorer classes — especially the so-called depressed classes — political reforms including free and compulsory education and facilities for higher education.[4] The same year the Indian Buddhists of Madras Presidency met in the vihara at Perambur, Madras. They issued statements to the following effect: In the last twenty years, three thousand converts to Buddhism had been made. The Buddhists were very poor and their position in Hinduism was bad, as they were Untouchables and unlike the Sudras could not enter temples and had to endure social ostracism. They had "their own form of Hinduism" and claimed "there is little doubt that these Panchamas are the descendants of the original inhabitants of India." If they became Buddhist, they would lose untouchability and achieve a "recognized status in the community." The statement ended with an accusation that most Buddhists of other countries were selfish, narrow, and indifferent to them, coupled with an appeal for monks to come to work among the poor.[5] This same pattern of distress, aspiration, and frustration was to be repeated many times later.

In 1924, the All-Kerala Buddhist Conference was held in Calicut, a town in Kerala where small pockets of Buddhists still exist. The speeches on this occasion also appealed for social justice, a "democratic religion," and the Buddhist "principles of brotherhood and equality" — the very terms later used by Dr. Ambedkar. In 1937, the *Modern Review* of Calcutta announced that "a low caste in Southern India had decided to adopt Buddhism; this event in any case was instigated chiefly by social motivation" (Glasenapp 1937: 221). It was not only in Hinduism that Untouchables in the south found discrimination. In 1944, Dr. Ambedkar was handed a memorandum from the Tamilnad Depressed Class Christian Association alleging that Christians maintained caste after conversion and ill-treated Depressed Class Christians; they appealed to him for help (Pressler 1964: 10). It would have been at about this time that the Madras union leader, Mr. Aryashankar, as a young man of eighteen, left the Catholic church to become a Buddhist in the tradition of Pandit Ayoti Das, founder of the South India Buddhist Association.

In a booklet published in 1954, two years before the conversion of Dr. Ambedkar, the South India Buddhist Association claimed nine branches in Madras State: Pudapet and Royapettah in Madras City; Vannivadu, Valathore, Gudiyatham, Thirupathore and Palikondai in North Arcot District; and Angambakam and Enathore in Chingleput District. The three branches in Mysore State were located at Champion Reef and Marikuppam in the Kolar Gold Fields, Bangalore City, and Hubli. Branches were claimed outside India in Indonesia and Africa: "Nattal," Durban, and "Zcluland"—areas presumably where Tamil-speaking laborers had emigrated. The Madras State census of 1961, however, lists only 777 Buddhists out of a total population of 33,686,953. This discrepancy may be due to a high concentration of South Indian Buddhists in Mysore State, and the decline of proselytizing in the area during the previous two decades. Another likely factor, as in all India, is that Scheduled Castes lose government aid in education, housing, and reserved jobs if they register as Buddhists in the census returns. There is also ignorance; a young man in Bangalore who claimed to be a Buddhist, and who said he knew where the Coxtown vihara was located, directed me to a Seventh Day Adventist institution.

By 1967, the main center of the Buddhist movement in the South was to be found at Kolar Gold Fields, Mysore State, under the leadership of C. M. Arumughum. He was head of the Miners Union as well as the regional head of the three organizations founded by Dr. Ambedkar: the People's Education Society, the Buddhist Society, and the Republican Party. Mr. Arumughum maintained close contact with Buddhists in North and South Arcot Districts, Perambur in Madras city, and Coxtown, Bangalore. Until recently the Buddhists of Kolar Gold Fields and Bangalore had enjoyed friendly and profitable relations with monks in Ceylon, especially Ven. T. Aryawansa Nayaka Mahathera and Ven. Saranandkara Thera. The monks came to teach and preach to the people, sometimes staying for years, living among them, training them in Buddhist practices, providing Buddhist images and pictures for the viharas. Elsewhere in Mysore State, new developments and conversions in 1917 were being led in Bijapur by S. S. Arakeri and in Belgaum by D. A. Katti. These two regions are linked to the Buddhist movement in Maharashtra as all three areas were formerly part of the Bombay Presidency. Many Mahars still live there, although, according to Mr. Katti, conversions are not limited to them.

The Buddhist Society of India

The Buddhist Society of India, founded in May of 1955 by Dr. B. R. Ambedkar, had attained little formal organization at the time of his death in 1956. In 1967, the formal structure of the society was still somewhat amorphous. Yeshwant Ambedkar, Dr. Ambedkar's son, served as president of the society with his headquarters in Bombay. The praesidium, or governing council, was composed in large part of such political leaders as B. K. Gaikwad of Nasik.* Branches of the society appeared to act independently, their success depending upon the initiative of local leaders who were usually engaged in political action — although the society was theoretically separate from the Republican Party. The society's membership was concentrated in Maharashtra, where many converts were drawn from the ranks of the Mahar caste to which Dr. Ambedkar belonged.

Extensions of the society and loosely affiliated organizations are to be found in the states of Gujarat, Rajasthan, Madhya Pradesh, Andhra Pradesh, and Uttar Pradesh with especially active groups in the cities of New Delhi, Agra, and Hyderabad. In 1967, the Buddhist movement was spreading north from Jullundar in the Punjab to Jammu and Kashmir

---

*President of the Republican Party in 1967.

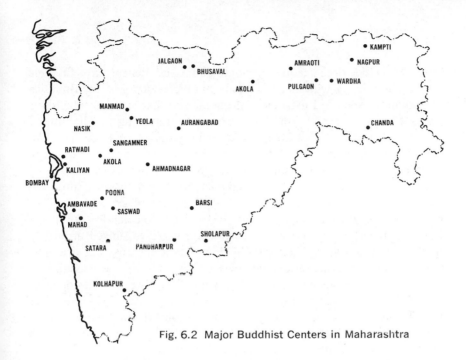

Fig. 6.2 Major Buddhist Centers in Maharashtra

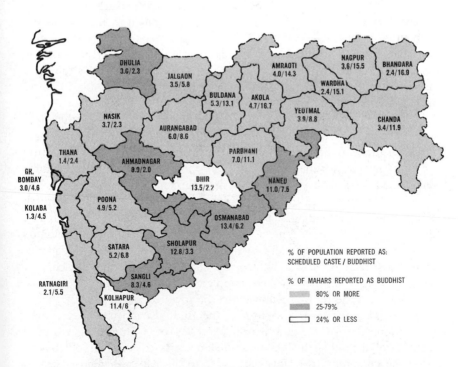

Fig. 6.3 Distribution by District of Scheduled Caste and Buddhist
in the Population of Maharashtra, 1961 Census

State. The older organizations in South India and Bengal have to some extent joined forces with it. There has been little evidence of any Buddhist activity in the state of Bihar. One informant said that in Bihar "the lower castes who had become Buddhists were now returning to Hinduism." Others, including Shri Jai Dva Prasad, deputy mayor of Patna (an Untouchable), deny that there have been any conversions to Buddhism in Bihar, although expressing devotion to Dr. Ambedkar.

The major centers of the Buddhist Society in Maharashtra are Nagpur, Poona, and the Bombay metropolitan area where 244 branches have been organized, according to the society's official list. In many instances the Bombay branches of the society are organized according to the region of origin of Untouchable migrants to the city. For example, there are three separate residential areas, each with its own small Buddhist temple, for the Bhandupa factory workers from Nagpur, Aurangabad, and Uttar Pradesh. Such groupings reflect the importance of kinship ties and regional differences in language and custom in the composition of neighborhoods in Bombay and other major cities heavily populated with migrants. There is little formal organization linking the various branches to one another and to the parent society. The activities and organization of a particular branch are more likely to be determined by the personality and interests of local leaders than by programs or policies emanating from the society's headquarters. The same loosely structured relationship also exists between urban and rural units. An example of the role of a regional leader and organizer, and the varied strands that bind diverse units together may be seen in the activities of D. T. Rupwate of Poona.

Mr. Rupwate, a barrister and active leader in politics, education, and religion, resided in Poona. He served in 1967 as an organizer and guide for many Buddhist centers located in such nearby towns and cities as Ahmadnagar, Dhulia, Nasik, and Sangamner. Each of these centers maintained links with villages in its area, in some instances established by organizers sent from the towns. Sometimes contact was made through village children attending school in town. Often, villagers interested in the movement initiated contact with the urban centers and maintained liaison through visits. Leaders such as Mr. Rupwate visited the smaller units on special occasions to provide encouragement and advice, but most organizational matters were handled at the local level.

A visit made by Mr. Rupwate to the town of Sangamner in March of 1967 illustrates several aspects of the Buddhist movement. He went there to preside at the graduation exercises of a Buddhist-sponsored high school, the Siddarth Vidalaya, which owes its existence largely to him. After the ceremony, Mr. Rupwate went to his parental village, Akola, where he met with all the local Buddhists, including women, in their *chawadi* (common hall). Mr. Rupwate delivered a religious talk followed by a brief group recitation of Buddhist texts. Later in his family house, now serving as a boys' hostel, he held a political meeting for men that included an exhortation by Mr. Rupwate on the value of education. He directed much of his speech to boys from other villages residing in the hostel while attending the Akola school. This was followed by a series of informal discussions with village leaders. Mr. Rupwate ended his day by visiting in the house of a neighbor the bride and groom whose wedding he had attended the previous day in another village. Mr. Rupwate's round of activities indicates the manner in which social, educational, and political activities of the Buddhist community are interrelated, and urban-rural ties sustained. His position as a regional leader of the Republican Party illustrates the overlapping of leaders and members belonging to several Untouchable organizations, a phenomenon found in other regions as well.

In 1967 there were a Buddhist Young Men's Association and a Buddhist Women's Association in Poona that drew members from the thirty or more branches of the Buddhist Society situated in the city. Approximately 5,000 members of the society were residents of the Kirkhi section of Poona. Most of the men were lower echelon employees of the ammunition factory or military ordnance center located in Kirkhi. None of them seemed to view these occupations as unsuitable for Buddhists. Many of the Buddhists had migrated to Poona from villages, settling with their families in quarters provided by the factory. Numerous neighborhood Buddhist associations, or *mandals,* had developed, each with its own president and weekly meetings held in its own vihara or in a member's home pending the erection of a small vihara. Plans were being made in 1967 to erect a central vihara, large enough for resident monks and a school, but land for this purpose had not been purchased. Mr. Kawadi, head of the Buddhists in Kirkhi, was a government employee and therefore not involved in politics. In his free time Mr. Kawadi, with the help of a team of friends, ran a library and night school. He also arranged lectures and wrote articles for newspapers. He has published three books in Marathi. One treats technical terms in Buddhism; another is entitled, *Wrong vs. True Interpretation;* and the third is a Marathi translation of Ambedkar's *Marx or Buddhism.*

In Aurangabad the People's Education Society, also founded by Dr. Ambedkar, has established the Milind College of Arts and Sciences. A Buddhist center existed in 1969 on the campus with a resident Ceylonese *bhikkhu,* Ven. Shanti Bhadra, professor of Pali. Students are instructed in methods for teaching Buddhism which they apply in their own villages during vacation. The P.E.S. also maintains some connection with, but does not claim to control, a college in Nagpur — the place of Dr. Ambedkar's *diksha* ceremony. Nagpur serves as the center of a web of formal and informal contacts with smaller towns and villages. Dr. D. P. Meshram, former mayor of Nagpur, has been an outstanding leader of the Buddhists in this area. However, there have been other Untouchable leaders in Nagpur, including the fiery M. D. Pachbai, who advocated solutions to the problems of the Untouchable that differed from those advanced by other Buddhists. He was openly critical of the Republican Party's leaders and their policies, "because the religion is in the hands of the politicians we are getting more Hinduized and the bhikkhus exploit the Buddhist masses." In the same interview, Mr. Pachbai wanted a movement of social workers who were also householders, from whose ranks Indian monks would eventually emerge.

The tendency towards fragmentation, inherent in the Buddhist Society's weak central organization and dependence on inspired local leaders, has led to two major breaks from the parent society in Maharashtra. The earliest was led by Mr. Rajbhoj, who is accused of having exploited his position as a trusted lieutenant of Ambedkar: "He went from village to village; he would tell them anything — talk like a prophet and live like a lord." Critics of Mr. Rajbhoj say that after being reproved by Dr. Ambedkar, he turned to the "Gandhians," who used him against Ambedkar. After being "discarded by Congress" he established a Buddhist Society of his own — the Bharat Dalit Sevak Sangh. Mr. Rajbhoj's own views on this matter were not obtained in spite of efforts to meet him. Others indicated in 1967 that Mr. Rajbhoj's organization might rejoin the Buddhist Society of India.

The second break from the society in Maharashtra was led by R. D. Bhandare of Bombay, who founded the Society of Buddhists in August of 1966. Mr. Bhandare's Buddhist Society did not concern him very much as of the late 1960s, as he had a "twenty-year plan" in which his efforts during the initial ten years were to be directed towards the economic betterment of his people. The next five years were to be devoted to cultural development, with religious training reserved for the final five-year period. Mr. Bhandare's views were based on the belief, shared by many other Untouchables, that his people might best be helped by working within the political party in power — the Congress — rather than by participating in a politically ineffectual opposition group such as the Republican Party. In 1967 Mr. Bhandare was elected to the Lok Sabha, the lower house of the National Parliament, as a member of the Congress Party. In the fall of that year he was sent to the United Nations as a member of a legal advisory committee. When interviewed in New York, in December of 1967, Mr. Bhandare expressed his conviction that a law enabling Buddhists to receive all the government benefits reserved for Scheduled Castes would be passed in the spring of 1968.

The amorphous nature of the Buddhist Society, even in Maharashtra where it was most active, may be attributed in part to the absence of a strong central organization and the lack of communication between local units. An example of the latter was observed in Poona in the fall of 1966 where a *diksha* ceremony was held for the conversion of thirty persons in front of the statue of Dr. Ambedkar. None of the members of the Buddhist Society of Poona knew the identity of those converted. D. R. Maheshkar, president of the Young Men's Buddhist Association, heard a rumor that the ceremony had been performed by a Tibetan lama who occasionally resided at the Dehu Road vihara, but nothing more was known. An interview with Y. Ambedkar, national president of the Buddhist Society, indicates an approach to communication that does not lend itself to a highly integrated or coordinated organization. When asked how he establishes contacts with fellow Buddhists in other areas, Mr. Ambedkar said: "When the newspaper says I will be in a certain place, the people write and call me to come and convert them; it is spontaneous, from the bottom of their hearts." Although the society has published a weekly paper and books, these publications have emphasized inspirational and religious content rather than organizational aims.

The Buddhist Movement Outside Maharashtra

Although the Buddhist Society has listed officers in at least a dozen states outside Maharashtra, much of the proselytizing in these areas has been conducted by other loosely affiliated organizations. The caste base for such organizations has often differed from one region to another. While the Mahars have been in the forefront of the movement in Maharashtra, members of the Chamar caste have taken the initiative in many areas of Uttar Pradesh and the Punjab. The importance of caste and kin ties in furthering recruitment and organization has often affected coordination and cooperation between organizations and regions.

In the neighboring state of Rajasthan, the Maha Bodhi Ashoka Mission of India was founded in Ajmer in 1961. The first president of this organization, Mrs. Freda Bedi, later became a Buddhist nun of the Kadgyupa sect in Dalhousie of Himalchal Pradesh state. It is not clear from its publications whether this organization is formally a branch of the Buddhist Society. The name of the mission suggests closer bonds to the Maha Bodhi Society which claims a branch in Ajmer, but its membership and activities have been among the Koliyas, an underprivileged group in Ajmer and adjacent areas. It overlaps territorially with the Buddhist Society as both organizations list centers in Ajmer, Akola, Bombay, Calcutta, and Nagpur. The mission also has claimed centers at Mukteshwar (Nainital) and Ceylon.

The Maha Bodhi Ashoka Mission of India has stated as its functions "to promote peace, love, harmony, fraternity, equality, and the right views among the human beings through Educational, Physical, Social, Cultural, and Spiritual Services." Its ceremonies are on full moon days and other feasts, and it has maintained a vihara and health center in Ajmer, giving free medical aid. Social welfare centers of the mission, also in Ajmer, are said to distribute vitamins, food, biscuits, and milk to "the poor, sick, disabled, and expectant mothers."[6] The mission publishes and distributes free Dhamma leaflets, setting forth the tenets of Buddhism. It also has published a periodical for converts, *Samyak Dristi (Right View)* in English and two vernacular languages.

The spearhead of the Buddhist movement in the north has been the Ambedkar Buddhist Mission founded in 1966 by L. R. Balley and others, with headquarters in the Punjab town of Jullundar. In an interview conducted in July of 1967, Mr. Balley said that he had been a member of the Buddhist Society's governing body (praesidium), but left that organization, "When I saw it was not doing its work." However, information received from India in 1969 indicated that the Ambedkar Buddhist Mission had amalgamated with the Buddhist Society of India.

According to Mr. Balley, in July of 1967, the Ven. Anand Kausalyayan was planning at that time to leave his teaching post in Ceylon in order to reside permanently in India as president of the Ambedkar Buddhist Mission. The Ven. A. Kausalyayan was originally from the Punjab where he was an active member of the Arya Samaj in his youth. Later, he joined the Maha Bodhi Society as one of three young Indian intellectuals who enhanced the society's prestige in the early twentieth century. These three eventually left the society: Rahul Sankrityayan of Uttar Pradesh, deceased; Jagdish Kashyap of Bihar, director of the Buddhist Institute at Nalanda; and A. Kausalyayan, who has identified himself with the Ambedkar-inspired movement. Kausalyayan appears to have lived in Nagpur at one time, as others in the Buddhist movement credit him with having trained six or eight young monks while residing there.

In the far northern state of Jammu, the mission organized mass meetings of the Batwal and other Scheduled Castes in 1966, and in 1967 at Bashnah and Dalhousie, to celebrate the Buddha's *Jayanti* (enlightenment), Freda Bedi, ex-president of the Ajmer Maha Bodhi Society and later a Buddhist nun, participated in the organization of these meetings. The only English-speaking leader of the mission in Jammu, Milkhi Ram, was a Chamar and former member of the Harijan Mandir Party. Although the Jayanti meetings were reported in the press as mass conversions, Milkhi Ram and L. R. Balley stated that the participants did not become "legal Buddhist." They viewed the meetings as part of a long-term program for the preparation of those who will become full converts when conversion will no longer involve the loss of government benefits accorded the Scheduled Castes.

The aims and intentions of the organization are set forth in a mimeographed copy of the Constitution of the Ambedkar Buddhist Mission received from L. R. Balley in April, 1967: "Preaching and spread of Buddha Dharma. to strengthen the spread of Buddha Dharma in different states, tehsils, districts and colonies of India as well as in other countries."

Specifically the organization hopes "to be helpful to the interested boy and girl students studying Buddha Dharma as well as to those interested men and women who have a desire to work for the spread of Buddhism." This indicates a concentration on potential leaders. The means chosen are the same as elsewhere: the publications of Dr. Ambedkar's works and Buddhist literature in different Indian languages, erection of new viharas and rest houses to help pilgrims, and "improvements in matters of marriage, death, naming ceremony, according to Buddhism and the scientific way." In line with this last is a somewhat ambiguous statement: "To allocate wealth and property of the forefathers of the people inclined towards Buddhism and try to refine their old traditions and customs." The mission also plans to arrange classes and examinations for the spread of Buddhism and "to maintain and spread such institutions like industries and hospitals which could promote the well-being and prosperity of the society." Finally, it specifies cooperation with related institutions of Buddhism. In the spring of 1967, plans were being made to open centers in Jullundar, Delhi, Nagpur, and Jammu. However, the only place where the organization was active at that time was Jullundar.

The mission, non-political in conception, emulates the Hindu Ramakrishnan Mission in its primary concern with social welfare and religion. It also uses propaganda techniques employed by the Arya Samaj, a militant Hindu organization actively hostile to the Buddhist movement in the Punjab. One technique used by both groups is the public lecture accompanied by the projection of slides; an especially effective means for conveying information to illiterates. One set of hand-painted slides used by the mission depicts episodes from the life of Dr. Ambedkar, the Lord

Buddha, and saints popular in the Punjab. Some indication of the content of these slides appears in the following captions and comments made during their presentation:

Dr. Ambedkar

1) Ambedkar as a child at school, isolated because of untouchability.
2) Ambedkar, forced to drink water through a bamboo pipe to avoid polluting the source.
3) Ambedkar insulted and rejected by a barber.
4) Ambedkar insulted by a peon when he was secretary to the Maharaja of Baroda.
5) Ambedkar driven out of his lodging by a Parsee. "This is the turning point of his life, the day he took a vow to elevate his people."
6) The Mahad tank Satyagraha. [On March 19, 1927, Ambedkar and his followers drank water from the Chawadar-Tala in the town of Mahad in an effort to establish the Untouchables' right to use this tank, or pond.]
7) The Nasik Kalaram Mandir Satyagraha. [In 1930, Ambedkar led Untouchables in their demand for the right to enter the temple of Prabhu Ram.]
8) The Round Table Conference in London. "This is the man who got your rights for you."
9) Signing of the Poona Pact in the jail at Poona.
10) Presentation of the Constitution. "A man from your own community has risen so high."
11) Ambedkar holding a copy of his book, *The Buddha and His Dhamma.*

The Buddha

12) Ananda, Buddha's disciple, and the Candala girl.
13) Buddha and Angulimala, a peasant, a dacoit, a laborer, a cobbler, a landless worker [people of the lowest groups].
14) Buddha's debate with the Brahmans who claimed to be gods, not born as other men.
15) Buddha begging at Rajgiri while Sunit, a Bhangi [sweeper], hides behind a tree to watch him.
16) Buddha embracing Sunit and asking him why he hides. "My religion does not teach untouchability."

Regional Saints

17) Pictures of Ravidas, Kabir, and Guru Nanak [all popular in the Punjab] as teachers of equality.
18) Ravidas in jail for having blown the sacred conch.
19) The Three Refuges, written in Hindi, Punjabi, and Urdu.

In 1967, Mr. Balley used these slides in several lectures delivered in Amritsar and Ambala. He also trained a team of five paid workers to present illustrated lectures in other areas of the Punjab.

South of the Punjab, in the capital of New Delhi, there existed in

1967 a number of Buddhist organizations affiliated in varying degrees with the Ambedkar Bhavan on Rani Jhansi Road. The Bhavan contains a Buddhist shrine, rooms for guests, meeting rooms, a library-reading room, and permanent quarters for a caretaker and his family. These facilities are used by young Buddhists for evening classes and weekly meetings. Mrs. S. Ambedkar, widow of Dr. Ambedkar, resided near Ambedkar Bhavan and served as head of an autonomous Buddhist group with a branch in Lucknow. Bhikkhu Pradhyanand of Ceylon administered the Lucknow branch which maintained a free school for 700 students. This school was said to serve 500 villages.

Elsewhere in Delhi, meetings and related activities for Buddhists were held in the Maha Bodhi *mandir* of the interdenominational Birla temple, and in the Ashoka Mission vihara on Mehrauli Road directed by the Ven. Dharmavara, a Buddhist monk from Cambodia. This independent center with vihara and hostel is primarily a religious institution. The venerable director sought to educate the Indian Buddhists in their religion with compassion and discretion, while disassociating himself from their political involvements and from intra-Buddhist dissension.

Headquarters of the Republican Party of India, and its president, B. K. Gaikwad, were also situated in New Delhi. Although much of his time was given to political activity, Mr. Gaikwad was held to be almost a Bodhisattva by some of his supporters, especially in his home town of Nasik in Maharashtra. Political leaders of Untouchable origin, particularly those serving in the central government, for example, Shankaranand Shastri from Maharashtra, an official in the Indian civil service, had their own following in New Delhi. The personal and regional biases of many Buddhist groups, confounded in some instances by caste loyalties, have tended to create separate Buddhist units within the city. Consequently, Buddhists from Maharashtra and the Punjab rarely seem to meet or act in concert on issues of common concern.

In central India the Buddhist Society of India has established an active branch in Hyderabad, the capital of Andhra Pradesh. A publication entitled, *Review of Our Activities* in 1964–65, claims the society has grown to a "mighty organisation" with the earnest desire to propagate Buddhism "by establishing Buddhist Study Centres, Viharas, Educational Institutions, Orphanages, Health and Relief Centers and etc." In 1965 this branch had acquired a site for a vihara near Osmania College on the outskirts of Hyderabad. Plans were being made to establish offices in Hyderabad and to found a residential high school and vihara in another city of Andhra Pradesh, Nagarjuna Sagar, "one of the greatest Buddhist Centres in India" (Satyanarayana 1965: 6-7).

In the far south, Buddhist organizations founded prior to the Buddhist Society of India were beginning in the 1960s to expand their activities, due in part to the Ambedkar-inspired movement. Efforts were being made to reconstruct old Buddhist temples, some built as early as 1907, and there was much interest in the founding of schools. In Madras City one of the oldest Buddhist organizations, the Maha Bodhi Society, collaborated with Buddhists of Untouchable origin in the Perambur section of town. But members of the Society tended to view this relationship with little enthusiasm, and the Perambur group generally organized and conducted their own weekly meetings. Mr. Aryashankar, head of the Cycle Rickshaw Drivers and Transport Coolies Union, has established in the Periamet section of Madras a Buddhist center completely independent of the Maha Bodhi Society. They advocate a simple form of Buddhism. According to Mr. Aryashankar, he and his fellow workers "tell the ladies not to worship stones and trees," and they train children to recite the Three Refuges and the Panch Shila.* The Periamet Buddhists consider Pandit Ayoti Das, founder of the South India Buddhist Association, to be their spiritual father. Mr. Aryashankar expressed more concern for the economic betterment of his people than for their religious development. He has succeeded in having several statues of Dr. Ambedkar erected in Madras City and areas nearby.

The rules of the South India Buddhist Association convey its objectives, at least as ideally conceived. The first is "to preach Buddhism among Indian masses and to add *upasakas* and *upasikas* [members of the laity] to its fold." Steps to propagate Buddhism are listed as lectures, meetings, publications, reading rooms, and libraries. Failure to attend weekly meetings is penalized. The rules distinguish between those who embrace Buddhism openly and those who do not. The latter are not to be excluded or ostracized, but considered as sympathizers. Full members are expected to master the Eightfold Path of Classical Buddhism:

Sarvam Anityam — everything is impermanent
Sarvam Anatman — nothing contains an immutable principle
Sarvam Pratitya Samutpada — everything has a cause-effect relationship
Sarvam Nirusvaram — nothing in the world has a creator
Sarvam Skandamayan — all things result from a combination of Skandhas
Sarvam Karmajan — everything arises as a result of action
Nirvanam Santham — mental detachment is peace

This degree of concern with the actual content of traditional Buddhism is not often found in more recently established Buddhist organizations.

---

*The Three Refuges are the Buddha, the Dharma and the Sangha; the Panch Shila is the Buddhist moral law: no killing, no stealing, no forbidden sex pleasure, no lying, no intoxicants.

However, this association's rules for marriage, naming, and funeral ceremonies are much the same as those practiced by other Buddhist groups.[7]

Two individuals residing in Madras City in 1967 identified themselves as Buddhists engaged in improving the lot of the Untouchable.
These reformers did not belong to any of the Buddhist organizations
involved in similar work. Mrs. Minambal Shivaraj, widow of an eminent
political figure, has done much for the betterment of the Scheduled
Castes. In the 1967 election she was an unsuccessful candidate for a
seat in the Lok Sahba or national parliament. The other reformer, an
elderly poet, V. V. Murugesa Bhagavadan, maintained an orphanage and
free hospital in the slum area of Villirakkam. He said that although not
a member of "the Mahabothi Sabha or the Bharatheeya Buddhist Society,"
he had been associated for the past fifteen years with the "South Indian
Buddhist Scholars." No additional information was obtained regarding
this organization.

Buddhist Activities

According to its president, Yeshwant Ambedkar, in 1967 the activities of the Buddhist Society of India were manifold. It published a weekly
paper and books; it arranged large-scale *diksha* ceremonies and provided
financial support for the follow-up work after such conversions. The
society lobbied for legislation beneficial to the Buddhists. It provided
education in family planning, and trained bhikkus (monks) and lay
leaders, sometimes called *baudhachariyas*. In most areas such lay leaders
officiated at life-cycle rites including the naming ceremony held for young
children, weddings, funerals, and *diksha* or conversion ceremonies. While
every branch of the society did not perform all of these functions, the
most effective work of the organization was performed at the local level.

Some idea of the working of a local group may be inferred from the
following regulations posted in the Dehu Road temple in Poona:

Every Sunday from five to seven p.m., all children, ladies and men
should assemble.
They should first wash, and wear no *chappals* [leather sandals] in the mandir.
They may not smoke, drink, chew betel in the mandir.
They should first bow three times to the image of the Buddha, then to the
presiding monk.
All must keep silent.
Men sit on the right, ladies on the left.
Any who wish to smoke, etc., must go at least ten feet away from the temple.
No one must damage the temple.

Parents must keep their children from disturbing the ceremonies.

No one can sleep in the temple, nor fight nor abuse one another there.

Parents must send their children from five to ten years of age regularly to the temple for instruction.

All must help those who are "socially weak," according to the orders of the committee.

"He who disobeys this will not count as a Buddhist and the others should have no relations with him."

Apart from the somewhat harsh concluding decree, this list is similar to the printed or handwritten list of rules seen in small *mandirs* or viharas in city slums and villages. The terms mandir and vihara are often used interchangeably by these Buddhists in reference to their meeting places and ritual centers. The former is the common Hindu term for temple, while the latter is used in classic Buddhism to designate a monastery.

Every local unit has a committee or governing board of laymen that works with a monk or, in the absence of a monk, leads group prayers and services. Very few communities in 1967 had a resident monk. For example, none of the villages within forty miles of Poona maintained a monk in residence. Some villages in this area, including Lolanala, Lolikand, Ranha, and Kirkitwadi, with fifteen to seventeen Buddhist families each, had never been visited by a monk.

There were very few monks in Poona proper. The presence of a monk is usually associated with much Buddhist activity and piety, judging from the influence of Venerable Sheelaratana in the Nagpur Chawl section of the city. Although this monk spent part of his time in Sholapur, Buddhist activity in Nagpur Chawl was much greater than in the nearby Public Works Workshop settlements of Tapoori, or the very small and destitute group, unvisited even by lay workers, located near the Papal Seminary.

A major Buddhist center in Bombay was under construction in 1967 and completed in 1969 on the site of Dr. Ambedkar's cremation. Located on the seashore in Shivaji Park, the Ambedkar Memorial Shrine is shaped like a *stupa* and designed to provide meeting rooms and lodging for monks and pilgrims. In 1967 the resident monk was Ven. Vajir Buddhi from Burma.

There were also two substantial Buddhist temples located in the Worli and Parel sections of Bombay. The former temple, directed by a Japanese monk, Ven. Tenjo Watanabe, followed the Japanese pattern for daily and weekly rituals. Young men of the Buddhist Society of India organized regular meetings in halls in the crowded *chawls* (tenements) of the Worli area. On such occasions people gathered around a table on

A typical neighborhood shrine — Bombay

which were placed the image of Lord Buddha and a picture of Dr. Ambedkar. They listened to talks explaining Buddhism, based on the *Dhammapada* and Dr. Ambedkar's book, *The Buddha and His Dhamma*. Naming ceremonies were held in the same way, but weddings were held in the Worli temple. In the Bahujan temple of Parel the Venerable Dhammananda held well-organized meetings with instructions and simple ceremonies.

Elsewhere in the innumerable *chawls* of Bombay, in large blocks of one-room apartments or squalid conglomerations of hutments, thousands of Buddhists had only a lay leader or none at all. Examples of this were found on Moses Road in Pathan Chawl, a labyrinth of narrow, twisting lanes between little patchworks of huts. A similar situation prevailed in a cluster of more solid sheds in a Christian cemetery, also on Moses Road. In each of these areas there was a small vihara for meetings and ceremonies, and in each lived sickly Tibetan monks, unable to speak the people's language but supported by their charity. A more ambitious vihara was located on Bapti Road in Karmati Pura, a unit of six residential blocks for municipal workers, five reserved for Buddhists, one for Hindus. This vihara had been built on the former site of a Hindu temple to Maruti.

Resident monk in the Paltan Road vihara, with paintings of Buddha and Ambedkar

Owen Lynch

On Paltan Road a one-room hut served as a temple, meeting place, and library as well as the living quarters of Bhadant Sivali Bodhi, a professor of Pali at Siddarth College. An older and more impressive vihara was also located within the compound of the Nair Hospital. The Venerable Anand, a monk of the Maha Bodhi Society, was in charge of this temple.

Small temples and attendant Buddhist associations were also found in the Buddhist sections of Nagpur in 1967. A particularly active group in the Nagasena area had D. H. Shende, L.L., as their president. He was also president of the Scheduled Caste Welfare Association in that area. The Nagasena Buddhists held ceremonies on various religious occasions, sponsored lectures and debates, and maintained a kindergarten and night school for Untouchables. Another active group in Nagpur was the Dr. Babasaheb Ambedkar Adhyayan Mandir, a study circle composed of eighty young government workers of Untouchable origin. They had collected a substantial library of books on Buddhism and books about or by Dr. Ambedkar. Their library was open to the public on Wednesday, Saturday, and Sunday and served as the meeting place for monthly study groups and for the quarterly meetings of the general membership. Although they had a president, R. M. Rangari, and a vice-president, B. S. Rangari, "every member helps and is devoted whether he has a post or not." The study circle published an annual review of its program and accomplishments.

Throughout Maharashtra, the provision of housing and education for Untouchables was an important activity that sometimes involved members of the Buddhist Society even though such efforts were not listed as part of the Society's formal functions. Buddhists have established primary and secondary schools and associated hostels for boys and girls. The primary purpose of these schools was secular education even though the institutions were often referred to as Buddhist. In only a very few instances government-sponsored housing projects for Untouchables had a Buddhist temple, such as the Dr. Ambedkar Center of Buddhist Religion and Culture in Nasik.

A variety of Buddhist activities were begun some years ago in Atit, a village of Satara District, ninety miles from Poona. The moving spirit behind this movement was Nivrittie Ragho Kamble, a clerk in the Irrigation Department of Maharashtra State. Mr. Kamble decided to organize a Buddhist association, The Ashtasila Upasaka Sangh, after studying twenty books on Buddhism by Dr. Ambedkar and the work of the following authors: Dharmananda Kausambi, Bhadant K. Anand, Venerable Silaratana, Venerable Satdharmacharya, V. G. Apate, S. S. Khanwelkar, K. V. Kedari, L. B. Kesakar, and Dr. S. Radhakrishnan. He also read translations of such classical Buddhist texts as the *Dhammapada* and *The Questions of Milind*.

After completing this course of self-instruction, Mr. Kamble conceived the idea of forming an association (*sangh*) of lay devotees (*upasakas*) based on the precepts of classical Buddhism's Eightfold Path (*ashtasila*). He sought to establish a disciplined religious community possessing some features of a monastic order while actively participating in society. The association's records show that all the Mahars of Mr. Kamble's parental village of Atit, consisting of twenty-three men and twenty-six women, embraced Buddhism and became *upasakas* and *upasikas*. They committed themselves to a regime of fasting and devotional ceremonies. According to an account provided by S. D. Gaikwad of Bombay, the laity fast at least four days of each lunar month on: *Paurnima,* Full Moon Day; the eighth day, *Ashtami,* of the first and second fortnight; and the New Moon Day. Their fast begins at noon on the designated day and continues until noon of the next day. Nothing is consumed, not even water, during the initial nine hours. At 9 p.m., fruit juice, milk, coffee, tea, or some other liquid may be taken in moderation. Shortly before breaking their fast, they recite the *ashtasila,* or precepts of the Eightfold Path. Other calendrical rites are performed on every full moon day and new moon day when the devotees assemble in the evening for *vandana,* a recitation of the Three Refuges. Sometimes, "I take refuge in Bhim Rao Ambedkar" is added to this recitation. Later the same night they gather to sing songs in praise of Dr. Ambedkar and Lord Buddha.

Festivals celebrated by this association include three commemorating events in the life of Dr. Ambedkar: his birthday *(Bhim Jayanti)* on April 14; the day of his conversion (on *Dasara,* a major Hindu holiday observed in the fall); and the date of Ambedkar's death, December 6. Excepting the last event, for which they fast, these occasions are celebrated by the preparation and consumption of sweets as part of the ceremonial activity. Although the dates of three other calendrical rites observed by the group correspond to popular Hindu holidays, they are observed without worship of Hindu deities. These rites are: Diwali (the Hindu festival of lights), the Bull festival of Bendur (held on the full moon day of the month of Shravana), and Naag Panchami (festival of snakes). The Buddha *Jayanti* is also a major occasion in their cycle of festivals.

Mr. Kamble has also drawn on the ancient and much loved Indian tradition of religious singing to form a singing group in Atit known as the Rajaratna Gayan Mandal. This Buddhist "choir" became very popular among the Buddhists of other villages who called upon them to perform on various occasions. Mr. Kamble was instrumental in the organization of similar groups of singers in three other villages of Satara District. The names of these groups and their villages are: Siddarth Gayan Mandal of Nandgaon, Rajkamal Gayan Mandal of Mattyapur, and Sankar Gayan Mandal of Kashila.

Mr. Kamble's proselytizing zeal has lead to the establishment of similar associations in seven other villages, including the three with singing groups, near his parental home of Atit. All the Buddhists in these villages have joined the Upasaka Sangh of their village. The names of these villages and the number of resident Buddhists are: Gondavale (20), Katapur (12), Taragaon (9), Apasinge (8), Nandagaon (50), Mattyapur (10), and Kashila (30). The Buddhists in the first-named village, Gondavale, have built a *mandir* at Mr. Kamble's suggestion.

In addition to his achievements as an innovator and organizer of religious activities, Mr. Kamble was responsible for the founding of the Karmaveer Vidyarthi Sanghatana in Atit. This organization provides free text books to students of Untouchable origin. Mr. Kamble also officiated at various life-cycle rites including: marriage, recognition of conception *(garbha mangal),* an infant's first feeding *(anna prashana),* the naming of a child, and the funeral offering of water to the dead *(jaladana vidhi).* He also performed the *mahapuja* of Lord Buddha, a ceremony that honors without implying worship, and initiated converts to Buddhism through the *dhamma diksha* ceremony.

Although Mr. Kamble was transferred to the town of Pandharpur, Sholapur District, the organizations that he left behind were still flourishing in 1967. He continued his proselytizing work in Sholapur by organizing a Buddhist "choir," the Siddarth Gayan Mandal, among the residents of Pili and Malshiras villages. In the latter village he initiated another type of organization, the Bhim Sanchar Majur Sahakari or Labour Contract Society.

Mr. Kamble's success illustrates the ready acceptance of new ideas and activities in rural India when such innovations are introduced in accordance with traditional religious practices. Fasting, calendrical rites, and singing groups are ancient features of the Hindu tradition from which the Buddhists seek to disassociate themselves. While Buddhism repudiates many aspects of the caste system, much of the strength of Mr. Kamble's organizations is drawn from the kin and caste ties emanating from his parental village. While the florescence of Buddhist activity in Atit could be attributed in large measure to the unique personality, learning, and zeal of Mr. Kamble, the enthusiastic response of the Untouchable community to his program indicates the latent forces in this stratum of Indian society that might readily respond to trained and dedicated leaders.

Training of Leaders

A common concern voiced by Buddhists in all the groups visited in India in 1967 was the need for more leaders, be they monks or trained laymen. While the older organizations, founded prior to 1956, had a few monks, most of them were non-Indians, trained in the classical Buddhist tradition. Some members of the Ambedkar-inspired movement consider these monks to be aloof and indifferent to the needs of the Untouchable whom they sometimes treat "as Brahmans would treat them." Dr. Ambedkar's conception of the sangha (monastic community) differs markedly from the traditional view of their role as contemplatives dedicated to spiritual pursuits. In his book, *The Buddha and His Dhamma,* Ambedkar argues that monks should serve as social workers and missionaries (Ambedkar 1957: 434-55).

Buddhist monks from other countries have played a minor role in the mass conversion movement of the past decade. Differences in rite, custom, and language have hampered the efforts of monks from Japan, Tibet, Burma, Cambodia, and Ceylon. Several laymen said, "We are Indians, we do not want to adopt Japanese or Ceylonese ways." Others indicated that monks should be recruited from Scheduled Caste communities so they would know the language and mentality of the people. Some Indian Buddhists expressed their preference for the development of lay leaders, fearing the emergence of a sangha that would become an end in itself. This concern, and the choice between monks or lay leaders, was of minor importance as there appear to be few provisions for the training of monks in India and little interest in becoming bhikkus among the younger generation. Some very young boys were sent from Nagpur to Ceylon in the early sixties to be trained as monks, but according to several reports, they were neglected and eventually sent back to India. Most Indian monks are recruited from among older men and even they frequently return to lay life. An attempt to establish a "nunnery" in Nagpur in the sixties was abortive even though many Mahar women possessed the motivation and essential qualities of character. Lack of trained leaders was the major reason cited for the failure of this project.

Apart from a devoted lay worker at the Worli temple in Bombay, most of the young Buddhists queried in 1967 expressed little interest in becoming monks. However, Ven. Shanti Bhadra, professor of Pali at Milind College in Aurangabad, said that some of his "matured students" were thinking of becoming bhikkus. The director of the Maha Bodhi Society center in Sarnath stated that his organization was prepared to maintain and train those aspiring to be monks of the traditional type, but none of the candidates that he had known were willing to spend the time and effort required for adequate training. Although other members of the Maha Bodhi Society claim a number of ordinations in recent years, the numbers cited varied from fifteen to thirty or forty. In contrast to the more traditional Buddhist organizations, the program of the Buddhist Society of India as described by its president, Yeshwant Ambedkar, requires only six months of training for its monks. While this brief period affords only enough time for a superficial acquaintance with the traditional role of the bhikku, it may serve the society's needs for ritual specialists and missionaries, since most of its members are unversed in even the rudiments of Buddhism.

Information pertaining to training facilities, and the number of monks active in India, was difficult to obtain. In 1967, one person stated that two monks of Nagpur, Venerable Dharmasheela and Venerable Sumedha, were soon to become *mahatheras,* a title conferred ten years after ordination, and therefore qualified to train and ordain monks. Fragmentary information was provided in a letter dated March 28, 1967, from Venerable Shantarakshak, a young monk of Chamar origin residing in Ambedkar Bhavan, the Delhi center of the Buddhist Society of India. His letter states:

A few of our monks have gone abroad for higher studies, . . . Nagsen to Thailand and Anand Kausalyayan and Megkar to Ceylon. We are unable to provide them with any assistance whatsoever from India.

The other monks are working in India at different places. I meet them on a few occasions. Their names are: (1) H. Rastrapal, (2) Aryadev, (3) Shili Bhadra, (4) Vimal, (5) Mahanam, (6) Sangpal, (7) Gyanprabkhar, (8) Sheelanand, (9) Shampriti, (10) Bodhanand, (11) Sadanand, (12) Vishudanand, (13) Sumedh.

Only two of these monks, other than Venerable Shantarakshak, were encountered during this study. One of them was a young man engaged in studying under the direction of Venerable Dhammananda of the Parel temple in Bombay. The other, trained in Bangalore by Venerable Buddharakkhita, was Venerable Sheelaratana, a most active and effective leader of Buddhist communities in Poona and Sholapur. Ven. A. Kausalyayan was also credited with having trained six or eight young monks while residing in Nagpur. The statement in Venerable Shantarakshak's letter regarding Ven. Anand Kausalyayan differs from the account of others who said that he went to Ceylon to teach Pali, not to study. In July, 1967, L. R. Balley said that Ven. A. Kausalyayan was planning to leave his teaching post in Ceylon and return to India to serve as president of the Ambedkar Buddhist Mission being organized in the Punjab town of Jullundar.

There appear to be more active and successful programs for the training of Buddhist lay leaders. In the early 1960s an English monk concerned with the plight of the Indian Buddhists, the Venerable Sangarakshit, used to spend half of each year in Poona. He taught a one-month course for the laity designed to lead them more deeply into the teachings of Buddhism. Several individuals who had successfully completed the course spoke with great pride of the certificate that he had awarded to them at the end of the course.

Several of the Buddhist organizations offer a course of training, usually of one-month duration, to prepare laymen to serve as *baudhachariyas*. Completion of this training qualifies these men to officiate at weddings and other ceremonies for which they are usually paid. Although some Buddhists disparage the *baudhachariyas* as being motivated by monetary rewards for their services, most groups are in dire need of these ritual specialists. This provision of specialists to officiate at family life cycle rites is in keeping with the Hindu tradition and differs markedly from Buddhist practices in other countries (Morgan 1956: 398). In 1966 a six-month program was begun at the Worli temple in Bombay to prepare young men to serve as *baudhachariyas*. An account written in November of 1967 describes this course of training — it was prepared for the author by S. D. Gaikwad, a Mahar Buddhist, who teaches history at Siddarth College in Bombay.

The young people who participate in the activities of the Japan Buddha Mandir at Worli have started "Sat Dharma Sangh" at the temple. The Japanese Bhikkhu, Rev. Tenjo Watanabe is the president of the Sangh and Mr. Y. H. Kamble is the secretary. The Sangh has started a training centre for men only to qualify them as Baudhachariya. . . . Only adults are admitted to the training centre without charging any fees. A course of six months is prescribed. After completing the studies and practical training (course) an examination is held and certificates are given to the successful candidates.

The examination consisted of three parts: written, oral, and "experiment" for which equal credit was given. Reference was made to Sunday classes held to "polish the language of Baudhachariyas." This account also stated that five persons had successfully completed the course during the previous year. Similar training was reported to have been given to two persons by Bhikkhu Dhammananda of the Bahujan Vihara in the Parel section of Bombay.

Another type of training, a religious retreat, was also described by S. D. Gaikwad in his report of November, 1967:

On 12th October 1967 (Dasara festival) Shri Yeshwantrao Ambedkar, the son of Babasaheb Ambedkar, C. M. Wagh, the Assistant Secretary of the People's Education Society, Aurangabad, and three more [sic] school-going children namely Gautam Gangurde, Anil Gangurde and Prakash Wagh joined the Order as Samaner and stayed ten days from 12th to 21st October at the Ambedkar Memorial (Ambedkar Smaraka) at the sea face, Shivaji Park, Bombay, under the guidance of Bhikkhu Vajir Buddhi, a Burmese monk. The memorial is nearly completed and the Burmese monk is staying there. . . .

The *samaners* (novices) participating in the retreat were given special names for the ten day period. Yeshwantrao Ambedkar was called Bhadant Maha Kashapa; C. M. Wagh, Dhammakirti; Gautam Gangurde, Rahul; Anil Gangurde, Buddhapriya; and Prakash Wagh, Sangharatan. Initially this retreat was planned for high ranking leaders of several Buddhist organizations who were to meet at the Maha Bodhi Society Center in Sarnath for a month of meditation and religious training. The change of location, from Sarnath to Bombay, may have been due to some conflict with the Maha Bodhi Society, whose facilities were to have been used. Although leaders of only two organizations attended this retreat, similar efforts to bring together the top leaders of various Buddhist groups might well serve to unify the movement and further the development of a common body of rite, belief, and practice.

The establishment of Buddhist institutes for advanced religious study and research has been advocated by many leaders of the movement including Mr. Rupwate of Poona and Mrs. S. Ambedkar of Delhi. In the 1950s, the Maharaja of Mysore donated five acres in Bangalore to Dr. B. R. Ambedkar for this purpose. Although the Bangalore institute was described by Benz (1966: 24) as already built and functioning, in 1967 it was still only a pious hope. Litigation, lack of funds, and the absence of capable scholars had delayed the creation of the proposed Institute for the Study of Comparative Religions and Buddhist Studies. Several leaders in Mysore State including C. M. Arumughum, D. A. Katti, and S. S. Arakeri asked how government or private foundations in the United States might be persuaded to provide financial support for the Institute. Queries of this kind often reflected an awareness of the American concern for combating Communism: "If the U. S. does not want India to go Communist, why does it not help us? We are the bulwark against Communism. If Dr. Ambedkar had led the masses to Communism, where would India be today?"

While there are several institutes for Buddhist studies in India, none of them are associated with the Buddhist Society of India and very few of their students are from the Scheduled Castes. In 1966, Milind College in Aurangabad was one of the few institutions providing advanced training for "new" Buddhists. In 1966–67, more than 300 students were enrolled in a course on the Pali language that forms part of a successful program in Pali studies established at Milind. The Marathwada University, of which Milind is a part, authorized the college to inaugurate an M.A. degree program in Pali studies to begin in 1967–68. It was anticipated that students completing this degree would be able to go to Buddhist countries for advanced training, research, and ordination as monks. The Buddhist Centre at Milind College, directed by Ven. Shanti Bhadra, began publishing an international Buddhist quarterly, *Bodhisattva,* in October of 1965. Although the first issue of this publication indicated its affiliation with the People's Education Society, no mention was made of the Buddhist Society of India. Judging from the ten-year plan of the Centre, its aims and activities were directed to the education of leaders and the recruitment of *bhikkus*. The Centre's program was more intellectually oriented than any of the other courses of Buddhist training encountered in this survey.

While the training of monks and lay leaders is one of the most pressing problems confronting the Buddhist movement in India, the need for education at the elementary and secondary levels is also of major concern. The latter view was expressed by a lay leader of a small slum area in Poona whose response, when asked whether the children were being educated in Buddhism, was: "They *are* Buddhists, first let them get a good education, then they will be able to learn about Buddhism." There is wisdom in this.

Conclusion

Although an editorial published in the first issue of *Buddhist India* in 1927 called for the formation of an all-India Buddhist organization, and at least fifteen Buddhist groups existed prior to Dr. Ambedkar's conversion in 1956, little evidence was found of inter-organizational communication and cooperation during the course of this survey in 1966–67. Even among the component units of the largest of the Buddhist organizations, the Buddhist Society of India, there was little coordination of programs, publications, and related activities. An assessment of the situation in 1964 was provided by D. C. Ahir in a form letter distributed in 1966 to Buddhist leaders and organizations throughout India.

Though there are more than 3 million registered Buddhists and over 20 million potential Buddhists in India — Buddhism has not so far attained national status in this country. This was reflected to a great extent at the time of the 7th Conference of the World Fellowship of Buddhists held at Sarnath in November, 1964. From India as many as ten delegations participated in this conference but most of them had no or little knowledge about each other before reaching Sarnath. The reason being that there does not exist an active All India Body of Buddhists and information about numerous Buddhist Societies and Organisations in the country is not available from any one place.

This statement was accompanied by a request for information concerning the existence in each locality of "Buddhist Societies and Organizations, Schools, Colleges, Viharas, Customs and Festivals and Buddhist Literature etc." Responses to this query were to be published in the *Bhartiya Buddhist Directory* established by Mr. Ahir, the managing editor, in collaboration with Ven. Anand Kausalyayan. In spite of the obvious usefulness of such information for the furthering of communication and integration within the movement, as of June, 1967, Mr. Ahir had received very few replies, and as of 1970, this work had not been published.

An explanation for the lack of unity within the Buddhist movement was presented in an article written in 1965 by S. S. Arakeri of Bijapur, Mysore State:

Now the conversion movement is somewhat at a standstill due to lack of cooperation and unity among the leaders of the Buddhist Community. At present no leader commands the respect of all the Buddhists throughout India due to internal quarrels, differences of opinion and narrow outlook . . . the other reason is political motive and gain. The present leaders are fighting for political leadership. . . . The political stability will be achieved alone if there is religious stability. So first preference should be given to religious propaganda and then to political propaganda. [Arakeri 1965: 44-46]

While the divisive forces described by Mr. Arakeri no doubt inhibit the development of a national organization, the findings of this survey indicate that inspired local leaders, and the adaptation of Buddhism to parochial interests and tradition, have served as a major source of strength as well as giving rise to "differences of opinion and narrow outlook." Lacking the financial base and personnel for large-scale organization, local leaders and their often autonomous following have played a crucial role in the rapid spread of Buddhism since 1956. Although religious considerations no doubt motivate many of these leaders, some of the most effective organizers of Buddhist activities have based their efforts on experience and contacts acquired as members of the Scheduled Castes Federation during the 1940s and its counterpart since 1956, the Republican Party of India.

Although this attempt to locate and delineate the organizational framework of the Buddhist movement was often frustrated by the elusive nature of the ties that link leaders and groups within the movement, when one is in actual contact with a particular group, at an evening meeting in a village hut or a naming ceremony in a Delhi slum or a large assembly gathered to celebrate the Buddha's Jayanti, one feels a dynamic vitality. While there are "many organizations, but no organization," the intangible network linking the different groups, their leaders, and the masses, possesses a power that is difficult to deny.

NOTES

1 An account of the aims and activities of the People's Education Society is provided by K. B. Talwatkar, Secretary of the Society, in the initial issue of *Bodhisattva* published in 1965. According to this account the Society supports seven colleges, three high schools, and two hostels. In 1966, three of the seven thousand students enrolled in these schools were from the "Backward Classes."

Location of PES schools and date founded
Colleges: Bombay: Siddarth College of Arts & Sciences (1945)
Siddarth College of Commerce & Economics (1953)
Siddarth College of Law (1956)
Siddarth College of Mass Communications and Media (1965)
Aurangabad: Milind College of Science (1950)
Milind College of Arts (1963)
Dr. Ambedkar College of Commerce (1960)
Mahad (District Kolaba): Dr. Babasaheb College of Arts, Science and Commerce (1961)

High Schools: Bombay: Siddarth Night High School, Bombay (1948)
            Aurangabad: Milind Multipurpose High School (1950)
            Osmanpura (Aurangabad): People's Education Society High
             School (1960)
Backward Class Hostels:
            Pandharpur: Shri Gadge Maharaj Backward Class Hostel
            Dapoli (District Ratnagiri): Devi Ramabai Ambedkar Vidyarthi
            Ashram
            Bombay: Siddarth College students are accommodated in the
            Siddarth Hostel located in Wadala.
Grants-in-aid to Backward Classes Hostels are provided in:
            Poona, Nandurbar, Chaalisgaon, Manmad, Dholka, Patan, Nipani.
Other high schools, apparently supported locally, exist in several places including Nasik and Nagpur where there is also a college.

[2] Editorial, *Buddhist India*, 1, 45–46. (1927)

[3] P. Lakshmi Narasu wrote a book, *The Essence of Buddhism*, that was admired and cited by Dr. Ambedkar, who arranged for its republication by Thacker of Bombay in 1948.

[4] *Mahabodhi and United Buddhist World*, 29, 213–216. (Calcutta)

[5] Ibid., 218–222.

[6] *Samyak Dristi*, 1961, 1–2. Published in Ajmer.

[7] *Objects and Rules of the South India Buddhist Association*. Perambur, Madras, 1954.

7.

LAWRENCE A. BABB

The Satnamis –
Political Involvement of
a Religious Movement

THE OBSERVER is often struck by what appear to be strong religious overtones in Indian political life. Not only do religious differences frequently provide a focus for political conflict, but many major figures on the political stage are religious figures as well.

An example of the fusion of religion and politics is the Satnami sect of the Chhattisgarh region of Madhya Pradesh. In the study that follows, examination in some detail of Satnami political involvement may reveal the critical determinants and the consequences of the political commitment of this sect.

The Satnami sect is confined mainly to the Chhattisgarh plain, a rice-growing area including roughly the present Durg, Raipur, and Bilaspur districts of eastern Madhya Pradesh. The Satnamis constitute at once a religious community and a caste — numerically the most important of the untouchable castes of Chhattisgarh.

How the Satnamis Began

To understand the Satnamis today, one needs to know something

This paper represents a revised version of a paper presented at the 20th Annual Meeting of the Association for Asian Studies at Philadelphia on March 22, 1968. Field work upon which the paper is based was supported by a grant from the Foreign Area Fellowship Program, administered by a Joint Committee of the American Council of Learned Societies and the Social Science Research Council. I am particularly indebted to Arnold L. Green and Owen M. Lynch for extremely helpful comments on earlier versions of the paper. All conclusions of the paper, however, are the responsibility of the author alone.

of their origin. The movement originated between 1820 and 1830 in Chhattisgarh. The founder was a Chamar called Ghasi Das. After the traditional sojourn in the wilderness, Ghasi Das returned to his caste-fellows bearing news of certain dramatic revelations. All men, he said, are equal irrespective of caste. He said further that there is but one god, of the "true name" or *satnam,* and he forbade the worship of Hindu deities. Ghasi Das proscribed the use of liquor and tobacco, and the consumption of meat and certain red vegetables (probably because of their resemblance to meat).

Finally, Ghasi Das laid the groundwork for an organized sect by naming himself head priest (guru) and stipulating that this office should devolve in the male line of his own family.*

As Stephen Fuchs (1965: 99) has suggested, it seems almost certain that Ghasi Das's revelations derived somehow from the doctrines of Jagjivan Das, founder of an earlier movement of the same name in North India. It seems likely also that the Kabirpanthi movement provided a model for the hereditary guru-ship and may have been a major source of Ghasi Das's doctrines as well. The Kabirpanthi movement was intro-duced into Central India by Kabir's disciple Dharm Das, and the authority of the *gaddi* (throne) of this division is said to have been transmitted to Dharm Das's descendants for forty-two generations (Westcott 1953: 72). It appears, indeed, that very little of what Ghasi Das said or did was without precedent, as the Dharm Das branch of the Kabirpanthis provided a model very close at hand. For present purposes, however, the source of Ghasi Das's teachings is not as important as their significance in the context within which they were taught.

Focus on Low Ritual Status

The impact of his doctrines appears to be in their common rele-vance to a single social issue — the low ritual status of the Chamars, which indeed accounts for the fact that Ghasi Das's teachings were quite explic-itly directed toward his own caste-fellows. Evidently, then, the important feature of Ghasi Das's monotheism was not the doctrine as such, but the correlative prohibition of Hindu image worship. The effect of this would be to remove from the lives of his followers many ritual situations in which their own low ritual status had traditionally been dramatized. Drinking and meat-eating are both hallmarks of low ritual status, and

Report on the Land Revenue Settlement of the Belaspore District in the Central Provinces, 1868. Nagpur: Oriental Press for the Chief Commissioner's Office, 1869, by J. W. Chisholm.

presumably, by giving up these habits, the Chamars would be in a better position to claim the higher status to which they aspired. Abstinence from tobacco was very likely an attempt to reinforce claims to higher status through the increased moral stature that comes from renunciation of sensual pleasures.

Unlike the "prophet" in Weber's sense (see Weber 1964: 58–59), Ghasi Das cannot be considered an agent for the "rationalization" of a full, religious tradition; indeed, he seems never to have concerned himself with such classical religious questions as those concerning the nature of the world, the problem of evil, the nature of and means to salvation. Ostensibly his one-god doctrine was an innovation with potentially profound religious implications. But Ghasi Das apparently never elaborated this doctrine beyond the assertion that the worship of images is wrong, nor did he ever prescribe any liturgy that might be appropriate to this seemingly new conception of divinity. Further, in his public pronouncements, he never tried to integrate his rules of behavior into a more general conceptual system. Thus the ideological basis of the Satnami movement has remained little more than a set of rules emanating from traditional conceptions of caste status founded on Hindu beliefs regarding ritual pollution. The movement has never approximated a "system of belief" distinct from its Hindu context.

The Satnami movement began with an evangelistic phase considered by the Satnamis today as an age of miracles. Ghasi Das is said to have effected many miraculous cures in his travels through rural Chhattisgarh, and early sources indicate that by the time of Ghasi Das's death in 1850, most Chhattisgarhi Chamars considered themselves Satnamis (Chisholm 1869: 47). The role of high priest rapidly became better defined as we see from this description published in 1869: "The high priest decides finally all questions involving social excommunication, and prescribes the penalties attending restoration. For those who can attend on him personally, or whom he can arrange to visit, he performs the ceremonies at marriage and on naming children. . . ." (Chisholm 1869: 47–8). Later a two-tiered organization appeared: at the top the high priest, known as the guru, and at the bottom a large number of village-level functionaries called *bhandaris* after Bhandar, a village which became the seat of the Satnami guru. The *bhandaris'* functions included very simple priestly duties and the mediation of certain types of disputes, and it seems very likely that this system represented a modification of the *jati panchayat* (caste council) system which still exists among other castes in the region. Apart from the addition of an intermediate level of *mahants,* the Satnami system has persisted up to the present time.

Separateness of Satnamis

No additions have been made to Ghasi Das's original teachings and since they never comprised a comprehensive religious ideology, the content of the Satnami religious life is essentially the rural variant of Hinduism practiced by most Chhattisgarhi villagers, even to the extent that most Satnamis worship Hindu deities. The critical difference between the Satnamis and other castes in the area is that while the Satnamis practice a variant of Hinduism, they do so within the framework of a sectarian organization, having its own priesthood, its own sacred centers, and its own calendar of major ritual events. This sets them apart from their Hindu neighbors — a separation symbolized by a white flag displayed prominently in almost every Satnami neighborhood. Such practices foster among the Satnamis an identity which crosscuts local boundaries. The Satnamis thus are at once a "caste" and a kind of regional religious community. No other major Chhattisgarhi caste can be called a regional unit in this or any other sense. The existence of this regional coherency provided one of the conditions for the intrusion of regional and state politics into Satnami affairs, as the Satnamis were a potential voting bloc of considerable size.

Another factor affecting political affairs of the Satnamis is the chronic instability within the sect's authority structure. Conflict over succession to the position of guru has been a major problem since the time of Ghasi Das's death. After his death (1850) Ghasi Das was succeeded for a brief period by his eldest son, and when the son died, the grandson assumed this office. Since this man was without issue, the line of succession shifted at his death to another of Ghasi Das's sons, a man called Agar Das. Agar Das, who had one wife, then married his elder brother's widow. He had a son by each of these wives, and at his death, both claimed succession. In the end each was accorded the title guru, and the competition between the lines fathered by these two men has persisted down to the present.

Though born in another village, Ghasi Das established his headquarters in Bhandar, a village that has become the most important sacred center of the Satnamis. The sect's property at Bhandar, and with it the most widely accepted claim to the leadership of the Satnamis, has been held by the line mothered by Agar Das's second wife, the widow of Ghasi Das's eldest son. The most recent member of the line to occupy this position was a man called Muktawan Das who died in 1966. During his lifetime he was styled *gaddi ka malik,* "the possessor of the throne," while all other male agnatic descendants of Ghasi Das were known simply as guru. Agar Das had one grandson in the line mothered by his first wife, a man called Agam Das. During his lifetime Agam Das was Muktawan Das's principal rival for the *gaddi*. Agam Das owned property in another part of Raipur district, and maintained a sphere of influence over a large area in which he functioned as *guru* and was acknowledged as the rightful leader of the sect.

By most accounts, Muktawan Das was never popular within the Satnami community. During the late thirties both his brother and Agam Das began to maneuver against him. In 1939, Muktawan Das was implicated in a murder arising from a land dispute and was jailed until 1947. This did little to increase his stature in the community. In fact, Muktawan Das's stay in jail enabled Agam Das to strengthen his own hand considerably. Although Muktawan Das still claimed the *gaddi* after his release from jail, he now faced an influential rival.

Victory of Agam Das

Probably the event most critical to the resolution of this conflict was India's attainment of independence in 1947. While Agam Das had actively supported the nationalist movement, Muktawan Das is said to have identified himself (and to have been identified by the Satnamis) with the interests of the pro-British local gentry. As the Satnamis represented a potential voting bloc of some importance in Chhattisgarh, the nationally dominant Congress Party decided to nominate a Satnami as their candidate for representative to Parliament from the area. Agam Das, as a loyal Congressman and a known quantity, was the logical choice. He ran on this ticket in the 1952 elections, his main opponent being Muktawan Das. Because of Muktawan Das's personal unpopularity, and the high prestige of the Congress Party in those days, Agam Das won by a considerable margin.

A most significant result of this contest, apart from Agam Das's victory, was the new arena provided for competition within the sect. The election crystallized latent conflict by providing a framework within which one competitor could gain a decisive victory over another. This was never possible within the restricted context of the sect itself, as the criteria for leadership were always ambiguous. While it was always understood that the leader of the sect should be a "sacred" figure, this "sacredness" was shared by all male agnatic descendants of Ghasi Das. Muktawan Das had the most legitimate claim to the *gaddi* largely because of his control of the sacred center at Bhandar, but his claim was never universally acknowledged. The 1952 elections resulted in the intrusion of new factors into the internal politics of the sect, namely, the prestige and political resources resulting from success in secular politics. As we shall see, this placed in sharp relief the question of who the holder of the *gaddi* should be, and at the same time provided a context in which the question finally could be resolved. Simultaneously it created the conditions for profound changes in the very nature of the sect.

Leadership of Minimata

Shortly after his election to Parliament in 1952, Agam Das died. In the by-election held to replace him, Congress supported Minimata, one of his co-wives, who ran against Muktawan Das and won by a margin of more than two to one. She then became Muktawan Das's principal rival and very formidable competitor. As of 1968 she had won all subsequent elections and remained a member of Parliament.

Minimata's initial success in the election, a political process external to the sect, has enabled her to bring about fundamental changes within the sect itself. Largely because of the prestige and resources of her office and the support of the Congress Party, she has become the single dominant factor in the internal politics of the sect where she controls a powerful Congress-oriented faction. Apart from the high prestige accruing to her office, Minimata possesses tangible political assets to a degree enjoyed by no other member of the Satnami leadership. For example, Minimata is able to get jobs for the more important Satnamis in the district and regional bureaucracy. Moreover, because of her influence within Congress circles, almost all the Congress tickets for Chhattisgarh District Scheduled Caste Reserve seats in the state legislative assembly have been given to Satnamis from her faction. This strongly reinforced her leadership within the sect throughout the region. In short, for some time Minimata held the Satnami *gaddi* in all but the formal sense, and was accepted by many Satnamis as their guru, and acknowledged by almost all as their leader.

Minimata's faction has thus in a sense become institutionalized as the authority structure of the sect — a structure whose core is a network of patron-client relationships centering on Minimata herself. It is significant, however, that Minimata has felt it necessary to legitimize her exercise of power in traditional terms. She has done so by claiming the *gaddi* for Bijay Kumar, Agam Das's son by another co-wife. This young man, still in his late teens in 1968, possesses the essential prerequisite for leadership of the sect — descent from Ghasi Das. By displaying Bijay Kumar at important ritual events, surrounded by all the symbolic trappings of the *gaddi,* Minimata effectively countered criticism based on her status as a woman and offset the claims of Muktawan Das's son, which were couched in the idiom of descent.

The supporters of Muktawan Das's son stress, of course, that he is the son of the last "legitimate" holder of the *gaddi.* Those supporting Minimata point to what they regard as marital irregularities in Muktawan Das's line. Regardless of the validity of either of the arguments, the question of succession is being settled on altogether different grounds — those of the control of external political power impinging on the sect. Owing to Minimata's dominant role within the Satnami community, based on her position in the regional political system, her candidate for the *gaddi* has enjoyed wide support and is expected to hold the *gaddi* upon the attainment of his majority.

The relationship between Minimata's faction and the local Congress organization has clearly been of practical benefit to both the Congress Party and the Satnami community as a whole. On the one hand, the largely self-interested loyalty to Congress maintained by Minimata and her followers has assured Congress of support from a sizable voting bloc in the Chhattisgarh Districts. This includes the Satnamis themselves, numerous everywhere in Chhattisgarh and highly concentrated in certain state legislative assembly constituencies. It includes also members of the other Scheduled Castes who over the years have come to look upon Minimata as their leader. In past years there have been attempts to establish the Republican Party and the Scheduled Castes Federation in Chhattisgarh, but largely as a result of Minimata's influence among the Satnamis and other Scheduled Castes, these rival organizations have never been a serious threat to Congress.

Restoration of Unity

At the same time, Minimata's involvement with Congress has had a unifying effect on the Satnami community as a whole. Since the latter half of the nineteenth century, the sect's unity had steadily deteriorated as a consequence of disputes over succession to the *gaddi* and the resulting creation of multiple gurus. During Muktawan Das's long tenure (from the early part of the century to 1966), a situation had developed in which each of the gurus operated more or less autonomously within a roughly defined territory of his own, the most important spheres of influence being those of Muktawan Das and Agam Das. By 1967 these problems seemed to be resolved, at least temporarily. Congress support, together with the resources and prestige of national office, had enabled

Minimata to dominate the internal politics of the sect, and she had successfully linked her interests with those of a legitimate candidate for the *gaddi*. In this case, secular political power and the "sacredness" of descent from the founder have complemented one another, Minimata having acquired a legitimate basis for her power within the sect, while at the same time Agam Das's son is widely acknowledged to be the heir apparent to the *gaddi,* a contingency which never could have come about from the simple fact of descent from Ghasi Das. Thus the éffect of the involvement of the sect in regional and state politics has been the creation of a degree of order in marked contrast to the confusion that disrupted leadership in the past. Simultaneously this involvement has made the Satnamis a force to reckon with in the politics of the region, and has provided an important link between individual Satnamis and centers of political authority.

Changing Character of Sect

Clearly, however, the character of the Satnami sect is changing. Celebrations that at one time were primarily ritual affairs – the major Satnami *melas* (festivals) at *Dassehra* (a Hindu holiday) and *Ghasi Das Jayanti* (Ghasi Das's birthday) — have become increasingly political in nature, providing public platforms for the new political elite. Many of those once considered purely local leaders and religious functionaries have become politicians in the larger sense of the word, politicians who seem perpetually to be jockeying against one another for Minimata's favor and for public office. Prior to India's independence, the sect was little more than a primitive caste-association with religious overtones. As of the 1960s, it seemed to be primarily secular with religious overtones increasingly muted.

Several conclusions to be drawn from the Satnami experience may aid in developing understanding of the political involvement of religious movements, a not uncommon phenomenon in the political life of post-Independence India. It is clear that the organization of a sect can provide an important vehicle of mediation between traditional relationships — in this case, caste — and modern electoral politics. A key feature in this process was that the Satnami sect provided a framework within which members of a widely dispersed caste attained group identity and a regional community. This community initially provided a medium through which external political interests could marshal votes. Ultimately it provided a basis for the political power which the Satnamis have collectively enjoyed. It is also evident that sectarian politics need not require the articulation of religious ideology with political issues. We have seen that in this case the critical feature of political involvement was the articulation of the internal structure of the sect with external political processes. The important factors, as we have seen, were the creation of a new political order in India and a condition of ambiguity with respect to the leadership of the sect. This allowed, and indeed encouraged, the contending factions to shift their competition from the restricted context of the sect itself to the larger arena of electoral politics.

It is also apparent that despite the "traditional" flavor of sectarian politics, the involvement of sectarian organizations in modern politics is not necessarily retrograde, or a reversion to traditional forms. Certainly pre existing elements were combined in the formation of the sect, but the very use of these traditional forms resulted in their transformation into something different. The articulation of the Satnami sect into broader political processes has not led to a deepening or strengthening of religious ties, but rather to an attenuation of the religious aspects, and to what appears to be a basic reformulation of the sect's organizing principles in which secular ties of political allegiance replace former reverence for a sacred leader. At the present time, however, religious or quasi-religious elements still play a role in maintaining a regional framework within which the new political elite may operate.

A central feature of the sect from its inception has been a concern with a narrow sector of the total range of experience of its membership, that experience which is related to questions of ritual status, especially in situations in which the Satnamis were treated as Untouchables. Accordingly, the development of the sect does not represent the formation of a truly comprehensive system of belief. Rather, it consists primarily of a re-shaping of traditional elements of belief and practice in a sectarian frame derived from the social structure of the sect and from the Satnamis' desire to dissociate themselves from the stigma of untouchability.

Ideological commitments are of minor importance in understanding the process of the sect's political involvement. The Satnamis were drawn into politics through manipulation by external political interests and a structural anomaly within the sect which favored such maneuvering. Far from having a disruptive effect, this political intrusion has set in motion certain internal processes which may have the ultimate effect of transforming what was once a religious movement into an effective political interest group.

8.

K. C. ALEXANDER

The Neo-Christians of Kerala

THE WORD "NEO-CHRISTIAN" is a translation of the Malayalam word "Putuchristiani" which means literally "new converts to Christianity." In the South Indian state of Kerala, however, the word is generally used to refer to Christian converts from the lower, especially untouchable, castes. Although many of these people were converted four or five generations ago, they are still referred to as Neo-Christians to distinguish them from the Syrian Christians whose church was founded in Kerala early in the Christian era. On the other hand, converts from the higher castes, even those recently converted, are never called Neo-Christians — they are referred to as "Syrian Christians." Hence the accepted rather than literal meaning of the term Putuchristiani is "lower-caste Christian." In this paper we shall examine the extent to which converts from one untouchable caste, the Pulayas, have been integrated into the Syrian Christian Church of Kerala.

The foundation for this study is work done by the author among the Pulayas of Central Travancore in Kerala between December, 1963, and May, 1964. For that investigation 450 persons were selected on the following basis: With the help of village officials the names of all adult Pulayas in several villages of Ambalapuzha, Tiruvalla, and Kunnathunadu *taluks* were extracted from the list of eligible voters maintained in the local office of each community. Ten to fifteen individuals were

An early version of this chapter appeared in *Man In India,* Vol. 47: 4, Oct.-Dec., 1967, 317–330, under the title "Problems of the Neo-Christians of Kerala."

randomly selected from each of these lists and other villagers helped to locate them. Although quite a few of those selected could not be found, only two individuals refused to be interviewed. In the total of 450 interviewees there were 130 Christians whose responses form the basis of the present study. All were from rural areas, and both male and female Pulayas participated.

Kerala society is noted for its exceptionally rigid caste system, one in which each caste occupies a fairly definite position. Brahmans hold the highest rank whereas Pulayas, Parayas, and Nayadis occupy the lowest positions in the hierarchy. Syrian Christians and Hindu Nairs are two important groups in the middle of the hierarchy. Ranked below the Nairs are the Izhavas and Mukkavans who were held to be Untouchables until recent times.

The Syrian Christians are mainly independent farmers, including substantial landowners, and merchants. Many of them follow "polluting" occupations such as dealing in fish, toddy, leather, and meat. They do not observe many of the traditional dietary taboos of Kerala including those pertaining to the consumption of beef, and they allow widows to remarry. Viewed in terms of traditional criteria based on ritual purity they should rank with the Untouchables since they eat beef and follow polluting occupations. But when evaluated by secular standards, the Syrian Christians rank rather high — more or less equal to the Hindu Nairs.

In the past the Pulayas, also known as Cherumas and Cheramars, occupied an extremely low status in society; ritually they were Untouchables and economically they were slaves. In the middle of the nineteenth century, due to British influence, slavery was banned. The abolition of slavery did not bring about any spectacular improvement in the economic status of the Pulayas and other Untouchables as they remained bondservants *(adiyans)* of the higher castes and there was no change in their ritual status.

With the establishment of English rule, Christian missionaries from various European countries came to work in Kerala. They obtained converts from high as well as low castes, but the former were comparatively few and the bulk of the converts came from lower castes, especially the Pulayas and Parayas. Although high-caste converts did not gain much in social status by conversion to Christianity, when the Pulayas and other Untouchables embraced Christianity they ceased to be Hindus and were no longer governed by caste rules. This change of identity was formally recognized by the government. Moreover, the missionaries endeavored to bring about an improvement in the life of the converts through education, employment in mission schools, and other means.

Despite such efforts by European missionaries, lower-caste converts continued to be treated as Untouchables by the long established Syrian Christians. Lack of integration between the Syrian Christians and converts from Untouchable castes was manifest at the social as well as denominational levels. Lower-caste converts became known as Neo-Christians, Cheramar Christians, Pulaya Christians, and by other caste-linked names. As recently as 1964 it was found that only Syrian Christians are generally referred to as "Christians" while Pulaya Christians are normally referred to as "Pulayas" even by the Pulaya Christians themselves. The Pulaya Christians have to address the Syrian Christians by such honorific titles as *Tampuran* and *Panikke,* whereas Syrian Christians add the suffix Pulaya when addressing a Pulaya Christian. For example, a man named Thoma is called Thoma-Pulayan and a woman named Maria is addressed as Maria-Pulakalli. This practice follows an ancient tradition borrowed from the Hindus. Even in the mid 1960s Pulaya converts were obliged to remove their headdress in the presence of rich Syrian Christians. While speaking with their Syrian Christian employers they had to conceal their mouths with their hands. Pulaya Christians are not given food inside the house of a Syrian Christian, but only outside the house in a broken dish or leaf. After eating food served on a dish the Pulaya must wash the dish before returning it.

Role of the Churches

In Central Travancore where this investigation was carried out, most of the Pulaya Christians are members of the Mar Thoma Church and the Church of South India (formerly known as the Church Mission Society). Even though the Mar Thoma Church and the Church of South India do not officially discriminate between their Syrian and Pulaya members, such segregation is actually prevalent. It was found that the Syrian and Pulaya members of the same church conduct religious rituals in separate buildings. The Syrian Christian priests who conduct rituals at the Syrian Christian churches do not perform rituals in Pulaya churches — instead a few Syrian Christian priests are appointed to serve the Pulayas. While there is no formal ban against Pulayas attending services in Syrian Christian churches, few Pulayas ever do so. In the organization of the church the Pulaya Christians are not given representation. For example, in the Mar Thoma Church every Syrian Christian parish is entitled to send a representative to the church governing council, called Mandalam, but the Pulaya parishes are not accorded this right. In other words, conversion to Christianity has not brought the Pulayas into the congregation of Syrian Christians. Consequently the Pulaya Christians have been relegated to a marginal position in society, standing on the periphery of the Hindu Pulaya and Syrian Christian communities.

India's Independence in 1947 had little effect on the Pulaya Christians' role in the Christian church as they continued to occupy a subordinate position. Subsequently they began reconversion to Hinduism on a large scale. This was abetted by some proselytizing Hindus who tried converting Christians to Hinduism by means of a purifying bath in temple tanks. An additional reason for the Pulayas' return to Hinduism was that only Hindu Pulayas were eligible for the special benefits provided by the government for members of the Scheduled Castes. Marriages between Christian and Hindu Pulayas were also found to be not uncommon.

Another important development taking place among the Pulaya Christians of Travancore is the emergence of the Prathyaksha Raksha Daiva Sabha (God's Church of Visible Salvation) popularly called P. R. D. S. It was founded in the 1930s by the late Poykayil Johannan, a Paraya convert to Christianity. He was first a member of the Mar Thoma Church, but later left it and joined the Brother Mission where he set forth the argument that caste differences should be done away with. Accordingly there was a proposal in his congregation to marry a Syrian Christian girl to a Pulaya Christian youth. When the local Syrian Christians heard about this proposed marriage they threatened severe sanctions and the intercaste marriage was abandoned. As an aftermath of this episode, Johannan established the P. R. D. S. with a majority of Untouchables and a few Syrian Christians.

Although an offshoot of Christianity the P. R. D. S. introduced new religious ideas among its members. These were not codified or printed in 1964, but may be summarized as follows: Every age has its paramount problems for the solution of which God becomes incarnate as man. The paramount problem of the present age is the emancipation of slaves from the fetters in which they have been suffering for ages, and to make them equal with others. For this purpose God became incarnate as Poykayil Johannan who is the savior of all slaves, and in the case of India, the Untouchables. Since God has come to earth as Johannan, heaven is like a cattleshed without cattle. Only those who believe and pray to Johannan and accept his teachings as the voice of God will be saved. Believing that the removal of untouchability and destruction of the caste system are the paramount needs of this age, Johannan and his followers abolished the observance of caste distinctions within the P. R. D. S. and advocated intermarriage between all castes. The teachings of the P. R. D. S. are becoming popular among Christians from the lower castes. Thousands of them have left Christianity in the past few decades and joined the P. R. D. S. where they are striving for the realization of the goal of their late leader — a casteless society.

The formation of the P. R. D. S. with God claimed as its founder was a revolutionary step. Less revolutionary phenomena are also taking place among the Pulaya Christians in Central Travancore. One is the formation of the Cheramar Daiva Sabha (Church of God of Cheramars-Pulayars). Its founder is a Pulaya Christian, Solomon Markose, who was an evangelist with the Church Mission Society until he began to question the Syrian Christians' treatment of the Pulaya Christians: Why should there be separate Pulaya Christians and Pulaya Churches? Why should the Pulayas occupy an inferior position in the Church? Solomon Markose received an answer to such questions in a revelation from God who instructed him to found the Cheramar Daiva Sabha for the social and spiritual uplift of the Pulayas. Solomon Markose began preaching his new ideals among the Pulayas in the 1950s and acquired enough followers to organize congregations that continue to flourish at six places in Central Travancore.

During the late 1950s a number of independent pentecostal churches having only Pulayas as members also came into existence. These groups differ little from other pentecostal denominations in theological matters, but they do not want a joint congregational life with Syrian Christians. The Pulayas prefer to have their own pastors, however unsophisticated, and the company of their own castefellows, however uncouth and uneducated, rather than being served by educated and sophisticated Syrian Christians who do not sit with them, take food with them, or marry members of their group.

In 1964 a large number of lower-caste Christians left the Church of South India and formed a new church under the leadership of Bishop Stephen, previously a priest in the Church of South India. In an interview with the author, the Bishop said that the main reason for this separation was the discrimination that low-caste Christians suffered at the hands of the Syrian Christians.

Domestic Customs

Conversion to Christianity for many Pulayas consisted merely of their adoption of a Christian name without a corresponding modification in religious beliefs and mode of life. For many the dominant motive for conversion was the material benefits gained. This may be a major reason why conversion often failed to bring about any marked change in their religious beliefs and practices. Many converts continue to have faith in the power of such Hindu deities as Mallam, Madam, and Kali, and many of them make use of shamans *(matravadi)*. About 8 percent of the Pulaya Christians interviewed in this study reported their worship of Kali and/or their reliance on shamans to cure illness. Typical statements of this kind:

I rely on *mantravadam* (propitiatory rites which may include offerings of fried rice, liquor, and chicken or sheep blood) in order to cure those diseases caused by evil spirits.

When my son was sick, I asked a shaman to find the cause of his illness and the means for curing him.

When our children became ill through fright caused by malevolent spirits, we resorted to shamans two or three times as the illness could not be cured by medicine. Afterwards I was afraid that God would punish us in retaliation for our use of shamans.

In order to prevent my daughter-in-law from losing her child during the fifth month of pregnancy, we did some *mantravadam* along with medical treatment.

The incidence of such practices is certainly higher than 8 percent as many people conceal such behavior since it is looked down upon.

Behavior affecting the family is strictly regulated among the Syrian Christians who prohibit polygamy and divorce. Those who break such norms are excommunicated from the Church. The relationship between husband and wife is considered to be sacred, sex relations outside the family are condemned, and premarital chasity is highly esteemed. The husband is the head of the family, and his wife and children must obey and respect him. In all these respects the Syrian Christians emulate the Nambudiri Brahmans who occupy the highest status in Kerala society.

The Pulaya legacy of customs relating to marriage and the family, though markedly changed in recent years, stands in sharp contrast to those of the Syrian Christians. A well-to-do man was allowed to marry sisters as well as to practice non-sororal forms of polygamy. The payment of bride-price used to be required in contrast to the upper-caste custom of giving a dowry. Divorce and remarriage were permitted and quite common. Today polygamy is disdained and fast disappearing, and dowry has replaced bride-price. However, divorce is still practiced, and the bonds of marriage remain comparatively weak. In the sample selected for this study, sixteen (15%) of the 106 married Christian Pulayas had divorced at least once and several of them had divorced four times. Six of the fifty-three married couples in this sample had married first cousins, a practice prohibited in the Syrian Christian Church. The role of the Pulaya father is also relatively weak in that he does not command the respect nor does he exercise the control characteristic of upper-caste fathers. One manifestation of the Pulayas' relatively weak parental control may be seen in the high incidence of Pulaya marriage in which children select their own mates, and elopement is not rare. Such practices are disdained by the Syrian Christians.

Status of Pulayas

Equally great is the distinction between the Pulaya and Syrian Christians in socio-economic status as may be seen in a comparison of their levels of education, occupation, dress and personal appearance, housing, and general standard of living. In the sphere of education Syrian Christians are among the most educated communities in Kerala, while the achievement of the Pulaya Christians, especially in Western education, has been very low. Many Pulayas are illiterate, and persons with higher education are exceptions among them. Syrian Christians are for the most part landowners, independent farmers, traders, and businessmen. They have also entered many kinds of white-collar occupations as clerks, teachers, nurses, doctors, and engineers. These are all prestigeful occupations assuring a relatively high standard of living.

In the past Pulayas were slaves of the higher castes including the Syrian Christians. When slavery was banned in 1862, the Pulayas became bond-servants of their previous masters and continued to live on the land of others serving the same landlord generation after generation. Although the landlord provided his Pulaya servant with gifts of food on festive occasions, and helped pay the expenses entailed when a marriage or death occurred, the bond-servant was paid a wage less than the market rate, and he did not have the freedom to serve another person. While conversion to Christianity facilitated the improvement of a few Pulayas, it did not bring about a radical change in the socio-economic status of most members of this caste as the resources of the missionaries were not sufficient to meet the needs of the large number of lower-caste converts. Consequently most of the converts continued to be landless laborers working on the land of higher castes. Few had the education or capital to follow any other occupation. The type of occupations followed by Pulaya Christians today may be seen in the following table.

Table 8.1

Occupations of Pulaya Christians interviewed in this study

Occupation	
Agricultural Laborers	80%
Tenant Farmers	3
Shopkeepers	2
Housewives	7
White-collar Workers	3
Social Service and Evangelical	5
Total	100%

It is evident that the great majority of these Pulayas are laborers bound to the land. Those who said they were farmers or merchants were found to be rather poor people, cultivating a small piece of land as tenants or keeping a small shop. Only three persons were enaged in "white collar" jobs providing a steady income. Two of them held menial office positions requiring minimal literacy, while the third was a primary school teacher.

Regarding dress and personal appearance, Syrian Christians are generally neat and well dressed while Pulaya Christians often appear in dirty and shabby clothes even though sumptuary laws regulating Pulaya dress no longer exist. Several Pulaya Christians said that because of their poor dress they felt hesitant to sit beside Syrian Christians at church services. Similarly, while the houses of Syrian Christians are generally well furnished and equipped with wells, bathrooms, and latrines, Pulaya Christian houses are seldom furnished or equipped in this manner. Most of the Pulaya Christians interviewed in this study were found living in huts made of adobe and plaited coconut leaves; only a few of their houses were built with stone walls or tiled roofs. Not one of these Pulaya Christian houses had electricity, a bathroom, or a sanitary latrine. Household equipment was scarce in most of their houses and many of those visited could offer no more than a piece of mat for a visitor to sit upon.

In summary it may be said that there remains a great distance between the Pulaya and Syrian Christians in all spheres of life. In religious matters many Pulayas are only nominal Christians and continue to rely on shamans and other non-Christian means for manipulating the supernatural. The Pulaya mode of family life differs markedly from Syrian Christian ideals and practices. In the economic sphere the gap between these groups differs little from the past. What then are the possibilities for the integration of such disparate groups into a single Christian community?

Even though most converts to Christianity in Kerala are from Pulaya and other low castes there are a few converts of high-caste origin. In contrast to the Pulaya, most converts from the higher castes were readily accepted as equals by the Syrian Christians. This indicates that prior commitment to Hinduism does not prevent integration into the Syrian Christian church. Nor does untouchable ritual status appear to be a decisive factor as there are converts to Christianity from the Izhava (toddy-tapper) caste who were considered Untouchables due to their occupation involving preparation of liquor from the toddy-palm. In the early twentieth century, they were accepted as members of the Syrian Christian community. The key difference in the case of the Izhavas seems to be their relatively high economic status. Consequently it appears that the reason for the non-integration of the Pulaya Christians must be due to considerations other than their identity as Untouchables.

A similar phenomenon also exists in the Catholic church of Kerala in which there are a large number of converts from the Mukkava (fisherman) caste. These converts are considered to be an inferior group by other Catholics, known as Romo-Syrian Christians, who refer to Mukkava converts as "Latin Christians." In spite of their low-caste origin, some economically successful Latin Christians are treated as Romo-Syrians and allowed to enter into marriage with Romo-Syrian Christians. According to Kathleen Gough:

For the prosperous Latin-Catholic there were, however, gradual avenues of mobility upward into the Syrian Caste. In any case, Latin Catholics tend to call themselves "Syrians" where they are not known, and in cities often pass as such. Inside the Catholic church, which in theory does not uphold caste distinctions, a wealthy and educated Latin Catholic family may eventually intermarry with Romo-Syrians of another area and assimilate itself to them. [Gough 1963: 196]

The process by which Latin Christians have been assimilated into the Romo-Syrian Catholic community will probably be repeated in the case of those Pulaya Christians who have acquired wealth and attained a style of life approximating that of the Syrian Christians. In this study it was found that the few Pulayas employed in white-collar jobs and those who are university graduates are rarely treated as Untouchables. They are never called by such derogatory names as *"Eda"* and *"Nee"* nor do these Pulayas address Syrian Christians with such honorific titles as *Tampuran* and *Panikke*. Educated and well-to-do Pulayas who have attained the appropriate life style are given food inside Syrian Christian homes and they need not wash their plates as other Pulayas are expected to do. Syrian Christian neighbors and friends attend and participate in the wedding feasts of such well-to-do Pulaya Christians, and one case of intermarriage between the two groups was found. Judging from these findings it may be inferred that the integration of these two Christian groups is dependent upon the Pulayas attainment of equality in the secular sphere of life. While wealth and education seem to be the principal determinants of one's status within the Christian church and community in Central Travancore, it is in this sphere of life that the gulf between the Syrian Christians and the Neo-Christians is the widest.

PART III

Government Efforts To Abolish Untouchability

Statue of Dr. B. R. Ambedkar — Bombay

Owen Lynch

9.

LELAH DUSHKIN

Scheduled Caste Politics

INDIA'S SYSTEM of official discrimination in favor of the most "backward" sections of her population is unique in the world, both in the range of benefits involved and in the magnitude of the groups eligible for them. Since the system had its origins in the nineteenth century and has existed on an important scale for thirty-five years, an assessment of its operation and impact seems long overdue. One assessment, which regards the system primarily as a means of giving extra help to those who need it most, holds that despite its imperfections the system has had some notable success, and members of the affected groups are playing a more prominent role in public life than they would be without it. The contrary assessment regards the system primarily as the tool of those who control it, holding that from its inception the politicians of the Congress Party have learned to dominate it and through it to control a minority which might otherwise have proved troublesome. As with any issue so large and complex, there is evidence on both sides. The present study attempts a review of such evidence, beginning with a sketch of the rationale, history, and features of the protective discrimination system itself as the official policy toward the "Untouchables" and some other minorities. The operation of a crucial part of the system, guaranteed political representation, is then examined through a study of the four elections since Independence. The final section discusses some implications and consequences of the system in terms of leadership roles, public opinion, and prospects for the future.

[165]

I

"Scheduled Caste" is a bit of legal jargon developed by the British, as was the theory behind it. The term was first adopted in 1935, when the lowest-ranking Hindu castes were listed in a "schedule" appended to the Government of India Act for purposes of statutory safeguards and other benefits. The term is appropriate only in this context of legal provisions, government action, and politics. Otherwise it is meaningless. The minority it designates is not a single, undifferentiated group but a huge, diverse population, approximately 80 million in 1971. The members are born into numerous castes, each of which has its own identity, traditions, and characteristic set of relations with other castes. To treat the hundreds of castes on the list as a single Scheduled Caste category is simply to deal with aspects of a common relationship their members have with government.

Two Sets of Problems

Whenever these castes are lumped together as a single category, whether it be called "Scheduled Caste," "Exterior Caste," "Depressed Class," "Outcaste," "Untouchable," "ex-Untouchable" or "Harijan," the category is based on a problem or set of problems they are believed to have in common.* Two basic types of problems may be distinguished: the problems of untouchability and the problems of poverty and lack of power. Some would call this a distinction between the ritual and secular statuses of the castes concerned. While others say the distinction is artificial, as the two aspects are so much a part of one another, it is necessary to draw such contrasts if one is to sort out the strands and paradoxes of official policy.

---

*A note on terminology. Like everyone else, I must choose amongst a batch of unsatisfactory terms which have come into popular use at various times. Each has something wrong with it. Educated Indians are offended by the term "Untouchable," which they feel is derogatory and ignores the abolition of untouchability by the Constitution. But their choice, "Harijan," is offensive to the educated Untouchables, who use the term "Untouchable" freely themselves. "Scheduled Caste" is used here wherever possible, but in some cases it is not adequate because it excludes the Buddhists. Isaacs' solution, "ex-Untouchable" was accurate enough for the people he interviewed, but for most of the others it is artificial, possibly misleading. Thus, where "Scheduled Caste" will not do, I use "Untouchable" and hope it will not be regarded as derogatory either to the people concerned or to India.

For non-Untouchable Hindus, I follow common usage in employing the term "caste Hindus." Strictly speaking, it is meaningless, since all Hindus, including Untouchables, belong to castes. Gandhi's term for "caste Hindu" was more accurate: *savarna*, or member of one of the four *varnas* of Brahmanical legal and social theory.

Secular status is not a status of the caste as such but an aggregate statistical profile of the *class* characteristics of the caste's members at any one moment in history: their actual distribution of occupations and related roles, their levels of literacy and education, of wealth, income, and debt, their positions of political dominance or dependence, their health and living conditions, their individual and family prestige. If the norms we deal with here are statistical, those concerned with ritual status are moral and are concerned with the ranking of castes *as castes*. For the individual this latter status is ascribed by birth into the caste and cannot be changed except insofar as the caste itself can change its position relative to other castes. The caste hierarchy is pervaded by a concern with pollution and purity; although its symbolism is important in many areas of life, it is enacted in clearest detail in social rituals invested with sacred significance.

"Untouchability" has to do with the caste ritual status side of the coin. First used only in the twentieth century, the term has never been adequately defined, and now that untouchability has been abolished by the Constitution, any official attempt to define it would be fraught with legal difficulties. In common parlance the term is used in two senses: as a social stigma and as a set of disabilities, the latter usage being much more common than the former. As a stigma, an inherited mark of Cain which can never be washed away by rite, dispensation, or individual achievement, its use is connected with the notion that the pollution associated with the very lowest castes is so deep that their touch and proximity must be avoided. They are therefore relegated to the periphery of established settlements and denied access to the wells, temples, schools, and other facilities used by other people. The most common use of the term "untouchability" comprises these customary restrictions and other practices, which segregate the lowest castes and symbolize their inferior status. Untouchability is rarely defined in a sentence; it is usually described by civil, social, and religious disabilities which vary in detail by time, place, and the particular castes concerned.

Although the primary meaning of "untouchability" is behavioral — the practice of customary disabilities — one other idea seems to have influenced the men who first formulated Scheduled Caste policy. This is that since it is only Hinduism that confers moral legitimacy and sacred significance on pollution and the hereditary caste hierarchy, untouchability is a Hindu phenomenon: only Hindus practice it and only Hindus are its victims. This notion flies in the face of obvious facts, but it is the legal position adopted. By this view, an Untouchable who converts openly to Christianity, Buddhism, or Islam ceases thereby to be an Untouchable (and therefore a member of a Scheduled Caste) even though the majority continues to discriminate against him as before. This legal technicality has had important political and religious consequences.

More important for our present purposes is that the role assigned government varies according to whether the ritual status or the secular condition of the castes is emphasized. Those who say the key problem is untouchability, as Gandhi did, tend to downgrade the role of government in solving it. Gandhi, for example, concentrated on persuading the caste Hindus to give up excluding and humiliating the Untouchables voluntarily and felt that the coercive power of government would not help in bringing about the "change of heart" he desired. Those who say the key problem is poverty and the lack of power place more responsibility on the government. However, they differ over the type of responsibility and the form it should take. Nehru, and with him probably most of those in the upper echelons of government service, stressed government's role in effecting major structural changes in society as a whole. Only such changes could provide a cure; doling out special benefits was a political sop which provided only a palliative at best. Other leaders, including the British policy makers and Untouchable spokesmen prior to Independence, believed it necessary to grant temporary safeguards and benefits to the "weaker sections" until such long-range structural changes bear fruit.

Turning to the official definition of the problem, insofar as it can be put together from statements made over the years, we find that the distinction between the ritual and secular aspects is ignored. Indeed, it must be ignored. The official model — the set of assumptions and beliefs that underlie protective discrimination for Scheduled Castes — assumes a one-to-one correlation between the ritual status of the caste and the secular condition of its members. It assumes that the most polluted castes contain the most destitute people, the least educated, the weakest and most dependent politically. Whether or not it is correct, the entire structure of benefits rests on this assumption.

Protective Discrimination

Protective discrimination is but one of three ways in which government attempts to deal with the problems confronting the Scheduled Castes. First, there are several constitutional and other legal provisions which remove discrimination against Untouchables and grant them the same rights as other citizens. Second, general development and welfare programs to aid landless agricultural laborers, municipal slum dwellers, or other low-income groups benefit Scheduled Caste individuals since they are found in large numbers in such populations. In these programs the criteria of eligibility for benefits vary with the kind of benefits involved. To such criteria the third alternative adds another criterion of eligibility — caste membership — which protects the Scheduled Castes' interests by making other persons ineligible. That is all it does, for benefits of the third type are not automatically given to anyone. The jobs, scholarships, loans, and grants must still be applied for on the proper forms, and the applicant must present evidence that he possesses the minimum qualifications prescribed for them. In addition, he must present proper written certification that he belongs to one of the castes on the schedule, a requirement that protects his right to be considered for the benefit by making non-members ineligible. Because of this protective character, the system is called "protective discrimination" by some scholars, though it should be understood that the phrase is not used by the government of India.

Another major feature of the system is that it is by definition temporary and is supposed to last only as long as it is needed. In theory, the protective caste criterion is used to ensure members of the lowest castes a share of power and opportunity for advancement until they can hold their own without it. However, no guidelines have been established for determining when this goal has been reached, and the only provision with a legal time limit on it has been extended each time it was about to expire. The benefits obviously build a vested interest in their own perpetuation. To the extent that the correlation breaks down between caste membership and actual levels of income, education, and power, the system which relies on such a correlation becomes less workable and more subject to criticism. We shall return to these problems in the final section of the paper.

A British Legacy

The policy of protective discrimination was developed by the British over several decades, and it was the British who drew up the list of castes. The post-Independence government has expanded and modified both the policy and the list since 1947, but with few substantive changes.*

The scheduling of various minorities and the award of statutory safeguards were political acts, adopted in part for political reasons, and

---

*The remark applies only to the Scheduled Castes. There have been major changes concerning other groups entitled to protective discrimination.

with political implications. The political reasons have not yet been studied in detail by historians. Presumably the utility of "divide and rule" influenced the policy, since it gave the British an opportunity to embarrass and perhaps reduce the nationalist majority by giving representation to the "neglected section" of Hindus. In addition to being an imperial style of doing business, this policy seems to have been adopted in the belief that it was the only just way to deal with pluralism of the kind that existed in India.

Viewed as a political act, the provisions for Scheduled Castes embodied in the Government of India Act, 1935, applied precedents already adopted for other minorities. A number of safeguards or privileges had been granted to special interest groups and communal minorities, including representation in legislative councils by nomination or electoral concessions. In 1906, separate electorates were granted to the Muslims, who claimed that such safeguards were necessary to assure them a fair share of any power to be transferred from the British to the Indians. With each devolution of power from Britain, similar claims were advanced by other communities as well.

The Depressed Classes, as they were then known, were latecomers to this process. It is true that special schools and scholarships had been established for them in Madras, Baroda, and Travancore in the 1880s, and additional benefits granted since then, in these states and elsewhere. But in the political field, the Depressed Classes began to receive benefits several years after other minorities. Few of them could qualify for the restricted franchise, and those who could were politically so weak as to be of negligible importance. It is doubtful that their spokesman would have been heard at all but for the encouragement of the British and such princes as Baroda, Kolhapur, and Travancore. Under the Montagu-Chelmsford reforms of 1921, Depressed Class representatives were nominated to the provincial legislatures. A decade later, when further reforms were pending, it was evident that additional safeguards were likely to be granted.

The Schedule

It was in this context that an effort was made to distinguish the Depressed Classes more precisely and to enumerate their population. In contrast to earlier efforts, in which the criteria for preparing lists varied by region and circumstance, an attempt was made for the first time in the early thirties to determine standards which could be applied on an all-India basis. This also entailed an appraisal of the appropriate role of government. The 1931 census officials, the Franchise Committee, and the provincial authorities all discussed such matters at length, and the various lists were revised more than once before being finalized in 1936. The outcome had some peculiar features.

In the minds of the authorities was an official view of the nature of caste which has been aptly described by Cohn.

. . . a caste was a "thing," an entity, which was concrete and measurable; above all it had definable characteristics — endogamy, commensality rules, fixed occupation, common ritual practices. These were things which supposedly one could find out by sending assistants into the field with a questionnaire and which could be quantified for reports and surveys. . . . [1968: 13]

The authorities had to determine what definable caste characteristics would warrant inclusion on the list and which castes possessed them.

One approach to the problem was suggested by Sir Edward A. H. Blunt in a memorandum he submitted to the government of U. P. "A depressed class," he said,

is one whose social, economic, and other circumstances are such that it will be unable to secure adequate representation of its political views or adequate protection of its interest without some form of special franchise concession. [India 1931, Bengal: I: 498–99]*

This definition is imprecise but fits the purpose for which it was issued — the impending award of some form of special franchise concession. According to this reasoning, the census ethnographers and the several commissions which took testimony on the subject would compile data on caste literacy rates, poverty, and other indices of political disadvantage. A study of available sources led the author to conclude that indeed this was often the *de facto* procedure adopted in the provinces. (Dushkin 1957, 1961, 1967)

The official *de jure* definition, however, took a completely different tack, one which caused a political crisis in 1932 and continues to pose difficulties. The Depressed Classes were defined in terms of the religious concept of pollution as "Hindu castes, contact with whom entails purification on the part of high-caste Hindus." Yet the British did not then construe pollution and purification as legitimate objects of government action. They had a long-standing policy of non-interference in social and religious practices and, though there were laws against imposition of civil disabilities, they were not vigorously enforced. Another peculiarity of this choice

---

*Parenthetical references in the text to India, followed by a date, refer to Census of India publications.

was that it required the provincial ethnographers to compile data, not on the objective characteristics of the castes, but on their customary relations with other castes. These, in turn, were assumed to be fixed, consistent for all members, and well known. The assistants sent to the field with questionnaires therefore consulted some learned Brahmans for authoritative information on which castes entailed purification on the part of high-caste Hindus.

As already noted, an effort was made to employ systematic standards in this process. The 1931 census commissioner, J. H. Hutton, wrote a long essay in defense of the definition adopted in which he set forth the specific criteria to be employed by the provincial superintendents (India 1931, India: I: 472; reprinted in Hutton 1963: 195; Singh 1947: 2; and RCSCST 1956: 10) The primary test, he said, was whether the caste suffered such civil disabilities as denial of access to roads, ferries, wells, and schools. In practice this was the least workable test, as the castes generally had limited, variable access to such facilities. Other tests consisted of well-known religious and social disabilities, namely: whether members of the caste caused pollution by touch or proximity, were denied access to the interior of ordinary Hindu temples, were denied the services of "clean Brahmans" or the same water-carriers, barbers, etc., who served high-caste Hindus, and whether high-caste Hindus would refuse to accept water from them. The remaining criteria were of a different sort. If an educated member of the caste were treated as a social equal by a high-caste man of equivalent education, or if the caste were depressed "merely" because of its occupation, ignorance, illiteracy, or poverty "and but for that would be subject to no social disability," it was apparently supposed to be excluded from the list. It is doubtful that information enabling these tests to be used as Hutton intended was available, and in practice they served instead to extend the range of eligible castes and tribes.

The criteria worked well enough in many areas, but in parts of South India they would have included too large a portion of the Hindu population, so illiteracy and poverty were applied to select the most depressed. In the northernmost provinces, Hutton's standards broke down for the opposite reason. Social disabilities were milder and so variable in detail that strict application of the criteria would exclude many of those the authorities felt should be included, so again the secular criteria of illiteracy and poverty were used. This problem was most acute in Bengal and U. P., which emerged with the largest Scheduled Caste populations in the country. Of the 8.4 million people included in Bengal, 2.2 million were included by an "ad hoc criterion," Blunt's definition given above. And in U. P., 1.4 million were officially listed as "Touchable but depressed" (India 1931, Bengal: I: 498–99, 502–503; U. P.: I: 628).

This was not the end of the problem. Further adjustments in the lists were made in the years between the census and the promulgation of the Schedule in 1936. The reasons for these changes are difficult to trace, but in at least one case, political pressure is suggested. The Rajbanshis, a very large caste of Bengal, were not included in the census list, even by the "ad hoc criterion" partly because they themselves claimed that inclusion would degrade them. Five years later they appeared on the official schedule, and they remained there. In the interim, during 1932, political safeguards were agreed on for the Scheduled Castes. The Rajbanshis evidently opted for power rather than status, to use Béteille's distinction (1967), and won their case.

Seats and Electorates: the Basic Equation

The most important concessions made to the Scheduled Castes had to do with political representation. Why the authorities felt it necessary to define and list the poorest and most powerless castes in terms of the religious concept of pollution has yet to be properly analyzed. The procedure was apparently adopted on analogy with the earlier provision of safeguards for Muslims and other religious minorities.

It was precisely here that Gandhi took issue with the British position. In his famous speech before the Minorities Committee of the Second Round Table Conference on November 13, 1931, Gandhi said, "Sikhs may remain as such in perpetuity, so may Muslims, so may Europeans. Would 'untouchables' remain untouchables in perpetuity? I would far rather that Hinduism died than that untouchability lived." Separate electorates and reserved seats, he argued, would —

create a division in Hinduism which I cannot possibly look forward to with any satisfaction whatsoever. . . . I cannot possibly tolerate what is in store for Hinduism if there are those two divisions set up in every village. Those who speak of political rights of "untouchables" do not know India and do not know how Indian society is to-day constructed. Therefore, I want to say with all the emphasis I can command that if I was the only person to resist this thing, I will resist it with my life. [Sitaramayya 1947, I: 538–539]

A year later Gandhi resisted it by fasting. Under the Communal Award, the Scheduled Castes were to vote in the general electorate and also to choose a few representatives of their own by separate electorates. The British would adopt this provision unless the Indians concerned could agree on an alternative. In response to Gandhi's objections, the British acknowledged that the Scheduled Castes were different from the other communal minorities. In an August 8, 1932, letter to Gandhi, Prime

Minister MacDonald said the government was anxious not to perpetuate the separation of the Untouchables. He emphasized that the Communal Award required the abolition of separate electorates in twenty years and allowed such abolition in ten (Sitaramayya 1947: I: 646 ff.). Gandhi rejected these protestations, and on September 21 he began his Epic Fast against separate electorates. Having conceded the provision of reserved seats, he won deletion of separate electorates from the award.

The drama of the time is often treated as a clash of personalities and viewpoints between Gandhi and B. R. Ambedkar, the leading Depressed Class spokesman. To some extent it was, but one point has not received due recognition. Caste Hindu leaders of all political parties took part in the negotiations, and still more leaders signed (and thereby committed themselves to support) the Poona Pact that emerged. These included various Liberals, C. Rajagopalachari and other Congressmen not in jail at the time, and such prominent Mahasabha leaders as Pandit Malaviya. In the supercharged atmosphere of the nationalist movement, most of these leaders would have ignored Dr. Ambedkar and the political claims of the Depressed Classes, had not the British initiative and the necessity of saving Gandhi's life forced them to reach a settlement conceding representation to the Untouchables. Under such pressure, it took only five days to arrive at a compromise: the number of seats reserved for Scheduled Castes was increased to equal their proportion of population, and the representatives were to be chosen in general, joint electorates including caste Hindus as well as Untouchables. This basic equation remained in effect as the 1970s progressed.

Untouchability and Protective Discrimination

Before turning to an analysis of how this system has worked, let us examine whether protective discrimination is, in fact, a means of removing untouchability. The question may seem startling in view of much public rhetoric which takes for granted that this is the purpose of the concessions. It should be remembered, however, that several other communities received such concessions, and they were not "untouchable." These communities were defined by traits, such as religion, mixed ancestry, and tribal culture, which they were expected to retain "in perpetuity." There was never any idea that protective discrimination would be a means of removing those traits.* The Scheduled Castes are doubly peculiar: first,

---

*The Tribes were not Scheduled until after Independence. Some of their defining traits, such as "isolation," are expected to be eliminated by the benefits and other development programs, but, in theory at least, their tribal culture is supposed to be retained and encouraged.

as we noted above, they are not defined by their own social traits but by their customary relations with other people. Second, only in their case is there even the pretence that the purpose of protective discrimination is the elimination of the criteria by which they were defined. There are many paradoxes in this, as Gandhi pointed out. More recently, some have alleged that the presumed connection with untouchability means only that evidence of continued disabilities, easy enough to obtain, is a convenient excuse to keep the benefits flowing. (Cf. Committee on Untouchability, 1969, including Achutan dissent, pp. viii-ix.)

There is, in addition, the practical question of what protective discrimination can do to remove untouchability even if this is in fact its goal. The evidence suggests that, at best, the benefits can reduce the disabilities only indirectly and in the long run; in the short run they may have the opposite effect. The "stigma of pollution" is not removed by forcing people to call attention to it every time they apply for a job or run for office. If "untouchability" is a set of disabilities traditionally imposed on certain castes, then "removing untouchability" means ending the exclusions and humiliations practiced by others. It has nothing to do with granting benefits to individual members of those castes.

A good illustration of this point is provided by the princely state of Travancore. The 1931 census superintendent, whose list seems to have been adopted by the state government, decided that the only sure test of untouchability was the traditional distance which each caste had to maintain from the inner sanctuary of a temple. Those who could not enter the outer compound walls were listed as Depressed Classes and came to 57 percent of the Hindu population (India 1931, Travancore: 379–80, 430–31). If the criterion is related to the purpose, and the purpose is the removal of untouchability, one would expect the list of Depressed Classes to be used to secure admission to the temples for these castes. This was not the case, however. Temple entry was provided by the Maharajah's famous Proclamation of November 12, 1936 opening some 1,600 temples in the state. The Proclamation does not allude to any list of Depressed Classes. It says that "there should henceforth be no restriction placed on any Hindu by birth or religion on entering and worshipping at temples controlled by us and our Government." One does not need a list for this since it consists in the removal of a restriction rather than the grant of a special benefit. Instead, the Maharajah's list of Depressed Classes was used for scholarships and other educational benefits, for land grants and other economic concessions, and for nominations to his legislative council.

The same principle has applied since Independence even though the government has assumed much more responsibility for social and religious change than did its British and princely predecessors. Government has been able to deal with untouchability directly only in limited ways, primarily by measures opening facilities and opportunities to everyone and by efforts to change the attitude of non-Untouchables, not by special benefits granted to Untouchables. Except for the Untouchability (Offences) Act of 1955, which requires a list (Section 12. Cf. Galanter 1969), no one of the government's programs aimed directly at the removal of untouchability has been a protective discrimination measure. They have provided subsidies to voluntary agencies for propaganda and welfare work, grants to municipalities to improve the conditions of the scavengers in their employ and to change attitudes toward the dirty occupations, prizes to the villages doing the most to remove untouchability, and so on. Such measures attempt to influence the caste Hindu majority and have not involved the award of benefits to members of the Scheduled Castes. All these programs put together have accounted for only a small part of the Scheduled Caste welfare budgets — perhaps Rs. 1 *crore* of the Rs. 28 *crores* shown in Table 9.1.

Whether by protective discrimination or by other measures, government has continued as before to deal more with the secular condition than the untouchability of the Scheduled Castes. By design or by happenstance, it has been more concerned with power and poverty, education and employment, than with pollution and related disabilities.

The Benefits

The benefits may be classified as two main types: reservations — applied to political representation, government employment, and higher educational admissions — and financial assistance, administered through a wide variety of welfare schemes.

The Constitution requires the reservation of seats in the legislatures, a provision subject to renewal every ten years, and permits but does not require it in education and government service. The time limit for reserved seats has been extended twice and can be again. There is no time limit on any other concession. The reservation of seats in proportion to population means that one out of seven members of the lower houses of the central and state legislatures is an Untouchable. Most states also either provide reservations or require co-option of Scheduled Caste members onto village *panchayat* councils. Reservations also exist, usually not in proportion to population, for admission to many, though not all, higher educational institutions. Reservations in proportion to population, and sometimes in excess of it, are applied by both Centre and states for direct recruitment and some types of promotional posts in government service; a number of other provisions go along with them. In both educa-

Table 9.1

Expenditure by the Centre and States for Scheduled Caste Welfare Schemes,
1961/2–1964/5, Cumulative

Sector and Subject	Expenditure (Rs.)
Central Sector*	
Education	55,180,600
Improving Working Conditions of those in Unclean Occupations	9,808,900
Housing Subsidies and Provision of House Sites	21,475,500
Completion of Second Plan Schemes (incomplete figures)	690,000
Total	87,155,000
State Sector	
Education	118,004,500
Agriculture	16,915,500
Cottage Industries	18,048,600
Cooperatives	9,597,000
Animal Husbandry	774,000
Medical and Public Health	11,786,400
Housing	14,157,900
Rehabilitation	206,000
Community Centres	1,768,700
Publicity	46,000
Aid to Voluntary Agencies	1,413,600
Miscellaneous	1,679,200
Total	194,397,400
Grand Total	281,552,400

*Plus some expenditure out of a Third Plan outlay of Rs. 12,500,000 for Non-Official Agencies
for the Scheduled Castes and Tribes and Other Backward Classes.

SOURCE: **Report of the Commissioner for Scheduled Castes and Scheduled Tribes,
1964–65,** pp. 29–30, 33–34, 39.

tion and government jobs, the reserved quotas must be filled by qualified
candidates; if there are none available, the seat or the job goes to someone else.

The Constitution also requires the appointment of a Commissioner of
Scheduled Castes and Scheduled Tribes to oversee the implementation of
the benefits, check on abuses and grievances, and report on the operation
of both the reservations and the financial grants. His office is usually
understaffed, and he is dependent in large part on what other officials
tell him, but his annual reports to the President are an invaluable source
for any student of the subject.

Financial grants have been made for a wide variety of Scheduled
Caste welfare schemes, as can be seen from Table 9.1 showing the
reported expenditures for the four-year period 1961/2–1964/5. As these

figures were incomplete, Table 9.2 shows the expenditure for the same
four-year period reported two years later, though no itemized breakdown
was given in that report. If the amounts for most of the state programs
seem small, it should be remembered that most of government's efforts
in these areas have been through general development schemes not
restricted by caste and financed under other budgets. The special Scheduled

Table 9.2

Expenditure by Centre & States for Scheduled Caste Welfare
for the same 4-year period, as reported in 1967

(Rs. thousands)

	Education	Economic	Health, Housing, Other Schemes	Total
Central Sector	110,639		32,041	142,680
State Sector	123,902	36,213	38,504	198,619
Total	234,541	36,213	70,545	341,299

SOURCE: **Report of the Commissioner for Scheduled Castes and Tribes, 1966—67**, p. 121.

Caste welfare schemes have indeed been small and quite scattered. The
only programs of any real size or importance have been in education.

Education

Education has been the major field of endeavor, as shown in its
accounting for Rs. 234,541,000 out of Rs. 341,299,000 (69 percent)
reported spent on Scheduled Caste schemes. In general, state funds for
education have covered the period through matriculation from high school.
They provide tuition freeships and often ancillary grants as well for books,
slates, midday meals, and other expenses. The central government effort
has been devoted mainly to post-matric scholarships. In 1964/5, 75,000
students received such scholarships. In 1966/7, the figure was 90,000,
and it rose to 103,000 in 1967/8. The amounts paid averaged about
Rs. 500 per student (India, RCSCST 1964/5: 44; 1966/7: 112–13.
Deccan Herald, 10 Dec., 1969).

The trouble with such figures is that we do not know what relationship they bear to the total Scheduled Caste population of school and
college age or to the total Scheduled Caste enrollment at different levels.
Presumably the 103,000 receiving post-matric scholarships account for
most of the Scheduled Caste college students, but at lower levels increasing numbers of Untouchable children have been educated under general
programs, particularly with the expansion of universal free compulsory
education.

In view of the enormous importance of education to virtually all other opportunities for the Scheduled Castes, it seems worthwhile to present some background data in this field. The source is the 1961 census, now out of date but still useful. Table 9.3 indicates that 6.6 million Untouchables, about 10.3 percent of their population, were literate in contrast to the national literacy rate of 24 percent. This difference would be even greater if the Untouchables were subtracted from the computation of the national rate. About 176,500 had matriculated from high school, but only 6,300 of these held college degrees. Two-fifths of the latter were accounted for by Delhi, the capital, and Uttar Pradesh, with its huge Scheduled Caste population. Table 9.4 gives the literacy rates of the different states in rank order. A comparison with the data given in Table 9.9 reveals that states with the highest Untouchable literacy rates are those with the smallest proportion of Scheduled Castes in their population.

Government Jobs

In a country where unemployment of the educated is chronic, educated Untouchables have long felt themselves dependent on government for employment and have done little to pressure private employers to hire them. Government is associated with greater security, and penetration of the upper levels of service has become a measure of general advancement. Moreover, such penetration provides a form of power that can outlast reserved seats in the legislatures. Most Scheduled Caste leaders are extremely reluctant to consider doing away with protective discrimination until they are "adequately represented" in the upper echelons of government service. "Once we have our fair share of power in the offices where decisions are made," several informants told the author, "we will be the first to recommend doing away with Scheduled Caste concessions. We won't need them any more."

Under these circumstances, a few facts are in order. First, while reservations have had some impact on clerical posts, the Scheduled Castes have entered higher ranks only very slowly, as Tables 9.5 and 9.6 show. The figures are for the central government only, as data for most states are not available. Even excluding the sweepers (who are almost all Untouchables) the Scheduled Castes accounted for 13.3 percent of the central employees in 1966, a figure which compares fairly well with their 14.6 percent of the population. But their distribution was extremely lopsided: over two-thirds were menials and all but 1,335 of the rest were clerks (Table 9.5). The number in senior administrative (Class I) posts

Table 9.3

Scheduled Caste Literacy and Educational Levels by
State, Rural and Urban, 1961 Census

State	Urban or Rural 1	Sch. Caste Population 2	Literate** 3	Primary** Education 4	HS Matric** 5	Degree** 6	Total of Cols. 3-6 7
ALL-INDIA	Urban	6,869,697	966,459	457,447	67,854	6,307	1,498,067
	Rural	57,547,669	3,850,435	1,165,369	102,332		5,118,136
	Total*	64,417,366	4,816,894	1,622,816	176,493		6,616,203
Andhra Pradesh	Urban	552,088	67,138	45,449	6,593	509	119,689
	Rural	4,421,528	211,841	83,605	5,962		301,408
Assam	Urban	60,670	14,077	5,788	782	100	20,747
	Rural	672,086	121,327	35,255	1,515		158,097
Bihar*	Urban	349,607	39,585	10,399	2,577	192	52,753
	Rural	6,155,359	277,676	51,989	4,965		334,630
Gujarat	Urban	334,182	37,064	63,066	2,639	257	103,026
	Rural	1,033,073	90,652	112,058	1,398		204,108
Jammu & Kashmir*	Urban	20,895	1,692	391	162	4	2,249
	Rural	263,236	9,068	1,749	343		11,160
Kerala*	Urban	121,845	30,255	11,402	1,926	208	43,791
	Rural	1,312,972	236,675	63,556	6,654		306,885
Madhya Pradesh	Urban	455,294	72,595	14,767	1,731	129	89,222
	Rural	3,797,730	198,994	46,097	1,093		246,184
Madras*	Urban	925,840	150,397	83,625	9,454	469	243,945
	Rural	5,141,487	535,679	101,330	8,561		645,570
Maharashtra	Urban	485,453	70,874	62,258	6,023	500	139,655
	Rural	1,741,461	137,800	71,838	2,012		211,650
	Urban	508,487	77,078	24,649	6,901	392	109,020

	Rural	2,637,832	270,909	25,615	1,485	24	21,662
							298,009
Punjab (& Haryana)	Urban	480,398	39,035	30,157	4,744	258	74,194
	Rural	3,658,708	182,121	127,590	15,073		324,784
Rajasthan	Urban	413,045	54,327	5,227	1,796	141	61,491
	Rural	2,946,595	139,504	13,714	1,537		154,755
Uttar Pradesh*	Urban	1,067,700	142,616	46,069	13,196	1,329	203,210
	Rural	14,332,181	669,689	197,383	29,681		896,759
West Bengal*	Urban	673,073	102,689	38,056	5,328	432	146,505
	Rural	6,217,241	570,101	201,861	17,389		789,351
Delhi	Urban	272,243	44,958	11,534	3,338	1,350	61,180
	Rural	69,312	7,045	2,561	473		10,079
Himachal Pradesh	Urban	12,142	1,998	1,200	188	6	3,392
	Rural	357,774	19,882	7,620	419		27,921
Tripura	Urban	6,745	951	577	62	6	1,596
	Rural	112,890	10,482	3,799	187		14,468
Manipur, Dadra & N.H.,	Urban	3,964	430	260	49	1	740
Pondicherry, Nagaland	Rural	67,369	7,079	1,701	80		8,860

SOURCE: **Census of India, 1961,** Vol. I, India. Part V-A(i), Special Tables for Scheduled Castes.

*The total Scheduled Caste populations for these states obtained by adding the rural and urban figures given here do not agree with the figures given in Table 9.10. The discrepancies are minor, however.

**Explanation of column headings:
Literate = able to pass a simple literacy test, no educational level specified.
The remaining headings refer to the highest examination passed:
Primary = Primary School or Junior Basic School.
HS Matric = Matriculation from High School and/or Diploma not equivalent to a University degree (Combines 3 columns in the Census source)
Degree = University degree (BA, BS, or better) and/or Diploma equivalent to a degree.

Separate figures for university degree-holders are given only for the Urban Scheduled Caste populations. For the rural populations, they are combined in a single column with High School matriculates and diploma-holders. Presumably there are very few Scheduled Caste BA's living in rural areas.

Table 9.4

Percentage of Scheduled Caste Population which is
Literate/Educated, by State, Rural and Urban, 1961 Census*

State	Total S. Caste Percent	Rank	Rural S. Caste Percent	Rank	Urban S. Caste Percent	Rank
Kerala	24.44	1	23.37	2	35.94	1
Assam	24.41	2	23.52	1	34.20	2
Gujarat	22.46	3	19.76	3	30.83	3
Delhi	20.86	4	14.54	4	22.47	8
Maharashtra	15.78	5	12.15	8	28.77	4
Madras	14.66	6	12.56	7	26.35	6
West Bengal	13.58	7	12.70	6	21.77	9
Tripura	13.42	8	12.82	5	23.66	7
Orissa	11.57	9	11.30	9	17.19	14
ALL-INDIA MEAN	10.27	—	8.89	—	21.81	
Punjab	9.64	10	8.88	10	15.44	15
Mysore	9.06	11	6.65	13	21.44	11
Himachal Pradesh	8.46 }	12	7.80	11	27.94	5
Andhra Pradesh	8.46 }	12	6.82	12	21.68	10
Madhya Pradesh	7.89	14	6.48	14	19.60	12
Uttar Pradesh	7.14	15	6.26	15	19.03	13
Rajasthan	6.44	16	5.25	17	14.89	17
Bihar	5.96	17	5.44	16	15.09	16
Jammu & Kashmir	4.72	18	4.24	18	10.76	18
4 Union Terr.**	13.46		13.15		18.67	

*In this table the totals given in column 7 of Table 9.3 are expressed as a percentage of the
S.C. populations given in column 2 of Table 9.3.

**Manipur, Dadra & Nagar Haveli, Pondicherry, & Nagaland.

SOURCE: **Census of India, 1961,** Vol. I, **India.** Part V-A(i), Special Tables for Scheduled
Castes.

had tripled since 1959, but the number of such posts had doubled, so the
proportion remained very low. Most Class I and II posts and a large number in Classes III and IV are filled by promotion, where reservations
do not apply unless the department or ministry adopts special rules. The
only one to do so was the Railway Board, in the early 1960s when the
Railway Minister was an Untouchable. In July 1968, reservations were
liberalized elsewhere for certain promotional posts, but it is doubtful that
they will have an appreciable effect on the administrative cadres. It is
the clerical and other petty white-collar posts in the Class III category
that are most affected by reservations, as the striking contrast between
the central services and undertakings shows (Table 9.6). Few public
undertakings have adopted reservations for recruitment or promotion.

Table 9.5

Scheduled Caste Employment In Central Government Services,
January 1959 and January 1966

Class of Post	Total Employees	1959 S. Caste Number	1959 S. Caste Percent	Total Employees	1966 S. Caste Number	1966 S. Caste Percent
I: Senior administrative	10,403	123	1.18	20,379	361	1.77
II: Other administrative	20,501	488	2.38	30,001	974	3.25
III: Clerical stenographic	829,471	57,625	6.95	1,117,754	99,017	8.86
IV: Attendants, peons (Excluding Sweepers)	914,705	157,704	17.24	1,176,826	211,073	17.94
TOTAL	1,775,080	215,940	12.16	2,344,960	311,425	13.28

SOURCE: **Report of the Commissioner for Scheduled Castes and Scheduled Tribes,
1966–67**, p. 15.

There is some indication that where no reservations are adopted, the
resistance to hiring the burgeoning number of qualified Scheduled Caste
matriculates is greatest at the Class III level (Cf. Elayaperumal Committee, 1969).

Table 9.6

Scheduled Caste Employment In Class I-III Posts of Public Sector
Undertakings, March 1965, and Class III Posts of Central
Government Services, January 1966

Employer	Type of Post	Total Officials	S. Caste Officials	S. Caste Percentage
Public Sector Undertakings	Class I	35,512	73	0.20
	Class II	15,820	274	1.07
	Class III	1,261,166	11,608	0.92
Central Government Services	Class III	1,117,754	99,017	8.86

SOURCES: For Public Undertakings: **Report of the Committee On Untouchability, Economic
and Educational Development of the Scheduled Castes and Connected Documents** [Elayaperumal Committee], 1969, p. 275.
For Central Government Services: **Report of the Commissioner for Scheduled
Castes and Scheduled Tribes, 1966–67**, p. 15.

Further, even for direct, initial recruitment where reservations do
exist, the actual proportion of jobs reserved is far from the percentage
supposedly reserved because of the fine print in the recruitment orders.
Table 9.7 gives the figures for the employment exchanges in 1966. Only
1.13 percent (9,605) of all vacancies reported to the exchanges were
notified as reserved for Scheduled Castes, and less than half of these were

actually filled by Scheduled Castes. The data are combined for central and state governments, other departments and private employers. For the Centre only, 6,621 out of 172,227, were notified as reserved — 3.84 percent of the vacancies. This compares with statutory provisions of 12½ percent reservation of posts recruited by open competitive exams and 16⅔ percent of other direct recruitment. The reservation orders do not

Table 9.7

Performance of Employment Exchanges During the Year 1966, by State: Scheduled Caste Applicants & Placements; Vacancies Notified, Reserved for, and Filled by Scheduled Castes

| State/ Territory 1 | Scheduled Caste Applicants | | | Vacancies Notified to Exchanges | | |
	Registra- tions 2	Place- ments 3	On Live Register at end 1966 4	Total Notified 5	Notified Reserved for S.C. 6	Reserved Vacancies Filled by S.C. 7
Andhra Pradesh	17,288	2,022	12,430	42,212	307	280
Assam	3,110	519	2,429	15,135	341	148
Bihar	19,635	2,261	15,967	52,117	512	137
Gujarat	17,971	1,493	12,514	30,510	134	53
Haryana	9,731	1,119	6,398	9,337	118	63
Jammu & Kashmir	1,868	184	683	4,847	40	18
Kerala	8,909	735	12,889	24,115	211	76
Madhya Pradesh	28,709	3,865	17,511	72,072	1,057	519
Madras	33,160	6,681	30,668	77,507	969	597
Maharashtra	54,695	6,603	42,128	95,387	949	409
Mysore	19,105	2,047	16,933	29,953	758	293
Orissa	12,247	1,899	6,473	34,276	112	57
Punjab	37,353	5,709	8,220	85,510	673	334
Rajasthan	13,915	1,460	7,019	25,111	290	175
U.P.	101,407	12,160	53,348	103,683	927	372
West Bengal	26,246	4,109	34,409	74,605	752	215
Chandigarh	2,333	296	1,364	1,706	220	73
Delhi	16,078	2,017	10,473	43,545	555	234
Goa	—	—	—	1,639	1	—
Himachal Pr.	7,084	1,062	3,385	18,445	127	91
Manipur	21	—	16	1,345	196	—
Pondicherry	432	184	241	1,673	70	22
Tripura	407	66	316	1,638	6	4
Central Employ- ment Exchange	—	—	—	9,099	280	9
TOTAL	431,704	56,491	295,814	852,467	9,605	4,179

SOURCE: **Report of the Commissioner for Scheduled Castes and Scheduled Tribes, 1966—67,** pp. 102—103 .

apply to a service but only to replacements; they do not apply when the service is being set up but only when vacancies in it arise. The great majority of the Untouchables who obtained jobs through the exchanges filled unreserved vacancies with government and private employers, presumably as menials.

Table 9.8

Distribution of Scheduled Caste Applicants on Live Registers of Employment Exchanges on December 31, 1966 According to Education and Jobs Applied for

Occupational Category	Non-Matric	Matriculate	Graduate & Postgraduate	Total
Doctors & Engineers	—	—	34	34
Typists & Stenographers	65	2,366	63	2,485
Assistants/Clerks	1,136	25,828	1,715	28,679
Teachers	1,215	2,943	171	4,329
Craftsmen & Production process workers	10,077	2,353	9	12,439
Unskilled Office Work	61,079	1,811	75	62,965
Unskilled Labour other than Office Work	80,379	424	14	80,817
Other	78,123	24,545	1,399	104,067
Total	232,074	60,260	3,480	295,814

SOURCE: **Report of the Commissioner for Scheduled Castes and Scheduled Tribes, 1966–67, p. 107.**

Also, although the reason that less than half the reserved vacancies are filled by Scheduled Caste applicants is always given as "a dearth of qualified candidates," this, too, must be modified. Evidently it often does not mean a dearth of candidates with the minimum qualifications (exam marks) stipulated for the job, as Table 9.8 indicates. It apparently means that they have not demonstrated the *additional* qualifications deemed desirable for the maintenance of efficient operations. It is difficult to regard the 60,260 high school matriculates and 3,480 college graduates still seeking jobs in 1966 as a "dearth" of any other sort. The fact that Scheduled Caste candidates sometimes passed the written qualifying exams and then failed the oral personality tests suggests that they were still suffering from the very class differentials which reservations are intended to overcome.

These data are only a fragment of the voluminous statistics published annually by the Commissioner and read, apparently, only by the Scheduled Caste representatives. Not surprisingly, they tend to suspect caste prejudice, sabotage of the rules, and other collusion against them by the appointing officials. In the absence of systematic studies, no one knows to what extent such factors may be operative.

The job concessions are worth noting because they illustrate a principle that applies to almost all other forms of protective discrimination as well. Even on paper, in the actual legal provisions and administrative rules, the concessions are much more limited than they seem to be at first glance. And this is only what is on paper. Poor implementation reduces them still more. (Cf. Galanter 1969, for another case in point, the Untouchability Offences Act).

The data on employment also make it abundantly clear that even with much better implementation and a vigorous recruitment drive, it would be a very long time before the Scheduled Castes are able to gain their "fair share" of power through appointments to decision-making posts. If the key factors in the situation are the power factors, it is evident that power just has to be developed and exercised in other ways. It behooves us, then, to study what has happened under the system of reserving the Scheduled Castes a "fair share" of seats in the legislatures.

II

At the time of this study, thirty years had elapsed since the first elections were held under the system established by the Poona Pact and twenty years since Independence. Four general elections had been held since the reservation of seats was combined with universal adult franchise. How had the system worked? What processes and patterns had developed? Were the Scheduled Caste MP's and MLA's dependent on protective discrimination, or might they withstand the lapsing of reservations? Were the Untouchables in the reserved constituencies any better off than those in the unreserved? Had they developed the means to assert themselves in local power structures?

The answers to be gleaned from available field studies provide a very mixed picture. André Béteille, for example, tells us (1967: 113) that "there are now many village *panchayats* where Harijans have a large representation," and that conflicts between them and non-Harijans are increasing. But in his village of Sripuram, Tamilnad, he found them so weak and shy that they were "unable to participate fully in the affairs of the *panchayat*" (1965: 153 and passim). In Bailey's village of Bisipara, Orissa, the Pan Untouchables had so improved their condition that their assertiveness became the major issue in the 1957 elections, and the resultant voter backlash defeated the Congress incumbents (1963: 13–68; 1957: 211–227). But in his coastal village of Mohanpur, the Scheduled

Castes were still very poor and weak and provided no issue in the election (1963: 86–89). In some cities, Untouchables have been able to win

Table 9.9

Scheduled Caste Population by State, 1961 Census,
and Seats Reserved in the Legislatures, 1967

State/Union Territory	Total Population	Scheduled Caste Population		Reserved Seats '67	
		Number	Percent*	Lok Sabha	Legislative Assembly
Andhra Pradesh	35,983,447	4,973,616	13.82	6	40
Assam	11,872,772	732,756	6.17	1	8
Bihar	46,455,610	6,536,875	14.07	7	45
Gujarat	20,633,350	1,367,255	6.63	2	11
Haryana**	—	—	—	2	15
Jammu & Kashmir	3,560,976	268,530	7.54	—	6
Kerala	16,903,715	1,422,057	8.41	2	11
Madhya Pradesh	32,372,408	4,253,024	13.14	5	39
Madras	33,686,953	6,072,536	18.03	7	42
Maharashtra	39,553,718	2,226,914	5.63	3	15
Mysore	23,586,772	3,117,232	13.22	4	29
Orissa	17,548,846	2,763,858	15.75	3	22
Punjab**	20,306,812	4,139,106	20.38	3	23
Rajasthan	20,155,602	3,359,640	16.67	4	31
Uttar Pradesh	73,746,401	15,417,245	20.91	18	89
West Bengal	34,926,279	6,950,726	19.90	8	55
Delhi	2,658,612	341,555	12.85	1	—
Himachal Pradesh**	1,351,144	369,916	27.38	1	14
Manipur	780,037	13,376	1.71	—	—
Tripura	1,142,005	119,725	10.48	—	3
Dadra & Nagar Haveli	57,963	1,184	2.04	—	—
Nagaland	369,200	120	0.03	—	—
Pondicherry	369,079	56,861	15.41	—	5
Remaining Territories***	1,051,192	—	—	—	—
INDIA	439,072,893	64,504,113	14.69	77	503

Notes

*As the two sources used disagree on the percentages, I have computed these independently. The discrepancies are very slight.

**Population figures = before creation of Haryana and enlarged Himachal Pradesh. Reserved seats = after creation of Haryana and enlarged Himachal Pradesh. After these changes, the Scheduled Caste population percentages were: Haryana, 17.97%; Punjab, 22.33%; Himachal Pradesh, 22.90%.

***Andaman & Nicobar Is.; Laccadive, Minicoy & Amindivi Is.; Goa, Daman & Diu; NEFA.

SOURCES: **Reports of the Commissioner for Scheduled Castes and Scheduled Tribes, 1961–62,** II, p. 74 and **1966–67,** pp. 108–111.

unreserved as well as reserved seats; in others they have not set up their own candidates but have learned to build and deliver "vote banks" to the highest political bidder.

These examples suggest the range of variation; what is lacking is a sense of proportion. In the absence of sufficient local studies to give us a balanced comparative view from the field, we shall attempt an overview by turning to the election returns and press reports for the country as a whole. The analysis based on such material, though admittedly superficial, examines the party returns under the double-member constituency system of the first two elections, the abolition of this system, the questions of voter turnout and elections to unreserved seats, the fate of the only party founded and led by Untouchables, the reserved-seat party distribution in the third and fourth elections, and some developments in the legislatures following the 1967 elections.

The First Two Elections, 1952 and 1957

The Scheduled Castes account for one-seventh of the electorate (Table 9.9). Their geographical distribution is relatively so even that they form less than half the voters in all constituencies from which members are elected to the Lok Sabha, lower house of the national Parliament

Table 9.10

Distribution of Lok Sabha Constituencies by Percentage
of Scheduled Caste Population, 1962

Scheduled Caste Percent of Population	Type of Constituency*			
	Reserved for Sch. Castes	Reserved for Sch. Tribes	Unreserved	Total
Under 10	4	22	113	139
10 — 19.9	25	8	210	243
20 — 29.9	33	1	61	95
30 — 39.9	10	0	3	13
40 — 49.9	3	0	0	3
Total	75	31	387	493

SOURCE: Galanter, n.d., Chapter II, Table II-C-2, p. II-43, using data collected by Henry Hart, University of Wisconsin.

*These are all single rather than double-member constituencies, as the double-member system was abolished in 1961. The percentages refer only to the Scheduled Caste populations in the three types of constituencies.

(Table 9.10), and in all but three of the constituencies at the state assembly level. Usually the Scheduled Caste percentage of population in a reserved constituency is quite close to the state average (Table 9.9) and perhaps five or six percentage points higher than the proportions in the unreserved constituencies. Thus, even in some reserved constituencies their proportion drops below 10 percent, and there are many constituencies with over 20 percent Scheduled Castes which are not reserved for them. The great majority of Scheduled Caste voters, like the great majority of other voters, live in unreserved constituencies.

For all of these reasons, a system of double-member constituencies was used in the first two general elections. Wherever a constituency could be demarcated in which either Scheduled Castes or Scheduled Tribes constituted a majority, it became a single-member reserved constituency. Where these groups were in the minority, the constituency was doubled in size, two seats were created, and one was reserved, one open to all. This led to several single member tribal constituencies but only three for Scheduled Castes, all in the West Bengal legislative assembly. In the double-member constituencies, each voter had two ballots which he had to give to two different candidates. When the votes were counted, the leading Scheduled Caste candidate got the reserved seat, and all the remaining candidates, including Scheduled Caste, were then regarded as contesting for the general seat, which went to the top vote-getter among them. Thus, if two Scheduled Caste candidates came in first and second, they got both seats. This provision was adopted with the intention of encouraging the integration of the Scheduled Castes.

An example of how the double-member system worked may be seen in the results of the 1957 elections. The party distribution in the reserved seats, omitting Jammu and Kashmir and one assembly seat in Andhra created after the elections, but including the three single-member seats in West Bengal, is given in Table 9.11.

The overwhelming preponderance of Congress party winners in the reserved seats is readily apparent. Table 9.12 shows that not only did Congress run better in the double-member constituencies by comparison with the single member, but also within the double-member constituencies Congress ran better in the reserved than in the general seats.

It was rather widely asserted that in the double-member constituencies the two winners were almost always of the same party because the Scheduled Caste winner rode in on the coattails of his party running mate. The reasons given for this assertion were that the caste Hindu running mate was likely to be much better known to voters to begin with, usually did more campaigning, raised and spent more money, and therefore won more votes. An inspection of the number of votes polled by the two

Table 9.11

Party Distribution of Scheduled Caste Reserved Seats, 1957

Party	Lok Sabha	Legislative Assemblies
Congress	64	351
Communist	3	24
Scheduled Caste Federation	2	17
Praja Socialist Party	1	13
Ganatantra Parishad	1	9
Jan Sangh	1	5
Five other parties		14
Independents	4	36
Totals	76	469

SOURCES: India, Election Commission, **Report of the Second General Elections in India, 1957**, v. II (Statistical).

——————, **Report of the Third General Elections in India, 1962**, v. II (Statistical).

R. Chandidas, et. al., editors, **India Votes** (New York, 1968), pp. 362—77, 400—408, and 700—717.

Table 9.12

Seats Won by Congress in the Lok Sabha and Legislative Assemblies, 1957, by Type of Constituency

Type of Constituency	Total Seats	Won by Congress Number	Won by Congress Percent
LOK SABHA: Total seats, all Constituencies	494	371	75.0
Double-Member Scheduled Caste Reserved	76	64	84.2
Double-Member General	76	58	76.3
Sub-Total	152	122	80.3
Remainder* (Tribal & Single-Member)	342	249	72.8
LEGISLATIVE ASSEMBLIES: Total seats	3098	2008	64.8
Single-Member Scheduled Caste Reserved	3	2	66.7
Double-Member Scheduled Caste Reserved	466	349	74.9
Double-Member General	466	315	67.6
Sub-Total	932	664	71.2
Remainder* (Tribal & Single-Member)	2163	1342	62.0

*By subtraction

SOURCES: India, Election Commission, **Report of the Second General Elections in India, 1957**, v. II (Statistical).

——————, **Report of the Third General Elections in India, 1962**, v. II (Statistical).

R. Chandidas, et. al., editors, **India Votes** (New York, 1968), pp. 362—77, 400—408, and 700—717.

winners in every double-member constituency provides one test of these beliefs. Although there are some gaps and inconsistencies in the data available, the results are summarized in Table 9.13.

Table 9.13

Scheduled Caste Double-Member Constituencies, 1957

Outcome in Double-Member Constituencies	Lok Sabha		Legislative Assemblies	
	No.	Percent	No.	Percent
Total Scheduled Caste Reserved	76	100.0	466	100.0
The two winners were of different parties (counting two Independents as of same pty)	18	23.7	103	22.1
A Scheduled Caste candidate polled largest number of votes	26	34.2	134	28.5
Scheduled Caste candidates came first and second and won both seats	3		7	

SOURCES: India, Election Commission, **Report of the Second General Elections in India, 1957**, v. II (Statistical).
_____, **Report of the Third General Elections in India, 1962**, v. II (Statistical).
R. Chandidas, et. al., editors, **India Votes** (New York, 1968), pp. 362–77, 400–408, and 700–717.

The results indicate that the above assertions, generally true, are not quite as true as seem to have been believed. In slightly more than three-quarters of the cases, the two winners were of the same party (counting two Independents as of the same party.) Usually the non-Scheduled Caste candidate did lead the party ticket, but in roughly one-third of the contests the coattails flapped the other way, at least insofar as number of votes were concerned. It seems reasonable to suppose that the non-Untouchable candidate did have more money to spend on the campaign, perhaps also more personnel, jeeps, loudspeakers, and other equipment. We have no way to measure this or the degree of dependency it may have created in the Scheduled Caste running mates. But regardless of whether assistance supplied by the non-Scheduled Caste candidate was crucial, the common belief that it was, combined with the generally weaker Scheduled Caste financial and other power resources, meant that the Scheduled Caste winners usually had a second-class status in the legislatures once the elections were over.

The three Parliamentary constituencies where Scheduled Caste candidates won both seats were in Kerala, Maharashtra, and West Bengal.

The seven Assembly constituencies included one each in Andhra, Assam, Madras, U. P. , and West Bengal, and two in Kerala, where the two Communist first-place winners seem to have lost their seats in the midterm elections of 1960. Ten does not seem a large number where the maximum is 542, and one wonders why it did not happen more often. There was a strong tendency to vote on party lines. It also appears that a number of non-Scheduled Caste voters simply threw away their reserved seat ballots. Some also may have cast both their votes for general candidates: this was not supposed to happen but was difficult to prevent.

Abolition of Double-Member Constituencies

Although the system was set up partly to favor the election of Scheduled Caste legislators to unreserved seats, and the actual occurrence of this was quite rare, the fact that it happened at all seems to have given the non-Scheduled Caste politicians a nightmare. Since the double-member constituencies were twice as large, campaigning in them was more difficult and more costly than in the single-member constituencies. Having (by their own estimate) done most of the work, spent most of the money, and mobilized most of the vote for the party ticket, non-Scheduled Caste politicians faced the prospect of being edged out of the contest by Scheduled Caste bloc voting. If Untouchables gave both of their votes to Scheduled Caste candidates regardless of party affiliation, a non-Untouchable candidate might be defeated for the general seat by his own party running mate.

The case that administered the major shock occurred in a tribal Parliamentary constituency, Parvathipuram in Andhra, where the Labour Minister, Mr. V. V. Giri (India's President in 1969) was defeated for the general seat by an unknown Scheduled Tribe candidate, Dippala Suri Dora. The figures:

		votes
1.	Congress Scheduled Tribe candidate	126,792 awarded reserved seat
2.	Independent Scheduled Tribe (Dora)	124,604 awarded general seat
3.	Congress general (Giri)	124,039 lost
4.	Independent general candidate	118,968 lost

Mr. Giri sued for the seat, but in 1959 the Supreme Court upheld Dora's election. (See Galanter's analysis of other aspects of this case, 1967b: 97–105)

The first bill to abolish double-member constituencies was introduced by a private member at the end of that year. His stated reason was that the old system was costly, cumbersome, and marked by "confusion among voters and misunderstanding among candidates of the same political parties" (*Hindu,* Dec. 1, 1959). Similar reasons were cited when the official bill was introduced a year later. During the fall of 1960, heated debate went on within the Congress Party, whose high command changed its mind more than once. The debate, however, seems to have been mainly among the politicians most directly concerned, and when the Congress Parliamentary Party finally met in December to decide what to do, only half of its MP's attended (229 of 555). They voted to introduce the bill by a margin of 124–95 (10 invalid), and it was passed at the next session of Parliament, in February 1961 (*Statesman,* Dec. 15, 1960; Dushkin 1961: 1737).

The general public seems to have been singularly unaware of the existence or the provisions of the bill. Interviews conducted in India by the author during this period reveal a general lack of awareness or concern even among those whom one would expect to be well informed. The Congress Party debate went on behind closed doors, and the press gave the issue absent-minded coverage, not making it clear that the bill would simply bifurcate the constituencies, leaving one single-member reserved and one single-member unreserved. One paper editorialized in favor of the bill on grounds that it would probably end reservations (*Free Press Journal,* Nov. 29, 1960). Individuals who knew it would not end reservations assured the author that the new single-member reserved constituencies would be in "Harijan majority areas," unaware that such areas are almost non-existent. Once the newpaper editorialists had done their homework, they were generally disapproving, but by this time the Bill's passage was assured (cf. *Hindustan Times,* Nov. 25, 1960 and Feb. 24, 1961). Eventually some citizens' groups in the constituencies concerned began to speak up, universally against the bill, but only after it was passed (cf. *Hindustan Standard,* Feb. 22, 1961).

Voter Turnout

Once double-member constituencies were bifurcated, how did the ordinary voter react? Contrary to predictions in some quarters, there was little overt expression of resentment by caste Hindus in the new single-member reserved constituencies at the discovery that they could no longer set up their own candidates. Instead, there is evidence that many of them simply withdrew from participating in these elections. Even under the double-member system fewer votes seem to have been cast for reserved seat candidates, but there is no adequate measure of how extensive this practice was. For the elections of 1962 and 1967, we do have a measure in the percentage of electors voting, and the pattern is very clear indeed. Table 9.14 compares the percentages of voter turnout for the Scheduled Caste Reserved (SCR) and the unreserved seats, state by state.

In the national Lok Sabha elections, there is little difference in turnout between the Scheduled Caste and the general constituencies, but in the state Assembly elections, a marked difference appears. As the Parliamentary constituencies are five or six times as large and frequently contain both reserved and unreserved Assembly constituencies, one might expect little difference here. Local variations in voting rates are likely to be cancelled out and obscured in such large, heterogeneous constituencies. The Assembly results are less diluted. For the country as a whole, a modest spread of 3 percent in favor of the unreserved Parliamentary contests becomes a spread of 11 percent at the Assembly level in 1962, and in 1967 a spread of 1 percent widens to 10 percent. The difference, moreover, widens on *both* sides: for the Assembly elections there is both a higher turnout for the unreserved seats and a lower turnout for the Scheduled Caste seats. This happens with striking consistency in every state and union territory except Kashmir.

Two types of explanation for these discrepancies have been suggested. The first attributes the lower turnout in the reserved constituencies to the Untouchables, on the ground that since their illiteracy and poverty are much greater, they are less likely to vote in any election than are the caste Hindus. Quite apart from its presumption that Untouchables are indifferent to who wins the reserved seat, the major flaw in this argument is the assumption that there is a significantly higher proportion of Untouchables in the reserved constituencies. We have already noted that this is not so: the population difference between reserved and unreserved constituencies in any state is normally only a few percentage points.* The second type of explanation attributes the lower turnout to the attitudes of the caste Hindu voters, who form the overwhelming majority of the electorate in both the Scheduled Caste reserved and the general constituencies. The ordinary voter usually is more interested in the identity of his state representative (MLA) than of his national representative (MP). The former is more likely to deal with the kind of state investments, laws, and executive measures that matter to the voter while the latter, himself more remote, is less likely to deal with

---

*Although this line of reasoning is rejected for the Scheduled Caste constituencies, it may be quite applicable to the Scheduled Tribe constituencies, which are sociologically and politically different. The tribals form a higher proportion of the population in them; they tend to be more isolated; their voter turnout is even lower; and their percentage of rejected ballots higher.

Table 9.14

Percentage of Electors Voting in General and Scheduled Caste Reserved Constituencies, 1962 and 1967

State	1962 Lok Sabha			1962 Leg. Assembly			1967 Lok Sabha			1967 Leg. Assembly		
	Gen	SCR	Net*	Gen	SCR	Net*	Gen	SCR	Net*	Gen	SCR	Net*
Andhra	66	62	−4	66	55	−11	70	67	−3	71	61	−10
Assam	53	58	+5	56	51	−5	59	64	+5	64	59	−5
Bihar	48	49	+1	49	39	−10	53	50	−3	55	43	−12
Gujarat	57	60	+3	59	49	−10	64	67	+3	65	63	−2
Haryana**	n.a.	n.a.	n.a.	n.a.	n.a.	n.a.	73	72	−1	74	68	−6
Jammu & Kashmir**	72	62	−10	n.a.	n.a.	n.a.	55			58	64	+6
Kerala	46	48	+2	49	36	−13	76	72	−4	77	69	−8
Madhya Pradesh	69	69	+	72	65	−7	55	54	−1	58	48	−10
Madras	61	60	−1	62	52	−10	76	78	+2	77	74	−3
Maharashtra	60	56	−4	61	49	−12	65	61	−4	66	52	−14
Mysore	26	23	−3	n.a.	n.a.	n.a.	63	64	+1	65	52	−13
Orissa	66	64	−2	67	60	−7	47	48	+1	49	42	−7
Punjab	52	54	+2	55	44	−11	71	71	+	73	66	−7
Rajasthan	52	48	−4	54	42	−12	58	59	+1	60	51	−9
Uttar Pradesh	57	50	−7	58	48	−10	55	53	−2	57	47	−10
West Bengal	68	71	+3	n.a.	n.a.	n.a.	66	66	−	68	63	−5
Delhi**	37	33	−4	n.a.	n.a.	n.a.	70	69	+1	n.a.	n.a.	n.a.
Himachal Pradesh**	n.a.	n.a.	n.a.	n.a.	n.a.	n.a.	51	53	+2	54	40	−14
Tripura**	n.a.	n.a.	n.a.	n.a.	n.a.	n.a.	76			76	76	+
INDIA	57	54	−3	59	48	−11	62	61	−1	64	54	−10

*Where the difference is less than 1 percent after rounding, only the direction of difference (+ or −) is given.

n.a. Not given in the sources used.

**Does not apply. Haryana did not exist in 1962. Jammu and Kashmir and Tripura do not have any Scheduled Caste Reserved seats in the Lok Sabha. Delhi does not have a legislative assembly, nor did Himachal Pradesh in 1962.

SOURCES: India, Election Commission. Report of the Third General Elections in India, 1962, vol. II (Statistical), pp. 9–10, 83–84. ———, Report of the Fourth General Elections in India, 1967, vol. II (Statistical), pp. 11–18, 113–118.

"bread and butter" issues. If the constituency is reserved, however, the caste Hindu voter is evidently much less concerned with the outcome of the Legislative Assembly election and may decide not to vote at all.

One is tempted to call this percentage difference a "boredom rate," or perhaps an "indifference index," on the assumption that apathy is the main explanation. The extent to which it may also be a "barometer of backlash," the expression of active resentment at the Scheduled Castes and the system, is purely a matter of conjecture as there are no local studies or public opinion polls on this point. The matter would seem to be well worth further investigation.

Elections to Unreserved Seats

If the percentages of voter turnout lead us to speculate on backlash, boredom, and apathy in the reserved constituencies, a look at the holders of unreserved seats suggests another, contrary set of speculations. Every year, the Commissioner for Scheduled Castes and Tribes reports the number of Scheduled Caste and Tribe legislators holding unreserved seats in the belief that this is of psychological importance. Table 9.15 provides a summary of these reports. As the figures vary slightly from year to year, the maximum and minimum number of seats are shown. In the upper houses, the Rajya Sabha and Legislative Councils, there are no reserved seats. Here, the number of Scheduled Caste members

Table 9.15

Scheduled Caste Members Holding Unreserved Seats, 1952–1967

Years	Rajya Sabha	Legislative Councils
1952–1956	5–7	5–8
1957–1961	6–11	9–19
1962–1965	11–13	15–17
1967	10	15
	Lok Sabha	Legislative Assemblies
1952–1956	4–5	5–7
1957–1961	6	7–9
1962–1965	1	12
1967	none	4

SOURCE: **Annual Reports of the Commissioner for Scheduled Castes and Scheduled Tribes** for the years **1953, 1955, 1956–57** through **1964–65**, and **1966–67**.

has increased steadily. Most of them were elected rather than nominated. The fifteen sitting in state Councils in 1967 were distributed as follows: 4 in Bihar, 3 each in Andhra and U.P., 2 in Mysore, and 1 each in Maharashtra, Punjab, and West Bengal.

In the lower houses, the contrast between the Lok Sabha and the state Assemblies is intriguing. In 1957 the number holding unreserved seats at the centre reached a high of six, of whom three were in double-member constituencies, and fell to one lone MP from West Bengal in 1962, after the constituencies were bifurcated. This would be expected from the data presented earlier. In the states, however, the nine cases reported for 1961, at least five of whom were in double-member constituencies, increased to twelve in the 1962 elections. It seems most significant that in 1962 twelve Untouchables were elected to state Assemblies without benefit of reservations or double-member voting devices. The state distribution of the successful candidates was as follows:

	1962	1967
Uttar Pradesh	4	2
West Bengal	4	1
Kerala	1	—
Madras	1	—
Orisssa	1	—
Punjab	1	—
Manipur	—	1

Unfortunately, it is not possible to assess the factors involved in the victories of 1962 or the poor showing of 1967. The Commissioner does not list the holders of unreserved seats by name or by political party, so that in all but one case (a Republican in U.P.) the necessary data cannot be collected. The sharp drop from twelve to four in 1967 suggests that the 1962 results were an aberration rather than a trend, and this may be the case. Such an inference, however, ignores one important element in the picture, the Buddhists. The Untouchables who declare themselves Buddhist are left out of the Commissioner's reckoning, as they are technically no longer Scheduled Caste. For example, the Buddhist MP elected from Aligarh in 1962 is not included in Table 9.15, derived from the Commissioner's data. If we add on the Buddhists who successfully contested for unreserved seats on the Republican party ticket, the total for 1962 is not twelve but sixteen, and the corresponding Assembly figure for 1967 is not four but twenty.* The Republican successes in the unreserved contests are paralleled by a consistently dismal showing in the reserved seat elections, quite the reverse of the pattern we would expect for the only national party founded and led

---

*The 1962 figure includes three Buddhists in U. P. and one in Maharashtra. The 1967 figure may not be correct, as the sixteen successful Republicans in unreserved contests might not all be Buddhists. The writer does not know the religious affiliation or caste membership of these MLAs, but the presumption that the majority are Buddhist Untouchables seems reasonable.

by Untouchables. For this and other reasons, it is worthwhile to discuss the electoral history of the Republican Party in some detail.

The Republican Party

The chequered electoral history of the Republican Party of India illustrates the liabilities, contradictions, and potentialities of Scheduled Caste politics. The Party's predecessor, the Scheduled Caste Federation, was founded in 1942 by B. R. Ambedkar, the Untouchables' leading spokesman. For many years the bulk of its supporters were to be found among his own caste-fellows, the Mahars of Maharashtra (cf. Zelliot 1969). In 1946, Dr. Ambedkar and his party were buried at the polls in the reserved seat elections of the Hindu-majority areas, where Congress won a landslide victory. The same thing happened in 1952 in the first elections held under the Constitution of independent India, which Ambedkar himself, as Law Minister, had piloted through the Constituent Assembly. He was defeated again in 1954, in a by-election for a reserved seat, and entered Parliament only through the courtesy of a seat given him in the Rajya Sabha. Again and again, the Scheduled Caste Federation got out the Mahar vote in large numbers; again and again its candidates were defeated by the votes of the caste Hindu majority.

The first break in this pattern occurred in 1957. Late in 1956, Dr. Ambedkar initiated large-scale conversions to Buddhism and reorganized the Federation, renaming it the Republican Party. He died in December 1956, two months before the elections: the new name did not become official, and the conversions did not gain political prominence until after the elections. What provided the change in the electoral situation was an alliance with other opposition parties in Bombay and a strong upsurge of opposition sentiment demanding the creation of Maharashtra State. The Federation profited from this alliance and won four Parliamentary seats,* and 17 Assembly seats. The Parliamentary seats and 12 of the Assembly seats were in the Maharashtra region.

In the 1962 elections, the Republicans contested 68 Parliamentary

---

*Two reserved and two unreserved. One reserved seat was purely a product of the double-member system: in Latur the leading vote getter was a Congressman, who got the reserved seat. The S.C.F. candidate came in second and got the general seat. This may have happened in one of the Assembly contests as well. The sources are not clear and there may be some typographical errors. The other unreserved seat was won by B. K. Gaikwad in a single-member constituency, Nasik. (India, Election Commission, *Rep. of the 2d Genl. Electns., 1957:* II (Statistical); *Rep. of the 3d Genl. Electns., 1962:* II (Statistical) seats and won 3, all in U.P. They contested 301 Assembly seats and won 11, 3 in Maharashtra and 8 in U.P. These two states represent two quite different patterns of electoral effort, one which proved a failure, the other a harbinger of success, as Table 9.16 shows.

Table 9.16
Reserved and Unreserved Seats Held by the Republican Party, 1962 and 1967

Year	State	Lok Sabha		State Assemblies		
		SC Res	Unres	SC Res	Unres	Total
1962	Uttar Pradesh	1*	2	1	7	8
	Maharashtra	—	—	2	1	3
	Totals	1*	2	3	8	11
1967	Uttar Pradesh	1	—	1	9	10
	Maharashtra	—	—	—	4	5**
	Punjab	—	—	2	1	3
	Haryana	—	—	1	1	2
	Andhra Pradesh	—	—	1	—	1
	Mysore	—	—	1	—	1
	Bihar	—	—	—	1	1
	Totals	1	—	6	16	23**

*Election later declared void. By-election lost to Congress candidate.

**Total Includes one seat in a Scheduled Tribe reserved constituency.

SOURCES: India: Election Commission. **Report of the Third General Elections, 1962,** II (Statistical). **Report of the Fourth General Elections, 1967,** II (Statistical).

In Maharashtra, the party continued its history of militancy as an assertive opposition force and did poorly in the elections. The basis on which it had won sufficient caste Hindu votes for victory in 1957 had disappeared with the creation of Maharashtra State, and no comparable issue could be found. In addition, while the Buddhist conversion movement served important psychological functions for the Mahars and furthered their cohesion as a political force, it undoubtedly alienated many caste Hindus from the Republican Party with which it was identified. The party polled enough votes to come in second in the state in total votes polled (12 percent), yet it won only three of the 66 seats contested.

In western U.P. the party followed a more complex strategy and achieved notable success in the unreserved constituencies. For these elections we have some excellent field studies to draw on (Brass 1965,

Ch V, esp. 103 – 110; Lynch 1966: 139 – 143, 156 – 167) as well as the election reports *(Rep. 3d Gen. Elec. in India 1962,* II; Chandidas et al, *India Votes,* 1968: 245, 678 – 79, 693, 706). Since the factors involved in winning these unreserved seats were probably similar to those involved elsewhere in India when Scheduled Caste candidates won unreserved seats in 1962, they are worth itemizing.

The Republicans contested 22 Parliamentary seats in U.P. and won 3, all near each other in the western region: Hathras (SCR), Moradabad, and Aligarh. The election to the Hathras reserved seat was later declared void, and a 1965 by-election returned the previous Congress incumbent. The winner in Aligarh was a militant and charismatic Buddhist, B. P. Maurya, who was the architect of the Republican victories. Maurya benefited, first, from the numerical importance of his own caste, the Jatav Chamars (skilled leatherworkers) who are the leading exponents of Buddhism in the area and increasingly numerous and assertive in the cities. Most of the Republican victories were in urban areas. Secondly, Maurya formed an alliance with locally important Muslims, whose community is also numerous in the cities. The Moradabad Republican MP was a Muslim. Thirdly, Congress was split into numerous factions, thus enabling the combined Buddhist-Muslim communal vote bank to gain the margin of victory in these constituencies.

The same factors appear in the Assembly contests. Of the eight winning MLA's: three were Muslim, one won a reserved seat, one is recorded as "SC" holding an unreserved seat, and three, who also won unreserved seats, are presumably Buddhist Jatavs. The reserved seat contest had a voter turnout of only 44 percent. The "SC" who won the unreserved seat of Fatehabad, Banwari Lal Bipra, did so by only 47 votes in a nine-way contest. In the Firozabad unreserved constituency, a Republican named Bhagwan Das won with only 20 percent of the vote in competition with 16 other candidates — the largest number of contestants of any Assembly constituency in India in 1962. Thus, we should add one more factor of success in addition to factionalism in the dominant party: the extreme fragmentation of the total caste Hindu vote, enabling a well-organized Untouchable minority to gain the edge by its own votes alone.

In the 1967 elections, the Republicans continued to do poorly in the reserved seats and to make further gains in the unreserved seats. The strategy of contesting unreserved seats was doubtless foreshadowed by the 1962 successes in U.P. but was also a necessity. Court cases occurring in the interim had made it clear that converts to Buddhism could not contest the seats reserved for Scheduled Castes, and most of the better-known Republican leaders were Buddhists. While they won only one Lok Sabha seat — reserved — they doubled their seats in the Assemblies, winning 6 reserved, 16 unreserved, and one Tribal seat (Table 9.16). The sources of their victories are presumably similar to those mentioned above, in various permutations, helped considerably by a national swing away from the Congress.

The significance of the Republican victories in the unreserved constituencies lies in the fact that they happened at all and that they represent a gain over the previous election. Numerically they are insignificant by comparison with the total of 378 Assembly seats contested by the party. In 285 of these, Republicans failed to poll enough votes to keep from losing their deposits. In their U.P. stronghold they lost all but one of the seats they held in 1962; those they won in 1967 were in neighboring constituencies.

The electoral history of the Republican Party illustrates the hard facts of political life that have to be faced by any group of Untouchables who seek power under their own leadership. First, they must obtain a substantial number of caste Hindu votes to win. The only exception to this rule is a case such as Fatehabad and Firozabad mentioned above, but 47 votes is not a safe plurality for anyone (both seats were lost in 1967). Normally they must win caste Hindu support as well as mobilizing their own members. The risk they run is that the very activities they must engage in to mobilize their own supporters will alienate the caste Hindu voters, as the Republicans did in earlier elections. Second, opposition alliances run the risk that, if successful in one election, the Congress will accommodate them, so the issue that made them possible will disappear by the next election. The Samyukta Maharashtra movement of 1957 illustrates this: by 1962, after the creation of a Maharashtra state, the Republicans lost virtually all they had gained. Third, more stable intercaste alliances based on common class interests are extremely difficult to effect under Untouchable leadership. The Republicans have tried this many times, going all the way back to Ambedkar's Independent Labour Party of 1937, but any successes have been extremely short-lived. Non-Untouchable laborers are very unlikely to follow Untouchable leadership: the successful labor movements and political parties have been led mostly by non-Untouchables.

Apart from the problem of sustaining intercaste alliances, even among Untouchables, and the generally poorer financial resources of Untouchables, the other factors mentioned are also true of all opposition parties in one form or another. Indeed, in the shifting sands of Indian politics in the 1960s, no party was in a secure position, not even the Congress, as the elections of 1967 and 1969 demonstrated.

The Fourth General Elections and their Consequences

The major fact of the 1967 elections was the erosion of Congress strength. This has given party distribution in reserved seats far more importance than it had previously, and, in turn, seemed likely to have more bearing on Scheduled Caste policy than any other set of factors. The election results are given in Tables 9.17 and 9.18. The abbreviations used in Table 9.18 are indicated in Table 9.17.

Table 9.17

Party Distribution of Scheduled Caste Reserved Seats in the Lok Sabha, 1967

47*	Cong	Indian National Congress
6	DMK	Dravida Munnetra Kazhagam
5	BJS	Bharatiya Jana Sangh
3	Swa	Swatantra Party
3	Soc/SSP	Socialist Party and Samyukta Socialist Party
2	PSP	Praja Socialist Party
2	CPI	Communist Party of India
2	CPI(M)	Communist Party of India (Marxist)
1	Rep	Republican Party of India
1		Akali Dal
1		Bangla Congress
1		Forward Bloc
3		Independents
77	Total	

*Congress' own statistical analysis of the elections (pp. 108–9) gives 46 because it gives 13 for U.P. rather than the 14 listed in the official **Report of the Fourth General Elections in India 1967**, II (Statistical), used as the source for this table.

Since the 1962 elections, Congress strength in the Scheduled Caste Reserved seats declined in the Lok Sabha from 60 to 47 and in the Assemblies from 341 to 237, for net losses of 13 and 104 seats, respectively. The number of successful Independents remained relatively constant. The most striking feature of these results is that the parties that gained at the expense of Congress in the reserved seats were the same as the parties that gained at the expense of Congress in the general seats, irrespective of ideology. Parties making the greatest gains in the reserved seats included two whose political philosophy appears antithetical to the interests of Untouchables: the conservative Swatantra Party and the

Table 9.18

Party Distribution of Scheduled Caste Reserved Seats In the Legislative Assemblies, by State, 1967

State	SCR Seats	Cong	BJS	Swa	SSP Soc	PSP	CPI M	CPI	Rep	Ind	Other Parties
Andhra	40	24	—	7	—	—	1	3	1	4	—
Assam	8	4	—	—	—	—	—	—	—	4	—
Bihar	45	23	3	—	7	2	2	3	—	5	—
Gujarat	11	4	—	7	—	—	—	—	—	—	—
Haryana	15	10	—	1	—	—	—	—	1	3	—
Jammu & Kashmir	6	6	—	—	—	—	—	—	—	—	—
Kerala	11	1	—	—	1	—	4	3	—	1	1 Muslim League
Madhya Pradesh	39	20	16	1	—	—	—	—	—	2	—
Madras	42	5	—	2	—	—	2	1	—	1	31 DMK
Maharashtra	15	14	—	—	—	—	—	—	—	1	—
Mysore	29	18	—	3	1	3	—	—	1	2	1 Jana Congress
Orissa	22	3	—	7	—	4	—	—	—	1	7 Jana Congress
Punjab	23	11**	—	—	—	—	—	2	2	2	6 Akali Dal
Rajasthan	31	10	4	13	—	—	—	1	1	3	—
Uttar Pradesh	89*	47	23	3	10	1	—	1	—	2	—
West Bengal	55	23**	1	—	3	1	8	—	—	2	10 Bangla Congress 6 Forward Bloc
Himachal Pradesh	14	11	1	—	—	—	—	—	—	2	—
Tripura	3	3	—	—	—	—	—	—	—	—	—
INDIA Total	498	237**	48	44	22	11	17	14	6	35	62

*One election was postponed.

**The Congress' The Fourth General Elections: A Statistical Analysis, pp. 110–111, gives 12 for Punjab, 24 for West Bengal, and a total of 239. Figures in this table are from the official election report.

SOURCES: India, Election Commission. Report on the Fourth General Elections in India, 1967, II (Statistical). R. Chandidas et al, eds. India Votes (New York, 1968), pp. 533–643.

militant Hindu Jana Sangh. The various Socialist and Communist parties, whose views would seem to be more appealing to Untouchables, made only modest gains in the number of reserved seats.

We may make two inferences from these election results. The first is the by now familiar point that it is normally caste Hindu voters who decide the winners in the reserved constituencies. A right-wing communalist party which appealed to a majority of these voters could win a reserved seat even if every Untouchable voted against its candidate. Secondly, insofar as the results represent the choice of the Untouchables, the choice seems to be based on local factors and organizational strength rather than ideology. It is probably a mistake to assume, on the basis of four general elections, that the Scheduled Caste candidates have been invariably the passive tools of the parties which gave them tickets. In the multisided contests typical of Indian elections, anyone with a demonstrated ability to bring out ten or fifteen percent of the vote is likely to be sought as a supporter, possibly as a candidate, by more than one party. Untouchable leaders with such abilities, whose caste-fellows account for vote banks of this size, are therefore in a position to bargain. Apparently they strike their side of the bargain less on the basis of ideology or legislative promises than on the basis of their assessment of the party's chances for winning and their own prospects for power. Such considerations have long been mentioned as reasons for locally important Untouchables to throw in their lot with the Congress. By the 1960s it seemed they were increasingly making such calculations in favor of other parties, as were politicians of other communities.

Nevertheless, Congress has remained the dominant party at the centre and in most states. In 1967 it still held well over half the reserved seats at both levels. Indeed, it was the combination of its weakened overall majorities with the large number of reserved seats retained that created quite a new situation in Scheduled Caste politics. It has long been avowed that Scheduled Caste Congressmen need the party's funds, organization, and patronage. The question that now arises is to what extent the Congress needs its Scheduled Caste members for the retention of its majorities in the legislatures. This question is dealt with in Table 9.19, computed from Congress' own analysis of the 1967 elections.

In the legislative assemblies, the Congress' advantage in the Scheduled Caste reserved seats was lost and its percentage, as of March 1967, was identical with that in the general seats. Both Congress and non-Congress governments were formed in the states, frequently with such narrow margins that the Scheduled Caste MLA's held the balance of

Table 9.19

Percentage of Seats Won by Congress in the Legislative Assemblies,
By State, and in the Lok Sabha, 1962 and 1967

	1962				1967			
State	Gen	R SC	R ST	Total	Gen	R SC	R ST	Total
LEGISLATIVE ASSEMBLIES								
Andhra Pradesh	54	77	91	59	56	60	82	57
Assam	80.5	100	52	75	63	50	40	58
Bihar	61	80	9	58	37	51	48	40
Gujarat	70	100	81	73	54	36	73	55
Haryana	58	56	—	57	58	67	—	59
Jammu & Kashmir	—	—	—	—	78	100	—	80
Kerala	28	18	0	27	7	9	0	7
Madhya Pradesh	50	56	43	49	57	51	57	56
Madras	66	73	100	67	23	12	50	21
Maharashtra	80	94	79	81	75	93	62.5	75
Mysore	64	79	100	64	58	62	50	58
Orissa	59	72	45	59	24	13	24	22
Punjab	58	57	—	57	44	52*	—	46
Rajasthan	50	46	55	50	51	32	57	48
Uttar Pradesh	57	62	—	58	45	53	—	47
West Bengal	61	71	53	62	44	44*	69	45
Himachal Pradesh	78	86	50	80	51	79	33	57
Manipur	67	—	11	50	52	—	56	53
Tripura	67	100	21	57	100	100	67	90
Goa, Daman, Diu	3	—	—	3	0	—	—	0
Totals	58	69	47	59	48	48*	53	49
LOK SABHA Totals	71	79	58	71	53	61**	89	55

*If the figures from the official **Report of the Fourth General Elections, 1967:** II are used,
the percentage for Punjab is 48%, for West Bengal 42%, and for India 47.5%.

**Adjusted to 47 Congress MP's, as given in official Report, rather than the 46 given in the
Congress source. (See note to Table 9.17).

SOURCE: Indian National Congress. **The Fourth General Elections, a Statistical Analysis**
(New Delhi, 1967) pp. 108–111.

power. Congress governments would fall if all or most of these Congress
MLA's defected in Andhra, Haryana, Madhya Pradesh, Rajasthan, and
Himachal Pradesh, and in Mysore if the Congress Tribal MLA joined the
defection of all Scheduled Caste MLA's. Non-Congress governments
would fall if all the opposition Scheduled Caste members defected to the
Congress in Punjab, U.P., and West Bengal. Nearly all of the governments
just mentioned did fall, and in most of these states midterm elections had

to be held in February 1969. Some of the governments set up after that time have also proved unstable. The extent to which Scheduled Caste MLA's were involved in the defections which brought about these changes, however, is not known. The most prominent "floor-crossers" do not seem to have been Untouchables, but the matter seems well worth investigating.

In the Parliamentary polls of 1967, Congress still ran strong in the reserved seats, but its overall governing majority dropped from 71 to 55 percent. Depending on the sources used, the Congress plurality was only 48 to 50 legislators, and 46 or 47 of these were Scheduled Caste members holding reserved seats. The defection of little more than half of them would bring down the government, a fact which gave them far more opportunity to assert themselves, though the narrow margin did the same for other groups and blocs as well. In November 1969, following a protracted power struggle, the party split up, with the "syndicate" group joining the Opposition against Mrs. Gandhi. She retained a governing majority only with the help of some Socialist and Communist parties and the continued loyalty of her own reserved-seat-holders. In this fragmented situation, actual defection entails numerous risks, but the implicit threat to defect seems to provide a leverage the Untouchables have not previously had. Even before the 1969 party split, the Congress' dependence on its Scheduled Caste MP's was effectively demonstrated in an incident that occurred in August 1967.

The occasion was a routine debate on the report of the Commissioner for Scheduled Castes and Tribes. Since a report had not been presented in the previous year, there were two to consider. In the past, the discussions had become an annual ritual, in which the Scheduled Caste and Tribe members trotted out standard grievances, other MP's said the appropriate words of support, and the government spokesman described the current programs and declared government's good intentions to do more. Little attention was given to a recurrent complaint in the reports — that while their recommendations were accepted in principle, they were seldom implemented: few people ever read them. In 1967 the Scheduled Caste MP's presented the usual grievances and objected to a cut in the Scheduled Caste welfare budget, part of an across-the-board reduction. Some also voiced dismay that the new commissioner, appointed a month before, was a well-known Gandhian anthropologist who had long been opposed on principle to protective discrimination. At the conclusion of the debate, the Congress spokesman moved the routine motion stating that the House had discussed the reports. Then came the surprise (*Statesman,* August 11 and 13, 1967).

Congress was defeated on a snap vote for the first time in the twenty years since it came to power. The opposition moved an amendment stating "the opinion of the House [that] safeguards provided in the Constitution for the Scheduled Castes and Tribes are not being fully implemented" which passed by 91 to 89 votes. This sent "a wave of jubilation through the opposition camp" (*Deccan Herald,* August 9, 1967). In the ensuing uproar and confusion, compounded by a failure in the electronic voting device, Congress whips managed to round up some more MP's. Congress immediately demanded another vote and found itself in the acutely embarrassing position of voting down its own innocuous original motion, 115 to 107.

The Congress Scheduled Caste members did not cross the floor. They apparently deliberately refrained from voting, which in this case had a similar effect (*Deccan Chronicle,* August 9, 1967). According to the *Statesman* of August 13, 1967, the Scheduled Caste MP's

. . . have now formed what is virtually a separate bloc and are holding meetings of their own to voice their grievances; one of their demands is said to be greater representation in the Cabinet. At least one result of the snap vote has been increased pressure from one more pressure group.

The demands bore fruit: on November 13, four new deputy ministers were appointed and a fifth was added a few days later. Three of the five were Scheduled Caste MP's (*Deccan Herald,* November 14, 1967).

During the Congress party crisis of mid-1969, one of the major figures was Jagjivan Ram, leader of the Scheduled Caste MP's. A durable politician who came to prominence at an early age, Jagjivan Ram first entered the Cabinet in 1946, replacing Ambedkar as Labour Member, and had been in it almost continuously ever since. His support of Indira Gandhi in her struggle with the "syndicate" leaders in the party was probably critical to her success. Later that year he was elected President of the Congress Party, the second Untouchable to hold the post,* and he has been given increasingly important Cabinet ministries.

In sum, then, the 1967 elections and their aftermath produced a power configuration new to Scheduled Caste politics. At the center of the Congress (R) Party, which as of 1970 maintained a governing majority only with the support of various other parties and factions, was a tough, highly experienced Scheduled Caste politician, and in Parliament were enough Congress reserved seat holders to bring down

---

*The first, D. Sanjeeviah, was elected when Nehru was still alive and the post was less important. Sanjeeviah became party president again in 1971, when Jagjivan Ram held a major cabinet ministry.

the government, should they ever be sufficiently angered to quit the party as a group.*

III

Any discussion of the empirical prospects of Scheduled Caste policy has to begin with this power reality. Despite the elements of artificiality in the situation, it is clearly observable that it brought results: in July 1968, reservations for promotions in government service were liberalized. In the fall of 1969, Buddhists became eligible for Scheduled Caste post-matic scholarships. In December the Constitution was amended again, by unanimous vote, to extend reserved seats another ten years. In January 1970, government proposed to stiffen the Untouchability (Offences) Act. In April, reservations for direct recruitment to the central services were raised from 12½ to 15 percent for Scheduled Castes. If the political pressure were to be sustained long enough, better implementation of provisions already on the books might result.

Besides such predictions, hazardous in the extreme, there remains another set of questions. These have to do with the implications and consequences of protective discrimination itself — the kinds of role behavior it seems to call for, the attitudes that have come to be associated with it. Though the analysis is necessarily somewhat speculative, it will deal with the leadership roles associated with the reserved seat system, with the "new class" of educated Untouchables and the "Harijan" image, and with the outlook of the bureaucrats who administer the system.

Reserved Seats and Leadership Roles

The political goals of the reserved seat system were two: power and integration. A minority was to have its fair share of power to "secure adequate representation of its political views [and] adequate protection of its interest" and to provide opportunities for its members to participate fully in political life on more honorable terms than before. Let us consider these goals in terms of processes of political mobilization.

The Rudolphs ˙(1967: 15ff.) have identified three types or stages of mobilization: "vertical" mobilization from above by local not-

---

*The present volume was in press during the national elections of March 1971, when Mrs. Gandhi led the Congress (R) to an overwhelming victory and a two-thirds majority in Parliament. One reason for her success was her ability to win the support of Untouchables and Muslims. Thus, although the Scheduled Caste leadership within Congress could no longer bring down the government through defection, their position seems to have been strengthened by the elections, as seen in the important party and ministerial posts they received.

ables, "horizontal" mobilization by caste blocs over larger regions, and "differential" mobilization, also over larger areas but by alignments that cut across caste. If we apply these types to Scheduled Caste politics, the first would require the Untouchable leader to play the part of the loyal "Harijan," analogous to the "Uncle Tom" of American parlance. Under this arrangement, locally powerful upper-caste notables mobilize the vote to fill the reserved seats with their own men, whom they manipulate and control. These men are bound to them by traditional ties, as well as political debts, and the kind of leadership expected of them is good followership. Their reward for loyalty is the opportunity to distribute the Scheduled Caste benefits to their own followers. This is the type of mobilization the Rudolphs find prevailing in Rajasthan (personal communication), and is a type which has probably occurred in all parts of the country at one time or another. As of the late 1960s, however, after more than two decades of experience with universal franchise in several elections, evidence was that the actual patterns of Scheduled Caste mobilization are normally far more complex and variable, and that there is also a complexity built into the reserved seat system itself.

The legal model of protective discrimination seems, in fact, to call for the second and third types of mobilization. It suggests a stage theory, more or less as follows: Stage 1: the British create a category, Scheduled Caste, which, through horizontal mobilization of its component groups, presses upward as a bloc. The leadership skills called for here are those needed to turn the legal category into an organized bloc, no small task. The tactics would presumably include emphasis on Scheduled Caste communal loyalties, symbols, and objectives as overriding those of locality, party, and particular caste of birth. Stage 2: as the members move into new fields of endeavor and gain differentially in prosperity, education, and more favorable links with a larger society, an "elongated" structure develops, and with it a tendency to mobilize on the basis of economic, ideological, and personal interests through parties, associations, and factions that cut across caste.

To state the above as a stage sequence called for by protective discrimination is to assume that of the two goals of the reserved seat system, power is the means and integration is the end. More satisfactory is the view that both goals have been pursued simultaneously, each serving in part as a means to the other. This is, after all, what much of the argument was about during Gandhi's Epic Fast crisis of 1932. The simultaneity of the two goals in the existing system calls on the Scheduled Caste legislator to play a dual role — not to exercise first one kind of leadership and then the other, but both at once. The system calls on him to represent two constituencies: the collection of castes in the Scheduled category and the territorial. Superficially, there may have been a kind of stage sequence between the double-member system of the first two elections, when he was assumed to represent his caste interest, and the present single-member system, which stresses the territorial constituency. In fact, the present arrangement requires him to play both roles, and, where they conflict to reconcile them as best he can.

There is little information on how the Scheduled Caste legislators handle these two identities. The impression is that they tend to compartmentalize them, emphasizing each in different arenas. H. M. Heidenreich (personal communication) reports from Bihar that in the arena of the territorial constituency, the Scheduled Caste MLA's behave the same way other MLA's do. They seek to get roads, schools, irrigation works, and other state investments for their districts, to manipulate patronage, and generally to build a power base for themselves. They may have fewer resources and less influence, but the political style is the same. Here they tend to underplay their caste identity and to present themselves as representatives of the population as a whole. But in the arena of the legislature, they often belong to a group of Scheduled Caste legislators, a fact they were not anxious to publicize back home.

Possibly the first role is more important to the MLA than it is to the MP. The MLA has more direct access to the kind of state investment and patronage sought by the local interests in his area, and therefore more incentive and opportunity to seek their support in this manner. The MP may find himself putting greater stress on caste concessions because he has less opportunity to play the other role effectively. This is another area of speculation that would repay investigation.

Within the legislatures, virtually all members align themselves with groups of varying stability on grounds of caste or community, economic interest, sub-region, party ideology, or mutual convenience. The possibility of multiple memberships for Scheduled Caste legislators should not be ruled out. It seems implicit in the system that they should also form Scheduled Caste groups in the legislatures and within the dominant party. The statement quoted earlier that the Scheduled Caste MP's "have now formed" a bloc is misleading, for a group of this sort had existed for several years. For example, in February 1961, two weeks before Parliament reconvened to pass the Bill abolishing double-member constituencies, Jagjivan Ram, prime supporter of the Bill, convened an "All-India Legislators' Convention of Scheduled Castes and Tribes." The combination of the bill and the convention suggested an effort both to strengthen the participants in their elective constituencies and to build an effective power bloc in the national legislature. Though its effectiveness was limited at first, Jagjivan Ram has for some time presided over a group of such legislators (Galanter, personal communication).

In the states, the pattern seems quite mixed, the data fragmentary. Ad hoc Scheduled Caste groups seem to exist in every assembly, although they vary in their degree of organization, continuity, and effectiveness. These MLA's belong to different parties and to different castes, often deeply at odds with each other. If a cross-caste, cross-party Scheduled Caste bloc is to exist and function at all effectively, it has first to be created, and this takes skillful leadership. It is more likely to succeed if virtually all the members belong to one party or most of them belong to one caste.

There is also the question of whether the existence of such a bloc can be translated into real power with the voters. Andhra Pradesh may be a case in point. A Scheduled Caste leader, D. Sanjeeviah, was able to develop a bloc, exploit a rivalry between the dominant non-Brahmans, and become Chief Minister for a while in the early 1960s. But the state's per capita expenditure on Scheduled Caste welfare was the lowest in the country (Schermerhorn 1969: 399), and in 1968 its politicians proved singularly indifferent to Andhra's Kanchikacherla "Harijan burning" incident that caused a furor elsewhere (*Statesman Weekly,* April 13, 1968; *Deccan Herald,* April 26 & 30, 1968; *New York Times,* May 3, 1968). It is difficult to believe that either condition could have existed if the Scheduled Caste MLA's were an effective force in the state. Possibly, blocs like the one that Mr. Sanjeeviah led rest more on reservations — on statutory numbers in the legislature — than on a power base with the voters. Possibly also, an effective bloc cannot survive the departure of its leader for a political role at the center.

Insofar as the Scheduled Caste MLA's act in a bloc, they tend to concentrate their efforts on those items of the protective discrimination system that are of most concern to their more prosperous caste constituents: more ministries for themselves, more scholarships and reservations in higher educational institutions, and above all, more government jobs. The direction of so much of their effort at gaining concessions in government services may obscure the full picture. If our analysis is correct, this is only one half, the more visible "Scheduled Caste" half, of their dual role as representatives.

Just as the system leads the MLA to play a double role, so it gives the ordinary Untouchable a dual choice. There is no evidence available concerning whether Untouchables in reserved constituencies get more from their MLA's than those in the unreserved. To whom does the

Untouchable in an *un*reserved constituency appeal for favors or redress of grievances? His own MLA or the Scheduled Caste MLA in another constituency who may be a caste-fellow? Would the Untouchable go to that other MLA if he were a member of a different Scheduled Caste? The available evidence suggests that if his objective is to obtain a government job he would turn to the Scheduled Caste MLA for help, but for most other favors he would turn to his own MLA. In most instances of this kind, he would probably turn first to local leaders, but if access to them were strained or precluded by the tensions that often accompany Untouchable assertiveness, the fact that he had two alternative higher representatives to whom to appeal would seem to be important. Until we have a better idea as to the Untouchable's choices and how he makes them, it is difficult to assess whether and in what manner the system facilitates his access to political power or his political integration.

Protective Discrimination and the "New Class"

If the reserved seat system has created special political roles, protective discrimination as a whole seems to have fostered the growth of a "new class." As noted already, protective discrimination has been utilized in some form in almost every branch of government activity, but certain types of concessions lend themselves to it more readily than others. These concessions are precisely the ones mentioned above as being of interest to the more fortunate Untouchables. The kind of people who can even contemplate running for the Legislative Assembly or holding a post-matric scholarship or seeking admission to an engineering college or applying for an upper-division government clerkship have already reached a level of education and prosperity well above that of the great majority of Untouchables. To what extent they owe this prosperity *initially* to protective discrimination is difficult to determine, but there is no doubt that they are the main beneficiaries of the system.

With the operation of the system over the years, the gap between these more fortunate ones and the rest of the Untouchables seems to have widened. The gap exists *within* castes, in that some families are much better off than others. They are also unevenly distributed *by* caste, being found far more freqeuntly in some castes than in others. Those who belong to large caste-aggregates with experience in organized political effort behind them, like Chamars and Dhobis in northern India, Namashudras and Rajbanshis in Bengal, Malas in Andhra, Mahars in Maharashtra, have a distinct advantage. It is members of such castes that are most likely to hold the reserved seats and, allegedly, to manipulate the benefits to their own advantage and that of their caste-fellows. We have no hard data whatever on this point, but such allegations are often made by the officials who administer the benefits. For example, the Rajbanshis, who were regarded by the 1931 Bengal Census Superintendent as too advanced to be listed as a Depressed Class, but were nevertheless later Scheduled, are said to have always had a disproportionate share of the scholarships, jobs, and other benefits awarded by government (Interview with N. K. Bose, Commissioner for Scheduled Castes and Tribes, April 3, 1968).

Public Opinion and the "Harijans"

The Rajbanshis have paid a price, however, and so have all the other beneficiaries of protective discrimination. In 1931, it will be remembered, the Rajbanshis were among the castes attempting to validate claims that they were not Untouchables at all, and thus to escape the stigma of such a designation. Far from allowing them to do this, protective discrimination requires them to call attention to their Untouchable caste membership in order to obtain benefits. Gandhi was neither the first nor the last to point out that this is no way to eliminate untouchability. The prejudicial attitudes and the disabilities have diminished to more subtle forms today, but their survival, in modified form, has also been fostered by the nature of government involvement since Independence.

There appears to be a widespread belief on the part of people with some education that government's commitment to the Scheduled Castes is total and that the number of people who receive such favored treatment is enormous. We noted in the first part of this paper that if one pores through the official reports, regulations, and statistics, one discovers that the actual benefits and the number of recipients are much more modest than they are believed to be. The belief is honestly held, however, and has had a considerable impact on public attitudes, for it provides an excellent rationale for inaction. Both by design and by default — responsibility for the Scheduled Castes is assigned to the government and the educated public is not concerned. Often there is little awareness even of policy matters that affect non-Untouchables as well, as shown by the history of the bill to bifurcate constituencies in 1960. It is true that both ritual and power relationships among castes have become *local* issues of some intensity in various parts of the country, sometimes leading to outbreaks of violence. But the problems of the Scheduled Castes cannot be said to have become important *national* issues. Statistics showing markedly lower voter turnout in reserved constituencies reinforce the impression of widespread public indifference to the Scheduled Castes and their fate.

We noted at the outset that attempts to cope with problems of the

Scheduled Castes differ, both in measures adopted and in the role assigned government, depending upon which of two sets of problems is given emphasis: the problems of poverty and lack of power or the problems of untouchability. Those who identify the key problem as the lack of opportunities for education, better employment, and political power will concentrate on providing such opportunities to the deprived population. Those who say the key problem is untouchability must aim to change the attitudes and practices of everybody else. Government has been assigned primary responsibility for both sets of problems, but it should surprise no one that the bulk of its effort has been directed at the first rather than the second.

Gandhi, on the other hand, directed his energies at the second, the "eradication of the sin of untouchability." Only the sinner could expiate the sin, he felt, and throughout his public career he exhorted the caste Hindus to do so, concentrating so much on them that he has been criticized for giving the Untouchables no leadership role in their own "uplift." Yet, aided by the political conditions already described, he did more than anyone else to make untouchability a public issue and to create public opinion against it. He pushed the issue to the "forefront" of the Congress platform in 1921 and did his best to keep it there for twenty-five years, despite the objection of his colleagues that it sometimes diverted public energies away from the top priority goal of achieving independence (cf. J. Nehru 1942: 236–239 on his unhappiness over the Epic Fast). Gandhi also reinforced his propaganda by numerous symbolic gestures, such as adopting an Untouchable girl, living in the Bhangi (sweeper, scavenger) colonies of the big cities, and insisting that the inmates of his ashrams be their own Bhangis.

Gandhi felt that the reform work he wanted should go on outside government and should not rely on official initiative or legal sanctions. Government should simply give legal recognition to reforms once they occurred. Although some argued that a little judiciously applied coercion might accelerate the "change of heart" (Galanter 1969), Gandhi felt such coercion to be inimical to it. Since independence Gandhi's views have been set aside, his idea that reform work should go on outside government serving only in the form of routine official subsidies to voluntary agencies.

As of 1970, nothing in the system would prevent mounting a public opinion campaign against untouchability similar to those led by Gandhi. Although such a campaign would complement rather than compete with official programs, none has occurred. The very existence of all the governmental provisions, or the belief that they exist, seems to justify inaction by private citizens. Again and again we are told that untouchability does not exist any more because it was abolished over twenty years ago by the Constitution. The Untouchability (Offences) Act, 1955, "takes care of the few places where it may still exist." Besides, the Scheduled Castes "have all those benefits now."

While the laws and the benefits appear to be accepted with little overt expression of resentment, the other side of the coin is, perhaps inevitably, a set of prejudicial assumptions made about the Scheduled Castes. For example, there is the widespread assumption that every Untouchable job- or scholarship-holder obtained his position because he is Scheduled Caste, rather than individually deserving. Not only is the Scheduled Caste job-holder assumed to be incompetent until proved otherwise, but where there is incompetence it is often assumed to be Scheduled Caste in origin. Isaacs (Chapter 13 this volume) reports the case of a bungling railway ticket clerk who was assumed to be Scheduled Caste because he had bungled.

A number of these attitudes appear to be summed up in the image of the "Harijan." Gandhi first publicized the term, meaning "God's folk" or "children of God" in the early 1930s as part of his propaganda against untouchability. It was not only a nice-sounding euphemism for a despised group, but a bit of propaganda in itself: the Untouchables are people of God *too,* and therefore entitled to worship in temples and receive decent treatment just like anyone else.* But whatever Gandhi's intentions, the word has taken on other connotations. Even in his lifetime the term also came to express condescension. Since then it has become universally adopted as the proper modern term by everybody except the educated "Harijans" themselves.

In the process, it has not become a term of abuse the way the caste names often are, but it does connote inferiority. It seems that the "Harijan" today is by definition a dependent, whether the dependency is on local patrons, as in the past, or on the more impersonal system of state benefits. The point is not that Scheduled Caste people are actually dependents, but that they are believed to be, and that this is part of the "Harijan" image. Marriott (1968) tells us that in the traditional food and service exchanges of a village, the lowest castes rank low, not

---

*Gandhi went further than this, saying that it was his object to have all Hindus become Harijans. Only by removing untouchability could *they* deserve to be called God's children. And if Hinduism can "purify" itself of untouchability, he said, "there will be only one caste, known by the beautiful name Bhangi, that is to say, the reformer or remover of all dirt." (*Harijan,* July 7, 1946, quoted in Gandhi 1954b: 85)

because of the polluting character of their occupations or customs, but because they are receivers. They receive not only food but polluting substances from everybody else and are unable to persuade or manoeuver others to receive from them. Some of this carries over to the modern "Harijan" image, the transactions in this case having to do with politics, jobs, and scholarships rather than ritual interactions. The Harijan still ranks low as a receiver, even though he is not as degraded as his fore-fathers were.

That the word "Harijan" is so widely used despite the feelings of educated Untouchables against it may be but another sign of the public lack of concern already referred to.* Many persons seem genuinely sur-prised to learn that educated Untouchables almost never use it and tend to resent it. Lest it seems callous to go on using the term, it should be acknowledged that any other word would very likely undergo a similar fate and take on the same set of meanings. The image of the dependent who is the object of pity or contempt is presupposed by the system of protective discrimination and is part of the justification for the system. To challenge the accuracy of the "Harijan" image today is to challenge protective discrimination itself. To argue for the continuation of the benefits is, in effect, to say that they are worth the price.

Officials, Politicians, and the Future of Protective Discrimination

Protective discrimination is supposed to be temporary, and in assess-ing its prospects, one should note that different actors in the system typi-cally hold different views of the price to be paid and the risks involved. One view, favored especially by caste Hindu and foreign scholars, is closely related to the considerations just discussed. Here the price is essentially psychological: a payment in continued quasi-untouchability — the dependency image of the Harijan — for employment and other benefits received. One form is the alleged cost of switching mobility tactics from claims for the symbols of higher prestige to claims for benefits on grounds of low prestige and "backwardness." This switch is associated with some emotional ambivalence and humiliation, possibly with lowered self-esteem. Another common way of expressing this view is that pro-

---

*It is an easy mistake to make. An early work of the author's (1961) used the term frequently because it drew heavily on official reports and interviews. When she later studied material exclusively from Scheduled Caste informants, she found that they rarely used the term, and then only when they alluded vaguely to all the "downtrodden," not just Untouchables. On further inquiry, the same annoyance was found at the word that Isaacs reports from his informants (Ch. 13 this volume).

tective discrimination is a "crutch," and in the long run no substitute for a healthy leg: once the beneficiary gets his post or his seat he may thereafter fear the withdrawal of reservations, believing himself unable to compete without them. This is one meaning of the commonly voiced danger of "building a vested interest in the survival of untouchability."

Although there are psychological problems (cf. Isaacs 1965) these are not identified as the principal risks by the beneficiaries themselves. As Galanter says, the alleged "cost to the self-respect of these groups" entailed by being "singled out for special treatment is . . . rarely raised by Scheduled Caste or Tribe spokesmen," who tend to be more "troubled by the considerable potential for manipulation in the arrangements for reserved seats" (Galanter, n.d.: II 78). We have already noted the vertical mobilization pattern, in which the Scheduled Caste politicians are the junior partners, and risk becoming merely the puppets, of the non-Untouchable leaders who dominate political parties and local power structures. Along with this goes a concern that the arrangements for government jobs simply siphon off and silence the ablest young men, who might otherwise provide effective leadership to less fortunate caste-fellows. Both of these risks would exist if there were no protective discrimination, but some Untouchables believe that the system accentuates them. It is on such grounds that B. P. Maurya, the Buddhist ex-MP from Aligarh, opposes protective discrimination. Isaacs (1965: 125–126) quoted him as saying:

This system does the Scheduled Castes no good because the people in the reserved seats belong to the party in power and are often incapable persons. Although they are educated, they dare not speak out against the party in power. They do not represent their people to the party and government, but represent the party in power to their people. . . . As for the school benefits, we do not need them in this form either. If there is free compulsory education for all, then every person will have access to it anyway. In higher education let scholarships be given where there is economic need. All our people are poor and the party in power is not solving the problems of poverty. As for the quotas in government service, these are only one to three percent filled and they take our best people. In government service, the educated people are kept out of politics and we are left with illiterate workers. We say end these reservations. They are just a way of keeping the weaker section weak. . . .

If Maurya is right, the political scientists of the future may look back upon protective discrimination as an efficient and inexpensive mechanism for social control. This line of reasoning would also suggest that protective discrimination has been extended not simply because Jagjivan Ram and the other Congress reserved-seat-holders can play political football, but because the caste Hindu leaders find it useful.

A third school of thought emphasizes the dangers of manipulation from another quarter: the "new class" of recipients. This point of view is particularly concerned with the dangers to national integration. The central issue is the granting of benefits to members of certain castes and tribes and the consequences believed to stem from this emphasis on community of birth. For one thing, caste/tribe loyalties and interests are believed to be inherently divisive, thus contributing to the "fissiparous tendencies" endangering national unity. A spate of publications and judicial decisions reflecting this view occurred during the decade 1956–65. Claims for caste benefits are also often regarded as extremely opportunistic. From 1917 to 1965, all the committees and commissions charged with investigating the "backward" and with drawing up or modifying lists of beneficiaries (and there have been many of them) have expressed dismay at the large number of petitions and deputations proclaiming backwardness in order to be listed for benefits. We have already noted that once a caste is on the list, its more fortunate members are likely to receive most of the benefits and, allegedly, to manipulate the system to their own advantage. This is another aspect of the oft-cited danger of a "vested interest in the survival of untouchability."

It is the third of the three viewpoints mentioned above that seems the most characteristic of officials who administer the Scheduled Caste benefits. Neither the psychological difficulties of the Scheduled Castes nor their vulnerability to co-option by the system or manipulation by caste Hindu politicians looms very large in the comments of the officials. Some officials who do not seem very sympathetic to the Scheduled Castes are full of stories of the incompetence of Scheduled Caste job-seekers and the corruption of their politicians. These stories seem to arise from the distrust civil servants have of politicians generally, the preju-dicial assumptions made about the Untouchables discussed earlier, and a feeling that claims on grounds of caste are somehow anti-national, even unpatriotic.

In addition to these attitudinal factors, however, there are numerous other difficulties. Even the conscientious official sympathetic to the Scheduled Castes is faced with problems stemming from the growing dis-crepancy between the caste and class variables with which he must deal. We noted at the outset of this paper that the justice of protective discrimination for Scheduled Castes rests logically on the assumption of a one-to-one correlation between the ritual status of the castes and the secular condition of their members. To the extent that the correlation breaks down between caste membership and individual levels of income, education, and power, the system which relies on it is perceived as being unjust. Moreover, a case could be made that one of the purposes of protective discrimination is to break down this correlation. The protective safeguards are granted to castes, it is true, but the specific benefits go to individuals, so that their low caste status — the slowest of the variables to change — will not serve as an obstacle to their education, their assumption of office, or any other form of mobility. Protective discrimination therefore becomes unfair to others precisely as it becomes successful in breaking down the correlation. The administering officials find it more and more difficult to do justice to the "weaker sections" through the mechanism of caste benefits: some of the neediest people do not happen to belong to the listed castes, and many of those who do cannot be reached because there are middle-class Scheduled Caste persons with better political con nections who are adept at getting the benefits for themselves. In the area of reservations, at least, it is difficult to imagine how it could be otherwise, given the nature of the benefits and the qualifications they require. Since such persons are precisely the ones the administrators are most likely to see, one suspects that the latter may be exaggerating both their number and their manipulative skill.

Nevertheless, this imbalance, wherever it occurs, is regarded as an unfortunate consequence of protective discrimination, one which should be avoided wherever possible. Many of the non-Scheduled Caste members of the relevant committees, commissions, and advisory boards seem to feel this way. The recommendations they make for coping with the problem are usually couched in terms of the long-range goal of eliminating protective discrimination, and are presented as steps or stages in the gradual phasing out of the system.

Four ways to eliminate protective discrimination have been proposed from time to time: shifting the concessions to bases other than caste, imposing time limits on them and gradually letting them lapse, stratifying the castes on the schedules into less and more backward, with the concessions adjusted accordingly, and taking the more advanced castes off the lists of those eligible for benefits. The first has always been the most appealing, but it has been tried almost entirely in connection with the Other Backward Classes rather than the Scheduled Castes and Tribes. There are two main difficulties: the use of a means test or some other economic criterion than caste would not seem feasible for defining eligibility for political seats or government jobs. Secondly, in the field of education, where it has been tried for the Other Backward Classes, it has been difficult to apply and subject to abuse. If there are cases of fraudulent certification of caste membership for the Scheduled Caste concessions, there are apparently even more cases of fraudulent certification of family income and father's occupation for the Other Backward Classes concessions.*

As for the remaining alternatives, we have already seen that the one time limit imposed on a Scheduled Caste concession has been extended both times it was about to expire. A precedent does exist — the Anglo-Indian concessions were successfully phased out several years ago — but it seems unlikely to be applied in the foreseeable future for obvious political reasons. The division of lists into compartments or layers of more-and less-backward has been widely utilized in various forms for the Other Backward Classes; the courts have rejected some of these arrangements but allowed others to stand (Galanter, n.d., Ch. VI, Sec. C, pp. VI–20–32). The procedure has been recommended sometimes for the Scheduled Castes but had not yet been attempted at the time of this study. It is possible, however, that the authorities had something of this sort in mind, leading to de-scheduling of some communities, when they decided to collect detailed data on all of the Scheduled Castes and Tribes in the 1961 census. These have been published in thick volumes for every state and territory, the data being given caste by caste, tribe by tribe, district by district.

As this study goes to press, the removal of castes from the schedule on grounds that they are now sufficiently advanced would seem to be a political impossibility. It has, however, been suggested from time to time, and one high-level official committee actually got to the point of naming names, albeit in a curious way. This was the Advisory Committee on the Revision of the Lists of Scheduled Castes and Scheduled Tribes, known as the Lokur Committee (Dept. of Social Security, 1965). The nature of its suggestions and their fate merit some discussion.

The committee was appointed in June 1965 with the essentially technical task of adjusting the lists "in a rational and scientific manner" (p. 29). Its members were all experienced civil servants: the chairman, B. N. Lokur, was the Law Secretary; the other two members were the Joint Secretary in the Ministry of Home Affairs and the Director of Backward Classes Welfare, Department of Social Security. The lists issued in 1950 were derived from those of 1936, modified by the re-drawing of state boundaries in 1947–49. They were modified further by more

---

*Galanter (n.d. IV-xxix-xxx note 177) reports that "In an investigation of a sample 15,438 beneficiaries of the income test in Maharashtra it was found that 4,491 (29.1%) had given false statements. False income statements were as high as 58.9% in one district." See also his analysis of the cases filed under the Mysore income-cum-occupation test adopted in 1963 (Ch IV, Sec F, pp IV–78–IV–84).

boundary changes in 1956 and later years, and by several additions made by Parliament in 1956. As no names were deleted, the lists for each state became more and more cumbersome. Several court cases brought out some of the many anomalies in the lists, particularly the area restrictions and the problems of alternate and new names, phonetic variations, sub-tribes and sub-castes. A Supreme Court opinion of September 1964, which seemed to indicate that all of these variants, groups and sub-groups within each listed caste or tribe had to be specified, was a major reason for the committee's appointment (pp. 19–20). In addition to rationalizing the existing lists, the committee had to recommend action on proposals received by the government. As soon as its appointment was announced, it began receiving the usual deluge of representations concerning the lists. It had to investigate over 800 castes and tribes "with a view to determining their eligibility" (p. 3). It was an enormous task, but the committee met its three-month deadline. It advised inclusion of 9 castes, all small, and the deletion of 171 names for the following reasons: 120 castes either did not exist in the state or had fewer than 10 members, 12 were not caste names, 1 was Muslim, and 38 "do not suffer from untouchability" (these being also quite small). The committee expected these changes to have no appreciable effect on the Scheduled Caste population. The 19 tribes to be added and 131 to be deleted from the Scheduled Tribe list would add a population of 2 million. Had the committee contented itself with these technical revisions, most of its recommendations would probably have been accepted without further ado.

In its opening remarks on "principles and policy," however, the committee went further than this. ". . . in the interests of national integration," it said,

We feel that the time has come when the question of descheduling of relatively advanced communities should receive serious and urgent consideration. Consistently with this approach, several persons who appeared before us, including some eminent social workers, brought the following communities to our notice, which, in their opinion, are relatively advanced and could forthwith be descheduled. . . . Some of the State Governments concerned, however, do not favour exclusion of these communities from the lists; strong representations have also been made by or on behalf of the affected communities for their retention. . . . In these circumstances and also as we have not been able to make a closer investigation into the conditions of these communities in the short time at our disposal, we are unable to make a specific recommendation in regard to these communities" (pp. 10–11).

The committee suggests but does not recommend, endorses but disassociates itself from this de-scheduling. The Scheduled Castes on this list of the relatively advanced are given in Table 9.20. Even a cursory glance

Table 9.20

Castes Suggested for Removal from Scheduled Caste List by the Lokur Committee on Ground that they are Sufficiently Advanced, Population and Literacy Rates, 1961 Census

State	Caste	Population	% of State's Sch. Caste Population	Caste Literacy Rate (%)	State SC Literacy Rate (%)	State Total Literacy Rate (%)
Andhra Pradesh	Mala*	1,745,466	35.09	10.12	8.46	21.19
Assam	Jhalo-Malo	15,503	2.12	13.76	24.41	27.36
	Jalia Kaibartta	199,590	27.24	27.65		
	Dhupi/Dhobi	19,589	2.67	22.97		
Bihar	Chamar**	1,895,179	29.13	6.32	5.96	18.40
	Dhobi	332,245	5.11	9.97		
Gujarat	Vankar/Dhed***	585,298	42.81	27.65	22.46	30.45
Kerala	Vannan	10,711	.75	46.36	24.44	46.85
	Mannan	15,667	1.09	44.21		
	Perumannan	4,702	.33	51.89		
	Velan	33,581	2.34	49.64		
Madhya Pradesh	Chamar/Jatav/ Satnami**	2,506,356	58.93	6.59	7.89	17.13
	Mahar/Mehra	209,794	4.93	15.26		

State	Caste	Population				
Madras	Mannan	16	—	nil	14.66	31.41
	Velan	8	—	25.00		
	Vannan	13,079	.22	25.40		
Maharashtra	Mahar	782,008	35.12	15.69	15.78	29.82
Mysore	Bhovi	268,141	8.60	7.57	9.06	25.40
Orissa	Dhoba/Dhobi	265,360	9.60	15.71	11.57	21.66
Punjab	Chamar**	1,596,030	38.56	10.63	9.64	24.22
Uttar Pradesh	Chamar**	8,693,327	56.45	7.41	7.14	17.65
	Dhobi	888,466	5.77	7.20		
West Bengal	Dhoba/Dhobi	154,791	2.25	13.11	13.58	29.28
	Namasudra	729,057	10.58	21.03		
	Rajbanshi	1,201,717	17.44	14.75		
	Sunri	106,870	1.55	28.58		
INDIA	TOTAL	22,272,551	34.58		10.27	24.02

*Figures are for the single "Mala" listing and exclude nine other castes with "Mala" as part of the caste name. These would add another 102,101 people.

**Most Chamar listings also include a large number of "synonyms," "alternates" and "subcastes." In Madhya Pradesh, for example, the four Chamar listings are clubbed with 15 other names, including "Jatav" and "Satnami," listed separately by the Lokur Committee.

***Three census listings, clubbed with five "synonyms."

SOURCES: States & caste names: The Report of the Advisory Committee on the Revision of the Lists of Scheduled Castes and Scheduled Tribes [Lokur Committee] (New Delhi, 1965), p. 11.

Census data: Census of India, 1961, vol. I, India, Part II-A(ii): Union Primary Census Abstracts, p. xlvi; and Part V-A(i): Special Tables for Scheduled Castes.

at the caste names will alert the reader to the inevitable fate of the committee's cautious suggestion. That it was quickly and firmly squelched by an angry delegation of MP's who called on the Minister for Law and Social Security in December, as soon as the Lokur report was available, should come as no surprise (Galanter, n.d., p. III–31). What seems a bit curious is that the committee made no use of the abundant 1961 census data for this list, relying instead on the impressions of "several persons who appeared before us." The writer, therefore, computed the caste literacy data appearing in Table 9.20, with the state literacy rates of the Scheduled Caste and total populations for comparison.

The de-scheduling of these castes would remove 22.3 million people from the list — more than a third of the total Scheduled Caste population. If literacy is used as an index of advancement, and a better measure is hard to find, only three of the castes have literacy rates higher than those of the total populations in their respective states, two in Kerala and one in Assam; only the latter is a caste of any appreciable size. Presumably those castes could justifiably be regarded as sufficiently advanced to be de-scheduled. But seven of the castes, some 3,746,404 people, have literacy rates lower than the Scheduled Caste averages in their states. It is difficult to justify removing them on grounds of "advancement." Seven huge caste-clusters, accounting for over 16 million people, have literacy rates lower than the all-India Scheduled Caste rate of 10.3 percent. There seems little justification for removing them, either. If the all-India total literacy rate of 24.02 percent were used as the standard, nine of the castes would be removed, a population of 969,506.

Even if the list had been accurate and the castes significantly more "advanced" than the other Scheduled Castes, the committee's suggestion would have met the same fate. The Congress, principal beneficiary of reserved seats, obviously would never remove one-third of the Scheduled Caste population from the list a year before a general election. That the de-scheduling in so many of the cases was unwarranted compounded the problem. Reportedly, this list was not only firmly repudiated, but the Law Minister was forced to repudiate all the committee's recommendations, including the technical changes mentioned earlier. On August 12, 1967, only four days after the reserved-seat-holders had demonstrated their political muscle in the snap vote incident, a bill to amend the lists was introduced by the government. The proposed new list would include every group recommended for exclusion by the Lokur committee, and a Joint Parliamentary Committee was established to review it (Galanter, n.d., p. III–32).

There, in the lap of the politicians rather than the civil servants, rests the matter of list revision and any other proposal to phase out protective discrimination. Significant changes, particularly toward reduction, are not likely to be made unless forced by a court case. The steps taken by politicians tend toward blurring rather than sharpening distinctions, accommodating and including aggrieved groups rather than rationalizing and excluding "advanced" groups. One example of this political trend of the post-1967 period is the handling of religious converts.

One of the anomalies noted at the beginning of this paper was the position of those Untouchables who were not Hindu. They were excluded from the Scheduled Caste category in the thirties, even though the authorities must have been well aware that within Christianity, Islam, Sikhism, and Judaism certain castes were discriminated against, not only by the Hindu majority but by high-caste members of their own communities in a manner that would fit all of Hutton's criteria. The technicality employed was that these faiths did not give theological recognition or legitimacy to untouchability, but one suspects that the reasons were political. Similar considerations applied to the position of converts from the Scheduled Castes, who ceased to be Scheduled even though their other circumstances had not changed. One effect of this was to nip in the bud a number of conversion movements that were gaining headway in the 1930s.

The primacy of political factors continued after Independence, particularly in the turbulent Punjab. In 1936 Untouchables who were Sikh, by birth or conversion, were excluded from the list of Scheduled Castes. After Independence, four castes were included, and in 1956 the remainder were added to the list, though converts to other religions were not. Here, as in so many other areas of communal relations, the "rational and scientific" logic of officials seems superficial — the underlying logic was political logic. As political circumstances change, that same logic seems to dictate further adjustments. Since the 1969 party split, the Congress (R) appears to have moved toward closer political accord with non-Hindu religious minorities regarding the status of their converts from the Scheduled Castes. In November of 1969 the central government, at Mrs. Gandhi's initiative, extended its post-matric scholarships scheme to Buddhist and Christian converts of Untouchable origin. The state governments had for several years been granting some educational benefits to these converts, but this was the first time that the centre had done so.

The fact that educational benefits, rather than reservations in politics and government jobs, were involved in this political adjustment is also characteristic. Expenditures in education, health, housing, and other welfare fields lend themselves more readily than reservations to the fine art of political patronage, an art which the present leaders evidently find essential to sustaining themselves in power. But this is not to say that the reservations have not also been made to serve political ends.

Our material indicates that whether the motive is to "keep the weaker section weak" as Maurya says, or simply to accommodate the conflicting claims and pressures of numerous groups and interests in a heterogeneous society, protective discrimination as a whole has become a mechanism for social control, an instrument of distributionist politics. This type of politics is a game played by both sides, recipients as well as donors. Its outcome — the inelegant but practical adjustments that are the politician's forte — will be determined by what the various actors perceive to be the realities of power. Our evidence suggests that reserved seats do not in themselves confer an effective form of power except under the singular circumstances that prevailed as of mid-1970, in the Lok Sabha. The kind of power that will be respected in the long run will have to be generated outside the legislatures and beyond the devices of protective discrimination.

10.

MARC GALANTER

The Abolition of Disabilities –
Untouchability and the Law

*After all, there is only one thing worse than injustice,
and that is justice without her sword in her hand.*
                                    —Nirod Mukherji

THIS PAPER IS concerned with the relationship between the law and the practices which came to be known as "untouchability." Part I depicts

This paper is part of a larger study of the relation of law, caste and religion in modern India, which has been generously supported by the Committee on Southern Asian Studies of the University of Chicago. Part of the research reported here was carried out while I was in India on a Faculty Fellowship of the American Institute of Indian Studies in 1965–66. An earlier version of the essay appeared in the *Economic and Political Weekly* Annual Number of January, 1969 (Vol. IV, Nos. 1 & 2). Law report citations are explained at the end of this chapter.

[227]

the way in which the legal system of British India supported certain aspects of the caste order. Part II traces the piecemeal withdrawal of this support in the years preceding Independence and the undertaking by independent India of a commitment to eradicate old patterns of caste relations. Part III describes the constitutional setting of these efforts to abolish disabilities. Part IV reviews the reception of anti-disabilities measures by the higher courts. Part V attempts to assess their effectiveness in operation. Part VI explores the prospects for making the law more effective in abolishing disabilities.

For the most part this paper is concerned with the "lawyer's law" — the official and unauthoritative legal rules found in statutes and in the judgments of the higher courts. There is, of course, no exact correspondence between this higher law and the behavior that it purports to regulate, nor even with the day to day operations of the magistrates, officials, lawyers and police who staff the lower levels of the legal system. Some gap or discrepancy between the most authoritative legal pronouncements and patterns of local practice, both lay and professional, is a typical, perhaps universal, feature of any complex multi-layered legal system. Obviously many factors other than legal rules influence behavior regarding caste. We shall review the "lawyer's law" as a set of rules for governmental intervention in caste behavior, in order to settle disputes, to maintain patterns or establish new ones. After determining the changing scope and nature of this intervention from the point of view of the lawyer's law, we shall then attempt to ascertain its extent and character in practice.

I. Caste Disabilities and the Law in British India

During the period of British rule in India, the practices which came to be called "untouchability" received limited and for the most part indirect support from the law. The establishment of a nation-wide legal system brought a general movement of disputes from tribunals responsive to the locally powerful into the government's courts and spread a consciousness of rights which might be vindicated independently of local opinion.[1] The government's courts espoused a norm of equality before the law and, with few exceptions, applied the same rules to all. As *shastric* and customary law was supplanted, the use of caste as a criterion in the application of general criminal, civil, and commercial law was restricted and eventually discarded. In the application of Hindu law to family and ceremonial matters, *varna* and caste distinctions remained relevant in some areas, but these legal categories did not spread to other fields. The abolition of slavery in the middle of the nineteenth century extended elementary rights to many Untouchables.[2] These lowest orders, then, enjoyed equality in the eyes of the law and had access to it, at least formally. In practice legal institutions often adapted themselves to prevailing patterns of disability.[3] However, the general features of the legal system were not articulated to a social system of graded inequality. The overall British policy toward caste was a policy of non-interference. In this section we shall trace the judicial response to caste from the consolidation of the modern legal system, which can be dated roughly at about 1860, to the advent of Independence.[4]

DIRECT ENFORCEMENT OF CLAIMS FOR PRECEDENCE AND FOR THE IMPOSITION OF DISABILITIES

With respect to use of religious premises, caste groups did enjoy the active support of the courts in upholding their claims for precedence and exclusiveness. Courts granted injunctions to restrain members of particular castes from entering temples — even ones that were publicly supported and dedicated to the entire Hindu community.[5] Damages were awarded for purificatory ceremonies necessitated by the pollution caused by the presence of lower castes; such pollution was actionable as a trespass to the person of the higher caste worshippers.[6] It was a criminal offense for a member of an excluded caste knowingly to pollute a temple by his presence.[7] These rights to exclusiveness were vindicated by the courts not only where the interlopers were "Untouchables" but also against such "touchables" as Palshe Brahmans and Lingayats,[8] whose presence in the particular temple was polluting.

In these cases the courts were giving effect to the notion of an overarching, differentiated Hindu ritual order in which the various castes were assigned, by text or by custom, certain prerogatives and disabilities to be measured by notions of *varna,* pollution and required ceremonial distance.[9] Thus, in *Anandrav Bhikaji Phadke* v. *Shankar Daji Charya,* the Bombay Court upheld the right of Chitpavan Brahmans to exclude Palshe Brahmans from worshipping at a temple, on the ground that such an exclusive right "is one which the Courts must guard, as otherwise all high-caste Hindus would hold their sanctuaries and perform their worship, only so far as those of the lower castes chose to allow them."[10] In *Sankaralinga Nadan* v. *Raja Rajeswara Dori* the Privy Council upheld the exclusion of Shanars from a temple and granted damages for its purification after a careful scrutiny of their social standing. Finding "their position in general social estimation appears to have been just above that of Pallas, Pariahs, and Chucklies (who are on all hands regarded as unclean and prohibited from the use of Hindu temples) and below that of the Vellalas,

Maravars, and other cultivating castes usually classed as *Sudras,* and admittedly free to worship in the Hindu temples," the Court concluded that the presence of Shanars was repugnant to the "religious principles of the Hindu worship of Shiva" as well as to the sentiments and customs of the caste Hindu worshippers.[11] As late as 1945, Nair users of a public temple were granted damages for pollution for the purificatory ceremonies necessitated by Ezhuvas bathing in tanks.[12]

Indian criminal law is extraordinarily solicitous of religious sensibilities. Defilement of places of worship, disturbance of religious ceremonies and outrage and wounding of religious feelings are serious criminal offenses.[13] These protections applied among Hindus inter se as well as between members of distinct religions. Punishable defilement included ritual defilement; physical impurity was not required.[14] Untouchable Mahars who entered the enclosure of a village idol were convicted on the ground that "where custom . . . ordains that an untouchable, whose very touch is in the opinion of devout Hindus pollution, should not enter the enclosure surrounding the shrine of any Hindu god, . . ." such entry is a defilement in violation of Section 295 of the Penal Code.[15]

These cases reveal a judicial notion of a single articulated Hindu community in which there were authoritative opinions (supplied by custom and accepted texts) which determined the respective rights of the component groups.[16] This conception of an overarching Hindu order is revealed clearly in the refusal of the courts to enforce claims for exclusiveness among Christians. In *Michael Pillai* v. *Barthe,* a group of Roman Catholic Pillais and Mudalis sued for an injuction to require the Bishop of Trichinopoly to re-erect a wall separating their part of the church from that entered by "low-caste Christians" and to declare plaintiffs' exclusive right to perform services at the altar. The Court characterized the claim as one for "a right of freedom from contact which can have but one origin . . . that of pollution."[17] The Court refused to recognize pollution as either a spiritual or a temporal injury among Christians. Not being Hindus, plaintiffs "cannot . . . invoke the authority of accepted sacerdotal texts for perpetuating the distinction between touchables and untouchables during a particular life solely by reason of birth."[18]

Practices of exclusion in religious premises were further reinforced by the civil laws regarding religious trusts which obligated the trustees to administer the trust property in accordance with the terms of the trust and the usage of the institution.[19] Thus even if a majority of the worshippers at a temple were willing to allow excluded groups to enter, the trustee was subject to civil suit by the hold-outs, prohibiting such action. If trustees still persisted, they might be removed from office or made liable for damages. Thus the law made trustees responsive in this matter to the most intractable of their constituents.

Exclusionary practices did not enjoy the same active judicial support — at least not from the higher courts (see below) — in regard to "secular" public facilities such as schools, wells and roads.[20] The courts declared that no right could be maintained to exclude other castes or sects from the use of streets and roads.[21] The situation was more complicated in regard to the use of water-sources. For a low-caste person to take water from a public well was held not to be the offence of corrupting or fouling a well under § 277 of the Indian Penal Code. It was held that the "defiling" or "corrupting" in the statute referred to "some act which physically defiles or fouls the water."[22] The Lahore Court held other users had no right to prevent Chamars from drawing water from a public well.[23] However, other courts conceded that a right to exclude might be upheld if a custom of exclusive use by higher castes could be proved. However, such customs were difficult to prove. In *Marriappa* v. *Vaithilinga,* Shanars obtained an order allowing them to use a large tank on the ground that no custom of exclusion was proved. A right of exclusion in regard to one well in the dispute was upheld where such a custom was proved. The absence of a custom of exclusion from the large tank, as distinguished from the well, was indicated by textual passages to the effect that precautions for impurity can be less intense in a body of water of this size.[24] In *N. D. Vaidya* v. *B. R. Ambedkar,* the Court found it unproven that there was any long-standing custom of exclusion in a municipal tank. Textual provisions indicating that no elaborate precautions against pollution are required in a tank of that size rendered it "doubtful whether any attempt would have been made to secure exclusive use of the water until such time as the tank came to be surrounded by the houses of caste Hindus."[25] The Court distinguished the temple cases on the ground that "in such cases long practice acquiesced in by the other castes and communities may naturally give rise to a presumption of dedication to the exclusive use of the higher castes, and may throw on the 'untouchables' the burden of proving that they are among the people for whose worship a particular temple exists. No such presumption of a lawful origin of the custom can be said to arise here."[26] And were such an immemorial custom established, said the Court, it would be necessary to consider whether such a custom was unenforceable because it was unreasonable or contrary to public policy.

In dealing with exclusionary rights the courts tried to confine themselves to claims involving civil or property rights as opposed to mere claims for standing or social acceptance. Thus the courts refused to penalize such defiance of customary disabilities as failure to dismount from a wedding palinquin[27] or failure to concede another caste an exclusive right to *mampam* or ceremonial deference.[28] The prevailing notion was that social and religious prerogatives did not give rise to enforceable legal rights unless the right was the sort of thing that could be possessed and made use of. Thus we find gradation from the temple cases, where there was ready enforcement of exclusionary rights, to water-sources, where it seems enforcement might be forthcoming if difficult technical requirements were met, to customs in no way connected with the use of specific property, where there was no enforcement at all. Where the courts intervened to uphold custom, this custom was evaluated and rationalized in terms of notions of ceremonial purity and pollution — existing in different degrees among different groups of Hindus.

INACTION WHERE DISABILITIES WERE ENFORCED BY "SELF-HELP"

A second variety of judicial support is found in instances where members of higher castes undertook themselves to "enforce" their prerogatives against lower castes and the latter responded by attempting to invoke judicial protection. It is clear that courts were reluctant to interpret the law so as to provide remedies against such "self-help."

Where Sonars, excluded from social intercourse and from use of the village well by other Hindus, brought criminal charges against leading villagers, the Court found the villagers' conduct amounted neither to a nuisance nor an insult with intent to provoke breach of the peace.[29] Where members of the Nilgiri Mahratta caste assembled and resolved that others were members of an inferior caste, it was held not to amount to criminal defamation.[30] Where Reddis asserted their superiority over Balijas and resolved to have no social intercourse with them and that village servants should not serve them, the Balijas brought charges of criminal defamation. The Madras High Court held that this conduct was not criminal defamation.[31] "The evidence discloses only the combination of one caste against another . . . and however inconsiderate and oppressive such a combination may be it is not penal unless it is for one of the purposes specified in § 141, Indian Penal Code."[32]

When the excluded group were not Hindus and the difference was one of religion rather than (or as well as) caste, judicial assistance might be forthcoming. Thus the Madras High Court found that where a breach of the peace was threatened as a result of village Hindus' exclusion of Christians from rightful use of a well (on grounds of their low caste), the magistrate "must give such relief as the circumstances admit of," and might forbid the Hindus to interfere.[33]

Those parts of the criminal law protecting religious sensibilities did not serve to protect lower castes from enforcement actions of higher castes. Where Brahmans tore the sacred thread from the neck of an Ahir who had lately taken to wearing it, the Court ruled that since he was a *Sudra,* the wearing of it was not "part of his religion" vis-à-vis other Hindus. To them it was an assertion of a claim to higher rank. Therefore the injury was not an offense to his religious susceptibilities — but only to his dignity. Had it been torn by non-Hindus, it might have been an insult to his religion itself.[34]

Thus it appears that lower-caste litigants (and their lawyers) explored a number of possible avenues of relief against such "self-help" but could find none that paid off. It may be surmised that those lower castes who wanted to carry their struggle into the legal arena probably diverted their efforts to bringing charges of ordinary crimes (assault, trespass, etc.) against their opponents.[35] Success in such litigation would depend only on the competitive struggle to produce convincing evidence, not on securing from the judiciary favorable interpretations of existing law. Even here, success was not readily to be had. Cohn concludes that:

The lower castes have generally been unsuccessful when, through the use of police or of the urban courts, they have sought to redress what they believe to be the corporate wrongs done to them by upper castes. The upper castes maintain their economic position; their knowledge of the courts and the intricacies of the law and better access to officials have thwarted attempts to change the position of the lower castes in the village society and economy.[36]

The potentialities of "self-help" were enhanced by the British policy of loosening legal control over the provision of services by village artisans and servants. It was early established that there was no right to enforce the provision of customary services,[37] even where receiving them was a requisite for retaining good standing in one's caste.[38] The service castes' exclusive right to serve was similarly unenforceable.[39] "The claim is against common sense and could never be upheld in a country where the law allows the freedom which is enjoyed under British government."[40] Dominant groups could now threaten diversion of patronage without fear of legal redress. Untouchable groups dependent for their livelihood on service relations might be subjected to pressure and find little relief in the courts, even where their offices were semi-governmental.[41] Sweepers, whose natural monopoly might have afforded them some protection, were often excluded from the general voluntarism and bound into their service relations by criminal penalties.[42]

One of the most powerful tools of enforcement of disabilities against lower castes was secondary boycott, i.e., depriving the offender of the services of village servants.[43] The British policy of making traditional

service relations unenforceable deprived those subjected to secondary boycott of avenues of relief at the same time that it made the service castes
more available to the power of the dominant groups. Service relations
were now fully susceptible to the exercise of local political and economic
power.[44]

Self-help need not take the form of overt violence to be effective.
Their economic dependence and lack of resources made the Untouchables vulnerable to economic and social boycott. The Starte Committee
concluded:

We do not know of any weapon more effective than this social boycott which
could have been invented for the suppression of the Depressed Classes. The
method of open violence pales away before, for it has the most far-reaching
and deadening effects. It is the more dangerous because it passes as a lawful
method consistent with the theory of freedom of contact.[45]

Boycotts might effectuate not only the withdrawal of economic relations
— opportunities for earning, buying food, borrowing money — but also
extend to areas where Untouchables possessed enforceable legal rights
— the use of footpaths, their remuneration as village servants, etc.[46] Indeed
the power of boycotts led some observers to despair of the possibility
of government vindication of these rights.

No legislative or administrative action can restore to the depressed class
people the right to use public wells. This disability of theirs springs from their
abject dependence on the land-owning high castes. Concerted pressure is often
brought to bear on them to dissuade them from exercising their right. The
Zamindar may refuse to employ them; the Bania may refuse to sell them
provisions; the Zamindar may let loose cattle on their crops destroying them;
and if that does not suffice, the dwellings of such obdurate people may also
be demolished. The depressed classes have neither money nor influence to
assert their right.[47]

UPHOLDING CASTE DISCIPLINARY POWER
AGAINST REFORMERS

We have seen that where lower castes were not themselves subject
to governmental enforcement of the claims of higher castes, the criminal
law was interpreted to give a broad immunity to the efforts of higher
castes to keep the lower castes in their place. Judicial doctrine also provided a third line of protection, by upholding the disciplinary powers of
castes against avowed reformers and others who would soften the imposition of disabilities.

This was an application of the general doctrine of caste autonomy.[48]
Generally courts held themselves disqualified to intervene in the internal
affairs of castes, even where internal disputes led to the outcasting of a

person or a faction. The only exception was where the outcasting led to a deprivation of civil or property rights or to defamation. Even here the courts undertook a merely supervisory jurisdiction, emphasizing the procedural regularity of the excommunication.

Thus reformers who provoked severe response from caste authorities found no protection in the courts. A spiritual superior might excommunicate someone associated with widow remarriages for the spiritual benefit of his sect.[49] It was not defamation to dismiss a *purohit* on the ground that he associated with persons involved in widow remarriages.[50] This rule clearly applied to anti-disabilities reformers. The head of a Math was not guilty of criminal defamation for outcasting a Gowda Saraswat Brahman on the grounds that the latter had attended a Brahmo Samaj dinner at which Pariahs were present.[51] The same privilege attached, of course, among Untouchables themselves. It was not defamatory for Gharagapur Julahas to excommunicate a member for associating with Jaswara Chamaras.[52]

A caste could excommunicate one for associating with sweepers and shaking hands with them. But it was defamation for individuals to impute that a Bhurji had become a sweeper by joining a procession in which some sweepers were included where no properly convened caste panchayat had formally made such a decision.[53] Similarly, it was defamation to allege that a social reformer among the Powars of Bhandara was outcasted for marrying a daughter among the Powars of Chanda when the panchayat had stopped short of outcasting.[54]

SUPPORT FROM SUBORDINATE OFFICIALS

Active judicial enforcement of rights of precedence was confined mostly to cases involving religious premises. There was, though, passive support in the form of unwillingness to employ the civil or criminal law in ways that interfered with "self-help" of higher castes, whether directed against lower castes or against reformers within. But while at the High Court level support for disabilities was thus mainly indirect and passive, there is some indication that at the lower levels of the legal system there was often active governmental support of the claims of the higher castes.[55]

Thus we find the Allahabad High Court reversing the conviction of Doms who were arrested for carrying a bride and groom through a village contrary to custom. The Doms had requested police protection and had been ordered by the police to observe the custom.[56] We find the Lahore High Court upbraiding a magistrate for issuing a succession of orders intended to keep Chamars from using a public well and expressing a hope that the magistrate will "refrain from taking any action under any other section of any Act or Code with a view to stultifying this order."[57] We find the Nagpur High Court expressing incredulity at the magistrate and subordinate judge who had required one caste to post security to an undertaking to recognize the exclusive rights of a higher caste to *mampam* at a festival.[58] In Madras, we find the High Court cautioning a magistrate that Adi-Dravidas have the same civil rights as others to take a procession through the streets. The magistrate had forbidden the procession, noting that they were putting forth "fresh claims." The High Court observed that "the fact that the Adi-Dravidas have been exercising restricted rights in the past was rightly taken into account; but it is not in itself a sufficient ground for refusing them protection in the exercise of their full rights."[59]

As the last three instances attest, the support secured by the higher castes was not necessarily in the form of a recognition of substantive rights, but rather by use of the power of the magistracy to preserve the public peace by issuing restraining orders against those who challenged the status quo.[60] The power to issue such restraining orders to prevent danger, disturbance and injury provided a powerful means for higher castes to elicit help from sympathetic police and magistrates. "Fresh claims" by lower castes especially when they elicited stiff resistance might indeed be seen as emergencies justifying the issuance of such orders, while assertions of exclusiveness by higher castes would be less likely to convey the same quality of urgency.[61] It is difficult to estimate the extent of such active intervention by the lower courts. One knowledgeable observer reported (in 1929):

It often happens that even when a well has been dug at public expense or is maintained in the same manner the higher castes claim the well as their own and let in evidence that they have all along been using it to the exclusion of others. Sometimes they are able to obtain an order under Section 144 of the Criminal Procedure Code preventing others from interfering with such wells. More often on the ground of such exclusive use and enjoyment, they are able to assert their prescriptive rights and obtain orders under Section 145 of the Criminal Procedure Code.[62]

A reformer, writing fifteen years later, observes that Untouchables are "unable to exercise their rights" because when they are obstructed by the higher castes "Section 144 of the Code of Criminal Procedure is resurrected and untouchables are restrained from exercising their lawful rights."[63]

*   *   *

The overall impact of the law on untouchability in the British period is difficult to assess. The law opened some possibilities for advancement and change to the lowest castes, as it did to others. But it did not provide any special leverage for Untouchables to use these opportunities, so that use of them tended to correspond to the existing distribution of power. That is, those who already had other resources could make use of new legal opportunities. The law did not provide an instrument for aggressively suppressing the Untouchables (as e.g., Jim Crow laws in the Post-Reconstruction southern United States)[64] but the law provided a resource with which higher castes could protect their claims and in some instances perhaps even tighten their hold on valued resources to the exclusion of lower castes.[65]

II. From Support to Abolition

LEGISLATIVE INTERCESSION

Isolated governmental action to protect the lower castes from disabilities may be found as early as the mid-nineteenth century. At the turn of the century, the "depressed classes" became an important focus of concern among reformers. It was only after 1909 that fears of diminished Hindu majorities and proposals for special legislative representation for "Untouchables" propelled "untouchability" from the realm of philanthropy into the political arena.[66] In 1917 the Indian National Congress reversed its long-standing policy of excluding "social reform" from its program to pass a hesitant anti-disabilities resolution.

The Congress urges upon the people of India the necessity, justice and righteousness of removing all disabilities imposed by custom upon the Depressed Classes, the disabilities being of a most vexatious and oppressive character, subjecting those classes to considerable hardship and inconvenience.[67]

As reform activity on behalf of Untouchables and political activity by Untouchables multiplied,[68] resolutions and orders confirming the right of Untouchables to equal use of governmental facilities, schools and wells were passed in Bombay and Madras as well as in several of the progressive princely states. In 1923 the Bombay Legislative Council resolved that Untouchables be allowed to use all public watering places, wells, schools, dispensaries, etc. The Provincial Government did not however undertake direct responsibility for enforcement as to local facilities, but requested "collectors . . . to advise the local bodies in their jurisdiction to consider the desirability of accepting the recommendations made in the Resolution so far as it relates to them."[69] The flavor of enforcement activity is conveyed by the action of a District Board which, seven years later, resolved to post notices that facilities were open to Untouchables "at only those villages in the district where the public opinion is favorable for such action."[70] At that time the Starte Committee concluded that the policy was a "complete failure" when it could not "find a single instance where Depressed Classes are continuously using the same public well as the higher classes. There may be such wells, but if so, they must form an infinitesimal proportion of the hundreds of thousands of public wells in the Presidency."[71]

In 1931, the annual meeting of the Indian National Congress at Karachi propounded a program of fundamental rights for future republican India which included:

(vi) no disability to attach to any citizen by reason of his or her . . . caste . . . in regard to public employment, office of power or honours, and in the exercise of any trade or calling.

(vii) equal rights of all citizens in regard to public roads, wells, schools and other places of public resort.[72]

It was only after Gandhi's 1932 fast in opposition to the Communal Award's provision of separate electorates for Untouchables that Congress leaders were willing to countenance the affirmative use of law to abolish disabilities — and in particular to obtain by law the admission of Untouchables to Hindu temples, thereby symbolizing their inclusion within the Hindu community.[73] A conference of caste Hindus, convened in Bombay on September 25, 1932, to ratify the Poona Pact, unanimously adopted the following resolution:

This Conference resolves that henceforth, amongst Hindus, no one shall be regarded as an untouchable by reason of his birth, and that those who have been so regarded hitherto will have the same right as other Hindus in regard to the use of public wells, public schools, public roads and all other public institutions. This right shall have statutory recognition at the first opportunity and shall be one of the earliest Acts of the Swaraj Parliament, if it shall not have received such recognition before that time.

It is further agreed that it shall be the duty of all Hindu leaders to secure, by every legitimate and peaceful means, an early removal of all social disabilities now imposed by custom upon the so-called untouchable classes, including the bar in respect of admission to temples.[74]

Between 1932 and 1936 a number of temple-entry and anti-disabilities bills were introduced in the Central Legislative Assembly and in the Madras and Bombay Legislatures.[75] Temple-entry bills in Madras were denied sanction by the Government on the ground that the subject was of an all-India character. A similar bill and an anti-disabilities bill, introduced into the Central Legislative Assembly in 1933, enjoyed only limited support within Congress and met stiff resistance from the orthodox and a decidedly cool reception from the Government. The bills never came to a vote and were withdrawn when new elections impended and their Congress support dissolved.[76]

None of these bills contained any penal provisions. The temple-entry bills provided for trustees opening temples to Untouchables if a majority of the Hindu voters of the locality approved. The anti-disabilities bills declared the general right of Untouchables to use all public facilities, and outlawed any enforcement to the contrary by courts or public authorities.

The new popular governments which took office in 1937 avowed their opposition to the imposition of disabilities. Governmental posture at this point is typified nicely in a statement of policy sent in May, 1938 to all District Magistrates in the United Provinces.

Public wells are as much free and open to these (untouchable) castes as to the high caste Hindus and other sections of the community. Government cannot possibly recognize any distinction on any ground whatsoever in the case of users of public wells and will do their utmost to enforce such right. All people are entitled to a free and unfettered use of all public property, such as public highways, public wells, public parks, and public buildings. While Government will not fail to do their duty in regard to this matter, it is obvious that public and social opinion must exercise the greatest influence in the solution of any difficulties which may arise in any part of the province. Government appeals most strongly to all sections of the public to ensure full support to the members of the scheduled castes in the peaceful enjoyment of their fundamental rights in this respect.[77]

In 1938 the Madras legislature passed the first comprehensive and penal act to remove social disabilities, making it an offense to discriminate against Untouchables not only in regard to publicly supported facilities such as roads, wells, and transportation, but also in regard to "any other secular institution" to which the general public was admitted, including restaurants, hotels, shops, etc.[78] The Act also barred judicial enforcement of any customary right or disability based on membership in such a group.[79] Violation was made a cognizable offense[80] with a small fine for the first offense, larger fines and up to six months' imprisonment for subsequent offenses.[81]

It will be recalled that it was in regard to the use of religious institutions that Government had most readily intervened to support the exclusionary rights of the higher castes. In the 1930s, temple-entry was proclaimed in a few progressive princely states, notably Baroda (1933) and, most spectacularly, Travencore in 1936.[82] In 1938, for the first time in British India, did governments intervene to secure the opening of temples when Bombay and Madras passed temple-entry acts. The Madras legislation began with an act providing that temples in the Malabar District might be opened by majority vote of the caste-Hindus of the locality and an ordinance indemnifying officials and trustees against liability arising out of the opening of certain Malabar temples.[83] This was followed by a comprehensive province-wide act authorizing trustees to open temples to excluded classes if, in their opinion, "the worshippers of such temple are generally not opposed."[84] When a temple was so opened, both trustees and the formerly excluded groups were protected from legal retaliation. The Bombay act is similar and contains a penal provision, making it an offense to obstruct Harijans from worshipping in an opened temple.[85] Similar bills were in process in the Central Provinces and Berar and in the United Provinces when the Congress Governments resigned.[86]

Between the end of the Second World War and the enactment of the Constitution, with power passing entirely into Indian hands, acts removing civil disabilities of Untouchables were passed in most of the provinces and in many of the larger princely states.[87] With some variation in detail, these statutes followed the general lines of the Madras Removal of Civil Disabilities Act. Enforcement of disabilities against Untouchables,[88] variously described as Harijans, Scheduled Castes, excluded classes, backward classes or depressed classes, was outlawed in regard to public facilities like wells and roads and places of public accommodation like shops, restaurants and hotels. Violations were made criminal offenses, in most cases cognizable.[89] Judicial enforcement of customs upholding such disabilities was barred.

During the same period, the provincial legislatures were active in the temple-entry field. The pre-war temple-entry legislation had been only permissive. It protected trustees and excluded groups from legal penalties if the former chose to ignore the customary practices of exclusion. But trustees were under no obligation to do so and excluded groups had no enforceable right to enter temples. As late as 1945 the Madras High Court had upheld an award of damages to high-caste worshippers for pollution caused by Ezhuvas entering a temple.[90]

Also, in spite of the symbolic victory, the results of the earlier temple-entry legislation were not at all impressive. Surveying the progress in 1945, a reformer noted that as a result of the Madras enactments "several small temples in the province were thrown open to Harijans. The Kallal-agar temple in Madura, the temples under the control of the Tanjore Prince, the Courtallam and Palani temples were thrown open. But most of the major temples in the land continue to be still closed to Harijans."[91] However, another reformer found the results "marvellous beyond imagination" and estimated that "in all about a hundred big temples including one dozen prominent ones are now [ca. 1946] accessible to...Harijans."[92] In Bombay, early returns were equally disheartening. In 1938, the Bombay Government reported 23,362 Hindu (and Jain) temples receiving state grants, of which 510 were open to Harijans.[93] In 1939, after a year of voluntary temple-entry, 142 temples were reported to be thrown open, but only 21 of these were temples with trustees; apparently the others were wayside shrines in little need of such opening. Of the 142,[94] 102 were in Poona and Dharwar Districts, none were in Gujerat. A. V. Thakkar's report in the mid-1940s, which lists 37 temples in Maharashtra and a few in other parts of the Province does not seem to record appreciably greater progress.[95]

Madras again took the lead in enacting a comprehensive temple-entry act,[96] making it a criminal offense for any person to prevent any Hindu from entering or worshipping at any temple to the same extent as Hindus generally.[97] Similar acts, varying slightly in detail, were passed in most of the provinces and a number of the larger princely states.[98] These acts withdrew any judicial enforcement, either civil or criminal, of customary rights of exclusion and gave Untouchables[99] an enforceable right of entry in temples.[100]

Thus in 1950 when the Constitution came into force, the exclusion of Untouchables from public facilities and Hindu temples, previously recognized and to some extent enforceable as law, had been transformed into statutory offenses throughout most of India.[101] The Constitution itself carried the prohibition on this conduct a step further, by entrenching freedom from such disabilities as a fundamental right.

CONSTITUTIONAL ABOLITION

The Constitution of 1950 enacts as justiciable fundamental rights a battery of provisions designed to eliminate caste discrimination on the part of governmental bodies.[102] Most of the Fundamental Rights conferred by the Constitution are restrictions solely on the actions of the state.[103] But several provisions, including those concerning untouchability, go beyond this to regulate private as well as official behavior. Article 17 provides that:

"Untouchability" is abolished and its practice in any form is forbidden. The enforcement of any disability in arising out of "Untouchability" shall be an offense punishable in accordance with law.[104]

It is further provided in Article 15(2) that:

(2) No citizen shall, on grounds only of religion, race, caste, sex, place of birth or any of them, be subject to any disability, liability, restriction or condition with regard to
   a. access to shops, public restaurants, hotels and places of public entertainment; or
   b. the use of wells, tanks, bathing ghats, roads and places of public resort maintained wholly or partly out of State funds or dedicated to the use of the general public.

Article 29 (2) forbids persons in charge of "any educational institution . . . receiving aid out of state funds" to deny admission to an applicant "on grounds only of religion, race, caste, language or any of them." Article 23 prohibits *begar* and forced labor.

Article 25, which guarantees freedom to profess, practice and propagate religion is specifically made subject to the other fundamental rights provisions and is explicitly qualified by the proviso that:

(2) Nothing in this article shall affect the operation of any existing law or prevent the State from making any law . . .
    (b) providing for social welfare or reform or the throwing open of Hindu religious institutions of a public character to all classes and sections of Hindus.

Thus a broad range of disabilities is directly outlawed and government is empowered to take corrective action.

Article 17 not only forbids the practice of "untouchability" but declares that "enforcement of disabilities arising out of 'Untouchability' shall be an offense punishable in accordance with law." Article 35 provides that "Parliament shall have, and the Legislature of a State shall not have, power to make laws . . . prescribing punishment for those acts which are declared to be offenses under this Part" [i.e., the Fundamental Rights section of the Constitution]. Parliament is specifically directed to "make laws prescribing punishment" for acts declared offenses in Part III "as soon as may be after the commencement of this Constitution." Until Parliament discharged this duty, existing laws prescribing punishment for such acts were continued in force "until altered or repealed or amended by Parliament."[105] Thus existing state (i.e., provincial) law was continued in force,[106] but was frozen in its then-existing form, beyond the power of the state legislatures to modify or repeal.[107]

In 1955 Parliament exercised this exclusive power and passed the Untouchability (Offences) Act,[108] which remains the culmination of anti-disabilities legislation to the early 1970s. The UOA outlaws the enforcement of disabilities "on the ground of untouchability" in regard to, inter alia, entrance and worship at temples, access to shops and restaurants, the practice of occupations and trades, use of water sources, places of public resort and accommodation, public conveyances, hospitals, educational institutions, construction and occupation of residential premises, holding of religious ceremonies and processions, use of jewelry and finery.[109] The imposition of disabilities is made a crime punishable by fine of up to Rs. 500, imprisonment for up to six months, cancellation or suspension of licenses[110] and of public grants.[111]

The power of civil courts to enforce any claim or recognize any custom, usage or right which would result in the enforcement of any disability is withdrawn.[112] The previous provincial enactments had also withdrawn all governmental sanction, but they did not venture into the area of "caste autonomy" or behavior indirectly supporting the practice of untouchability. But the UOA punishes not only the enforcement of disabilities, but indirect social support of untouchability. The use of social boycotts against persons who exercise rights under the Act,[113] the use of sanctions, including excommunication, against persons who refuse to practice untouchability,[114] and the instigation of the practice of untouchability in any form[115] are likewise prohibited and penalized. The Act contains one further novel and notable feature: it provides that where any of the forbidden practices "is committed in relation to a member of a Scheduled Caste . . ." the Court shall presume, unless the contrary is proved, that such act was committed on the ground of "untouchability."[116]

III. *Constitutional Context of Anti-Disabilities Legislation*

Having traced the development of anti-disabilities legislation in Part II, we now turn to its reception in the courts. Before examining the specific problems of the UOA in the higher courts (Part IV) and in the lower courts (Part V), we shall consider the judicial treatment of three general issues which relate to the constitutional foundation and limits of anti-disabilities legislation: (A) the constitutional meaning of "untouchability"; (B) constitutional challenges to anti-disabilities legislation; (C) the constitutional position of the caste group.

CONSTITUTIONAL MEANING OF UNTOUCHABILITY

The Constitution does not define "untouchability," nor is it clear what constitutes its "practice in any form" or "a disability arising out of 'untouchability.'" The English term "untouchability" is of relatively recent coinage; its first appearance in print was in 1909 and as it gained wide currency it did not gain clarity.[117] Although the meaning of the constitutional command still remains unclear in some important respects, the work of the courts so far provides some guidelines.

In its broadest sense "untouchability" might include all instances in which one person treated another as ritually unclean and as a source of pollution. In this sense, women at childbirth, menstruating women, persons with contagious diseases, mourners, persons who eat forbidden food or violate prescribed states of cleanliness or are subjects of social boycott might be considered to be Untouchables. But it was not intended to make observance of such temporary or expiable states of untouchability subject to the constitutional ban.[118] The Mysore High Court, the first to address itself to the problem, pointing out that the word "untouchability" appears in Article 17 between inverted commas, inferred that "the subject matter of that Article is not untouchability in a literal or grammatical sense but the practice of it as it had developed historically in this country."[119] Other courts concur that the untouchability referred to does not include that which arises from incidents of personal history. The ban on "untouchability" has not convinced any court that excommunication is thereby unconstitutional, although it makes a person, in the words of the Orissa High Court, "for all practical purposes an untouchable."[120] Indeed the Supreme Court held that the power to excommunicate may in some circumstances be the constitutionally-protected right of a religious sect,[121] notwithstanding the dissenting judge's argument that forbidding such excommunication was only carrying out "the strict injunction of Art. 17. . . ."[122]

Nor does untouchability refer to situational or relative impurity, such as that between ordinary worshipper and priest or temple attendant. Thus the Kerala High Court suggested that refusal to admit a worshipper to a *thidappally* for preparation of a *nivedyam* on grounds that his entrance would be polluting was not a refusal on ground of untouchability.[123] Consonant with this understanding, temple-entry legislation puts Untouchables on a parity with ordinary worshippers but does not attempt to erase distinctions between worshippers and priests or attendants.[124]

A second, somewhat narrower sense of the term would include all instances in which a person was stigmatized as unclean or polluting or inferior because of his origin or membership in a particular group — i.e., where he is subjected to invidious treatment because of difference in religion or membership in a lower or different caste.[125] Such untouchability might be on grounds of membership in a group other than those ordinarily deemed untouchable.[126] However, this view too has been rejected by the courts. The use of *varna* classifications in the personal law continues without judicial censure.[127] The Mysore High Court held that the classification of Lingayats as Sudras for purposes of the law of adoption was not a violation of Article 17.[128]

In *Devirajian* v. *Padmanna,*[129] an orthodox Jain issued a pamphlet contending that complainant, a non-Jain, had no right to enter or offer worship in Jain temples or to take food with Jains, since admission of non-Jains to commensality and common worship was contrary to the tenets of Jainism. He was prosecuted under the Untouchability (Offenses) Act for urging that Jains forbear from social and religious intercourse with "others of the same religion" as the complainant. The Mysore Court held that this "instigation of a social boycott" did not constitute an attempt to enforce a disability "arising out of untouchability." The Court indicated that the untouchability with which Article 17 is concerned is that which "refer[s] to those regarded as untouchables in the course of historical development" and which is related to the relegation of persons "beyond the pale of the caste system . . . on the ground of birth in certain classes."[130] For Jains, then, to regard non-Jains as "untouchable" in certain respects would not be within the scope of untouchability whose practice in any form is forbidden by Article 17. Enforcement of disabilities against non-Jains would not be a disability "arising out of untouchability" within the meaning of Article 17. (Thus it would presumably not matter whether complainant was actually a member of a group traditionally "regarded as untouchables" or not, since the disability enforced against him would not be *on grounds of* the kind of untouchability forbidden by the Constitution.)

Thus we arrive at a third and still narrower sense of the term "untouchability" — as referring only to those practices concerned with the relegation of certain groups "beyond the pale of the caste system." That is, confining it to those disabilities imposed on groups commonly regarded as "Untouchables."[131] This narrower sense does not include invidious treatment due to difference in religion or difference in caste, except insofar as the caste was traditionally considered "untouchable."

The meaning of untouchability then is to be determined by reference to those who have traditionally been considered "Untouchables." But it is no easier to define precisely "Untouchables" than it is to define "untouchability." "Beyond the pale of the caste system" is an imprecise and unworkable formulation. Even the lowest castes are within the system of reciprocal rights and duties; their disabilities and prerogatives are articulated to those of other castes. Presumably the Mysore Court means by this phrase "outside" the four *varnas* of the classical law books. In reference to their customary rights, Untouchables have sometimes, particularly in southern India, been referred to as a fifth *varna*, below the *Sudras*.[132] But in other places they were regarded as *Sudras*.[133] For purposes of personal law, the courts have never attempted to distinguish Untouchables from *Sudras*; all Hindus other than the twice-born have been lumped together as *Sudras*.[134] Even where Untouchables are popularly regarded as *Sudras*, they cannot be equated with them since there are non-untouchable groups which belong to this category. Thus, the tests used for distinguishing *Sudras* from the twice-born for purposes of applying personal law, cannot be used as a satisfactory measure of untouchability. In attempting to identify untouchable groups for the purpose of giving them benefits and preferences the Government has not tried to apply general criteria, but has adopted the device of compiling lists of castes in each locality.[135]

"Untouchability," then, as used in Article 17, is confined to invidious discriminations against certain not readily definable classes of persons.[136] The Article refers to two overlapping classes of conduct: acts constituting the "practice [of 'untouchability'] in any form" and acts which are the "enforcement of any disability arising out of 'untouchability.' "[137] The first is apparently broader than, but not fully inclusive of, the latter. While all of the former are "forbidden," only the latter are declared an "offense punishable in accordance with law."

The "practice" of untouchability is not confined literally to avoidance of pollution by touch or to practices based on such avoidance.[138] It would seem to include any invidious treatment associated with the victim's membership or origin in an untouchable group, even if the treatment did not involve avoidance of pollution — for example, restrictions on the dress or ceremonial of Untouchables. It would seem to extend to such private social conduct as avoidance of commensality and observance of purification after contact.[139] Yet it is not clear that all of these would be included in the "enforcement of disabilities." The latter would seem to be confined to some narrower class of acts which involve more than mere denial of private social acceptance. The "practice" of untouchability "in any form" would also seem to include the kinds of indirect support of untouchability proscribed by the Untouchability (Offences) Act, 1955 — e.g., the use of sanctions against a caste-fellow to induce him to uphold untouchability, or the incitement of forms of discrimination which are not themselves offenses. Since this conduct would not directly involve any "Untouchables" it is not clear whether it would be considered the "enforcement of a disability arising out of untouchability."[140]

The enforcement of disabilities includes more than actual physical prevention of the use of facilities or compulsion of customary deference. The Untouchability (Offences) Act makes it an offense to molest, injure, annoy, obstruct or attempt to obstruct the exercise of any right accruing to a person by reason of Article 17.[141] Loud words by a worshipper frightening an untouchable boy out of a temple have been held to constitute an offense under an earlier Bombay Act.[142] Similarly, vulgar abuse and insult on the ground of untouchability has been held to constitute enforcement of a disability.[143] It is not clear whether it would be "enforcement" of a disability to persuade an Untouchable voluntarily to abide by an invidious usage.[144]

CONSTITUTIONAL CHALLENGES
TO ANTI-DISABILITIES LEGISLATION

Anti-disabilities statutes have survived challenges to their constitutional *vires*. An early challenge to a state act on grounds that it violated the freedom to carry on one's occupation or trade was rejected by the Calcutta High Court, along with contentions that the act was discriminatory (under Article 15) and denied equal protection (Article 14).[145] Since then, a number of challenges have been directed to the constitutionality of temple-entry provisions in the light of the guarantees of freedom to religious denominations in Article 26. However, the courts have uniformly decided such challenges in favor of the temple-entry power.[146] Article 26 provides that:

Subject to public order, morality and health, every religious denomination or any section thereof shall have the right . . .

(b) to manage its own affairs in matters of religion[.]

At first glance it may be difficult to see how such denominational autonomy can be reconciled with governmental power to provide for temple-entry. Denominational rights would seem to represent the outermost constitutional limit of the temple-entry power; the two could be reconciled by excluding denominational institutions from the "Hindu religious institutions of a public character" mentioned in Article 25(2)b.

However, the courts have been unwilling to impose such a limitation on the temple-entry power. *Sri Venkataramana Devaru v. State of Mysore*[147] involved a denominational temple, founded for the benefit of the Gowda Saraswat Brahman community. The general public were admitted on most occasions, although non-GSB's were excluded from some ceremonies. Under the Madras Temple-Entry Act,[148] which defined a temple as a "place which is dedicated to or for the benefit of the Hindu community or any section thereof as a place of public religious worship," the temple was a public one and subject to temple-entry laws. The trustees resisted the application of the Act on the ground that as a denominational temple they enjoyed freedom to manage their affairs in "matters of religion."

Is the exclusion of all or some other communities a "matter of religion"? The Supreme Court conceded that religion embraces not merely doctrine and belief but also "practices which are regarded by the community as part of its religion."[149] The Court allowed that under the Hindu law of ceremonial, "the persons entitled to enter into [temples] for worship and where they are entitled to stand and worship and how the worship is to be conducted are all matters of religion."[150] Thus the claims of the denomination here fall squarely within the ambit of Article 26(b).

The Court concedes that if the issue were to be decided on grounds of 26(b) alone, the application of the Act to denominational temples would be unconstitutional.

Does Article 25(2)b authorize the state to provide for temple-entry at denominational temples? The Court holds that the Article extends not only to those temples dedicated to the Hindu community as a whole and not merely those used by *all* "touchable" Hindus, but even to denominational institutions. For "public" institutions include those founded for only a section of the public and thus include denominational temples. Textual arguments that the temple-entry power is subordinate to the denominational rights are rejected on the ground that they ignore the true nature of the right conferred by Article 25(2)b.

That is a right conferred on 'all classes and sections of Hindus' to enter into a public temple, and on the unqualified terms of that Article, that right must be available, whether it is sought to be exercised against an individual under Article 25(1) or against a denomination under Article 26(b). [Although] Article 25(1) deals with the rights of individuals, Article 25(2) is much wider in its contents and has reference to the rights of communities, and controls both Article 25(1) and Article 26(b).[151]

Article 26(b) must then be read as subject to the temple-entry proviso. Thus the Court reconciles denominational rights with temple-entry power by what amounts to forthright judicial amendment. In order to preserve the temple-entry power from attrition by denominational rights, it treats the temple-entry provision as if it appeared in Article 26 as well as in Article 25.[152] It also reads the temple-entry provision as conferring rights on individuals instead of merely powers on the government. The Court repeatedly speaks of the "rights" conferred by Article 25(2)b. It is clear that if this proviso actually confers any rights, they are considerably broader than those enforced by the criminal sanctions of the UOA. They would be rights as extensive as the full ambit of the power which the proviso seems to authorize.[153]

But to read Article 25(2)b as conferring "rights" is somewhat paradoxical. Unlike Article 17, it does not speak in tones of prohibition. It does not seem to confer any rights on excluded groups, nor of itself to extinguish any existing exclusionary rights. On its face, it is merely an enabling provision, insuring that the guarantee of freedom of religion does not remove governmental power in this field. If the Supreme Court were taken literally, it would represent a major piece of judicial legislation. But what the Court presumably means is that the rights conferred by the state pursuant to this provision have constitutional status comparable to those granted in Part III itself. It is not necessary to infer that the section creates new rights of access in all classes and sections of Hindus, but only that the rights of entry given to particular classes by temple-entry legislation are rights of constitutional status and of such weight as to overcome the rights granted in Article 26(b).

Although the temple-entry rights have overriding force, the denominational rights may be exercised so long as they do not "substantially reduce the right conferred by Article 25(2)b."[154] The denomination may exercise its rights to exclude others and confine certain services to initiates so long as "what is left to the public of the right of worship is something substantial and not merely the husk of it."[155] The Supreme Court found that other occasions of worship were sufficiently numerous and substantial that temple-entry rights could be exercised compatibly with the denomination's right to exclude all non-GSB's during certain ceremonies.

The courts, then, have preserved anti-disabilities legislation against challenges of conflict with other fundamental rights. They have read the constitutional provisions in a manner that provides broad scope for legislative implementation of the constitutional commitment to abolish untouchability. However, as we shall see, the legislatures have been hesitant to employ the full ambit of this power.

THE CONSTITUTION AND THE CASTE GROUP: THE POSSIBLE LIMITS OF ANTI-DISABILITIES LEGISLATION

We noted earlier (Part I above) that during the British period, the chief legal support of untouchability was not through affirmative enforcement of disabilities, but through the broad area of immunity enjoyed by the self-help of higher castes in enforcing disabilities. This self-help might take the form of sanctions imposed on Untouchables directly, or of "secondary boycott" against third parties, or of disciplinary action against those within the caste group who defied the norms of untouchability. The Constitution of its own force makes illegitimate any affirmative legal enforcement of disabilities. In *Aramugha Konar* v. *Narayana Asari,* two communities claimed a customary right to use a public well to the exclusion of Asaris and Thevars of a village.[156] The purported reasonableness of a custom of exclusive use of public property, held the Madras Court "can straightaway be disposed of by reference to Art. 15 of the Constitution. . . ."[157] However, even after the passage of the Constitution, indirect enforcement of disabilities by boycott or excommunication was not per se illegal. The earlier anti-disabilities legislation passed by the states did not undertake to control this indirect enforcement of disabilities. The ordinary law still provided little protection for the anti-disabilities reformer. Abusing a reformist priest as a "chandal," and accusing him of associating with Untouchables and lacking a sense of purity was held not to be a criminal defamation, since it was merely admonition and abuse but not an imputation on his reputation.[158]

In spite of legislative[159] and judicial[160] expressions of a desire to minimize the impact of caste in public life, the doctrine of "caste autonomy," which before Independence gave caste groups a broad measure of immunity from judicial interference has remained in large measure unimpaired. Courts still refuse to entertain suits involving caste questions and castes retain their disciplinary powers over their members.[161] The caste group still retains its power of excommunication.[162] In spite of the changing social order, said the Madras High Court,

> where an individual has done something wrong or prejudicial to the interests of his community, the members of this community which, by virtue of custom or usage is competent to deal with such matters [can] take a decision by common consent; and so long as such a decision does not offend law, it can be enforced by the will of the community.[163]

It is still a good defense to a criminal action for defamation to assert the privilege of communicating news of an excommunication to one's caste fellows.[164] Indeed, the Supreme Court has held in *Saifuddin Saheb* v. *State of Bombay*[165] that the power to excommunicate for infractions of religious discipline is part of the constitutional right of a religious denomination to manage its own affairs in matters of religion.

The Untouchability (Offences) Act attempts, for the first time in any anti-disabilities legislation, to reach boycotts and caste disciplinary power. It provides that:

Whosoever

(i) denies to any person belonging to his community or any section thereof any right or privilege to which such person would be entitled as a member of such community or section, or

(ii) takes any part in the excommunication of such person, on the ground that such person has refused to practice "untouchability" or that such person has done any act in furtherance of the objects of this Act, shall be punishable with imprisonment which may extend to six months, or with fine which may extend to five hundred rupees, or with both.[166]

The constitutional protection afforded to excommunication in *Saifuddin's* case would not appear to reach the excommunication banned by the UOA. In *Saifuddin's* case, the Bombay Prevention of Excommunication Act, which made any excommunication a criminal offense, was held to violate the rights of a Muslim sect to manage their own affairs in matters of religion by excommunicating dissidents in order to preserve the essentials of their religion. This does not imply similar constitutional protection for the caste group as such. Even if a caste group could meet the first requirement and was recognized as a religious denomination (or section thereof) — and some have been —[167] it is unlikely that the enforcement of untouchability would be regarded as an essential part of its religion, within the protection of Article 26. In the *Venkataramana Devaru* case the Supreme Court held that the denomination's exclusion of outsiders from temple services was indeed a matter of religion.[168] But the recent decision in *Sastri Yagna Purushdasji* v. *M. B. Vaishya* indicates that the Supreme Court would not be likely to take that view today.[169] There, the Court suggested that a sect's apprehension about the pollution of their temple by Untouchables "is founded on superstition, ignorance and complete misunderstanding of the true teachings of the Hindu religion. . . ."[170]

But even if the Court did not take an activist stance in estimating the religious character of the practice,[171] and was willing to recognize the claim as a religious one, it is clear from the *Venkataramana Devaru* case that the religious rights would run subordinate to the rights conferred by the temple-entry power and by Article 17.[172] In *Saifuddin,* the Supreme Court refused to give such overriding force to the Bombay Prevention of Excommunication Act. The majority there refused to see the measure as one of social reform insofar as it invalidated excommunication on religious grounds. However, they conceded that the "barring of excommunication on grounds other than religious grounds, say, on the breach of some obnoxious social rule or practice might be a measure of social reform and a law which bars such excommunication merely might conceivably come within the saving provisions of . . . [Article 25 (2)b]."[173] By drawing a strict distinction between religious grounds and obnoxious social practices, the Court avoided the question of deciding which would prevail in case of conflict. But it seems clear from the *Venkataramana Devaru* case, that it is the anti-untouchability policy which would prevail. For the temple-entry power reaches even those practices considered essential to a sect.[174]

The case of excommunication for failure to uphold untouchability might, however, be distinguished from *Venkataramana Devaru* on the ground that the excommunicated party is, unlike the Untouchable in the *Devaru* case, not the beneficiary of the constitutional right: he is asserting no constitutional right of his own but is only vicariously asserting the Article 17 right of the Untouchable. However, the language of Article 17, which outlaws the practice of untouchability "in any form" seems broad enough to be read to confer directly on every person a right to be free from caste action against him for the purpose of enforcing untouchability.[175] The abolition of untouchability was presumably meant to liberate all Indians from this evil, not only Untouchables.

The boycott and excommunication provisions of the UOA are

little used. As we shall see (Part V), this reflects the limited effectiveness of the UOA when faced with the resistance of coherent social groups, whose own internal sanctions are both stronger and more certain of application than those threatened by the law. Would the Constitution permit some form of anti-disabilities regulation directed at the caste or village group as a whole, rather than at specific individuals?

In this respect autonomy of the caste group seems to be enhanced by the Constitution. One of the basic themes of the Constitution is to eliminate caste as a differentia in the relation of government to individuals — as subjects, voters or employees. The Constitution enshrines as fundamental law the notion that government must regulate individuals directly and not through the medium of the caste group. The individual is responsible for his own conduct and cannot, by virtue of his membership in a caste, be held accountable for the conduct of others. Thus the imposition of severe police restrictions on specified castes in certain villages on grounds of their proclivity to crime was struck down as being unconstitutional, since the regulation depended upon caste membership rather than individual propensity.[176] Similarly, in *State of Rajasthan* v. *Pratap Singh,* the Supreme Court struck down a punitive levy upon certain communities on the ground that it discriminated against the selected communities on grounds of caste and religion, in violation of Article 15.[177] The State had stationed additional police to 24 villages on grounds that they were harboring dacoits, receiving stolen property, etc. In assessing the villagers for costs, the State had exempted the Harijan and Muslim inhabitants on the ground that the great majority of members of these communities were not guilty of the conduct which necessitated the stationing of additional police. The Supreme Court said that:

even if it be that the bulk of the members of the communities exempted or even all of them were law-abiding, it was not contended that there were no peaceful and law-abiding persons in these 24 villages belonging to the other communities. . . .[178]

Thus the State discriminated unconstitutionally against the law-abiding members of the other communities and in favor of the Muslim and Harijan communities on the basis only of caste or religion.

It is not clear whether the *Pratap Singh* case would rule out any anti-disabilities measures which attempted to impose collective responsibility. It may be that collective penalties are unconstitutional per se, not only when they involve classifications forbidden by Article 15. On the other hand, if Article 15 is the obstacle, measures imposing collective responsibility along village lines might be constitutional.[179] Thus, several states have announced a policy of withholding grants from villages where Untouchables are not accorded equal rights.[180]

Again, anti-disabilities measures which attempted to utilize caste solidarity by imposing collective responsibility might be thought distinguishable from, e.g., dacoity, inasmuch as the commission of anti-disabilities offenses by their very nature involve assertions of caste solidarity. Such offenses are in many cases not the acts of isolated offenders, but the expression of patterns which are maintained by the active and passive support of one or more caste groups.[181] It is an open question whether the Article 15 rights of members of such groups would prevail against the rights under Article 17 to be free of such patterns of disabilities.[182]

IV. The Untouchability (Offences) Act in the Higher Courts

Having examined some aspects of the larger constitutional setting of anti-disabilities legislation, we shall now proceed to see how the Untouchability (Offences) Act has operated in practice. In this section we shall describe its reception in the appellate courts; in the next section we shall deal with it on the ground, as applied by the trial courts and police.

No case involving the UOA has reached the Supreme Court and, since few petty criminal appeals do, it is not likely that the Supreme Court will play a significant role in interpreting the UOA.[183] It seems fair to say that the UOA has not fared well in the High Courts, in contrast with the earlier state legislation, which generally received favorable interpretations from these courts. A very crude measure of the shift of judicial response is provided by Table 10.1, which compares the outcomes of High Court cases involving the UOA and the earlier state legislation.

Table 10.1

Disposition by High Courts of Appeals Concerning Temple-entry and Anti-disabilities Legislation

Legislation	Decision	
	In favor of Untouchables' rights	Against Untouchables' rights
State Acts	12	6
UOA	2	9

Note: This table includes all cases which could be found in the more prominent Indian law reports and in the local reports available to me, and two unreported judgments in my possession. Each case has been treated as a unit and scored as favoring the Untouchables' rights if the overall result is in their favor (i.e., conviction affirmed, act held applicable, relief granted) even where there are elements in the case that detract from the result, as, e.g., acquittal of some parties, reduction of fine, etc.

This unfavorable reception by the High Courts seems to involve three problem areas: the requirement that the forbidden act be committed "on the ground of untouchability"; the uncertainty about coverage of private property; and the limitation of rights to those enjoyed by members of the same religious denomination.

THE "GROUND OF 'UNTOUCHABILITY'" PROBLEM

The principal substantive sections of the UOA forbid the denial of facilities and services "on the ground of 'untouchability.'"[184] This requirement of specific intent makes it difficult to secure convictions, since states of mind are difficult to prove. The drafters of the UOA attempted to obviate this difficulty by reversing the onus of proof; the Act provides that where any of the forbidden practices "is committed in relation to a member of a Scheduled Caste . . . the court shall presume, unless the contrary is proved, that such act was committed on the ground of 'untouchability'."[185]

Even accompanied by this presumption, the "ground of untouchability" requirement restricts the operation of the UOA to instances in which the accused's act proceeds from or is accompanied by a specific mental state. However, as we have seen (IIIA above) the nature of this mental state is far from clear. Neither the Constitution nor the UOA defines untouchability; judges required to define it find it no easy matter. Government, the legislature and the courts all tend to define it denotatively — by pointing to well-known examples of its practice rather than connotatively by specifying boundary criteria. How then can the judge as trier of fact decide whether this complex and obscure notion of untouchability was a component of the mental state of the accused at the time of the purported offense? States of mind can only be inferred from observed behavior. And observed behavior may involve a complex admixture of motives: economic, religious, social and psychological. Making this imponderable mental state a part of the offense makes it difficult to deal with those patterns of discriminatory conduct whose incidence does not correspond precisely and directly with the touchable-untouchable distinction. For example, let us take the situations we may call "tokenism," "over-discrimination" and "intervening motives."

The potentialities for evading the UOA by "tokenism" are demonstrated, if not exemplified, in the case of *Kandra Sethi* v. *Metra Sahu*,[186] where a dhobi complained of exclusion from a village kirton. The defense was that dhobis as a class were not excluded, since the kirton had been attended by a dhobi (apparently the dhobi headman). The Court upheld the defense that the exclusion of the complainant was not, then, on the basis of his caste. The mere admission of one Untouchable was taken to defeat the "ground of untouchability" requirement. The Kerala High

Court was much more sensitive to the problem of tokenism when it took the contrary view in *Ramachandran Pillai* v. *State of Kerala*.[187] Where the headmaster of a girls' school constituted a separate division exclusively of Harijan students, the fact that there were some Harijan students in other classes did not overcome the illegality of this segregation, for each individual student had an equal right not to be singled out.

Another situation, the reverse of "tokenism," might be called "over-discrimination." Suppose a discrimination is aimed not only at Untouchables but also at other low castes? The Allahabad High Court reversed the conviction of a hotel proprietor who had put up a sign intimating that the hotel would serve only Brahmans, Thakurs, Vaishyas, Kayasths and Yadavanshis.[188] The Court held that since many other communities besides Harijans were not served, refusal to serve the latter was not on grounds of untouchability and therefore not an offense. The reversal of the burden of proof attempted by the UOA would not suffice to correct this anomalous result, for it is clear that the ground of discrimination here is broader than "untouchability" as defined by the courts. However, individuation (as suggested by the Kerala High Court) would at least enable the Court to focus on the case of the Untouchable complainant undistracted by the other exclusion.

A third problem with the "ground of untouchability" requirement is what we might call the problem of the "intervening motive." Suppose dhobis or restauranteurs who refuse service to Untouchables assign as their motive fear of loss of trade or of social standing? *State* v. *Banwari,* decided under the United Provinces Removal of Social Disabilities Act,[189] graphically and dramatically presents this problem:

On the passing of the Act the Chamars served notice on the barbers and dhobis of the village calling upon them to render services to them. When they did not agree, a Panchayat was called by the Chamars; it was attended by . . .[the dhobis]. In the Panchayat, the Chamars and other people assembled there asked the [dhobis] to render service to the Chamars. The Chamars brought bundles of clothes to be washed. At first the [dhobis] agreed to render service and even accepted the bundles of clothes for washing. Then they said that they would reconsider the matter and held consultation with one another at some distance from the Panchayat, returned and told everybody that they had decided not to render service to the Chamars and returned the bundles to them. They were pressed to reconsider that decision but they remained adamant and the Panchayat broke up.[190]

Appealing their conviction under the UP Act, the dhobis asserted that their refusal was not merely on the ground that the Chamars were Untouchables, but also that if they rendered service to these Chamars, they would lose the trade of other Hindus. The UP Court held that since this loss of custom would be the consequence of the fact that the Chamars were Scheduled Castes, the reason for refusal of service reduced to their untouchability and was forbidden.

The U.P. statute involved in *Banwari* did not contain "on the ground of 'untouchability' " language, but provided that no person should refuse to render services "to any person merely on the ground that he belongs to a Scheduled Caste. . . ." A less resolute court might easily have allowed the "merely" to elevate the loss of trade argument into a good defense. (The language of the UOA is stronger in this respect, since it omits the restricting "merely" or "only" found in some state statutes.)

Again, in *Ramachandran Pillai,* it was claimed that the segregation of Harijan students was on grounds of their intellectual deficiency and with the intention of providing them better coaching. Although finding that the evidence did not support this assertion, the judge there made clear that an admixture of other motives for discrimination would not excuse the act, since there was no requirement that untouchability be the "only" ground. Nor did he find any requirement of *mens rea.* The fact that untouchability was one of the grounds of discrimination was sufficient to establish a finding of guilty.

The "ground of 'untouchability' " requirement, then, does not prevent convictions under the Act, but it acts as a slope, inclining toward a restrictive interpretation of the Act. Judicial attentiveness, resoluteness, sympathy and inventiveness are required to isolate this imponderable state of mind and resist the pull toward restrictive interpretation. Resistance of the kind displayed in *Banwari* and *Ramachandran Pillai* may sometimes be forthcoming, but a statute is not likely to be effective where it is dependent on extraordinary exertions of judicial energy to carry out its policy.

THE PRIVATE PROPERTY PROBLEM

A second weakness in the UOA is the equivocation in its coverage of facilities which are used by the "public" but are not, technically, public. In *Benudhar Sahu* v. *State,* two Pano boys were prevented from drawing water from a privately owned well used by most villagers.[191] The High Court reversed the conviction of the owner of the well on the ground that the boys had no right to use the well. The Court was unwilling to measure their access to the well by the access of other villagers, but insisted that it be shown they had a right to use the well.

Merely because he was permitting other people to draw water from his well, it cannot be said that every villager had a right [to use] . . . the well. The prosecution must affirmatively establish that the public had a right [to use] the well in question before the offence . . . is established.[192]

It is not clear here that this conclusion is required by § 4 (iv) of the UOA, which provides:

Whoever on the ground of "untouchability" enforces against any person any disability with regard to

(iv) the use of, or access to, any river, stream, spring, well . . . which other members of the public have a right to use or have access to. . . .

It seems equally plausible that only a showing of public "access" is needed, not a showing of "a right to use" in the public. In any event, this seems to leave the Untouchable with a remedy only against exclusion from places used by the public as of right. Since there is no exact correspondence between facilities ordinarily used for public life in villages and those which the public has an enforceable right to enter, Untouchables are left with restricted rights.[193]

The court below had convicted the well-owner for violation of § 7 of the UOA which makes it an offense to prevent or obstruct "any person from exercising any right accruing to him by reason of the abolition of 'untouchability' under Article 17 of the Constitution." The High Court found there was no offense since "no right accrued to the Pano boys to use the well . . . merely by reason of the abolition of 'untouchability' under Article 17 of the Constitution."[194] However, since Article 17 establishes a right not to be the subject of untouchability "in any form," it might be argued that it includes disabilities respecting use of privately owned property which is part of the "public" life of the village. There is no limitation in Article 17 which restricts its operation to property that the public has a "right" to use.[195]

A similar situation is found in *State of M. P.* v. *Tikaram,* where a villager organized a recitation of the *Ramayana* in an open space (of unspecified ownership) and invited the public to come and make offerings over the book.[196] Untouchables were refused permission to make offerings admittedly on the grounds of untouchability. The High Court held that this was not a violation of the UOA since this was not a "place of public worship." Again, the UOA failed to secure to Untouchables the same rights of everyday use that were enjoyed by the public in general.

THE "SAME DENOMINATION" PROBLEM

Crucial sections of the UOA provide that an Untouchable can enter and use premises open to other persons "professing the same religion or belonging to the same religious denomination or any section thereof." Section 3 of the UOA provides that:

Whoever on the ground of "untouchability" prevents any person:

(i) from entering any place of public worship which is open to other persons professing the same religion or belonging to the same religious denomination or any section thereof, as such person; or

(ii) from worshipping or offering prayers or performing any religious service in any place of public worship, or bathing in, or using the waters of any sacred tank, well, spring or water course, in the same manner and to the same extent as is permissible to other persons professing the same religion or belonging to the same religious denomination or any section thereof, as such person;

shall be punishable with imprisonment which may extend to six months, or with fine which may extend to five hundred rupees or with both.

The scope of the rights conferred by this provision (and other crucial sections of the Act) depends on the meaning of the qualifying phrases, "the same religion or the same religious denomination or section thereof." The lawmakers, presumably for the purpose of clarifying these terms, added an explanation that:

persons professing the Buddhist, Sikh, or Jaina religion or persons professing the Hindu religion in any of its forms or developments including Virashaivas, Lingayats, Adivasis, followers of Brahmo, Prarthara, Arya Samaj and the Swaminarayan Sampradaya shall be deemed to be Hindus.

In spite of this explanation, the courts have resisted the implication that temple-entry provisions obviate denominational and sectarian distinctions. In *State* v. *Puranchand*[197] it was held that denial to Untouchables of entry to Jain temples is not a violation of Section 3 of the UOA, since those excluded are not of the "same religion" as those admitted. The UOA, according to the Court, does not abolish the distinction between Hindus and Jains, nor does it create any new right — either in Untouchables or in caste Hindus — to enter Jain temples. It only puts the rights of Untouchables on a parity with the right of "others of the same religion"; i.e., Untouchables have the same rights to enter a Jain temple that were previously enjoyed by caste Hindus. If the temple was not open to the latter before, it is no offense to exclude Untouchables from it now. Jain Untouchables, if there are any, would of course now have the right to enter Jain temples since the latter are open to persons of the "same religion."

This interpretation of the temple-entry provisions is supported by the absence in the UOA of any evidence of intent to confer any new rights on non-Untouchables. The Act penalizes exclusion only "on grounds of untouchability," not on grounds of caste or sectarian exclusiveness. It would be, as the High Court points out, anomolous if Untouchables were given rights of entry more extensive than those enjoyed by their high-caste co-religionists.

What, then, was the purpose and effect of including this expansive definition of Hinduism in the UOA? One of the judges in the *Puranchand* case attributes its presence to a desire to "bring the Act in line" with the Explanation appended to Article 25(2)b and to preserve the distinctions between places of public worship belonging to different religions.[198] Since the power saved to the State by Art. 25(2)b is clearly confined to Hindus and Hindu institutions, the desire to provide against narrow construction of this power is readily understandable. But this does not account for the Explanation found in the UOA.

According to the High Court in the *Puranchand* case, the sum effect of the Explanation is twofold: first, to insure that the exclusion of their respective co-religionists is forbidden among Jains, Sikhs, Buddhists and sectarians as well as among Hindus in the narrower sense; second, to extend to Hindu Untouchables whatever rights caste Hindus might enjoy regarding entrance and worship at Jain, Buddhist, Sikh and sectarian shrines. But both of these objectives are accomplished by the wording of Section 3 itself; the Explanation, as interpreted, is not required for either purpose. For, first, the Act is not on its face limited to Hindus in either the narrow or broad sense.[199] Its language would seem to cover exclusion on grounds of untouchability even when practiced by those beyond the widest possible definition of Hinduism.[200] And secondly, parity of rights in sectarian temples is accomplished without the Explanation, for the rights of entry are measured not by the sectarian character of the premises, but by the affiliation of those who use it.[201]

It appears, then, that the Court has read the Explanation right out of the UOA. But the result would not be much different if it were taken in its most direct and plausible meaning — as lumping all of the named groups into the "same religion." For the "same religion" qualification is followed by the further requirement that the excluded persons belong to the "same religious denomination or section thereof" as those admitted. Even if all of the different faiths and sects mentioned in the Explanation are deemed to be the "same religion" they would still remain distinct denominations or sections within it.[202] And these denominational lines would set the boundary of the rights conferred by the UOA.[203]

In *State of Kerala* v. *Venkiteswara Prabhu*,[204] Untouchables were prevented from entering the Nalambalam of a temple belonging to the Gowda Saraswat Brahman community. Finding no evidence that persons other than members of this community ordinarily entered this part of the temple, the High Court held that exclusion of Untouchables from it was not a violation of Section 3, since those refused entrance did not belong to the same "denomination or section thereof." While enlarging the rights of Untouchables to a parity with other caste Hindus, the UOA did not increase the rights of the latter. Since members of other communities enjoyed no right of entry to this part of the temple, no such right was conferred on Untouchables.

The acceptance by the courts of denominational lines within Hinduism as limiting the operation of temple-entry provisions may produce some unanticipated results.[205] For the "religion" and "denomination" qualifiers also appear in other provisions of the UOA relating to: use of utensils and other articles kept in restaurants, hotels, etc.; use of wells, water sources, bathing ghats, cremation grounds; the use of "places used for a public or charitable purpose"; the enjoyment of benefits of a charitable trust; and the use of dharmasalas, sarais and musafirkhanas.[206] Given the reading of "religion" and "denomination" generated by judicial solicitude for sectarian prerogatives, the rights granted by some of the central and crucial provisions of the UOA seem to be seriously limited.

There is thus a wide gap between the extent of the power conferred by Article 25(2)b, as interpreted by the Supreme Court in the *Venkataramana Devaru* case and the exercise of this power in the UOA, as interpreted by the High Courts. The UOA, as interpreted, uses only part of the power conferred by the Constitution, for it recognizes denominational and sectarian differences as limiting the extent of rights of entry. But the Constitution empowers the state to confer cross-denominational rights to enter and use premises not only of the same religion or denomination, but *any* Hindu institution.

Aware of the denominational limitations of the UOA and also troubled by the anomalous situation that while it is an offense to exclude Untouchables from temples, classes of touchable Hindus could be excluded with impunity, several states have enacted supplementary legislation.[207] A Bombay Act makes it an offense to prevent "Hindus of any class or sect from entering or worshipping at a temple to the same extent and in the same manner as any other class or section of Hindus."[208] An Uttar Pradesh Act, inspired by judicial barriers to entry of Harijans at the Vishwanath temple in Benares, declares the rights of all sections of Hindus to offer worship at any Hindu temple.[209] These laws apparently utilize the full ambit of the constitutional power regarding temples.[210] They extend protection to non-Untouchables and they overcome the sectarian and denominational limitations which the courts read into the UOA. Although the states are limited in their power to legislate directly on untouchability,[211] this legislation will substantially broaden the rights of Untouchables as well. For the rights of the latter under the UOA are automatically

elevated to a parity with the new rights which the state legislation confers
on caste-Hindus.

*   *   *   *

These problems in the Act are by no means insurmountable. As we
have seen, the UOA demands constant inputs of judicial energy, sympathy,
and inventiveness to resist the pull toward a weak, restrictive interpretation. It may be expected that, as the Act becomes older and the consciousness of the evils that inspired it becomes less vivid, this pull will
be even stronger. The Act will be used less often (see V below), techniques of evasion will become more sophisticated; defense lawyers, with
more experience of its provisions, will become more plausible. The more
acquittals, the less the Act will be used; and the less it is used, the more
difficult it will be for judges to make the extraordinary exertions required
to carry out its original policy of abolishing untouchability "in any form."

V. The Effectiveness of Anti-Disabilities Legislation

We have discussed the way in which the UOA and kindred measures
have been interpreted and applied by the higher courts. However, in order
to estimate the effectiveness of this legislation in implementing the national
policy of abolishing disabilities, we must examine working of this legislation on the ground. What kind of impact does it have on the officials
who are to administer it and on the ultimate "consumers" who are supposed to be regulated by it? Does this legislation clearly enunciate public
policy regarding the practice of untouchability? Does it promote new
patterns of behavior? Does it deter offenses? When offenses occur, does
it provide an efficacious remedy for the aggrieved Untouchables?

Assessment of the impact of anti-disabilities legislation is rendered
exceedingly difficult by the absence of any reliable measure of recent
changes in the condition of the Untouchables. Some notable advances
are evident. Untouchables have succeeded in participating in public life
to an extent unimaginable a few decades ago. Increasing numbers of
Untouchables have succeeded in securing employment in the higher
reaches of government and in attaining political office. There has been
a marked increase in the number of Untouchables receiving education
at all levels. But the vast majority of Untouchables remain poor, rural,
landless, uneducated, indebted and dependent.[212]

There is reason to believe that there has been some decline in the
level of disabilities suffered by Untouchables. In cities, anonymity, indifference and changing attitudes have freed many from public exhibition of

disabilities. Even in rural areas, there has been, with wide local variation, a general softening in the rigor of disabilities. However, resistance to change is very great, though it is often indirect and is rarely articulated publicly.[213] Although the decline in disabilities varies from locality to locality and from one aspect of untouchability to another, a few generalizations may be tendered on the basis of scattered reports. Disabilities have, it seems, declined more in urban than in rural areas; they have declined more in public and occupational life than in social and family matters; they have declined more among the educated than among the uneducated; more among men than among women. The highest castes are, it seems, generally more accepting of change than the middle groups.[214] The higher groups among the Untouchables are the greatest beneficiaries of these changes; their disabilities have declined more than those of the lower groups, especially the sweepers.[215]

Official reports almost invariably overstate the progress that has been made. That the continued existence of disabilities should be understated should be of no surprise in view of the timidity of Untouchables in calling attention to them, the unwillingness of caste Hindus to admit their presence, and the reluctance of officials to discover them.[216] Occasionally a note of frankness obtrudes, as when the Chief Secretary of Uttar Pradesh wrote to all magistrates in 1959 that there had been:

no appreciable improvement in the treatment given by members of the so-called higher castes to the persons belonging to the Scheduled Castes. The practice of untouchability continues unabated. . . . The provisions of the Untouchability (Offences) Act are being disregarded on a large scale.[217]

From a variety of sources, we may conclude that most Untouchables continue to suffer under disabilities which are both onerous in themselves and which severely restrict their life chances.[218] The public disabilities most often reported are exclusion from restaurants and hotels (and restrictions on the use of utensils), restrictions on the use of wells and other water sources, denial of services by barbers, *dhobis,* etc. and, in rural areas, denial of equality in seating arrangements, and exclusion from accommodation.[219] Exclusion from schools and government offices is rarely reported of late and entry into Hindu temples is common, although restrictions within temples are not unusual. All of this exists against a background of widespread harassment of those who assert their right to equality and a pervasive discrimination which bars even the more fortunate urban and educated Untouchables from full social acceptance and full participation in society.[220]

Many concurrent influences have had a share in producing the changes that are taking place. The far-reaching commitment of the Indian government to elevation of the Untouchables includes not only anti-disabilities legislation but also a variety of other policies and programs. The other programs may be divided roughly into three types which we may label redistribution, uplift, and symbolic inducements.[221]

Redistributive programs include all those arrangements aimed at securing to Untouchables a larger share of tangible resources and opportunities — political, occupational, educational, etc. Along with tribals, Untouchables are the only group which are guaranteed representation in legislative bodies; a share of government jobs is reserved for them; scholarships and other educational advantages and a variety of other welfare schemes are provided for them. All of these efforts are directed at improving the conditions of Untouchables themselves.

Second, there are efforts, declining in recent years, to increase the Untouchables' cultural achievements and moral status in Indian society by inducing them to give up drink and drugs and "unclean" or polluting practices. Government has especially attempted to reduce the pollution of castes engaged in work as sweepers and scavengers by introduction of equipment that will reduce contact with the offending substances.

Both of these types of program aim at changing the conditions of Untouchables directly. A third type is aimed at bringing about a change in the behavior of others toward them, so that they cease to impose disabilities and admit Untouchables to the benefits of community life. Directly and through the medium of private agencies which it subsidizes, Government has engaged in a wide array of activities intended to persuade people to change their attitudes toward untouchability. Harijan Days and Weeks are sponsored by state governments, often celebrated by inter-caste dining, entertainments, and speeches by politicians denouncing untouchability. The end of untouchability is proclaimed by the traditional method of drumbeat through the village. Fairs, exhibitions, lecturers, posters, films and broadcasts, school textbooks, meetings and conferences are utilized to carry the message of equality. Intercaste dinners are sponsored and the mixing of castes in hostels, meetings, and fairs is subsidized. Some states have even required that Untouchables must be employed to prepare and serve meals in every canteen, tea shop, and hotel maintained by the government. Some governments provide monetary rewards for intercaste marriages. Prizes are awarded to villages which succeed in ending disabilities. Some states attempt to put pressure on local bodies by announcing that grants will be withdrawn from villages where Untouchables are not allowed equal rights. It is in the setting of these government policies that the working of anti-disabilities legislation must be examined.

THE INCIDENCE OF ANTI-DISABILITIES LITIGATION

The official reports do not usually record the subject matter of anti-disabilities cases. However, there are some scattered breakdowns by subject matter which give us a rough indication of the kinds of situations in which these acts are invoked.

Table 10.2

Subject-matter of Cases Registered Under Anti-disabilities Acts in Ten States During 1953.

Subject-matter	Number of cases	Percentage
Shops, restaurants, hotels, places of public entertainment	232	64.1
Wells, tanks, bathing ghats	50	13.8
Temples, other religious places	22	6.1
Sumptuary regulations (refusal to allow use of ornaments, eating of ghee, etc.)	9	2.5
Public conveyances, horseriding	8	2.2
Public roads and resorts	4	1.1
Other	37	10.2
TOTAL	362	100.0

Source: **Report of the Commissioner for Scheduled Castes and Scheduled Tribes, 1953: 244—45.**

Table 10.2 suggests that the preponderance of cases are directed against restaurants, tea shops, hotels and similar places. Smaller but appreciable groups of cases concern wells (and other water sources) and temples; only a scattering are directed at other forms of disabilities. The general distribution suggested here is confirmed by other reports.[222] It appears, then, that the Act has been used mostly to deal with exclusion from commercial establishments and less with invidious treatment in looser settings. It appears that exclusion from such prominent and delimited establishments lends itself more readily to bringing of cases, since these establishments can be more readily exposed to the social workers or other outsiders who are, as we shall see, often involved in the invocation of the Act. Also, these opponents may be less likely than fellow villagers to have at their disposal formidable counter-sanctions.

Although reports are far from complete, it is possible to make an informed estimate as to the prevalence of cases under the UOA and the predecessor state acts, which covered most of India by 1949. In the early 1950s there were probably more than four hundred cases registered each year under these state acts.[223] A tabulation of the available information

Table 10.3

Cases Registered Under State Anti-Disabilities Acts* 1952–55

Year	Source (RCSCST)	Andhra	Bihar	Bombay	Coorg	Hyderabad	Kutch	Madhya Bharat	Madhya Pradesh	Madras	Mysore	Orissa	Punjab	Saurashtra	Travencore-Cochin	United Provinces	West Bengal	All-India
1952	1952: 28	1	N.I.	35	0	N.I.	1	73	28	174	N.I.	N.I.	6	8	3	2	0	330
1953	1953: 243		10	60	1	5	3	67	29	161	N.I.	N.I.	N.I.	N.I.	25	N.I.	1	362
1954	1954: 101		76	N.I.	1	N.I.	N.I.	N.I.	7	N.I.	N.I.	N.I.	1	N.I.	N.I.	N.I.	N.I.	89
(5 mos. only) 1955	1955: II, 15	N.I.	N.I.	17	N.I.	N.I.	N.I.	26	11	78	8	4	N.I.	9	2	19	N.I.	174
Projected Annual Average		1	43	45.3	0.7	5	2	67.5	22.6	173.7	19.2	9.6	3.5	14.8	8.2	23.8	.7	440.6

*Totals comprise cases under Temple Entry acts as well as civil disabilities acts.

EXPLANATION: Wherever different figures appear in successive reports, the later figures have been used. All-India totals may be higher than the sum of the state totals due to the inclusion of Union Territories in the former.

N.I. = No information

Table 10.4

UOA Cases Registered 1955–1964

Year	Source (RCSCST)	Andhra Pradesh	Assam	Bihar	Bombay	Jammu & Kashmir	Kerala	Madhya Pradesh	Madras	Mysore	Orissa	Punjab	Rajasthan	Uttar Pradesh	West Bengal	All-India**
†1955 (7 mos.)	1955: II, 16	N.I.	N.I.	N.I.	168+* (1955–56)	N.I.	N.I.	N.I.	N.I.	11+	2+	2+	N.I.	30	N.I.	N.I.
1956	1957-58: II, 29	N.I.	N.I.	11	(incl. above)	0	23	227	N.I.	69	32	13	106	N.I.	5	693
1957	1958-59: II, 102	12	0	10	68	N.I.	33	162	N.I.	36	23	10	104	20	9	492
1958	Do.	1	0	5	133	N.I.	95	158	N.I.	46	10	8	70	16	8	550
1959	1960-61: II, 8	12	0	2	N.I.	1	40	139	68	99	20	8	59	23	2	481
1960	1961-62: I, 7	17	0	8	73 / 45 (Guj Mh.)	1	17	N.I.	47	N.I.	N.I.	N.I.	58	13	3	502
1961	1963-64: II, 2	10	0	N.I.	87 / 27	4	22	74	58	88	20	1	69	10	3	489
1962	Do.	4	0	N.I.	69 / 17	2	33	56	52	58	12	6	60	9	3	389
1963	1964-65: 85	3	0	N.I.	72 / 35	2	6	31	86	56	N.I.	4	59	35	3	393
1964	Do.	4	N.I.	0	63 / 8 (incl)	N.I.	12	N.I.	190	31	N.I.	8	53	N.I.	1	371
Projected Annual Average		7.6	0	6.2	53.5 / 31.0	2.0	31.2	105.9	83.5	60.4	19.5	7.2	71.1	18.0	4.2	501.3+ Union Territories

* = 18 months only

** All-India totals are slightly higher than totals of horizontal columns due to inclusion of a few cases from Delhi and Union territories. Challaned cases have run 86% of registered.

† 1955 figures are understated, since they are figures challaned rather than registered.

about the number of cases registered is presented in Table 10.3. From these figures, we may project an average annual total of about 440 cases registered from 1952–55.[224] The data from Bombay from 1947–50 (See Table 10.4) suggests that the number of cases before 1952 may have been larger than during 1952–55, a supposition reinforced by the decline observed later under the UOA.

The Untouchability (Offences) Act came into force on June 1, 1955. It made more things punishable; it made all offenses cognizable; it extended throughout India. It provided heavier penalties and contained a presumption designed to make proof easier. It was accompanied by a great deal of publicity. One would then expect that there would be more enforcement activity on the basis of this stronger and more extensive statute. This was anticipated both by its proponents and by critics who considered it too far-reaching and harsh. The available data on prosecutions under the UOA is tabulated in Table 10.4.

During the first few years that the UOA was in force, there was a slight increase in the number of prosecutions registered, but this tapered off in the early 1960s. By a rough projection from the data available, we arrive at an average of approximately 520 cases a year during 1956–64.[225] This is probably a slight overstatement, since it does not take into account the decline in recent years. But for the moment we may take this figure as representing roughly the level of use of the Act. Most of the "increase" in reported cases over the period 1952–55 is accounted for by the inclusion of Rajasthan, which had no earlier state act. Population increases more than offset the remainder of the increase. So we may conclude that, contrary to expectations, the UOA does not have a significantly higher level of use than did the predecessor state acts. In those areas covered by the state acts, there were more anti-disabilities prosecutions in the early 1950s than in the early 1960s.

If we break up this overall rate and consider the rate of use for each state, the trends become somewhat more clear. Setting aside Assam, in which there has been no use of the UOA, we find that the average number of cases registered annually ranges from 2.0 in Jammu and Kashmir and 4.25 in West Bengal to 72.8 in Gujarat and 105.87 in Madhya Pradesh. To provide a clearer notion of the extent to which Untouchables avail themselves of the Act, we can adjust these totals according to the size of the Scheduled Caste population in each state.[226] We can then restate the rate of use of the UOA in terms of cases registered annually per million Scheduled Caste population. The discrepancies in the use of the Act from state to state emerge even more dramatically. The rate (excluding Assam again) varies from 0.6 cases per million in West Bengal and 0.9 per million in Bihar to 28.5 per million in Madhya Pradesh and 53.5 per million in Gujarat — a difference of nearly ninety times.[227] These state rates are set out in Table 10.5.

Table 10.5

Rates of Use of UOA by States 1956–1964

State	UOA Years Reporting	Total Cases Registered	Avg. No. of cases Registered per year	Millions of Scheduled Castes, 1961	Cases per year per million Scheduled Castes
Andhra Pradesh	8	61	7.62	4.97	1.5
Assam	6	0	0	0.73	0
Bihar	6	37	6.15	6.53	0.9
Gujarat	5	364	72.80	1.36	53.5
Jammu & Kashmir	5	10	2.0	.26	7.7
Kerala	9	281	31.22	1.42	22.0
Madhya Pradesh	7	847	121.0	4.25	28.5
Madras	6	501	83.50	6.07	13.8
Maharashtra	4	124	31.0	2.22*	13.9
Mysore	8	483	60.37	3.11	19.4
Orissa	6	117	19.5	2.76	7.0
Punjab	8	58	7.25	4.13	1.8
Rajasthan	9	638	70.7	3.35	21.1
Uttar Pradesh	7	126	18.0	15.41	1.2
West Bengal	9	37	4.16	6.95	0.6

* = Buddhists not included.

Source: Derived from information in reports of Commissioner for Scheduled Castes and Scheduled Tribes at sources cited in Table 10.4.

If we were to arrange the results of Table 10.5 on a map, we could transect India by a line running roughly from northwest to southeast — north of Rajasthan, around Madhya Pradesh and Mysore, and north of Madras. Below the line lie the states with "high use" of the UOA; above the line are the "low use" states. The "high use" states below the line (Rajasthan, Gujarat, Maharashtra, Madhya Pradesh, Mysore, Madras and Kerala) together contain only about 40 percent of the Scheduled Castes population, but they account for about 80 percent of the cases registered under the UOA. The Scheduled Castes in these "high use" states invoke the UOA more than eight times as frequently (on a population basis) as do those northwest of the line in the "low use" states.

On the basis of available data, it is not possible to suggest a single explanation for the high and low groupings. It would seem that several factors are at work, with different intensities in different states. The general

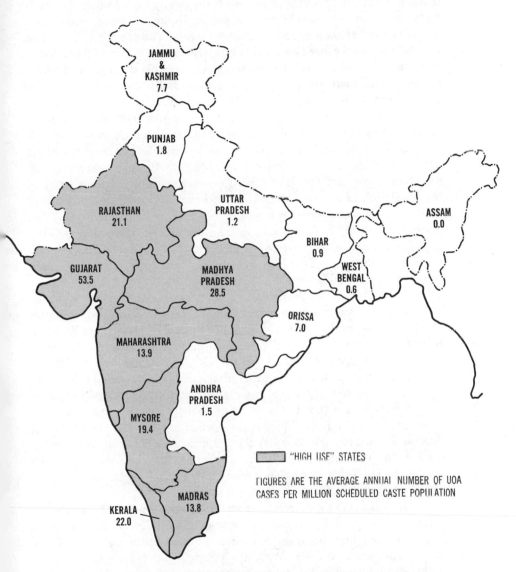

Fig. 10.1 Untouchability (Offences) Act: Average Annual Number of Cases
Per Million Scheduled Caste Population

division seems to correlate closely with the degree to which caste dominance has been expressed in terms of public display of distance and touch avoidance rather than in more economic terms. Thus in the 1930s when lists of Scheduled Castes were being established, it was found that criteria of avoidance and exclusion from temples served to distinguish the Untouchables in southern, western, and central India, but not in northern and eastern India.[228] It is roughly in those areas where Untouchables were readily identified by these pollution criteria that the Act is used.[229] However this does not account for all of the variation. Another factor is the prevalence of activities by uplift organizations who have social workers helping to bring cases[230] (Gujarat and Madhya Pradesh). Some of the variation seems attributable to other factors. For example, the novelty of the legislation in an area which did not have any prior state legislation and where the initial impetus is still in the course of running down (e.g., Rajasthan). Another factor may well be the degree of literacy, political organization and other resources at the disposal of Untouchables (Kerala). Neither of the states in which Scheduled Caste politicians have been prominent in the ruling party is a "high use" state (Andhra Pradesh, Bihar).

The decline in anti-disabilities prosecutions which can be seen in the overall figures emerges even more clearly upon inspection in the course of affairs in any of the states with sizable numbers of cases (e.g., Bombay, Rajasthan, Madhya Pradesh). It is sometimes claimed that the decline in prosecutions reflects the success of the UOA in eradicating disabilities, a claim labelled "fantastic" by the Commissioner of Scheduled Castes and Scheduled Tribes.[231] If there is any merit at all to the "success" explanation it is only a partial explanation of the decline. By itself, such an explanation would have difficulty in accounting for the course of the decline. For example, in Bombay there appear to have been two separate declines in prosecutions, one under the earlier state acts and one under the UOA (see Table 10.6). Nor could the "success" explanation account for the dramatic increase in cases in Madras in 1964.

The "success" hypothesis rests on the assumption that the number of cases is directly related to the quantum of disabilities. This assumption is improbable, first, because such a minute fraction of instances of disabilities eventuate in cases. Whatever progress has been made in eliminating disabilities, there is no doubt that there are more offenses against the UOA in a good-sized village in a week than there are UOA prosecutions in all of India in an entire year. Second, the nature of the UOA makes it unlikely that the relationship would be direct. Because of its level of penalties, the UOA is addressed only to what we might call the middle

Table 10.6

Anti-Disabilities Cases Challaned in Old Bombay
(and its Successor States)

		PROSECUTIONS		
Period	Source	State Anti-Disabilities Act	State Temple Entry Act	Total
1947–48	a	262	3	265
1948–49	a	161	31	192
1949–50	a	85	6	91
1951		N.I.	N.I.	N.I.
1952	b	N.I.	N.I.	35
1953	c	N.I.	N.I.	47
1954		N.I.	N.I.	N.I.
1955 (5 mos.)	d	N.I.	N.I.	17
		UOA	Temple Entry Authorization Act, 1956	
1955–56 (18 mos.)	e	148		148 (18 mos.)
1957 (incomplete)	f	68	3[x]	Incomplete
1958 (2 districts missing)	f	132	5[y]	139
1959		N.I.	N.I.	N.I.
		MH. Guj.	MH. Guj.	
1960	g	35 66	N.I. 0*	111
1961	h	27 82	N.I. N.I.	109
1962	h	17 65	N.I. N.I.	82
1963	h	18 54	N.I. N.I.	72
1964	i	8 (incom) 54	N.I. N.I.	Incomplete

Sources: a = Publications Division, 1952; **Harijans Today**: 35
      b = RCSCST 1952: 28
      c = RCSCSI 1953: 243
      d = RCSCST 1955: II; 15
      e = RCSCST 1956–57: I, 33, II, 30
      f = RCSCST 1958–59: II, 102
      g = RCSCST 1960–61: II, 8
      h = RCSCST 1963–64: II, 2
      i = RCSCST 1964–65: 185

      x = RCSCST 1957–58: I, 13
      y = RCSCST 1958–59: I, 31

* 2 districts missing

range of imposition of disabilities, between the subtle and covert on the one hand and the violent and repressive on the other. The latter impinge on the legal system in the major crime categories, if at all. Thus the most serious cases having to do with the imposition of disabilities come up in other forms than UOA cases, e.g., in prosecutions for rioting, assault, arson or murder that may ensue when new rights are exercised by Untouchables.[232] The UOA is, in effect, aimed at a low level of resistance and use of the UOA may be taken as an indication that resistance is relatively mild. A rise in UOA cases may reflect not an increase in disabilities but a decrease in the severity of repression. Conversely a decline in UOA cases might indicate not the disappearance of disabilities, but that resistance to the assertion of Untouchables' rights is either more subtle or more violent. Third, since the bringing of cases requires an expenditure of resources on the part of an Untouchable complainant and of the police, variations in the number of cases may involve changes in available resources or in judgments about their best use.

An alternative to the "success" hypothesis might be called the "initial impetus" explanation of the decline. In this view, the factors which induced the bringing of cases during the early years of the statute's life have waned with time. The state anti-disabilities acts and later the UOA were passed with a great deal of attendant publicity and public excitement. In the initial years there was a backlog of ready complainants and vulnerable targets. News of the Act might be expected to hearten potential complainants and impress them with a sense of the possibility of change. Police would be responsive to the exhortations of their superiors who urged them to enforce the Act vigorously. In the initial impetus view, public excitement faded, the backlog got used up, potential complainants were uninspired by the results of prosecutions, and new contenders would have stronger call on police efforts. This explanation leads to further questions. For an upward spiral of increasing use can be imagined as readily as a downward spiral of decreasing use. Why should the level of police activity fall off rather than become routinized as police gain experience in successful prosecution under the Act? Why has the experience of early complainants not induced others to follow in their course by emboldening new groups of Untouchables and orienting them toward change? What evidence (besides the decline in the number of cases) makes the downward spiral more plausible?

THE DISPOSITION OF CASES

During the period when the state anti-disabilities acts were in force, about 80 percent of all the cases registered were challaned by the police. Fully half of those challaned ended in conviction. There were few compounded cases and even fewer acquittals (see Table 10.7). During the first eight years of the UOA, the percentage of registered cases challaned by the police rose slightly (to about 86 percent).[233] But there has been a drastic shift in the pattern of dispositions. The percentage of cases ending in conviction has dropped steadily: from 70.8 percent in 1952–55 (under the state Acts) to 42.8 percent during the first three and a half years of the UOA's operation, to a mere 31.1 percent during the next four years.[234] The number of cases compounded increased with the coming of the UOA and has grown slightly since.[235] The percentage of cases ending in acquittal has grown steadily larger.

Table 10.7

Disposition of Cases under State
Anti-Disabilities Acts and UOA

Legislation	Time	Total Disposals	Disposition		
			Convicted	Compounded	Acquitted
State Acts (41 mos.)	Jan. 1952– May 1955	508	360 (70.9%)	58 (11.4%)	90 (17.7%)
U.O.A. (55 mos.)	June 1955– Dec. 1959	1,281	548 (42.8%)	427 (33.3%)	306 (23.9%)
U.O.A. (48 mos.)	1960– 1963	1,124	350 (31.1%)	421 (37.5%)	353 (31.4%)

SOURCES: Derived from information found in Reports for Commissioner for Scheduled Castes and Scheduled Tribes at Sources cited in Tables 10.3 and 10.4.

Thus, in the early 1950s the conviction rate in anti-disabilities cases was close to the average rate of convictions for all criminal trials in India.[236] But by the early 1960s the convictions in anti-disabilities cases fell to less than half of the former rate. In part this decrease represents an increase in the number of cases compounded. But we may view this as a sharp decline in the number of cases in which the outcome is successful for the Untouchable complainant.[237]

Figures for 1964, the last year for which data are available, seem to belie this downward trend of convictions. Figures for the ten states reporting show a conviction rate of 60.4 percent of the cases disposed of. However, on closer inspection we may see that for the first time more than half of all cases reported as registered during the year were in a single state, Madras. If we separate the Madras figures from the all-India figures, we see that the long-term trend is accentuated outside Madras. But in Madras we see a dramatic reversal.

In Madras there are approximately 31 cases registered for each million Scheduled Castes;[238] in the other nine states reporting, there are about 7 cases per million Scheduled Castes. In Madras, 97.9 percent of the registered cases are challaned, compared to only 82.8 percent in the other nine states. The Madras courts disposed of 93.4 percent of these cases within the year; in the other nine states only 58.3 percent were disposed of. Of the cases disposed of, fully 78.7 percent lead to convictions in Madras,

Table 10.8A

UOA Cases, 1964

	Registered	Challaned (as % of registered)	Convicted (as % of disposed)	Acquitted (as % of disposed)	Compounded (as % of disposed)	Disposed	Pending	Pending (as % of Challaned)
Total	371	336 (90.6)	157 (60.4)	53 (20.4)	50 (19.2)	260	76	(22.6)
Madras	190	186 (97.9)	137 (78.7)	32 (18.4)	5 (2.9)	174	12	(6.4)
Nine Other States	181	150 (82.9)	20 (23.3)	21 (24.4)	45 (52.3)	86	64	(42.7)

SOURCES: RCSCST 1964–65: 185.

Table 10.8B

UOA Cases Brought by Workers of Harijan Sevak Sangh 1966–67

	Registered	Convicted (as % of disposed)	Aquitted & Dismissed (as % of disposed)	Compounded (as % of disposed)	Disposed (as % of registered)	Pending (as % of registered)
Total	215	97 (65.1)	10 (6.7)	42 (28.2)	149 (69.3)	66 (30.7)
Madras	114	89 (84.0)	7 (6.6)	10 (9.4)	106 (93.0)	8 (7.0)
Five Others	101	8 (18.6)	3 (6.9)	32 (74.4)	43 (42.6)	58 (57.4)

SOURCE: Harijan Sevak Sangh, Annual Report 1966–67: 25.

while only 22.3 percent end in convictions in the other states. The downward trend in the use of the Act and in the rate of convictions is accentuated in the other nine states, while both of these are reversed in Madras.[239] This striking disparity between Madras and the rest of the country still prevailed two or three years later (see Table 10.8B). Madras provides a picture of prosecutory initiative, investigatory vigor, judicial toughness and dispatch that contrasts starkly with the other states. This contrast suggests that with sufficient inputs of governmental initiative, the UOA can result in vastly higher rates of prosecution and higher rates of conviction.

THE LOGISTICS OF UOA LITIGATION

Although the Untouchability (Offences) Act is a central law, responsibility for its enforcement, like that of virtually all central laws, lies with the states. There is no separate central enforcement apparatus for this or (typically) for other national policies. Nor is there any central agency which actively coordinates or directs enforcement activity in the various states. Within each state, the same decentralized pattern is replicated. There is no special agency or staff for the enforcement of these laws or coordination of the enforcement activities of local officials.[240] There is not at any level any agency which systematically gathers information about the problems and policies of enforcement.[241] Thus, initiative is extremely decentralized.[242]

The total expenditure of law enforcement resources on anti-disabilities enforcement is miniscule compared, e.g., with prohibition. For example, in Bombay from 1946–54 there were over 100,000 prohibition cases registered (and over 44,000 convictions obtained).[243] It will be recalled from Table 10.6 that there were far less than 1,000 anti-disabilities prosecutions during the comparable period. While dry states typically have special squads, task forces, coordinating officers and intelligence bureaus for prohibition enforcement,[244] there are no special squads or staffs for enforcing laws against Untouchability.

There are no non-governmental organizations which systematically undertake a purposeful role in the development of anti-disabilities legislation or in its enforcement. There is no group (like, for example the American Civil Liberties Union or the legal staff of the National Association for the Advancement of Colored People) which concerns itself with the strategy or tactics of anti-disabilities litigation. Social uplift organizations, especially the Harijan Sevak Sangh, are involved in a large portion of the cases brought under the UOA. But their involvement is typically initiated by their local workers in response to a particular situation, not as part of a coordinated program of litigation. The Sangh has no specialized legal staff and ordinarily does not engage lawyers to handle these cases. There are no lawyers with specialized expertise in such matters. Untouchable lawyers, particularly those in politics, are involved in some UOA cases. But again, there is no coordinated program of action nor are there any channels for sharing of experience. It should of course be added that opposition to anti-disabilities laws appears if anything more unorganized. Except in a few disputes involving major temples, there has been no organizational support to defendants in such cases.

Among the educated strata, untouchability is generally a dead issue. Aside from occasional flashes of interest when it temporarily assumes some political import, it evokes little attention from politicians, administrators and intellectuals — with a few notable exceptions. Except for intermittent atrocity stories the sparse public discussion and disconnected press coverage are mostly confined to political issues (or to misgivings about the government policies of preferential treatment).[245] While the political scene is subject to waves of concern about regional, religious and caste cleavages, there has been little sustained concern about untouchability. There is no interest in the intellectual community in the mechanics of programs for attacking untouchability, no debate about alternatives, no assessment of prospects.[246] The problems of anti-disabilities policies, their tactics and strategy, receive little systematic consideration.

Anti-disabilities prosecutions depend on the initiative of the local police and the sympathy of local magistrates, both of whom have obvious reason to be disinclined to antagonize the dominant elements of the local community. If they are not themselves members of the latter,[247] they are heavily dependent upon their cooperation in order to do their jobs and gain promotions. (As an Untouchable Ph.D. succinctly put it, "law means police and police means higher caste people.")[248] Police are often uninformed of the provisions of the UOA — or even of its existence.[249] The vast majority of potential cases that come to the attention of the police are ignored or at best "compromised" without being registered. Even if the police were sympathetic — and they often are not — limited resources and career pressures would keep them from expending much effort on this unrewarding line of activity.

Initiative then must be supplied by the Untouchable to press his claim for police time and resources. Complainants and the witnesses they need to prove their cases are extremely vulnerable to intimidation and reprisal. Very often they are economically dependent upon the higher castes. They may face social boycott or reprisal in the form of eviction or denial of grazing rights, when they do not meet with physical coercion in the form of beatings, house burnings or worse. Except in cases where outsiders are involved, witnesses other than their caste fellows are not ordinarily forthcoming. A High Court judge, rebuking a magistrate for discounting the evidence of the complainant and his friend as interested, observed that "in such cases it would be idle to expect disinterested witnesses to support the complainant's case."[250] If the complainant does have witnesses and a good case, he is likely to be subjected to pressure to compound it.[251]

Although boycotts and reprisals are themselves offenses, they are by their very nature extremely difficult to prove. They involve the behavior, often covert, of a large number of people and successful prosecution requires proof of motivation. Witnesses will be even harder to find. So these secondary offenses are even more difficult to prove than the original offense. As a social worker active in anti-disabilities campaigns put it:

In the case of a boycott we apply to the Collector and he will go out and settle the matter. We do not look to the judiciary in such cases because it is too difficult to prove the existence of a boycott in court.[252]

If the complainant manages to withstand these pressures, there is often considerable delay in the disposition of cases. The Elayaperumal Committee analyzed 70 completed cases and found that the average time elapsed was more than six months.[253] Repeated court appearances are time-consuming and expensive. The accused almost always have greater resources and can hold out longer. With the passage of time, witnesses may be less persuasive and less inclined to cooperate with the prosecution. As Table 10.9 suggests, protracted delay substantially reduces the chances of conviction.

Table 10.9

Relation of Delay and Disposition in UOA Cases

Time elapsed from registration to disposition	Disposition		
	Convicted	Compounded	Acquitted
Less than 6 Months	15 (37.5%)	10 (25.0%)	15 (37.5%)
More than 6 Months	8 (26.7%)	6 (20.0%)	16 (53.3%)

n = 70

SOURCE: Derived from Department of Social Welfare 1969: 51.

In at least some cases there is a disparity of legal resources.[254] Prosecutions in magistrates' courts are ordinarily handled by the police prosecutor. Usually this official is a lawyer but with little prestige in the profession, and as a civil servant whose superior is a police official, he does not represent a strong and independent prosecutory initiative. (In a few cases, state prosecutors have been deputed or private lawyers engaged to assist in the prosecution of UOA cases.) The accused are often represented by counsel, a circumstance that is credited by knowledgeable observers with increasing their chances of obtaining an acquittal.[255] Untouchables are often too poor to engage lawyers, and local lawyers, who are themselves drawn from the higher castes and dependent upon the landowning classes for patronage, may be reluctant to take such cases. Most of the states extend some legal aid to Untouchables, although usually not to help them prosecute criminal cases. However, legal aid is so inadequate and so poorly distributed that it is completely insignificant.[256]

Once the case is presented to the court there are formidable obstacles due to the ambiguities and loopholes of the Act. These defects are, as we have seen, difficult to overcome in the High Courts where there is a higher level of skill, more time for preparation and greater insulation from local pressures. It may be surmised that in the magistrates' courts the tendency of the Act's ambiguities and of the difficulties of proof to reduce chances of conviction are amplified. It is, simply, very hard to win one of these cases. Some indication of the difficulty of winning one of these cases is presented in a recent report of the Harijan Sevak Sangh. The Sangh, an organization of mild reformist outlook, prefers uplift and persuasion to litigation. However, its workers are involved in a large proportion of cases registered under the UOA. The Sangh's policy is that only "when all persuasive measures fail and workers feel themselves at bay and there is no way out they very hesitatingly seek the help of law."[257] One may assume that the cases with HSS sponsorship should be fairly good candidates for securing convictions. There should not be many false cases or abuses of the UOA for harassment or complainants who misunderstand the law. There would typically be an outside witness, an experienced social worker with previous experience with the law, and there would be some organizational resources to insure tenacity against dilatory tactics. Yet with all of these advantages, of the 476 HSS cases that were disposed of in the five-year period 1961–66, only 90 (18.9 percent) resulted in convictions.[258]

Even if a conviction is secured, the penalties imposed are so light as to have little deterrent effect (and to generate little favorable publicity). "Ludicrously low" fines of only three or four rupees are not uncommon.[259] The Elayaperumal Committee gathered information on 22 cases in which convictions were obtained and found that the median penalty was a fine of Rs. 10. Judicial tolerance of this level of penalties is suggested by a

Table 10.10

Disposition of UOA Cases Brought by Harijan Sevak Sangh Workers, 1961–62 to 1965–66

Period	Registered	Convicted (as % of Disposed)	Comprised, Acquitted, or Dismissed (as % of Disposed)		Total Disposed (as % of Registered)	Pending (as % of Registered)	Source: H.S.S. Annual Reports
			Compromised	Acquitted or Dismissed			
1961–62	196	24 (27.6)	63 (72.4)		87 (44.3)	109 (55.6)	1961–62:18
1962–63	202	21 (15.6)	114 (84.4)		135 (66.8)	67 (33.2)	1962–63:36
1963–64	181	10 (8.6)	106 (91.4)		116 (64.1)	65 (35.9)	1963–64:25
1964–65	146	15 (28.3)	37 (69.8)	1 (1.9)	53 (36.3)	93 (63.7)	1964–65:25
1965–66	161	20 (23.5)	48 (56.5)	17 (20.0)	85 (52.8)	76 (47.2)	1965–66:22
Total 1961–66	886	90 (18.9)	386 (80.1)		476 (53.7)	410 (46.3)	

recent case in the Allahabad High Court, where the Judge upheld the conviction of a couple who had been fined Rs. 20 each.

Taking into account the strong prejudices which are still continuing in that part of the State, coupled with the fact that [complainant] had come to the tap after responding to the call of nature and while attempting to take water had touched the utensils of the [defendants] which in the natural course of events must have given them the cause of provocation, I think the ends of justice will be met if the . . . fine imposed on them is reduced to Rs. 10 each.[260]

In the event of an appeal, there is a high probability that a conviction will be reversed.[261]

Table 10.11

Penalties Imposed in 22 Cases of Conviction Under the UOA

Penalty	Cases
1 week rigorous imprisonment	1
1 week simple imprisonment	1
Fine: Rs. 100	2
Fine: Rs. 50	3
Fine: Rs .25	3
Fine: Rs. 10	2 (median)
Fine: Rs. 5 + imprisonment to rising of the court	1
Fine: Rs. 5	4
Fine: Rs. 3	2
Fine: Rs. 1	1
Warning only	2

SOURCE: Department of Social Welfare 1969: 52.

In view of the trouble and expense, often accompanied by economic hazard and physical danger, the uncertainty of securing a conviction and the tiny effect of such a conviction, it is not difficult to see why few Untouchables would feel that there is anything to be gained by instituting a case under the UOA. It is sometimes suggested that the failure to invoke the Act or to abide by its provisions is due to lack of awareness of its provisions. There would seem to be little merit to this explanation. The Act has been widely publicized. A national survey, the reliability of which cannot be ascertained, found that 77 percent of the non-Scheduled Castes and 66 percent of the Scheduled Castes were aware of the existence of an act outlawing untouchability.[262] In any event, there can be no doubt that vast numbers of Untouchables are aware of the UOA. It is not unawareness of its existence that inhibits its use, but awareness of its hazards and weaknesses. Untouchables are, quite sensibly, more deterred by the formidable difficulties of using the UOA than caste Hindus are deterred by the remote and mild penalties that it threatens them with. Any moderately astute Untouchable, finding himself with the strategic resources to invoke judicial power in a dispute with his caste Hindu neighbors, might, one supposes, be far less attracted to the UOA than to the ordinary criminal law.

In view of the difficulties of using the UOA, it is not surprising that Untouchables who seek extra-local support may not find the Act a promising means of redress and may instead resort directly to executive officers or political figures rather than to the police and the courts. A very crude index of the extent of such recourse is given by the Commissioner for Scheduled Castes and Scheduled Tribes who has noted in his annual report the number of "complaints" made directly to his office in New Delhi by aggrieved Untouchables. Even as the number of prosecutions under the UOA has declined, the number of complaints to this remote and relatively powerless official has continued to increase.[263]

The Commissioner could offer nothing more than an attempt to sting local and state officials into action, a process subject to delays of years before getting even a satisfactory reply.[264] To many, even this cumbersome and remote procedure seemed a more attractive remedy than the UOA. It is safe to assume that persons sophisticated enough to communicate with a high administrative officer in New Delhi are not ignorant of the existence of legal remedies close at hand.

The question, then, is not why so few cases are brought, but rather why any cases are brought! Probably very few are brought without the intervention of some "outsider" to the local situation — usually political leaders, social workers or religious reformers. For example, a single organization, the Harijan Sevak Sangh helped to bring 721 cases in the four-year period from 1961–62 to 1964–65.[265] This is somewhere over 40% of the cases registered during that period.[266] This intervention tends to concentrate on certain kinds of facilities. Temple-entry has often, particularly in the early years of anti-disabilities legislation, involved political sponsorship.[267] Social workers tend to concentrate on public accommodations like tea shops, hotels and barbers. Such conspicuous and fixed establishments appear to be most vulnerable to anti-disabilities litigation.[268] The identifiable offender with a fixed establishment and a public license cannot melt away like the crowd at the village well or return later to intimidate the complainant.[269] Where, however, disabilities are supported by self-help of coherent social groups it is unlikely that they will be deterred by the UOA, even when the presence of transient intervenors increases the probability that it will be invoked. In these settings, the problem is not that the UOA depends on outside intervention

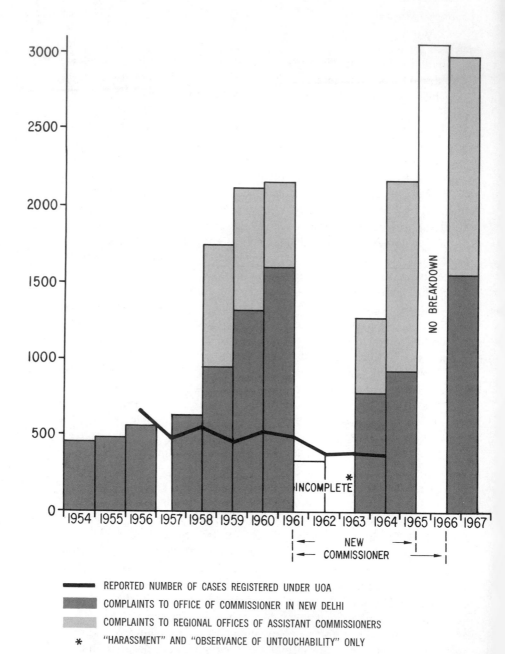

Fig. 10.2 Complaints to the Commissioner for Scheduled Castes and Scheduled Tribes, 1954-1967.

for its invocation, but rather that it is such a poor vehicle for getting intervention of the requisite strength and tenacity. It leaves Untouchables vulnerable to itinerant reformers who often cannot deliver the goods that they promise, after Untouchables have risked their well-being.[270]

The conjunction of use of the UOA with outside intervention calls for two cautions in interpreting its impact. First, in many instances the successful use of facilities has a purely ceremonial and symbolic character. Under the wing of a politician, social worker, or government officer, Untouchables enter a temple, draw water from a well or are served in a tea shop with much fanfare. After Harijan Week is over and the outsiders have departed, the situation reverts to normal, perhaps until the next special occasion when the ritual of acceptance is re-enacted.[271] This performance cannot be dismissed without significance, but it is of a different order than the free access contemplated by the law.[272] Second, assertion of their rights by Untouchables, especially when reinforced by outside intervention, may result not in sharing of common facilities but in provision of separate facilities for Untouchables. This may happen when Untouchables are successful and their entry is met by withdrawal of others. It also may happen through diversion of governmental resources to provide a separate well or meeting hall, etc. Thus, while the Act takes equal access to common facilities as its aim, it often serves to provide leverage for increase of separate facilities for Untouchables.[273]

THE IMPACT OF ANTI-DISABILITIES LEGISLATION

The impact of anti-disabilities legislation is not to be measured merely by the few cases that are brought. The aim of such laws is not to prosecute offenders, but to promote new patterns of behavior. Undoubtedly the total effect of the UOA as propaganda, as threat and as leverage for securing external intervention outweighs its direct effect as an instrument for the prosecution of offenders. To some extent, however, its effectiveness at an educational device and as a political weapon depends upon its efficacy as a penal provision. The power of the law to elicit widespread compliance depends in part on its ability to deal with obvious cases of non-compliance.[274] A law that permits effective prosecution of offenders may, of course, not succeed in inducing widespread compliance, but surely a statute which fails to enable effective prosecution is less likely to secure general compliance.

This is especially so in the case of laws like the UOA. For successful legal regulation depends upon what might be called the "halo-effect" — the general aura of legal efficacy that leads those who are not directly the targets of enforcement activities to obey the law. The "halo" may be generated by self-interest, approval of the measure, generalized respect for the law-making authority, the momentum of existing social patterns, expectation of enforcement — or a combination of these. In the case of anti-disabilities legislation which runs counter to the sentiments and established behavior patterns of wide sectors of the public, the "halo" of efficacy depends very heavily on the expectation of enforcement. By this measure, the UOA appears an unwieldy and ineffective instrument; its shortcomings as a penal provision vitiate its capacity to secure general compliance.

However, even where there are massive inputs of governmental enforcement, the other components of compliance (approval, self-interest, momentum of existing patterns) must be successfully mobilized to some extent. In the case of the UOA, there is little in the way of these other components, except for generalized respect for government. The law goes counter to perceived self-interest and valued sentiments and deeply ingrained behavioral patterns. Thus the difficulties of securing general compliance in the case of anti-disabilities legislation are so formidable that to measure the Act in these terms sets too high a standard. A more modest approach would be to ask how the Act stands as an enabling measure. First, to what extent does it enable Untouchables to improve their position vis-à-vis disabilities? Does it provide useful leverage for those willing to expend their resources and take risks? Second, does the level of enablement sustain itself? Is the Act effective enough so that its use as an enabling measure is cumulative and self-reinforcing?

Perhaps the greatest "enabling" feature of anti-disabilities legislation is its general symbolic output. This legislation has an effect on the morale and self-image of Untouchables, who perceive government action on their behalf as legitimating their claims to be free of invidious treatment. By providing an authoritative model of public behavior that they have a right to demand, it educates their aspirations. More generally, such legislation promotes awareness of an era of change in caste relations. Specifically it provides an alternative model of behavior; it puts the imprimatur of prestigious official authority upon a set of values which are alternative to prevailing practice.[275] Thus it presents a challenge to social life based upon hierarchic caste values. As Henry Orenstein observed in a Maharashtrian village, "The villagers knew that there was a prestigious alternative to the traditional values of caste."[276]

Although mere knowledge of the existence of such legislation does not in itself bring about changes, there are instances in which these laws have contributed to "widespread change in daily behavior."[277] For at least some groups the Act provided leverage for securing favorable changes.[278] However, this successful use did not lead to widespread use of the legislation.

We have seen that the UOA followed a "downward spiral" of ineffectiveness rather than an upward spiral of increasing use.[279] Obviously this downward spiral has happened to a different degree in different places and perhaps there are some places where it has not happened at all. But the overall pattern seems to be that both inputs from the government side (official concern, police initiative, judicial sympathy, etc.) and those from potential complainants and their supporters have declined. As the press and higher officials have diverted their exhortations to the new problems of the day, the police have ceased to make whatever special efforts they made in such cases, which are costly to them in terms of their normal functioning. Offenders become more subtle, lawyers find the soft spots in the Act and courts become less vigilant in protecting the Act against restrictive interpretation. There are fewer convictions and smaller penalties. Potential complainants and their supporters are discouraged from using the Act. The few outsiders who might get involved are heavily overcommitted to many programs and projects. As instances of the use of the Act become rarer, they seem less matter of course. And insofar as the law's halo of efficacy depends heavily on expectation of enforcement, the law loses its ability to secure compliance from those who are not themselves the direct target of enforcement activity.

The present situation, then, is characterized by a wide gap between the law on the books and the law in operation. As in many other areas, the government's commitment to change greatly outruns its power to effect it. This disparity between aspiration and performance, between great commitments of principle and small deployment of resources, itself transforms the symbolic as well as the practical uses of anti-disabilities legislation. Symbolically, it blurs what the Government's commitment is. The law's equivocation is institutionalized: in the ceremonial character that attends the admission of Untouchables to many facilities; in the fact that anti-disabilities measures become leverage for increasing separate facilities for Untouchables; and, generally, in the law's provision of remedies without relieving the dependence which prevents them from being used.

For power-holders, intellectuals and educated urban dwellers, the law's equivocation permits them to maintain favorable images of their society and to believe that untouchability is gone or going, without paying the political cost that a strenuous attack on it would entail. Thus the UOA serves as a screen which helps those who prefer to ignore the continued existence of untouchability to convince themselves that it is not there. It provides a foundation for official optimism: untouchability is "on its last legs."[280] Thus the Government of Andhra Pradesh recently reported that:

the small number of cases reported by the Inspector General of Police is itself indicative of the disappearance of this evil and the rapid economic advancement of the former untouchables. . . . There are no pockets where untouchability is practised in [the] state.[281]

The ineffectiveness of the law means that the new national norms are not conveyed — or rather, tolerance of their violation is communicated at the same time that they are espoused. Thus Peter Rowe observes of district town lawyers:

The gap between knowledge and practice is especially true of the prohibitions of the Untouchability (Offences) Act, where a fairly high percentage of persons, particularly in the upper and dominant castes, know about the rules, but have not changed their practice regarding untouchables.[282]

This is not confined to the more sophisticated. The Commissioner of Scheduled Castes and Scheduled Tribes reports of a village just outside Delhi that:

The villagers expressed a view that untouchability was being practiced in that village to a lesser extent than in any other surrounding village . . . they did not consider the practices like denial of the use of drinking water, wells, entry into common shrines and temples, and smoking and eating along with others, as untouchability. In their opinion, these practices were a way of their life.[283]

At the same time, the law's equivocation serves to disillusion reformers and Untouchables who are convinced that the law is totally useless and without effect. While the complacent look only to the law on the books, overlooking that its performance in practice falls far short of its promise, the cynical focus on the modest results of the law in operation and tend to dismiss it as mere lip service, overlooking the pressure that this law might exert on local practice. Both the complacent and the cynical concur in equating the present legal accomplishments with the law's potential. There is widespread agreement that all that might be done by law has been done and that only a "change of heart" can secure further gains to the Untouchables.[284] The Study Group on the Welfare of the Weaker Sections of the Village Community (1961) expressed a widely shared opinion when it asserted that social disabilities:

is a sphere in which legislation and administration cannot accomplish much. Basically it is a matter of how people think, and what their values are.[285]

This estimate of the law's potential is sustained by a number of features of the current Indian scene. One is the absence of controversy about the working of anti-disabilities laws: all of the laws (if not all of the law's enforcers) are on the "side" of the Untouchables. There is no articulate public opposition to these laws, and Untouchables do not exert much pressure for their enforcement or their improvement, preferring to divert their efforts into search for tangible gains through protective discrimination. All of this takes place in a milieu which puts great store on the symbolic aspects of the law and where a tradition of conceptualistic legal thinking is shared by lawyers and the educated public, who are both equally innocent of any tradition of looking at legal institutions empirically.

The notion that untouchability cannot be dealt with by legislation, but must await a change of heart on the part of its perpetrators, comports with a great deal of evidence on the difficulty of inducing social change by penal regulation. The dangers of law becoming ineffective when it moves too far from prevailing public opinion are well known.[286] It may be even more difficult to induce change in behavior which is not merely instrumental but is invested with deep expressive meanings for those concerned.[287]

The ultimate argument against the efficacy of law in changing relations between groups is that law cannot affect the deepest values and attitudes of the target group. However, this assumes that there is a direct relationship between the "prejudiced" attitudes of the target group and their discriminatory behavior. But there is evidence (from other settings) that the relationship is not direct; that specified behaviors can be changed without waiting for change in underlying attitudes, and that legal regulations can be effective in changing these behaviors in the field of intergroup relations.[288]

The problem of a "change of heart" is not one of waiting upon a wave of moral edification, but rather of changing specific behaviors that have their roots in a variety of attitudes about pollution, hierarchical grading, indignity of manual labor, etc. The problem is how the law might be used to induce changes in these behaviors. There is no reason to conclude that patterns of caste interaction are exempt from the general human capacity for acting at variance from belief. Also, there is evidence of great pliability in caste behaviors in the past and at present.[289] If caste will not break, it is known to bend. The question is: How can law be used to induce it to bend more quickly and without inordinate cost?

VI. Prospects and Options

The picture we have drawn of the working of the anti-disabilities legislation shows that it is of limited effect in eliminating disabilities. We have argued that this is not because the legislation has reached the utmost limits of effective legal action, but because it stops far short of these limits. One would be foolish indeed to believe that legal measures alone could secure the elimination of untouchability from society, but it is possible to envision a policy of anti-disabilities legislation and enforcement which might contribute more effectively to this end.

The improvement or upgrading of anti-disabilities law can be analyzed into four stages of increasing difficulty and increasing significance. First there is the task of closing the loopholes and eliminating the ambiguities that plague the UOA.[290] This is a job that does not lie beyond the present capabilities of the draftsman's art. Such re-drafting might eliminate throughout the UOA the requirement that the accused be proved to have acted "on grounds of untouchability." (And the presumption that helps to offset the requirement.) The various forbidden acts could be transformed from common law offenses with a required showing of *mens rea* to an offense of strict liability. In order to prevent the conviction of persons whose actions do not contravene public policy (e.g., the restauranteur who excludes a drunk), a saving clause might be added to forestall application in such situations.[291] Admittedly, this kind of readjustment may not make a great difference where the magistrate is unfriendly to the purpose of the Act, but it at least permits the magistrate who is friendly or indifferent to avoid being distracted by the *mens rea* question.

Such a broadening of the Act's scope would seem to be well within the policy of Article 17 which declares it an offense to enforce "any disability *arising out of* 'untouchability' " — not merely those where the disability is enforced *on grounds of* "untouchability." The subjective limitation interposed by the UOA is not required by the Constitution.[292]

Similarly, the provisions describing the coverage of the Act could be re-drafted to insure that the scope of the rights granted by the Act is not measured by an artificial rigor. Thus it could be made clear that the Act applies to any property, by whomsoever owned, which is used by the public — not only to property that the public has a legal right to use.[293] Regarding religious places, the Act could be extended along the lines of the legislation now in force in several states to cover places which are used by any section of the Hindu public. This could be accomplished simply by replacing the "same religion or same religious denomination thereof" language on the order of "open to Hindus in general or any section thereof."[294]

These changes would extend the scope of the rights conferred by the Act, making ordinary usage rather than enforceable rights the measure of their scope — a measure which comports with the broad language of Article 17's abolition of the practice of "untouchability" *in any form* and with the broad powers conferred upon the Government by Article 25(2)b. Again, such changes would not guarantee a favorable determination in any particular case, but they might serve to enunciate policy more clearly to those concerned and to reduce the outlay of judicial exertion required to carry out this policy.

Secondly, there are a number of improvements possible in the enforcement of the UOA. Changes of this kind would require greater and continuous inputs of administrative attention, and willingness to divert some resources. These might include measures for reducing delay, either by priority on court calendars or by appointing special magistrates to try offenses;[295] redress of any disparity of legal talent by deputing public prosecutors to prosecute these cases (or, perhaps, generous legal aid to attract high-level legal talent); making outcomes more visible by making anti-disabilities offenses non-compoundable; provision of mandatory higher fines or prison sentences;[296] providing exceedingly heavy penalties for interfering with complainants or witnesses in UOA cases. Such measures would not solve the fundamental problems of the Act, but they would go some way to reduce the cost and risk to the complainant while assuring that the return on his cost and risk is not entirely negligible.

Third, the effect of these improvements might be greatly augmented by the establishment of machinery to guide and coordinate enforcement activity. Such an establishment might gather and disseminate information on enforcement problems and techniques; it might develop coordinated strategies of enforcement, using both the UOA and other legal provisions now largely unused. (E.g., writ petitions,[297] civil suits, preventive police action,[298] etc.) By assigning priorities, providing continuity and encouraging development of specialized skills in this area, such a coordinating body could promote the best use of resources allocated to enforcement.

But even these improvements in the clarity, scope and rigor of the UOA would not touch the major weaknesses of the UOA — for these flow from the very nature of the remedy it provides. The simple penal sanction, dependent upon detection and investigation by the regular police, trial by the regular magistrate, and punishment by fine or imprisonment of guilty individuals is probably not capable of delivering the goods.

The effectiveness of ordinary penal sanctions is dependent upon several conditions which typically do not obtain in the case of anti-disabilities measures. These conditions are, first, that the victim of the offense will have widespread community sympathy — or at worst indifference — and that he (and those who cooperate with him) will be able to invoke the law without being subject to community sanctions. Second, that the offender will be an identifiable and isolable individual who will, as a result of his infraction, be subject to community censure and isolated from community support. Third, that the enforcing officials will be independent of the accused and his supporters and that the total outcome for the enforcing official will be positive.[299] (The sort of situation in which the UOA is most frequently invoked is one which approximates these conditions: the offender is an identifiable and relatively isolated tea shop or cinema owner, not the villagers at the well; and outside support reduces the likelihood of reprisal and increases the cost to the police of inaction.) What is needed then is a way to build these favorable conditions — or surrogates for them — into the enforcement machinery. In order to do this, it is necessary to move away from the ordinary penal law process.

One way to do this would be by means of an administrative agency.[300] For example, imagine an agency, consisting of a tribunal and an investigative branch, which could, on its own initiative, depute examiners to investigate suspected cases of persistent imposition of disabilities. The purpose of the investigation would be to determine the existence of patterns of discrimination, not to establish individual instances. If a prima facie case of discrimination were established the examiner's findings would be presented (after opportunity for voluntary compliance) to the tribunal, where all parties would have a right to appear and contest the investigator's findings. Both investigator and tribunal would be free of the judicial standards of evidence; the tribunal could operate by a rule of preponderance of evidence rather than by the "beyond a reasonable doubt" standard required in criminal proceedings.

Upon the tribunal making a finding that a pattern of disabilities existed, it could, if compliance was not forthcoming within a fixed time, approach the High Court for an order to named persons to desist from practicing untouchability in specified forms. Violations of this order might be punished by the contempt power, by resumption of government grants to the village, etc.[301] The agency might devise penalties which would mobilize the leverage of caste discipline and village solidarity against the continuance of disabilities, rather than in support of them — e.g., disqualifications for government service or contracting.[302] The agency might undertake periodic checks to see that compliance was permanent.

Such an administrative remedy would conform more closely to the conditions of effectiveness than do the present remedies. It would place the burden of initiative on someone other than the local Untouchables or the police. Initiative would lie with those immune to retaliation or pressure and whose careers would be helped, not hindered, by enforcement.[303] The agency would have a continuing interest and would be able to exercise continuing scrutiny, affording outside support of a persistence not available at present. As such a body it could develop expertise and might articulate anti-disabilities enforcement with other measures for the welfare of the Untouchables.[304] Were such an administrative procedure to prove effective, it might be possible for investigators to operate principally by arranging settlements, with formal undertakings by responsible village parties and periodic re-checking by the investigatory staff.[305]

Just how much could be accomplished even by such an amplified machinery for enforcement depends on things beyond enforcement itself, that is, to what extent government programs for distributing resources and opportunities succeed in liberating Untouchables from economic dependence on higher castes. Surely, though, there are even now at least some groups of Untouchables who are in a position to use the leverage of amplified enforcement to improve their position, and there are some villagers who would modify their behavior when faced with this kind of enforcement.

It may be argued that a higher level of enforcement in such a sensitive area would lead to negative results by provoking greater resistance, more circumvention, more pressure on Untouchables. On the other hand, there is the opposite danger that if the law moves too slowly and is too solicitous of those who resist, it will lose its ability to secure compliance from those who are not themselves the direct targets of enforcement activities.

Obviously, machinery along these lines, designed to meet all the contingencies of rural Indian life, would be both financially expensive and politically costly to operate. Whether the political system is capable of mobilizing support for such legal initiative — or whether it should do so — are beyond the scope of this paper. India's decision-makers may decide that scarce resources can be put to better use than stronger anti-disabilities legislation. It should be clear, though, that the limited success of anti-disabilities legislation is the result of choices among political alternatives, not of the inherent inefficacy of legal controls.

Looking back, we can see that the posture of the lawyers' law toward disabilities has followed the course of political concern with Untouchables. The emergence of the Untouchables as a factor in the struggle for power in India was soon reflected in the first glimmerings of political concern about their legal position. From 1917 to 1947, they enjoyed a strategic political position, due to their role as a potentially crucial swing group in the three-way struggle among the Congress, the Muslim League and the British to determine when the British would withdraw and what would replace them. During this period, the cause of the Untouchables was taken up by the nationalist movement (and to some extent by its rivals) and became an integral part of the Congress program for an independent India. Opposition to untouchability became a warrant of commitment to modernity and development and it remains an unchallenged (at least overtly) premise of public life in India. The force of this commitment continued into the middle 1950s, culminating in the passage of the Untouchability (Offences) Act, which confirmed and consolidated at the national level what had been done by the state legislatures in the late 1940s. But after 1947, the structural conditions of their influence were changed; Untouchables were no longer a crucial group at the national level. From the late 1950s the government's many programs for the amelioration of the Untouchables' condition continued in force, but were not significantly augmented. Untouchability became a dead issue.

However, by the late 1960s several factors suggested that this eclipse for more than a decade was only temporary and that untouchability was due for another round of prominence as a public issue. The first of these was the new political situation. The 1967 elections (and the subsequent split in the Congress) eroded the great Congress majorities and left Congress (and others) dependent for pluralities on the Scheduled Castes representatives who occupy reserved seats. Untouchables again occupy a strategic position from which they can make demands for further governmental action in their behalf. Second, the government's redistributive "compensatory discrimination" policies (especially in education) are producing a growing number of educated Untouchables, who are less economically dependent and who have greater political resources and higher aspirations. Sooner or later they will provide a leadership to whom the equivocation of the present legal situation will not be acceptable. [306] Third, as government is more responsive to these demands, we may expect the opposition to the government's policies of special treatment for Untouchables to become more overt, more articulate and more powerful. We may anticipate that before too long the earlier (1938–56) generation of anti-untouchability measures will be subjected to a more thorough scrutiny than they have in the past.

NOTES

[1] On the general character of the legal system, see Galanter 1968b.

[2] Legal enforcement of slavery was outlawed by the Indian Slavery Act (Act V of 1843); possession of slaves was made a criminal offense by the Indian Penal Code (Act XLV of 1860) § 370. On the way in which agrestic slavery in Southern India compounded the disabilities of the lowest castes, see Adam 1840: 171 ff.; Banaji ca. 1933: 85; Kumar 1965.

[3] On the incidence of exclusion of Untouchables from courts, see O'Malley 1941: 375; Government of Bombay (Starte Committee) 1930; 56–7.

[4] For a discussion of the impact of law on caste organization, see McCormack 1966. It should be pointed out that the "law" regarding caste set forth here is to

some extent an artifact of the present study. Except for the area of "caste autonomy" (which was the subject of a technical literature during the period 1900–1920) caste was not a salient legal category. The separate strands were familiar (and the context and details better understood) but practical motives and difficulty of retrieval make it unlikely that the composite pattern was widely grasped. In a sense, then, hindsight provides us with more learning on the subject than would have been available to any but the most indefatigable (and prophetic) lawyer. The first attempt at a full statement of the relation of law to untouchability in historical and comparative perspective was published by Borale in 1968.

5 *Anandrav Bhikiji Phadke v. Sankar Daji Charya,* I.L.R. 7 Bom. 323 (1883); *Sankaralinga Nadan v. Raja Rajeswara Dorai,* 35 I.A.C. 176 (1908); *Chathunni v. Appukuttan,* A.I.R. 1945 Mad. 232.

6 See cases cited, note 5 above. Cf. *S. K. Wodeyar v. Ganapati* A.I.R. 1935 Bom. 371, where damages were awarded although the parties agreed there should be no finding on the question of pollution.

7 *Atmaran v. King-Emperor,* A.I.R. 1924 Nag. 121.

8 *Anandrav Bhikiji Phadke v. Sankar Daji Charya,* I.L.R. 7 Bom. 323 (1883); *S. K. Wodeyar v. Ganapati,* A.I.R. 1935 Bom. 371.

9 On this and contrasting conceptualizations of caste, see Galanter 1968a.

10 7 Bom. 323 at 329.

11 35 I.A.C. 176 at 182.

12 *Chathunni v. Appakuttan,* A.I.R. 1945 Mad. 323.

13 Indian Penal Code, §§ 295–298 (Act XLV of 1860) and § 295A (introduced by Criminal Law Amendment Act [XXV of 1927] § 2).

14 In *Sivakoti Swami,* I Weir 253 (1885), a division bench of the Madras High Court divided over whether these sections were applicable to Hindus inter se and whether to defile included ritual defilement caused by a goldsmith pouring coconut-water over a lingam — Muttusami Aiyar, J., upholding the affirmative on both propositions. His position prevailed subsequently. *Bheema Goundan,* I Weir 256 (Mad., 1891).

15 *Atmaram v. King-Emperor,* A.I.R. 1924 Nag. 121. Borale 1968: 223 cites a similar case, unreported, decided in 1880.

16 This approach did not always work to the disadvantage of the excluded class. In *Gopala v. Subramania,* A.I.R. 1914 Mad. 363, members of the Elaivaniyar community obtained a declaration of their right to enter the outer hall of the temple and an injunction restraining other worshippers from ejecting them. The Court declared that each group enjoyed a prima facie right to enter that part of the temple assigned its caste by the *Agamas* (texts on use of temples), that these texts authorized the entry of Sudras in this part of the temple, and that the plaintiffs were "at least Sudras." Their right could only be overcome by proof of a custom of exclusion. Similarly in *Kuti Chami Moothan v. Rama Pattar,* A.I.R. 1919 Mad. 755, where Moothans were convicted for defiling a temple by entering the part open to "non-Brahmins" the Court reversed the conviction on the ground that Moothans are Sudras, no lower or more polluting than the Nairs who were allowed in the temple.

17 A.I.R. 1917 Mad. 431 at 433.

18 Ibid., at 442. This dispute was still going strong twenty years later. See Anon. 1935–37: 211 passim.

19 See Madras Hindu Religious Endowments Act (II of 1927) § 40.

20 Nevertheless, such exclusion was widespread. There was official enforcement of exclusion from such facilities in many of the princely states. See O'Malley 1932: 150; O'Malley 1941: 374.

21 *Sadoppachariar v. Rama Rao,* I.L.R. 26 Mad. 376 (1902). aff'd 35 I.A. 93; *Sambalinga Murti v. Vembara Govinda Chetti, Vejiaragavooloo Chettiar* 1858: 302 (Mad., 1857). Cf. the resolution of the Madras Government after the Tinnevelly riot of 1859 that "the public high streets in all towns are the property not of any particular caste but of the whole community; and every man . . . has a right to the full use of them." Quoted at II Weir 83.

However, local restrictions on the use of thoroughfares had sometimes elicited official support. See, e.g., the finding of the Sessions Court in South Malabar in 1879 that for a Tiyan Sub-magistrate to go through Brahman *granoms,* contrary to custom, except on bona fide official business, was an unwarrantable intrusion. Ramachandra Aiyar 1883: 131. Aiyappan reports that the willingness of the British courts to vindicate the rights of those excluded from thoroughfares "in test cases on the subject . . . strengthened the early movement against untouchability" among the Iravas of Malabar. Aiyappan 1965: 134.

[22] *Queen Empress v. Bhagi Kom Nathuba,* 2 Bom. L. Reporter 1078 (1900) (Magistrate had convicted a Vanjari woman of "corrupting water in a public cistern and causing the water less fit for drinking purposes" under § 61 of the District Police Act when she had contravened the repeated "directions" and "objections" of higher castes not to touch it.) *Empress v. Pandia Mahar,* 3 C.P.L.R. 92 (1890). Cf. the narrow interpretation of "defilement" here with the broad interpretation in the temple cases discussed above.

[23] *Kazan Chand v. Emperor,* A.I.R. 1926 Lah. 683.

[24] 1913 M.W.N. 247.

[25] A.I.R. 1938 Bom. 146 at 148.

[26] *Id.*

[27] *Jasnani v. Emperor,* A.I.R. 1936 All. 534.

[28] *Govinda Amrita v. Emperor,* A.I.R. 1942 Nag. 45; *Tirumalai v. Ponmari,* 1861 S.U.D. (Mad.) 3.

[29] *Ramditta v. Kirpa Singh,* 1883 Punjab Record (Criminal) 3. The Sonars here were members of the Shumsee sect (followers of a *pir* named Shums-Tabrez) and had "peculiar customs" like burying their dead. The Court suggested that if they had a right to use the well, they should seek a remedy by civil suit rather than criminal prosecution.

[30] *Salar Mannaji Row v. C. Herojee Row,* I Weir 614 (Madras High Court, 1887). The magistrate had found infirmities in the caste proceedings, but the High Court reversed the conviction on the ground that the matter was within the exclusive cognizance of caste assemblies and the Court was debarred from going into the merits.

[31] *Venkata Reddi* (Criminal Revision case No. 265 of 1885, decided 12 June 1885, Muttusami Aiyar, J.) Reported I Weir 575 [Madras High Court, 1885].

[32] § 141 of the Indian Penal Code makes unlawful assemblies for such objects as intimidating public servants, resisting the execution of law, committing mischief or trespass and "by means of criminal force" to take another's property or "compel any person to do what he is not bound to do or to omit to do what he is legally entitled to do."

[33] *Hindus of Kannampalaiyam Village v. Koi Kola Christians,* 8 I.C. 848 (Madras, 1910). In an earlier phase of the dispute the Court had held that the magistrate could not issue an order under Criminal Procedure Code § 144. *Venkatroya Gowondan v. Very Rev. N. Rondy,* 7 I.C. 343 (1910).

[34] *Sheo Shankar v. Emperor,* A.I.R. 1940 Oudh 348.

[35] For some instances of unsuccessful use of criminal law by Untouchable groups in their attempt to throw off the domination of higher castes, see Cohn 1955: 70; Lewis 1958: 73 ff.; Pradhan 1966: 163.

[36] Cohn 1965: 108.

[37] *Phagoona Nayee v. Menya Matha,* 1854 S.D.A. (Bengal) 465.

[38] *Raj Kisto Majee v. Nobaee Seal,* I Weekly Rep. 351 (H.C., Cal., 1864).

[39] *Coopa Mootoo v. Baupen,* II S.U.A. 77 (Mad., 1844) (barbers); *Parythy Caytholah Madey v. Toonery Ryoo,* II S.U.A. 83 (Mad., 1844) (midwife). But cf. *Hunnappa v. Hunmunna,* Bellasis Reports 8 (SDA Bom., 1840) where a village ironsmith recovered his "bulootee hucks" for the year in accordance with "the rules of the village communities." The right of a priest to fees from his hereditary jajmans was upheld in the early 19th century, e.g., *Narana Bhut v. Ganapa Bhut.,* 1853 S.U.D. 206 (Mad.) but was later rejected as inconsistent with "those principles

of religious liberty which govern the policy of the British government as respects all subjects of the State. . . ." *Anna Bassettappah v. Mattam Mariah,* 1862 S.U.D. 33, 34 (Mad.).

40 *Cooppa Mootoo v. Baupen* II S.U.A. 77 at 78 (Mad. 1844).

41 Consider the case of the Mahars, who early experienced difficulty in enforcing their rights to the traditional perquisites of their office (here, skins of bullocks). *Suntoo Wulud Madnak v. Babajee Bin Shriputrow,* Morris (Part 2) 68 (1849). When villagers removed them from village service and extorted Rs. 300 in exchange for restoring them, the participation of the *patel* was indeed unlawful, but only technically so. (Sentence for taking gratification for official act reduced from four months imprisonment to Rs. 10 fine.) *Imperatrix v. Appaji,* I.L.R. 21 Bom. 517 (1896). Civil courts had no jurisdiction to enforce the right of Mahars to perform village services; such determinations could be made only by the collector. *Bhiva v. Vithya,* 2 Bom. L. Reporter 869 (1900). An award in favor of Mahars by a panchayat convened to settle their claims against villagers was unenforceable because the collector had unlawfully delegated his power of appointment. *Mahadu Kashiba v. Krishna Tatya Mahar,* 24 Bom. L. Reporter 918 (1922).

42 E.g., the U.P. Municipalities Act (Act 2 of 1916) § 85(1) makes it an offense for a board-employed sweeper to absent himself without reasonable cause or to resign without the permission of the board. Sweepers were convicted of work-stoppage in *Baswa v. Emperor,* A.I.R. 1935 All. 216; *Angnoo v. Crown,* A.I.R. 1924 All. 188.

43 E.g., Majumdar 1958: 76 ff.

44 See, e.g., *Sheikh Jinaut v. Sheikh Khusen,* 7 C.W.N. 32 (1902), where it was held that the use of defendants' influence "to stop the services of the village barber, washerman and others from being rendered to the complainant" was not sufficient to justify an order requiring defendants to post security under § 107 of the Code of Criminal Procedure.

45 Government of Bombay (Starte Committee) 1930: 58.

46 *Id.* For classic instances of upper castes using boycotts and violence to secure economic advantage and to enforce detailed restrictions, see Hutton 1961: 205–6; Ambedkar 1945a: 6–8.

47 M. Singh 1947: 144.

48 On "caste autonomy" see Mulla 1901; Kikani 1912; Ramakrishna 1921.

49 *Queen v. Sankara,* I.L.R. 6 Mad. 381 (1883).

50 *Venkayya v. Venkataramiah,* A.I.R. 1915 Mad. 908.

51 *Sri Sukratendar Thirtha Swami v. Prabhu,* A.I.R. 1923 Mad. 587.

52 *Desai v. Emperor,* 33 Crim. L.J. 472 (Allahabad, 1931).

53 *Khamani v. Emperor,* A.I.R. 1926 All. 306.

54 *Babulal v. Tundilal,* 33 Crim. L.J. 835 (Nagpur, 1932).

55 There is evidence that government officials assisted in returning runaway indentured servants long after slavery was formally abolished. See Harper 1968b: 47.

56 *Jasnani v. Emperor,* A.I.R. 1936 All. 534.

57 *Kazan Chand v. Emperor,* A.I.R. 1926 Lah. 683; A.I.R. 1927 Lah. 430.

58 *Govinda Amrita v. Emperor,* A.I.R. 1942 Nag. 45.

59 *Shanmuga Pandaram v. Ponnuswami,* A.I.R. 1938 Mad. 714.

60 Criminal Procedure Code (Act V of 1898) §§ 144, 145, 147.

61 E.g., *Venkatroya Gowondan v. Rondy,* 7 I.C. 343 (1910).

62 Appasami 1929: 151.

63 Venkatraman 1946: 11.

64 See Woodward 1957.

65 Chidambaram Pillai (1933) argues that British law recognized and promoted more restrictive claims of exclusiveness regarding temples in South India than had prevailed earlier.

[66] Lajpat Rai 1932: 263–4; Natarajan 1959: 119.

[67] Quoted in Natarajan 1959: 144. The Congress resolution omitted several passages of the original, as submitted by the Depressed Classes Mission Society, which specified "disabilities imposed by *religion and* custom. . . ." (Italics supplied.)

[68] On the growth of reform activity during this period, see Natarajan 1959; Heimsath 1964; Dushkin 1957. On Untouchable politics see Keer, 1962.

[69] Government of Bombay (Starte Committee) 1930: 52.

[70] Quoted at Senjana 1946: 237.

[71] Government of Bombay (Starte Committee) 1930: 52. On Madras during the 1920s, see Hutton 1961 208 ff.; Ghurye 1961: 184. The Madras effort to secure the admission of Untouchables to government-aided schools eventuated in an order withholding grants from non-complying schools. G. O. No. 1446, Law (Education), dated 16 July 1935.

[72] All-India Congress Committee n.d.: 66. For a brief survey of the position of Untouchables at this time, see Hutton 1961: 198 ff.

[73] On the fast, the Poona Pact (or Yeravda Pact) which ended it, and reaction to these developments, see Pyarelal 1932.

[74] Quoted in Rajagopalachari 1933: 1.

[75] Information on these bills is available in Venkatraman 1946, Rajagopalachari 1933, Bakhle 1939. In November, 1932, the Madras Legislative Assembly passed without opposition a resolution favoring temple-entry, introduced by Dr. P. Subbaroyan.

[76] Ambedkar 1946: 117 ff. For a defense of the Congress shift, see Rajagopalachari 1946.

[77] Quoted at Santhanam 1949: 45–6.

[78] Madras Removal of Social Disabilities Act, 1938 (XXI of 1938). Baroda enacted a similar measure, the Social Disabilities Removal Act, formalizing earlier proclamations, in 1939. Government of Baroda 1949: 105.

[79] Madras Removal of Social Disabilities Act, 1938 § 2.

[80] I.e., an offense for which a police officer may arrest without a warrant. Code of Criminal Procedure (V of 1898) § 4(f).

[81] Madras Removal of Social Disabilities Act, 1938 § 6.

[82] See Venkatraman 1946: 26 ff. It should be noted that this famous temple-opening extended only to temples controlled by the State.

[83] Malabar Temple Entry Act (XX of 1938); Madras Temple Entry Indemnity Ordinance (I of 1939).

[84] Madras Temple Entry Authorization and Indemnity Act (XXII of 1939).

[85] Bombay Hindu Temple Worship (Removal of Disabilities) Act (XI of 1938).

[86] Venkatraman 1946: 58 lv; Santhanam 1949: 45. For a critical account of the accomplishments of the Congress Governments of 1937–39 in respect of disabilities, see Coupland 1944: II, 144.

[87] Orissa Removal of Civil Disabilities Act, 1946 (X of 1946). Bombay Harijan (Removal of Social Disabilities) Act, 1946 (X of 1947), and Amendment Act of 1948 (LXXVII of 1948). Central Provinces and Berar Scheduled Castes (Removal of Social Disabilities) Act, 1947 (XXIV of 1947). Uttar Pradesh Removal of Social and Religious Disabilities Act, 1947 (XIV of 1947). East Punjab (Removal of Religious and Social Disabilities) Act, 1948 (XVI of 1948). West Bengal Hindu Social Disabilities Removal Act, 1948 (XXXVII of 1948). Bihar Harijan (Removal of Civil Disabilities) Act, 1948 (XIX of 1949) and Amending Act of 1951. The Bombay Act was later extended to Delhi and Kutch, the W.B. Act to Tripura; the U.P. Act to Ajmer, Bhopal, Bilaspur, Himachal Pradesh and Vindhya Pradesh.
Mysore Removal of Social Disabilities Act, 1943 (XLII of 1943) and Amendment Acts of 1948 and 1949: Saurashtra Harijan (Removal of Social Disabilities) Ordinance (XL of 1948), Hyderabad Harijan (Removal of Social Disabilities) Regulation (LVI of 1358 Fasli [1948–49]). Coorg S.C. (Removal of Disabilities) Act,

1949 (X of 1949). Madhya Bharat Harijan Ayogta Nivaran Vidhan, Samvat 2005 (XV of 1949) and Amendment Act of 1950 (LXIII of 1950). Travancore-Cochin Removal of Social Disabilities Act, 1125 (VIII of 1125 [1950]).

88 Some of these acts conferred rights explicitly on "Untouchables." See, e.g., U.P. Removal of Social and Religious Disabilities Act (XIV of 1947). But others were more broadly worded to confer rights on non-Untouchable groups as well. E.g., Travancore-Cochin Removal of Social Disabilities Act (VIII of 1125 [1950]) outlawed discrimination against any person on grounds of belonging to a particular caste or religion. §§ 3, 4, 6.

89 The Orissa and U.P. Acts were the only ones in note 87 above under which offenses are *not* cognizable.

90 *Chatunni v. Appukuttan,* A.I.R. 1945 Mad. 232. The Court found that the temple was a public one, but upheld the right of Nairs to exclude Ezhuvas.

91 Venkatraman 1946: 56.

92 A.V. Thakkar in Santhanam 1949: 86.

93 Figures reproduced in Bakhle 1939: 89-90.

94 Senjana 1946: 33.

95 Santhanam 1949: 87.

96 Madras Temple Entry Authorization Act, 1947 (V of 1947) and Amending Act of 1949 (XIII of 1949).

97 For an example of efficacious use of this act by local militants as leverage to effect temple-entry, see Aiyappan 1965: 144.

98 Bombay Harijan Temple Entry Act (XXXV of 1947); Central Provinces and Berar Temple Entry Authorization Act (XLI of 1947); Orissa Temple Entry Authorization Act (XI of 1948). Some of the social disabilities removal acts, note 87 above, contain temple-entry provisions: e.g., § 3(d) of the United Provinces Act, § 3 of the East Punjab Act.

Mysore Temple Entry Authorization Act (XIV of 1948) and Amending Act of 1949 (V of 1949); Hyderabad Harijan Temple Entry Regulation (LV of 1358 Fasli [1948–49]); Coorg Temple Entry Authorization Act, 1949 (II of 1949); Travancore-Cochin Temple Entry (Removal of Disabilities) Act, 1950 (XXVII of 1950).

99 Like the social disabilities acts (see note 87 above) some of these temple-entry acts concerned only rights of "Untouchables," making it an offense, e.g., to exclude "members of a scheduled caste" [United Provinces Removal of Social and Religious Disabilities Act (XIV of 1947) § 3(d)] or "excluded classes" [Central Provinces & Berar Temple Entry Authorization Act (XLI of 1947); East Punjab (Removal of Religious and Social Disabilities) Act (XVI of 1948); §§ 3–5]. See *Bhaichand Tarachand v. State of Bombay,* A.I.R. 1952 Bom. 233, holding the Bombay Act so confined. Other acts were more broadly phrased to confer rights even on groups not Untouchable. E.g., the Travancore-Cochin Act, note 98 above.

100 Except for the United Provinces and Coorg Acts, all created cognizable offenses.

101 The only areas which did not have such regulation at the time of the enactment of the Constitution were Assam, Manipur, PEPSU, and Rajasthan.

102 Article 15(1) forbids discrimination by the State on grounds of caste. Other provisions deal with specific areas of governmental activity: Art. 16(2) with government employment; Art. 23(2) with compulsory public service; Art. 29(2) with admission to state-aided educational institutions. Cf. Art. 325 which forbids separate electorates for Parliament or State legislatures on caste lines.

The restrictions on state use of these forbidden classifications are qualified to allow special provision in favor of women (Art. 15[3]) and Backward Classes, Scheduled Castes and Scheduled Tribes (Art. 15[4], cf. Art. 46). For a discussion of the scope of State power to make special provision for these groups, see Galanter 1961b.

103 *Shamdasani v. Central Bank of India,* A.I.R. 1952 S.C. 59. The "State" includes all governmental authorities, local as well as central. Art. 12.

[104] Only two other provisions in the Fundamental Rights section of the Constitution regulate private as well as public conduct: Art. 24, which forbids child labor in hazardous employment; and Art. 18(2) which prohibits acceptance of titles from foreign states.

[105] Art. 35b.

[106] *State v. Gulab Singh,* A.I.R. 1953 All. 482; *State v. Banwari,* A.I.R. 1951 All. 615.

[107] Where an act was, after the Constitution, amended by the State legislature to provide heavier penalties, it was held that Art. 35 saved only existing state law and withdrew state power to legislate further in the area, even by amending an existing act. *State v. Kishan,* A.I.R. 1955 M.B. 207.

[108] XXII of 1955. For discussion of the scope of exclusive central power and continuing efficacy of state power, see Galanter 1961a.

[109] §§ 3–6.

[110] § 8. Where the offense is committed in relation to a trade or profession in respect to which the convicted person holds a license. Imposition of such sentence by the court is to have the same effect as if the license was suspended or revoked by the authority competent to cancel or suspend it.

[111] § 9. Where the convicted person is manager or trustee of a place of public worship receiving grant of land or money from the government. This penalty cannot be decreed by the court itself but requires action by the appropriate government authority. Some states have debarred persons convicted of UOA offenses from contesting elections to village *panchayats.*

[112] Cf. *Shelley v. Kraemer,* 334 U.S. 1 (1948) in which the Supreme Court of the United States held that enforcement by a state court of a racially restrictive covenant between private parties amounted to state action prohibited by the 14th Amendment.

[113] § 7(1)b.

[114] § 7(2).

[115] § 7(1)c.

[116] § 12.

[117] Use of this term in print can be traced with fair precision to the year 1909. The Maharaja of Baroda in his remarks to the Depressed Classes Mission of Bombay on 18 Oct. 1909 uses the term and provides an explanation to his audience. (Sayaji Rao 1928: 244–245). The adjectival form, "untouchably," is used by Shridhar V. Ketkar (1909: 86) in a footnote to his study of the caste system; the preface of the volume is dated September, 1909. The text of the volume suggests that the author did not have this term at his disposal when he wrote the text. Cf. pp. 99 and 121–22. The Maharaja of Baroda was the patron of Mr. Ketkar and supported him during the years at Cornell University when he wrote this book. (See Ketkar 1911: xxvi.) Weitbrecht-Stanton 1920: 173 attributes the term's prominence to the Gaikwad.

[118] Cf. the bizarre (and perhaps facetious) claim that a wife's denial to her estranged husband of access to his infant child amounted to "instigating the practice of untouchability," which served as the basis for issuance of search warrants by a Magistrate. His handling of the case was severely castigated in *Banaris Lal* v. *Neelam,* A.I.R. 1969 Del. 304.

[119] *Devarajiah v. Padmanna,* A.I.R. 1958 Mys. 84, at 85. Cf. remarks of Professor K. T. Shah, VII CAD 668 and Mr. Nazirrudin Ahmad at VII CAD 665.

[120] *Hadibandhu v. Banamali,* A.I.R. 1960 Or. 33. The court found it unnecessary to decide whether "untouchability" in Art. 17 included that produced by excommunication, the excommunication here not being proved. The court suggested that the shastras made a sharp distinction between "jathi chandalas" and "karam chandalas" and that the ambiguity of Art. 17 could be cured by an enactment outlawing excommunication, such as then existed in Bombay.

[121] *Saifuddin Saheb v. State of Bombay,* A.I.R. 1962 S.C. 853.

[122] B.P. Sinha, C.J., dissenting, *id* at 866.
Several years after the *Saifuddin* case was decided, the Judge who decided the *Hadibandhu* case had occasion to comment on the scope of Art. 17 and suggested

that "some *via media* should be found so that while maintaining the disciplinary powers of the religious head of a caste or sect, his power of ex-communicating members of his sect or caste and thereby reducing them to the position of untouchables, should be taken away. Perhaps an inclusive definition by way of an explanation in Art. 17 to the effect that its scope is not limited only to those who are untouchables by birth may be somewhat effective." R. L. Narasimhan 1964: 145–7.

123 *Parameswaran Moothathu v. Vasudeva Kurup*, I.L.R. 1960 Ker. 73.

124 All temple-entry legislation confers rights to enter and worship "in the same manner and to the same extent" as is permissible for other persons professing the same religion, etc. On several occasions the Supreme Court has implied that the ambit of the temple-entry power would not extend to erasing the distinction between ordinary worshippers and temple functionaries (*Sastri Yagnapurushdasji v. Muldas Bhundardas Vaishya*, A.I.R. 1966 S.C. 1119) or sectarian initiates (*Sri Venkataramana Devaru v. State of Mysore*, A.I.R. 1958 S.C. 255).

125 An attempt to explicitly attach this meaning by amending Art. 17 to read "no one shall, on account of his religion or caste, be treated or regarded as an 'untouchable' " was defeated in the Constituent Assembly. VII CAD 665, 669.

126 Krishna Shetty (1969: 180) reads "untouchability" in Article 17 as extending to all discrimination, exclusion or disassociation "not because of conduct or certain physical conditions but because of his caste, group, class, religion." I.e., he would include all invidious treatment on grounds of group membership.

127 E.g., *Ajit Kumar v. Ujayar Singh*, A.I.R. 1961 S.C. 1334. The classification of the offspring of a Sudra and his Brahman concubine as a *chandala*, the lowest of Untouchables in the classical scheme, did not strike the court as unconstitutional in *Bachubhai v. Bai Dhanlaxmi*, A.I.R. 1961 Guj. 141.

128 *Sangannagouda v. Kalkangouda*, A.I.R. 1960 Mys. 147.

129 A.I.R. 1958 Mys. 84.

130 *Id.*, at 85.

131 A district magistrate in Tiruchirappalli (Madras) is reported to have held that the UOA did not apply where the party excluded from a village well was not a Harijan. *Times of India*, May 1, 1956.

132 See, e.g., *Sankaralinga Nadan v. Raja Rajeshwari Dorai*, 35 I.A.C. 176 (1908).

133 See, e.g., *Atmaram v. King-Emperor*, A.I.R. 1924 Nag. 121.

134 See, e.g., *Muthusami v. Masilimani*, I.L.R. 33 Mad. 342 (1909); *Maharajah of Kolhapur v. Sundaram Ayyar*, A.I.R. 1925 Mad. 497, 521. This explicitly included "Untouchables": *Manickam v. Poongavanammal*, A.I.R. 1934 Mad. 323 (Adi-Dravidas); *Bhola Nath v. Emperor*, A.I.R. 1924 Cal. 616 (Doms); *Sohan Singh v. Kabla Singh*, A.I.R. 1928 Lah. 706 (Mazhabis).

135 Such lists derive from earlier attempts (in the 1930s) to find a single set of criteria to measure "untouchability." (These included such tests as whether the caste in question was "polluting" or "debarred" from public facilities – which may admit of no unequivocal answer – and whether they were served by "clean" Brahmans – which has only a local and comparative reference.) All attempts to set up tests based on the assumption that "Untouchables" were set off by some uniform and distinctive pattern of practices proved inadequate to isolate the groups which local administrators felt deserving of inclusion. Additional criteria of poverty and illiteracy had to be added. The government lists then give little guide to the meaning of untouchability. There is no adequate inclusive list of all groups considered untouchable or any set of criteria for identifying them. For a discussion of the problem of identifying the "Untouchables," see Duskhin 1957, 1961.

136 Lelah Dushkin has observed that the term "untouchability" is ordinarily used in two senses: first, to refer to the pollution-stigma imputed to "Untouchables"; second, to refer to "the set of practices engaged in by the rest of society to protect itself from the pollution conveyed by the Untouchables and to symbolize their inferior status." (Dushkin 1967: 628). The first sense describes an attribute of Untouchables; the second refers to the social relations imposed by the non-untouchables. Article 17 is clearly concerned primarily with the second or relational sense.

The "practice" that is forbidden by the first sentence of the Article is invidious treatment by the higher castes, not the performance by lower castes of acts which might be considered polluting or expressive of pollution. Presumably the quotation marks are intended to refer to the imputation of uncleanliness without subscribing to it. They further serve to resist restriction to any narrow meaning of literal avoidance of touch.

[137] This distinction has been pointed out by Kelkar (1956). It is criticized as difficult to maintain by Krishna Shetty (1969: 176).

[138] It is not clear whether "the practice of 'untouchability' " includes all instances of avoidance of pollution associated with Untouchables — at least where none of the latter are directly the subject of the behavior. An interesting theoretical problem is raised by the situation in *Bharat Airways v. Their Workers*, 1953 L.A.C. 450 (L.A.T.). Caste Hindu loaders were dismissed for insubordination when they refused to load hides, a job for which "other workers" were available. The Appellate Tribunal held the dismissals wrong on the ground that the orders were "unreasonable."

[139] Krishna Shetty (1969: 175–6) argues that the broad phrasing of Art. 17, "in any form," should not be construed to reach acts which take place in the domestic sphere, such as invidious separation at private functions and observance of purificatory rites at home after contact. "In any form" he suggests, means all kinds, but it does not mean "in any place." He argues that broad reading would interfere with the privacy, sanctity and peace of the home. The coverage of Article 17, then, should be confined to "the public sphere, where citizens have equal right to enjoy the public facilities." Thus a discriminatory act would come within Article 17 only if "in regard to public institutions, public places and public facilities."

The exclusion of intra-household activities from the coverage of Article 17 is surely unexceptional. But the proposed dichotomy between domestic and public spheres might unduly constrict Article 17's coverage, by assimilating to the domestic everything that is not formally public. (Cf., the restrictive interpretations of public discussed below in Part IV and text at note 293). The public/domestic distinction is not clear about the intermediate social space between the household and the formally public (e.g., facilities that are widely used but privately owned). One might, instead, read the broad language of Article 17 as announcing that public norms will prevail in that intermediate realm — i.e., that social facilities beyond the household cannot be monopolized by groups on the ground that they are an extension of their domestic arrangements.

[140] I.e., if we assume that disabilities can be "enforced" only against the person who suffers from them. But cf. note 173 below.

[141] § 7(b).

[142] *State v. Kanu Dharma*, A.I.R. 1955 Bomb. 390.

[143] *State v. Kishan*, A.I.R. 1955 M.B. 207.

[144] Persuasion was held outside the scope of the prior U.P. Act. *State v. Gulab Singh*, A.I.R. 1953 All. 483.

[145] *Banamali Das v. Pakhu Bhandari*, A.I.R. 1951 Cal. 167. On earlier litigation concerning the power of provincial legislatures to pass anti-disabilities legislation, see Galanter 1961a.

[146] The leading case here is *Sri Venkataramana Devaru v. State of Mysore*, A.I.R. 1958 S.C. 255. See also *Sastri Yagnapurushdasji v. Muldas Bhundardas Vaishya*, A.I.R. 1966 S.C. 1119; *P. S. Charya v. State of Madras*, A.I.R. 1956 Mad. 541; *Ramamirtha Ayyar v. Narayana Pillai*, A.I.R. 1956 Mad. 528.

[147] A.I.R. 1958 S.C. 255. The Madras High Court in an earlier case, *P. S. Charya v. State of Madras*, A.I.R. 1956 Mad. 541, suggested several alternative lines of resolution, none of which were followed by the Supreme Court when it finally dealt with the issue. Perhaps the most interesting of the Madras High Court's holdings is that Art. 26(b) is subject to the exception of "public . . . morality," and that Art. 17 makes the complete abolition of "untouchability" a standard for public morality. Thus, it is immoral to exclude any class of pious Hindus from entering religious places. The Court does not indicate how it determined that exclusion from denominational premises is the practice of untouchability.

[148] Madras Temple Entry Authorization Act, 1947 (V of 1947) and Amending Act of 1949 (XIII of 1949).

149 A.I.R. 1958 S.C. at 264. On shifting judicial views of what are the "matters of religion" protected by Article 26(b), see Subramaniam 1961; Parameswara Rao 1963; Tripathi 1966.

150 A.I.R. 1958 S.C. at 265.

151 *Id.*, at 268.

152 The textual difficulty is the result of the distribution of subordinating qualifiers. Article 25(2)b expressly exempts the temple-entry power from limitation by the rights granted in Article 25(1), but is silent concerning the effect of the rights granted by Article 26. The whole of Article 25 is expressly made "subject to the other [Fundamental Rights] provisions. . . ." (including, of course, Article 26), while Article 26 is subject only to "public order, morality and health." Subramaniam 1961: 334 notes that Article 26 rather than Article 25 would appear the appropriate location of the temple-entry proviso and calls its appearance in Article 25 a "defect in drafting."

153 The constitutional power extends not only to temples, but to all "Hindu religious institutions." Presumably this includes institutions of instruction, meditation and hermitage as well as the places of public worship and the sacred waters dealt with by the UOA. The temple-entry power is not confined to the exclusion of "Untouchables" but empowers the state to confer rights on "all classes and sections of Hindus." If Article 25(2)b does confer rights, then presumably these rights can be used defensively, even without legislative implementation. Since they would be Fundamental Rights, civil proceedings (including writ petitions) would be available to enforce them.

154 A.I.R. 1958 S.C. at 269.

155 *Id.*

156 A.I.R. 1958 Mad. 282.

157 *Id.*, 283.

158 *Sarat Chandra Das v. State*, A.I.R. 1952 Or. 351.

159 Thus the use of caste as a legal identification has been discouraged. Indian Registration (Amendment) Act, 1956 (XVII of 1956) § 2; Appeals to caste loyalty in electoral campaigning are forbidden. Representation of the People Act, 1951 (XLIII of 1951) § 123. Promotion of enmity between castes is a serious criminal offense. Penal Code § 153-A as amended by Indian Penal Code (Amendment) Act, 1961 (XLI of 1961).

160 See, e.g., *Bhau Ram. v. Baij Nath*, A.I.R. 1962 S.C. 1476, where the Court struck down (as unreasonable restrictions on property rights) laws providing for pre-emption on the basis of vicinage. The Court held that the real purpose of these laws was to promote communal neighborhoods, a purpose which could no longer have force as public policy since the desire to promote such exclusiveness could no longer be considered reasonable.

161 *Kanji Gagji v. Ghikha Ganda*, A.I.R. 1955 N.U.C. 986.

162 Subject to the provisions of the UOA, § 7(2), discussed below and the provision of § 123(2) of the Representation of the People Act, 1951 (XLIII of 1951) which forbids excommunication for purposes of influencing voters, discussed in note 172 below.

163 *Varadiah v. Parthasarathy*, I.L.R. 1964(2) Mad. 417, 420.

164 *Panduram v. Biswambar*, A.I.R. 1958 Or. 256; *Manna v. Ram Ghulam*, A.I.R. 1950 All. 61. Cf. *Hadibandhu v. Banamali*, A.I.R. 1960 Or. 33. However, composite groups such as "caste Hindus" and "non-Brahmans" do not enjoy the privilege when they undertake to outcaste for caste offenses. *Ellappa v. Ellappa*, A.I.R. 1950 Mad. 409.

165 A.I.R. 1962 S.C. 853.

166 § 7(2).

167 *Sri Venkataramana Devaru v. State of Mysore*, A.I.R. 1958 S.C. 255; *State of Kerala v. Venkiteswara Prabhu*, A.I.R. 1961 Ker. 55. Cf. *Commissioner, H.R.E. v. Shri Lakshmindra Thirtha Swamiar*, A.I.R. 1954. S.C. 282.

168 A.I.R. 1958 S.C. 255 at 265.

169 A.I.R. 1966 S.C. 1119.

[170] *Id.*, at 1135.

[171] Since the *Venkataramana Devaru* case, the Supreme Court has indicated that it is moving away from the view that what are matters of religion are to be decided by the views of the religious groups themselves. See *Durgah Committee v. Hussain Ali*, A.I.R. 1961 S.C. 1401, 1415; *Shri Govindlalji v. State of Rajasthan*, A.I.R. 1963 S.C. 1638; authors cited note 149 above.

[172] Cf. the Supreme Court's treatment of the anti-excommunication provision of the Representation of the People Act, 1951, which makes it "undue influence" and a corrupt election practice if one ". . . (i) threatens any candidate, or an elector, or any person in whom a candidate or an elector is interested, with injury of any kind, including social ostracism or excommunication or expulsion from any caste or community. . . ."

In *Ram Dial v. Sant Lal*, A.I.R. 1959 S.C. 855, the Court declared void an election in which the religious head of the Namdhari sect of Sikhs issued a Farman to his followers, threatening them with expulsion (and with divine displeasure) if they did not vote for a specified candidate. The Court noted that a religious leader enjoys the right of free speech to exercise his influence on behalf of a candidate, but that if he leaves voters no choice by implying that disobedience will entail divine displeasure or spiritual censure, it is a corrupt election practice. The denominational freedom to excommunicate was not argued in this case, but it is difficult to believe that it would prevail.

[173] A.I.R. 1962 S.C. 853 at 870.

[174] This is explicitly the position of the concurring judge in *Saifuddin*, who distinguished the *Venkataramana Devaru* case there (*Id.*, at 875). "As regards the position of the 'Untouchables' Art. 17 . . . had to be recognized as a limitation on the rights of the religious denominations, howsoever basic and essential the practice of the exclusion of Untouchables might be to its tenets and creed."

[175] Cf. *Barrows v. Jackson*, 346 U.S. 249 (1953) where the Supreme Court of the United States permitted a white defendant, sued for breach of a covenant not to sell to Negroes, to invoke the constitutional rights of the Negro purchaser who was not a party to the action.

[176] *Sanghar Umar Ranmal v. State*, A.I.R. 1952 Saur. 124.

[177] A.I.R. 1960 S.C. 1208.

[178] *Id.*, at 1210.

[179] Collective fines (in the form of payment for extra police) were recently recommended to the States by the Central Home Minister as a method of dealing with communal violence and were employed by at least one state government. *Hindu Weekly Review*, March 25, 1968.

[180] Bombay announced this policy. RCSCST 1958–59: 41.

[181] See, e.g., *State v. Kanu Dharma*, A.I.R. 1955 Bom. 390, where a meeting of villagers ordered the father of an untouchable boy who entered a temple to pay for its purification. Compare another instance from Madras:

"At Pathinettangudi, the Harijans were summoned to the chavadi (community hall) for taking water from the common well and a collective fine of Rs. 50/- was imposed on them. Harijans paid this fine for fear of economic boycott being declared against them. The Harijans are so afraid of the Ambalagars that they would not complain to the authorities about this fine. They have also stopped taking water from the well." Harijan Sevak Sangh 1953–54; 44.

[182] Even if Article 15(1) would ordinarily invalidate such classifications, the further question arises whether such collective responsibility might be imposed after an undertaking by members of a community acting in some representative capacity. See, e.g., *Nanhe Mal v. Jamil-Ur-Rahman*, A.I.R. 1925 All. 316; *Lachman Singh v. Diljan Ali*, 43 I.C. 955 (Patna, 1918).

[183] Criminal cases, other than capital ones, reach the Supreme Court only by certificate of fitness for appeal from High Court or because a substantial question of constitutional interpretation is involved. (Articles 134, 132.) Only two cases involving anti-disabilities legislation have been decided by the Supreme Court; both

were appeals against applications of state temple-entry laws. *(Sri Venkataramana Devaru v. State of Mysore,* A.I.R. 1958 S.C. 255; *Sastri Yagnapurushdasji v. Muldas Bhundardas Vaishya,* A.I.R. 1966 S.C. 1119.)

184 UOA, §§ 3–6.

185 UOA § 12.

186 XXIX Cuttack L.T. 364 (1963).

187 (1964) K.L.R. 226.

188 High Court at Allahabad, 6 February 1957. Reported in Indian Civil Liberties Bulletin, Vol. IV, p. 255 (March 1957). The prosecution here was under the United Provinces Removal of Social and Religious Disabilities Act, § 3(1)c, which prohibited refusal of services "on grounds that . . . [customer] belongs to a Scheduled Caste."

189 A.I.R. 1951 All. 615.

190 *Id.,* at 616.

191 I.L.R. 1962 Cuttack 256.

192 *Id.,* at 258.

193 It seems clear that in other contexts the "public" character of a well is determined by use, not by legal right. *Ramkaranlal v. Emperor,* A.I.R. 1916 Nag. 15 (unconvincingly distinguished in *Ramekwal Singh v. State,* 1954 Crim. L.J. 998). Eminent commentators have no hesitation about stating flatly that " 'a public place' is a place where the public go, no matter whether they have a right or not." Ratanlal and Thakore 1948: 634 (commentary on I.P.C. § 277).

194 I.L.R. 1962 Cuttack, at 258.

195 Since Untouchables are protected from caste discrimination specifically in regard to wells supported by or dedicated to the public by Art. 15(2), it might be thought that Art. 17 would avoid superfluity in this regard only if it covered facilities beyond those covered by Art. 15(2). Such a reading would comply with the general principle of giving effect to all provisions of an enactment, so that none of them are nugatory. See Basu 1965: I, 38–9.

196 1965 M.P.L.J. (Notes of Cases) 7.

197 A.I.R. 1958 M.P. 352. The same reasoning was applied to a similar provision of the Bombay Harijan Temple Entry Act (XXXV of 1947) in *Bhaichand Tarachand v. State of Bombay,* A. I. R. 1952 Bom. 233.

198 Nenaskar, J., A.I.R. 1958 M.P., at 354.

199 Cf. the remarks of Pandit Pant, then Home Minister, to Parliament: This Bill does not apply to Hindus alone. It applies to all. . . . It will apply not only to scheduled castes, but probably to Christians in the South who are not allowed to enter Churches by those who consider themselves as belonging to higher classes. There are certain Muslims who are treated in the same manner by the followers of Islam. They will have the benefit of this provision. It is for their benefit that the word "untouchability" has been left undefined. *Lok Sabha Debates,* 27 April 1955, Cols. 6545, 6672.

200 Unless, of course, "untouchability" is to be taken as coterminus with Hinduism. This would accord with the scope of the temple-entry power conferred by Art. 25(2)b, which is confined to Hindu institutions.

201 See the definition of "place of public worship" in UOA, Sec. 2(iv).

202 "Religion" and "religious denomination" have shifting meanings. Adopting the dictionary definition of denomination as "a religious sect or body having a common faith and organization and designated by a distinctive name," the Supreme Court (*Commissioner v. Laxmindra Thirtha Swamair,* A.I.R. 1954 S.C. 282) concluded that every sect and sub-sect within Hinduism would qualify. Jains and Parsis are also religious denominations. *Ratilal v. State of Bombay,* A.I.R. 1954 S.C. 388. Hinduism as a whole is a "denomination" and each school within it and every territorial or doctrinal sub-group within such a group is a "section thereof." *Laxmindra Thirtha Swamiar v. Commissioner H.R.E.,* A.I.R. 1952 Mad. 613, 639.

[203] This reading turns on the interpretation of the word "or" in the phrase "same religion or same denomination or section thereof." In effect, the courts read it as meaning "and" — i.e., the excluded person must be a member of the religion and (if there are denominational lines) of the same denomination as well. This perfectly proper construction is not the only possible one. An equally plausible interpretation would read the religion and denomination requirements as alternative rather than additive. Thus the Act would apply if the excluded person were a member of the "same religion" and, in the event that he were not, it would then be sufficient if he were a member of the "same denomination" or the "same section." Most cases would be covered by the "same religion" condition and the few cases of sects whose memberships cut across lines between Hinduism and other religions would be covered by the "denomination" or "section" language. This would seem to comport with the provision of an expansive definition of Hinduism and with the UOA's avowed purpose of opening facilities to Untouchables.

[204] A.I.R. 1961 Ker. 55.

[205] To the extent that these qualifications represent a desire to preserve denominational prerogatives and the rights of Muslims, Christians, Jains, etc., to control access to their premises, they are superfluous, since it is only exclusion on "grounds of 'untouchability' " that is outlawed and "untouchability" has been interpreted not to include religious exclusiveness. *Devarajiah v. Padmanna*, A.I.R. 1958 Mys. 84.

[206] §§ 4(ii), 4(iv) and 4(ix). Strangely enough the qualification is omitted from § 4(x) regarding the "observance of any . . . religious custom, usage or ceremony or taking part in any religious procession." Thus Untouchables seem to have legal access to the religious processions of Hindu denominations and sects, but not to their wells, etc.

[207] Besides the statutes referred to in notes 208 and 209 below, the "denomination" limitations of § 3 of the UOA are overcome by the Madras Temple Entry (Authorization) Act, 1947. This is the only one of the earlier anti-disabilities acts which was not repealed upon passage of the UOA. (See Schedule to UOA.) The Madras Act is in force in part of Andhra Pradesh. RCSCST 1959–60: 29. No other states have enacted remedial legislation. The Central Law Minister and the Minister of Home Affairs declined to recommend any central legislation to solve this problem. RCSCST 1958–59: 3.

[208] Bombay Hindu Places of Public Worship (Entry Authorization) Act, 1956 (Act 31 of 1956). (The Supreme Court has held that this legislation extends even to sectarian groups, historically connected to Hinduism, which presently claim to be distinct from it. *Sastri Yagna Purushdasji v. Muldas Bhundardas Vaishya*, A.I.R. 1966 S.C. 1119.) Kerala has recently passed similar remedial legislation. The Kerala Hindu Places of Worship (Authorization of Entry) Act 1965 (Act 7 of 1965).

[209] United Provinces Temple Entry (Declaration of Right) Act, 1956 (Act 33 of 1956). This act contains no penal provision, but declares the rights of all sections of Hindus to participate in worship in Hindu temples and prohibits the courts from recognizing any custom, usage or practice to the contrary. After passage of the Act, criminal prosecutions under ordinary law were instituted against those who obstructed Harijans from entering the Viswanath temple at Benares.

[210] The power conferred by Art. 25(2)b is wider than that exercised by the UOA in another respect. The constitutional power extends not only to temples but to all "Hindu religious institutions." It includes the full array of institutions of instruction, meditation and hermitage as well as the "places of public worship" and the sacred tanks and waters dealt with by the UOA. See VII CAD 828–9.

[211] See Galanter 1961a.

[212] The following observations rely heavily on the annual reports of the Commissioner for Scheduled Castes and Scheduled Tribes, the annual reports of the Harijan Sevak Sangh and its quarterly Supplement, *Harijan Seva*. A useful compilation of a variety of data can be found in Planning Commission 1965; Dept. of Social Welfare, 1969.

[213] For some instances, see Ghurye 1961: 235 ff.

There is virtually no articulate defense of the *ancien regime*. Anything even suggesting it is liable to provoke a widespread and engaged outcry. Cf. the fuss about the remarks of the Sankaracharya of Puri in late March, 1969. Opposition to government policy is always couched in terms of liberty, equality and merit, never as an assertion of traditional prerogatives. Cf. Morris-Jones postulation of two contrasting political "idioms" or "styles" in contemporary India: the "modern" idiom of national politics with its plans and policies; and the "traditional" idiom of social status, customary respect and communal ties, ambitions and obligations. He notes that "Indian political life becomes explicit and self-conscious only through the . . . [modern] idiom. . . . But this does not prevent actual behavior from following a different path." 1962: 142.

214 Cf. the suggestive opinion survey of Oommen 1968. In a social-distance study Phillips 1967 suggests that among the higher castes, the higher the class the greater the acceptance of Untouchables.

215 RCSCST 1962–63: 1-14.

216 See, e.g., RCSCST 1955: 79.

217 Quoted at RCSCST 1960–61: 25.

218 Committee on Plan Projects 1959: 189.

219 No overall pattern of continuing disabilities emerges on cursory inspection of the various local surveys reported in the annual Reports of the Commissioner for Scheduled Castes and Scheduled Tribes and those in Harijan Seva (especially Nos. 44, 46, 47 and Oct.–Dec. 1967). Available data distinctly suggest that wells are the most intractable of public facilities. Cf. the rank ordering of resistance to acceptance found by Oommen 1968 in his Rajasthan attitude survey: intermarriage/temple/well/political leadership/economic concessions/education.

220 See Isaacs 1965.

221 For a review of these programs and their impact, see Dushkin (1961, 1967); Béteille (1965); and the annual reports of the Commissioner of Scheduled Castes and Scheduled Tribes.

222 Of the 70 cases subjected to detailed analysis by the Elayaperumal Committee, 40.9% concerned service of tea, water, utensils, etc.; 24.2% concerned wells and taps, 6.1% concerned temples. Department of Social Welfare 1969: 51. Compare, e.g., the breakdowns at RCSCT 1957–58: I, 14; Harijan Sevak Sangh 1955–56: 82. The suggestion of Table 10.2 as to the proportion of cases that involve temples is borne out by Table 10.6. Of the 448 anti-disabilities cases registered in Bombay during the three-year period 1947–50, 40 (8.9%) were under the Temple-entry Act.

223 The "case" is the basic unit of our analysis in the following pages, but it must be admitted that it is not entirely clear just what a "case" is. Is a prosecution involving multiple defendants one case or is each defendant's fate a separate case? Throughout the record-keeping (both that of the state governments which appear in the Reports of the Commissioner for Scheduled Castes and that of the Harijan Sevak Sangh, see below) the count of convictions and acquittals and compoundings adds up to the total of cases. Perhaps each individual defendant is scored as a separate case — but the frequency of multiple defendants, as may be gathered from the reported cases on appeal, makes the totals improbably small. So apparently each registered complaint is counted as a unit and we are provided with a single "score" for the total outcome. We have no assurance that the scoring process has remained constant. But then again, there is no reason to assume that this scoring has been an exception in a field marked by administrative inertia or that changes would have gone unrecorded.

224 On the basis of the data in Table 10.3, it is possible to derive an ideal rate for each state, assuming that the activity during the periods reported is representative of the activity during the entire period. On this basis, we get an average rate of 384.4 cases per year. This probably amounts to a slight overstatement since it is more likely that active years would be found more worthy of report than inactive ones. Nevertheless, the relative constancy of the all-India totals (excepting the poorly reported 1954) indicates that the rate was not too far below this.

[225] This is computed by figuring an ideal rate for each state, as explained in note 224 above.

[226] Of course, the correspondence between Untouchables and Scheduled Castes is not exact. There are groups which are treated as untouchable which do not appear on the lists of Scheduled Castes. See Backward Classes Commission I: 28. Notable among these are recent converts to Buddhism. On the exclusion of converts, see Galanter 1967: 105 ff. Therefore the rates in Table 10.5 somewhat overstate the frequency of recourse to the UOA, especially in the case of Maharashtra where most of the Buddhists are to be found.

[227] The UOA is relatively little used as measured against, e.g., recourse by American Negroes to administrative remedies. Compare the following figures for employment complaints only:

FAIR EMPLOYMENT PRACTICE COMPLAINTS IN SELECTED AMERICAN STATES

State	Year	No. of Cases	Cases Per Million Negro Population
California	1962	705	800
Kansas	1964	57	580
Massachusetts	1963	182	1620
Minnesota	1963	30	1360
New Jersey	1962	120	230
New York	1962	611	430
Pennsylvania	1963	220	260

Source: Adapted from Lockard 1968: 92.

[228] See Dushkin 1957: Chap. V. One may speculate that such ritual expression of untouchability is correlated with the elaboration of caste ranking in various areas. Cf. Marriott 1960.

[229] Andhra Pradesh is the striking exception to the regional pattern. Other indicators suggest that the Andhra government gives low priority to the interests of the Scheduled Castes. Measured by Schermerhorn's two indices of ministerial assignment and per capita expenditure (adjusted for affluence level of state) on Scheduled Castes welfare, Andhra ranks at the bottom. Schermerhorn 1969: 399. This suggests that a low commitment on the government side may be one factor in low use of the UOA.

[230] The Harijan Sevak Sangh reported that its workers in Gujarat brought 127 cases in 1963–64 and 55 cases in 1964–65. Similarly, in Madhya Pradesh HSS workers brought 35 cases in 1963–64 and 51 cases in 1964–65. In the latter year, there were 62 HSS "sevaks" in Gujarat and 52 in Madhya Pradesh. Of an All-India total of 280 sevaks, 227 (81%) were in our "high use" states, which have been the scene of approximately 86% of the cases under the UOA. Harijan Sevak Sangh 1963–64: 25; 1964–65: 14.

[231] RCSCST 1963–64: I, 25.

[232] For an instance which led to imposition of fourteen death sentences, see Harijan Sevak Sangh 1963–64; 86. For a more typical case, see RCSCST 1960–61: I, 42.

[233] This may be due in part to the insistance of the Commissioner of Scheduled Castes and Scheduled Tribes that state governments forward reasons why registered cases were not challaned.

[234] These percentages are based only upon those cases disposed of in the year that their registration was reported by the various states. If we may assume that prosecutions subjected to prolonged delay are less often successful, then these conviction rates should be taken as overstatements.

[235] § 345 of the Code of Criminal Procedure (Act. V of 1898) provides for the compounding or composition of specified offenses: (Some are to be compounded automatically upon petition by the parties; others require "the permission of the court.") The UOA § 15(b) provides that every offense under the Act may be

compounded "with the permission of the court." The prevailing view is that discretion is entirely in the court whether to permit such a case to be compounded. The magistrate is not to refer to a higher court or to act on the advice of the police. Generally he should permit compounding unless the offense is so serious that punishment is considered absolutely necessary. § 345(6) provides that composition "shall have the effect of an acquittal of the accused." Once approved, the composition cannot be withdrawn, the case cannot be tried and fresh charges arising out of the same facts are barred. There is no form of judicial supervision to see that the agreement between the parties is carried out. See Ramanatha Iyer 1956: II, 1237 ff.

236 The average rate of convictions in criminal trials in India is near 70%. Cases of cognizable crime in 1951 led to 124,350 convictions (65.9%) and 65,945 (34.1%) acquitted or discharged. Statistical Abstract of India 1953–54: 212. In 1960 there were 2,715,446 (63.9%) convictions for all crimes and 1,534,266 (36.1%) acquitted or discharged. Statistical Abstract of the Indian Union 1963–64: 641–42.

In the Punjab between 1955 and 1964, the annual percentage of cases in which there were convictions ranged from a low of 63% to a high of 76%. Govt. of Punjab 1966: 13. In 1957, all the courts in Bombay disposed of a total of 1,529,131 defendants. Of these, 1,127,638 (73.7%) were convicted and only 367,446 (24.0%) were discharged or acquitted. Govt. of Bombay 1962: 62.

237 It is not clear whether compounded cases should be regarded as a disposition favorable to the Untouchable party or not. Obviously the compounded category covers a variety of situations from full compliance by a penitent accused to intimidation by a party who continues flagrant disregard of the UOA. But there is reason to believe that it should be scored as generally not favorable to the Untouchable party, or somewhat closer to an acquittal than to a conviction. For some years the Harijan Sevak Sangh's annual report divided cases into "convicted" and "compromised or dismissed" and clearly identified only the former as "decided in favour of Harijans." (1963–64: 25; 1962–63: 36). Cf. fear of observers that Untouchables were pressured into compounding (Committee on Plan Projects 1959). Strategically, compounding provides little leverage for the weaker party to the agreement. There is no form of judicial or police supervision to see that the agreement between the parties is carried out. Presumably the only sanction available to the weaker party is the threat of a new prosecution on new facts. But in a setting where the chances of conviction are not high and where penalties are not severe, this may have little force. For this reason, I feel justified in regarding compounded cases as situations in which Untouchables broke even at best. I consider it doubtful that these compounded cases mark the employment of the UOA to break decisively the pattern of disabilities.

238 Unlike the situation in other states with sizable numbers of cases registered, these cases in Madras have no known connection with organized social workers. In contrast to its active role in Gujarat and Madhya Pradesh, the Harijan Sevak Sangh reports that its workers in Madras brought only four cases in 1963–64 and two cases in 1964–65. Harijan Sevak Sangh 1963–64: 25; 1964–65: 25.

239 No information is available to explain conclusively the distinctness of Madras. One element in the situation is that from 1963 on, the Home Minister in Madras was a Scheduled Caste member; increased police activity may perhaps be credited to his sense of priorities.

240 The closest approximation is provided by the procedure under § 6 of the Madras Temple Entry Act (Madras Act V of 1947 as amended by Madras Act XIII of 1949) for governmental determination that a temple falls within the purview of the Act.

241 The Office of the Commissioner for Scheduled Castes and Scheduled Tribes is required by the Constitution "to investigate all matters relating to the safeguards provided for the Scheduled Castes . . . under this Constitution and report to the President upon the working of those safeguards. . . ." The President is directed to "cause all such reports to be laid before each House of Parliament." Art. 338(2). The Commissioner's Office has its headquarters in New Delhi and has seventeen regional field offices, each in the charge of an Assistant Commissioner. While the Commissioner's office has conducted several sample surveys on the continuing

incidence of disabilities, it has not undertaken any independent investigation of enforcement activity, but has merely collated reports sent to it (sometimes after many reminders) by state officials.

The Elayaperumal Committee found that only two states had followed the recommendation of the 1954 Untouchability Offences Bill Joint Committee to establish committees to look into the implementation of the Act. As of 1963, the Advisory Boards on Harijan Welfare in the various states did not include implementation of the UOA in their agendas. Dept. of Social Welfare 1969: 46–7.

[242] A distinguished American lawyer described the general problem of enforcement of Indian regulatory legislation as "rather like what OPA would have been up against if it had no Enforcement Department in the national and field office and had to depend for enforcement on state and local police bringing violations to the attention of the county D.A.'s." Cavers 1964: 8.

[243] Government of India, Prohibition Inquiry Committee 1955: 132–33.

[244] Planning Commission 1964: 367 ff.

[245] The English-language press and the educated classes share an exaggerated notion of the amount of preferential treatment that Scheduled Castes actually receive and are inclined to attribute the flagrant abuses that have characterized some schemes for other backward classes to the relatively modest and innocent schemes for Scheduled Castes.

[246] A recent exception is Oommen 1968; Shukla 1969; Oommen 1969.

[247] Under British rule, Untouchables were barred from the police. Curry 1932: 68. In 1956, Scheduled Castes comprised 5.4% of all police personnel. RCSCST 1956–57: II, 172–3.

[248] Interview (Bombay, 1958).

[249] The Elayaperumal Committee concluded that some police officials were not aware of the provisions of the UOA. Dept. of Social Welfare 1969: 47. In a survey of one U.P. district, almost half the police were unaware of the existence of the UOA and almost all were unaware of its important provisions. Id. The Committee found that State Governments had been remiss in distributing copies of the Act in regional languages and that copies were not available at many district offices, Id. 43.

[250] *State v. Kanu Dharma*, A.I.R. 1955 Bom. 390 at 393. An attempt to impeach witnesses on the ground that they belonged to the same community as the party for whom they testified was condemned as against the spirit of the Constitution in *Kashiram v. Lakmichand*. A.I.R. 1958 M.P. 407.

[251] See Committee on Plan Projects 1959: 193. This problem was anticipated by the Commissioner of Scheduled Castes and Tribes prior to the passage of the UOA and led to his opposition to the provision allowing offenses under that act to be compounded. RCSCST 1952: 29.

[252] Interview (Madurai, 1958).

[253] Department of Social Welfare 1969: 51.

[254] See Goyal 3. See, e.g., *Benudhar Sahu v. State*, I.L.R. 1962 Cuttack 256, where an important and arguable interpretation of the UOA was promulgated in a case where the complainant did not appear by counsel before the High Court.

[255] Interview (Delhi, 1968).

[256] In the first three years of the Third Five Year Plan, only 9% of the funds allotted for legal aid to Scheduled Castes were utilized. RCSCST 1963–64: I–27.

[257] Harijan Sevak Sangh 1964–65: 25. Cf. 1962–63: 37.

[258] Until 1964–65, the reports lump compromised and acquitted cases as a single category. The pattern of dispositions shifted radically in 1966–67. See Table 10.8B.

[259] RCSCST 1958–59: I-30; 1959–60; I-28-9. Committee on Plan Projects (1959: 193) recommended enactment of a minimum fine of Rs. 50 for a first offense, with Rs. 200 fine and a month's imprisonment for a second offense.

[260] *Behari Lal v. State*, A.I.R. 1967 All. 131.

[261] See Table 10.1. There is no way of determining how many UOA cases have been appealed, since minor criminal cases decided by the High Courts often go unreported.

[262] RCSCST 1958–59; I-32; Committee on Plan Projects 1959: 189. The village studies conducted by the 1961 census did some inconclusive polling and found that awareness of the act varied from 3% to 100%. RCSCST 1963–64: I-21.

[263] Many of the matters involved in these complaints (e.g., services, scholarships) are not within the purview of the UOA, but many seem to concern the enforcement of disabilities and to lie within the scope of the Act. The following table represents the available information:

Period and Source RCSCST	Land	Drinking Water	Harassment	Housing	Services Employment	Observance of Untouchability	Miscellaneous	Total (New Delhi)	Total (Reg Offices)	Grand Total
1954:105-07	85	20	126	38	92		91	452		
1955:I,80	65	10	180	20	120		90	485		
1956:I,20	71	17	84	19	173		195	559		
1957-58:I,23	72	9	347	46	89	53		616		
1958-59:I,49	202	18	136	120	222	117	127	942	800	1742
§1959-60:I,40	242	15	107	†	485		347	1301	805	2106
§1960-61:I,41	314		188	†	630	27	252	1591	551	2146
1961-62:I,10			53			287		340		
1962-63:I,23			316			83		399		
1963-64:I	223	7	209		128	70	140	777	} 480	1257
	82	15	56	†	99	10	206			
1964-65:I,25	188		130	†	109	46	129	902	} 1251	2153
	158	10	111	237	233	36	380			
1965-66:83	784	*	434	†	765	116	952			3051
1966-67:33	219	*	147	†	697	43	443	1549	} 1432	2981
	389		192		229	45	577			

§1959-60 Financial Help 75; Scholarships 30
§1960-61 Financial Help 163; Scholarships 27
*included in miscellaneous
– – – – – – – – – – Change in Commissioner
†included in land

[264] RCSCST 1960–61: I-43. Cf. RCSCST 1963–64: I-26–27, where the Commissioner notes that complaints against government officials are often forwarded to those same officials for a report!

[265] See Table 10.10 above. In 1955, the Bharatiya Depressed Classes League reported that its workers brought "about 100 cases" under the newly passed UOA. RCSCST 1955: I-73. Subsequent reports of this organization's activities have not included any reference to litigation.

[266] The periods are not strictly comparable since the HSS does not go by the calendar year.

[267] See, e.g., *Sridhar Krishnarao v. Crown*, A.I.R. 1949 Nag. 383.

[268] Compare Lockard's findings of the greater success of American anti-discrimination laws in regard to similar public facilities and his explanation that this is due to the greater ease of proving discrimination in such cases.

DISPOSITION OF ANTI-DISCRIMINATION CASES IN SELECTED AMERICAN JURISDICTIONS

Type of Cases	No. of States/ Cities	Total Years Covered	Total Cases Closed	DISPOSITION					
				Satisfactorily Adjusted		No Probable Cause, No Jurisdiction, Dismissed		Withdrawn or otherwise Terminated	
Employment	10	108	14,036	4467	32%	8969	64%	600	4%
Housing	10	47	3,085	1378	45%	1591	51%	117	4%
Public Accommodations	7	50	2,123	1211	57%	781	37%	131	6%

SOURCE: Adapted from Lockard, 1968: 91, 122, 138.

[269] Even in favorable settings, social workers report that the UOA is more useful in cleaning up "hold outs" as, e.g., where a majority of tea shop owners have agreed to end disabilities, than it is breaking down a solid barrier of opposition. Interview (Madurai, 1958).

[270] For a poignant example, see Epstein 1962: 183 ff.

[271] The Office of the Commissioner of Scheduled Castes and Scheduled Tribes conducted a survey on the accomplishments of the *pracharaks* of non-official anti-untouchability agencies in five villages in Rajasthan and found "the impact of propaganda conducted by the *pracharaks* was obviously not of a lasting nature; the services of barbers, tea-stall holders, etc., made available to the Scheduled Castes through their efforts were stopped as soon as the *pracharaks* left the villages." RCSCST 1966–67: 45.

[272] See, e.g., the suggestion of the Commissioner for Scheduled Castes and Scheduled Tribes that such "opened" facilities be periodically rechecked. RCSCST 1959–60: I, 31.

[273] The whole governmental program of welfare measures tends to operate not to share common facilities, but to create separate ones for Scheduled Castes. Separate housing developments lead to separate schools, wells, meeting halls. Karve 1958: 886; Indian Conference of Social Work 1955: 41.

[274] Andeneas 1966.

[275] Lynch (1968: 26) observes that anti-disabilities legislation communicates government support for the greater salience of citizen roles over caste roles in interaction.

[276] Orenstein 1965: 253.

[277] Id.

[278] E.g., Aiyappan 1965.

[279] The downward spiral here seems somewhat analogous to that in the use of the Reconstruction Civil Rights Acts in the United States, where interaction between local prejudice, lack of facilities, and restrictive interpretation of the laws occurred in a context of declining national interest and political support. See Davis 1914.

[280] Publications Division 1963: 19–20.

[281] Quoted at RCSCST 1963–64: I, 25.

[282] Rowe 1968: 37.

[283] RCSCST 1963–64: I, 19. Orenstein's (1965: 249) description of Maharashtrian villagers' assessment of legal changes a decade earlier: "Many villagers interpreted these legal phenomena more broadly; they thought that all caste proscriptions were 'against the law,' even in private interaction. For instance, some believed the law required that they not object to sitting beside Harijans, even in their own courtyards."

[284] The feeling that everything that might be done has been done may be maintained at any level of activity. As early as 1923 an authoritative publication observed that "everything that can be done by legislation has now been done; and so far as the letter of the law is concerned, the Depressed Classes might rise unimpeded." Government of India, Home Department 1923: 223.

[285] Ministry of Community Development and Cooperation 1961: 31.

[286] The classic formulation is by Sumner 1960. The most dramatic evidence of legal inefficacy is drawn from two areas: "crimes without victims" (i.e., penal prohibition of commodities and practices which are not disapproved by their purchasers, such as liquor, drugs and abortion) and family law. For recent and vivid documentation, see Schur 1965; Massell 1968. The analogy of these areas with the regulation of intergroup relations is not, however, conclusive. Unlike "crimes without victims" the proscription of untouchability has a class of beneficiaries who have a tangible interest in enforcement. And, unlike family law, the beneficiaries are coherent social groups capable of coordinated action, protection and support in the use of such legal advantages.

[287] Dror 1959 suggests that laws have more difficulty in changing expressive and evaluative areas of activity than emotionally neutral and instrumental ones. Chambliss 1968 suggests that the effectiveness of deterrence varies with the expressive nature of the act and the degree of commitment to "crime" as a way of life. Untouchability offenses would seem to rank high on both counts. For the villager there would seem to be high commitment to a way of life that puts a positive value on the proscribed conduct and which provides group support for it. For the tea shop keeper, cinema owner or school principal there may be less expressiveness and less commitment, which clearly comports with the greater effectiveness of the UOA in these settings than in dealing with wells and housing.

[288] Berger 1952: chap. V; Raab and Lipset 1959. Cf. Mayhew's (1968) finding of greater impact of an anti-discrimination law in the field of housing than in the field of employment (in spite of greater opposing sentiment in the housing area), suggesting that institutional features may be more important than sentiment in determining the effectiveness of anti-discrimination legislation.

[289] See, e.g., Srinivas 1966; Rudolph and Rudolph 1967.

[290] The Elayaperumal Committee suggested one substantive area that should be included in the UOA: protection against exaction of menial services (carrying death news, etc.). Dept. of Social Welfare 1966: 59.

[291] A saving clause along the following lines has been suggested to the writer by a distinguished Indian lawyer:
No person shall be deemed to be guilty of an offense under this Act if he proves that the act alleged to constitute the offense was committed by him solely on grounds other than the "untouchability" of the complainant, and that such grounds were reasonable under the circumstances and not adverse to public policy.

[292] Compare the "arising out of" language of Article 17 with Article 15(2) which forbids discrimination "only" on grounds of caste, etc. Clearly the rights conferred by Article 17 are more ample and the State is empowered to go beyond those disabilities accompanied by a subjective animus against Untouchables.

[293] Cf. the broad inclusive definition of "public" in the Indian Penal Code, § 12.

[294] If this were done, it would be necessary to append a suitable disclaimer in order to preserve the ritual prerogatives of the priests and temple attendants. In regard to facilities other than temples which are now subject to the "same religion and denomination" qualifier, it would be necessary to provide explicitly for whichever intra-Hindu rights of exclusiveness it was desired to save.

[295] This has been suggested by Goyal 1965.

[296] Cf. the recommendations of the Elayaperumal Committee for making offenses non-compoundable, minimum sentence of three months imprisonment, disqualification from public office, government service and doing business with the government. Dept. of Social Welfare 1969: 63.

[297] The power of the Supreme Court and the High Court to issue "directions or orders or writs" to enforce the Fundamental Rights would seem to include those Fundamental Rights which run against individuals [Articles 15(2), 17, 23] as well as those which run only against the Government.

[298] The police are authorized to intervene actively to prevent the commission of cognizable offenses. Code of Criminal Procedure (V of 1895) §§ 149, 151.

[299] It is for this reason that nothing can be expected from the suggestion (RCSCST 1961–62: I, 8) that the Village Level Worker be made responsible for reporting offenses under the UOA. Even more than the policeman, the VLW is dependent upon the locally powerful for the successful performance of his job. The notion of transferring UOA cases to village panchayats has the virtue of setting the fox to guard the henhouse. RCSCST 1958–59: I, 41.

[300] Useful analysis of the strengths and weaknesses of administrative commissions in effectuating anti-discrimination policies may be found in Lockhard 1968; Mayhew 1968; Witherspoon 1968.

[301] Such sanctions would represent the extension of a principle already incorporated in existing schemes, e.g., Bombay made grants to local bodies conditional upon equal treatment of Scheduled Castes. RCSCST 1958–59: I, 41. Gujarat gives money for projects only where there is a resolution that Scheduled Castes will share it. RCSCST 1962–63: I, 23.

[302] Cf. The Elayaperumal Committee's proposals. Dept. of Social Welfare 1969: 63.

[303] Goyal 1965: 4 suggests deputing special police officers of high rank and "missionary zeal" to handle enforcement and prosecution of UOA cases. The proposal here concurs in the need for an agency independent of the local police, but prefers to reinforce "zeal" by career incentives rather than depending exclusively upon sustained personal commitment. It would, of course, be necessary to make the remuneration sufficiently high to enable these agents to resist any inducements that might be offered by offenders. Prohibition serves as a warning here, but there is this difference – the untouchability offender is not making his livelihood by his offense.

[304] In doing so, an agency would encounter some vexing problems of resolving the ambiguities of current government policy. For example, should priority be given to providing Untouchables with an adequate water supply – or to affording them the social honor attendant upon using the same well as the other villagers. To what extent should this turn on the convenience or cost of a separate well? Is it acceptable to trade-off commonness of wells for other gains of more value to a group of Untouchables?

[305] The thoughtful proposals of the Elayaperumal Committee for the formation of social disabilities Boards at the taluk (i.e., sub-district) level take up some of these possibilities in detail. Setting up Boards at this level would undoubtedly have the advantages of accessibility, responsiveness and knowledge of local conditions. It also suggests countervailing dangers of accessibility to local political pressures and the need for some way of building in safeguards against pressures from dominant local interests.

[306] Cf. the American experience that the bulk of anti-discrimination complaints are filed by more highly educated middle-class Negroes and that their complaints are more often successful. Lockard 1968: 78, 130.

LAW REPORTS CITED

Citations of the reported judgments of courts are given in standard Indian legal form. Thus citations of official reports give the names of the first party on each side, the notation I.L.R. (indicating Indian Law Reports), the volume number, the title of the series (indicating the court), the page on which the case begins, and, finally the date of publication; for example *Gopal* v. *Hanmant,* I.L.R. 3 Bom. 273 (1879). Citations to the *All-India Reporter,* the most popular series of unofficial reports, follow a slightly different pattern; for example, *Sunder Devi* v. *Jheboo Lal,* A.I.R. 1957 All. 215 (names, A.I.R.-series, year of publication, name of court, page on which case begins). There is a separate A.I.R. volume published each year for each court. The coverage of A.I.R. and I.L.R. is overlapping but not identical. Occasionally cases not found in either of these series are reported in a local or specialized series. The citation of these follows a similar pattern. In citations of pre-1860 reports I have tried to approximate the modern style to facilitate location.

A.I.R. *All India Reporter.* Nagpur: D. V. Chitaley, 1914–.

Bellasis *Reports of Civil Cases Determined in the Court of Sudder Dewanee Adawlut of Bombay,* compiled by A. F. Bellasis, Esq., 1840–1848. Bombay: printed for the government at the Bombay Educ. Soc's. Press, 1850.

Bom. L. Reporter *Bombay Law Reporter.* Bombay: The Bombay Law Reporter Office, 1899 .

C.W.N. *Calcutta Weekly Notes;* reports of important decisions of the Calcutta High Court. 1896–.

C.P.L.R. *Central Provinces Law Reports.* 17 Vols. 1886–1904.

Crim. L.J. *Criminal Law Journal:* a monthly legal publication containing full reports of all reportable criminal cases of the High Courts and Supreme Court of India. Nagpur: All India Reporter, Ltd., 1904–.

Cuttack L.T. *Cuttack Law Times.* Cuttack: H. P. Bhagat, 1935–.

I.A.C. *The Law Reports . . . Indian appeals:* being cases in the Privy council on appeal from the East Indies. London: Council of Law Reporting, 1874–1950.

I.C. *Indian Cases.* Containing full reports of decisions of the Judicial Committee of the Privy Council, the High Courts of Allahabad, Bombay, Calcutta, and Madras, the Chief Courts of Lower Burma and Punjab, the Courts of the Judicial Commissioners of Central Provinces. Oudh, Sind and Upper Burma. 231 Vols., Lahore: Law Publications Press, 1909–1947.

I.L.R. (Bom.) *Indian Law Reports,* Bombay series, containing cases determined by the High Court at Bombay and by the Judicial committee of the Privy council on appeal from that court. Bombay: Superintendent, Government Press, 1876–.

I.L.R. (Cuttack) *Indian Law Reports,* Cuttack series, containing cases decided by the Orissa High Court and by the Supreme Court on appeal therefrom. Cuttack: Superintendent, Orissa Government Press, 1950–.

I.L.R. (Kerala) *Indian Law Reports,* Kerala series, containing cases determined by the High Court of Kerala and by the Supreme Court of India on appeal from that court. Ernakulam: Government of Kerala, Government Press, 1957–.

I.L.R. (Madras) *Indian Law Reports,* Madras series, containing cases determined by the High Court at Madras and by the Judicial committee of the Privy council on appeal from that court. Madras: Government Press, 1876–.

K.L.R.   *Kerala Law Reporter.* Weekly, containing judgments of the Travancore-Cochin High Court and of the Supreme Court on appeal
therefrom. Ernakulam: V. Seshan, 1928–.

L.A.C.   *Labour Appeal Cases.* Decisions of the Labour Appellate Tribunal
and of the Supreme Court on Appeal from the Tribunal. Delhi:
Manager of Publications, 1951–.

M.W.N.   *Madras Weekly Notes.* Madras: N.R.K. Tatachariar, 1910–.

M.P.L.J.   *The Madhya Pradesh Law Journal.* Nagpur: Central Law House,
1956–.

Morris   *Selected Decisions of the Court of Sudder Dewanee Adawlut of
Bombay* compiled by James Morris. Bombay, 1852.

P.R.   *Punjab Record.* 1866–1919.

S.D.A.   (Bengal)   *Decisions of the Sudder Dewanee Adawult at Calcutta.*
18 Vols., 1845–62.

S.U.A.   (Madras)   *Sudr Udalut Appeals.* Decrees in Appeal Suits determined
in the Court of Sudr Udalut. Madras: Pharoah & Co. 2 Vols., 1853.

S.U.D.   (Madras)   *Sudr Udalut Decisions.* Decisions of the Sudr Udalut.
1849–62.

U.S.   *United States Reports. Official reports of the Supreme Court.* Washington, U. S. Government Printing Office.

Vejiaragavooloo Chettiar   *Rulings of the Court of Sudr Udalut* contained in
the decisions passed by them during the years 1850 to 1857. Compiled by S. Vejiaragavooloo Chettiar. Madras. 1858.

Weekly Rep.   *The Weekly Reporter.* Calcutta: Thacker, Spink, 25 Vols.,
1864–77.

Weir   *The Law of Offenses and Criminal Procedure* (Criminal Rulings) as
expounded by the High Court of Judicature, Madras. Thomas Weir,
comp. and annotator. 4th ed. (K. Jagannatha Aiyar, ed.) 2 Vols.,
Madras: Srinivasa Varadachari and Co., 1905.

PART IV

Social and Psychological Response To Change of Status

Owen Lynch

Parade marking the second Religious Conference of Indian
Buddhists — Bombay, December, 1970

11.   ROBERT J. MILLER
                                           & PRAMODH KALE

The Burden on the Head
Is Always There

> *What must we do? Where are to be found*
> *The manifold potencies of being?*
> Aryadeva, A.D. *Seventh Century*

THE BUDDHIST CONVERSION movement initiated in 1956 by Dr. B. R. Ambedkar spread rapidly among the Mahars of Maharashtra, one of the largest Untouchable castes in India. The ready acceptance of Buddhism by several million Mahars raises many questions as to the nature of their role in Hindu society and the social and psychological consequences of their decision to abandon a status based on social, political, and economic ties of great antiquity as well as religious beliefs and practices. The identity given these Untouchables, by those who considered themselves the Mahar's superiors and masters, was couched in ritual and philosophical terms. It was an identity maintained by stringent restrictions that included physical as well as ideological separation from the greater society. Viewed from a modern Western perspective, such restrictions would place severe limitations on the individual's "potencies of being." In psychological terms such treatment should have been utterly destructive of the individual's ego-strength.

The bold and assertive response of the Mahars to Ambedkar's call seems out of keeping with the common assumption that the Untouchable

The author wishes to thank the National Science Foundation and the American Institute of Indian Studies for grants permitting himself and his wife, Beatrice D. Miller, to work with Mahar Buddhists in Maharashtra during 1963–64.

[317]

generally accepts his "place" in society. The radical changes inherent in religious conversion of this kind might also be expected to create a Mahar "crisis of identity" (see R. Miller 1967). Efforts to explore such questions, however, are severely hampered by a paucity of material that might elucidate the Mahar's "self-image" prior to conversion and their social and psychological reactions afterwards. A promising, though little used, avenue of enquiry is literature created by members of depressed groups. Such material is rare, due in part to the illiteracy that accompanies low status. Fortunately, the recent emergence of Mahar writers, and a new interest in depicting the lower classes in Marathi literature,* afford a unique opportunity to examine aspects of the Mahar "self-image" and some of the consequences of their conversion in the context of village life, where the role of Mahar is most clearly articulated.

This study is based on seven short stories written in Marathi that depict various facets of being a Mahar. Six of these works of fiction were selected from a collection of short stories published in 1965 by Sankarava [Shankarao] Kharat, a Mahar. The author of the seventh story, V. Madgulkar, is a Brahman. His work, published in 1966, and the stories by Kharat, appear to have been written in the late 1950s or early 1960s. Pramodh Kale, a native speaker of Marathi, translated these stories into English and provided many insights into the meaning and implication of the text. In the preparation of this translation, some descriptive material was deleted, and in some instances original paragraph structure was broken into segments that lend greater clarity to the English version.

Each story is prefaced with a brief sketch of the plot and definitions of untranslated Marathi terms and titles whose meaning is not clear from the context. Since the enumeration of a general number is standardized in Marathi, conventional expressions such as "eight-sixteen Mahars" are used, rather than "eight to sixteen" to avoid the implication that specific numbers are intended.

Following the translation, an effort is made to explicate the Mahar's traditional role, his self-image, and his relations to others. Themes relating to this analysis are indicated in the preceding title and poetic excerpts.† Through comparison and contrast, themes derived from one story are amplified in succeeding analyses. While each story is complete in itself, the order of their presentation approximates the sequence of major devel-

---

*Mahadeo L. Apte, "Contemporary Marathi Fiction," *The Journal of Asian Studies,* Volume XXIX, No. 1, November, 1969, pp. 55–56.

†The poetic excerpts have been taken from "The Rebel" by Padraic Pearse. This poem appears in *The Poetry of Freedom* edited by William R. Benét and Norman Cousins. New York: Random House, 1945.

opments that occurred in the Mahar community during the post-Independence period.

The initial story to be examined, "Daundi," serves as the title story of Kharat's collection. Here we find reference to various facets of the Mahar's traditional role in rural Maharashtra — that of town-crier, messenger, remover of dead cattle, and maintainer of the cremation grounds. Rama, a Mahar, is summoned to the village *chavadi* (headquarters or office) where the *patil* (village headman) and *talathi* (village accountant) conduct official business with the assistance of two other minor officials, the *chaugula* and *ramoshi*. The occasion is a smallpox epidemic, and Rama is called upon to announce the arrival of a doctor to treat the villagers, which he does in spite of his own illness. Untranslated Marathi terms used in the story include *arrey*, an ejaculated utterance of varied meaning whose use approximates that of "hey there" in English: and two terms of address, *"anna"* and *"leka,"* which denote high and low status respectively. *Johar*, the traditional mode of salutation used to greet deities and men of high status is referred to in "Daundi" and later stories.

Daundi (The Town-crier's call)

The sky is full. Hanging down. Leaking all the while. The rain drips forever, seeping in. The slushy mud bubbles audibly. The soul feels sick. The villagers feel out of sorts. Rama Taral feels low. He is lying down in his house.

The air in the village is oppressive too. For the last eight—ten days, daylight has not shown its face. The air has become close and chilly. Rama does not want to leave his house and go out. He doesn't even feel like poking his head out of the house. He wants to sit by the threshold here, warming himself. He feels like gulping down a warm potful. He wants to eat hot *bhakar* crushed in gravy that is hot. He feels like filling his belly with hot tea, warming all his inner linings.

Rama feels that he should wrap himself all over in a woolen blanket and sleep by the warmth of the wood-burning stove. Ask the wife to cover him with a double-folded quilt. Burrow deep into it.

Then he could sleep. This feverishness would go. The heavy limbs would become light. Feel good. The heavy eyes become clear. The drowsiness would leave. The burning would go. The tired feet would feel rested. A new strength will enter them. Feel good again. . . .

I shall go out with new breath, new vigor. Finish all the work.
Listen — there she is. The bitch lizard crying tschkk-tschkk. Beat it.
It feels bad enough and her vicious words are making things worse. Arrey!
Sprinkle some water on the roof. Yes, Yes, sprinkle some water. . . .

Rama feels tired. His hands and legs are heavy. The stomach feels
like it is being sucked into itself. A strange pain shakes through his
stomach to the head. It goes up and down. The head is gripped, losing
its sensation — cold like a stove.

For the last eight days, to tell the truth, Rama had not slept a wink.
Work in the day. Work at night. A huge heap of village work. He had
sunk into it, was buried under it.

*Now tell me — how can a man carry on? How can a man live? Not a job or
two. A whole big mountain of jobs to do. People dying all around. Make
arrangements for wood and cowdung cakes for burning someone. Take the
death-message to his kith and kin. Attend at the chavadi. Obey the patil's
orders. Carry his messages to farms and places in and around the village.
Do other things they ask you to. Bring a man to the chavadi, make him
appear before the patil and the talathi. If anybody's cattle dies, drag it out
of the village. Watch all the strangers going in and coming out of the place.
And then the watchman's job at night. Take rounds through lanes and bylanes
of the village. Calling "Husshar — who goes there — husshar." The whole village sleeps. Only I am standing. At dawn, no sooner does the body touch the
ground than the day breaks. The sun shows its face. Get up and go running
home. Spit and gargle and come back to the chavadi.*

*Like the oil-presser's bullock. Nothing else. Eyes covered by blinders.
Work all the time. No rest. No one to say, you are tired. No one to say
"Come. Sit down. Stop dragging yourself to death."*

"Yes brother. All's work, nothing else. So good to meet you. Someone
who knows how I work."

"Take rest. Let things go for awhile."

*True. But who's going to say that to me? Who is mine here? Whom
can I tell of this pain in my stomach?*

*"Brother. No one here is mine. No one's heart would feel sympathy for
me. I have got to live in this village. My wife and children have to live.
And for that I do all this, suffer all this.*

Mouth gagged.
Hands and feet chained
A mountain of work to face . . . .

*This is the way things go. You cannot see it. You are moving to your own
rhythm, your own intoxication . . . .*

"Oh *Ma!* Oh — Oh *Dev* Parameshwara!"

"Now, now — don't get worked up. Why are you babbling so? Sleep quietly
for a while — you will feel lighter." Rama's wife Savubai aproached. She
felt his forehead. Caressed the face with her hand. Her face dropped,

darkened. Holding her forehead she sat down. Releasing with a sigh the long abated breath, she felt Rama's forehead again.

"Please, why are you talking like this in your sleep?" Savubai's voice woke Rama up. He moved a little. With great effort he lifted the heavy eyelids. Peeping at her with half-closed eyes, from under them he said in a sunken voice, "Has somebody come?"

"No it's only me."

"Sit. Sit here by me. See, I am not feeling well."

"Why are you speaking like this? You have been talking in your sleep as if you were talking with someone."

"When? No."

"See now. I have been listening for a long time. — to your muttering and plaints."

"What for? And who is going to listen to it? Only God! And he knows all. He sees all. All things are recorded. Then tell me why should I say anything to anybody." Saying this, Rama kept quiet for a little while and muttered, "God, oh Lord! Now my trust is in you. You are the support of my children and babies."

He folded his hands to God and wiped his tear-filled eyes. Seeing this, Savubai quickly spoke in a lowered voice — "Why do you say that and feel bad? The work has tired you. Rest for a couple of days and you will feel good. Don't worry yourself unnecessarily. God has given enough — children by the basketloads."

"I am worried about them."

"God will care for them. What's the use of you worrying about them?"

"Yes, True."

"Now don't talk crazy like this. Lie down quietly. When you get a little sleep you will feel better." Saying this Savubai got up. Folding the quilt she covered him with it and set about preparing food and fetching water.

It is long past breakfast time. The day has come a long way but is hidden in the overcast sky. It is impossible to know what hour of the day it is. The sheep and the cattle are let out. The cowherd boys have set out on their chilly way. The squishy mud stretches all around. The air is oppressive.

The air has become bad in the village. In all the neighboring villages are the same complaints. Men are sick in bed. The air is bad. People have become worried. The same wind blows in so many villages. Word is passed, the message spreads. Guests and visitors stay indoors — depressed, worried. All are stricken. All are sucked into a whirlwind.

The sky above droops down in fullness. At a blow it may fall down on a person. The gnats are singing. The roofs are leaking. Mud is everywhere.

The air stands still, sad, desolate.

Half my life is gone. Summer and rain. I bore heat and thirst — suffered. Rain and wind on my body. Times hard and bitter.

Ate my bite, fresh and stale. Never waited for something to eat it with. But always worked for the village. Yes, of course, you did. So what — a favor to someone? Wanted to live here in the village, didn't you? This is my mother, this pandhari land. I should serve her, so it was ordained. I fulfilled it. A constant sacrifice performed.

"Rama, oh Rama Taral —" Someone calling from outside. No answer within. "*Arrey,* anyone there at home or not?" All quiet. Cold. Not the littlest sound.

"By mother! Where are all the people in Rama's house gone?" An angry muttering followed by a loud shout — "Rama, *Arrey* Rama. Are you in the house? I am here."

Rama thought this was God's call — his shout. God has come to see him . . . . .

Lord, I am yours. I was born to serve you. Let me serve you without a break.

Rama heard someone calling. Once more he was awakened. He removed the blanket from his head. Once again the words hurled themselves at his ears.

"*Arrey* RAMA! I am here outside."

So someone has really come outside. Rama removed the blanket, rubbed his heavy eyes.

"Oh — oh — mother. . . ." He squirmed up and replied, "Please, who is there outside?"

"*Arrey,* it is me — *patil.* Can't you recognize a man's voice?"

"Oh my god — so you did come." Rama muttered to himself and said aloud, "Coming, master."

"Sleeping in ease?" The *patil's* words forced themselves into his eardrums like molten lead.

Now what shall I tell this patil? How can I tell him — by breaking my head and splattering my hands in the blood — ? Patil, I am not sleeping in ease. My body is aching. My intestines are shrivelled. The limbs twist. Chill has entered the bones, biting like a snake all the time . . . . . Let that be.

His lips moving wordlessly, moaning in pain — "*Age, Aya, ayas ga —*"
Rama came over the threshold and bowing a low *johar* to the *patil* said,
"Yourself! Here!"

"What else can I do?"

"You should have sent a *chaugula* or *ramoshi*," Rama said, rubbing
his eyes.

"Who am I going to get at the right time?"

"Yes, true."

"Why are you lying down? See how far the day has come up."

"Yes, very far, indeed." Rama began to think. Never before had the
patil himself come to his place. What's wrong? Someone must have died
in his house. Possibly. The air has become so sick. He asked *patil* —

"Has some urgent work come up suddenly?"

"See, the air has become bad in the village — " No need for Rama
to be told this. It was playing all around him. "Yes, don't I know that."

"The doctor is coming to help."

"Is that so? Good!"

"This should be announced in the village, to nearby farms and
homesteads."

"Yes."

"For that there should be a *daundi*."

"Certainly. Without that it would not reach all houses and homesteads."

"Make a *daundi* that the doctor has come to the village and all should
come to the *chavadi* to get treatment."

"Yes, that should be the call."

"Then why waste time? Start immediately. Come with me."

"*Anna*, you lead the way. I shall follow you immediately."

"Follow me? Come, right now."

"Let me wash my mouth."

"What were you doing 'til now?"

"*Anna*, my body feels so heavy. I am not feeling very well today."

"*Leka!* If you feel like this what can the village do? This *daundi* must
be made!"

"How can one not make it? God himself is coming to the village. The
village must be saved, let anything happen to me."

"Bravo! You are leaving immediately, aren't you?"

"Yes, certainly. I shall be there in the *chavadi* as soon as you arrive
and set yourself down there."

"See, Rama. Don't fall. Don't lie down."

"No, no — no. How can that be!"

Assured by Rama's words, the *patil* left. The noise of his hobnailed shoes accompanied him as he went in the direction of the village. Aching, Rama came back into the house. His stomach was upset. Flashes of lightning struck through his head. The eyes swam in darkness. The head had turned into a stone. He came into the house, laid himself down for a little moment, but soon, gathering all energy, got up —

No, no. I mustn't lie down. I must go and make the daundi *in the village. Summon all the people to get inoculated. The sick must be saved. If the village lives, I live — Get up now. Don't fall down."*

Talking thus to his own mind Rama gets up. Gets a small potful of water from the big pot. Sits down, and rinses his mouth. Wipes his mouth with the end of his *dhoti*. Asks his son to give him his turban. Winds it around the head. Throws the tattered blanket across his shoulder. As he steps out of the house with a stick in his hand, he calls out to his wife —

"See here. I am going to the *chavadi.*"

Savubai was taken aback. All of a sudden, the master of the house in the doorway. Standing. She thought it was his delirious talk which made him act so. She rushed forward to stop him.

"Why? Where?"

"See, the doctor is coming to the village in the afternoon."

"Did you dream or what?"

"No. The *patil* came and told me. I have to make a *daundi* in the village." "What for?" "The doctor is coming. People should come to the *chavadi* for inoculation."

"But you are feverish, aren't you?

"Yes, but what am I to do?"

"Didn't the *patil* realize you were not feeling well?"

"Yes, but the whole village is down."

"But how about you?"

"See — if the village is saved, we are saved."

"Come now. Lie down quietly. If one's life is well, the village is well. The *patil* comes and you are ready to go. Is there anyone to ask about your health?"

"I know you are right. But it won't do to act like that. Many people in the village are sick with smallpox."

"That's enough talk. Get back into the house."

"No, no. I must go to the *chavadi*. The *patil's* gone ahead."

"Get your children out of house and home with such doings, won't you."

"Don't speak evil like that. I shall make the *daundi* and be back soon." Saying this Rama stepped out of the house and set himself on his way to the village gate.

Rama stepped inside the village gate. As he walked his arms and legs began to cramp. His stomach began to rumble. The nerves began to bind the body like tight pieces of cord. He came to the *chavadi* somehow. He got the order for *daundi* from the *patil*. Sambya Horal, the drumbeater, accompanied him. Walking a few steps away from the *chavadi*, Rama gave out the call for the *daundi* in his sharp voice —

"The doctor is coming to the village. Everyone should come to the village to get inoculated —."

Rama intoned the call. The flat drum sounded. The air was filled with even greater sadness because of the *daundi*. It pierced the sky like the flight of a lone gull. Folks in lanes and byways were roused by it. Some came to the threshold, some to the door. Some stared with worried faces in the direction from which the sound came.

Rama was lifting his feet slowly. The stick in his hand supported him. His body was getting cold. The stomach was rumbling. Someone, he felt, was sapping the strength from his hands and legs. He came to the temple of Maruti. He again gave the call. The flat drum sounded.

The heavy, full clouds sagged. Drizzle. Slushy mud. Blowing wind. Oppressive air. The shout of the *daundi* brought the people to their doors. With dry mouths some approached Rama and asked —

"Rama, what's this for?"

At this, the breathless Rama would stop, take a breath, and explain the announcement. Then he would sit down. Try to suppress the shooting pain in his stomach. Spit out the saliva which filled his mouth. Lean against the stick in hand to get up and lift the feet again to walk.

Sometimes he would hear cries and moaning in a house along the way — pyre burning. Hearing that Rama's heart would sink into his feet. Heart beat faster. Hands and legs tremble. Cramps rise up the legs. Intestines tighten. Eyes swim. Head whirling like a wheel, and the houses spin around.

Lurching, tottering, Rama walked with the help of the stick, counting every step. Gave the call for *daundi*. Gathering his soul together, shouted the news. Each time the ball in the stomach would surge up and eyes become white.

People sunk in worry were asking Rama. He replied to them in his fading voice. Hold the ground with the stick first and then take a step. Some caste fellows said to Rama

"Rama — " "Yes," Eyes spoke.

"You have become very weak. It's not good."

"No, nothing, It's all right."

"You are lying. You are lurching as you walk."

"No" — with a shake of the head.

"Your voice is fallen." "No, no."

"The call of the *daundi* does not come sharp."

"No, not that — "

Mouth dry, face sunk — "um, um" — too tired to say no.

With all his strength Rama tried to lift his leg. But the cramps spread, climbed up. The veins became stiff like ropes, like cords began to bind the body. The head became numb. The stomach turned and twisted madly. The intestines flowed, the mouth watered. Vomit thrust itself up the throat, but he held it back.

Somehow, Rama walked a few steps. Gathering his life and soul together, he gave a shout of *daundi*. The flat drum sounded. The noise brought people rushing up.

Rama Taral fell. He began to vomit. Bloody liquid. Diarrhea. His *dhoti* soaked in white fluid. Blood vomit, blood retching.

Rama's arms and legs began to twist and turn. Eyes began to whiten. His arms and legs grew cold. The crowd of people around him increased. The noise of the *daundi* was stilled. The flat drum was cold.

Themes of Duty, Sacrifice, and Honor

*The Children with whom I have played, the men and women with whom
    I have eaten,*
Have had masters over them, have been under the lash of masters,
And, though gentle, have served churls.

— Pearse

In "Daundi" we are thrust into an atmosphere of heaviness, one of inescapable weight bearing down on the protagonist, Rama Taral, and the village in which he lives. Rama is ill, the "world" is ill — the link between Mahar and village is established in a single moment. The weight of the village, of the illness, of the oppressive atmosphere is summed up in Rama Taral's complaint — "How can a man carry on? . . . A whole big mountain of jobs to do." As Rama Taral recounts his many unfinished tasks we find that he is a vital communication link between village officials and the populace, and between the dead and the living. He is called upon to transmit official orders to the villagers, and he must inform those relatives of the dead who live outside the village. He must also gather fuel for the many cremations occasioned by the smallpox epidemic. When not engaged in such tasks, he is expected to be present at the village office, the *chavadi,* in case an official wishes to send a message or make an announcement. All these duties are part of "what we must do" to be a Mahar.

Another aspect of the Mahar identity is highlighted immediately: the Mahar is a village guardian — a watchman — who protects the village by his wakefulness while others sleep. He must be observant of strangers, must "protect" the villagers against the "pollution" of dead cattle lying in the fields.

A striking analogy is drawn by the Mahar between himself and the oil-presser's bullock. The bullock is long-suffering, mute and stolid. Attached to the yoke, the bullock moves round and round the press, with blinders to prevent his attention from wandering, goaded when his pace is too slow. There is, in effect, no beginning and no end, only constant movement in the same place. The image is reinforced in the account of Rama's delirium in which his mouth is gagged, his hands and feet are in chains, and he confronts a mountain of work — never to be diminished or surmounted.

Despite his many contributions to the community, Rama has not become "part" of the village. He is still separated, alone. Although Rama's ties are ostensibly to the "village," his contacts in this story are limited to village officials, the *patil* and the *talathi,* for whom the Mahar is not one whose feelings warrant consideration. The Mahar is only part of the system, a system which moves inexorably along its own path. As Rama Taral puts it: "This is the way things go. You cannot see it. You are moving to your own rhythm, your own intoxication. . . . " Though he serves as a communicator, he has no opportunity to transmit his own feelings, desires, observations. No one listens to him or attempts to understand his views. Only God is able to grasp the meaning of his "aloneness." Even his wife, though she feels his pain, does not truly understand his sense of separation from all others. His realization that he is bound to the system, but not integrated into it, is indicated by his concern for wife and family — it is clear that should he die, the village would not aid them in any way.

To understand this sense of aloneness it is necessary to recall that in Maharashtra, few villages harbor more than a few Mahar families. Irawati Karve, in *Hindu Society, An Interpretation,* makes the point that although Mahars constitute over 70 percent of the Untouchable castes in Maharashtra, they are so widely scattered that any given village rarely contains more than twenty Mahar households, and villages with a single Mahar family are not uncommon. Though perhaps the author exaggerates Rama Taral's sense of aloneness for literary effect, the feeling of social isolation evoked in "Daundi" may not be far removed from reality.

Why then does he continue to serve, to guard, to help maintain the system? Slowly the image begins to take shape — the Mahar is bound to a particular location. He has no choice. He must stay; and staying, must live, must protect his family, must maintain strength to confront whatever is demanded of him.

The Mahar's link to the land, rather than to people, is suggested in a passage where Rama Taral describes the work that he has done for the village: "So what — a favor to someone? Wanted to live here in the village, didn't you? This is my mother, this *pandhari* land. I should serve her, so it was ordained. I fulfilled it. A constant sacrifice performed." Although this passage suggests an element of personal choice in Rama's selection of his village, the Mahar's position in one village is little different than in another. Rama's statement implies that he belongs to the land and that only through his continuing sacrifice is the land sustained. The author's portrayal of this relationship may echo also a belief common to many Untouchable groups — that they were the original inhabitants of the land and were conquered, degraded, and oppressed. This belief is reminiscent of the old *Amrutnak* tale, an origin myth of the Mahars, in which faithful and self-denying services freely given by Mahars in ancient times are later redefined by others as caste duties. Both interpretations are possible, and are part of the Mahar self-image (Miller, 1966).

The Mahar's ability to sustain his sense of self-esteem, despite the treatment accorded him by others, may be attributed in part to the psychological phenomena characterized by Anthony Wallace as "internal cognitive manipulation." Wallace defines this concept as "physical or mental effort which is designed to bring into perception evidence which will justify the cognitive resetting of real identity as a more desirable state."* Ample evidence of cognitive manipulation appears in "Daundi" where the Mahar's self-image is one of courage, perseverance in duty, pride, loyalty, and sacrifice. Similar themes are to be found in "Bhara."

Rama's view of his service to others as "a constant sacrifice" also is in keeping with the Hindu belief that freedom from rebirth may be attained through the proper performance of one's dharma or duty. The interruption of Rama's thoughts by the shouts of the *patil* outside his house, shouts which Rama in his delirium mistakes for the voice of God, introduces a possible touch of irony — in that the *patil* was in one sense the Mahar's "secular god" (Miller, 1967). The image of the *patil's* words forcing themselves "into his eardrums like molten lead" is also reminiscent of the punishment advocated in the *Laws of Manu,* an ancient Brah-

---

*Anthony C. Wallace, "Identity Processes in Personality and Culture," in *Cognition, Personality and Clinical Psychology,* ed. by Jessor and Feshbach. 1967, p. 67.

manical work, for Shudras who dare to listen to the recitation of the sacred *Veda*.

The theme of the warrior resounds throughout the story from the initial call to duty to the end. This recurrent motif in Mahar folk-history appears in Rama's pride in being in the forefront of action, courageously ignoring his own "wounds" to aid others. The soldier's bravery and willingness to give his life in battle is evoked by Rama's heroic struggle to overcome pain in order to deliver the call to the village — an effort that ends only with his death.

Rama Taral, the village Mahar, falls as he has lived, alone. Though his last shout brings many people, he does not see them — just as they did not "see" him when he was alive. The contrast of images is stark. The Mahar self-image: A soldier who fought heroically to the last in defense of his village, who is the strength of the village, the eyes and ears and voice of the village — but is not considered a *man* of the village. And what is the image held by the villagers who come in response to the Mahar's call? Rama Taral expresses it: "No one here is mine. No one's heart would feel sympathy for me."

Bhara (The Burden)

"Bhara" reveals that not only is the Mahar isolated from other castes in rural communities, he is separated even from those Mahars (like the narrator, an educated Mahar official) who have broken free of the confines of village life. Once again we are made to feel that the "essence" of being Mahar is related intimately to service. In this instance, two village watchmen, or *kotwals*, assist officials by carrying their luggage on a visit to the ancient fortress of Sajjangadh. This duty is carried out under duress without flinching and without expectation of appreciation — with the soldier's pride and commitment to duty. At the outset, Kharat develops a powerful image of overpowering darkness, offset by the Mahar, who carries the burden, and lights the way for others — metaphorically for all of society. Perhaps Kharat is prophetic here: when Hindu traditions crumble and the Mahar self-image is accepted by society at large, then the Mahar may remove "the burden on the head."

BHARA

The month of Asadha. The sky was brimming. The water streamed down all the time. Brooks and streams were overflowing. The sound of swelling water could be heard in the pitch darkness of the night. We were passing through a town on our way to Sajjangadh. We had decided to camp there that night.

Around nine or ten at night only, but the whole town seemed to be fast asleep. The falling rain had chilled all. The doors were closed. Sometimes a window showed a faint glimmer of light. An occasional word from inside a house could be heard. The place had become uneasy from the rain.

Through that somnolent village we set on our way to the fort. Now and again the light showed the white figure of a man walking. A cat would cross the street in a flash. The dogs raised hell barking at the light of our lanterns. A whole tribe of them barking furiously accompanied us. They were all there around us. The garish light of the lanterns, seven — eight people walking and the barking of the dogs awakened people in the roadside houses, who peeped out and closed the doors firmly when they saw us departing.

The barking dogs drummed and trumpeted us right out of town. The town was left behind. After walking through an open wilderness, the climb to the fort began.

We had two *"kotwais"* accompanying us. One of them was Samba Kotwal, like a stick, bent because of the chilly rain. He felt his way along in the light of the gas lantern. On his head our bedding and blankets. In his right hand he held a gas lantern. Shaking with cold, tottering under the burden he walked along. He wore a cotton vest-jacket. From the elbows down his dark hands were exposed. The turban on his head was hidden under the burden on his head. His *dhoti* was tucked up, showing the dry wooden logs of his legs. Nothing on his feet. Barefoot. A rag of a sackcloth, which he had thrown on himself because of the rain, was soaked through and through. In the light of the lantern the water dripping down it stood out. Looking down and in front he walked. He was leading the way, showing us the way in the light of the lantern.

The stunted shrubbery on the road, the ground covered with stones and rocks, the stealthy movements and sudden creepings in the shrubs. . . . Samba walked on, turning himself into a stone.

This Samba Kotwal had a burden on his head, a lantern in his hand and the rag on his body was soaked. So I thought I should walk a little with him. Hold my umbrella over his body. Protect him a little at least from the rain. And so I went to him. Held my umbrella over him. The patter of the rain on the umbrella woke up Samba who was walking along lost in his own thought. Ashamed to see a Sahib holding an umbrella, he stepped quickly aside as if burned, and turning around a little, glanced with narrow eyes at his Raosahib. The shadow of his feet approached Samba, who noticing it, kept moving away.

Walking a little faster, I again reached Samba's side. His observant eyes were watching the shadows of the feet under the light of the lantern. He saw the shadow of my feet and stepped quickly aside.

What needless trouble! Why is this Sahib holding the umbrella over me? I am already drenched. I always get drenched. Is this something new for me? Samba Kotwal always works like this in heat and in rain. The talathi knows this. The patil knows this. The circle-officer sees it. And the Mamlatdar knows.

Mamlatdar Raosahib will impale me because of this umbrella-holding! What, Kotwal! Become too arrogant, have you? Swaggering along with us officers, making my guest hold an umbrella over you. Aren't you ashamed of yourself, you so-and-so, dishonoring us in our midst.

Raosahib, sir, why do I need an umbrella? I am Mahar by caste — Kotwal. Am I an officer? I should hold an umbrella over an officer in the sun. I should hold an umbrella over his head in the rain. It is your luck that I should hold an umbrella over you — so you don't feel heat, so a drop of rain doesn't touch you. In our forehead, it is natural to soak in rain, This is our share. Don't I know this? More than half my years are gone. Are you telling me these things? I should tell you rather.

Samba's mind became confused, for no reason. Thoughts began to whirl madly. . . .

Rip-rap. The rain falls. The muddy water by the way. Pitch darkness in front. Mountain of darkness. Black all around.

Samba kept moving further away, watching the shadow of my feet. Walking with speed. And then walking with heavy steps. Noting the pace of my steps, moving quickly away. Stopped. He was avoiding me.

And now and again he would look at the shadow of the Raosahib's feet. As it ran near him Samba would become jittery with fear. His speed would increase. He moved away from my umbrella.

How this man is soaking! The rain's falling all the time! There is a burden on his head. Maybe, this soaking will make him ill tomorrow. Maybe this will chill him to the bones. This may give him the shivers. He may have fever. What will he do? What would his children do? Who would take care of his household?

The hill and the darkness became one. Impossible to know the end of the climb or fathom its depth. Immeasurable height. Immeasurable depth. All darkness. Darkness behind, darkness in front.

I was climbing the steps of the fort. Tight knots moved in my legs. Still I walked fast. Getting near Samba Kotwal. Trying to hold my umbrella over him. He saw the shadow of my feet, started by them, moved quickly away.

At a distance Raosahib is walking. The shadow of his feet comes near in long strides. There is speed in it. Force in it. He reaches him. He

hangs on to him. Samba's chest begins to palpitate. He feels heavy —
as if a stone has been put down on his chest. His breath catches.
Breathing becomes quick. He escapes from the umbrella. Becomes free.
Then the stone on his chest is put aside. His nostrils relax. He feels free
— so very free. Taking the whole burden he walks easily in the open rain.

Soon I brush by him. His free, unimpeded pace is disturbed. He
gets jittery —

*Sarkar! Why do you hold this umbrella on me! The rain doesn't touch me
even in the middle of a torrent. But your umbrella is a burden to me. It may
keep me dry on the outside, but I shall have Raosahib's burden on me forever.
You don't understand this. The climb is not steep for me. The burden is not
heavy for me. My feet don't get cramped as I walk. The shivers don't run up
my body as the rains wet me. The rain may soak my clothes but I am dry
within! Fresh within. In such cold my body feels warm. In such a rain when
I climb the gadh I feel strong.*

*Why do you hold the umbrella over me! This is the way I soak in rain. This
burden on the head is always there . . . do you understand?*

*And that man over there . . . my 'husband.' He stares at me angrily. His guest
himself holds an umbrella over me . . . what would he feel! Would that
make him feel good? Tomorrow I have to deal with him. I am bound to his
rope. He will skin me. Grind me with work. It's all right for you. You are
here today. Gone tomorrow. You came today, leave as you will tomorrow.
I am here in this cage for good. In this trap — I am. I have to live with
Raosahib every day. Do you understand now? Why do you pile more burden
on my head by holding that umbrella over me? It's burden, just more burden.*

We have come up a long way. Still more to go. Steep climb. Legs get
heavy. The bellow of the chest works fast.

I happened to look down. A deep, big chasm. Full of darkness.
Bottomless. That's the way things are. Immeasurable depths. Immeasurable heights. We travellers walk on. Climbing with difficulty each single
step. The legs had become tired. We were climbing the fort.

Raosahib's step quickened. He began to walk fast. He started toward
Samba. Shadow touched shadow. Samba's pace slackened. Overtaking
him, Raosahib quickly climbed the steps in front and started ahead.

*— His honor is angry with me? Why be angry with a poor man like me? I
did not ask your honored guest to hold an umbrella over me. What wrong
did I do? Truly, I used to move away whenever the umbrella was held over me.
I move forward. Hold back. Stretched three ways. My heart pounds. Caught
in a trap. Swirling in the whirlpool. Moving round and round like the potter's
wheel. Go down and come up with the whirlpool. Floundering like a drowning
man. Suffering hard to bear. God! what a burden on the soul. Stone-heavy
burden.*

*Like they were chained, legs become heavy. The whole body becomes heavy.
Not a step more. What a burden.*

The cliff of darkness hangs all around and in the middle the dazzling brightness of the gas lantern. The hide and seek of footsteps can be seen clearly in that light. Shadows chasing each other. Shadows brushing against each other. Separating. Going ahead. Lagging. Quick steps and slow. One, two, three. The footsteps alone talk. The language of shadows. The light of the lantern the only witness. Yes, in this murky darkness, the true witness — light.

The shadows of footsteps ran across Samba Kotwal's mind at every step. He was getting hints. His steps quickened. Slackened as well. He forgot the rain. The burden on his head was not felt. Keeping a strict watch with his eyes he walked on.

The light of the lantern suddenly stood up. The wall of the *gadh* stretched wide, standing erect. The firm and solemn fortification could be seen clearly now. Suffering rain and heat these walls have stood gloomily for hundreds of years. They have watched over the fort, have borne all the burden.

Better to be at the back. Better to walk at the rear. The companion Kotwal is there in the front. He too has a gas lantern in his hand. In that light Raosahib and the other guests are walking.

The walls of the fort became visible. The burden on my mind became less heavy. My steps lingered. The climb had already made them heavy. They were weary. Cramps were rushing up my legs. I slackened my pace. I tarried behind. Samba Kotwal was also behind. Lifting heavy footsteps. "Let me catch this man," I thought, "and talk the four things."

Arrey baba! I am your caste and kin. Like you I have done village service as a village Mahar. Day and night. Rain and heat. Light and heavy like this. Like the cattle.

No one pities. No one feels sympathy The Mahar dies under the burden of work. Let him die. Baba, today it is you who are Kotwal. The burden on your head gets heavy for me. The rain hits you but I get drenched. Chills me to the bones. When your climbing steps became slow my legs got cramped and I cannot climb the fort any more. You and I are one. I have suffered this all. And so my guts break into bits. Thought I should reduce the burden on your head and so I was holding the umbrella over your head. Do you understand . . . now at least?

I stopped by Samba. Samba trembled as he walked, then stopped and stood like a stone. Thrusting my umbrella over his head I asked

"Samba . . . you know me?"

The rain was coming down in torrents. Samba was soaked to the skin. He lifted up his burdened head. Looked at me. His face brightened. He said to me happily:

"Yes Sahib, I know."

"How do you know?"

"We had a message that you were coming."

"What was it?"

"We heard that our Sahib was going to come here to see the fort. We were happy. All of us know this."

"Did you come to know my name?"

"Yes, your name. As soon as the *gramsevak* said it I knew. It felt good. Our man is coming to our village. You are not Raosahib's guest, you are our guest. And so we came at night . . . in rain. So happily. Today's burden was so light . . . !"

"*Baba!* You were drenched. The rain kept pouring. And so I tried to hold the umbrella over your head but you kept hedging."

"Yes, true. You felt my pain and that's why you held the umbrella over my head in this soaking rain. It's all very well. You may hold the umbrella over my head now. But what about tomorrow. Rain is there. Heat is there. The burden on the head is always there. Yes."

Samba's words which came from the depth of the stomach were true. Tonight he might be sheltered under the umbrella for a little while, but tomorrow it was going to rain for sure and he was going to be drenched for sure.

Samba began to walk. I began to walk. But Raosahib stopped. His shadow rushed at Samba who stopped and then began to walk, keeping a little distance. The burden on Samba's mind began to increase. He began to get soaked in the pouring rain. The chill began to cut through. He began to shake, to totter. All the strength he had gathered together was let out like air from a tire. And at the very next step Samba collapsed. Fell down like a sack. The burden on his head fell in the muddy water. The lantern broke. The light was gone. Quickly the darkness blossomed, and with its tendrils wound around, bound and gripped everything —

Themes of Perseverance and Courage

Like "Daundi," "The Burden" evokes a mood and reveals aspects of the Mahar identity. One is thrust into threatening darkness, constant rain, people tense and closed-in. The story revolves about a single episode, a visit to the fortress of Sajjangadh by local officials and their guests. The author may well have chosen this site with the realization that it is the location of the Ramdas Math, a shrine erected in honor of a seventeenth century Hindu saint, Ramdas, who, though he believed in the inherent superiority of Brahmans, attacked them for their spiritual failings in his time. He also asserted that spiritual leadership had passed to the lower castes.

. . . The lower castes have attained to spiritual leadership; the Sudras are demolishing the social status of the Brahmins. The Brahmins, unable to understand this work of destruction are yet retaining their social arrogance. . . . This kingdom of the spirit has fallen to the lot of the base people in society, and the Brahmins are nowhere. [*Dasabodha*, Chapter XIX]*

Ramdas established a school that sought to make the Brahmans true spiritual leaders of society, while at the same time accepting disciples from all castes. Perhaps Kharat, through his choice of setting, is suggesting that contemporary conditions are similar to those of Ramdas' day, and that it is the Mahar who should take the lead, difficult though it may be.

Samba Kotwal, the Mahar in the story, is set apart — fearful. He is "free" only when untouched by those around him — including the young government official of Mahar origin. Samba feels "entrapped." He shies away from the touch of shadows — particularly the shadow of the village official, the Mamlatdar Raosahib. Even the umbrella held over Samba's head by the Mahar official is viewed as a burden, one from which he must escape to avoid later reprisals from the Mamlatdar. The failure of the Mahar official to comprehend the full consequence of his friendly gesture reveals the gulf that exists between himself and his caste brethren who remained enmeshed in the traditional system of hierarchical authority and prescribed behavior. As Samba explains: "Your umbrella is a burden to me. It may keep me dry on the outside, but I shall have Raosahib's burden on me forever. . . . Tomorrow I have to deal with him. . . . You came today, leave as you will tomorrow. I am here in this cage for good. In this trap. . . . "

Entrapped, alone, strong enough to bear the weight of an uncomprehending society, the Mahar is like the walls of the fort. "Suffering rain and heat these walls have stood gloomily for hundreds of years. They have watched over the fort, have borne all the burden." Other aspects of the Mahar self-image, that of protector and guide, also appear in the story: "Better to be at the back. Better to walk at the rear. The companion Kotwal is there in front. He too has a gas lantern in his hand. In that light Raosahib and the other guests are walking."

The self-conception of Samba evokes Ramdas' classic characterization of the ideal man:

The Ideal Man loves to put forth effort, enters boldly on any enterprise, and does not shun work. He can live in the midst of difficulties, bear the brunt of action, and yet keep himself away from contact with it. He is everywhere, and yet nowhere. Like the Atman, he hides himself. . . . In the midst of

---

*Selections from the *Dasabodha* of Ramdas were taken from *Pathway to God in Marathi Literature* by R. D. Ranade. Bombay: Bhavan's Book University, 1961.

difficulties, he knows the way out. A man of courage is a great support to all. This indeed is what he has become through the grace of God. [*Dasabodha*, XI, 6.12–19]

Again, like Rama Taral of "Daundi," Samba falls in the course of duty. He is alone, like Rama Taral, at the end, having led his followers to safe haven. Darkness envelops him as he is stalked by the shadow of the Mamlatdar. The author's termination of this tale seems in keeping with Ramdas' advice to the ideal man:

If we meet a bad man, and if the limits of forgiveness are reached, then we should leave the place in silence. [*Dasabodha*, XII, 2.15–26]

Gaonkusachya Ant (Inside the Village Womb)

Some of the obstacles confronting the Mahar seeking to break free of the "system" are presented in this account of Shankar, an educated Mahar, who returns to the village of his father, Rama. The story also suggests a marked change in inter-caste relations during the generation following India's Independence. Also evoked are echoes of the past, and the emotional ambivalence towards the past of Mahars who only recently have attained a new role in society.

Marathi terms appearing in the text include the titles of village officials, *talathi* and *chaugula,* and the village headquarters, *chavadi.* The Mahar quarter, situated outside the village proper, is referred to as the *Maharwada* or *vasti.* The term, *takia,* meaning platform or meeting place, is also used. A high caste village elder, Desai Nana, encountered by the Mahar narrator at the outset of the story, alludes to the Kali Yuga — the last age in the Hindu cycle of time, in which the disruption of the caste system is held to portend the end of the world. The temporal setting of the period recalled by the narrator — a time of harvest — should also be kept in mind for then the demands of the upper castes become especially onerous in that they prevent the Mahar from earning supplementary income as a harvest hand.

GAONKUSACHYA ANT

The sun had shown its face. The tender light of the sun was sprinkled all around. My village was shining bright with it.

I had started from my house in that tender sunlight. I was on my way to the village to meet friends of old. My hamlet — outside the village gate, far out in the direction of the rising sun — was now far behind and I could see the gate. I went on. The old banyan tree facing the village gate still stood. Its branches looked chopped. New shoots were growing from the old chopped wood. They bloomed with new tender leaves. The islands of thorny, snake-hooded cactus near the banyan tree seemed to have been destroyed. In their place neat level ground was seen. There used to be piles of stones from tumbled-down houses near the mouth of the gate. Snakes and reptiles lived there. I could not see that stone-pile today. Around the pile the *dhotra* shrub with its white and yellow flowers grew vigorously. I could not see that yellow and white shrubbery today.

When I used to go to the village from my house . . . from my vasti — the dirt road used to throw up dust by buckets into your eyes. Now it was a 'pukka' road, hard with stones and 'murum.' The old village gate, brightened by the tender sunlight, blinked at me with a new gleam. I felt good to see the changed, new look of things near the mouth of the village gate, and passing the red Maruti temple I saw Desai Nana sitting on the terrace of the temple. I heard him calling as I walked on. . . .

"*Arrey,* who is going?"

"It's me." I stopped and answered. Desai Nana looked me over closely and quickly recognizing me asked, "When did you come from Poona, Shankar?"

"Came yesterday," I replied, looking at Desai Nana, who seemed to have grown so old. He remarked with a little sympathy, "Good thing you did. You came. It's good — But after so many days!"

"Yes, came to see my father. He doesn't feel well."

"Yes, so did I hear. Wasn't I on my way to see your father now? Heard your Rama is in the house lying down?"

"Yes, he is bedridden."

"The man's tired now. Your Rama worked very hard — See?"

"True," I said and kept quiet, on which Desai Nana continued, looking straight at me, "See here Shankar! you raised the banner of your name there. Made your father's name. Spread the name of our village. Did good things. Yes, you did."

Admiring me thus, Desai Nana said easily,

"But Shankar, your Rama spent his whole lifetime in the village and never acted once above his level. Now the 'Kali' has turned around — our time's — gone."

Addressing these last words, the "Parthian shot" from the depth of his mind, to me thus, Desai Nana moved from the terrace and set on his way to visit my father, leaning against the stick in his hand. His last words pierced my eardrums like arrows. . . .

"— Rama never acted once above his level. . . . Now the 'Kali' has turned round — our time's gone —"

The words began to dance before my eyes again and again. They began to circle around in my mind . . . and that time, those old days. . . .

The clouds in the sky rushed together and came down on me. . . .

— Those were days of harvest. The village fields were loaded with fall crops. Those were days to earn your living by laboring on daily wages in the fields and pastures.

Our *Maharwada,* to begin with, was outside the village gate. Caught as it were, in mourning for someone's death. But even it got up very early that day, drawn by the prospect of bread and water. The cooking fires were lighted even before the day broke. Smoke was reaching for the sky from every house and door. Bare, naked children came out of the dwarf doors of the houses. Womenfolk dipped and washed vessels in the water brought from the streams. Their dry locks of hair forced themselves out of the torn covering on their heads. They pushed them back with their wrists. A crying, fussing child had his back slapped by the flour-smeared hand of his harassed mother, sitting in front of the fire, shaping the dough into *bhakars.* As the hand imprinted itself in the flour on his back, the child would wail and scream with renewed vigor, stamping his feet madly. Then the mother would hold him close, lovingly seat him on her lap, feed him pieces of hot *bhakar.* And that child ate those pieces of *bhakar* with great enjoyment and taste.

Seeing the day come up with so much activity, my father left the house and set on his way to the village. As I had morning school, I too followed him with my slate and satchel. Nevara Mahar called him from the community *takia* of the Mahars —

"Rama, oh Rama, where are you going at such an early hour?" As he heard the call my father stopped in his track and said,

"Oh! on my way to chop the wood for Rangoba Vani."

"All right, all right. Be quick. We can go to the winnowing field when you come back."

"Very good, very good!" Saying this my father and I started on our way from the lemon tree in front of Dai's *takia.*

On a branch of the lemon tree the raw hide of a dead ox was stretched. Its stench filled the nostrils. Crows were fluttering around the hide. Their crowing tired the ears. Flocks of hawks, lured by the smell of the flesh, were floating above. Now and again a hawk would swoop down on the hide. The nostrils of thin dogs followed the smell of flesh as it floated around on the wind. The dogs ran in the direction indicated by the cawing of the crows and swooping of the hawks. They stopped when they reached the lemon tree near the *takia.* They drew in the smell of the wet flesh with their dilated nostrils. Gazed at the branch above and barked angrily at the crows. With their nails they furiously dug the ground near the trunk of the tree and growled at the crows above.

My father walked with quickened steps. I was walking with him. The *takia* fell behind. We were walking through the last lane of the *Maharwada*. By the side of the lanes and byways were tumble-down flat-roofed houses. Dogs had dug up the ground, made puddles and turned those houses into their homes. The neighbors had made latrines in the privacy of the tumble-down walls. The owners of some houses had gone out to live in the uncultivated land. Some had run away to the cities for work. They had settled there for good. The family lines of some had sunk — those houses were vacant. There was an increase in the population of dogs and cats. The grass which had grown on these half-fallen houses was now dry. The nests of sparrows and bats could be seen in many places on posts and pillars.

The *Maharwada* fell back and my father and I started on the way to the village gate.

Just outside the village gate there was a huge banyan tree. On its tall branches were nests of hawks and crows. Hawks were floating above. They swept down on the little chicks pecking food under the roofs of the houses in the *Maharwada* and flew to their nests with their prey. Now and again a crow would chase and harass a hawk.

As we were walking, a sudden gust of wind threw up buckets of dust. My eyes were filled with earth. My father began to rub his eyes with the end of his turban. With our eyelids fluttering we reached the mouth of the village gate —

The village *chaugula* crossed our way right in the middle of the gate. My father did *johar* to him and asked —

"*Dada*, which way so early in the morning?"

"Ah! To call the Mahars and what else? The *talathi* is sitting in the *chavadi*. Revenue-payers should be called early."

The *chaugula* said this and my father replied, fidgeting with the end of his *dhoti* on his shoulder . . .

"All of them you will get right now. They are in the *takia*. I will go ahead to the *chavadi*."

Thus did my father make the best of things and escaped for the time being. He took a step and turned quickly around and said to the *chaugula* —

"*Dada*, please give a little lime, enough for two betel leaves. . . ." Without saying anything, the *chaugula* took out his pouch of tobacco. Taking out the box he pulled out the lid with a 'phat'-sound. Putting the thumb of his right hand into the box he scratched at the lime with his nail. In the meanwhile my father had taken out his pouch. There was hardly any tobacco in it . . . a little bit of tobacco dust. Tasteless. Feeling it with his finger my father said again to the *chaugula* —

"Oh *Dada,* there's just dust in my pouch. So please to give a bit of tobacco."

"Come, take this lime first." Saying this the *chaugula* put out his right hand. My father spread out his left palm. . . . "Now, Now! Don't touch my hand! Get back a little!" At this my father drew back quickly. I too got back a couple of steps with him. Spreading his hand my father said,

"How could I touch. . . . Don't I know? But the lime will fall down — please drop it right into my hand."

The *chaugula* dropped that lime on my father's palm and putting his hand into his pouch took out a little tobacco.

"Hold your hand a little further down." Saying this the *chaugula* dropped some tobacco into my father's hand. A gust of wind blew half of it into the dust.

"Now Rama. Your hands are tattered or what?" said the *chaugula* looking at the tobacco spilled on the ground.

"No *Dada,* it's not like that. You are dropping it from far above and the wind doesn't allow it to get into the palm."

"Then what do you say, I should touch you in this morning hour of God and put it right on your palm — What nonsense!"

"Good, good — throw it down." Saying this my father cupped his hands and the *chaugula* put some tobacco on it.

"High hopes you hold in your mind. One should observe one's rules." Saying this the *chaugula* went out of the gate and we came in.

The temple of Maruti is the first thing inside the gate. Around the temple are the houses and *wadas* of the *Deshmukh-patils.*

Morning and evening there is someone sitting in the Maruti temple . . . either on the step or on the patio or reclining against a pillar. Never can a Mahar miss a *johar* outside the temple. We were walking a little fast. My father did not notice the step of the temple. Overtaking the people in the temple we went a little further. Then my father remembered; turned round quickly. He made *johar* to the *patils* and *desais* sitting in the patio and on the steps. He put his head on the step and had a *darshan* of Maruti. Smeared his forehead with the dust on the step. He was about to go when from the patio where he was sitting — Desai Nana cracked at him — "What's that, Rama?"

"Nana, what's — please?"

"Trying to escape without making *johar,* weren't you? Which great man are you going to, brushing us off like this?"

"It's not like that, Nana. I have to chop wood at the *vani's* house. He called me early so I was hurrying." My father answered, putting his head down like a guilty person and remarked — "How can we do like that? We have to live at your feet."

"I have to spread a manure-cart. Are you free tomorrow?" Desai Nana had this new work for him. My father was a little taken aback and blurted out —

"There are some government jobs for the village to be done tomorrow. I shall certainly do it if I find a little time."

"Now, how do you say that? Don't say no tomorrow."

"All right Nana. . . ." My father agreed and we were about to set on when Desai Nana asked my father —

"Arrey, this is your boy, Rama?"

"Yes, mine."

"Goes to school?"

"Yes."

"What does he learn?"

"He is in the seventh standard, *Marathi."*

"Bring him to carry manure-buckets tomorrow."

"He has school. He doesn't like to cut his classes."

"You son of a . . . are you going to raise your banner or what, making him a *mamlatdar-foujdar* (officer-soldier)?"

"Not like that —"

"Why do you talk about his school then? If there are two of you to help each other, you can finish sooner."

"What you say is right, but I will come by myself."

". . . your mother! See how worried he is about his boy's school. We know what sort of lamp he is going to light in the future."

My father pretended not to hear his words. We set on our way and reached the village *chavadi.*

The *patil* was sitting on a cotton carpet in the *chavadi.* Aba Ramoshi was sitting outside in the courtyard. My father was about to go, avoiding the *patil's* eye when he saw him and called out — "Hey, Rama Mahar!"

His call entered my father's eardrums. He turned back quickly and came to the *chavadi.* Holding to its post he said — *"Johar, kaka* [uncle]. I shall be back in a moment, chopping four sticks for the *vani."*

The *patil* fixed the turban on his head at the proper angle, coming out to the patio, spit out the chewed betel leaves and said angrily —

"Ha! Ha — Ha! Coming back, you say. You were trying to run

away. When do you see people . . . when you get eyes in your head or what?"

"How can I do like that, *kaka?* I met the *chaugula* in the gate. He is going to bring the other Mahars. I will be back by then."

My father pleaded humbly. On which the *patil,* raising his voice said:

"See here Rama! If you don't come back on time — I shall hit you right in the face. You Mahars are trying to make me lose my *patil's* office. Here this husband is sitting on my chest!" The *patil* held forth angrily, turning toward the *talathi.* Again my father pleaded in utmost humility —

"I shall be back immediately. Chopping the *vani's* wood." On which the *talathi,* showing his teeth said mischievously —

"Now, whose job first — government's or *vani's?*"

"We are tied to the rope of both — see, we have to work for both." Time was flying. My father's legs were impatient to go. The first bell of my school had begun to ring when the *patil* said:

"Go! Go! But finish the work and return soon."

My father nodded his head. In a jiffy we reached the shop of Rangola *vani.* Father was asking the *vani* about the wood. I was standing nearby. Nana Baman who was entering the shop looked at my face and said:

"Hey, you son of a Mahar. Touch the platform, will you? Get back. Don't you understand — people come and go out of the shop."

His words made me draw back quickly. I looked up at his face, eyes blinking. The second bell of the school began to ring and I began to run toward the school . . .

All this rose before me like a suddenly overclouded sky. In that darkened sky a sudden flash of lightning frightens a man. That happened to me. Standing within the village gate my mind trembled. I looked back at the old Desai Nana walking away from the gate, leaning heavily on his stick. Turning, I took a step forward.

On the way, the upper-caste residents of the caved-in tumbled-down houses beyond the Maruti temple were staring at my neat dress. They began to whisper into each other's ears — "Look at that educated son of Rama, our village Mahar!" I quickly passed the Maruti temple. I thought someone called me — I was startled.

Was someone calling me because I passed that temple without making *johar?* I looked back. There was no one there . . .

I walked in front of the *chavadi.* As I walked I heard the *patil's* shout. It began to strike against my ears again and again. I looked back at the *chavadi.* It was empty now. I could not see my father sitting in the courtyard.

I walked through the bazaar area to go to the school. The *vani's* shop had collapsed — it had turned into a cave. The platform of the shop had fallen, broken into pieces. Lifting my steps quickly I passed that shop. That tumbled-down cave of a shop was staring at me in wide-mouthed amazement.

My old school was a little bit further. I went on. As I walked, those tumble-down houses, that empty *chavadi,* that collapsed shop . . . rushed down on me. I threw them off and hastened on to the school. I was wet with perspiration . . .

Themes of Shame, Hope, and Rebirth

The very title of this story, "Inside the Village Womb," alerts us to the theme of the Mahar "tied" to the village, a theme variously expressed in previous stories as: ties to village official, ties to the land, ties to duty and honor. Here, Shankar, an educated Mahar youth, returns to his father's village after having cut the "umbilical cord" of tradition. His "rebirth" from the ruins of the old system has been painful and the trauma of his early years almost unnerves him. There is a suggestion that were it not for the ties of family and kin, Shankar would not have returned to the village. Throughout the story there runs a counterpoint, as the changes in social relations play against the subtle persistence of attitudes and feelings.

In contrast to the previous stories, the opening scene is one of sunlight, new plant growth, the destruction of old thorny cacti, and a smooth road in place of the old. Although the brooding, oppressive feeling of "Daundi" and "Bhara" are absent at the outset, as soon as the Mahar narrator enters the village and meets an old upper-caste villager — Desai Nana — the atmosphere begins to change. Echoes of the past and a rejection of the present are introduced by Desai Nana:

See here Shankar! you raised the banner of your name there. Made your father's name. Spread the name of our village. Did good things. Yes, you did. . . . But, Shankar, your Rama spent his whole lifetime in the village and never acted once above his level.

The praise is hollow: Shankar knows what is meant. In traditional terms his success was attained through the "raising of his banner" — defiance of village authority. Although the Mahar's father is praised for conformance to tradition, the son's recollection of an earlier day reveals that his father's deference masked a bold and courageous struggle, a struggle that enabled Shankar to acquire the education needed to free himself from the village.

With this confrontation between the educated Mahar and an upper-caste elder, the atmosphere of tension, pressure, and oppression closes in.

We are given a capsule description of a *Maharwada,* Mahar quarters, located outside the main village walls. Hints of change, due to deteriorating economic conditions, are conveyed by the deserted houses whose inhabitants have died without offspring or have moved elsewhere in search of employment.

The oppressive role of the village is evoked by the hawks perched on a banyan tree near the village entrance. Soaring above the *Maharwada,* the hawks now and then swoop down to capture those chicks who dare to venture into the open. Another metaphor may also be intended in an earlier reference to a sweet-smelling lemon tree in the *Maharwada,* a tree whose pleasant scent is obliterated by the stench of an ox hide. Since the removal of dead cattle is one of the Mahar's traditional duties, a duty whose performance is held to be a major source of his pollution, this scene suggests that the services Mahars are forced to perform for the "clean castes" prevent the recognition of the Mahar's true nature.

An example of the behavioral consequences of belief in pollution, and the "bonds" that enmesh the Mahar, appears in the encounter of the father and son with a minor official at the village gate. The *chaugula* tells the Mahar that he is summoning revenue payers to the village office. The Mahar agrees to comply, and then exercises the "prerogative" of the poor by asking for some tobacco. Fear of pollution prompts the *chaugula* to drop the tobacco from a distance into the Mahar's hand, but the wind spills some of it on the ground. The exchange that ensues prompts the *chaugula* to impart a "lesson" — directed most likely at the son — "Then what do you say, I should touch you — What nonsense! . . . High hopes you hold in your mind. One should observe one's rules."

The policing role of the upper castes appears also in the next episode when Shankar's father momentarily forgets to salute some village elders and to put his head on the step of the village temple — required acts of obeisance. An upper-caste observer taunts the Mahar for this lapse and reiterates the *chaugula's* criticism that the Mahar is arrogant and "uppity." Presumably, these men and the other villagers appearing in the story are aware of the Mahar's attempt to educate his son. Many of the demands made upon the Mahar may be viewed as an attempt to dissuade him from this bold break with tradition, either by calling for his son's services during the time when school is in session or by heaping more work upon him than one man can do without assistance. This harassment is further compounded by the fact that it is the time of harvest, an occasion when the Mahar can normally supplement the meager income of a government servant by working as a harvest hand.

The Mahar's position as a pawn in the never-ending battle for prestige and power among the upper castes is also illustrated in the varied and often conflicting demands for his services. Although he sets out from the *Maharwada* to chop some wood for the village merchant, others stop him on the way and insist that he work for them. The constant need for tact and evasion in coping with such demands, and the possibility of physical punishment if one fails to maintain a proper balance, is exemplified in the Mahar's encounter with the *patil*. "Ha! Coming back, you say, you were trying to run away. . . . See here Rama! If you don't come back on time . . . I shall hit you right in the face." The Mahar's dilemma is voiced by the *talathi:* "Now, whose job first — government's or *vani's?*"

Shankar's instruction in the Mahar's role, imparted as he and his father run the gauntlet of demands and derision, culminates at the merchant's shop when the child touches the platform on which customers sit.

"Hey you son of a Mahar! Touch the platform will you? Get back. Don't you understand, people come and go out of the shop."

The boy runs off in response to the school bell. We are carried forward in time once more. The boy, now grown to manhood, recalls the events of that not so distant day. Although his recollections begin on a pleasant note, when he enters the village, ghosts of the past in the person of Desai Nana return to haunt him. He feels the subtle tug of ancient bonds as he nears the village temple. His sense of assurance is threatened by imagined sounds of the past that strike his ears as he approaches the village office where his forefathers had attended to the beck and call of officials. But the structure of tradition, symbolized by the dilapidated platform of the merchant's shop, has lost its strength. Hastening by this last reminder of the past, the youth makes his way to the sanctuary of the school — the point of entry into a new way of life.

Nirvana (Enlightenment)

In the preceding stories by Kharat, the transition from the old Mahar self-image to the new is incomplete — only a few young Mahar men are shown to have broken free of the system and even they continue to feel the shame and restrictions that impinge upon their caste fellows in the context of village life. In "Nirvana," written by a Brahman, the forces of change, whose initial manifestations are described by Kharat, find fruition in the conversion of a group of Mahars to Buddhism.

The catalyst in this conversion is an educated Mahar from outside the village whose message, delivered in the course of one night, precipitates a complete break between the *Maharwada* and the rest of the village. Only one Mahar, an elderly man named Bavarya, refuses to accept Buddhism and all that conversion implies. Much of the story centers about his dilemma, which is shared by many Mahars of the older generation who are unable to comprehend or adjust to a new self-image and role in society. While this account touches on many themes encountered in Kharat's stories, it also provides a view of the Mahar as seen by others that may well reflect the caste background of the author. Marathi terms used in this story include *par,* a gathering place for men, often a raised platform or porch; and *tamasha,* or entertainment, which in this instance refers to the festive role of the Mahar in a community celebration.

NIRVANA

Panchayats were established in the villages of Maharashtra. New-comer *talathis* began to handle the record folios of *kulkarnis. Patils'* jobs became the property of thieves. The *nayaki watans* of Ramoshis were abolished. The *maharki* jobs of Mahars were taken over by the government. A brazen brat could dress himself up in coat-pant, sit in the *chavadi* to scold well-to-do farmers. The flat-top village school donned a cap of Managhre tiles. Poles with square lanterns on top were raised all around the village. Down in the village dell every *bigha* of land could now boast of a farmer of its own. There was talk of a canal and five hundred spades started digging in the red mewses on the west. White-capped leaders began to visit the village. All this happened and yet the village cart of Arangaon creaked on through the same old ruts of its ancient wheels. Bavarya Mahar still went around the village, calling for his rightful bread from house to house. The sharecropper, cursed by litigations about the barriers, still waited patiently at Appajipant Kulkarni's door to rub off the line of law. The house of Janu *patil* still received the first invitation to any auspicious occasion from every home in the village. A police gate was installed in the village and yet the Ramoshi *nayaks* did their job of watching over the village. The eight-sixteen Mahars in the *Maharwada* still ploughed the straight and curved furrows in the lands of village farmers and sharecroppers. The village carpenter still made and joined the *kuni* of the village plough. The village smith repaired the iron *mot* used for irrigation. The village *gurava* still walked the village distributing betel leaves. The potter's wheel still spun for the sake of the village. The cobbler had not yet gathered courage enough to ask for cash in return for mending the villager's footwear. The sign on the tile-roofed structure at the center of the village called it the "Community Temple," but the villagers still called it the *chavadi.* The Block

Development Officers were happy with the development of Arangaon, but the place itself was what it always had been.

One evening a passenger dressed in yellow clothes got down at Arangaon from the bus going to Pandharpur. Asking directions of people, he finally found his way to the *Maharwada* on the outskirts of the village. The *Maharwada* rejoiced at his coming. As usual after the long days toil, trouble, and sweat the *Maharwada* gathered in front of the *takia*. The yellow-robed young man poured some new medicines into the Mahar ears. The *Maharwada* was disturbed. That whole night the Mahar community kept awake. "Victory to Bhagawan Buddha" — the cry dashed against the sleeping villagers' ears some five-ten times that night.

In the morning the news spread. The *Maharwada* had converted to Buddhism. No one really knew or understood what had happened. Appajipant Kulkarni who sat with bundled knees on the village *par* in the center of the village, sunning himself happily in the mild early morning rays, prophesied "Now the *Maharwada* will break away from the village." Well, as a matter of fact, it always had. Ever since the village got settled, the Mahar dwellings were separate from the village and so the audience listening to Appajipant did not at all understand what he meant when he said that the *Maharwada* was going to break away.

The rays of the sun had become quite warm now. Old Bavarya Mahar came into the village from the *Maharwada*. That old pair of *patil-kulkarni*, made respectable and idle by age, still sat on the *par*. A few small farmers on their way to work were sitting around them. Old Bavarya approached them, touching his forehead with the raised four fingers of his right hand, he bowed down and called,

"*Johar, Maybap.*"

"Ram Ram," the toothless Appajipant said, pounding the *pan* in the stone *khalbatta*. Janu Patil and the farmers looked questioningly at the bent figure of the old Mahar. It was customary for the Mahar to sit politely on the dusty ground below when the villagers started their gossip session on the village *par*. Occasionally he could even join the conversation. But Bavarya could not even sit down today. Awkwardly he stood there. He locked the top of his stick with two hands and put his long, wrinkled chin on the gripping hands. With eyebrows contracted, mouth agape he just stood there staring at the villagers. He wanted to say something. He wanted to tell them something. He wanted to empty his heavy heart at the feet of the villagers. The brazenness to begin the conversation unasked was not in his blood. He thought that someone would ask him and then he would answer. For a long time the villagers did not speak to

him. Their talk went on. Finally, when tall Sitaram from Chahur farm-
stead rose and begged leave to go, he was stopped by Appajipant Kulkarni.
Appajipant said,

"Wait a while, Sitarambapu. Let's ask this Bavarya what was going
on all night in the *Maharwada*."

This remark gave Bavarya the opportunity he was waiting for. In
a pained voice he said,

"Strange things happened."

"What, what happened?" asked Janu Patil in his thick voice. He
asked the question first and then raised his eyebrows and chin.

Bavarya began to intone in his tired voice,

"Some mendicant-monk had come from *taluka* place. But he talked
nothing of God and faith. He kept talking how the villagers trouble
us Mahars. It wasn't untrue what he was saying and so the young boys
immediately were swayed. They asked the holy man for remedy. He said,
'Become Buddha.' Mahars nodded their heads. The man stood them in
a row and like our Ramu Bhat asked them to say something in some
difficult tongue. All the Mahars said that as they could, after which the
man said, 'You are Buddha.' "

"Very good — good riddance. The Brahmans lost their Brahmanness; why should the Mahars want their Maharness?" Appajipant said.

"How can you say that, Pant? They gave up their dharma-faith.
These Mahars." Bavarya said miserably.

"As if you can give up your dharma by saying so," said the *patil* in
his thick voice, gesturing wildly with his hands. Bavarya's wound began
to bleed again. This was the very thing he had told his brothers.

"What are they going to do, giving up their dharma? They have to
feed their bellies. They will have to do the work they have been doing.
What's there to this change? If Gomya changes his name to Somya,
the sky is not going to shower down magic food for his hunger and thirst!"
Sitaram, who was about to leave, said easily.

"It's not like that," said Appajipant, struggling through the chew-
spit of his *pan*-filled mouth.

"Then?"

The question which Janu Patil asked was the question uppermost
in the minds of all the assembled villagers. Appajipant did not say anything. Without rising up he moved toward the edge of the *par*. He put two
fingers and jettisoned a stream of spit to the ground under the *par*.
Sitaram standing below the *par* released his foot from the *vahan*. With
his foot he pushed some earth on the chew-spit. Putting his foot back into

the *vahan,* he stood looking expectantly at Appajipant's face. Appajipant who was sitting in a rather relaxed fashion, held up his knees and tightened the scarf around them. Caressing the growth on his unshaven cheeks with his two hands, he asked Bavarya.

"Were you with them all night, Bavarya?"

"Yes, please."

"Did they swear any oaths or anything after becoming Buddha?"

"Yes, please they did."

"What were they?"

"All very strange — keep your homes neat and tidy. Teach all children. Put clothes on them — all this is good — but — Bavarya faltered.

"Speak — speak on —"

"They swore not to remove cattle carcasses — not to eat carrion flesh. Well, that's all right. But if the Mahars don't drag away dead cattle who's going to do that?"

"Each one should do his own," Appajipant said. Well, it was exactly the same thing the yellow-clad man had said.

"What else have the Mahars decided to do?"

"What grace in telling all that? They have made up their minds not to do all the things we've been doing since our forefathers. I snorted a lot. But who is going to care for an old man? That man was from another place. He talked to them, made them swear, and went away by bus this morning. But we have to stay in the village — or don't we?"

"Hum — " said Appajipant, sighing deep, "This is what's going to happen now, Bavarya. It's happened in every village in the region. We didn't have it till now. Well, now it's happened —"

Appajipant was going to hold forth on the subject but he heard the call of his granddaughter, shouting from his *wada* near the *par* — "Appa, your bath water is warm" — Appajipant released himself from the *jetha* position, straightened himself with the support of his own knees and saying, "Well and good —" moved toward the steps of the *par.* As he rose, Janu Patil too got up. The other farmers also removed themselves. Only Bavarya was left behind in the middle of the village under the hot, dazzling sun. His whole body felt sour because of last night's lack of sleep. He felt unhappy as he felt the obstinacy of the Mahars and the indifference of the villagers. The simple soul sincerely felt that what happened shouldn't have. Up until now there was a mere distance between the village and the *Maharwada;* from now on he feared there would be a burning pit between them. His mind felt the heat of that fire. It burned his heart. For a long time Bavarya just stood there. Like a tired donkey, he just stood there.

After a while, sighing deeply, he went away, taking care of the stick in his hand and the blanket across his shoulder. He went away — who knows where.

From the next day the Mahars from the *Maharwada* stopped coming to the village for work. They simply wouldn't hear the villagers' calls. The villagers fretted and fumed. Cursing the Mahars, they began doing their own work. In like manner, the farms were ploughed. Green crops were seen growing in the irrigated land. The leaves of onion and garlic plants grew full. Eggplants were loaded with fat and luscious fruit. The sweet-potato patches were rich with their green and red leaves. The non-irrigated land was still being worked. Transporting manure had been the Mahars' job. But the villagers took it into their own hands. Each one did his own building and repairing of bunds and barrages.

It was the middle of the month of Vaisakh but the Mahars had not come to the village even once. Not a Mahar man stood in the barrier to beg a sweet-potato of a farmer in the farm, and not a Mahar woman came to the vegetable patch to request for "a bit to go with dry bread."

The *Maharwada* changed within a night and changed for good. In a month-fortnight, five-twenty-five Mahars from the *Maharwada* left to work in the sugar factory at Akluz. Some began to work for the government canal-building project. The Mahar women began to report in flocks at the canal for work. None of them cared for the good will or ill will of the villagers. Only Bavarya choked and gulped in the strange circumstances. He could not walk along with his community. He wished to walk with the village. Alone he would come to the village. Alone he would wander around. His usual work, which no one asked him to do now, he did still to the best of his capacity. When the lamps were lighted he went to the courtyards of the bigger houses of the village and pounded his stick. He got his bread of honor. He ate it at the foot of the *par*. The leftovers he kept for the next day. The *Maharwada* gave up coming to the village and Bavarya gave up going to the *Maharwada*.

Sometimes a villager asked him nastily, "Why, Bavarya, why don't you go home?"

Bavarya would keep quiet. Some other villager answered the first one, "Why should he go to *Maharwada*? Like Bibhishan in Lanka!"

On a dark Vaisakh night Bavarya was lying down in a piece of ragged blanket at the foot of the *par*. He was homeless though he had a house. Because of the mistake of his community the villagers also did not treat him with old-time affection. Well, true it was. No one thought the other behaved as in the old days. Who knows what it was? The fact was Bavarya was unhappy. He was miserable. These days he even could not sleep well. His sleep had become light like a watchdog's. He was lying down that night but his eyelids hardly touched each other. He suffered tortures thinking of things as they had been in other times and as they were now.

For the last few days there had been a great deal of activity in Appajipant Kulkarni's *wada* near the *par*. Guests came and went. Dinners and feasts were eaten. Today poles were erected in the courtyard. But not a single person from that *wada* had so much as said anything to Bavarya. No one had even asked him to do the sure and special work of chopping the wood. He had heard that Appajipant's daughter was to be married off. He felt very unhappy that there should not even be the shadow of a Mahar in a wedding in his village. Once he even thought of going to Appajipant's courtyard on his own to ask for his rightful work. But it was dishonor to do this work alone! It was appropriate, he thought, that all the eight-sixteen Mahars should present themselves together and ask for their rightful share of work in the Brahman wedding. It was impossible for this to happen now. He feared that alone he would be bluntly brushed aside. He was unhappy. Very unhappy —

He yearned that God himself would give Appajipant the mind to call him. The flower and the wood met. He heard himself being called for from Kulkarni's *wada*.

"Bavarya, Bavarya, hey —"

Overjoyed Bavarya got up. He gathered the ragged blanket on which he was lying down and put it on his shoulder.

"Coming — I'm coming —"

"Pant wants you." Mhamu Chaugula, who had called him from the door, told him. Bavarya approached the rectangular yard of the *wada*. A *pandal* was being erected there. Gas lanterns were shining brightly on all the four verandahs on the sides of the yard. Appajipant was seated on a cotton carpet spread in the yard. Prominent people from the village like Janu Patil, Pawar, Krishna Master were sitting around him.

"*Johar*," Bavarya shouted.

"So you are there Bavarya?" Appajipant tried to look at him but the radiance of the lanterns forced him to shut his eyes tight.

"Yes, please, I'm here."

"Sit down."

"Yes, please — I'm fine." Bavarya did not sit down.

"See, I called you. . . ."

"Yes, please —"

"See, we have a wedding."

"Yes, please, I know —"

"None of the Mahars came."

Bavarya did not say anything.

"It is not the custom in our village to send invitations to Mahar folks." Bavarya did not say anything.

"You are elderly. You have worked as a *taval* — the villagers managed to do all other things somehow or other. Only one thing remains to be done. You folks have been doing it for generations. The day after tomorrow the bride and the groom go out in procession. Who is going to carry the gas lanterns?"

"The Mahars must carry them," Bavarya said.

"They should. Shouldn't they? Remember things of old! The lanterns are new. We used to have torches — and flares — the Mahar folks carried them. What?"

"Yes, please."

"At least seven-eight men are needed."

"Yes, please,"

"Go, ask your people and let me know. Otherwise we will have to hire people from another place."

"Why should that be? I will ask."

"You've been in touch with them?" Janu Patil interrupted.

"What of that? I'll go and ask."

"Bavarya —"

"Yes, please." "Get that hole here," a villager busy erecting the posts said to him. Bavarya's heart danced with joy. He took off his turban and shirt. Took the crowbar and started resolutely to dig a hole in the yard. A new energy flowed through his tired old body with the thought that he had not broken away from the village like the rest of the *Maharwada* — he had not left the road while the other pilgrims had turned back. He began to dig with the speed of a lusty young man. In no time he dug five-six holes of a good size hand-span. In those holes poles stood up for the *pandal*.

After a very long time Bavarya was about to enter the boundaries of the *Maharwada*. Between the village and the *Maharwada* nothing stood now except a tumble-down house of rough-hewn stone. He had not crossed it since the *Maharwada* became "Buddha." It was early in the morning when he entered the *Maharwada*. The *Maharwada* was as it was. The same grass-walled huts. The same brood of chickens digging up dirt. The same naked, bare children. The same unclean women. The same smoke. The same noise. Bavarya walked to the *takia*. The Mahar folks who had slept there the night before were now getting up. Their bedding rolls were lying against the back wall of the *takia*. Some rubbed their teeth with the burnt-black powdered tobacco. Some washed their mouths at the well across from the *takia*. Not a person heeded his presence there. He felt very bad. He felt like going back. But he did not. Whatever it was, the *Maharwada* was his home. These Mahar folks who had turned away their faces were people of his own blood. He sat on the patio of the *takia*. He looked at the walls. There were a few new letters painted in red on the walls. He recognized the photograph of Babasahib Ambedkar on the wall. He had no acquaintance with them. Well, he never had even a nodding acquaintance with any kinds of letters throughout his life. A young man returning to the *takia* from the well after washing his mouth, stopped to look at Bavarya.

"Why — It's hard to recognize acquaintances, isn't it Fakira?" Bavarya said bitterly.

"It's a long time and so —"

"What's there left by you people for me to come?"

"So, why are you here today?"

"For some work."

"With us?"

"Yes."

"What kind?"

"Let all come."

"Are you going to lecture?"

"Child, I'm not Buddha yet, I am still Mahar."

"What has a Mahar to do here?"

Fakira's rude answer cut Bavarya to the quick. Struggling with the fire in his heart he said, "I've come with a message from the villagers."

"What villagers?" Another Mahar approached them. Soon a crowd gathered around them. Realizing their attitude Bavarya said,

"Don't you try to frighten me like that — there's a wedding at Appajipant's house. For years and years we have been doing the work of holding the torches and flares for wedding processions. I've come to ask if you are going to come for this wedding!"

"Hasn't that *kulkarni* a mouth to ask or legs to come here?" Fakira burst out.

"Why did you come with the message?" Another shouted.

"By mother! Why doesn't the old fool mind his own business?" A third one breathed through spread nostrils.

It did not take long to have a Mahar melee around Bavarya. Women and children from every hut came out and crowded around Bavarya. No one would let him speak. The whole community barked at him, attacked him. A barrage of questions began. Bavarya could not speak any more. His eyelids became wet, breathing heavy, limbs began to shake and tremble. Soon as he heard the news, Bavarya's son came running from his hut. Elbowing his way through the crowd he came to the center. Putting his arms under Bavarya's armpits he raised him up. In a scornfully sympathetic tone he scolded his father. "Come — now. Or you will pop off. Put your wisdom into storage some place. Live in ease what few days remain. When you die tomorrow the village won't carry you on its shoulder, it will put that on our head."

The son walked the father to the hut.

Bavarya did not return to the village. The wedding in Appajipant's house was celebrated as elegantly as ever. Realizing that the Mahars had entered into enmity with the village the *Mangawada* offered itself into village service. The *valers* played the drums. The Mangs carried the lanterns. The procession went around in pomp. The whole village ate the feast. Huge cauldrons of wheat *kheer* were emptied. Barring the *Maharwada*, the whole village was fed by the *kulkarni*.

In his hereditary hut, in a dark hovel, Bavarya suffered. His body burned. Blood rushed to his head. Very often he suffered fits of apoplexy. In such fits the old Mahar rose up, rushed against the closed door, showering it with kicks and fists. He kept repeating, *"Arrey, arrey,* let me go, I am *taral* of the village. I have the *babul* log to chop in *Patilwada*. Parar's bullock is dead. . . . Let me go. . . . I have to take the revenue to the *taluka* place. . . . There's a wedding in Appajipant Kulkarni's house. It's time for the procession —"

But there was no one to hear him. After all he was babbling in his fit. The door of Bavarya's room remained shut till the end of Vaisakh. The village knew nothing. None had any reason to go to a Mahar house. Bavarya was alive only because death did not claim him. His son showed humanity enough to place a plate of food in front of him at meal time but he did not respond. His screaming and shouting made Bavarya hoarse. He went on crying hoarsely. But his shouts had no more the color of wrath. The burning of the body and the fire in the head both cooled. He now looked like a mad mendicant. The whole *Maharwada* knew that Bavarya had gone mad. In the grip of his madness he sat for hours singing and clapping his hands.

> *The body's filth everyone knows*
> *But the soul is spotless, pure, Buddha . . .*

"Buddha! I have become Buddha!" He laughed madly. The village never worried itself about what had happened to Bavarya. *Maharwada* gave up taking him into account. Vaisakh was over. Jyestha went away. At the beginning of Akhad, the rain painted green over the black fields.

With no help from the Mahars, the village cart rolled on. Like every year the usual crops swayed their heads in the wind. The farmer's fortune bloomed up in the field. The *Maharwada* organized its own separate existence and thrived on it. Young boys returned for a day's vacation. They sat in the *takia* and talked of the pleasures of the new jobs. Bavarya had begun to move around now. As he was not right in his head, no one stopped him, talked with him. His eyes, however, were open. They carefully noted everything. He still could not understand what exactly happened when the *Maharwada* became "Buddha." The grassmat huts were there. The hens and chickens ran around digging up dirt. The unclean women still made the *bhakar*. The only change was the sound of cash which could be heard from a few huts. But this was the gift of the Akluz factory. If the Mahars had remained Mahars and worked in the factory, the same money would have found its way into the *Maharwada*.

One evening, on the full moon day of Akhad, crazy Bavarya sat on the Nandarki *par* by the side of the *takia*. The sky was bursting red. The wind smelt of wet earth. The noise from the *Maharwada* dashed against the ears. Bavarya's head was cool. His limbs had no strength. When the moon was about to rise he heard the quick beat on the *halgi* drum. The sound of *lezim* began to spin. The bellowing of bulls echoed. Shouts of men burst out. Bavarya remembered suddenly. He saw even without looking. It was the *Bendar* procession in the village. A herd of choice bulls was on its way to the Maruti temple near the village gate. Their horns were painted with *hingul*. Bright-colored paper was stuck around the horns. The points of the horns were decked with shiny bright brass thimbles. The quilts on their backs were ornamented with small mirrors. In front of this herd *halgi* drums were beating. Horns were sounding. The young boys of the village were playing *lezim*. The ends of their turbans tossed in the air. Walking proudly with the bulls were their owners. The pride in their eyes was for the handsome cattle. Now and again an uncastrated young bull bellowed passionately. Angered by it, another breathed through his nostrils. It was the wealth of the village which was being taken around the village. As it was the month of Akhad, there was no saying when the clouds would gather to cover the moon. The procession was accompanied by gas lanterns. Mangs were carrying them. Mahars had refused that job. Not a single Mahar had gone to carry lanterns at the wedding in Appajipant's house. When he came with the message, they had beaten him, shut him up. Now it was a good opportunity. The village did not care for the Mahars. The relations between the village and the *Maharwada* had snapped. If the village wouldn't come to the *Maharwada* why should a Mahar go to the village? The procession today is not the procession of the village. It is the procession of bullocks.

Why should the Mahars have animosity to the bullocks? The bullocks toiled for generations. Crops grew. The village fed itself on the crops. The *Maharwada* fed itself. The village is indebted to the oxen. The *Maharwada* is indebted to the oxen. A Mahar must carry a lantern in their procession. The bullocks never erred or shirked in doing their hereditary job. Why should the Mahar err?

With the shock of this thought, Bavarya got up. Who knows how he mustered strength, like the gusty wind he rushed toward the village. A youngish Mahar caught hold of his arm as he ran.

"Where are you going grandpa —"

"To the *Bendar* — to carry a lantern — leave me." With a push Bavarya released himself. He jumped across the mud and mat wall. In no time he reached the procession. He took off the lantern on the head of a Mang from behind. He put it on his own head. He began to dance to the rhythm of the *lezim*. The Mang gaped at him. What's the use of complaining against a madman's antics? The *lezim* players danced on. The drums beat their rhythm and Bavarya danced along. None paid any attention to this mad Mahar in the procession of five hundred choice cattle.

The *lezim* dancers went on dancing. The drums kept on beating. Bavarya kept dancing. In the proud procession of five hundred bullocks, no one paid any attention to the crazy Mahar. As the procession came to the village gate the whole *Maharwada* had gathered itself behind the stone walls. With fiery eyes they stared at Bavarya. The procession came in front of the temple. It rested there. The shepherds' sheep exceeded themselves in jumping across the stretched turbans. The villagers clapped. Every year there used to be a Mahar *tamasha*. It did not take place this year. The bullocks returned and the villagers sat down in front of the temple. The tune of the *bhedic* songs sung by the Daraveshi filled the air till dawn. The village audience wrapped in rough woolen blankets dozed as they listened. Some lay down. Bavarya still stood. Till dawn he stood with the lantern on his head. His legs did not stiffen, his hands did not cramp.

With the red of day-break, all the lantern holders sat down on the *par*. One of them lightly removed the lantern from Bavarya's head. Bavarya was pleased today. Obstinately he had done his hereditary duty. But with lantern on his head lifted he felt himself hanging in the void. He did not know where he should go. For almost two months he had tossed in feverless pain and not a villager had so much as inquired. The village did not need him. He had done his job. He was free now to go back to his own people. But were those people really his own people? All of them had become "Buddha." He had no one in the village. He had no one in the *Maharwada*. Still he started. With a mind benumbed he started. He started for the place where he had come from.

With the morning rays he came to the stone walls. His kith and kin surrounded him. Sticks fell against his head. With his life clasped in his fist he ran away. Running across the wilderness he came to the homestead of Jagu Patil. He remembered. Patil's old woman knew the art of healing. From the courtyard of the homestead he gathered his strength to call, "Mother."

"Who's that?" The old woman's voice was heard.

"It's me — Bavarya Taral. I'm beaten, Mother. I've come for medicine."

"Come up, Baba, I can't see."

"How can I come up? I'm a Mahar."

"The sick have no caste. Come, come up." The old woman shouted.

With the old woman's words Bavarya's soul cooled. In a moment the gap between castes was closed. For the first time in his life he was going to climb the steps of the *patil's* house. A horrible pain shot through Bavarya's chest. He sat down on the step. He had hardly sat down when he collapsed. All the movements of that wounded Mahar stopped. Leaving the ragged rough blanket there, his unsoiled soul went away.

"We would not even touch Bavarya's body." This message from the *Maharwada* met with an angry reaction from the prominent people of the village. Determination fired them. The body of that old Mahar was bathed in the warm water in the *patil's* courtyard. There it put on the fragrant garland and black powder. Men such as Appajipant Kulkarni, Janu Patil, and Sitaram Pawar gave their shoulders for carrying his last palaquin. "It was his merit, the poor soul," the blind woman of Patil said. In front of his last procession people from the *bhajan* group sang. "We are on our way to our own place."

Accept our last farewell, "Ramarama."

The whole village had gathered to send off this visitor going back to his place. The whole village walked behind the funeral procession. The red and black fragrant powder was being freely thrown into the air.

From behind the stone walls the *Maharwada* stood watching the whole ceremony. Moved by that scene, perhaps, Bavarya's son shouted,

"Look, you sons of guns — what you couldn't ever get by living my old man got by dying." Someone stopped him by putting his hand over his mouth.

The whole *Maharwada* stood watching silently. Bavarya's last procession had moved them too.

The Theme of "Enmeshment"

In Madgulkar's story, we enter the period of widespread conversion to Buddhism initiated by Dr. Ambedkar in 1956. The central character in this story, an elderly Mahar named Bavarya, does not understand what conversion means. He cannot accept this break with the past. Bavarya is not the Rama Taral or Samba Kotwal type of Mahar "soldier" — he is dependent on the village, feels intimately a part of it, and does not feel his isolation until it is forced upon him. Like Rama and Samba, he glories in service — but it is the glory of the faithful dog who wags happily in appreciation of a kind word or a pat on the head. In contrast to Kharat's tales, the Mahar's self-image as portrayed by Madgulkar contains little evidence of cognitive manipulation. Rather, Bavarya conforms to the upper-caste image of a Mahar, one who willingly identifies himself with the bullock whose "noble labor" is performed without thought or fantasy regarding the Mahar's "true" role as guardian or protector.

As the story unfolds, Madgulkar develops a view very different from Kharat's of the Mahar's relationship to the village. In "Nirvana" the Mahar is not portrayed as "sustaining" the village — rather, it is the village that sustains the Mahar. It is not the village service relations and ties to village officialdom which distinguish the Mahar as Mahar. It is his position within, and commitment to, an ideological system — the traditional Hindu social order — that gives meaning to his role. Once the break has been made, when the Mahars "raise their banner" in defiance of tradition, it becomes clear that the villagers no longer need the Mahar — nor does the Mahar need the village.

This abrupt break with the past is presumably made possible by the post-Independence economic and political changes touched upon at the outset of the story. The construction of factories, canals, and other innovations enables the Mahars to obtain employment outside the village. These changes, however, also enable the villagers to supplant the Mahar's service. Economic tasks traditionally done by Mahars are now performed by others, including their former employers. Despite this disruption of economic ties, one attempt is made to retain the Mahar's ritual service — but this gesture is rejected by the Mahars due to the haughty manner of the Brahman who requests their assistance, and the connotation of inferiority associated with the role the Mahar is asked to perform. The willingness of the Mang, low-caste rivals of the Mahar, to undertake Mahar ritual duties and prerogatives allows the village to sever its last link with the *Maharwada*.

In the work of both authors one finds a lack of communication between Mahar and villager. In Kharat's stories the Mahar repeatedly calls out for understanding, for recognition — "Who is mine, who knows me?" Madgulkar presents another instance of this barrier to understanding — the inability of all but one of the villagers to comprehend the implications of the *Maharwada's* conversion. While other villagers are shocked and mystified by the conversion, Appajipant, the Brahman, realizes: "Now the *Maharwada* will break away from the village." It is clear that Appajipant is aware of the ideological link tying the Mahar into the system, and of the transformation of tradition that has taken place — "The Brahmans lost their Brahmanness; why should the Mahars want their Maharness?" Appajipant's awareness suggests a curious kinship between Brahman and Mahar. Both castes seem to share a common perception of what it is that constitutes the essence of "Maharness." In a way, they are mirror-images of each other in that both castes have served the village as "protectors," one by performance of ritual, the other by the removal of pollution. Unlike the Mahar, however, the Brahman has received recognition and appreciation from the other castes.

The villagers' lack of concern and appreciation for the Mahar is exemplified in Madgulkar's portrayal of Bavarya. Despite Bavarya's adherence to tradition, and his service to the village, only in death does the village acknowledge his loyalty. While Madgulkar describes the upper-caste woman's offer to assist the injured Bavarya as having briefly "closed the gap between castes," this appears to be wishful thinking. Even the villagers' performance of Bavarya's funeral rites is viewed by the *Maharwada* as an affront, since it expressed the villagers' willingness to accept as a *person* only those Mahars who adhere to tradition. Both authors seem to agree that, for the Mahar, death in service brings honor denied in life.

The prospects for accommodation of the new Mahar within the village community are rather remote, judging by Madgulkar. The same conclusion seems to underly Kharat's observation: "Until the village crumbles, there cannot be an end to Maharness." Kharat's stories, however, especially "Return to the Village Womb," imply that the old system is crumbling, that profound changes intimately linked to the "defection" of the Mahar are in the offing. If this is true, and if the old image of the Mahar is ultimately overcome, the new image may be forged as expressed by the poet, Pearse:

And now I speak, being full of vision;
I speak to my people, and I speak in my people's name to the masters
*   of my people.*
I say to my people that they are holy, that they are august, despite their
*   chains,*
That they are greater than those that hold them, and stronger and purer. . . .

12.   BEATRICE MILLER

The Man Inside

THIS STUDY IS offered as an exercise, or an experiment, in the application
of psychiatric insight to the type of literary materials presented in the
preceding chapter, supplemented by one other Marathi short story written
by Bhaurao Sathe. The analysis explores differences in the image of the
Mahar as portrayed in the writings of S. Kharat, a Mahar, and V. Madgulkar, a Brahman. The Sathe story, written by a member of the Untouchable
Mang caste, affords an opportunity to investigate possible differences in
the self-image held by Untouchables of different caste origin. This choice
of a Mang author was prompted in part by Madgulkar's story, "Nirvana,"
in which members of the Mang caste are described as having assumed
ritual roles rejected by Mahar converts to Buddhism.

In this attempt to obtain some insight into "the man inside," short
stories written by natives of Maharashtra for a Marathi audience are
used to elucidate phenomena sometimes studied by means of Rohrschach
and similar psychological projective devices. In contrast to the findings
of such techniques, literary materials afford a measure of values, ideals,
and emotional reactions as expressed by individuals *seeking to communicate with other members of their society*. The use of this approach,
however, is severely limited by the paucity of available literary works by
Untouchable authors. It should also be noted that the selection of the
stories used in this analysis was dictated by their ready availability,
rather than by any systematic sampling or by adherence to any formal
methodological criteria. It is to be hoped that others more versed in Indian
literature will pursue this line of enquiry through the application of the

same or similar approaches to a more representative sample of literary accounts treating Untouchables, including works by authors of diverse caste backgrounds. The prospect for such enquiry seems most promising in the light of Apte's survey of post-Independence Marathi fiction in which he finds strong interest in depicting life among the lower classes.*

This exploratory venture was made possible by the generous assistance of Dr. Arnold Ludwig, psychiatrist at the Mendota State Hospital, Madison, Wisconsin. In addition to his formal training in psychiatry, Dr. Ludwig's long-standing and close association with anthropologists provided him with an interest in and appreciation of cultural diversity and a conceptual orientation well-suited to the task. Dr. Ludwig was also willing to accept a reversal of the psychiatrist's usual role in that the technique employed here entailed tape-recording his own train of thought. His lack of any substantive knowledge of Maharashtrian society, or more than a layman's acquaintance with India, enabled Dr. Ludwig to approach the stories relatively "blind" in so far as their cultural content is concerned.

Dr. Ludwig's examination and interpretation were carried out in several stages. Initially he read the tales without benefit of supplementary information. In this phase, he attempted to comprehend the personalities of the characters, and the perspective and perception of the authors, solely in the light of his own experience and analytical training. Consequently the impressions recorded at this time were relatively subjective and untempered by cultural clues. Dr. Ludwig's further reactions to the stories were recorded after he was informed of the authors' caste identities and provided with specific information about the social position of Untouchables in rural Maharashtra and the relevance of contemporary events to their lives. Before turning to his analysis, however, the reader should review the stories provided in the preceding chapter and the translation of Sathe's story given below.

SAVALA MANGA†

The day was leaning toward the setting side. The fire in the rays had become faint. The cool rays came down like a shower on the thick green forest wealth. The green of the trees glittered bright. It dazzled the eye. A cart trail which came from Vategaon entered that thick forest. After many a curving twist, climbing the side of a hill, it descended on Tabgaon.

---

*Mahadeo L. Apte, "Contemporary Marathi Fiction," *The Journal of Asian Studies,* Volume XXIX, No. 1, November 1969, pp. 55–56.
†Translated from Marathi by Pramodh Kale, University of Minnesota.

Savala had set himself on that trail for Vaghadari. His frisky caravan horse trotted quietly today. Savala, the outlaw, the rebel, had been
to see his wife and children. His rebellious soul still lingered in the midst
of his young ones.

Savala's figure, large and imposing, matched his action. A large
head, topped with a turban equally large — broad face, sharp eyes, thick
eyebrows, pointed nose, full curving "gulchabi" mustache, thick neck, a
heavy chest like a dovecote. With a bright shining axe, its blade as big
as a frying pan, in his hand, Savala rode the horse. He looked like a hill
set on a hill. His sharp eyes looked far ahead of him.

Savala saw two persons coming down the mountain ahead. One
of them was a woman and the other a man. Savala wondered who these
two were. He spurred his horse. He flashed around turn after turn of that
curving trail. He rode forward fast as the two ran down the hill.

Savala had declared rebellion against the British. The British in
order to make firm their rule had passed a new law called the *Criminal
Caste Law*. According to this law all the Mangs in Maharashtra had to
present themselves for a check three times a day. Twice during the day
the Mangs had to present themselves at the *chavadi* for check. At night
the *police-patil* of the village had to go to the *Mangawada* for check and
roll-call. If a Mang remained absent he was sentenced to three months of
hard labor in prison. The whole Mang community had opposed this
oppressive law. Fakira, Mura, Chinchanikar, Pira, Ghonechikar, Bali
Sajurkar, Nilu Mang and Bhiva of Khujagaon in Varana — these Mangs
had declared rebellion against this law. Savala was looked upon as a
general of the rebels.

The one thought that possessed Savala's mind was to gather together
all the Mang-Ramoshis in the province and cut down all the British army
posts. His fighting men had armed and readied themselves in the ravines
of Vaghadari. His mind was made up. He was determined to destroy
the British Raj.

Savala rode ahead. His eyes reached even further. They moved
around the two figures.

The two came down fast. At one turn Savala could see them, at the
next they disappeared.

Only a single turn separated Savala from those two. He spurred his
horse, expecting to intercept them.

He was disappointed. Those two whom he saw for such a long time
had disappeared all of a sudden. How did this happen? Where did the
two hide? Why did they hide? The thought disturbed Savala. He got off
the horse and fired by an obstinate determination set himself to trace

them down. He observed the footprints amongst the fallen leaves. He got off the main road where the two had done the same. He started looking for them in the thick forest. He looked for them in shrubs and trees, streams and hollows but he could not find them. How could this be? Wherever did they go? Disappointedly, Savala walked back to his horse. As he walked his eyes fell on the tall *ganjani* grass on the side. Surprised, he stopped in his track. The grass stalks stood tall and still except for a few the tips of which were shaking and trembling. He felt happy. He called: "Now come out."

At that the two came out trembling and like offenders stood shaking before Savala. One of them was a young girl. The water from her mouth had run away. Savala looked at her with his penetrating eyes. She had only recently stepped down into the courtyard of youth. Her full body quivered uncontrollably. Fear overflowed from the pools of her dark liquid eyes. Her fearful state made her even more attractive. She tried hard to control the tremulousness of her body. Again and again she moved her tongue over her dry lips and stared at Savala with unbatted eyelids. Her thighs trembled but she did not allow the *padar* on her breasts to fall down. She thought she was going to be raped. She was going to lose her honor. Till that time at least she should cover her body at any cost. This thought swirled through her mind. She had a silk saree but not an ornament was seen on her body.

Savala observed the young girl carefully from top of the head to the nail on the toe and then turned his gaze to the man. The man stood erect. He had crossed fifty. There was grey in his moustache but it still retained its twisting curl. His body looked rugged and his anger showed itself on his face. Making his face devoid of any expression he just stood there with a bundle under his arm. Holding his axe straight, Savala asked:

"Who're you? What's your name?"

"I'm Dada Patil from Jaisinghpur."

"Who's she to you?"

"That's my daughter Kashi." Putting down the bundle under his arm, Dada Patil folded his hands in *namaskara*. "I have heard your name. I know your reputation. Take all this jewelry. But Savala don't lay hands on me or on my daughter. I'm a man of honor. For my daughter's honor I'll gladly give a thousand or two but don't lay hands —"

A powerful slap from Savala flashed against Dada Patil's mouth. He fell down. Kashibai screamed. Savala raised his axe and shouted:

"Get up."

"Don't hit me now." Dada Patil got up rubbing his cheek.

"Don't hit you? Why not? You should be killed, nothing else. A man of wealth you are and that's why you are auctioning your daughter's honor. Only you are a man of honor and we have given up our honor. Who told you that? Speak up —"

"I was wrong," Dada Patil said sadly, "But the whole world says that the Mang people rob young girls of their honor."

"I'll burn that whole world," Savala said taking a step forward. "Stand up straight. Where have you been?"

"To Talagaon. To take Kashibai to her husband's house."

"Then why did you bring her back?"

"My son-in-law won't let her in the house."

"Why wouldn't he let her in the house?"

"I had agreed upon a dower in the marriage. I wasn't able to make good the whole amount."

"How much dowry had you agreed upon?"

"Fifteen thousand."

"Why did you agree to such an amount?"

"For my daughter's happiness and to make ties with a family of substance."

"You are a devil," Savala said in a burning voice. "What is your son-in-law's name?"

"Rajaram Patil from Talagaon." Dada Patil replied in a fallen voice.

"Come on then." Savala shouted.

"Where?" Dada began to tremble. Savala's anger burst out,

"Follow me without a word."

"I'll follow you."

The three came to the main path. The horse was standing there. Looking at it Savala ordered, "Put your daughter on that horse and start." Dada Patil put Kashi on the back of the horse. Kashi's life gathered itself in her throat thinking of what sort of things she would have to face. She was sure that she was not going to be able to save her honor that day.

The horse had trotted a few steps when Khandu Mang, who was on the watch, came running. Savala said to him:

"Khandu, I'm on my way to Talagaon. Wait for me until midnight, tell Fakira. When the starspread hangs overhead, start and enter Talagaon. Burn the place. Turn it into ashes."

Khandu ran in the direction of Vaghadari and Savala set himself for Talagaon with Kashi. The day drowned. Darkness fell. Face recognition was lost. At such time Savala entered Talagaon with Kashi. He was angry because of the bad name given to Mangs, making them not rebels but mere robbers of women's and girls' honor and ornaments. As he came to Rajaram Patil's *wada* he gave a shout like the bellowing of a tiger.

"Rajaram Patil, come out."

Rajaram Patil was taken aback to hear this. Who could call him so arrogantly? He was angered. He jumped up and took an axe. In the light of the lantern its blade gleamed. He shouted:

"Who's that?"

"It's me, Savala Mang," said Savala. "Leave that axe there and come out. Or your head will travel to Vaghadari. Out, now."

The axe dropped out of Rajaram's hand to hear the name Savala and the awful words. His heart began to jump. His mother and sisters shook and shivered and his old man got a fright. Rajaram came down to the courtyard and stammered:

"Na — na — naik — What do you say?"

"Who is this woman?" Fire was burning in Savala's head. His axe gleamed.

"My wife — Kashi." Rajaram replied with a mournful face.

"Why won't you let her in the house?" Savala asked in a sharp voice and took a step forward. The atmosphere became tense. Rajaram was frightened out of his wits. He said:

"It was a mistake. Pardon me — I'll never give any trouble to Kashibai." Quickly he bowed to Dada Patil and held his feet. His mother and sister took Kashibai into the house. Then Savala calmed down. He said:

"This Kashi is my daughter. Don't make her unhappy, or I'll butcher your head. I'll pile a mountain of sorrow on your house and home."

"Such a mistake would never happen hence." Rajaram folded his hands. Savala stepped back. Rajaram said.

"Naik, eat dinner and go."

"Eat? No, never," Savala said. "At this hour you are my enemy. If I eat your salt today and if you turn against me tomorrow, I'll have to butcher your head. People then would call me disloyal to self. You be straight. Take care of Kashi. Then I'll come and eat your food." With these words he jumped on his horse and rode toward Vaghadari fast as the wind.

It was past midnight. The time for Savala's return had passed, and so Fakira, Mura, Bali, Nilu had saddled the horses and readied themselves with swords tied at their sides. The Mangs had made up their mind to burn Talagaon to ashes.

But when Savala came, everybody became calm. Addressing them all, Savala said:

"Listen, my brave friends. True, we have rebelled against the British.

But our enemies have raised the jungle against us. We rob and loot. We abduct people's daughters and take their honor. This is the bad name we have got. People with such a bad name have no right to hold a sword. A sword should be raised only in good cause. It should strike only in good cause."

"Nana, what you do is agreeable to us," said Fakira. "I won't mind if five — no, five hundred — Mangs die of starvation to make our name good. But let the whole world know that the Mang rebel is after all a human being — "

The rebellion of the Mangs was growing. Fakira, Mura, Bali, Nilu worked hard for their reputation. Savala strove harder to spread the good name. He was death to the treacherous and disloyal. The sons-in-law who mistreated their wives were his special targets. A new age had begun in that valley since Kashibai was taken back to live in her in-laws' house. Fathers from distant villages came and saw Savala to give him full accounts of their sons-in-law's misbehavior. Savala then visited each village to dry up the mischievous arrogance of each son-in-law. Many girls now lived a family life bright as gold and many daughters blessed Savala.

Kashi was absolutely dazzled by Savala's goodness to her. Every morning and every evening she folded her hands to God and said silently in her mind: "God, give long life to Savala. Give him mighty power. Give sharpness to his sword — Let me know of his happiness every day. My mother's place is not in Jaisinghpur but in Vaghadari. Protect it forever —"

During the same time many respectable people had become angry. They did not like the Mang rebellion. They helped the English. Mathaji Dabhade of Karungali was the maternal uncle of Rajaram. He had become almost crazed with rage. He told his kith and kin that a Mang had oppressed his nephew.

"We are Marathas. Our ways are different. Our customs are different. We can do anything. I'll never agree to a Mang ruling over us. I'll never agree to bowing my head before a Mang. We too have swords." In this manner he kindled fire against Savala. His kith and kin listened to him. For in this valley Dabhade was known to be a powerful man. He was powerful in might and wealth. His word had value.

Mathaji Dabhade once came to Talagaon. Rajaram politely requested him to be seated. But the obstinate man fired up. Trembling with rage, he said:

"You are my nephew. You bowed your head before a Mang to take Kashi back into the house. You didn't act well. You soiled our *kuli*.

Now my saying is this. Drive off Kashi. Don't be afraid of Savala, that Mang. Let that Savala come, my sword is ready."

Kashi was frightened to hear this. Her mouth dried up. And she said in a humble voice:

"Uncle, it won't be good to anger Savala thus. You will say Harahara and step aside, and I'll have to become a 'sati.' "

"This son of Dabhade won't let you down," said Dabhade with his eyes spread: "I'll pick up the 'Bel-Bhandara' and vow that I won't leave you alone. Drive off Kashi."

"But why?" Rajaram asked. To this Mathaji replied:

"I want to test Savala's strength. Dada Patil put his tongue into hell by mustering that Mang's power. He cheated you of fifteen thousand. And so we don't want his daughter in the house. If you don't listen to me and drive off Kashi, our ties are burnt. We'll meet henceforth only in heaven."

Rajaram was helpless. Kashi could not control her sobs. She cried aloud in pain. Her living with her husband was ended. The next day Rajaram set her on the way with a sari and a couple of bhakars in her hand. Mathaji said to her then:

"Girl, go back to your mother's place. If you want your in-laws' place come back with fifteen thousand. Or bring Savala Mang. I want to see his strength."

The hot sun of Vaisakha was blazing overhead. It was midday. Taking the hot sun on her head, Kashi was on her way to her mother's place. As she came near Vaghadari, the Mang on the watch accosted her and said:

"Where are you going, lady?"

"To my mother's place," Kashi replied.

"What's the name of your mother's house?" the Mang asked.

Kashi replied, "My mother's house is in Vaghadari." Her reply puzzled the Mang on the watch. He asked, "Whose are you?"

"I'm Savala Mang's," Kashi said. The Mang realized in a hurry. He climbed a tree, raised his axe and signalled with the rays shining on the blade. And Savala's caravan horse came galloping. Savala was stupefied to see Kashi. He asked:

"'Kashibai, what happened?"

"Nana, I was driven off." Kashi began to cry and Savala flew into a rage. "Who drove you off?"

"Mathaji Dabhade of Karungali." Uttering these words, Kashi sat down.

"Who is this Mathaji Dabhade?" Savala asked, to which Kashi replied, crying, "My master's maternal uncle. He said, 'Either bring fifteen thousand dowry or bring that Savala Mang. I want to see his strength.' "

"Is that so?" said Savala. For a moment he paused to think and then forcing a smile he said, "Now you go to your mother's place. I will show my strength to Dabhade. Don't cry. . . . "

"I won't go to my mother's place." Kashi said through her sobs. "For how many days is my life's misery to go on? I don't want my mother's place. I want nothing — "

"Where are you going to live then?"

"In Vaghadari." Hearing this Savala laughed like a falling rock. He took Kashi into Vaghadari and said, "Silly, my girl. Take rest today, I'll show my strength to Dabhade today, give the dowry to Rajaram and from tomorrow morning you go to your in-laws' place and rule happily like Rama's kingdom — " Kashi smiled.

The darkness slowly put a blanket over Sahyadri. The solemn mountain was standing still in that darkness and Savala was hurrying to go to Karungali.

At the middle of the night Savala dashed against the walls of Karungali village with his brave, fighting men. Blazing with torches and accompanied by the noise of drums and trumpets he rushed towards Dabhade's *wada* like a tornado. In the violent light of the torches Savala appeared flowering with rage. Armed Mang-Ramoshis were ready with their swords raised. With a quick stride some rushed through the main gate. As they entered the middle quadrangle Mathaji unsheathed his sword and ran into the field. All his five sons took up arms. The servants began to fight with the Mangs. Within moments the battle began to rage furiously. A servant opened the back door to let the villagers in.

Swords were dashing against each other there. Men were moving with the quickness of sword blades. Both sides were frenzied and Mathaji's sword had exceeded itself. The Mangs were stepping back. One of them shouted,

"Savalunana, Dabhade's sword is getting the upper hand. We can't get Dabhade."

Savala was gripped with rage to hear this. "Get aside," he shouted and rushed on to Dabhade. With a moment circumstances changed completely. Savala battled. Mathaji struck with all his might. Like death the two swords glittered brightly over their heads. Sparks flew. Blood flowed. Pushing Dabhade back, Savala shouted:

"Dabhadya, see now my strength."

Dabhade's eyes turned. Savala's sword struck him. Mustering all his energy, Dabhade returned the stroke. Maddened with fury, Savala struck Dabhade across the shoulder. The sword dropped down. Putting his back against the wall Dabhade said: "I lost my arm. . . . "

"Then sit down or you'll lose your head." Savala warned Mathaji. Mathaji sat down. Seeing that Dabhade was wounded the villagers ran away. Opposition ended. Savala said,

"Well done, my braves. Now strip the *wada*. Don't leave a cowry behind. Come."

The Mangs set about their business quickly. Tying the rupees into bundles they returned to Vaghadari. Savala had shown his strength to Dabhade by robbing him of fifty thousand rupees.

Light was flowering in the south. At that auspicious hour night was turning into day. The morning wind had got up. Its jolting had awakened Sahyadri. Trees and shrubs were awake and swaying. The birds were talking. The whole atmosphere had become auspicious because of their sweet talk. Kashi was happy to see Savala returned safely. She asked,

"Nana, what happened?"

"Nothing. I came back annexing Dabhade's kingdom." Saying this Savala poured all of Dabhade's wealth in front of Kashi and got ready to go to Talagaon.

But Khandu Ramoshi came running. He said:

"Nana, Rajaram from Talagaon has come."

"Go, bring him here." Savala ordered, and Khandu pushed Rajaram in front of him. Rajaram began to tremble to see Kashi, Savala, all that wealth and Savala's sword. He said:

"My uncle cheated me. Nana, forgive me. I'll never make trouble for Kashi — never make her unhappy or you can butcher my neck."

"I don't feel like making Kashi a widow by butchering your neck," Savala said. "But now don't listen to anyone. Look at your uncle's wealth. If you want dower, take this with you. But if you offend me again you'll die — "

"No, no," Rajaram said, "I'll live with Kashi. I don't want to die." Rajaram went back with Kashi and the British armies rushed on to Savala. Savala should be blown off from a cannon, the order said. Savala who strove for his name with the sword tied to his waist walked the path of death.

Bringing her life into her eyes, Kashi prayed to God. "God, give long life to my Nana. Give him mighty strength. Give sharpness to his sword. Let me know every day. Protect forever my fighting mother's place in Vaghadari."

Contrasts and Comparisons

After an initial reading, Dr. Ludwig's first reaction to the stories was that "Savala Mang" "stuck out like a sore thumb," Sathe's story appearing to have little in common with the others. It was a "modern Robin Hood" or "super-hero" folktale in marked contrast to Kharat's stories which were "very gloomy, very depressed, passive, and resigned." The portrayal of the hero of "Savala Mang" was viewed by Ludwig as in accord with his conception of the folk-hero: "A function of a folk-hero in folk literature is that he provides a common 'fantasy' which establishes the worth, self-esteem and basis for self-regard among the group to whom the hero belongs." Ludwig speculated that the "superficiality" of "Savala Mang" might be due to the author's personal involvement in a movement for which this tale of the Mang's glory served as an ego-enhancing myth. At this juncture, Ludwig did not know that when the story was written, Sathe was a professed "Communist man of action."

"Nirvana," written by the Brahman author, Madgulkar, was felt to be the most "realistic," even though the main character, Bavarya, exhibited a "delusional clinging to the past and a rejection of the present and those things he considered to be new." Bavarya's emotional reaction to the *Maharwada's* conversion to Buddhism was likened by Ludwig to the sense of loss often experienced by adolescents in the West after their rejection of the past. In both instances the individual finds the present untenable and seeks release from psychological pressures. Madgulkar's portrayal of Bavarya was felt to be akin to that of the Mahars by Kharat. Bavarya was unable to articulate his anger at being trapped between the old and the new, as manifest in the competing demands of the *Maharwada* and the village. Madgulkar, however, presents a resolution of this conflict. He shows the tangible conditions of sickness and bodily discomfort as psychologically meaningful responses to the amorphous pressures impinging on Bavarya. By contrast Ludwig initially was puzzled as to why Kharat stories did not express anger, hurt, and confusion in a "normal" manner. As these tales rarely provided a "direct expression" of actual emotions, he felt them to be lacking in reality. Also, Madgulkar presents the interplay between social and psychological forces, in contrast to Kharat's stories where little interaction of this kind is shown.

Ludwig's first impression of the authors was that Madgulkar, the Brahman author of "Nirvana," was a Mahar. On the other hand, the stories by Kharat, a Mahar, were thought to be far less perceptive, more dependent on stereotypes, and lacking in familiarity with the inner feelings of the subjects. Kharat's "Inside the Village Womb," however, did evoke a mood of uncertainty and psychological stress stemming from portents of change, a new beginning without direction or definite goals — "These are people who are somewhat lost and don't know why, nor how to find a way."

When Kharat's identity as a Mahar was made known, Ludwig re-examined his previous reactions to the author's work. Kharat's portrayal of Mahars, previously viewed as stereotypical and unfeeling, was reassessed as a possible reflection of the intensity of his anger and antagonism toward Hindu society's treatment of Untouchables. Such personal feelings might have prevented Kharat from attaining the more balanced overview of the Mahar's situation presented by the Brahman, Madgulkar. The anxieties and the sense of impending doom that pervade Kharat's work were seen by Ludwig as a clue to the author's incomplete suppression of anger and hostility. The inability of most of Kharat's characters to achieve release, other than through illness and death, and the absence of any attempt at overt rebellion, indicated to Ludwig that Kharat had written the stories prior to his own personal resolution of the problem.

After Ludwig was told that Sathe, author of "Savala Mang," was of Mang origin, and the traditional roles of Mang and Maratha were explicated, Ludwig reassessed "Savala Mang." His earlier impression, that this story stood apart from the others, was reinforced. In contrast to the portrayal of the Mahar by Kharat and Madgulkar, in which illness, death, and despair appear as a common response to their low-status — the Mang, as presented by Sathe, appear to have achieved a degree of psychological "peace" which might enable them to continue as an integral part of the present social order. Psychologically they did not need to break the bonds of tradition and reciprocal roles of the caste system. The means for their "escape" was that of fictional role reversal. Instead of attaining release through death, the Mang relied on fantasy — on the glorification of a folk-hero whose exploits represent a direct confrontation between the "noble Mang" and their Maratha masters portrayed in subservient, if not servile, roles. In contrast to the image of the Mang held by the upper castes, Savala is portrayed as a protector of women, one who magnanimously helps others regardless of caste, and disdains the avarice which he attributes to Marathas. The story implies that the unflattering stereotype of the Mang commonly held by Marathas more appropriately applies to the Maratha. If such fantasy, as expressed through role-reversal, is widely shared by the Mang, it might help account for their behavior in "Nirvana," where they are depicted as having accepted their place within the Hindu social order. Also the Mang's relative indifference to the Buddhist conversion movement, so popular among the Mahar, may be related to such acceptance.

In contrast to Sathe's portrayal of the Mang, the Mahars presented by both Kharat and Madgulkar appear to see no escape from the psychological stress of their low status other than through a complete rejection of the caste system and all that it implies. The Mahar solution would entail a breakdown of traditional patterns of inter-caste relations and their disengagement from any involvement with others in the community. As Ludwig observed: "There is only one resolution possible for the Mahar — breaking away. Those who do not break away can only turn inward — differences are wiped out by physical ailments which all men can have, or by death which also affects all men."

The Mang's acceptance of traditional "Untouchable" roles, at a time when Mahars are seeking to break free of the past, suggests the need to qualify the common assumption that all Untouchables, regardless of caste, share a common fate and world view. It may further suggest that the choice of what might be called a "target" caste or castes, against which a particular group measures its worth, may also affect the psycho logical mechanism necessary for survival. As an indication of that sug- gestion, the reader might notice that the main "target" in the Mahar stories was Brahman. Even when the Brahman was not physically present in a tale, the Mahar protagonist's self-image and role — as guide, selfless protector and even, to some extent, outsider — has its Brahmanical parallels. For the Mang, the story shows the "target" as Maratha, whose position in the hierarchical order was closer, and in a sense more attainable. The Mahar resolution of conflict was to move out. The Mang, seeing a vacuum, moved in.

13.

HAROLD R. ISAACS

The Ex-Untouchables

IN 1946–47, the year before Indian Independence, the country's school population stood at 18,200,000 and the literacy rate at about 10 percent. Twenty years later, the school population was well over 50 million and the literacy rate was nearing 25 percent. In this widening spread of popular education, India's Untouchables — made ex-Untouchables by constitutional fiat in 1949 — have shared in steeply rising proportions. In 1948–49, there were about half a million members of the Untouchable castes in Indian schools. In the next fifteen years while the total school population doubled, the figure for Untouchables in school swelled about tenfold to some 6 million, including more than 4 million in primary schools, about 1,500,000 in middle and high schools, and nearly 60,000 in colleges and universities and various other technical and other higher schools. These members of a new generation, representing nearly 10 percent of India's 65 million Untouchables or members of the so-called Scheduled Castes, are on their way to new levels of life in the Indian society. They are coming up, moreover, alongside millions of other young Indians who are caste Hindus who also were never part of an educated class in India before. One can only guess at how these new groups of educated people will relate to each other and what their future

Excerpted and slightly edited from *India's Ex-Untouchables,* John Day Co., N.Y., 1965. The interviews quoted were conducted in 1963 and the statistics used are in most cases 1963 figures. More recent figures, available in subsequent reports of the Commissioner for Scheduled Castes and Tribes, would change quantities without, expectably, altering their substance as reported here.

roles will be in a changing India. This will depend on the pace and manner of India's conquest of its backwardness and this in turn will depend heavily on what happens elsewhere in the world. Meanwhile these masses of young people coming up out of the schools add grievously each year to the already grievously high numbers of India's educated underemployed or unemployed. Those who are ex-Untouchables, coming up from so much farther down, have a longer and harder way to rise, because as they come up, they find all the entrenched sanctions and habits of the Indian caste system standing in their way.

The central government in India, itself caught in a great deal of ambivalence and conflict over the caste system, is committed to giving the ex-Untouchables special help. It is doing this not only by helping them through school but in opening the way afterward to jobs. Since ex-Untouchables cannot hope to find jobs in a society still dominated by caste-bound Hindus, the government has opened its own services and has set up quotas of reserved places for them to fill as they qualify. This system of "reserved places" or "reservations" began well back in the British time, mainly for the benefit of the non-Brahman lower castes, and came partly as a result of the non-Brahman fight against Brahman domination. It has been enormously expanded by the government of independent India. It is now the lifeline by which more and more people are pulling themselves — or are being pulled — out of the cesspools of untouchability.

Of the earlier generation of Untouchables who made their way upward through the educational opportunities opened up in the British time, some found places in politics, in Maharashtra through Ambedkar and his Scheduled Castes Federation, and many more elsewhere in India via the patronage of Gandhi and the Congress Party. In Gandhi's party — Gandhi was in this, as in all things, *bapu,* or father — the ex-Untouchables came to occupy a peculiarly favored position as wards, individuals specially selected for advancement in the political and government machinery. Untouchables have served as president of the All-India Congress Party, ministers and deputy ministers in the cabinet, and as occupants of the 72 reserved seats in the House of the People in the Central Parliament and 477 seats among the 3,283 in the various state legislatures. Many of these seats are already occupied by younger arrivals on the political scene, products of the post-Independence system of aided education and promotion by preferment.

No comparable visibility has been achieved by ex-Untouchables in the academic profession. "There are no Harijan intellectuals," flatly said one well-informed caste Hindu scholar and educator. "The older men who came up became politicians. A new group now coming up is moving into the universities, but they will be found still in fairly junior positions and almost all in the traditional branches of learning, not moving into fields where one might do research, for example, on the problems of the community. I would guess, however, that there may be as many as 100 Scheduled Caste Ph.D.'s now, where 10 years ago there were none." At the University of Mysore — where unusual opportunities opened earlier for the Scheduled Castes when it was a princely state —I was told there were 10 ex-Untouchable Lecturers (equivalent to an American Assistant Professor) out of a total of 100, three Readers (equivalent to Associate Professor) one Professor, a dean of a medical college, and a college principal who holds a Ph.D. in botany. The University of Bombay, I learned, had produced two Ph.D.'s in sociology and was about to produce a third, and 10 M.A.'s in this field since 1951. In this matter too, however, as in so many others, the numbers get vague. There are instances in which ex-Untouchables who attain faculty positions sometimes become less easily identifiable. I met one high administrative officer at one university who had been specifically named as an ex-Untouchable, but he never so identified himself to me. Farther down the line in the educational system there are now great numbers of ex-Untouchable teachers, many thousands of them, but, as we have already remarked, no one knows just how many. Most of them are still humble graduates themselves of little more than the primary grades or secondary schools, but they are playing a key role in widening the path up which they had traveled and along which vastly greater numbers are following them.

In the world of business and professions there is still, by all accounts, only the tiniest trickle of ex-Untouchables. Employment in private business firms in India is still heavily determined by regional, caste, and family connections. Mobility in this respect is only just beginning in the larger enterprises to cut across these lines. The chances are, I was told, that the rare few ex-Untouchables who have moved successfully into business and commerce have managed in some way to conceal their identities. This was the case in the two very modest examples I myself ran into, one a man who was working for a trade association, and the other the father of a student who had made his way to a white collar position in a department store. As to other professions, I gathered only a few fragmentary indications. I asked staff members of several newspapers if there were any Scheduled Caste journalists and drew only blank stares of surprise at my question. There is apparently quite a scattering, however, of doctors and lawyers. In Bombay, I was told that there are nine Scheduled Caste lawyers trying to practice privately but only one practicing physician, and that one a young woman whom I met, Dr. Shinde. She holds the degree

the British call "Bachelor of Medicine and Bachelor of Surgery" — the
M.B.B.S. — and has set up her own clinic in the city. In Madras, a caste
Hindu journalist friend told me, "There are 10 Harijan doctors who seem
to be getting along all right." There are larger numbers who hold medical
and law degrees and others qualified as engineers and chemists but they
are all, I was usually told, working for the government.

At the lower occupational levels considerable change has come
in the shift of great numbers of ex-Untouchables from village to city.
Figures on this would probably show that relatively impressive numbers
of former Untouchables have moved into industrial occupations, although
large numbers have remained within the boundaries of their traditional
occupations. Among those whose individual experiences I explored
directly, the pattern of migration was a common one. The father, sometimes the grandfather, had come into the city from the village, and such
people are in their many thousands the scavengers and sweepers who
carry away the waste of India's great cities and who continue in their new
situations many of the conditions and divisions they brought with them
from their villages. Many others have gone to work in industry, though
still as menials, as sweepers, as common laborers, dockworkers, steve-
dores, and the like. But many who have had some education, if only a
few grades, have moved up, becoming truck and bus drivers and workers
on the railroads — where they moved into the slots vacated by many
Anglo-Indians at the time of Independence — and have begun rising
through the grades of firemen on the way to becoming engine drivers. For
those who are more enterprising and push up higher on the educational
ladder, there is always the magic step up and out of manual labor
altogether — the goal of goals for the aspiring Indian. Any manual labor
in India is still held to be part of a low estate and it is the primary function
of education, many still think, to emancipate them from it. In Bombay,
the law stipulates that no one who has passed the matriculation examination may be kept in a manual job.

Following individuals on their way up, one pattern became familiar
through its recurrence: the higher a father went, the higher a son could
reach. The case of the Class 1 civil servant who was the son of a Class 3
civil servant was characteristic. In a group of youngsters I met in the south,
there was one lad whose father works in a railway boiler shop who told
me he wanted to become an engineer. Another was the son of a farmer
who had managed to acquire a piece of land of his own; he wanted to
become a doctor. The one ex-Untouchable I met in Bombay who is in
private business is the son of a man who came to the city from the village
and found a new kind of work in the railway paintshops. Quite a few

high-aimers were the sons of men who had gone far enough in school themselves to have become teachers.

One also got from these individual family stories a quite literal sense of the swelling numbers of young people moving swiftly beyond their parents to higher and higher levels. Where the father had begun to move up, not one son but four or six moved higher, and so did his daughters. One student of law, who is the son of a tanner, has one brother who is a government clerk, another a factory inspector, and a younger brother now in his second year of science. The son of the department store employee has one brother with a Bachelor of Commerce degree who is now working in the government sales tax office, another brother who passed his matriculation and is working for the same firm as his father does, and two sisters moving up the school grades. The son of a primary school teacher has an older brother who holds a Master of Science degree and works for the government. Ubale, whose home we visited in Rawaly Camp, is the son of a Grade C fireman on the railway. Of his four brothers, one, a matric, now works for the railroad; another, a B.A., is in the government service; the third, who was about to appear for his B.A., meanwhile was holding a job in a private insurance company. His youngest brother has taken a step beyond them all by entering the University of Bombay.

But this rule too had its exception. Probably the most spectacular example of self-generated forward drive I came upon in this quest was that of Khadtale, the solidly chunky young man who had become a pilot for Indian Airlines. The son of a laborer who had never gone to school at all but whose children had, Khadtale made his way up to an engineering school in Poona along with 30 other Scheduled Caste boys. He failed several times, but kept trying. All his classmates of that time are now working for the government, he told me, with one exception who is working as an engineer in a private automobile concern where his employer does not know he is an ex-Untouchable. With his degree in science, Khadtale landed a job in the state aviation department and found himself working in the control tower at the Bombay airport. Here he conceived the ambition to learn to fly and with the help of government scholarships he did so, winning his wings as pilot of a single-engine plane in 1955. From there he pushed on to commercial pilot training. For this there were no scholarships, no reserved places — who would ever dream of an ex-Untouchable reaching so far up? Khadtale hoarded his own money and talked himself into loans and grants from a great variety of places and ultimately from the Ministry of Social Welfare. After several intervals when his money ran out, Khadtale finished his training in 1959 and got his first job with a private cargo plane company, Kallinga Airlines, flying old Dakotas (the Douglas DC3) between points in India, the Middle East and Africa; the son of an illiterate Untouchable laborer, born and raised in the town of Nasig, was spanning the continents. In 1961 he was taken on by Indian Airlines as a pilot, and a great astonished fuss was made in the newspapers over this man who had come all the way up from the bottom of the cesspool into the sky. Still flying co-pilot when we met, Khadtale was expecting his own two-engine command momentarily and was looking ahead to a move to four-engine aircraft and to jets.

Upward-moving ex-Untouchable boys obviously have to marry upward-moving ex-Untouchable girls. This is getting easier to do now than it was, but it still presents problems. Marriage out of caste is still quite rare and radical in all parts of Indian society, and all the more so, of course, where ex-Untouchables are concerned. In the beginning, only boys moved out onto the path of education and it has only been in more recent years, with the opening of public education on a large scale, that girls have joined the general movement across the great divide of literacy. Along this way, marriage has been a problem, often an unhappy tangle. A common Indian story of these years — and not only for the ex-Untouchable — is the story of the early marriage, made in the traditional way, that cannot survive the changed life that comes with education and the move out into the world. This happened to many young ex-Untouchables, as a Chamar from Uttar Pradesh told me:

Most of the boys are already married. These marriages might have been made at age six, though the wives do not come to join their husbands until they are sixteen. When the boys go to school and grow up and the time approaches for them to fulfill these marriages, it is then they often seek a divorce. They don't want to have illiterate wives. Their parents ask them to accept these wives but many refuse at this time. This is a kind of divorce, and the family has to pay a penalty because the marriage is not fulfilled. Others do obey their parents and go on with the ceremony and stay with their wives two or three years. But this leads to troubled lives and they finally also often get divorces. A penalty must be paid in this case to the panchayat [caste council] when the girl leaves. She will try to marry someone else in some other place. In some cases it is the other way around, the girls seeking the divorce, but this is very rare. If there are children and the father wants them, he keeps them, for this is the law, Hindu law and also government law. If the mother does not want them, the father must keep them in any case. This is also the law. I would guess that at least half of the 48,000 who received scholarships this past year are married in this manner.

But now it is becoming the custom not to marry early, because of this trouble with illiterate wives and because of the greater knowledge people have of the new opportunities. A new idea of change is going on in many villages where there is now compulsory education or where it is now more usual for everybody to go to school.

Girls are moving more and more into the channels of education and move up themselves to become teachers, nurses, and to higher education. This has been true longer for caste Hindu women, but ex-Untouchable girls are now getting their chance along with all the others. I met three such ex-Untouchable women, one who had earned a Ph.D. in England and had returned to the high post of Reader at her university; the practicing physician I have already mentioned; and the third, a bright young woman who was the only one of her sex among the competitors for Class 1 appointments at the coaching school I visited in Bangalore. Of the three only the physician was married. She was the daughter of an educated father but she married the son of a much humbler man of her community who had also risen through education and become a practicing lawyer. She was the only one I met who spoke up in a more positive way about marriages across different educational levels. "It is true," she said, "there are not enough educated girls and some men sometimes have to marry uneducated girls. There are many families like this. That would be like my father and mother who are absolutely happy!"

In both the other cases there was some discouragement about the outlook for marriage. Ex-Untouchable men in India are no different from caste Hindu men or their similars in many other modernizing countries: they want their mates to be educated but not *too* educated and certainly not more educated than they are. This is something of a handicap for the girl who is gifted and ambitious. The young lady I met in Bangalore who had set her sights on a Class 1 government post had apparently brushed aside the question of marriage altogether. She was a light-skinned, well-dressed young woman who was quite aware of her unusual situation and rather pleased with it. She told me that the women of her village in northern Mysore had said to her: "You study, and then you don't get married, what's the use?" She had more directly personal reasons for not wanting to think of marriage—her own parents were separated—but she said she had heard that educated girls had unhappy marriages and she preferred to think of making her life in community service. "High officials often do not care for the people," she said. "I want to go into welfare activity, in education for women. My own caste people are ignorant and do not know the importance of education." The Class 1 civil service takes qualified women — five had made it in the country the previous year, she said — but the rule is that if a woman marries while in the service, she has to resign, with the option of dropping down to a Class 2 post. "In any case,"

she said, "it is difficult to find a boy of our level of education in our caste.
I don't want to marry. I don't want to leave my mother, and men are not
good, they don't give freedom and equality to women."

Quite a few of the young men I met had not been caught in early
marriages arranged by their parents and they usually said they were
waiting to get more settled in their lives before finding someone to marry.
Among the Mahars, with their longer tradition of seeking education, there
seemed to be no great problem now of finding educated girls. "There are
many girl matriculates, even many graduates," I was told. In other caste
groups the difficulty is greater but hardly insuperable. "I want an educated
girl interested in social service," an Ada-Andhra boy told me in the south.
"In my village there is no one I can marry. I will have to find one."
He happened to be a very handsomely dark young man, as so many
are in south India, and I asked him whether color would figure in his
choice. "In my community all are dark," he answered. "Maybe the Brahmans are not quite so [colored] — [not quite so "colorful" is what he
actually said!] — but this is not a problem, this is not the way to distinguish people. In a girl I would prefer character and conduct and taste,
no matter what color." He laughed a nervous little laugh then, and
went on: "It is true that lighter girls will not prefer darker boys in any
community. This is a matter of personal taste. If a man is dark, he has
to be rich or educated. When parents arrange marriages, they compare
complexions. It has to be what we call 'edo-jodu' — equal as the equal
sign — in many things and color is one of the things. It is true that darker
boys prefer lighter girls. If we are educated and wealthy, nobody will
mind if we are dark. If you are poor, whether dark or light, people *will*
mind, no doubt about that!"

There was usually no question at all about marrying inside the
community. This was always assumed. For most of these young men
the radical change was not an out-of-caste marriage, but choosing their
own mates. "I will marry in my own community," said a Shangar boy
in Mysore in a typical answer, "but *I* will choose the girl. There are few
who are educated and I will have to find one of them somehow!" But in
a few instances boys did raise their sights above the caste line. "If my
father finds a girl for me," said the son of a politician, "it will be in our
own community. If I find a girl for myself, it might be outside." Another
young man thought intermarriage was the only way to solve the caste
problem. "I want to marry outside," he said, "because it is the only way
to abolish untouchability. If you come together in marriage, you forget
the past." The father of a growing son said to me somewhat musingly:
"I want to choose a wife for my son and I might seek a wife outside our

caste. This is not possible now in most cases, it's not likely, but I would like to." Then he added with vehemence: "I certainly will not choose a village girl for my son!"

The Name To Go By

In writing about ex-Untouchables in India it is needful to begin to clear up the knotty question of the name they go by. Here, as always, there is a great deal indeed in the name. To begin with, there is no general name of common acceptance that actually describes this large group of people. I have chosen to use "ex-Untouchable" as the most precisely descriptive term that can be applied at this time to people whose past names are no longer usable or acceptable and who hope in the future to need no special name for themselves at all. The dreamy vision of India's struggling nation-builders is that all the thousands of names by which people group themselves in India — by caste, by language, by region — will eventually be superseded by the single common name "Indian" in which all will meaningfully share. The sense of this new common identity still flickers only fitfully among the peoples of India, and I met some ex-Untouchables who would eagerly reach for it if it would meet their great need. Unfortunately it is still far from doing so. Right now ex-Untouchables do not know what to call themselves for they are people trying to cease being what they were and to become something else, though they are not sure what. As a result, all the names they now go by are matters of conflict and ambivalence and reflect in various ways their history and their status during this time of change.

I had noticed that in his writings, B. R. Ambedkar usually referred to his people simply as "Untouchables," that the official term for them was "Scheduled Castes," and that a third term in frequent use in the literature on the subject was "Harijan." From the very first conversations I had with anybody on the subject in India, certain nuances of usage quickly became apparent. The term "Untouchable" had disappeared from ordinary parlance; it was not only impolite to use it but illegal. The new Indian Constitution of 1949 legally "abolished" untouchability. There is no such thing legally as an "Untouchable" in India. I also began to note that the term "Harijan" was used freely in the main not by ex-Untouchables but by caste Hindus. Very rarely would an ex-Untouchable use it about himself, though it might flicker through his talk in some general connection. I also noticed that while it might be used to this extent by a supporter of the Congress Party, it was never used at all by the much smaller group of supporters of Ambedkar politically organized in the

Republican Party. In both cases they would much more commonly use the term "Scheduled Caste" both as noun and adjective, e.g., "He is a Scheduled Caste person" or "I am Scheduled Caste." This phrase, pronounced in variations of "she-dool'd caste," has grown less awkward with usage but has hardly acquired the sound of a name.

Except for the stark word "Untouchables" there never was any single name to cover this great mass of people. In the various Indian languages they were known by many versions of words that mean "Untouchable" or "outcast" or variations thereof: Pamchamas, Atishudras, Avarnas, Antyajas, Namashudras, etc. One also comes on "Pariahs," "Unseeables," and "Unapproachables." In British officialese sometime late in the last century the term "Depressed Classes" was introduced and remained the most commonly used, though vague, name of the group for many decades. In the Montagu-Chelmsford reforms of 1919 the first separate representation on a number of public bodies was given to members of the "Depressed Classes" and this included Untouchables along with quite a scatter of others, such as the aboriginal Tribes. It was not until 1932 that the term "Depressed Classes" was officially defined as meaning only the Untouchables. But it was just about at this time that "Depressed Classes" was replaced by "Scheduled Castes." This came about because the British government, already engaged in a number of programs for the benefit of this lowest group, was preparing to include it in the array of communal separate electorates (for Muslims, Christians, Anglo-Indians, etc.) through which it hoped both to appease and to weaken Indian nationalist pressure. Special effort was made in the 1931 census and by a special committee to draw up a "schedule" of the "castes" entitled to benefit from these various special arrangements (see Dushkin, Chapter 9 this volume). At the Round Table Conference in London in 1931, held to discuss future political concessions by the British in India, Ambedkar demanded a separate electorate for the Untouchables and he also made a special demand for "a change of nomenclature." He proposed that the Untouchables be called "Protestant Hindus" or "Non-conformist Hindus."[1] What emerged instead, when the electoral award was made and eventually incorporated into the Government of India Act of 1935, was the new official term "Scheduled Castes."

At this point the matter of the name gets entwined with some crucial history and the role of Gandhi in relation to untouchability. Gandhi had said from the beginning that it was one of his aims to purge Hinduism of untouchability. Indeed, at the outset of his career in Indian politics in 1920, he declared that swaraj or self-government would be "unattainable without the removal of the sins of Untouchability." He saw this as a reform to be brought about by exhortation and example. In his own ashram, or retreat, he and his immediate entourage demonstratively cleaned their own latrines as a symbolic way of "cleaning the Hindu society," and Gandhi also adopted an Untouchable girl as a daughter. He saw untouchability as an "excrescence" or an "appendix in the body of Hinduism" which had to be removed, leaving the rest of the caste system intact and purified. Gandhi preached on this persistently enough to disturb some of his caste Hindu followers, but Ambedkar charged him with being weak and equivocal at best in his pursuit of this aim. "How can [Untouchables] believe," he asked, "in the earnestness of a man who does nothing more than indulge in giving sermons on the evil of Untouchability?"

The difference here was a fundamental one, for while Gandhi attacked untouchability and not caste, Ambedkar argued that the heart of the problem of untouchability was the caste system itself. "There will be outcasts as long as there are castes," he held. "Nothing can emancipate the outcasts except the destruction of the caste system." This was a view also held by some Congress liberals and radicals, including Nehru, but not by Gandhi, who wanted Hindu society to put an end to untouchability and revert to the original system of four varna, or large caste divisions, of the distant past. Although he long exhorted his fellow caste Hindus to give up sinning against the Untouchables, very little effect was ever given to his plea and he never directly forced the issue upon them. He saw it as a matter for long and patient correction and as a "lesser" issue within the "greater" one of freedom from British rule. Ambedkar was unwilling to accept either Gandhi's conception of the problem or his timetable. "There have been many Mahatmas in India whose sole object was to remove Untouchability and to elevate and absorb the Depressed Classes," Ambedkar said at the height of the 1932 crisis, "but every one of them has failed in his mission. Mahatmas come and Mahatmas have gone. But the Untouchables have remained as Untouchables." Hence Ambedkar sought political guarantees and political power to ensure they would be honored. To this end he sought and won a separate electorate for the Untouchables in the new arrangement with the British. Gandhi, who reluctantly accepted the political separateness of the other groups as a "necessary evil," absolutely opposed any grant of separate political power to the Untouchables. This would permanently sever the Untouchables from the main Hindu body, he said, and this he would not accept either as a matter of religion or of politics. He thereupon proclaimed a "fast-unto-death" to force revision of the electoral award. Ambedkar argued that the Untouchables were and always had been "separate" from the main body of Hinduism and that only separate political power would win for them rights that caste Hindus would never voluntarily yield to them. He observed bitingly that Gandhi never embarked on a fast to force caste Hindus to abjure the practice of untouchability but did so now to keep the Untouchables from getting a share of the power for their own. For more than a week as Gandhi lay fasting in Yeravda Prison in Poona, the uproar raged around Ambedkar's head, the Congress press charging that he had made himself the tool of a British plot to divide-and-rule. In the negotiated outcome, which became known as "the Poona Pact," Ambedkar yielded up the "separate electorate" which he won in the award, and accepted in its place a system of reserved seats for Untouchables under a "joint electorate" with the caste Hindu majority. This arrangement had the air of also being a concession by Gandhi — who had originally opposed any kind of special political representation for the Untouchables — but it had the effect, as events later showed, of keeping the legislative representatives of the Untouchables under the effective controlling influence of the dominant Congress Party.[2]

Following the fast and his pact with Ambedkar, Gandhi spurred his campaign among caste Hindus to mitigate the evils of untouchability and there was a brief spurt of response among some of his followers, mainly in the form of temple-openings which were reported for a time with great acclaim from week to week in the Gandhian press. (Ambedkar, who had little use for temple-entry if it was not linked to a fundamental assault on the caste system, commented scornfully later that most of the temples opened "were dilapidated and deserted temples which were used by none but dogs and monkeys." Over a celebrated temple-entry issue in 1933, Gandhi threatened to fast, but did not do so.) It was in the course of this campaign to promote improvement and uplift for the Untouchables that Gandhi bestowed on them the new name, "Harijan," a word meaning "children of God" which he took from a poem by a sage in his native Gujarat. His "Anti-Untouchability League" became the "Harijan Sevak Sangh" and he started a publication called *Harijan*. The new name was intended, it was said, to give new dignity to the Untouchables and to impress on caste Hindus the need to admit these unfortunates into the Hindu fold.

Gandhi's caste Hindu followers adopted the new name and it evidently soon passed into common usage among them. I have no way of knowing how it was among the Untouchables themselves in the beginning, but I do know that now it never takes long in any conversation with the most committed Congress Harijan to discover that he does not really like the term and by choice avoids it.³ Back in 1938 on one occasion Ambedkar's group in the Bombay state assembly challenged the Congress majority on this issue. They demanded that the term "Harijan" as used in a bill then before the House be changed to "Scheduled Castes." The chairman, a Congress caste Hindu, replied that he thought the name was intended to give dignity to the Untouchables and challenged Ambedkar to suggest a better name. "Ambedkar replied [recorded a biographer] that all he would say was that he was not in a position to suggest any better name."⁴ When the Congress majority voted them down on the subject of their own name, Ambedkar and his followers walked angrily out of the chamber.

In my own talks with ex-Untouchables I was given more than one reason for the discomfort felt, even by Congress followers, over the term "Harijan." A former member of Parliament and one-time member of the Gandhi entourage said:

We usually don't use the word "Harijan." In fact, most educated people don't like "Harijan." The word connotes Untouchability and I don't think anyone likes it. Before Gandhi introduced it we were simply known as the "Untouchables," or by particular group names, such as Mahar, Mala, Pulaya, and so on. But very few liked to be called "Harijan." Nobody took it in the right spirit. Gandhi wanted to remove the inferiority and give a sense of superiority. But people did not take it that way. It just meant getting another name instead of a caste name, but a name that meant the same thing: Untouchable.

A graduate student from Andhra described himself as a follower of Congress but said: "I do not like 'Harijan.' It means 'children of God.' Aren't all the other people children of God too? Why this particular name for us? I think it is very childish." The followers of Ambedkar in the Republican Party are rather more colorful in their explanations. One of them, a member of Parliament, gave me this crisp version:

"Harijan" is a bad word introduced by Mahatma Gandhi. In Hindi it means a boy whose father's name is unknown, hence "children of God." In the Hindu temples there were, as you know, the devadassi, the girls who took part in worship ceremonies and also served the priests. Sometimes they gave birth to children and these children were called "Harijan." That's why we don't like the name.

While this seemed to leave the unwieldy "Scheduled Castes" as the nearest thing to an accepted general name, I soon gathered that ex-Untouchables much more commonly referred to themselves, or thought of themselves, by their various "caste" or "community" names. But these too were a constant reminder of status. In the home village — still "home" even to most of those who have become city dwellers — the caste name itself was usually used by the caste Hindus as a derogatory expletive. " 'Chamar' is a word carrying contempt," said a Chamar from the Punjab, now a senior civil servant in New Delhi. "In school other children called us 'Dhor' as a way to dismiss us with contempt," said a young woman, a Dhor, who is now a physician in Bombay. The 27-year-old son of a prominent politician from Andhra remembered from his childhood some of the feelings surrounding the attempt to get rid of the shame of the group name by using Gandhi's recently bestowed substitute:

I came to know (from my father) that the word "Harijan" was for Malas and Madigas. I think at that time people like my father following Gandhi found it easier to say "I'm Harijan" than to say "I'm Mala." It was hard to say you were a Mala. I was in the 6th standard when the teacher asked me what caste I was. I said: "I'm Harijan." The whole class mocked at me when I said that. All the heads turned as though to look at a convict. I felt ashamed, embarrassed, and looked down on.

His younger brother, now 23, returned to that village a few years later — the family was living in Madras then but he would come back with his mother at vacation time. He discovered the shame of being "Mala" not from caste Hindu boys but from Madigas, another Untouchable group in the village which had located itself above the Malas and practiced some degree of untouchability toward them:

Those boys called me "Mala!" and said: "Don't talk to him, don't touch him!" The first time this happened, I must have been five years old or so. I went to my cousin, my father's nephew, and I asked him: "What is Mala?" He told me we belonged to the Mala caste. The next time I was called Mala I kept quiet. I didn't get annoyed. I just kept quiet. I would feel bad and go away. My cousin had not explained it all to me but I knew it was very low. . . . I never asked anybody about this. I assumed to myself this was the rule of society and we are all subject to the rules. When I went to someone's house, I would be asked what caste I was. When I said "Mala" I had to stand outside. Naturally one feels this. Having stayed in Madras, I felt it very bad to be in a village of mud huts where they made you stand outside. I wanted to run away, I felt insulted, and I wanted to run, but I didn't run.

Here is a boyhood recollection of a man of 50 who is a Paravan from Kerala:

My father's name was Kunjen and he would be called Kunjen Paravan. I was called Velu Paravan. The name Kunjen Paravan was not derogatory to my father but Velu Paravan was quite derogatory to me. I would not allow myself to be called this to my face, because I did not want to be called by my caste name which signified backwardness. . . . At school no caste names were allowed but the other boys still used it and I would quarrel or fight whenever I was called Velu Paravan. If we got into a fight, they would begin to call me by my communal name. They could call me "Paravan" but there was nothing I was allowed to say that could relate to their caste or group or their father's name. We were not allowed to call other groups by their names. We could only address others as "Acha," which means "sir" or "father." We could only use this term of respect. Even now in the village an old man would have to call even a caste Hindu child not by his name but by "Acha." But even a caste Hindu child could address my father as Kunjen Paravan. In this way the group name itself became an insult. The term "son of a Paravan" or "son of a Pulayan" [another Untouchable group] were all bad names. For someone simply to say "You are a Pulayan" was to call a bad name. The upper caste children used these names to insult us.

Thus the caste name itself became the common term of contempt and shame whenever it was used by others and could hardly avoid carrying this freight with it whenever one used it to identify oneself. For older people who stayed in the villages this had been and largely remained the accepted state of things. For the youngsters now going to school, it soon became a fighting matter. For the educated ex-Untouchable who went out into the world to go to more advanced schools, or those who came up in the big city and encountered these humiliations whenever they traveled out in any direction, it became the source of a constant harassment of spirit.

Although it is now frowned upon by more cosmopolitan Indians and it happens much less often now than it did in the big cities, the practice of asking a person to identify his caste is still a common practice for great masses of people in everyday life in India. For the educated ex-Untouchable, this common occurrence has become a maddening challenge to his conscience and his self-respect. If he answers truthfully when he is asked, he may still more often than not be denied a job, a place to live, a bed to sleep in, food in a restaurant, coffee or tea at a café, even a drink of water. On trains and buses especially, it seems, a frequent and familiar opening gambit of conversation is: "And what community do you belong to?" Each person has to devise his own way of meeting this question. If an ex-Untouchable tells the truth in reply, he is likely to feel, almost like physical impact, the sudden fall of silence in the crowded compartment, a pulling away from contact, a cutting off of further talk. "When I travel anywhere I am upset and discouraged by this," said a Master of Arts from Gujarat. "I have learned that if people you are traveling with know you are Scheduled Caste, they would never offer you water or a place to stay, and this is true even today. So I never declare my community or my name. Nobody among us does. We never talk about community, because the mentality of the people hasn't changed."

Among the Mahars I met in Bombay there was always the double edge to the dilemma: whether, if they chose to identify themselves at all, to say "Mahar" or "Buddhist," though the effect in both cases would be the same. A person would want to assert his aggressive rejection of Hinduism and say boldly "Buddhist!" while knowing that he would catch at once that quick glassy look in the other's eye and almost hear the thought clicking in his mind: "Oh, Buddhist-Mahar-Untouchable keep away!" One individual told me the effect was much the same if one said "Christian," even though the conversion of Untouchables to Christianity in any significant numbers goes back a long way. One young man, with some malicious enjoyment, told me that he always turned a cold gaze on his questioner and said severely: "And *why* do you want to know?" This had a freezing effect, he explained, because very often the question of caste would be put to a well-dressed and obviously educated young man by a fellow traveler on the lookout for a suitable husband for his daughter or other relative. In such cases, the cold answer was usually enough to reduce the questioner to embarrassed silence.

It was, of course, best when no one asked and no answer had to be made at all, no identity acknowledged. In most of the daily comings and goings of urban life nowadays no one does ask this question very much anymore — except that is, when it has to do with getting into school, qualifying for a job or getting hired, getting a place to live, getting married, or in the affairs of life surrounding a birth or a death. In the great common namelessness of crowded city streets or public places, there is respite. But to be engaged on any of the important business of life, to be traveling anywhere, to be mixing with people casually on trains or buses — to be in any of these situations is to face the still-recurring question: what community do you belong to? For most Indians it is still the most important question to ask a man, while for the ex-Untouchable it is the question above all that he does not want to answer.

Some of the same weight is attached also to personal names. Traditionally an Untouchable had no surname but would be known by a given name and after it, for further identification, the given name of his father. Indeed, by this tradition also, Untouchables did not choose their children's names; this was the prerogative of one's landlord or employer in the village, or some other local caste Hindu dignitary. Given names were often simply whatever day of the week it happened to be. Thus if you were born on a Tuesday in a Hindi area, your name might be "Mangala." Often caste Hindus would give the name of some lowly object, also an unclean one, like "Panami" which means "shoe." Often they might bestow what were called "bad names," such as a word which literally means "a person who should be dragged." Now, educated ex-Untouchables more usually do the naming themselves and of course they choose "good" names, which I gathered means Sanskrit-sounding names taken from among those used by the touchable castes, not uncommonly the name of some god, hero, or benefactor. Among the ex-Untouchable students I met in Bombay, I found a remarkable number of them all with the name "Gaikwar" and was puzzled until I learned that this was the family name of Maharajah of Baroda, who opened early opportunities for Untouchables in his realm and gave Ambedkar his chance for higher education abroad. There were also quite a few named "Shinde" — the name of a caste Hindu reformer in Maharashtra who had taken up the cause of the Depressed Classes around the turn of the century. But other names would be chosen mainly for their good upper-caste sound, "good" names like the recognizably Brahman Pande, Mehta, or Parshad, a Banya name like Vakil or Patel, a Kshatriya name like Singh (which could be either a Sikh or a Rajput name) and their equivalents in other language areas.

The choice of names has become part of the process of shedding the old identity and acquiring a new one. Sometimes this is quite literally a way of blotting out one's identity in order to "pass" as a member of some higher caste. But while for some the choosing of new names is a way of trying to erase the past, for a few it is a way of making a demand on the future. One of the small group of Ambedkar's successors in Parliament, a self-assured and roughly handsome young man of thirty-six from Uttar Pradesh, told me: "I have four children: a boy of eight whom I named Ajai, which means a person who can never be defeated; a girl of five I have called Anula, after a famous Buddhist princess of Ceylon; a son of three I named Kennedy because he was born in 1960, Kennedy's year; and the youngest boy, only five months old, I have named Lincoln."

Jobs by Reservation: The Quota System

Almost all educated ex-Untouchables move into government jobs. This has been up to now the open channel and it has led several hundred thousand former Untouchables to new and better places in the society. These places have been preserved for them by explicit percentage quotas at every level of government employment. This system had its beginnings in India at least forty years ago coming as part of the revolt against Brahman domination by the non-Brahman castes, especially in the south. The reservation of government posts for non-Brahmans led to the opening of some places for Untouchables who qualified, especially in some of the princely states, and some of them rose rung by rung to fairly high places.

In the state of Mysore there are now five or six district commissioners — senior administrative officers — who are members of Scheduled Castes. A small number of men of this generation have risen to senior posts in the central government services as well. Special benefits and reserved places for Untouchable and other groups were quite strongly established in the central and state governments in the closing decades of British rule. These were greatly enlarged after independence when the new Indian government set out to help raise the lowly by providing special channels of preferment both in education and in jobs.

This system of reservations was laid out for the benefit of the Scheduled Castes, the aboriginal Scheduled Tribes, and a third huge omnibus category called "Other Backward Classes." In its first years, this program was challenged in the courts and the new Indian Constitution, at first based on the premise of recognition of equality of all citizens before the law, was duly amended to give the government power to practice some inequality in reverse in order to give these lower groups a chance to rise more rapidly. The program was originally set for a period of ten years ending in 1960. It has since been renewed twice, and there is little likelihood that it will be terminated in the immediate future. The Indians did not have much difficulty overcoming the contradiction between their very new formal official doctrine of equality and their effort to practice discrimination-in-reverse for the backward classes. This kind of contradiction was, after all, a familiar part of the traditional system, although it usually worked in the opposite direction, against and not for the lowly. But they did run into a lot of trouble and great confusion over the matter of who in India was "backward." The criterion used was caste, the assumption being made that certain castes were by definition "backward." It quickly became clear, however, that the great bulk of India's multitude of castes considered themselves "backward" enough to be counted among the deserving poor and to share in any benefits that were being handed around. A government commission in 1953 named 2,399 such deserving castes and communities with an estimated total population of about 120,000,000. In many states a great clamor arose, with all kinds of groups insisting that they too should be classified as "backward" and these included, it must be said, some pretty forward castes who felt that their jealously guarded ritual or social superiority should not be allowed to interfere with their right to get on the government gravy train. One state tried to meet the problem by distinguishing between "backward" and "more backward" and another sorted out the "backward" from the "most backward." In the south these matters had long been wrapped up in the struggle of the lower castes against the Brahmans, who had managed to reserve everything for themselves for quite a few centuries. The revolt against the Brahmans, which goes back many decades, had gone far enough to make the Brahmans in many places the victims of considerable counter-discrimination, forcing many of them to migrate elsewhere or even to change *their* names to something less obviously Brahman in order to escape some of the exclusions practiced against them. In Mysore, for example, from 1921 to 1959, Brahmans could hold only three out of every ten government jobs. Revised rules issued in 1961 reserved a total of 64 percent of all jobs in the state for the Scheduled Castes, Tribes, and Other Backward Classes. Similar quotas operated against the Brahmans in Andhra, Madras, and Kerala.[5]

This issue caused a great confusion of political fights and court cases. The Supreme Court, denouncing some of these state arrangements as "a fraud on the Constitution," began pulling in the reins on what threatened to become a runaway absurdity imperiling the entire government program.[6] The Central Government and many of the states began to move toward imposing economic rather than caste criteria for defining "backwardness." These took effect during 1963, with cutoff points at annual income of Rs. 1,000 to Rs. 1,500 ($210 to $315) coming into more general use to screen out undeserving recipients of government help. "Four states in the south still have quotas in government jobs for 'Other Backward Classes,' " a high Home Ministry official in New Delhi told me. He went on:

"Backward" seems to have a special meaning down there. There is a stigma attached to being Scheduled Caste, but it was fine to get the money without the stigma simply by being "OBC." Everybody wanted to be "OBC" including the dominant groups in some states. Mysore has never had a chief minister who was not a Lingayat, a group whose name was removed from the "Backward" list, but they insisted and succeeded in getting it restored. On the other hand, you have the Anglo-Indians, who also got benefits but they protested against being called "backward." They wanted to get rid of this description while, of course, keeping the benefits.

None of this confusion and controversy over who else was "backward" affected the status of the Scheduled Castes and Tribes. No one could challenge *their* backwardness and very few of them in any case had broken through the income floor fixed as the bottom limit. The national and state programs were designed primarily to help them. Listed specifically by caste, they remained the prime targets of the special welfare programs and the beneficiaries of the quota system of reserved places in government jobs of all kinds and at all levels.

In the central government services in India, the quota for the

Scheduled Castes in jobs filled by competitive examinations is 12½ percent (five percent for Scheduled Tribesmen) and 16⅔ percent in all other jobs filled simply by appointment. The states operate on variations of these percentages according to differences in their local population figures. In theory, when jobs are filled from examination lists, the places go to the top competitors on the general list until the 12½ percent level is reached, at which point the remaining places go to the Scheduled Caste competitors with passing scores no matter how much lower these scores might be. In fact, up to now in government white collar jobs the actual percentages of ex-Untouchables employed has fallen far short of the quotas. In 1963 they were only one to seven percent filled. Government spokesmen said they could not fill the quotas because there were too few qualified applicants. Scheduled Caste spokesmen complain that the real reason is continuing discrimination, especially in cases where a personal interview is part of the appointment procedure and caste Hindu interviewers are able to exercise their prejudices. This argument goes on about jobs in the white collar categories only. At the lowest levels of manual or menial work, of course, the quotas are filled without difficulty.

As given by the Commissioner for Scheduled Castes and Tribes,[7] January 1963, figures show 329,046 ex-Untouchables in central government services out of a total over 2,300,000. The report adds that it was impossible to get a comparable total for those employed in the state service.

The top of the crop in the government are the members of the "I.A.S." or Indian Administrative Services, heirs to the highly prestigious "I.C.S." or Indian Civil Service of the British time. These are the top administrative posts, occupied at the most senior levels always by Englishmen in the old days, and since independence, of course, by Indians, as senior administrators and secretaries in the ministries and departments of the government. In 1963 there were 18,021 members of the I.A.S. Of these 237, or 1.3 percent, were ex-Untouchables. In 1962, the quota posts for Scheduled Caste applicants, 22 positions, were filled for the first time, and the same thing happened with the 11 positions open by quota in 1963. This marked a real turning point, my Home Ministry informant told me, for it showed that enough educated ex-Untouchables were now beginning to come out of the universities to produce enough applicants with the necessary qualifications. In 1961–62, 6,000 applicants, including more than 600 with 1st class degrees, took examinations for the 99 posts that were going. The competition was extremely close, with a margin of 200 points or "marks" out of a top possible score of 1,800 separating the lowest man on the general list from the top man on the Scheduled Caste list. At the narrowest point, this difference was a margin of only about 10 percent, he remarked, but as you moved on down the list, the margin widened and the difference between top man and low man became painfully wide. The successful candidates go into the ministries as third secretaries and the best of them will rise in 20 years or so to the top posts. "We are worried about this difference in quality," he said. "The effect on administration won't be visible for some years to come, but it will appear." The government actually goes to some lengths to help ex-Untouchables qualify for this top service, maintaining two coaching centers where candidates work for a fully supported year to prepare themselves for the examination.

The class 2 category of Indian government servants is the grade that leads to positions that have some executive responsibility plus a heavy portion of plain clerical work. As of January 1, 1963, there were 28,968 such officials in the service of the central government and of these 761, or 2.6 percent, were members of the Scheduled Castes. Class 3 is simple clerical work carried on by the lowest grade of white collar civil servants of whom there were 1,131,760 in the service on that date, and of these 79,336 or 7 percent, were ex-Untouchables. Class 4 consists mainly of manual workers and plain laborers in the government's agencies and enterprises, as well as the great masses of messengers, menials, and flunkeys who inhabit the corridors of all Indian government buildings and who are still universally called "peons" as they were in the British time. The total of such workers is 1,061,646, and of these 186,481, or better than 17.5 percent, are ex-Untouchables. It was rather striking to find, going through these figures, that just as there are four great varna or divisions or classes in the caste system, and then the Untouchables as a fifth group of but not in the system, the Indian government's services are similarly organized in these four main classes, plus the sweepers, who are listed quite separately outside the regular classifications — the tables in the record showing a separate group of 68,950 sweepers, of whom 62,231, a whacking non-quota 90 percent, are listed as ex-Untouchables.

In sum, it is clear that at the bottom of the widening pyramid of mass education in India, the ex-Untouchables, like Indians in general, are becoming literate at the rate of many millions of people every year, generating new but incalculable pressures for change in the society as a whole. At the top of the pyramid, among the 1,000,000 who are getting higher education, there are 55,000 ex-Untouchables and this number is also rising steeply each year. To the figure of some 330,000 ex-Untouchables who now hold central government jobs at all levels, one has to add unknown totals for teachers and for all who are working for the states, the municipalities, and the districts. Some figure has to be added in here also for the number of ex-Untouchables who have moved from the old sub-menial occupations into more or less semi-skilled industrial jobs in the private and public sectors of the economy. Counting only job-holding adults, all those who fall under these various headings might be guessed to be in the neighborhood of a million people. If we count in the children of these ex-Untouchables who are in school, we arrive at a total of nearly six million human beings who are by these means coming up out of the lowest estate into which any people have ever fallen anywhere at any time in human history, and are now moving into some new condition of life.

The Semi-Limbo

As the educated ex-Untouchables pull up and away from the sodden bleakness of their past estate, they do not quite get *nowhere,* but neither do they reach *somewhere.* They are people who want above all to become different from what they were and what their fathers were. They want to leave all that behind, to forget it, to blot it out, but they came into a situation where too little is changing too slowly; a society still governed by caste does not allow them to abandon their past, to forget it, to blot it all out. What they move into becomes a kind of semi-limbo.

Behind them a widening distance opens between them and the rest of their community, even their closest kin. This happens to those raised in the city and even more to those who come up in the village. One of the I.A.S. aspirants at the coaching school in Bangalore, a stocky, nearly jet-black young man, an Ada-Andhra from a village called Laddigan, described what it was like when he went home:

When I go back, they feel different toward me, even though I treat them all as equal to me. But I find I can only stay there two or three days. I need paper and books. I can't get anything there. Our house is a dilapidated house. Here I live in a room with friends and I eat in restaurants and I have friends to talk to. In the village I have no friends to talk to, no books to read, no papers to see. In our district very few children go to school. The parents are ignorant, there is no encouragement, no one insists. I talk about welfare. I tell things about myself to my mother. There is some reserve between father and son. Normally sons won't move freely with their fathers, only rarely do they talk freely. I talk to my father and brother only about family affairs. They are proud of me when I come, they celebrate and get me things, prepare special food, and insist on my staying longer.

In Bombay our airline pilot friend, Khadtale, took us one evening to have tea at the home of a friend of his, a senior government official, an ex-Untouchable who had been able to move his family of four daughters and two sons to a middle-class apartment block where they lived in plain but comfortable style. The people this man had left behind him as he moved up were very much on his mind because, it appeared, they were very much on his back. "We educated people form a separate group," he said. "We are seen as too high above the others." His voice began to take on a sharper edge. "We can't really bring *all* of them up!" He sighed and went on: "We cannot really get ahead. If we do not stay with them, then we are treated as outcasts by them, we become people who go on and get ahead, and leave them behind, when we should be *with* them. But if we try to do this and satisfy them, then we can't bring our own families out ahead." He looked around the modest room in which we were sitting. "We wouldn't even be able to change our place of living," he said. "Our poorer relatives say these things. We cannot satisfy *all* of them!" These feelings, apparently common in families from which some members have risen, are being exploited, he said, by some politicians within the group. "They side with the families against the educated ones," he said. "They criticize the educated for remaining away from their society. This is partly true, but partly it is jealousy, envy, and partly propaganda. There is very little opportunity to mix with our society. I have a brother who is farming and another brother who works in a machine shop and my sister's husband works for the railway. When would I mix with them?"

He felt generally unhappy about all the people below, feeling that the drive for advancement was disappearing and that people were descending into a new kind of morass of their own making:

The majority of people are now not as eager to learn as we were when we were young. They give up after the 4th standard. Education is free up to the 7th standard and yet we find working people with children not going to school, even in the cities. When I came to Bombay in 1940, every parent wanted his children to have education. But now parents send their children out on dirty business, begging, crime, illicit liquor — this happens among working people at the lowest levels who are making maybe Rs. 100 or Rs. 150 a month. Those who are educated feel frustrated about getting ahead, and the poorer people feel they can't afford education. The trend is against more education, I think. The mass has no power of thinking, no firm opinion about things. We are trying to do something for the masses but we get no cooperation. Faith in each other is lacking. Whom to follow? Nobody knows. Everybody followed Ambedkar, but now nobody knows whom to follow.

In the crowded world where they work at their white collar jobs, the educated ex-Untouchables move daily among masses of caste Hindus, and since these are the people they would rather be *like* than anybody else, they do their best simply to lose themselves in that white-shirted mass. In the great blur of people out on the city streets and in the public places, they can and do appear to be just about like everyone else of their class, and one would think it would be equally easy in the great mazelike offices where the Indian bureaucracy works, and indeed, up to a point, it is. In the busy-busy preoccupation of each one with his own concerns, and the trivialities that pass for talk between desks or over tea or soft drinks in the canteen, the prickly question of one's caste identity might just never arise, especially if one is careful to steer the talk away if it ever threatens to wander in that direction. Friendly associations can be maintained especially if they stay casual, if they are not allowed to carry over too far into the non-working hours, or to get too personal. In this way for a considerable time of every day and in a considerable area of life, one's identity as an ex-Untouchable can be quite largely effaced, or at least kept out of sight. It is not so much a matter of hiding one's caste but more a matter, as one person said, of not announcing it.

But from some accounts I heard, this insulation is fairly thin. In jobs where the competition for appointment or promotion has been sharp, identities are unavoidably known and caste Hindu rivals are often resentful, and show their feelings in all the nasty little ways that the situation readily provides. It is not unknown in some government offices for caste Hindus to insist that ex-Untouchables keep cups or glasses in a separate place away from the common supply. Wherever conflicts arise, mistakes are made, or competence brought into question, the appropriate jibes are ready on the lips of the resentful and the malicious, probably spoken out of one's hearing, or the thought conveyed by a taunting or superior look — and all of this, moreover, might really be there or just be imagined. Or, again, out in the public places, the anonymous surface can be suddenly lacerated and a man can be painfully unsure of what to say, how to react. One story:

Just yesterday I went to Victoria Terminus to book a first-class ticket for my superior. At one window the clerk made his entry on the wrong kind of slip. With that slip I went to purchase the ticket at the booking window and passed it in. The man there said with irritation: "This is the wrong slip." I said I didn't know, that the clerk back there had given it to me. And he said: "These Scheduled Caste people! The government is recruiting people who are not fit for their jobs!" I don't think the first clerk was Scheduled Caste at all, but this one just assumed he was, and he showed his contempt. Somebody had made a mistake and he attributed it to the Scheduled Caste. I felt it. But I didn't say anything.

By way of response to these slights, an ex-Untouchable can become what is called "aggressive" — which usually means insisting on one's rights, big and small, at every point, or even just being openly resentful of contempt or insult. This is the kind of person that a caste Hindu will sometimes describe as being "proud of being Scheduled Caste." Alternatively, he can choose to draw back into himself, back into the safety of his own group, or his own self, keeping away from all the others as much as he can. But it is best, is seems, to have his identity tacitly known without anybody openly taking note of it. A civil servant of high rank said: "I think the others in my office know that I am Scheduled Caste, but they don't express anything about it. My superior told some of them . . . but I have not taken the initiative to explain myself in any way, and I don't want to, because I think it is absolutely unnecessary." Another quite senior official said: "In government I never hid myself. Everyone knew I belonged to the Scheduled Caste but no one showed anything openly about it. . . ."

Another response is concealment. Some kind of *passing,* or hiding one's identity, becomes part of almost every educated ex-Untouchable's experience. At almost any point of personal contact with the caste Hindu world, the satisfaction of a man's simplest needs often depended on his readiness to conceal his caste identity and, if need be, to falsify it. We have seen young people concealing their caste to get food and lodging, to win acceptance or at least to avoid rejection. Anyone who moved out of the fixed patterns of the old untouchable existence soon had to learn how and when to engage in hiding his identity. A man who has managed to rise fairly high recalled that his own first such experience occurred at the initial crucial turning point of his life. A caste Hindu teacher had grown interested in him and took him to a district town 20 miles from their village to take an examination that was going to determine the shape of the rest of his life.

He told me not to say I was of my caste. He was traveling with me and did not want to have any problem at the hostel. He asked me not to tell and instructed me to say I belonged to another caste. So when I was asked, I said I belonged to the Ahir caste, an agricultural caste, very low but not Untouchable. There were three boys who took that examination that day. The other two failed.

Another person well on his way to high professional status recalled:

When I was eight or nine, my father told me: "If anybody inquires about your caste, tell him you belong to the Baria [a higher caste] so that you may not be hindered or insulted." When we went to visit the village, my father used to wear a Parsi gentleman's hat on the train. My brother and I put on khaki uniforms, something like a Boy Scout uniform, and we also wore Parsi caps, so that others would not know we were of the Scheduled Caste. I felt bad and awkward. I couldn't mix freely with other people. It was a hide-and-seek game. My father used to tell us we had to avoid all these things. He was not angry about it; in fact, he used to take pride that nobody questioned his identity or objected to his presence.

Many of those who have moved up in life have naturally continued to find it easier to "pass" in many situations than not to, and, as we have seen, this often meant not falsifying your identity but not proclaiming it either. If in some instances this was pushed to the point where you actually had to give the name of another caste as your own, well, it did not prove so hard to do. There were so many advantages in doing so, and it corresponded to one's deepest desires — "What we want, what we always wanted," said one person, "was to become something else, to be something higher." So wherever it was needful or possible, you would pass, whether while traveling or even, in a more consistent way, at your place of work where what other people did not know could never hurt you. The need to "pass" on a more consistent basis seemed to come most often out of the effort to get better housing. At the lower levels in the big cities, as we have indicated, caste groups tend to live quite separately in sandwiched layers through the great slum tenement blocks. As the economic level rises, some locations still remain caste-bound but more generally nowadays Hindus of various castes will be found living side by side. The higher the scale, the fewer the separations, even for Brahmans. Anybody can get in who has the price — anybody, that is, except an ex-Untouchable. Here the line remains quite rigidly drawn. Better housing will be open where it is public, in government colonies or government-supported apartment block locations. But in most privately owned housing, the ex-Untouchable is likely to be turned away if his identity is known. "That is why many hide their caste," a prominent Bombay ex-Untouchable told me. "They say they are some other caste, even Brahman, or some say they are Christians or Muslims. 'Why live like a dog in some other place?' they ask."

But there are serious limits to how far and for how long an educated ex-Untouchable can continue to pass successfully in India today. Some have tried to disappear from view entirely, only to be overtaken eventually by the demands of life in a society still dominated by caste. One man who is partially passing himself told me:

You may be able to go up yourself, but you can't take the whole family with you. I know of some people who go away from here and hide their identity entirely and try to solve their problems by themselves. I know one man who worked for a steamship company who hid his identity and called himself another name. He refused all help to Scheduled Caste people. He would say he just didn't belong to the Scheduled Castes. But then his family grew up and the time came to marry his daughters and he could not find anybody. He had to come back to the community after all to find husbands for them. You can't disappear entirely. There are always relatives and parents, always ceremonies, marriage, and death.

It was death that brought an end to another story of passing told to me:

If a man conceals his caste, sooner or later it is discovered, and then he suffers a lot. There was a Mahar, a contractor who got rich. He told everybody he was a Mahratta. He lived in a caste Hindu community and never disclosed his caste. But then his daughter died. The custom is that your relatives must come to prepare the body, not yourself or a stranger. But nobody came. No Mahrattas came of course. He had cut himself off from his relatives, so they didn't come. Some of his friends and neighbors came and said to him: "How is it nobody is here? Call your nearest relative now, right away!" In desperation he finally called on some of his old people to come to lift the body. When they came, the neighbors recognized them from their clothes, their language, the way they talked, and his caste was disclosed. He suffered. We say to such a man, "You see, you wanted to be a Brahman or a Mahratta, why should we feel sympathy for you?"

Marriage remains the most formidable barrier in the path of anyone who wishes to escape his caste. Intercaste marriage among caste Hindus is less infrequent in India now than it was a generation ago,[8] but such marriages involving Scheduled Castes are still extremely rare. Ambedkar himself married a Brahman woman late in his life, and some people I met were able to cite an instance or two that they knew of personally, but these were all cases in which concealment was not being attempted. One man said:

Just yesterday a Scheduled Caste boy married a Sonar girl, a caste Hindu, though both families objected. He is a clerk in my office. The girl is better off and better educated than he is. They met in a night school where they formed a friendship. I too objected and tried to dissuade him from it. These marriages do not work out successfully. I know a Scheduled Caste man married to a Brahman girl, but she is not at home in his family environment and every day their life gets worse. In the joint family, it is almost impossible. When a couple lives alone it is a little easier.

The point about marriage is that ex-Untouchables who pass are unlikely to find mates for their children outside their caste, and if they do, they are unlikely to be able to keep their own caste background hidden. "It is possible, but not very likely," said one informant. "In India everybody knows everybody's caste one way or another, sooner or later. The educated people can separate, yet they can't separate, for community is part of this society. You can't be without a community. Without a community, it is awkward for a man in all his relationships. This is the culture of the country. *In India you have got to be connected.*"

The inescapable facts of caste life in India have led some ex-Untouchables to devise an in-between style, a kind of semi-passing, as the solution to their problems. Put a bit roughly, it is a system for passing in public while not passing in private. In general it means that in all situations where self-advancement, comfort, and convenience dictate it, an ex-Untouchable passes as a member of some higher caste. At the same time, in all the circumstances that demand it — death, marriage, even voluntary work for the community — he leads a second or double life in the bosom of his community. I met several individuals who were trying to organize their lives this way and they did their best to explain to me just how they managed it. The technique is to take a name that might be common to more than one upper caste, so that by name alone, it might be assumed by people that you belong to any one of the possible castes it suggests. You are prepared if necessary to claim one of these castes as your own, but generally speaking, the appearance of things is hopefully enough for most purposes. As one of these individuals explained: "The idea is that you adopt the appearance of being of a higher caste through your name and your way of life. Your professional associates must not know about you in too much detail. You can have your social life with them, but you avoid having this social life grow too close. You go to tea, but you avoid having dinner, that's too close, and you avoid that." And why not dinner? I asked. "Well, when you take dinner," came the answer, "you take it in a particular manner. You might eat out of the pot, or do something that is not right, and spoil the whole relation. At the same time," he went on, "You keep your connections with your community in all such things as arranging marriages, family affairs, observing ceremonies. Thus in your public and professional life you appear to be of another caste while in your private, personal life, you are of your own community. This is difficult, but it is not so difficult as trying to disappear away from the community altogether."

It takes strong nerves to live in this fashion but evidently it can be done. My informant illustrated how it worked in one crisis that had occurred not very long before in his own life. "One of my relatives who was living with me died at the hospital," he said. "I should have taken her body to my own house, but I took her to my brother's house in the community in order to avoid any embarrassment with others where I lived. Any ceremony that might reveal to others we are of Scheduled Caste, we hold in a relative's home."

Among those I met who are engaged in this tightrope operation as a way of life was a lawyer who told me he had taken his name, a common upper-caste name, while he was still in law school. He went through the proper legal procedure, a formal application, publication in the gazette, and so on. It took two months. His diploma was made out in his new name, "and in this way," he said, "I started out fresh." Thanks to a "certain fraternity" of people engaged in this way of life, he was able to get started on his practice, intimating that some friends who knew who he was sent him some clients for a start.

I get caste Hindu clients, Mohammedan clients, and a few Scheduled Caste people who know me. About 90 percent of my clients do not know I belong to the Scheduled Castes. If they knew, they would not employ me, so naturally I have to conceal it. It is a problem. In the profession, people generally do not know I am Scheduled Caste, though some of my associates and a few lawyers do know. I mix with many non-Scheduled Caste advocates at dinner, lunch, tea, sometimes I even go to their homes. My wife — who is Scheduled Caste and is educated up to matric — does not go with me on such occasions. It is not the custom. They come to my home too, perhaps two or three times a year. I live in a neighborhood where all high caste people live. They do not know there that we are Scheduled Caste. I have some good friends whom I visit often, perhaps every week or so. Some of them know what I am, some do not.

He was able, it seemed, to keep a mental card file and always to know who knew what he was and who did not know. If this was a wearing business, he gave no sign of it. Indeed, it was when individuals were talking to me about things like this that I felt least sure that I had any idea how they actually *felt* about what they were telling me. I had to assume that on this subject, above all, they were guarding themselves psychologically as well as they could. There were confusions and contradictions and unclarities when we got down to details, but I had to be content with leaving most of them unexplored. This was especially true when I asked the most troubling question of all: What about the children, what do you tell your children?

Telling the Children

Whenever the subject of children came up in my talks with educated ex-Untouchables, things invariably began to get very confused. A father might say to me: "My son [or daughter] does not know about untouchability." Sometimes this turned out to mean that he was saying that his child had not actually experienced untouchability in its more traditional forms. But then he might also say: "He [or she] does not know we come of an Untouchable community." Even the most tentative pursuit of this statement would quickly show that the child, no longer an infant and often already an adolescent or not far from it, would have to be deaf, dumb, and blind not to know a great deal more about himself and his family than the father either would or could acknowledge. A father would frequently say that his child did not know any of this because the child had never asked and he, the father, had never told. When I would ask whether the child did not learn these things outside the home, from schoolmates or neighborhood children, I would sometimes get a blank stare, or a blank denial, or: "No, the matter has never come up." And this might be followed a few minutes later by details that showed that it had indeed come up in one way or another. What every one of these men wanted more than anything else was to blot out the legacy of the past and to give his children a new identity of their own. They seemed to feel that awareness of the past status was enough to instill "feelings of inferiority." In their own families and with their own children, they tried to deal with this problem by simply not talking about it. I never felt free to push too far into the confusions that always surrounded this question. This was the most sensitive ground I found myself on in all my encounters with educated ex-Untouchables, and I trod upon it softly.

In the case of one young man, still unmarried at thirty-four, the characteristic cloud of denial and/or confusion had settled in his own mind over his own childhood. His father was a motor mechanic and they lived in "two good rooms" in government quarters in Bombay. His father never told him anything about this, he said, and it was not until he got his leaving certificate at the end of the fourth standard when he was ten that he learned that he was "Mahar." But even this had no meaning to him, he said. "I did not take it to mean anything." He said he had never had any reason to think of himself as "Hindu" either. "I never heard of Scheduled Castes," he continued in this remarkable catalogue of non-awareness, "until I filled out the form for my first year at college. I had never heard of it before. That was in 1953." But a few minutes later he was telling me how his father was a follower of Ambedkar, how the whole family had gone to meetings, and how as a small boy he had heard of the Scheduled Castes Federation, though, he added, "I didn't know the meaning of it."

This was a rather extreme case, but it illustrated some of the complications involved in this matter. Several men with young children told me that they had never told their children anything about their background, and expressed the belief that their children knew nothing about it. But then they would go on to tell me how they had taken their youngsters back to their family villages for visits and I was left to wonder what they thought their children learned there. I met one father who emphatically declared he would never take his children back to the village for this very reason. "My son is fourteen," said this senior civil servant in Bangalore, "and I have never taken him back to the village. I don't want my children to have any experience of untouchability. They don't know what it is, they have never experienced it. I don't think they are clear about what it is, even though they have read about it in books. They do not identify themselves with it. My son goes to public school in a mixed class and it does not come up. He knows he is Adikarnataka, but he does not know his identity as an Untouchable."

A Congress M.P. acquaintance in New Delhi first said: "Up to now I have not told my children. I have sons twelve, ten, and nine, and a daughter, five. I have not told them all the things that have happened." But then he added: "Now my oldest son knows that he belongs to such a caste, though up to a year ago I avoided it. He asked me one day: 'Father, what caste do we belong to — the boys were saying that you are a Chamar — is this correct?' I said, 'Yes, this is correct.' But up to that time none of the children had known about these things. Now they understood that they belong to a lower caste, much lower than the others. Here in Delhi they feel no effect of it, they go to school here." Then, as if to complete the confusions in his account, he went on: "We get back to our village once a year. They still feel it there, living separately, not allowed into houses, and so on." His sons came in to be introduced and they shyly received some of my questions. The small boy said in English: "I want to be a leader." What kind of leader? I asked. He looked up at his father and said: "I want to be a Member of Parliament."

In Bombay a short, sharp-featured young man who aspires to become a professor of law was quite certain he was going to be able to start his children out quite fresh.

They don't know what the Scheduled Caste is. They will live in an advanced way. I now live among Catholics and Anglo-Indians. I will tell my daughter she is Buddhist. Why should I tell her about our community? I won't have to. It will just be forgotten. When my daughter grows up we will just be Buddhists.

A well-placed civil servant who lives in a caste Hindu neighborhood took me somewhat further into this business of what the children know.

My daughter (who is eleven) does not know she is Dhor. She has seen the tanning business in Dharabi, the section of Bombay where all the tanners, the Dhors and the Chamars live. We lived there until 1960 when we moved to a better place. She never asked. The question never arose. Most of the people there are Dhors, so they don't ask. When we moved, nobody questioned us. She has never asked. People elsewhere, as in Poona or Kholapur, still ask what community you belong to, and the children become conscious of it. If my children ever ask me, I'll tell them the truth. My brothers and sisters who stay with me in the same house, they know, but my children do not. Yes, it is a joint household, but the question never does come up. The children have gone to marriages but they are not conscious of caste or community. They don't know that untouchability exists. My young sister and brother do know, but my daughter does not. She will come to know it gradually. This is just striking me now, because you are asking me. I never had an idea about it. Most parents will avoid this discussion with their younger children because they think it will have an effect on their minds. They don't want their children to have a complex that we are lower and other people higher. We want our children to think that everybody is equal. I will have to explain to my children that when I was a child, I stood at the door of the classroom with the Scheduled Castes, that nobody mixed with us, but that I was first in the class. I will explain the history and my experience so that they won't feel inferior, that we should not feel inferior to any community in India. There *is* a stigma in belonging to the Scheduled Castes. Other people will think a Scheduled Caste person is inferior, and the other person's behavior changes when he finds out, like my superior when he learned I was Scheduled Caste. He was surprised I could come to such a position. As my daughter grows up, she must learn about our community, but she must have no complexes about it.

A school administrator began by giving me the familiar assurance his son "does not know he belongs to an Untouchable caste." He knows that their community was "Mahar" and that they are now "Buddhist," but he knows nothing at all about untouchability. "We take care that no inferiority complex should seep into his mind. Most people might not be so careful and their children might be able to tell that they belong to an Untouchable caste." But he was quite sure that his eleven-year-son did not know.

His boy, he then went on to tell me, goes to a private primary school run by caste Hindus — Brahmans, in fact — under the name Aryan Education Society. As I took in this almost indigestibly ironic bit of information, he was adding: "They know there he is a Scheduled Caste boy. There are only two Scheduled Caste boys in the school." I asked whether the other boys knew his son was Scheduled Caste. "I don't know," he answered. "Usually they don't inquire." What happened when there were fights or arguments, I wanted to know. He said he had not heard of any from his son. "He will learn of his past from *us,*" he offered and then continued, as if in a dialogue with himself:

But why should he learn it? He will only say he is Buddhist. This will tell others that he is former Scheduled Caste and this means they might see him from a special point of view, for they will understand he comes from the Mahar community. But those brought up on Ambedkar's teachings know about untouchability and will reject the inferiority coming from it. Others called us inferior, but *we* do not see ourselves as inferior, now or in the past.

He went on to repeat the Mahar-Buddhist view of the inherent inequality of Hinduism and how emancipation was achieved by leaving Hinduism altogether and becoming Buddhists. "Why not explain all this to your son?" I asked. "This is not the age to do so," he answered. "He might get a complex from the fact that his fathers were inferior. The development of his mind must come first." And when would that come? I asked. "He must gradually come to know," he insisted, ignoring my question. But when would he be ready? I insisted. He paused. Then unexpectedly he said: "You know the capacity of Indian boys to understand this kind of thing is different from boys of advanced countries." I asked: "Suppose your son gets into an argument with some caste Hindu boys and he learns that way?" He looked at me for a moment. "I don't know, I never thought about this question." I waited, and then he cried out with some anger. "But I don't see *why* we should tell our boys they belonged to such a caste!" Could it be concealed? "I do not want to conceal it!" he answered heatedly. "But if I tell him, he will get a sort of inferiority complex. He knows Mahar, but he does not know about untouchability. If he comes to know at a later stage, the knowledge won't affect him." Then he said, weakly, suddenly folding: "It is our problem. We are not sure ourselves when to tell our boys." He fell silent, and then: "I am not able to answer this question. I am not able to know."

For people who are "passing," it all gets even more complicated because they have to draw their children into their conspiracies of concealment. A man of the Mahayanshi community of Gujarat told me he has two baby sons, still too young for these confusions, but he also has a daughter of thirteen. His story:

She knows she belongs to the Mahayanshi community. She heard this word long ago but had no concept of what it meant until one time five years ago when we took her to our family village for a visit. It was the first time she had ever been there. We had to stay in our separate place. The other children asked her who she was and she said she was my daughter, and they said: "Oh, then you are Mahayanshi, as we are." She was very offended. They were very poor children and she learned she was in their caste. She could not go into any home in the village, or shop. She had to stand outside. That was in our village only five years ago, 156 miles from Bombay.

My wife was brought up in Poona in a cosmopolitan atmosphere. She came to our village when we were married. I was twenty-two then and she was eighteen and she learned of the village conditions that time. She had the same disappointing things happen to her when we came to visit my family. But she did not tell our daughter about it. She thought things might have improved. Now my daughter is in the seventh standard. At school she gives the name of a Gujarat caste, which is what we tell people who ask us, for if we disclosed our true caste people would frown on us and not give us respect. She knows that if she said she was Mahayanshi, there would be some sort of dislike toward her. Now people look on her with regard and affection. They would not do so if they knew she was Scheduled Caste. She is telling a lie, but it is not difficult. It is not a good idea, telling lies, but it is not difficult. In Bombay we live among non-Scheduled Caste people. The moment I disclosed that

I was Scheduled Caste, there would be some sort of non-cooperation. They would try to harass us until we left the place.

I asked how his daughter felt about all of this. He shrugged. "She's not worried now about the future. My daughter will be married in our community. Others will be bound to know one day. Some friends will continue their friendship with her, some will not, and those that keep on being friends, it will be a shallow friendship. In my own case, I feel that I will not be mindful what other people do. She will be mature enough also later on and will decide what to do." I asked if there was any chance that she might marry outside her community. "I think not," her father answered. "No one will be ready for that." Does she talk about this with her friends? "I don't think so," he said. I explained that I meant Maha-yanshi friends. "Oh no," he replied, "there aren't any Mahayanshi in the vicinity. She has no such friends. At school things will just go on. School friendships come to an end. Very few continue. Then she will go on to high school and make new friends. When I have to fill out the form for college, I will say she is Scheduled Caste to get the rights and facilities. As far as her student friends are concerned, she won't disclose our caste. If they come to know, yes, for example, from the notice of scholarships, well, all right, they will come to know!" He did not seem to think this would present much of a problem and when I asked whether he thought his daughter would be unhappy over it, he shrugged again. "Not neces-sarily," he said. "If the others take it in good spirit, it will make no difference. If they look at it with prejudice, then there will be some diffi-culty, because the prejudices are that we are ignorant people, with no ability. My own idea is that if people come to know I am Mahayanshi, I will not bother about it. They can adopt any course they like as far as I am concerned, but on my own account, I will not tell anybody I am of Scheduled Caste. This is how I hope it will be with my daughter."

When she got married, he went on, she would marry someone of their own caste, but at the wedding none of her friends would discover the bridegroom's caste. "Mahayanshis are married by Hindu rites," he explained, "and there is no clue to caste just by looking at the ceremony; you can't tell. There will be other non-Scheduled Caste guests and no one will discover anything about our caste. The priest may be under the impression that we are of some higher caste; he would not know. If he did know we were Scheduled Caste, it would probably make no difference if he agreed to come in the first place. The ceremony would not be any different. If he did not agree to come, I would get another priest who would."

All this was said in a vigorous, confident way. He gave the air of knowing just what he was about and having it all taped down well into the future. I wondered whether he really did or whether he was fooling himself, and I subsequently put the question to a number of others: would it be possible to have a wedding ceremony and reception without the guests learning the caste of the principals? Other Scheduled Caste people looked at me incredulously when I put the question. "Impossible!" came the reply again and again. "Why, the guests talk with each other, somebody is going to ask where the family comes from, there is always some curious person, and one way or another the name of the community will come out." Or again: "Even if they don't talk, the caste Hindu guests will be able to tell from the speech and dress of the relatives, because if there are relatives they are surely poorer relatives and you can always tell." It was suggested that if the host invited only those members of his family who were prosperous and could dress and talk well, he might just get away with it, barring that one curious guest who might ferret out the truth anyway. Against all this there was the testimony of one Parsi lady I asked who described her wedding-going experiences in a way that suggested that if this man chose his guests with care he might indeed carry it off just as he said he could. "Why, of course I never learn the caste of the people," said the Parsi lady. "I have often been invited to weddings in the families of associates at the university. I go and sit down and I'm quiet. I don't really know anybody there. All the other people talk some, but mostly they also just sit down. The ceremony takes about an hour. Then I go up and express my good wishes to the family, and I leave. I might not say more than a few sentences to anybody the whole time and I would certainly never know anything about their caste!" It is also possible, of course, that being a Parsi and not a Hindu, the question of their caste would be less likely to enter her mind.

Getting back to my original informant on this matter, besides the daughter who would figure in this problematic wedding, he had two small sons and I asked him what he thought about the outlook for their future. "We will see what development there will be in the society by 1970 and 1980," he calmly replied, and then went on:

If caste prejudice is wiped away, then no difficulty. If it is still here, then we will follow our practice. We will remain Mahayanshi in private and our higher caste in public. If there is no prejudice or hatred, then there will be no more problem about coming out with it. If there is no distinction between treatment of Brahman and Scheduled Caste, then fine. If all caste is abolished, that will be fine too. But I think the problems will remain. It is all not likely to change too much. The caste system will remain and we will find ways to deal with it, to show we are in no way inferior. Different people will give various caste names to hide their original caste. We can do this for years, and it may just go on and on.

NOTES

[1] B. R. Ambedkar, *What Congress and Gandhi Have Done to the Untouchables,* Bombay, 1945, p. 317.

[2] The authoritative Gandhian account of these events is given in Pyarelal, *The Epic Fast,* Ahmedabad, 1932, and is reflected in the account given by Louis Fischer, *The Life of Mahatma Gandhi,* New York, 1950, pp. 306–321 and similar works. Ambedkar's record appears in *What Congress and Gandhi Have Done to the Untouchables,* Chap. III and *passim,* and additional details giving Ambedkar's view will be found in his biographer's account in Dhananjay Keer, *Dr. Ambedkar, Life and Mission,* Bombay, 1962, pp. 204–216. Of the Untouchable legislators elected as a result of the Poona Pact, Ambedkar later wrote: "They were completely under the control of the Congress Party Executive. They could not ask a question which it did not like. They could not move a resolution which it did not permit. They could not bring in legislation to which it objected. They could not vote as they chose and could not speak what they felt. They were as dumb as driven cattle. One of the objects of obtaining representation in the Legislature for the Untouchables is to enable them to ventilate their grievances and to obtain redress for their wrongs. The Congress successfully and effectively prevented this from happening." — *What Congress and Gandhi Have Done to the Untouchables,* p. 102.

[3] In 1955, Jagjivam Ram, the Congress Party's highest ranking ex-Untouchable as Minister of Communications in the Nehru cabinet, gave a major address on the subject of caste and untouchability without ever once using the term "Harijan." — See "Address by Shri Jagjivam Ram," *Report of the Seminar on Casteism and Removal of Untouchability,* Bombay, 1955, pp. 25–39.

[4] Keer, *op. cit.,* pp. 301–302.

[5] Cf. M. N. Srinivas, "Pursuit of Equality," *Times Survey of India,* Jan. 26, 1962; also his "Changing Institutions and Values in Modern India," *Economic Weekly Annual Review,* February, 1962.

[6] Cf. Donald E. Smith, *India as a Secular State,* Princeton, 1963, pp. 316ff.; *Report of the Backward Classes Commission,* New Delhi, 1956. For an examination of the legal and judicial aspects of this matter, see the studies by Marc Galanter: "Equality and 'Protective Discrimination' in India," *Rutger's Law Review,* XVI:1, Fall, 1961; "The Problem of Group Membership: Some Reflections on the Judicial View of Indian Society," *The Journal of the Indian Law Institute,* IV:3, July-Sept. 1962; "Law and Caste in Modern India," *Asian Survey,* III: 11, Nov. 1963. (See also Galanter's contribution in this volume.)

[7] Supplied to the writer in mid-1964 from the figures being prepared for the Commissioner's report for 1962–63. Later figures as of January, 1966, presented by Dushkin in Table 9.5 of Chapter 9, this volume, indicate little dramatic change.

[8] Cf. C. T. Kannan, *Intercaste and Intercommunity Marriages in India,* Bombay, 1963.

14.

ANDRÉ BÉTEILLE

Pollution and Poverty

THE HARIJANS OR EX-UNTOUCHABLES are a large and important segment of the Indian population whose problems differ from region to region, from urban area to village, and among the various occupational spheres. Also, as a consequence of both spontaneous social currents and the purposive actions of planners and policy-makers, the social life and wider society of which the Harijans are a part have undergone many changes.

Because of the complexity of these changes, rather than attempt a single, systematic account of the Harijans' present position and future prospects, the editor of this volume has chosen to present a variety of disciplinary approaches and points of view, each embodied in an essay concerning a different aspect of the Harijan experience. Inevitably certain issues have been emphasized. The result is a series of interesting and varied explorations into the lives of the Harijans. In reading these it is important to remember that the different regions of India are not all equally represented here, and that the idea of pollution, so significant to the Harijan's place in society, varies greatly from one region to another. Again, although much has been said about the conversion of Harijans to different sects and religions, it should be borne in mind that the vast majority of them are neither Buddhists nor Christians but simply Harijans. From these diverse essays, however, each addressed to an important problem, much can be learned about the position of the Harijan in modern Indian society.

I am grateful to the Jawaharlal Nehru Memorial Fund for providing me with a fellowship during the tenure of which this piece was written.

[411]

In fact, this setting is of first importance in understanding the Harijans' problems, for the structure and values of the total society have a significant bearing on every aspect of the Harijans' lives. Two questions in this context arise at once: What, if any, are the distinctive features by which the Harijan can be differentiated from the lowest strata in other societies? And, to what extent are the theory and practice of untouchability an integral part of traditional Indian society?

In answer to the first question, not only are the Harijans at the bottom of Indian society, but in purely material terms their levels of living are far below those of comparable strata elsewhere. Although not all 60 million Harijans are destitute, the lives of a vast majority are characterized by uniform conditions of poverty. They tend also to be concentrated in rural areas, mainly as landless agricultural laborers. When they do own land, usually it is insufficient to provide their living and they must work on the land of others as well. Characteristically also, Harijans who own land do so in unfertile and non-irrigated regions.

The extreme poverty of the Harijans is related in great measure to general conditions in India where an economy of scarcity has given rise to acute inequalities. Backward classes tend to be doubly backward in poor countries where opportunities for economic advancement are limited. This generalization is relevant to the present topic since genuine attempts to raise the social position of the Harijans have so often been defeated by a variety of material constraints.

Besides suffering from a low level of material existence, the Harijans have experienced a number of other deprivations which can best be understood in terms of the emphasis on purity and pollution in Indian social life. These concepts, although most systematically elaborated in the Hindu religion, are not without influence beyond Hinduism, as illustrated by K. C. Alexander in Chapter 8 of this volume. First, as the dominant religion, Hinduism has influenced members of other faiths. Further, it seems likely that the low material status of Harijans has made them accept more readily the roles assigned to them by members of the dominant community.

We need a clarified assessment of the weight of pollution in the entire range of Indian society and not just among the Harijans. Those who seek to raise the status of the Harijans quickly — planners and policy-makers in particular — do not always realize the significance of values deeply rooted in religion. Liberal Indians are inclined to regard certain manifestations of these values as a kind of aberration. On the other hand, almost every reliable anthropological study of the Indian village shows how pervasive and tenacious these values are (See Opler Introduction).

There are some who have argued that the opposition of the pure and the impure is what gives Hindu social structure its distinctive character. According to them, the Brahman at one end and the Harijan at the other constitute the two fixed points of traditional Indian society. The links between Hinduism, the ideas of purity and pollution and the social situation of the Harijans are clear and beyond dispute. In the economically underdeveloped countries of Asia, where other religions predominate, poverty and destitution may be as acute as in India, but the poor — though often scorned and mistreated — are rarely regarded as "untouchable."

On this view, the polarity of purity and pollution (or Brahman and Untouchable) not only gives Hindu society its distinctive character, but also forms one of its essential elements in every region and during most of India's recorded history. Among liberal Hindus, on the other hand, untouchability today is described as an "excrescence," a "perversion," or an "aberration" — not as an essential part of the Hindu religion and social structure.

These disparate views of untouchability are represented by Ambedkar and Gandhi whose varying interpretations of Hinduism, each with its social ramifications, form the subject of Eleanor Zelliot's essay in Chapter 4 of this volume. Gandhi held that rather than being essential to Hinduism the practice of untouchability was a violation of its basic spirit. Ambedkar maintained that untouchability derived its real strength from the Hindu scriptures. Gandhi was seeking a new basis for the integration of the whole of Indian society whereas Ambedkar was chiefly concerned with a particular section of it.

It is only a step from the belief among Indologists and ethnographers that untouchability in theory and practice has been an important feature of Indian society to the argument that inequality in India is a question, not merely of unequal distribution of resources, but of basic ideas and values. In such terms scholars are sometimes inclined to find misleading any attempt to compare the lot of Harijans in India and blacks in the United States because the systems incorporating these two human elements are distinctively different. According to some scholars traditional Indian society embodied a harmony between existence and ideology which has not been present in the United States where genuine inequality co-existed with emphasis on equality as an ideal.

Although in India undoubtedly there is greater acceptance than elsewhere of inequality among the upper and lower strata, this observation should not lead to oversimplified conclusions. The theory of karma has probably been at all times less acceptable to Harijans than to Brahmans, as Joan Mencher indicates in Chapter 2 of this volume. She points out that "there has always been a large amount of hostility and resentment among the Harijans toward those higher in the social hierarchy."

Also a factor in the social outlook are changing attitudes toward social inequality among Indian leaders of opinion. Gandhi and Ambedkar, whatever their differences, agreed that the theory and practice of untouchability were wrong. In strengthening the legal and constitutional basis for the rejection of untouchability, Gandhi's ideas rendered ambivalent the defense of untouchability, even among the orthodox.

Nevertheless the attitudes and behavior of the upper castes toward the Harijans with whom they daily interact do not seem to have undergone radical change. Indeed, members of the urban intelligentsia, leading protagonists of change, have little direct contact with Harijans. As Harold Isaacs indicates in Chapter 13 of this volume, educated Harijans in the large cities either conceal their status or are treated with great circumspection.

In rural areas contemporary attitudes toward Harijans vary greatly. Particularly in the village setting, victimization of Untouchables has often increased with the intensity of their efforts to achieve equality. For a number of reasons traditional attitudes toward the Harijans have been difficult to modify. Pollution has deep roots in Hinduism. Also deeply imbedded, at least in the popular mind, is the notion of inherited inequality. These ideas have been reinforced by the vested interests of the upper castes in their day-by-day relationships with Harijans, concerning especially such matters as wages and agricultural employment. Although it may be unrealistic to argue that the concept of untouchability was invented to justify economic exploitation, it is nonetheless a fact that modern efforts to improve the condition of the Harijans have often been defeated by those who stood to gain from the Untouchables' social and economic inferiority.

It appears, therefore, that the Harijans owe their characteristic position in society mainly to two factors: material deprivation and the stigma of pollution. Intensifying this situation is the cumulative nature of inequality in India — more striking at the bottom than at the top.

Opinion varies as to the priorities to be assigned to material and ritual factors in explaining the plight of the Harijans. One side stresses the importance of ritual factors — Dumont and his school of thought, for example. The other side, exemplified by Walter Neale's essay in Chapter 3 of this volume, emphasizes the effect of poverty and deprivation on all underprivileged groups in all underdeveloped societies.

Problems of Agricultural Laborers

About 90 percent of the Harijans live in villages (as compared to about 80 percent of the total population). The vast majority of Harijans depend directly on agriculture for their living, and their position in the agrarian economy is generally weak and precarious. A few are owner-cultivators of small, unproductive holdings. Most are part owners and part tenants or sharecroppers and agricultural laborers. Their specialized occupational skills bring small returns and often carry the caste stigma of "unclean" occupations.

The problem of Harijan sharecroppers and agricultural laborers must be viewed in relation to the larger picture of Indian agriculture which includes such issues as ownership and distribution of land, mounting pressure of population on the land, and the low rate at which this population is being transferred from agriculture to industry.

Also, members of "clean" castes are sometimes sharecroppers and agricultural laborers, and in many of these cases the distinction between Harijan and non-Harijan loses relevance.

Recent changes in the system of agricultural production have brought little improvement in the position of Harijan sharecroppers and laborers. Despite land reform legislation aimed at giving land to the tiller, the majority of Harijans (and many others) continue landless or in possession of uneconomic holdings. This is explained in part by village landowners who continue to restrict the Harijans' ability to take advantage of their legal and political rights.

Any analysis of Indian agricultural labor in purely quantitative terms is likely to omit certain important aspects of the work process. Agricultural operations, particularly wet paddy cultivation, may call for labor that is arduous as well as onerous — a point to which economists may have given insufficient attention. In India, the differing types of work are elaborately graded, not only by occupation but by the diverse operations within one broad occupational sphere such as agriculture. The most onerous types of work are generally left to the Harijans. In wet paddy areas, for example, the so-called "cultivating castes" perform very few of the physically exacting tasks which are done by Harijans — or as in some part of West Bengal — by tribal migrants or settlers. In wheat-producing areas the situation is somewhat different, but even here status remains important. In Haryana, for instance, the Jats, a "cultivating caste," perform most of the difficult operations on their own land or on land they have leased, but are reluctant to become laborers on someone else's land. Here again, wage labor is performed largely by Harijan castes.

Also, for certain types of operation (again probably wet paddy rather than wheat) women are preferred, partly because they work for lower wages, and partly because they are more skilled. Although there is variation in this matter, in general the upper-caste women do not work in the fields.

Thus even among landless agriculturists there are differences in the economic activity of Harijans and caste Hindus although such differences are not equally great in every region. Where sharecroppers are Harijans, in some areas the resumption of land by the owners for "personal cultivation" has transformed them into daily laborers, demoting them one step on the socio-economic ladder. Elsewhere the threat of resumption of land is a constant factor in the sharecropper's assessment of his security.

As the poorest segment of the landless class, the Harijan suffers from the fact that in an agrarian economy land has a supreme value for the individual, giving him work, security, status, and a measure of independence. Where an individual has no land of his own he tries to acquire some as a tenant on more or less permanent lease. Among the landless Harijans today, however, the proportion of wage laborers to tenants is probably increasing. For a variety of reasons more landowners are cultivating with hired labor. Also, tenants who already own land are preferred because they are more likely to be able to pay the rent. The net result is that fewer Harijans are becoming tenants.

Although money wages have risen recently in India, in general the low rate of agricultural pay has not gone up faster than the cost of living. The tendency to change from wages in kind to wages in cash has also affected the laborer adversely. As for advances in technology, although some of these have pressed wages upward, to date the effects of power equipment and modern fertilizer practices have been felt only in a few selected areas.

Some of the problems of Harijan agricultural labor under conditions of technological change are illustrated in the Tanjore district of South India. With its large concentration of Harijan laborers and agricultural activity, Tanjore was one of the first seven districts selected for a program of intensive agricultural development. In the eastern part the few Harijans who had been tenants were in large measure evicted and had to become day laborers. Subsequently, medium-to-large landholders in many villages began relying solely on wage laborers, who were almost invariably Harijans, to cultivate their fields.

The intensive program has indeed led to an increase in the output of paddy and temporarily in the demand for labor, accompanied by organized pressure for higher wages from Harijan laborers and leaders. In Tanjore a large and fairly homogenous class of "pure" agricultural laborers who are almost all Harijans (and also oriented toward Marxian Communism) have raised the wage level somewhat. But this increase has been achieved at the cost of uncertainty, conflict, and violence. On December 25, 1968, following a protracted quarrel between landowners and wage laborers, the houses along an entire Harijan street were set on fire and forty-two women and children burned to death.

Elsewhere also, particularly in the southern and eastern regions of India, there have been sporadic conflicts between landowners and laborers over wages and other conditions of employment. Gains to the landless have, on the whole, been limited. At times, regardless of caste identities, the interests of wage laborers and sharecroppers (as well as small owner-cultivators) have been in conflict. At other times the cleavages between Harijans and landless caste Hindus have made united action impossible. Nevertheless, where landless laborers are mostly Harijans, as in East Tanjore, it has been easier for landowners to isolate and victimize them. In any case, widespread and substantial improvement in the Harijans' material condition through concerted political action has seemed unlikely.

In the Ludhiana district of North India, agricultural laborers in another program of intensive development seem to have fared better. Here the bulk of the "pure" agricultural laborers are Mazbhis, counterparts of the Harijans among the Sikhs. During the 1950s and 1960s, Ludhiana district experienced rapid growth both in agriculture and small industry, with increasing demand for labor, and wages among the highest in the area. Basic conditions evidently were more favorable than in other regions for simultaneous growth in agriculture and industry, and in addition the Ludhiana social system seems to have been less rigid. Even among Hindus the conceptions of purity and pollution have played a less important part in the Punjab than in South India, and the Sikhs in their turn have been more flexible in these matters than the Hindus. With the hiatus between top and bottom strata not too great, the lower castes apparently found more opportunity for material improvement.

Thus the general material conditions of the large mass of Harijan sharecroppers or landless laborers are variously responsive to changes in the agricultural economy. Without major changes in this economy it appears that the chances of the Harijans attaining a more viable economic situation will continue to be limited. There are nation-wide development programs aimed at raising the economic levels of the backward classes, but such programs by their very nature seem to bring only marginal improvement to small portions of the 60 to 70 million Harijan population.

Pervasiveness of Values

Just as improvements in the material conditions of Untouchables seem linked to wider economic development, so also do changes in ritual status seem to depend upon changes in the broader system of social and cultural values. Both Gandhi and Ambedkar were acutely conscious of this, Gandhi directing much of his energy toward bringing about a change of heart in the caste Hindus — a change which would enable them to see the high and the low-born as equal in the eyes of God. Ambedkar despaired that such a change could be brought about within the framework of Hinduism and sought escape for his fellows from the tyranny of caste through conversion to a different religion. Gandhi believed that untouchability could be conquered only by a return to the original spirit of Hinduism.

In a sense both leaders failed. Gandhi failed because the change of heart did not go far enough or deep enough. Ambedkar failed because conversion to Buddhism or any other religion has rarely led to escape from the stigma of pollution. Both failures testify to the weight and pervasiveness of hierarchical values in Indian society.

Viewed in this context the persistent attempts at sect formation among Harijans reveal both the acceptance of traditional Hindu values, loosely described as "Sanskritization" and the rejection of those values in the process of conversion, notably to Buddhism. Neither acceptance, nor rejection through conversion is confined to the Harijans, however, or to attempts to achieve upward social mobility. Hindu society has long encompassed such changes or attempts at change which have not necessarily led to formation of separate sects, for example, subdivisions within a caste or subcaste.

It is worth noting that untouchability is not merely something imposed by upper strata on lower, but is practiced by Harijans themselves. In Tanjore district, for instance, Pallas do not draw water from Paraiyan wells, nor do they allow Paraiyans to use their wells. On occasion it has appeared that the various Harijan castes are no less rigid in their observances among themselves than are Brahmans toward Harijans.

Apparently social movements among the lower strata not only create new ranks but develop these ranks from considerations of purity and pollution. The intense preoccupation in every section of India society with hierarchy, purity, and pollution helps to explain why all levels persist in an effort to raise status and why the lower levels have so rarely succeeded.

Conversion, it should be recognized also, has been motivated by factors other than the desire to escape the stigma of pollution. Material considerations have played their part. Christian missionaries in particular have provided incentives to conversion in the form of jobs, housing, and medical care. Education in mission schools has attracted Harijans as well as members of other castes. It should be noted, however, that many benefits accorded Untouchables under present government policy are lost through conversion.

A unique development — the conversion of Mahars to Buddhism — was organized by Ambedkar on the basis of two decades of conscious deliberation. Its primary objective was adoption of a religion rooted both in Indian tradition and in opposition to inequality. Although Ambedkar was wooed by leaders of various religious communities including Islam and Christianity, he chose Buddhism because it was not only Indian but egalitarian. In the process he tried to explain untouchability in India as a consequence of the forceful suppression of indigenous Buddhists by invading Hindus.

Yet the conversion of Ambedkar's followers to Buddhism seems to have had little impact on upper-caste Hindu society even in Maharashtra. For the great majority of rural people, a Mahar is still a Mahar, whether Buddhist or Hindu. As long as the Mahars continue in their traditional socio-economic position, it seems that Hindus will not be sensitive to their conversion. While Adele Fiske's study in this volume indicates that such attempts have increased greatly among Harijans in recent years, little is known as to resultant shifts in social rank. Changes in food habits and the abandonment of such occupational practices as flaying and tanning do not insure ready acceptance by other castes, as is illustrated in Chapters 11 and 12 of this volume by Robert and Beatrice Miller.

Nor is this unchanging attitude among the upper strata confined to Hindus. Upper-caste Christians in Kerala, as described by Alexander, are as jealous of their purity as Hindus anywhere. The "old" and the "new" Christians remain apart, with a gulf in their material condition so great that "passing" on any extensive scale would appear almost impossible within the local community.

Again one is impressed by the concern with material conditions governing such observable features as dress, grooming, and appearance. In India the differences between the well-to-do and the poor are not only large but extremely visible. A kind of cumulative causality keeps the poor isolated because of their "unclean" habits, and keeps the isolated poor because they lack access to the means of material advancement.

At the bottom of the hierarchy, material deprivation and ritual impurity reinforce one another. The poor are unclean, both physically and ritually. The very squalor in which the majority of Harijans live stands in the way of their establishing a new social identity. It is this and not ritual impurity alone which the upper castes have used to justify keeping the Untouchables at a distance, both physically and socially.

Poverty and squalor are everywhere the lot of the underprivileged and everywhere seem to justify their separation from the rest of society. In India this separation has acquired distinctive force because of the association of squalor with defilement. Although the defilement of Untouchables did not arise simply from squalor but from a much more complex set of factors in Indian society, the material conditions of the Harijans' lives have restricted severely their attempts to escape the stigma of pollution.

15.   J. MICHAEL MAHAR

Conclusion

UNDERLYING THE MULTIPLE approaches to the central theme of this volume is a recurrent concern with describing and assessing Indian government policies and programs affecting Untouchables. The complementary nature of these studies makes it possible to consider the role of the Untouchable from a variety of perspectives, and to evaluate the relative efficacy of divergent approaches to a common goal — improvement in the lot of the Untouchable — as represented by Mahatma Gandhi and Dr. B. R. Ambedkar. As shown in Eleanor Zelliot's account of the running debate between these two leaders during the decades preceding Independence, policies and programs may be profoundly affected by the difference in views on such key questions as: What is the ultimate goal — assimilation of the Untouchable minority or the establishment of separate but equal status in a reformed version of the traditional social order? If change is in order, who should change — the Untouchable minority or the Hindu majority? Given a commitment to change, how might it best be implemented — through voluntary means or government coercion? While these contrasting extremes barely touch upon the range of possible alternatives, it is evident that views approximating them have had considerable effect on the formulation and implementation of policies affecting Untouchables in recent decades. Decisions of this order also can be expected to confront those seeking to assist the Untouchables in the future.

Judging from Eleanor Zelliot's study, Gandhi's answers to such questions were rooted in his view that caste Hindus were primarily responsible for righting the wrongs done to the Untouchable. Meaningful change,

[421]

therefore, must arise from a change of heart on the part of the majority. Favoring private rather than government attempts at social reform, Gandhi's program called for little initiative or action by Untouchables. Though in accord with Gandhi's vision of the ideal Indian society— one rooted in the agrarian way of life — this approach found its polar opposite in the dynamic leadership of Dr. B. R. Ambedkar. Ambedkar advocated policies presuming marked change on the part of the Untouchable minority who he believed must equip themselves with the education and skills needed to compete effectively in a "modern" society. He assumed also that little fundamental change could be expected in the Hindu's treatment of the Untouchable without recourse to government intervention.

Marc Galanter's analysis of the Untouchability (Offences) Act of 1955 invites assessment of the relative effectiveness in the methods of Gandhi and Ambedkar. In 1955 the coercive power of the state, operating through police and courts, was called upon to curb the traditional social disabilities imposed on Untouchables. Judged on the basis of court action, such efforts appear to have had little effect. As noted by Galanter, the registration of approximately 520 cases annually, from 1956 to 1964, is but a faint measure of the actual incidence of such offences.

Mahar and Mencher report incidents from the context of village life during the same period, adding support to the view that these attempts to enforce change have had only minor direct effects. While the improvements suggested by Galanter may increase the number of cases brought to trial, the long-range consequences in all probability lie outside the courtroom. Mahar's and Mencher's accounts of village life, as well as the contemporary short stories analyzed by Robert and Beatrice Miller, indicate that the egalitarian principles embodied in the Indian Constitution and the Untouchability (Offences) Act are now generally familiar to all Indians. For Untouchables and caste Hindus alike, new ideals, advocated by men of power and authority beyond the milieu of village life, have become an important measure of appropriate behavior. While the courts may serve mainly as a symbolic source of sanctions emanating from the new view of the Untouchable's role, the rapid diminution of sumptuary laws in the Mahar and Mencher accounts, and the rejection of ritual roles depicted in such stories as Madgulkar's "Nirvana," point to a widespread acceptance of new rights for the Untouchables, despite the tempered acceptance of these rights by the upper castes.

Still another component of the ongoing process, far different from programs based on law or the other powers of the state, may be seen as an additional aspect of Ambedkar's strategy of change. His dramatic call for mass conversion to Buddhism was an attempt to create a new self-image for the Untouchable as an initial step toward self-improvement through education. As described in Fiske's account of Buddhist activity among the Untouchables, this attempt to break the bonds of tradition appears, paradoxically, to be rooted in the matrix of kin and caste ties from which the traditional social order draws much of its strength and tenacity. While the magnitude of recorded conversions to Buddhism is most impressive, the separateness fostered by the new identity and the regional basis of the Buddhist conversion movement suggest that it is an interim measure rather than an ultimate solution. A major feature of Buddhist activity — the creation of schools and hostels — affirms the importance of education as the Untouchable's way out of the rural communities in which their traditional plight is most firmly rooted.

The use of religion to organize people for a wide variety of purposes is quite in keeping with Indian tradition. Lawrence Babb's account of the Satnami sect in Madhya Pradesh offers another instance in which sectarian interests and identity, based on a caste network rooted in a particular region, may link rural communities to the national political system. In the Satnami case, the Congress Party was the mediating organization. According to Fiske, the Republican Party has served this function for many of the Buddhist communities who, as noted earlier, have developed organizations to further the higher education of their own. While adult education classes and community libraries have also been established as part of the Buddhist movement, there is little evidence that this organizational base has been used to create credit cooperatives, labor unions, or similar organizations for the fostering of Untouchable economic interests.

Economic prospects for the Untouchables seem most disheartening in the agrarian sector of the economy where they are heavily concentrated as landless laborers. Judging from Neale's economic analysis in Chapter 3, and the observations in Chapter 14 of sociologist André Béteille, the landless agricultural laborer has been one of the first to suffer from the pressures of over-population, and will continue in a position of prime vulnerability. Rapid expansion of agricultural production through improved farming methods in the 1960s appears to have increased employment for Untouchables in some areas, but long term gains have accrued chiefly to those owning land.

Mencher notes also the possibility of a shift in the caste composition of South Indian villages because of the urban migration of artisan and service castes. Such a shift might lead to further polarization of the haves and have-nots in village communities, a trend that, coupled with an increase in the ranks of unemployed agricultural laborers, bodes ill for the political peace of the countryside. Although urban migration of the kind and magnitude noted by Mencher were not found in the North Indian village described by Mahar, the relatively high employment rate of Untouchables in that area has deferred the potential problem of finding jobs for their progeny — a problem pressing upon the many artisan and service castes who have begun educating their children to prepare them for occupations outside the village. The paucity of such opportunities, however, is cruelly evident in the slums of the larger cities, and prospects for the educated Untouchable a decade or so from now are not likely to be any better.

The failure of the Untouchables to produce other leaders of Ambedkar's stature raises the question of what becomes of those Untouchables who do attain a college education and urban employment. Harold Isaacs' account indicates that many of these potential leaders retreat into anonymity. Few of them appear rooted in an urban community such as that provided by the Jatavs of Agra. Rather, they appear to be isolated by choice or circumstance from their village brethren. Some evidence to the contrary, however, is provided by Fiske's report that leaders in the Buddhist movement are often educated Untouchables living in provincial towns. In such instances the link between the "modern" man and his village counterpart is reaffirmed in a traditional manner — via an appeal in terms of religion rather than political ideology or class interest. Even though the prime mover in this case was the secular-minded Ambedkar, echoes of Gandhi are evoked by the reliance on religion as a group rallying point in support of programs to further education and political activity.

Turning to consideration of the city as the place of opportunity and escape from the confines of village tradition, we find much of interest in the accounts of Owen Lynch and Harold Isaacs. In Lynch's study of the Jatavs of Agra, there is evidence of a viable Untouchable community, sharing many village-like features of group solidarity, based on a caste exclusive industry — that of shoe manufacture. The economic base afforded by this caste monopoly has enabled the Jatavs to generate educated leaders capable of utilizing the political power of caste bloc voting to their individual and group advantage. Although the vitality of this group attracted Ambedkar's interest and support, their participation in his effort to develop an effective national party does not appear to have been in keeping with their potential. This account, and Dushkin's study of the recent composition and efforts of the Republican Party, show that the Jatavs have done little to further the lot of other Untouchable groups within their own region, let alone the nation.

The availability of political offices to Untouchables, despite their weak economic base, through the provision of reserved seats in legislative bodies, represents a major effort by the Indian government. Dushkin shows that this policy has not given rise to an effective Untouchable party — as envisioned by some — nor does it appear to have generated leaders of the heroic stamp of B. R. Ambedkar. The Untouchable population, constituting approximately 15 percent of the nation, would seem to afford an effective base for political organization, based on common interests in a polity divided by numerous caste and regional cleavages. Considering this, the failure of the Republican Party to attract widespread support might well puzzle the outside observer. As Dushkin points out, however, the wide dispersion of Untouchables within the population and the accompanying phenomenon of caste Hindu majorities in most constituencies, severely hampers those seeking to win office by an appeal to Untouchables alone. Considerations of political "realities" as they were manifest in the need for campaign funds, organizational support, and the dominant role of the Congress Party until recent years are also noted by Dushkin and supported by the views of Untouchable villagers recorded by Mahar and Mencher. Why waste a vote for a minor party when support of a broader based party dominant in regional or national politics may provide some tangible returns? Recruitment of Untouchable leaders by Congress, or regionally dominant parties, also serves to subvert the appeal of the Republican Party for aspiring politicians.

To apply some of Dushkin's conclusions to the Republican Party, the most successful of the parties dedicated primarily to Untouchable interests — its faltering fortunes may be attributed in part to the common fate which it shares with other parties seeking to grow in competition with the Congress Party. In addition to being associated with such national heroes as Gandhi and Nehru, the Congress and its local representatives are given credit by many Untouchables with initiation of most of the government assistance programs. The political dominance of Congress during the two decades following Independence has also given credence to the belief suggested earlier that it is better to support the party in control, whose major leaders have at least voiced their concern with Untouchables, than to waste support on a militant party committed to Untouchables — but with little prospect for attaining power. In those areas where Untouchables have left the ranks of Congress, they have generally switched to parties that have attained regional dominance such as the Dravida Munnetra Kazhagam in Madras — or to coalitions formed to contest a short-term regional issue — such as occurred in Maharashtra.

As noted by Dushkin, Untouchable politicians — including those elected to reserved seats — are beholden to the party that supports them with campaign funds and organizational assistance. Further, since virtually none of the reserved constituncies are composed solely of Untouchables, the interests of other groups must be served. Given these and similar considerations, prospects seem most unfavorable for the development of an effective national party dedicated primarily to Untouchable interests. Dushkin's analysis of recent developments in the Lok Sabha, however, does point out the potential power of Untouchable blocs in legislative bodies where the defection of Untouchable legislators could topple a majority party. Political leverage of this kind may well serve to attain objectives beyond the reach of a separate Untouchable party.

The government policy of protective discrimination — as manifest in reserved legislative seats, scholarship support, and quotas in government jobs — poses the dilemma of perpetuating Untouchable separateness through the creation of vested interests. Given the modest dimensions of this problem at the present and in the foreseeable future, it does not seem to be of major concern other than to those who view policy formulation in terms of ultimate solutions.

From several of the accounts in this volume it appears that an increasing number of Untouchables view formal education as their only avenue of escape from the restrictions of village life. As shown in Dushkin's account, the all-India enrollment of Untouchables has increased dramatically since India's independence, with the greatest gains at the elementary level. The same phenomenon was found in the village studies by Mencher and Mahar. The extent to which this development is due to the government scholarship program's financial supplement for Untouchables from the first grade through college is difficult to determine as the rapid expansion of schools since Independence has increased educational opportunities for all strata of society. As Isaacs notes, the effect of the government program is little known for want of systematic follow-up on what happens to scholarship recipients upon completion of their studies. Judging from scattered references in the studies here, Untouchables completing the tenth or higher grades turn to the government for employment in the lower echelons of the civil service. The creation of quotas for Untouchables in the Central Government services appears to be a critical complement here, as jobs in industry and business for all classes of educated Indians are far fewer in number than the qualified aspirants for employment.

As noted by Mencher the opening of schools to Untouchables and the provision of support by the government has not brought the Untouchables' participation in education up to the level of the general population.

Economic consideration undoubtedly accounts for this in part, as government stipends do not meet the full cost of education, and many families cannot afford the loss of income resulting from having a son in school. The story of "Daundi," presented in Chapter 11, also conveys some of the subtle and not so subtle social and economic pressures that can be brought to bear on an Untouchable seeking to educate his son. Regarding daughters, little if any evidence of a concerted effort or widespread interest in the education of Untouchable women is reported in these studies. The implications of this disparity are difficult to foresee but the two cases reported by Mahar of domestic tragedy, involving twelfth-grade graduates and their illiterate wives, underline the need to prepare women as well as men for participation in the new spheres of life opening up for Untouchables.

Returning to the question of what happens to the educated Untouchables, we find little evidence of their being accommodated within the rural areas other than Mahar's account of their employment as elementary school teachers in the region north of Delhi. It would be of interest to know the incidence and consequences of this practice as the schoolroom provides one of the few settings in a rural community where caste-based relations are subordinated to the awesome role of the "master." Judging from Mencher's account of a South Indian village, the younger generation also appears more susceptible than its elders to the "change of heart" sought by Gandhi. Turning to Isaacs' account of educated Untouchables interviewed in large cities, we find little indication of their active concern with bettering the lot of their less fortunate caste fellows. Their major preoccupation appears to be with meeting the needs of immediate family and kin, and few are to be found using their time and talents to form or further organizations for the betterment of Untouchables in general. On the other hand, Fiske's account of the Buddhist conversion movement reveals that Untouchable leaders, notably men in such professions as law, and those holding executive positions in labor organizations, have served as sustainers and catalysts in a wide variety of organizations. In many instances these men serve to link and coordinate city-based programs reaching out into the surrounding villages. The creation of such leaders, however, requires not only education, but a commitment to public service and an effective organizational base.

●   ●   ●

Turning from the perspective of plans and planners — how might the events of the past two decades be viewed by an Untouchable? If asked, what's happened in your lifetime? — the initial response would probably be — not much! Further discussion might reveal a slight relaxation of traditional restrictions on Untouchable behavior. An Untouchable woman might now discard her skirt for a sari in a North Indian village. In the South, a Paraiyan youth might don his best clothes and walk down a Brahman street. In both instances, while the age-old fear of a beating may be stilled — such behavior might elicit the more subtle sanction of upper-caste ridicule. The parents of such venturesome youths would most likely feel out of place, uneasy, in situations of this kind, and their upper-caste counterparts would note those among the young who are potential "troublemakers." In the context of village life, sanctions more powerful than scorn remain in the hands of the caste Hindu — sanctions beyond the reach of the law. While everyone knows that the village temple is supposed to be open to all, only a fool would enter its portals if he were a landless Untouchable in a village where the land-owning castes view temple entry as a transgression. A villager seeking to recruit members for the Republican Party, or to persuade his caste fellows to adopt Buddhism might well find himself branded as an agitator. At the end of the harvest, when land is leased for the coming year, such a militant might find that no one is willing to negotiate with him. If his livelihood depends on wages, it doesn't take very long for the refrain "no work today" — "no job this month" — to bring him to heel. So he bites his lip and bides his time. Hope centers on his son — if only he can get an education, leave the village, work for the government in some nice office in the city. But this means the loss of sorely needed income — the son's earnings. And never-ending expenses for books, paper, food and lodging — if he manages to gain admission to a college. Once this dream is attained, and only one out of 200,000 reach the goal — the struggle continues. Where to find a job? In all likelihood the government quota for clerical jobs — the only ones he can do — have been filled. Knowledge of officialdom, contacts, are needed in the rough competition for white collar jobs. Here his illiterate father and village kin can be of little help — he must turn for advice and assistance to the upper castes whose contacts reach beyond the confines of the village.

Success in acquiring a white collar job requires moving to the city — no easy matter for a villager, even a college graduate. The reassuring contacts with kith and kin are several traveling days removed. Housing is expensive, especially if he is married — and who will look after his wife while he's in his office? He seeks out a neighborhood where his caste fellows reside. The predictable patterns of intercaste relations in the village no longer exert their oppressive weight — but who knows when an office mate might object to his use of the water jar? Home at night, the freedom of the cinema and public restaurants is rarely savored on a clerk's salary. Better to turn to the local Buddhist temple where the ritual, devotional singing, and the presence of friends serve as a faint substitute for the close associations of village life. The teachings of the Buddha are good, but in times of crises his wife calls upon the more familiar mother goddess for help. Pleas from the village come in the mail — for money — to replace the family cow, to help finance younger sister's wedding. But the needs of his own wife and children grow daily, and visits to the village diminish after the death of his parents. Now his own boy wants to attend a school that may serve as a stepping-stone to a better position than the father will ever attain. Should he apply for a Harijan scholarship? Risk the embarrassment of having his name posted as an Untouchable on the school bulletin board? The problems of his village brethren and his caste fellows in the slums are remote — and there is little that he can do. A Republican Party organizer addresses a meeting at the Buddhist vihara — more pleas for money, time, energy — all in too short supply. If he is fortunate, promotion to a better-paying position, but prospects for the future are set — twenty years in the same office and then retirement on a pension providing less than his present bare subsistence. Return to the village? Not likely — the children have grown accustomed to city life. And if they marry — an illiterate village girl? Seek out a suitable wife in the labyrinth of the city? And what shall they tell their children, when they ask — to whom do we belong?

J. M. M.

ELEANOR ZELLIOT

Bibliography on Untouchability

References cited in this volume have been incorporated in the bibliography by the editor. All works cited are classified under subject headings. To locate any particular author, refer to the cross-reference beginning on page 481.

General: Pre-Independence

Adhicary, Radica Mohan
1922.   *The Suppressed Classes of India.* Dacca: A. C. Roy Chowdhury.

Agarwal, C. B.
1934.   *The Harijans in Rebellion.* Bombay: Taraporevala Sons.
[The liberal caste Hindu viewpoint, chiefly concerning Maharashtra.]

Anandan, P. M.
1911.   The Coronation and the Depressed Classes. *Hindustan Review* XXIV (138) December.

Andrews, C. F.
1933.   The Untouchability Problem. *Contemporary Review* 144: 152–60.

Anonymous
1912.   *The Depressed Classes: An Enquiry into Their Condition and Suggestions for Their Uplift.* Madras: G. A. Natesan. [Essays reprinted from the *Indian Review* on the problems and progress of Untouchables — exhibits a wide range of caste Hindu attitudes.]

Anonymous
1935–37. *The Depressed Classes: A Chronological Documentation.* Part I, Ranchi: Rev. Fr. J. Jans, S. J., Catholic Press. Parts II–XI, Kurseong: St. Mary's College. [An invaluable review of the 1935 conversion movement and its consequences.]

Baines, Sir Athelstane
1912.   *Ethnography,* (Vol. II, Part 5 of Encyclopedia of Indo-Aryan Research: 72–85.) Strasbourg: Karl J. Trubner.

Bhandarkar, Sir Ramakrishna Gopal
1913.   The Depressed Classes. *The Indian Review* XIV: 482–85.

Chakravartti, Vanamali
1912.   A Short Note on the Hinduization of the Aborigines: The Swelling of the Chandala Caste. *Indian Antiquary* 41: 75–76.

Dubois, Abbé J. A.
1959.   *Hindu Manners, Customs and Ceremonies.* 3rd ed. Translated by Henry K. Beauchamps. Oxford: Clarendon Press. [Originally written in 1815, the fifth chapter contains one of the earliest thorough descriptions of Untouchables.]

Farquhar, John N.
1917.   Help for the Depressed Classes. In *Modern Religious Movements in India.* London, New York: Macmillan. Reprinted in Delhi: Munshiram Manoharlal, 1967.

Fazal-ud-din, Joshua
1934.   *Tragedy of the Untouchables.* Lahore: Civil and Military Gazette.

Glotz, Marguerite
1912.   Les parias dans l'Inde d'aujourdhui. *Revue de Paris* 19: 401–28.

Gokhale, Gopal Krishna
    1903a.   Elevation of Depressed Classes. In *Speeches and Writings of Gopal Krishna Gokhale*. Vol. III. Edited by D. G. Kaine and D. V. Ambedkar. Poona: Servants of India Society, in collaboration with Asia Publishing House of Bombay. [Speech given at Dharwar Social Conference, 1903.]
    1903b.   *Treatment of Indians by the Boers and Treatment of the Low Castes in India by Their Own Countrymen*. London: Christian Literature Society for India.

Henrich, Rev. J. C.
    1937.   *The Psychology of a Suppressed People*. London: George Allen & Unwin. [An early comparison of the problem of untouchability with that of race.]

Kelkar, N. C.
    1909.   The Elevation of the Depressed Classes. In *Pleasures and Privileges of the Pen*. Poona: Kashinath N. Kelkar, ca. 1929. [Reprinted from *Mahratta*, Nov. 7, 1909.]

Lajpat Rai, Lala
    1909.   The Depressed Classes. *The Indian Review:* May.
    1909.   The Depressed Classes. *The Modern Review:* July.
    1913.   *Presidential Speech at the Depressed Classes Conference*. Lahore.
    1913.   The Depressed Classes. *The Indian Review* XIV: 485–92.
    1914.   *On the Upliftment of the Depressed Classes*. Lahore.

Mayo, Katherine
    1930.   Mahatma Gandhi and India's Untouchables. *Current History* 32: 864–70.

Molony, J. Chartres
    1932.   The Depressed Classes. In *Political India, 1832–1932*. Edited by John Cumming. London: Humphrey Milford for Oxford University Press.

Olcott, Henry S.
    1902.   *The Poor Pariah*. Madras. [pamphlet]

Ouwerkerk, Louise
    1945.   *The Untouchables of India*. London: Oxford University Press.

Rajah, Rao Bahadur M. C.
    1925.   *The Oppressed Hindus*. Madras: The Huxley Press. [An account by the first Untouchable to serve on the Central Legislative Council.]

Ramanujachari, K.
    1901.   The Present Condition of the Low Castes. In *Indian Social Reform*. Edited by C. Y. Chintamani. Madras: Thompson.

Rathnaswamy, A. M.
    1947.   *Harijans in a Changing India*. Madras: Author.

Rice, Stanley
    1934.   The Indian Untouchables. *World Unity Magazine* XIV: 232–38.

Sadasiva, Iyar, Sir T.
1923.   *Problems of the Depressed Classes.* Presidential Address, Cochin
         Pulaya Conference, May 14, 1923. Madras.

Sanjana, J. E.
1946.   *Caste and Outcaste.* Bombay: Thacker.
         [An outspoken Parsi viewpoint, critical of caste Hindus.]

Sauter, Johannes A.
1932.   *Unter Brahminen und Parias.* Leipzig: K. E. Koehler.

Sayaji Rao III, Maharaja
1928.   *Speeches and Addresses of His Highness Sayaji Rao III Maharaja
         of Baroda.* London: Macmillan.
         [Contains addresses to Depressed Classes Mission Conferences
         in 1909 and 1918 speech on untouchability.]

Singh, Mohinder
1947.   *The Depressed Classes of India: Their Social and Economic
         Condition.* Introduction by Radhakamal Mukerjee. Bombay:
         Hind Kitabs.
Singh, Saint Nihal
1913.   India's Untouchables. *Contemporary Review* 103: 376–85.

Suryanarayana Rao, R.
1936.   House Sites for Depressed Classes. *Servant of India* 19: 190.
Tandon (or Tondon), Laltaprasad
1934.   *Rationale of Untouchability.* Cawnpore: S. G. Rastoji.

Tilak, B. G.
1918.   The Emancipation of the Untouchable. *The Hindu Missionary*
         42 (April 15), [Published in Bombay.]

Underwood, A. C.
1931.   The Depressed Classes. In *Contemporary Thought of India.* New
         York: Alfred A. Knopf. [A brief review at an important time,
         evidently based on personal knowledge.]

U. S. Office of Strategic Services. Research and Analysis Branch.
1943.   *The Depressed Classes of India.* Washington, D. C., Ann Arbor:
         University of Michigan Microfilms.

Venkatraman, S. R.
1946.   *Harijans Through the Ages.* Madras: Bharati Devi Publications.

NOTE: *See also material on untouchability presented from time to time in:*

Indian Review. [Founded by G. A. Natesan in 1900, Madras.]

Indian Social Reformer. [Founded in 1890, Madras; moved in 1901 to Bombay. Organ of the Indian Social Conference.]

Social Reform Annual. [Founded in 1938, Bombay. Organ of Bombay Presidency Social Reform Association.]

General: Post-Independence

Abel, Elie
1959.   India's Untouchables — Still the "Black Sin." *New York Times Magazine.* March 1: 21, 38, 41–44.

Alexander, K. C.
1968.   Changing Status of Pulaya Harijans of Kerala. *Economic and Political Weekly* III (Special Number, July): 1071–74.

Anonymous
1968.   The Plight of Harijans. *Link.* June 2, 1968: 17–21.

Aurora, G. S.
1968.   Caste and the Backward Classes. *Man in India* 48: 297–306.

Barnabas, A. P. and S. Mehta
1967.   *Caste in Changing India.* New Delhi: Everest Press.

Berreman, Gerald D.
1960.   Caste in India and the United States. *American Journal of Sociology* LXVI: 120–27.
         [Includes comparison of the Indian Untouchable and American Negro.]

Béteille, André
1965.   The Future of the Backward Classes: The Competing Demands of Status and Power. *Perspectives.* Supplement to the *Indian Journal of Public Administration* XI: 1–39. Reprinted in *India and Ceylon: Unity and Diversity.* Philip Mason, ed. London, N.Y., Bombay: Oxford University Press, 1967.

1967.   Race and Descent as Social Categories in India. *Daedalus* 96: 444–463.

Béteille, André and M. N. Srinivas
1969.   The Harijans of India. In *Castes Old and New.* Edited by André Béteille. Bombay: Asia Publishing House.

Bhatt, Bharat L.
         The Scheduled Castes and Tribes of India: A Geographical Analysis. Dissertation in progress, Syracuse University.

         Distribution and Segregation of Scheduled Castes and Tribes in Indian Cities. To be published in proceedings of Syracuse Graduate Student Symposium, 1971.

Bhatt, G. S.
1961.   Trends and Measures of Status Mobility Among Chamars of Dehradun. *Eastern Anthropologist* 14: 229–41.

Bose, Nirmal K.
1970.   Scheduled Castes and Tribes: Their Present Condition. *Man In India* 50: 319–349.

Census of India, 1961.
1966.　Study of Customary Rights and Living and Working Conditions of Scavengers in Two Towns. (By Suman Bhatia, H. C. Hasit, and B. K. Roy Burman.) Vol. I, Part II-D. (Monograph Series.) Delhi: Manager of Publications. [The towns are Mathura in U.P., Bhiwani in Punjab.]

In Press. Bibliography on Scheduled Castes, Scheduled Tribes and Selected Marginal Communities of India. 5 vols. Edited by B. K. Roy Burman. New Delhi: Office of Registrar General of India.

Chauhan, Brij Raj
1969.　Scheduled Castes and Scheduled Tribes. Economic and Political Weekly 4: 257–263.

Cohen, Stephen P.
1969.　The Untouchable Soldier: Caste, Politics and the Indian Army. Journal of Asian Studies 28: 453–68.

Dave, P. C.
1966.　Voluntary Organizations and Welfare of Backward Classes. Vanyajati XIV: 156–64.

DeVos, George and Hiroshi Wagatsuma
1966.　Japan's Invisible Race. Berkeley and Los Angeles: University of California Press.
[See especially John Price, Outcaste Status and Untouchability in Asia, 6–10, and passim.]

D'Sousa, Victor S.
1958.　An Operational Definition of Backward Groups in India. Indian Journal of Agricultural Economics 13: 33–45.

1962.　Changing Status of Scheduled Castes. Economic Weekly 14: 1853–54.

Ghurye, G. S.
1959.　Caste and Race in India. 5th ed. Bombay: Popular Prakashan.
[Much newspaper material on untouchability.]

Gough, Kathleen E.
1963.　Indian Nationalism and Ethnic Freedom. In The Concept of Freedom in Anthropology. Edited by David Bidney. The Hague: Mouton.

Gould, Harold
1960.　Castes, Outcastes and the Sociology of Stratification. International Journal of Comparative Sociology 1: 220–38.

Government of India
1968.　Encyclopedia of Social Work. 3 vols. New Delhi.
[Contains relevant biographies, legislation, lists of backward classes, etc.]

Harper, Edward B.
   1968a.   A Comparative Analysis of Caste: The United States and India.
      In *Structure and Change in Indian Society*. Edited by Milton
      Singer and Bernard S. Cohn. Chicago: Aldine

Indian Conference of Social Work.
   1955.   *Report of the Seminar on Casteism and Removal of Untoucha-*
      bility. (Held in Delhi, Sept. 26–Oct. 2, 1955.) Bombay.

Isaacs, Harold R.
   1965.   *India's Ex-Untouchables.* New York: John Day.
      [Perceptive interviews with educated, urbanized Untouchables.]

Lambert, R. D.
   1958.   Untouchability as a Social Problem: Theory and Research. *Socio-*
      logical Bulletin (Bombay) VII: 55–61.

Lederle, M. B, (S.J.)
   1964.   The Untouchable's Claim to Human Dignity. *Journal of the Uni-*
      versity of Poona, Humanities Section, 19: 67–76.

Lohia, Rammanohar
   1964.   *The Caste System.* Hyderabad; Navahind.

Mahar, Pauline Moller
   1958.   Changing Caste Ideology in a North Indian Village. *Journal of*
      Social Issues 14: 51–65.

Mason, Philip
   1970.   *Patterns of Dominance.* London: Oxford University Press.

Mehra, D. S. and I. J. Kundra
   1966.   A Study of the Scheduled Castes and Scheduled Tribes' Working
      Force in India. *AICC Economic Review* 18 (Nos. 391 and 392):
      31–36, 39–41.

Mehta, Subhash Chandra
   1963.   Persistence of the Caste System: Vested Interest in Backwardness.
      Quest 36 (Jan.): 20–27.

Nagolkar, V. S.
   1969.   Removal of Untouchability — Goals and Attainments. *Indian*
      Journal of Social Work 30: 189–201.

Nanavathy, M. C.
   1955.   Seminar on Casteism and Removal of Untouchability: a Review.
      Indian Journal of Adult Education 16 (4): 41–50.

Natarajan, S.
   1962.   *A Century of Social Reform in India.* 2nd ed. Bombay: Asia
      Publishing House.

Oommen, T. K.
   1968.   Strategy for Special Change: A Study of Untouchability. *Eco-*
      nomic and Political Weekly III (June 22, 1968): 933–36.

   1969.   Strategy for Social Change: A Reply. *Economic and Political*
      Weekly IV (Jan. 25, 1969): 266.

Panchbhai, S. C.
1967.   The Levels of Regional and National Identification and Inter-
         group Relations Among Harijans and Adivasis. *Indian Anthro-
         pological Society Journal* 2: 75–84.

Paruj Sasanka Sekhar
1961.   Untouchability in the Early Indian Society. *Journal of Indian
         History* 39 (April): 1–11.

Parvathamma, C.
1968.   The Case for Untouchables. *United Asia* 20: 279–286.

Passin, Herbert
1955.   Untouchability in the Far East. *Monumenta Nipponica* 11 (3):
         27–47. [Untouchability in India compared to similar institutions
         in Japan, Korea, Tibet.]

Phillips, W. S.
1967.   Social Distance. *Eastern Anthropologist* 20: 177–96. [A study of
         the attitudes of the upper castes toward the lower castes.]

Radhakrishnan, N.
1965.   Units of Social, Economic and Educational Backwardness: Caste
         and Individual. *Indian Law Institute Journal* 7: 262–272.

Ram, Chandrika
1951.   *Plan for Harijans and Other Backward Classes.* (Foreword by
         N. V. Gadgil.) New Delhi: Bharatiya Depressed Classes League.

Ram, Pars
1955.   *A UNESCO Study of Social Tension in Aligarh, 1950–51.* Ahme-
         dabad: New Order Book Co. [See especially Chapter X, Attitudes
         of Harijans.]

Ramu, G. N.
1968.   Untouchability in Rural Areas. *Indian Journal of Social Work*
         29: 147–155.

Rao, P. Kodanda and Mary Campbell Rao
1951.   Critique of Group Prejudice with Special Reference to Harijans.
         In *Group Prejudices in India: a Symposium.* Edited by Sir Manilal
         Balabhai Nanavati and C. N. Vakil. Bombay: Vora.

Rath, R. and N. C. Sircar
1960.   The Cognitive Background of Six Hindu Caste Groups Regarding
         the Low Caste Untouchables. *Journal of Social Psychology* 51:
         295–306.

DeReuck, Anthony and Julie Knight
1967.   *Caste and Race: Comparative Approaches.* London: J. and A.
         Churchill Ltd.
         [Includes comparisons of pariahs in Japan and India.]

Rudolph, Lloyd I. and Susanne Hoeber Rudolph
1967.   Untouchability: The Test of Fellow Feeling. In *The Modernity
         of Tradition: Political Development In India.* Chicago: University
         of Chicago.

Santhanam, K.
  1949.   *The Fight Against Untouchability.* New Delhi: The Hindustan Times.

Sharma, R. S.
  1958.   *Sudras in Ancient India: a Survey of the Position of the Lower Orders down to circa A.D. 500.* Delhi: Motilal Banarsidass.

Shrikant, L. M.
  1964.   Education of the Backward Classes. In *The Indian Year Book of Education 1964. Second Year Book: Elementary Education.* New Delhi: National Council of Educational Research and Training, 173–94.

Shukla, S.
  1968.   Strategy for Social Change: A Comment. *Economic and Political Weekly* III (Dec. 14, 1968): 1918.

Silverberg, James (ed.)
  1968.   *Social Mobility in the Caste System in India.* The Hague: Comparative Studies in Society and History, Supplement 3. Mouton. [Many references to the mobility of Untouchables.]

Singh, Hari
  1959.   Scheduled Castes and Tribes in India. *New Age* VIII (6): 31–46.

Srinivas, M. N. and A. Béteille
  1965.   The "Untouchables" of India. *Scientific American* 213 (December): 13–17.

Subramanya Menon, K. P.
  1961.   *The Shame of Free India: A Study of the Social and Economic Disabilities of Scheduled Castes and Scheduled Tribes.* New Delhi. [pamphlet]

Thakkar, K.K.
  1956.   The Problem of Casteism and Untouchability. *Indian Journal of Social Work* XVII: 44–49.

Tripathi, B. D.
  1967.   On Minimising Social Distance Existing Between the Upper Castes and Harijans. *Interdiscipline* 4: 316–321.

University Education Commission
  1949.   Report of the University Education Commission. Vol. I. Simla: Government of India Press. [Contains development of education for Untouchables.]

Venkatraman, S. R.
  1952.   *Untouchables Liberation Movement.* Madras.
  1956.   Review of Seminar on Casteism and Removal of Untouchability. *Indian Journal of Social Work* XVI: 305–09.

Studies of Specific Castes

Balahi (Nimar Balahis of the Central Provinces)

Fuchs, Stephen
  1950. *The Children of Hari.* Vienna: V. Herold, 1950; New York: F. A. Praeger, 1951.

Bauri

Sarkar, R. M.
  1964. The Religious Activities of the Bauris and their Modern Trends. *Vanyajati* XII: 32–40.

  1966. Bahubir Sammelan, a Case of Social Mobility Movement. *Eastern Anthropologist* XIX: 225–229.

Shasmal, Kartick Chandra
  1967. Economic Conditions of Bauris of West Bengal. *Khadi Gramdyog* 13: 402–05.

  1967. Divorce and Its Causes among the Bauris of West Bengal. *Bulletin of the Cultural Research Institute* 6: 73–77.

Bhangi [Also known as Cuhra or Mehter.]

Fuchs, Stephen
  1951. The Scavengers of the Nimar District in Madhya Pradesh. *Journal of the Bombay Branch of the Royal Asiatic Society* 27: 86–98.

Mahar, Pauline Moller
  1960. Changing Religious Practices of an Untouchable Caste. *Economic Development and Cultural Change* VIII: 279—87.

Ratan, Ram
  1955. A Study in Magic and Medicine: Treatment by Poison-Sucking Among The Bhangis. *Vanyajati* III: 67–72.

  1961. The Changing Religion of the Bhangis of Delhi: a Case of Sanskritisation. In *Aspects of Religion in Indian Society.* Edited by L. P. Vidyarthi. Meerut: Kedar Nath Ram Nath.

Thaliath, Joseph
  1961. Notes on the Scavenger Caste of Northern Madhya Pradesh, India. *Anthropos* 56: 789–817.

Chamar

Bhatt, G. S.
  1954. The Chamar of Lucknow. *Eastern Anthropologist* VIII: 27–41.

  1961. Trends and Measures of Status Mobility among Chamars of Dehradun. *Eastern Anthropologist* 14: 229–41.

  1962. Urban Impact and the Trends of Intra-caste Solidarity and Dissociability as Measures of Status Mobility among the Chamar. *Journal of Social Research* 5: 97-108.

Briggs, George Weston
    1920.   *The Chamars*. London: H. Milford for Oxford University Press. Calcutta: Association Press.

Cohn, Bernard S.
    1954.   *The Camars of Senapur:* A Study of the Changing Status of a Depressed Caste. Ph.D. Dissertation, Department of Sociology and Anthropology. Cornell University. (Ann Arbor: University of Michigan Microfilms.)

    1955.   The Changing Status of a Depressed Caste. In *Village India: Studies in the Little Community*. Edited by McKim Marriott. Chicago: University of Chicago Press. Also Asia Publishing House, Bombay, 1961.

    1959.   Changing Traditions of a Low Caste. In *Traditional India: Structure and Change*. Edited by Milton B. Singer. Philadelphia: American Folklore Society.

    1961.   Chamar Family in a North Indian Village: A Structural Contingent. *Economic Weekly* XIII: 1051–55.

Crooke, W.
    1903.   Chamar. In *Census of India, 1901*. Vol. I. *India: Ethnographic Appendices*. Edited by H. H. Risley. Calcutta: Superintendent of Government Printing: 167–175.

Fuchs, Stephen
    1965.   The Satnami Movement of the Chamars. In *Rebellious Prophets*. Bombay, London: Asia Publishing House.

Goyal, Prem Prakash
    1961.   An Inquiry into the Impact of Urbanism on the Magico-Religious Beliefs and Practices of Raidas Chamars of Dehra Dun. Master's Thesis, Department of Anthropology, D.A.V. College, Dehra Dun.

Lynch, Owen M.
    1967.   Rural Cities in India: Continuities and Discontinuities. In *India and Ceylon: Unity and Diversity*. Edited by Philip Mason. London: Oxford University Press.

    1968.   The Politics of Untouchability: A Case from Agra, India. In *Structure and Change in Indian Society*. Edited by Milton Singer and Bernard S. Cohn. Chicago: Aldine.

    1969.   *The Politics of Untouchability: Social Mobility and Social Change in a City of India*. New York: Columbia University Press.

Sarana, Gopala
    1955.   Kinship among the Chamars of Dhanaura. *Agra University Journal of Research*, (Letters) III: 148–57.

Cuhra [*see Bhangi*]

Dhed

Stevenson, Mrs. Sinclair (Margaret)
  1930.   *Without the Pale: The Life Story of an Outcaste.* Calcutta: Association Press and Humphrey Milford for Oxford University Press. [The Dheds of Gujarat, with some description of other untouchable castes.]

Dom

Briggs, George Weston
  1916.   *The Doms and Their Relations.* Mysore: Wesley Press, reprint, 1953.

Clarke, C. R.
  1903.   *The Outcastes, Being a Brief Account of the Magahiya Doms.* Calcutta.

Das, Harish Chandra
  1963.   The Economic Life of the Doms of Barbaria (A Village in North Balasore). *Orissa Historical Research Journal* XI: 260–65.

Irava (Also spelled Iluvan, Ilava, Ezhava. See also *Tiya.* A Depressed Class in the Census of 1931, but later not listed as a Scheduled Caste.)

Aiyappan, A.
  1944.   *Iravas and Culture Change.* Madras: Supt. Government Press. Initially published as Madras Museum Bulletin, New Series, General Section, Vol. V, No. 1, 4. 1943.

  1965.   *Social Revolution in a Kerala Village.* Bombay: Asia Publishing House.

Census of India, 1931

  1932.   Swami Narayana and His Movement. In Appendix to Chapter XI, Vol. XXVIII, *Travancore,* Part I, *Report:* 353–54. Trivandrum: Supt. Government Press.

  1933.   Reform Among Iluvans. In Chapter XII, Vol. XXI, *Cochin,* Part I, *Report:* 260–61. Ernakulum: Supt. Cochin Government Press.

Banu, B. Vijaya and K. C. Malhatra
  1967.   The a-b Ridge Count in Palmar Detmatoglyphics of the Izhavas of Kerala. *Man in India* 47: 149–157.

Fuchs, Stephen
  1965.   Among the Ezhavas. In *Rebellious Prophets.* Bombay, London: Asia Publishing House.

Natarapan, P.
  n.d.   *The Word of the Guru.* Kaggalipura, Bangalore South, Mysore State: Gurukula Publishing House.

Madiga

Fishman, Alvin Texas
1941.   *Culture Change and Underprivileged: A Study of 'Madigas in South India under Christian Guidance.* Madras: The Christian Literature Society for India.

Rauschenbusch-Clough, Emma
1899.   *While Sewing Sandals. Tales of a Telugu Pariah Tribe.* London: Hodder and Stoughton.

Mahar (See also sections on Buddhism and Ambedkar and His Movement.)

Mann, Harold H.
1916.   The "Mahars" of a Deccan Village (Saswad). *Social Service Quarterly* (Bombay), II (1): 1–8. Reprinted in Harold H. Mann. *The Social Framework of Agriculture.* Edited by Daniel Thorner. Bombay: Vora.

Miller, Robert J.
1966.   Button, Button. . . . . Great Tradition, Little Tradition, Whose Tradition? *Anthropological Quarterly* 39: 26–42.

Robertson, Alexander
1938.   *The Mahar Folk.* Calcutta: Y.M.C.A. and Oxford University Press.

Thorat, Major General S. P. P.
1954.   *The Regimental History of the Mahar MG Regiment.* Dehra Dun: The Army Press.

Mala

Nicholson, Sydney
1926.   Social Organization of the Malas — an Outcaste Indian People. *Journal of the Royal Anthropological Institute of Great Britain and Ireland,* 56: 91–103.

Mazbhi Sikhs

Brander, Lt.-Col. H. R.
1906.   *32nd Sikh Pioneers: Regimental History.* Calcutta: Thacker & Spink.

MacMunn, Lt.-Gen. Sir George
1935.   *The History of the Sikh Pioneers.* London: Sampson Low, Marston.

Meghwal

Mehta, B. H.
1937.   *The Social and Economic Conditions of the Meghwal Untouchables in Bombay City.* Ph.D. Dissertation in Sociology. University of Bombay.

Namasudra

Census of India, 1931.
  1933.   Namasudra. In Appendix III to Chapter XII, Vol. V, *Bengal and
              Sikkim,* Part I, *Report,* Calcutta: Central Publishing Branch,
              528–29.

Nayadis

Aiyappan, A.
  1937.   *Social and Physical Anthropology of the Nayadis of Malabar.*
              Madras: Madras Museum Publication.

Rajbansi (Not considered a Depressed Class by the Government in 1931, but
              listed as Scheduled Caste today.)

Mitra, Sarat Chandra. Notes on the Godling Mahakala Worshipped by the
              Rajbansis of the Jalpaiguri District in Northern Bengal *and* A
              Note on the Rain God of the Rajbansis of the Jalpaiguri District
              in Northern Bengal. *Journal of the Anthropological Society of
              Bengal.* 15: 425–29 and 438–42.

Mukherjee, Bhabananda
  1963.   Caste-Ranking among Rajbanshis in North Bengal. In *Anthropol-
              ogy on the March.* Edited by Bala Ratnam. Madras: The Book
              Centre.

Tiya (See Irava)

Bhadra, Samanta.
  1963.   Recent Race Mixture in Kerala: Some Social Aspects. In *Anthro-
              pology on the March.* Edited by Bala Ratnam. Madras: The Book
              Centre.

Farquhar, J. N.
  1917.   The Tiyas. In *Modern Religious Movements in India.* London,
              New York: Macmillan. (Reprinted by Munshiram Manoharlal,
              1967, Delhi.)

Rao, M. J. A.
  1963.   Sanskritization among the Tiyas of North Malabar. In *Anthro-
              pology on the March.* Edited by Bala Ratnam. Madras: The Book
              Centre.

Surveys of Tribes and Castes

Anantha Krishna Iyer, L.
  1909–   *The Cochin Tribes and Castes.* 2 vols. Madras: Published for the
  1912.   Government of Cochin by Higginbotham and Co.; London:
              Luzac and Co.

  1928–   *The Mysore Tribes and Castes.* 4 vols. and appendix. Mysore:
  1936.   Published under the auspices of the Mysore University.

Crooke, William
    1906.   *The Tribes and Castes of the North-Western Provinces and Oudh.*
             4 vols. Calcutta: Office of the Supt. of Government Printing.

Enthoven, Reginald Edward
    1920–   *The Tribes and Castes of Bombay.* 3 vols. Bombay: Govern-
    1922.   ment Central Press.

Krishna Iyer, L. A.
    1937–   *The Travancore Tribes and Castes.* 3 vols. Trivandrum: Printed
    1941.   by the Supt. of Government Press.

Risley, Herbert Hope
    1891.   *The Tribes and Castes of Bengal.* 4 vols. Calcutta: Bengal Secre-
             tariat Press.

    1903.   *Ethnographic Appendices.* Calcutta: Supt. of Government Print-
             ing.

Rose, Horace Arthur
    1911–   *A Glossary of the Tribes and Castes of the Punjab and North-West*
    1919.   *Frontier Provinces,* based on the census report for the Punjab,
             1883, by the late Sir Denzil Ibbetson and the census report for
             the Punjab, 1892, by Sir Edmond Maclagan and compiled by
             H. A. Rose. 3 vols. Lahore: Printed by the Supt. of Government
             Printing.

Russell, Robert Vane
    1916.   *The Tribes and Castes of the Central Provinces of India.* 4 vols.
             London: Macmillan.

Sherring, Matthew Atmore
    1872.   *Hindu Tribes and Castes as Represented in Benares.* 3 vols.
             Calcutta: Thacker, 1872–1881. London: Trubner, 1872.

Thurston, Edgar
    1909.   *Castes and Tribes of Southern India.* 7 vols. Madras: Govern-
             ment Press.

Area Studies

Andhra

Census of India, 1961.
    1964.   *Special Tables for Scheduled Castes and Scheduled Tribes.* Vol.
             II, *Andhra Pradesh,* Part V-A. Delhi: Manager of Publications.

Reddy, N. (Reddi)
    1950.   Community Conflict among the Depressed Castes of Andhra.
             Man in India 30 (Oct.–Dec.): 1–12.

    1954.   *Transition in Caste Structure in Andhra Desh with Particular*
             Reference to Depressed Classes. Ph.D. Dissertation. University
             of Lucknow.

Assam

Census of India, 1931.
1932.   The Depressed and Backward Classes of Assam. In Appendix I
           to Chapter XII, Vol. III, *Assam,* Part I, *Report:* Shillong: Supt.
           Assam Government Press, 209–27.
Census of India, 1961.
1964.   *Scheduled Tribes and Scheduled Castes:* Reprints from Old Census
           Reports and Special Tables. Vol. III, *Assam,* Part V-A. Delhi:
           Manager of Publications.

Bengal

Census of India, 1931.
1933.   The Depressed Classes. In Appendix I, Vol. V, *Bengal and Sikkim,*
           Part I, *Report:* Calcutta: Central Publishing Branch, 494–513.
Census of India, 1961.
1966.   Tables on Scheduled Castes. Vol. XVI, *West Bengal and Sikkim,*
           Part V-A(i). Delhi: Manager of Publications.
Das, Amal Kumar, Bidyut Kumar Roy Chowdhury and Manis Kumar Raha
1966.   *Handbook on Scheduled Castes and Scheduled Tribes of West
           Bengal.* Bulletin of the Cultural Research Institute, special series
           no. 8. Calcutta: Tribal Welfare Department, Government of
           West Bengal.
Mitra, Asok
1953.   *The Tribes and Castes of West Bengal.* West Bengal Government
           Press.
Roy Burman, B. K.
1956.   A Note on the Scheduled Castes and Scheduled Tribes of West
           Bengal. *Vanyajati* 4: 60–73.
Roychowdhuri, B. K. and B. Bhattacharya
1967.   A Brief Record on Stagnation of Scheduled Tribes and Scheduled
           Caste Students. *Bulletin of the Cultural Research Institute* 6:
           86–87.
Simha, Hari Mohan
1902.   Notes on Koch, Poliya, Rajvamsi in Dinajpur. *Journal of the
           Asiatic Society of Bengal* 12 (Part 3): 20–25.
West Bengal State, Government of. Tribal Welfare Department.
1957.   *Backward Classes Welfare in West Bengal, 1952–56.* Calcutta.

Bihar

Census of India, 1931.
1933.   The Depressed Classes. In Appendix III, Vol. VII, *Bihar &
           Orissa.* Part I, *Report:* Patna: Supt. of Government Printing, Bihar
           and Orissa, 283–87.
Census of India, 1961.
1965.   *Special Tables for Scheduled Castes and Scheduled Tribes.* Vol.
           IV, *Bihar,* Part V-A. Bihar: Supt. of Census Operations.

Bombay Province (See Maharashtra)

Central Provinces and Central India Agency. (*See also* Madhya Pradesh)

Census of India, 1931.
1933.   The Depressed Classes. In Appendix III, Vol. XX, *Central India Agency*. Part I, *Report:* Calcutta: Government of India, Central Publication Branch, 280–82.

1933.   The Depressed Classes of the Central Provinces and Berar. In Appendix II of Vol. XII, *Central Provinces and Berar*, Part I, *Report*. Nagpur: Government Printing, Central Provinces, 386–96.

Hira Lal.
1923.   Caste Impurity in the Central Provinces. *Man in India*, 3: 65–73.

Cochin (See Kerala)

Delhi

Census of India, 1961.
n.d.   *Tables on Scheduled Castes and Scheduled Tribes.* Vol. XIX. *Delhi*, Part V-A. Delhi: Supt. of Census Operations.

Dodhra and Nagar Haveli

Census of India, 1961.
1967.   Special Tables for Scheduled Castes and Scheduled Tribes. In Vol. XVIII, *Dodhra and Nagar Haveli*, Part V: 187–214. Supt. of Census Operations, Dodhra and Nagar Haveli.

Gujarat

Census of India, 1961.
1964.   *Tables on Scheduled Castes and Scheduled Tribes.* Vol. V, *Gujarat*, Part V-A. Delhi: Manager of Publications.

Gujarat State, Government of. Social Welfare Dept. Backward Class Wing. *Annual Report.*

Oza, M. B.
1958.   Survey of the Economic Conditions and State of Health and Nutrition of Harijan Families of Baroda (abstract). *Journal of the Gujarat Research Society,* 20: M15.

Pandya, B. V.
1957.   Occupational Pattern of Scheduled Castes in Ahmedabad District. *Journal of the Gujarat Research Society* 19: 112–24.

1959.   *Striving for Economic Equality.* Bombay: Popular Book Depot.

1959.   Trends and Patterns of Indebtedness among Harijans. *Journal of the Gujarat Research Society,* 21: 99–115.

Patil, Gajanan M.
1958.   Harijans in Mehesana District (abstract). *Journal of Gujarat Research Society,* 20: S16.

Vyas, K. B.
   1938.   *The Untouchables of Kathiawar.* M.A. Thesis in Sociology. Uni-
            versity of Bombay.

Himachal Pradesh

Census of India, 1961
   1967.   *Report on Scheduled Castes and Scheduled Tribes: A Study of
            Gaddi Scheduled Tribe and Affiliated Castes.* (By William H.
            Newell.) Vol. XX, *Himachal Pradesh,* Part V-B. Delhi: Manager
            of Publications.

   1965.   *Special Tables of Scheduled Castes and Scheduled Tribes (Includ-
            ing Reprints)*: Vol. XX, *Himachal Pradesh,* Part V-A. Supt. of
            Census Operations, Himachal Pradesh.

Hyderabad

Census of India, 1931
   1933.   The Depressed Classes. In Vol. XXIII, *The Nizam's Dominions
            (Hyderabad State),* Part I, *Report.* Hyderabad: Government
            Central Press, 255–60.

Grigson, Wilfred Vernon
   1947.   *The Challenge of Backwardness:* Some Notes and Papers on
            Tribal and Depressed Classes Policy with Special Reference to
            Hyderabad State. Hyderabad: Government Publications Press.

Kerala (Including former Cochin and Travancore States)

Aiyappan, A.
   1965.   *Social Revolution in a Kerala Village: A Study in Cultural Change.*
            New York: Asia Publishing House.

Census of India, 1931.
   1932.   The Depressed and Backward Classes. In Appendix II, Vol.
            XXVII, *Travancore,* Part I, *Report.* Trivandrum: Supt. of Gov-
            ernment Press 430–41.

   1933.   Depressed Classes. In Appendix II, Vol. XXI, *Cochin,* Part I,
            Report. Ernakulum: Supt. of Cochin Government Press: 289–99.

Crowley, Eileen
   1941.   *Champion of the Outcaste: Lester Hooper of Travancore.* Lon-
            don: Highway Press.

Kerala State, Government of. Harijan Welfare Department.
            Annual Administration Report

Mateer, Rev. Samuel
   1884.   The Pariah Caste in Travancore. *Journal of the Royal Asiatic
            Society of Great Britain and Ireland* 16: 180–95.

Madhya Pradesh (See Central Provinces)

Census of India, 1961
  1965.   *Special Tables for Scheduled Castes.* Vol. VIII, *Madhya Pradesh,*
            Part V-A(i). Supt. of Census Operations, Madhya Pradesh.

Jayakar, Samuel.
  1952.   *Rural Sweepers in the City.* Mysore: Wesley Press and Pub-
            lishing House. [Study of Christian Sweepers in Jabalpur.]

Thaliath, Joseph
  1961.   Notes on the Scavenger Caste of Northern Madhya Pradesh,
            India. *Anthropos* 56: 789–817.

Vishwakarma, S. R.
  1963.   Opportunities for non-Farm Employment and Economic Progress
            of a Depressed Caste: A Case Study. *AICC Economic Review,* XV
            (July 15), 25–26. [Village near Gwalior.]

Madras and General Works on South India

Aiyappan, A.
  1948.   *Report on the Socio-Economic Conditions of the Tribes and
            Backward Castes of Madras Province.* Madras.

Census of India, 1931
  1932.   Depressed Classes. In Chapter XII, Vol. XIV, *Madras,* Part I,
            Report. Calcutta: Government of India Central Publishing Branch:
            342–47.

Census of India, 1961
  1964.   *Scheduled Castes and Tribes (Report and Tables).* Vol. IX,
            Madras, Part V-A(i). Madras: Supt. of Census Operations.

  1965.   *Scheduled Castes and Tribes (Tables).* Vol. IX, *Madras,* Part V-A
            (ii). Madras: Supt. of Census Operations.

Dolbeer, Martin Luther
  1929.   *The Movement for the Emancipation of Untouchable Classes in
            South India.* Master's Thesis. University of Chicago.

James, E. E.
  1930.   Outcaste Progress in South India. *Asiatic Review,* XXVI: 716–24.

Kumaraswami, T. J.
  1923.   The Adi-Dravidas of Madras. *Man in India,* 3: 59–64.

Madras State, Government of. Directorate of Information and Publicity.
  1959.   *Grant of Concessions to Harijans.* Madras.

Madras State, Government of. Harijan Welfare Department. *Annual Admin-
          istration Report.*

Moffatt, Michael
  1969.   *Untouchables in a Region of South India.* M.A. thesis in Anthropology. University of Chicago.

Murti, S.
  1927.   *On Behalf of the Oppressed: An Inquiry into the Past and Present Condition of the Depressed Classes in Southern India.* Ambur. [pamphlet]

Pandian, T. B.
  1899.   *Slaves of the Soil in Southern India.* Bound together with *Pandian and the Pariah.* Amsterdam, Holland.
            [Probably the earliest book on untouchability. Christian viewpoint.]

Rama Naidu, M. B.
  1921.   *The Adi Dravida: His Cult, Past and Present.* Chidambaram.
            [Presidential Address at the Adi Dravida Conference held at Chidambaram, April 21, 1921.]

Richards, F. J.
  1932.   From Pariah to Brahman in South India. *Man* 32 (17): 21.
            [Summary of a communication.]

Sivertsen, Dagfinn
  1963.   *When Caste Barriers Fall.* Oslo: Universietetsforlaget.

Maharashtra (including Bombay Province)

Bhagat, M. G.
  1935.   The Untouchable Classes of Maharashtra. *Journal of the University of Bombay,* IV (Part I) July. (Reprinted separately.)
  1938.   The Untouchable Classes of the Janjira State (Konkan). *Journal of the University of Bombay,* VII: 131–54.

Bhatt, Anil
  1963.   Caste and Politics in Akola. *Economic Weekly,* XV: 1441–46.

Bhatt, Vanamrai A.
  1941.   *The Harijans of Maharashtra.* Delhi: All India Harijan Sevak Sangh. [With a lengthy note by V. N. Barve.]

Bombay Presidency. Depressed Classes and Aboriginal Tribes Committee.
  1930.   *Report of the Depressed Classes and Aboriginal Tribes Committee.* (Chairman: O. H. B. Starte.) Bombay: Government Central Press. [A record of current practice and recommendations for governmental reform.]

Bombay State, Government of.
  1949.   *Privileges Provided by Bombay Government for the Backward Classes.* 2nd ed., revised to 30th Sept., 1949. [There is also a later edition, corrected to 31st March, 1954.]

Bombay State, Government of. Backward Class Department. *Annual Administration Reports.* Poona or Bombay.

Census of India, 1921.
    1922.   *Bombay Presidency.* Vol. VIII, Part II (Tables). Bombay: Government Central Press.

Census of India, 1931.
    1933.   The Depressed Classes. In Section V of Vol. VIII, *Bombay Province,* Part I, *General Report:* Bombay: Government Central Press, 383–84.

Census of India, 1961.
    1964.   *Scheduled Castes and Scheduled Tribes in Maharashtra — Tables.* Vol. X. *Maharashtra.* Part V-A. Delhi: Manager of Publications.

Kulkarni, M. G.
    1962.   Report on the Survey to Assess the Program for the Removal of Untouchability in Maharashtra State. Part I: Buldana. Part II: Nasik. Poona: Gokhale Institute of Politics and Economics. [Manuscript]

Maharashtra State, Government of. Social Welfare Department. Backward Class Wing.
    Annual Administration Report on the Welfare of Backward Classes. Bombay: Government Printing.

Mann, Harold H.
    1912.   The Untouchable Classes of an Indian City. *Sociological Review* (London) V: 42–55. Reprinted in Harold H. Mann, *The Social Framework of Agriculture.* Edited by Daniel Thorner. Bombay: Vora, 1967.

    1916.   The Housing of the Untouchable Classes in an Indian City (Poona). *Social Service Quarterly* (Bombay) I (3): 1–10. Reprinted in Harold H. Mann, *The Social Framework of Agriculture.* Edited by Daniel Thorner. Bombay: Vora, 1967, 192–203.

Pradhan, G. R.
    1938.   *Untouchable Workers of Bombay City.* Foreword by B. R. Ambedkar. Bombay: Karnatak Publishing House.

Shinde, V. R.
    1912.   The Depressed Class Mission. *The Theistic Directory.* Bombay: Depressed Class Mission, 61–73.

Manipur

Census of India, 1961.
    n.d.   *Tables on Scheduled Castes and Scheduled Tribes.* Vol. XXII, *Manipur.* Part V. Manipur: Supt. of Census Operations.

Mysore

Census of India, 1931.
    1932.   Depressed Classes. In Chapter XII, Vol. XXV, *Mysore.* Part I, *Report.* Bangalore: Government Press: 327–29.

Census of India, 1961.
1966.   *Special Tables on Scheduled Castes and Scheduled Tribes.* Vol.
           XI. *Mysore.* Part V-A. Delhi: Manager of Publications.

Epstein, Scarlett.
1959.   Industrial Employment for Landless Labourers Only. *Economic
           Weekly* XI: 967–72.

Harper, Edward B.
1968b.   Social Consequences of an "Unsuccessful" Low Caste Movement.
           In *Social Mobility in the Caste System in India: An Inter-disci-
           plinary Symposium.* Edited by James Silverberg. Comparative
           Studies in Society and History Supplement III. The Hague:
           Mouton.

Kadetotad, N. K.
1966.   Caste Hierarchy among Untouchables of Dharwar. *Eastern An-
           thropologist,* 19: 205–13.
1968.   The Untouchables of Dharwar and Their Festivals. *Journal of
           Karantak University (Dharwar);* Social Sciences 4: 143–151.

Kakade, Raghunath Govind
1949.   *Depressed Classes of South Kanara: A Socio-Economic Survey.*
           Poona: Servants of India Society.

Mysore State, Government of.
           Welfare of Backward Classes in Mysore State. Bulletin. Published
           quarterly. Bangalore: Director of Printing, Government Press.

Department of Planning, Housing and Social Welfare.
1961.   *The Welfare of Scheduled Castes in Mysore State.* Bangalore.

General Administration Department.
1962.   *Scheduled Castes and Scheduled Tribes Appointments Commit-
           tee Report.* Mercara.

Office of the Commissioner for Depressed Classes.
1957.   *Mysore State Depressed Classes Seminar: Summary and Main
           Recommendations.* [pamphlet]

Scheduled Castes and Scheduled Tribes Appointments Committee, 1960.
1962.   *Report.* Bangalore: General Administration Department (Chair-
           man: B. Birappa.)

Woodruffe, Gertrude M.
1959.   *An Adidravida Settlement in Bangalore, India: A Case Study of
           Urbanization.* Ph.D. Dissertation, Radcliffe College.

Orissa

Bailey, F. G.
1957.   The Boad Outcastes. In *Caste and the Economic Frontier.* Man-
           chester: Manchester University Press.

1960.   *Tribe, Caste and Nation.* Manchester: Manchester University
         Press. [Extensive description and comparison of tribal and Hindu
         Untouchables.]

Census of India, 1961.
    1965.   *Tables on Scheduled Castes and Scheduled Tribes.* Vol. XII,
             Orissa. Part V-A. Delhi: Manager of Publications.

Orissa, State Government of. Tribal and Rural Welfare Department.
    1958.   *Welfare of Backward Classes in Orissa.* Bhubaneswar. [This
             department also issues an *Annual Report.*]

Pondicherry State

Census of India, 1961.
    1964.   *Scheduled Castes — Tables.* Vol. XXV, *Pondicherry State.* Part
             III-C. Superintendent of Census Operations, Madras and Pon-
             dicherry.

Punjab

Census of India, 1931.
    1933.   Ad-Dharmi. Section 4, Chapter XI, Depressed Classes. Appendix
             III, Vol. XVII, *Punjab,* Part I, *Report.* Lahore: 310–11, 373–74.

Census of India, 1961.
    1965.   *Special Tables on Scheduled Castes and Scheduled Tribes.* Vol.
             XIII, *Punjab.* Part V-A. Supt. of Census Operations, Punjab.

Punjab State, Government of. Evaluation Committee on Welfare.
    1966.   *Report: Regarding the Welfare of Scheduled Castes. Backward
             Classes and Denotified Tribes in Punjab State* (for the period
             commencing from 15 August, 1947. Chandigarh. (Brish Bhan,
             Chairman).

Public Relations Department.
    1961.   *Harijan Welfare in Punjab.* Chandigarh.
Welfare Department. *Annual Report on the Working of the Welfare Depart-
         ment.*

Rajasthan

Census of India, 1961.
    1965.   *Special Tables for Scheduled Castes and Scheduled Tribes.* Vol.
             XIV, *Rajasthan.* Part V-A. Supt. of Census Operations, Rajasthan.

Chauhan, B. R.
    1955.   Recent Trends among Depressed Classes in Rajasthan. *Agra
             University Journal of Research,* (Letters), 3: 158–61.

Sikkim (See Bengal)

Travancore (See Kerala)

Tripura

Census of India, 1961.
1967. *Special Tables for Scheduled Castes and Scheduled Tribes.* Vol. XXVI, *Tripura.* Part V-A. Supt. of Census Operations, Tripura.

Uttar Pradesh

Anonymous
1957. Harijans of Uttar Pradesh. *Eastern Economist* 29:19–20.

Berreman, Gerald D.
1963. *Hindus of the Himalayas.* Berkeley: University of California Press. [Provides much information on the Pahari Dom castes.]

Bose, Anil Baran
1957. *Economic and Living Conditions of Harijans in Uttar Pradesh.* J. K. Institute Monograph, 5. Lucknow: J. K. Institute of Sociology and Human Relations, Lucknow University.

Census of India, 1921.
1923. The Depressed Classes of the Kumaun Hills. In Appendix C, Vol. XVI, *United Provinces of Agra and Oudh.* Part I, *Report:* Allahabad: Supt. of Government Press, 21–22.

Census of India, 1931.
1933. Notes on (I) Untouchables, (II) Depressed Classes, and (III) Backward Classes. In Appendix No. 2. Vol. XVIII, *United Provinces of Agra and Oudh.* Part I, *Report:* Allahabad: Supt. of Printing and Stationery, U. P., 626–38.

Census of India, 1961.
1965. *Special Tables for Scheduled Castes.* Vol. XV, *Uttar Pradesh.* Part V-A (i) and (ii). Delhi: Manager of Publications.

Gupta, S. C. and B. G. Prasad
1964. Socio-Medical Survey of Sweepers and Their Families in Lucknow Municipal Corporation. *Indian Journal of Social Work,* XXIV: 289–96.

1965. Note on Living and Working Conditions of Sweeper Community in Lucknow. *Eastern Anthropologist,* XVIII: 177–83.

Harijan Sevak Sangh
1934. *Report of the Committee Appointed by the Cawnpore Harijan Sevak Sangh in May 1933 to make a Survey of the Social and Religious Disabilities, etc., of the Harijans of Cawnpore.* Cawnpore: Harijan Sevak Sangh, Cawnpore Branch.

Kashi Vidyapitha
1955. *The Scheduled Castes in Eastern Uttar Pradesh; a Sample Survey.* Lucknow: The Director, Harijan Welfare Department.

Kolenda, Pauline Mahar
1964. Religious Anxiety and Hindu Fate. *Journal of Asian Studies* XXXIII: 71–81.

  455

Lucknow University. J. K. Institute of Sociology and Human Relations.
    1955.   *Survey of Living Conditions of Harijans in Uttar Pradesh: a
             Sample Survey.* Lucknow: Director, Harijan Welfare Depart-
             ment, U. P.

Mahar, Pauline M.
    1958.   Changing Caste Ideology in a North Indian Village. *Journal of
             Social Issues* XIV (4) : 51–65.

Neihoff, Arthur
    1959.   *Factory Workers in India.* Milwaukee, Wisconsin: Milwaukee
             Public Museum, Publications in Anthropology, No. 5. [Much
             material on untouchable industrial workers of Kanpur.]

Singh, K. K.
    1967.   *Patterns of Caste Tension.* London: Asia Publishing House.
             [Treats intercaste tensions in villages of Senapur and Borsar.]

Government Policy — Documents and Commentary.

Only all-India census reports and documents treating testimony and commentary on general policies are cited here. Census reports for provinces, and
similar documents are given in the preceding sections.

Pre-Independence

Barton, W. P.
    1937.   Indian Federation and the Untouchable. *Quarterly Review* (Lon-
             don), 268: 18–28.

Census of India, 1931.
    1933.   Exterior Castes. Appendix I in Vol. I, *India.* Part I, *Report:* 471–
             501. Delhi: Manager of Publications. (By J. H. Hutton.)

Coatman, John
    1933.   Reforms in India and the Depressed Classes. *Asiatic Review*
             (London), XXIX (97, January): 41–53. [Discussion of Coat-
             man's speech by James Crerar, Harold Mann, Maharajah of
             Burdwan, Arthur Blowers, Henry Lawrence, et. al., 54–70.]

Dushkin, Lelah
    1957.   The Policy of the Indian National Congress Toward the Depressed
             Classes: An Historical Study. Unpublished M.A. Thesis, Depart-
             ment of South Asian Studies, University of Pennsylvania.

Foot, Isaac
    1931.   The Round Table Conference, the Future, and the Depressed
             Classes. *Contemporary Review* 139: 282–90.

Great Britain. East India (Constitutional Reforms)
    1918.   *Addresses Presented in India to His Excellency the Viceroy and
             the Right Honourable, the Secretary of State for India.* London:
             H.M.S.O. Cmd. 9178. [Includes lists of the Depressed Classes and
             excerpts from their representations.]

Indian Statutory Commission (1928).
1929.   *Review of Growth of Education in British India* (Auxiliary Committee of Indian Statutory Commission. Chairman: Sir Philip Hartog.) London: H.M.S.O. Cmd. 3407. [See Chapter X: Education of the Depressed Classes, 217–28.]

Indian Statutory Commission (1928).
1929–   *Report of the Indian Statutory Commission* (Chairman: Lord
1930.   Simon.) 17 vols. London: H.M.S.O. Vol. I. *Survey.* Cmd. 3568. [Depressed Classes report, 37–41.] Vol. III. *Reports of the Committees appointed by the Provincial Legislative Councils to Cooperate with the Indian Statutory Commission.* Cmd. 3572. [Includes Report of Dr. B. R. Ambedkar as adjunct to Bombay Report.] Vols. XVI, XVII. *Selections from Memoranda and Oral Evidence by Non-Officials.* [Includes testimony from twenty Depressed Class groups or individuals.]

Indian Round Table Conference, 1st, London, 1930–31.
1931.   *Indian Round Table Conference, 12th November, 1930–19th January, 1931. Proceedings.* London: H.M.S.O. Cmd. 3778. [B. R. Ambedkar speaks on behalf of the Untouchables.]

Indian Round Table Conference, 2nd. London, 1931.
1932.   *Indian Round Table Conference, 7th September, 1931–1st December, 1931 Proceedings.* London: H.M.S.O. Cmd. 3997. [N. Srinivasan speaks on behalf of Untouchables.]

1932.   *Proceedings of the Federal Structure Committee and Minorities Committee.* London, H.M.S.O. [Controversy between B. R. Ambedkar and M. K. Gandhi.]

Indian Franchise Committee, 1932.
1932.   *Report of the Indian Franchise Committee, 1932.* (Chairman: Marquess of Lothian.) 5 vols. London: H.M.S.O. Vol. I. *Report.* Cmd. 4086. [Includes B. R. Ambedkar's note on the Depressed Classes, 210–20, and a chapter on the Depressed Classes, 112–30.] Vols. IV and V. *Selections from Memoranda Submitted by Individuals and Oral Evidence.* [Contains testimony of various Depressed Class groups.]

The Reforms Committee (Franchise, 1918).
1919.   *Evidence Taken Before the Reforms Committee.* (Chairman: Lord Southborough.) 2 vols. Calcutta: Government of India. [The earliest record of Depressed Classes representations on the idea of separate electorates.]

Stanton, H. U. Weitbrecht
1920.   The Untouchables of India and Their Enumeration. *Asiatic Review* 16: 171–84.

Post-Independence

Anonymous
1963.   Progress of the Backward. *Economic Weekly* XV: 1513–14.

Aryamane, R. V.
  1965.   Backward Classes in the Indian Constitution. *Political Scientist*
          II: 27–36.

Borale, P. T.
  1968.   *Segregation and Desegregation in India: A Socio-Legal Study.*
          Bombay: Manaktalas.

Census of India, 1951.
  1953.   *Papers, 1953, No. 4, Special Groups.* New Delhi.
  1960.   *Papers, 1960, No. 2, Scheduled Castes and Scheduled Tribes.*
          New Delhi.

Census of India, 1961.
  1966.   *Consolidated Statement Showing Scheduled Castes, Scheduled
          Tribes, Denotified Communities and Other Communities of Simi-
          lar Status in Different Statutes and Censuses Starting from 1921.*
          Vol. I, *India.* Parts V-B (ii) and (iii). New Delhi.

  1966.   *Special Tables for Scheduled Castes.* Vol. I, *India.* Part V-A (i).
          New Delhi.

Cohn, Bernard S.
  1959.   Some Notes on Law and Change in North India. *Economic
          Development and Cultural Change* VIII: 79–93.

Dushkin, Lelah
  1961.   The Backward Classes: Special Treatment Policy. *Economic
          Weekly* XIII: 1665–68, 1695–1705, 1729–38.

  1967.   Scheduled Caste Policy in India: History, Problems, Prospects.
          Asian Survey VII: 626–36.

Galanter, Marc.
  1961a. Caste Disabilities and Indian Federalism. *Journal of the Indian
          Law Institute* III: 3: 205–34.

  1961b. Equality and "Protective Discrimination" in India. *Rutgers Law
          Review* XVI: 42–74.

  1961c. "Protective Discrimination" for Backward Classes in India. *Journal
          of the Indian Law Institute* 3: 39–69.

  1962.   The Problem of Group Membership: Some Reflections on the
          Judicial View of Indian Society. *Journal of the Indian Law Insti-
          tute* 4: 331–58. (Reprinted in *Class, Status and Power.* Edited
          by S. M. Lipset and R. Bendix. New York: Free Press, 2nd ed.,
          1966.)

  1963.   Law and Caste in Modern India. *Asian Survey* III: 544–49.

  1966.   The Religious Aspects of Caste: a Legal View. *In South Asian
          Religion and Politics.* Edited by Donald E. Smith. Princeton, N.J.:
          Princeton University Press.

  1967a. Equality and Preferential Treatment: Constitutional Limits and
          Judicial Control. In *Indian Yearbook of International Affairs,
          1965,* XIV: 257–80.

1967b.   Group Membership and Group Preference in India. *Journal of Asian and African Studies* II: 91–124.

1968a.   Changing Legal Conceptions of Caste. In *Structure and Change in Indian Society*. Edited by Milton Singer and Bernard S. Cohn. Chicago: Aldine.

1968b.   The Displacement of Traditional Law in Modern India. *Journal of Social Issues* 24: 65–91.

1969.   Untouchability and the Law. *Economic and Political Weekly* (Bombay) Annual Number (January) 4: 131–70.

n.d.   "Equality and Compensatory Discrimination in India" [tentative title] Unpublished manuscript. Chapters II-VI.

Government of India.

Backward Classes Commission.
1956.   *Report of the Backward Classes Commission*. (Chairman: Kaka Kalekar.) New Delhi: Manager of Publications.

Commissioner for Scheduled Castes and Scheduled Tribes.
1956.   *Annual Report*. Delhi: Manager of Publications. [First issued in 1956 for the period 1950–55; issued annually thereafter.]

1968.   *Handbook on Scheduled Castes and Scheduled Tribes*. Compiled by Vimal Chandra, Deputy Commissioner. New Delhi.

Committee on Plan Projects.
1951.   *Report of the Study Team on Social Welfare and Welfare of Backward Classes*. (Chairman: Renuka Ray.) Vol. I. Delhi: Manager of Publications.

Department of Social Security.
1965.   *The Report of the Advisory Committee on the Revision of Lists of Scheduled Castes and Scheduled Tribes*. (Chairman: B. N. Lokur.) Delhi.

Department of Social Welfare.
1969.   *Report of the Committee on Untouchability, Economic and Educational Development of the Scheduled Castes, and Connected Documents*. (Chairman: L. Elayaperumal.) Delhi.

Displaced Harijan Welfare Board.
n.d.   *Rehabilitation of Displaced Harijans. Nine Year's Report, 1948–57*. Delhi. [pamphlet]

Ministry of Community Development and Cooperation.
1961.   *Report of the Study Group on the Welfare of the Weaker Sections of the Village Community*. (Chairman: Jayaprakash Narayan). Delhi: Government of India Press.

Ministry of Home Affairs.
1956.   *Memorandum on the Report of the Backward Classes Commission*. Delhi.

1960.   *Report of the Scavenging Conditions Enquiry Committee.* New Delhi.

1964.   *Report of the Special Working Group on Cooperation for Backward Classes.* 2 vols. New Delhi.

Ministry of Information and Broadcasting.
1952.   *Harijans Today.* Delhi.

1963.   *Welfare of the Backward Classes.* Delhi.

Ministry of Law.
1955.   *The Untouchability (Offences) Act.* (22 of 1955). [pamphlet]

Office of the Registrar General
1969.   *A Preliminary Appraisal of the Scheduled Castes of India.* Compiled by H. L. Harit. Supervised by B. K. Roy Burman. New Delhi. (Mimeographed.)

Goyal, C. P.
1965.   Eradication of Untouchability; Recent Legislation and Its Enforcement. [A four page mimeographed paper presented in a seminar on Harijan welfare and the process of integration and alienation held under the auspices of the Welfare Forum and Research Organization, Lucknow.]

Imam, Mohammed
1966.   Reservation of Seats for Backward Classes in Public Services and Educational Institutions. *Journal of the Indian Law Institute* 8: 441–49.

Jagannathan, R.
1962.   Weaker Sections of the Village Community and Panchayati Raj. *Indian Journal of Political Administration* VIII: 589–94.

Jain, M. P.
1961.   Comment: Reservation of the Posts for Scheduled Castes and Article 16 (4). *Journal of the Indian Law Institute* 3: 366–71.

Kelkar, R. V.
1956.   The Untouchability (Offenses) Act, 1955. *Vyavahara Nirnaya* (University of Delhi, Faculty of Law) V: 127–44.

Krishna Shetty K. P.
1969.   *Fundamental Rights and Socio-Economic Justice in the Indian Constitution.* Allahabad: Chaitanya Publishing House.

Mittal, J. K.
1965a.   Concept of Equality in Constituent Assembly. *Supreme Court Journal* XXXII (5): 65–84.

1965b.   Educational Equality and the Supreme Court of India. *Indian Advocate* V: 31–39.

Nigam, S. S.
1960.   Equality and the Representation of the Scheduled Classes in Parliament. *Journal of the Indian Law Institute* 2: 196–320.

Pillai, K. G. Janardhanan
1966.   Equality of Opportunity in Public Employment. *Supreme Court Journal* XXXIV (2) : 9–24.

Radhakrishnan, N.
1965.   Reservation to the Backward Classes. In *Indian Yearbook of International Affairs, 1964.* (University of Madras) XIII (Part I) : 293–345.

Ravenell, Barbara J.
1965.   *The Scheduled Castes and Panchayati Raj.* M.A. Thesis in Political Science. University of Chicago.

Revankar, Ratna G.
1971.   *The Indian Constitution — A Case Study of Backward Classes.* Cranbury, N. J.: Fairleigh Dickinson University Press.

Schermerhorn, R. A.
1969.   Scheduled Caste Welfare: Public Priorities in the States. *Economic and Political Weekly* IV (Feb. 22, 1969) : 397–401.

Religion

Hinduism, General, and Temple Entry

Briggs, George W.
1937.   The Harijan and Hinduism. *Review of Religion.* II: 33–59.

Census of India, 1911.
1912.   Shuddhi. In Chapter IV of Vol. XIV, *Punjab,* Part I, *Report:* Lahore, 148–52.

Chakravarti, Satis Chandra and Serojendra Nath Ray (compilers).
1933.   *Brahmo Samaj, The Depressed Classes and Untouchability.* Calcutta: Sadharan Brahmo Semaj.

Chidambaram, Pillai, P.
1933.   *Right of Temple Entry.* Nagarcoil.

Cochin, State Government of.
1935.   *Report of the Temple Entry Enquiry Committee, 1934.* Trivandrum: Supt. Government Press.

Desai, Valji G.
n.d.   *The Shastras on Untouchability.* Ahmedabad: Navajivan.

Galanter, Marc
1964.   Temple-entry and the Untouchability Offenses Act. *Journal of the Indian Law Institute* 6: 85–95.

Gupte, G. S.
1939.   Legislation for the Improvement of the Lot of "Depressed Classes" or "Harijans." *Social Reform Annual* (Bombay) : 86–90.

Indian National Congress. Anti-Untouchability Sub-Committee.
1929.   *Report of the Work Done by the Anti-Untouchability Sub-Committee April–December 1929.* (Jamnalal Bajaj, Secretary.) Reported in the *Indian Annual Register, 1929.* Part II: 276–80. [pamphlet]

Iyengar, G. Aravamuda
1935.   *The Temple Entry by Harijans.* 2nd ed. Nellore: Sanatana Dharma Printing Agency.

Krishnamacharya, U. P.
1931.   *Temple Worship and Temple Entry.* Chitoor (?).

Malkani, Naraindas Rattanmal
1934.   *A Critical Note on Hindu Temple Entry Bill.* Delhi.

Pillai, P. Chidamabaram.
1933.   *Right of Temple Entry.* Nagercoil: author.

Rajagopalachari, C.
1933.   *Plighted Word: Being an Account of the History and Objects of the Untouchability Abolition and Temple Entry Bills.* Delhi: Servants of Untouchables Society.

Sath Brahmana Ashram, Bezwada
1934.   *A Memorandum of the Real Indian Nationalist Congress Party, Bezwada, Submitted to the Government of India Regarding the Temple-entry Bill.* Bezwada.

Sorabji, Cornelia
1933.   Temple Entry and Untouchability. *Nineteenth Century and After* 113: 689–702.

Sundarananda, Swami
1922.   *Hinduism and Untouchability.* Foreword by Shyma Prasad Murkerjee. Calcutta: Udbodhan Office, reprint, 1946. (Originally published in 1922.) [Also reprinted in Delhi: Harijan Sevak Sangh, ca. 1945.]

Temple Entry Enquiry Committee
1935.   *Report of the Committee, 1934.* Trivandrum: Supt. of Government Press.

Tiwari, Chitra
1963.   *Sudras in Manu.* (Foreword by Jagjiwan Ram.) Delhi: Motilal Banarsidass.

Venkatraman, S. R.
1946.   *Temple Entry Legislation: Reviewed with Acts and Bills.* Madras: Bharat Devi Publications.

Wadia, Sophia
1932.   *Theosophy and Untouchability.* Bombay: Servants of Untouchables Society.

Christianity

De Meulder, E., S.J.
    ca. 1963 *They Have Not Spoken Yet.* Nagpur: author (Rev. Fr. E. Meul-
        der, S.J., Catholic Ashram, Raigarh P. O., Madhya Pradesh.)

Depressed Class Awakenings
    1936.   *Depressed Class Awakenings. News and Views of the All-India
                Depressed Conference.* Lucknow: C. O. Forsgren, June 24, 1936.
                [Newspaper, no further issues known.]

Hayter, O. C. G.
    1930.   Conversions of Outcastes. *Asiatic Review* XXVI: 603–11.

Hunt, William S.
    1929.   *India's Outcastes: A New Era.* London: Church Missionary
                Society.

Koshy, Ninan
    1968.   *Caste in the Kerala Churches.* Bangalore: Christian Institute
                for the Study of Religion and Society.

McGavran, D. A.
    1939.   *India's Oppressed Classes and Religion.* Jubbulpore.

Modak, R. V.
    1882.   History of Native Churches. In *Memorial Papers of the American
                Marathi Mission.* American Board of Commissioners for Foreign
                Missions, ed. Byculla, Bombay: Education Society's Press.

Philip, P. O.
    1925.   *The Depressed Classes and Christianity.* Calcutta.
    1935.   The Harijan Movement in India in Relation to Christianity.
                International Review of Missions 24: 162–77.

Phillips, Godfrey
    1936.   *The Untouchables' Quest: The Depressed Classes of India and
                Christianity.* Foreword by B. R. Ambedkar. London: Edinburgh
                House Press.

Pickett, J. Waskom
    1933.   *Christian Mass Movements in India.* New York, Cincinnati:
                Abingdon.

Whitehouse, Bishop
    1903.   The Gospel for Pariahs. *Missionary Review.*

Buddhism

Ahir. D. C.
    1962.   *Babasaheb's Message.* Delhi: Institute of Buddhist Thought.
                [pamphlet]

1964.   *India's Debt to Buddhism.* New Delhi: Maha Bodhi Society of India.

1964.   Seven Years of Ambedkar Era. *Maha Bodhi* 72: 69–72.

1966.   Dhamma Vijaya. *Maha Bodhi* 74: 205–08.

Ambedkar, Bhimrao Ramji
1950.   Buddha and the Future of His Religion. *Maha Bodhi* 58: 117–18, 199–206.

1956.   *Buddha and Karl Marx.* (Speech given November 20, 1956, to the Fourth Conference of the World Fellowship of Buddhists at Katmandu.) Nagpur: M. D. Panchbhai, reprint 1964. [pamphlet]

1957.   *The Buddha and His Dhamma.* Bombay: Siddharth College Publication I.

Anandamaitreya, Balangola (Thera)
1927.   The Dawn and Spread of Buddhism. *Maha Bodhi* 35: 274–78.

Arakeri, S. S.
1965   *The Burning Problem of Indian Buddhists,* In *Dharma Chakra Pravartan, Buddhist Souvenir.* Hyderabad: The Buddhist Society of India.

Benz, Ernest
1966.   *Buddhism or Communism: Which Holds the Future of Asia?* New York: Anchor.

Bhandare, R. D.
1966.   *The Problems of the Indian Buddhists.* Bombay: R. D. Bhandare. [pamphlet]

Bharatiya Bauddhajan Mahasabha
1963.   *Judgements and Buddha Religion.* Nagpur: Bharatiya Bauddhajan Mahasabha, Nagpur City Branch.

Chhawara, Koliya Putta Rahula Suman
1961.   On the Way Back to Buddhism. In *Right View (Samyak Dristi).* Ajmer: Maha Bodhi Ashoka Mission.

De, Gokuldas
1955.   *Democracy in Early Buddhism.* Calcutta: University Press.

Deva, Shanthi, and C. M. Wagh
1965.   *Dr. Ambedkar and Conversion.* Hyderabad: Dr. Ambedkar Publications Society. [pamphlet]

Dhammaratana, Bhikku U.
1955.   *Buddha and Caste System.* Sarnath, Banaras: Sarnath Publications.

Fiske, Adele M.
1966.   *The Use of Buddhist Scriptures in Dr. B. R. Ambedkar's 'The Buddha and His Dhamma.'* M. A. Thesis. Columbia University.
1969.   Religion and Buddhism Among India's New Buddhists. *Social Research* 36: 123–157.

Glasenapp, H. Von
1937.   *Brahman et Bouddha.* Paris: Payot.

Karve, Iravati and Hemalata Acharya
1962.   Neo-Buddhism in Maharashtra. *Journal of the University of Poona,* Humanities Section, 15: 130–33.

Korthurkar, V. K. and V. V. Pendse
1962.   A Study of Social Prejudice in Three Villages: the Problem of Neo-Buddhas. *Journal of the University of Poona,* Humanities Section, 15: 123–29.

Kulkarni, A. R.
1950.   Dr. Ambedkar and Buddhism. *Maha Bodhi* 58: 338–46.

Lokanatha, Salvatore
1936.   *Buddhism Will Make You Free!* Panadura, Ceylon: Harijan Publishing Society. [pamphlet]

Miller, Beatrice Diamond
Forthcoming. Revitalization Movements: Theory and Practice as Evidenced among the Buddhists of Maharashtra, India. (To be published in Verrier Elwin Memorial Volume.)

Miller, Robert J.
1967.   They Will Not Die Hindus: The Buddhist Conversion of Mahar Ex-Untouchables. *Asian Survey* VII (Sept.): 637–44.

Nair, Sheo
1927.   Prospects of Buddhism in India. *The Mahabodhi Society Journal.* 25: 204–06.

Nair, V. G.
1966.   The Buddhist Revival in India. In *Baba Sahab Dr. Ambedkar Jayanti Sandesh.* Agra: Ambedkar Bhavan.

Nalanda Education Society of India.
1964.   *The Neo-Buddhist Movement in India.* Bombay: Nalanda Education Society of India. [pamphlet]

Narasu, P. Lakshmi
1907.   *The Essence of Buddhism.* (Preface by B. R. Ambedkar.) Bombay: Thacker, reprint, 1948. (1st edition, 1907; 2nd edition, 1912.)

Newly Converted Buddhists' Problems Conference.
1960.   Background of Conversion and Future Effect, by R. B. More; The Problem of the Neo-Buddhists, by M. N. Wankhede. Poona: Gokhale Institute, (Mimeographed). [Two papers and some comments in English presented in reports of the Newly Converted Buddhists' Problems Conference held June 3–5, 1960, at Gokhale Institute in Poona.]

Niyogi, M. B.
  1963.   Problem of Nava Buddha in Maharashtra. *Social Service Quarterly* XXXXVIII: 97–105.

Parvathamma, C.
  1965.   Buddhism: Its Relevance to Buddhist Converts in India. *Dharma Chakra Pravartan, Buddhist Souvenir.* Hyderabad: Buddhist Society of India. 29–30.

Pressler, Henry H.
  1964.   The Neo-Buddhist Stir in India. *India Cultures Quarterly* 21: 4: 1–29. Jabalpur, Madhya Pradesh: Leonard Theological College.

Sangharakshita, Stavira
  1965a.   Mass Civil Disobedience in India by Ex-Untouchable Buddhists. *Institute of Race Relations News Letter* (London), March: 11–13.

  1965b.   Dr. Babasaheb Ambedkar and Buddhism. *Bodhisattva* 1: 1–2.

Satyanarayana, Y.
  1965.   Review of our Activities. In *Dharma Chakra Pravartun, Buddhist Souvenir.* Hyderabad: The Buddhist Society of India.

Shastri, Sankarananda
  1957.   A Report on the Conversion Movement. *Maha Bodhi* 65: 128–30.

Sheth, Jyotsna
  1970.   The Neo-Buddhists. *The Illustrated Weekly of India* May 24.

South India Buddhist Association.
  1954.   *Objects and Rules of the South India Buddhist Association* Perambur, Madras: South India Buddhist Association.

U Nu
  1958.   The Late Dr. B. R. Ambedkar. *Maha Bodhi* 66: 18–20.

Zelliot, Eleanor
  1966.   Background of the Mahar Buddhist Conversion. In *Studies on Asia.* Edited by Robert K. Sakai. Lincoln: University of Nebraska Press.

  1966.   Buddhism and Politics in Maharashtra. In *South Asian Politics and Religion.* Edited by Donald E. Smith. Princeton, N.J.: Princeton University Press.

  1968.   The Revival of Buddhism in India. *Asia* (New York) No. 10 (Winter): 33–45.

B. R. Ambedkar and His Movement

Ambedkar, B. R.
  1917.   Castes in India — Their Mechanism, Genesis and Development. *Indian Antiquary* XLVI: 81–95.

  1924.   Prantik Bahishkrit Parishad, Adhivershan Dusre. [Presidential address delivered at the second session of the district conference of the Depressed Classes held in Barshi, Solapur district, May 10–12, 1924. A handwritten manuscript in Marathi.]

1930.   Presidential Address, All-India Depressed Classes Conference. *Indian Annual Register*, 1930 II: 367–74. [Extracts.]

1936a.   Annihilation of Caste, with a Reply to Mahatma Gandhi. Bombay: Bhusan P. Press.

1936b.   *Mukhti Kon Pathe* [Which Way Freedom?]. Bombay: Bharat Bhushan Press. [A pamphlet in Marathi.]

1943a.   *Mr. Gandhi and the Emancipation of the Untouchables.* Bombay: Thacker.

1943b.   *Ranade, Gandhi and Jinnah.* Bombay: Thacker. Reprinted by Bheem Patrika Publications, Jullunur City (Punjab), 1964.

1945a.   *Annihilation of Caste, with A Reply to Mahatma Gandhi.* Amritsar: Katra Jaman Singh for Ambedkar School of Thoughts, 3rd ed. Bombay: Bhusan P. Press.

1945b.   *What Congress and Gandhi Have Done to the Untouchables.* Bombay: Thacker, 2nd ed., 1946. (First published in 1945.)

1946.   *Who Were the Shudras?* How they came to be the 4th Varna in the Indo-Aryan Society. Bombay: Thacker. (Reprinted in 1947.)

1947.   *States and Minorities.* Bombay: C. Murphy for Thacker.

1948.   *The Untouchables.* Who were they and why they became untouchables. New Delhi: Amrit Book Co. [A sequel to *Who Were the Shudras?* A 2nd ed. was published in Lucknow in 1969.]

1963.   *Thus Spoke Ambedkar. Selected Speeches.* Compiled by Bhagwan Das. Jullundur City: Bheem Patrika Publications.

Ambedkar Buddhist Mission.
1966.   Constitution of the Ambedkar Buddhist Mission. Jullundar, Punjab: Ambedkar Buddhist Mission [mimeographed].

Anonymous
1966.   The Greatest Social Reformer and Educationist of this Era. In *Baba Saheb Dr. Ambedkar Jayanti Sandesh.* Agra: Ambedkar Bhavan. 2–4.

Bhadra, Ven. Shanti
1966a.   Bodhisattva Ambedkar. In *Dr. Babasaheb Ambedkar Amrat Mahotsab Visesanka.* Nagpur: Dr. Ambedkar Adhyayan Man Mandal. 7–8.

1966b.   Bodhisattva Ambedkar. *Milind College of Arts, College Magazine.* Aurangabad. 4: 56–57.

Bharill, Chandra
1966.   Experiences of an Untouchable: Glimpses of Ambedkar's Early Life. *Political Science Review* 5: 323–31.

1969.   *Social and Political Ideas and Contribution of Ambedkar.* Ph.D. dissertation in Political Science. University of Rajasthan.

Bhole, R. R.
1944.   *An Untouchable Speaks.* London: Brittain Publishing Company.

1944.   The Untouchables on the Move. *Asiatic Review* XI: 146–50.
[Discussion of R. R. Bhole's speech: 150–57.]

Clark, Blake
1950.   The Victory of an Untouchable. *Reader's Digest* 56: 107–11.
(Reprinted from *Christian Herald*, March, 1950.)

Depressed Class Conferences, 1942.
1942.   *Report of the Depressed Class Conferences.* Nagpur: G. T.
Meshram. [Formation meeting of the Scheduled Castes
Federation.]

Deshmukh, A. S.
1963–64. Dr. Babasaheb Ambedkar as a Religious Reformer. *Magazine of
Dr. Babasaheb College of Arts, Science and Commerce.* Mahad.
2: 52–53.

Gajendragadkar, P. B.
1960.   *Speech by Hon'ble Justice P. B. Gajendragadkar* (at the unveiling
of the statue of Dr. B. R. Ambedkar at Poona, 26 January 1960).
Poona: Poona Municipal Corporation. [pamphlet]

Gandhi, Sham S.
1963–64. Dr. Ambedkar as a Religious Reformer. *Siddarth College of Law
Magazine.* 53–56.

Independent Labour Party
1936.   *Independent Labour Party: Its Formation and Its Aims.*
(Reprinted from *Times of India*, August 15, 1936.) Bombay:
Independent Labour Party Publications No. I.

Jatava, Daya Ram
1965a.   *Social Philosophy of B. R. Ambedkar.* Agra: Phoenix Publishing
Agency.

1965b.   *Political Philosophy of B. R. Ambedkar.* Agra: Phoenix Publishing Agency.

1966.   Ambedkar and Manu, in *Dr. Babasaheb Ambedkar Amrat
Mahotsab Visesanka.* Nagpur. 9–10.

Kausalyaayaan, Bhandant Aanand
n.d.   *Baabaa Saahab.* Vardhaa: Sugat Prakaashan Griha. [In Hindi.]

Keer, Dhananjay
1954.   *Dr. Ambedkar: Life and Mission.* Bombay: Popular Prakashan.
(2nd ed: 1962, with additional material.)

Khairmode, C. B. *Dr. Bhimrav Ramji Ambedkar.* Vol. I. Bombay: Y. B.
Ambedkar, 1952. Vol. II. Bombay: Bauddhjan Panchayat Samiti,
1958. Vol. III. Bombay: Pratap Prakashan, 1964. Vols. IV and V.
Bombay: Dr. Ambedkar Education Society, 1966, 1968. [In
Marathi.]

Mallik, Sima
1963. The Great Outsider: A Review of "Dr. Ambedkar, Life and Mission," by Dhananjay Keer. *Quest* 39: 95–7.

Nariellawalla, G. E.
1964–65. The Writings of Dr. B. R. Ambedkar. *Siddarth College of Commerce and Economics Annual.* 20.

Rajogopalachari, C.
1946. *Ambedkar Refuted.* Bombay: Hind Kitabs, 2nd ed.

Republican Party.
1957. *Election Manifesto of 1957.* Delhi: B. D. Khobaragade.

1964. *Charter of Demands.* Delhi: Dada Sahib B. K. Gaikwad, B. P. Maurya, B. D. Khobaragade.

1965. *Presidential Address by R. D. Bhandare.* Bombay: R. D. Bhandare.

Robbin, Jeanette
1964. *Dr. Ambedkar and His Movement.* Hyderabad: Dr. Ambedkar Publishing Society.

Scheduled Castes Federation.
1951. *Election Manifesto of the All-India Scheduled Castes Federation.* New Delhi: P. N. Rajbhoj, General Secretary. [pamphlet]

1955. *Resolutions Passed by the Working Committee of the All-India Scheduled Castes Federation on 21st August, 1955, Bombay.* Chanda: All-India Scheduled Castes Federation.

Scheduled Castes Students' Federation.
1947. *Report of the Second Session of the All-India Scheduled Castes Students' Federation.* (Held at Nagpur December 25, 26, and 27, 1946), Nagpur.

Thakkar, A. V.
1945? *Aboriginals Cry in the Wilderness: Their Education and Representation in Legislature.* Bombay: A. W. Thakkar, Servants of India Society. [Controversy between Dr. Ambedkar and A. W. Thakkar with facts and figures regarding aboriginals and hill tribes.]

Tope, T. K.
1964. *Dr. B. R. Ambedkar, a Symbol of Social Revolt.* New Delhi: Maharashtra Information Centre. [pamphlet]

Yaadvendu, Raamnaaraayan
1942. *Yaaduvansh Kaa Itihaas.* Agra, India: Navyug Saahitya Niketan. [In Hindi.]

Zelliot, Eleanor
1969. *Dr. Ambedkar and the Mahar Movement.* Unpublished Ph.D. Dissertation, University of Pennsylvania.

1970a.   Learning the Use of Political Means: The Mahars of Maharashtra. In *Caste in Indian Politics*. Edited by Rajni Kothari. New Delhi: Allied Publishers.

1970b.   The Nineteenth Century Background of the Mahar and Non-Brahman Movements in Maharashtra. *The Indian Economic and Social History Review* VII: 397–415.

See also sections on Government Policy — Pre-Independence, Buddhism, Mahars, Maharashtra.

Publications related to the Ambedkar Movement have been issued by the following institutions: Ambedkar Bhavan, Agra; Buddhist Society of India, Hyderabad; Dr. Babasaheb Ambedkar College of Arts, Science and Commerce, Mahad (Maharashtra); Milind College of Arts, Aurangabad; Siddharth Colleges of Arts and Sciences, of Commerce and Economics, of Law, all in Bombay. See also the *Andhra Republican*, Hyderabad.

A collection of materials on Dr. B. R. Ambedkar has been presented to the Library of the University of Bombay by Mr. C. B. Khairmode.

Gandhian Reform

Alexander, Horace G.
   1935.   Mr. Gandhi and Untouchability. *Contemporary Review* 147: 194–201.

Arokiaswami, M.
   1936.   The Birth of the Harijan Movement. *New Review* (Calcutta) 4: 175–83.

Asad, Mohamed
   1933.   The Jingo Mahatma. *Living Age*. 344: 489–95.

Bondurant, Joan V.
   1958.   *Conquest of Violence; The Gandhian Philosophy of Conflict*. Princeton: Princeton University Press.

Dalton, Dennis
   1967.   The Gandhian View of Caste, and Caste after Gandhi. In *India and Ceylon: Unity and Diversity*. Philip Mason, ed. London: Oxford University Press for the Institute of Race Relations.

Desai, Mahadev
   1937.   *The Epic of Travancore*. Ahmedabad: Navajivan.

   1953.   *The Diary of Mahadeo Desai*. (Translated from the Gujarati and edited by Valji Govinji Desai.) Ahmedabad: Navajivan. [Record of Gandhi's life March 10, 1932–September 4, 1932, a period of intensive concern with untouchability.]

Gandhi, M. K.

1932.   *The Bleeding Wound!* Being a most up-to-date collection of Gandhiji's speeches, writings and statements on untouchability. Compiled and edited by Shri Ramnath Suman. Introduction by C. Y. Chintamani. Foreword by G. D. Birla. Benares: Shyam Lal.

1932.   *My Soul's Agony.* Being Gandhiji's statements from Yeravada prison on the removal of untouchability among Hindus. Ahmedabad: Navajivan.

1944.   *Untouchability.* Lahore: Gandhi Publications' League.

1947.   *The Nation's Voice.* (Being a collection of Gandhiji's speeches in England and Sjt. Mahadev Desai's account of the sojourn — September to December, 1931), edited by C. Rajagopalachar and J. C. Kumarappa, 2nd ed. Ahmedabad: Navajivan Publishing House, 1947.

1948.   *Gandhi's Autobiography: The Story of my Experiments with Truth.* Translated from the Gujarati by Mahadev Desai. Washington Public Affairs Press, 1948.

1954a. *For Workers Against Untouchability.* Ahmedabad: Navajivan.

1954b. *The Removal of Untouchability.* Compiled and edited by Bharatan Kumarappa. Ahmedabad: Navajivan.

1964a. *All Are Equal in the Eyes of God.* Selections from Mahatma Gandhi. Delhi: Government of India, Publications Division.

1964b. *Caste Must Go and the Sin of Untouchability.* Compiled by R. K. Prabhu. Ahmedabad: Navajivan.

1965a. *My Varnashrama Dharma.* Edited by Anand T. Hingorani. Bombay: Bharatya Vidya Bhavan.

1965b. *None High: None Low.* Edited by Anand T. Hingorani. Bombay: Bharatiya Vidya Bhavan.

Harijan
1945.   *Gandhi or Ambedkar.* Foreword by Radhakrishnan. Madras: Gandhi Era Publications.

Harijan Sevak Sangh
        Annual Report (from 1933).

Kalwankar, S. R.
1934.   *An Appeal to Gandhiji.* (To desist from anti-untouchability campaign.) Malegaon: author.

Kaushik, P. Datt
1963.   Gandhiji and Congress vis-a-vis Untouchables. *AICC Economic Review,* XV (October 1): 27–30.

Mahadevan, S.
1936.   *Mahatma Gandhi's Warning and Flashes in Harijan Tour.* Madras: Journalists' Publishing House.

Malkani, N. R.
1933.   *Report on Conditions of Harijans in Delhi*. Delhi.

1963.   What Man Does to Man in India. *Gandhi Marg*, 7: 190–95.

1965.   *Clean People and an Unclean Country*. Delhi: Harijan Sevak Sangh.

Nehru, Rameshwari
1940.   *The Harijan Movement*. Delhi: Harijan Sevak Sangh. (pamphlet)

1950.   *Gandhi is My Star*. Patna: Pustakbhandar.

Pushparaj, P. K.
1933.   *As an Untouchable Feels Untouchability*. Delhi: Servants of Untouchables Society, Tract No. I. (pamphlet)

Pyarelal (Nair or Nayyar)
1932.   *The Epic Fast*. Ahmedabad: Mohanlal Maganlal Bhatt.

1958.   *Mahatma Gandhi: the Last Phase*. Ahmedabad: Navajivan Publishing House, 1958.

Rajagopalachari, C.
1933.   *The Impending Fast of Mahatma Gandhi: the Issues Explained*. Delhi: Servants of Untouchables Society.

1946.   *Ambedkar Refuted*. Bombay: Hind Kitabs.

Santhanam, K.
1946.   *Ambedkar's Attack*. New Delhi: The Hindustan Times.

Tagore, Rabindranath
1932.   *Mahatmaji and the Depressed Humanity*. Calcutta Visvabharati.

Tendulkar, D. G.
1952.   *Mahatma. Life of Mohandas Karamchand Gandhi*. Vol. I–VIII. Bombay: Vithalbhai K. Jhaveri and D. G. Tendulkar, 1952.

Thakkar, A. V.
1949.   *Thakkar Baba Eightieth Birthday Commemoration Volume*. (A. V. Thakkar) Compiled and Edited by T. N. Jagadisan and Shyamlal. Madras [Contains fifty pages of material on the Harijan Sevak Sangh.]

Thaware, G. M.
1948.   *Gandhiji's Letters Re: Untouchables*. Nagpur: L. P. Meshram and H. O. Dongre.

Many collections in book and pamphlet form of M. K. Gandhi's statements concerning social reform are drawn from the weeklies, *Young India* and *Harijan. Young India*, from 1919–1932, was edited by M. K. Gandhi, and others during his absence and published by Navajivan of Ahmedabad. *Harijan*, edited successively by Mahadev Desai, Pyarelal Nayyar, and K. G. Mashruwala, was published in Poona or Madras from 1933 to 1941, then in Ahmedabad by Navajivan.

Fiction, Biography, Autobiography

Anand, Mulk Raj
1947.   *Untouchable.* London, N. Y.: Hutchinson International Authors.
         [A novel.]

1967.   The Story of My Experiment with a White Lie. *Indian Literature*
         X. 28–43. [The story of writing *Untouchable.*]

Balakrishnan, P. K. (ed.)
1954.   *Sri Narayana Guru.* Cochin. [Treats the Irava Caste.]

Chandar, Krishan
1966.   Kalu Bhangi. In *Tales from Modern India.* Edited by K. Natwar-
         Singh. New York: Macmillan, 1966.

Doraiswamy Iyengar, N. A.
1922.   *A Pillar of Swaraj: Being a Collection of Three Short Stories on
         Untouchability.* Madras: Everyman Publishers.

Duggal, Kartar Singh
1967.   The Sins of Thy Fathers . . . *Indian Literature* X: 48–52.

Gupta, Captain M. R.
1948.   *The Untouchable.* Delhi: Rajkamul Publications. [A play.]

Hazari (pseud. of Marcus Abraham Malik)
1951.   *An Indian Outcast.* London: Bannisdale, 1951. Reprinted as
         I Was an Outcaste by the Hindustan Times, New Delhi, 1957.
         Reprinted as *Untouchable: The Autobiography of an Indian
         Outcaste* by Frederick A. Praeger, New York, 1969.

1957.   I was an Outcaste. *Social Welfare* 4: 8–11.

Kharat, Shankarava [Shakarao]. *Daundi.* Poona: Continental Publishers. [A
1965.   collection of short stories in Marathi.]

Kincaid, C. A.
1922.   The Outcastes Story. In *The Anchorite and Other Stories.* London
         and Bombay: Humphrey Milford for Oxford University Press.
         [A Mahar anchorite at Pandharpur.]

Madgulkar, V.
1961.   Planning a Feast. In *16 Modern Marathi Short Stories.* Bombay:
         Kutub Popular.

1966.   Nirvana. In *Tupacha Nandadipa.* Poona. [A collection of short
         stories in Marathi.]

Pillai, Thakazhi S.
1967.   *Two Measures of Rice.* (Tr. by M. A. Shakoor.) Bombay: Jaico.
         [A novel of Paraiyan and Puliya life in Travancore.]

Sathe, Bhaurao
1965?   Savala Mang. Poona. [A collection of short stories in Marathi.]

Sharma, Nalin Vilochan
 ca. 1957. A Biography of Jagjivan Ram. In *The Working Man*. Patna:
  Jagjivan Ram Abinandan Granth Committee.

Tagore, Rabindranath
 1933. Chandalika, in *Three Plays*. Translated from the Bengali by
  Marjorie Sykes. Bombay: Oxford University Press, 1950. [A play
  based on the Buddhist legend of an outcaste girl becoming a
  Bhikkuni, written in 1933.]

Thomas, Daniel
 1965. *Sree Narayana Guru*. Bangalore: Christian Institute for the Study
  of Religion and Society. [Treats the Irava Caste.]
NOTE: See also biographies listed under Ambedkar and His Movement.

Peripheral References Cited In Text

Adam, William
 1840. *The Law and Custom of Slavery in British India in a Series of
  Letters to Thomas Powell Buxton, Esq.* Boston: Weeks, Jordan
  and Company.

All-India Congress Committee.
 n.d. *Indian National Congress 1930–34: Being the Resolutions Passed
  by the Congress. . . During the Period Between January 1930 to
  September 1934. . . .* Allahabad.

Andenaes, Johannes
 1966. The General Preventive Effects of Punishment. *University of
  Pennsylvania Law Review* 114: 949–83.

Appasamy, Paul
 1929. *Legal Aspects of Social Reform*. Madras: Christian Literature
  Society for India.

Arakeri, S. S.
 n.d. *The Origin of the Caste-system and Its Role in Bringing Foreign
  Rule to India*. Bombay: Libertarian Social Institute.

Bakhle, P. S. (ed.)
 1939. *Social Reform Annual 1939*. Bombay: Bombay Presidency Social
  Reform Association.

Banaji, D. A.
 ca. 1933. *Slavery in British India*. Bombay: D. B. Taraporewala Sons & Co.,
  2nd ed., n.d.

Baroda, Government of
 1949. *Rural Baroda: A Monograph Drawn up by the Government of
  Baroda*. Bombay: Indian Society of Agricultural Economics.

Basu, Durga Das
 1965. *Commentary on the Constitution of India*. Vol. I. Calcutta: S. C.
  Sarkar & Sons, 5th ed.

Bayley, W. H. and W. Hudleston (eds.)
1892.   *Papers on Mirasi Right.* Madras.

Beidelman, Thomas O.
1959.   *A Comparative Analysis of the Jajmani System.* Monograph of the Association for Asian Studies, No. VIII. Locust Valley (N.Y.) : J. J. Augustin.

Bendix, Reinhard
1962.   *Max Weber: An Intellectual Portrait.* Garden City: Doubleday and Co. (Anchor Books).

Berger, Morroe
1952.   *Equality by Statute: Legal Controls Over Group Discrimination.* New York: Columbia University Press.

Béteille, André
1965.   *Caste, Class and Power.* Berkeley: University of California Press.

Bombay, Government of
1962.   *Report on the Administration of Civil and Criminal Justice in the State of Bombay for the Year 1957.* Bombay: Government Central Press.

Brass, Paul
1965.   *Factional Politics in an Indian State.* Berkeley and Los Angeles: University of California Press.

Cavers, David
1964.   *India's Need for Well-Trained Lawyers.* (Mimeographed memorandum.) New Delhi.

Chambliss, William J.
1967.   Types of Deviance and the Effectiveness of Legal Sanctions. *Wisconsin Law Review* 1967: 703–19.

Chandidas, R. et al, Editors
1968.   *India Votes.* New York: Humanities Press.

Chayanov, A. V.
1966.   *The Theory of Peasant Economy.* Homewood, Illinois: Richard D. Irwin, Inc., for the American Economic Association.

Cohn, Bernard S.
1965.   Anthropological Notes on Disputes and Law in India. *American Anthropologist* 67 (6) Part 2: 82–122.

1968.   "Notes on the History of the Study of Indian Society and Culture." M. Singer and B. S. Cohn, Editors, *Structure and Change in Indian Society.* Chicago: Aldine Publishing Company, pp. 3–28.

Constituent Assembly.
1947–50. *Debates.* 12 vols. Delhi: Manager of Publications.

Coupland, Reginald
1944.   *The Constitutional Problem of India.* Oxford: Oxford University Press.

Curry, J. C.
1932.   *The Indian Police.* London: Faber and Faber.

Davis, William Watson
1914.   The Federal Enforcement Acts. In *Studies in Southern History and Politics Inscribed to William Archibald Dunning.* New York: Columbia University Press.

Dobb, Maurice
1951.   *Some Aspects of Economic Development: Three Lectures.* Delhi: Delhi School of Economics.

Douglas, Mary
1966.   *Purity and Danger.* London: Routledge and Kegan Paul.

Dowson, John
1961.   *A Classical Dictionary of Hindu Mythology and Religion, Geography, History and Literature.* London: Routledge and Kegan Paul.

Dror, Yehezkel
1959.   Law and Social Change. *Tulane Law Review* 33:787–802.

Dube, Shyama C.
1958.   India's Changing Villages: Human Factors in Community Development. Ithaca: Cornell University Press.

Dushkin, Lelah
1957.   The Policy of the Indian National Congress toward the Depressed Classes. Unpublished M.A. thesis, University of Pennsylvania.

Epstein, T. Scarlett
1962.   *Economic Development and Social Change in South India.* Manchester: Manchester University Press.

Festinger, Leon
1957.   *Theory of Cognitive Dissonance.* Evanston, Illinois: Rowe Peterson.

Fürer-Haimendorf, Christoph Von (ed.)
1966.   *Caste and Kin in Nepal, India and Ceylon, Anthropological Studies in Hindu-Buddhist Contact Zones.* London: Asia Publishing House.

Geertz, Clifford
1966.   "Religion as a Cultural System," in *Anthropological Approaches to the Study of Religion.* Edited by Michael Banton. London: Tavistock Publications.

Georgescu-Roegen, N.
1960. Economic Theory and Agrarian Economics. Oxford Economic Papers (new series) 12(1): 1–40.

Ghurye, G. S.
1961. Caste, Class and Occupation. Bombay: Popular Book Depot.

Government of India.

Home Department.
1923. India in 1922–23. Calcutta.

Prohibition Enquiry Committee.
1955. Report of the Prohibition Enquiry Committee 1954–55. Delhi, Manager of Publications.

Planning Commission.
1964. Report of the Study Team on Prohibition. Delhi, Manager of Publications.

Gumperz, John J.
1958. Dialect Differences and Social Stratification in a North Indian Village. American Anthropologist 60: 668–82.

Heimsath, Charles H.
1964. Indian Nationalism and Hindu Social Reform. Princeton: Princeton University Press.

Hutton, J. H.
1961. Caste in India: Its Nature, Function, and Origins. Oxford: Oxford University Press, 3rd ed.

Ishwaran, K.
1966. Tradition and Economy in Village India. Humanities Press, Inc. New York.

Joshi, Ram
1968. Maharashtra, in Myron Weiner, Ed., State Politics in India. Princeton: Princeton University Press, pp. 177–212.

Kannan, C. T.
1963. Intercaste and Inter-Community Marriages in India. Bombay: Allied Publishers.

Karve, Irawati
1958. What is caste? (III) Caste as a Status Group. Economic Weekly, Special Number (July 1958): 881–88.
1961. Hindu Society: an interpretation. Poona: Sangam Press.

Ketkar, Shridhar V.
1909. The History of Caste in India. Ithaca: Taylor and Carpenter.
1911. An Essay on Hinduism: Its Formation and Future. London: Luzac & Co.

Kikani, L. T.
1912. *Caste in Courts: or Rights and Powers of Castes in Social and Religious Matters as Recognized by Indian Courts.* Rajkot.

Kothari, Rajni (ed.)
1970. *Caste in Indian Politics.* New Delhi: Allied Publishers.

Kumar, Dharma
1965. *Land and Caste in South India: Agricultural Labour in Madras Presidency in the Nineteenth Century.* Cambridge: Cambridge University Press.

Lajput, Rai
1932. *The Arya Samaj: An Account of Its Doctrine and Activities with a Biographical Account of the Founder.* Lahore: Uttar Chand Kapur & Sons.

Leach, E. R.
1960. "Introduction" in *Aspects of Caste in South India, Ceylon and Northwest Pakistan,* ed. E. R. Leach. Cambridge: Cambridge University Press.

1965. *Political Systems of Highland Burma.* Boston: Beacon Press.

Levi-Strauss, Claude
1963. *Structural Anthropology.* New York: Basic Books.

Lewis, Oscar
1958. *Village Life in Northern India.* New York: Vintage Books.

Lewis, W. Arthur
1954. *Economic Development with Unlimited Supplies of Labour.* The Manchester School of Economic & Social Studies (May) 23: 139–91.

Lockard, Duane
1968. *Toward Equal Opportunity: A Study of State and Local Anti-discrimination Laws.* New York: Macmillan.

Lynch, Owen
1966. "The Politics of Untouchability: Social Structure and Social Change in a City of India." Unpublished Ph.D. thesis, Columbia University [published 1969 by the Columbia University Press].

Majumdar, D. N.
1958. *Caste and Communication in an Indian Village.* Bombay: Asia Publishing House.

Malinowski, Bronislaw
1948. *Magic, Science, and Religion.* Garden City: Doubleday and Co. (Anchor Books).

Marriott, McKim
1960.   *Caste Ranking and Community Structure in Five Regions of India and Pakistan.* Deccan College Monograph Series, No. 23. Poona: Deccan College.

1968.   "Caste Ranking and Food Transactions: A Matrix Analysis." M. Singer and B. S. Cohn, Editors, *Structure and Change in Indian Society.* Chicago: Aldine Publishing Co., pp. 133–171.

Massell, Gregory J.
1968.   Law as an Instrument of Revolutionary Change in a Traditional Milieu: the Case of Soviet Central Asia. *Law and Society Review* 2: 178–228.

Mayhew, Leon
1968.   *Law and Equal Opportunity: A Study of the Massachusetts Commission Against Discrimination.* Cambridge: Harvard University Press.

McCormack, William
1966.   Caste and the British Administration of Hindu Law. *Journal of Asian and African Studies* 1:25–32.

Mencher, Joan P.
1964.   Possession, Dance, and Religion in North Malabar, Kerala, India, to be published in the *Collected Papers of the VII International Congress of Anthropological and Ethnological Sciences,* Moscow.

Minturn, Leigh and John T. Hitchcock
1966.   *The Rajputs of Khalapur, India.* New York: John Wilev.

Morgan, Kenneth W. (ed.)
1956.   *The Path of Buddha.* New York: Ronald Press.

Morris-Jones, W. H.
1962.   India's Political Idioms. In *Politics and Society in India.* C. H. Phillips, ed. London: George Allen & Unwin.

Mukerji, Nirod
1964.   *Standing at the Cross-roads: an Analytical Approach to the Basic Problems of Psycho-social Integration.* Bombay: Allied Publishers.

Mulla, Dinshah Fardunji
1901.   *Jurisdiction of Courts in Matters Relating to the Rights and Powers of Castes.* Bombay: Caxton Printing Works.

Narasimhan, R. L.
1964.   Chief Justice Sinha — A Review of Some of His Decisions. *Journal of the Indian Law Institute* 6: 145.

Nehru, Jawaharlal
1942.   *Toward Freedom.* New York: John Day.

Nurkse, Ragnar
1953.   *Problems of Capital Formation in Under-developed Countries.* Oxford: Oxford University Press.

Nurullah, Syed, and J. P. Naik
1951.　*History of Education in India.* Bombay: Macmillan.

O'Malley, L. S. S.
1932.　*Indian Caste Customs.* Cambridge: The University Press.

1941.　*Modern India and the West.* L. S. S. O'Malley, ed. Oxford: Oxford
University Press.

Orenstein, Henry
1965.　*Gaon: Conflict and Cohesion in an Indian Village.* Princeton:
Princeton University Press.

Panjabi, Kewal L.
1962.　*Indomitable Sardar.* Bombay: Bharatiya Vidya Bhavan.

Parameswara Rao, P.
1963.　Comment: Matters of Religion. *Journal of the Indian Law Institute* V: 509–13.

Pearse, Padraic
1945.　The Rebel. In *The Poetry of Freedom.* W. R. Benét and Norman
Cousins, eds. New York: Modern Library, Random House.

Place
1795.　Extracts from the Report of Mr. Place. In *Fifth Report from the
Select Committee on the Affairs of the East India Company.* Vol.
3. Firminger, W. K. ed. Calcutta: R. Cambray & Co., 1918.
149–67.

Pradhan, M. C.
1966.　*The Political System of the Jats of Northern India.* Bombay:
Oxford University Press.

Punjab, Government of
1966.　*Report on Police Administration in the Punjab for the Year Ending 1 December 1964.* Chandigarh: Controller of Printing and
Stationery.

Raab, Earl and Seymour Martin Lipset
1959.　*The Prejudiced Society.* New York: Anti-Defamation League of
B'nai B'rith.

Ramachandra Aiyar, Cuddalore
1883.　*A Manual of Malabar Law, as Administered by the Courts.*
Madras: Vest & Co.

Ramakrishna, C. S.
1921.　Caste Questions, Caste Customs and Jurisdiction of Courts. *Hindu
Law Journal* I: § IV, pp. 33–68.

Ramantha Iyer, P.
1956.　*Commentaries on the Code of Criminal Procedure* (Act V of
1898). 2 vols. (Revised by M. A. Krishnaswami Iyer.) Madras:
Madras Law Journal Office, 3rd ed.

Ranade, R. D.
  1961.   *Pathway to God in Marathi Literature.* Bombay: Bhavan's Book
           University, Bharatiya Vidya Bhavan, #89.

Ranis, Gustav & J. C. H. Fei
  1961.   A Theory of Economic Development. *American Economic
           Review* LI(4): 533–55.

Ratanlal, Ranchhoddas and Dhirajlal Keshavlal Thakore
  1948.   *The Law of Crimes.* Bombay: Bombay Law Reporter Office,
           17th ed.

Retzlaff, Ralph H.
  1962.   *Village Government in India: A Case Study.* New York: Asia
           Publishing House.

Rowe, Peter
  1968.   Indian Lawyers and Political Modernization: Observations in
           Four Distinct Towns. *Law and Society Review* III (Nov. 1968–
           Feb. 1969): 219–50.

Rudolph, Lloyd I. and Suzanne H.
  1967.   *The Modernity of Tradition.* Chicago: University of Chicago
           Press.

Schur, Edwin M.
  1965.   *Crimes Without Victims: Deviant Behavior and Public Policy.*
           Englewood Cliffs, N. J.: Prentice-Hall.

Sitaramayya, Pattabhi
  1946.   *The History of the Indian National Congress, Vol. I.* Bombay:
           Padma Publications (First published 1935).

Smith, Donald E.
  1963.   *India as a Secular State.* Princeton: Princeton University Press.

Srinivas, M. N.
  1962.   *Caste in Modern India and Other Essays.* Bombay: Asia Pub-
           lishing House.

  1966.   *Social Change in Modern India.* Berkeley: University of Cali-
           fornia Press.

Subramanian, N. A.
  1961.   Freedom of Religion. *Journal of the Indian Law Institute* III:
           323–50.

Sumner, William Graham
  1960.   *Folkways: A Study of the Sociological Importance of Usages,
           Manners, Customs, Mores, and Morals.* New York: New Amer-
           ican Library.

Tripathi, P. K.
  1966.   Secularism: Constitutional Provisions and Judicial Review.
           Journal of the Indian Law Institute VIII: 1–29.

Wallace, Anthony F. C.
1967.   Identity Processes in Personality and in Culture. In *Cognition, Personality and Clinical Psychology*. Richard Jessor and Seymour Feshback, eds. San Francisco: Jossey-Bass, Inc. 62–89.

Weber, Max
1958.   *From Max Weber: Essays in Sociology*, translated and edited by H. H. Gerth and C. Wright Mills. New York: Oxford University Press (Galaxy Book).

1964.   *The Sociology of Religion*. Translated by Ephraim Fischoff. Boston, Beacon Press.

Westcott, G. H.
1953.   *Kabir and the Kabir Panth*. Calcutta, Susil Gupta Limited.

Witherspoon, Joseph Parker
1968.   *Administrative Implementation of Civil Rights* Austin: University of Texas Press.

Woltemade, Uwe Jan
1967.   The Emergence of a Market Economy and Socio-economic Change in Rural India. Unpublished Ph.D. dissertation, University of Texas. [University of Texas Library and University Microfilms, Ann Arbor, Michigan.]

Woodward, C. Vann
1957.   *The Strange Career of Jim Crow*. New York: Oxford University Press. New and revised ed.

BIBLIOGRAPHIC AUTHOR CROSS REFERENCE

Pushparaj, P. K., 471
Pyarelal (Nair), 471

Raab, Earl, 479
Radhakrishnan, N., 438, 460
Raha, Manis Kumar, 446
Rajah, Rao Bahadur, M. C., 433
Rajogopalachari, C., 461, 468, 471
Ram, Chandrika, 438
Ram, Pars, 438
Rama Naidu, M. B., 450
Ramachandra Aiyar, Cuddalore, 479
Ramakrishna, C. S., 479
Ramanatha Iyer, P., 479
Ramanujachari, K., 433
Ramu, G. N., 438
Ranade, R. D., 480
Ranis, Gustav, 480
Rao, Mary Campbell, 438
Rao, M. J. A., 444
Rao, P. Kodana, 438
Ratan, Ram, 440
Ratanlal Ranchhoddas, 480
Rath, R., 438
Rathnaswamy, A. M., 433
Ratnam, Bala, 444
Rauschenbusch-Clough, Emma, 443
Ravenell, Barbara J., 460
Ray, Renuka, 458
Ray, Serojendra Nath, 460
RCSCST. *See* Commissioner of
   Scheduled Castes
Reddy, N. (Reddi), 445
Republican Party, 468
Retzlaff, Ralph H., 480
Revankar, Ratna G., 460
Rice, Stanley, 433
Richards, F. J., 450
Risley, Herbert Hope, 445
Robbin, Jeanette, 468
Robertson, Alexander, 443
Rose, Horace Arthur, 445
Rowe, Peter, 480
Roy Burman, B. K., 436, 446, 459
Roychowdhuri, B. K., 446
Rudolph, Lloyd I., 438, 480
Rudolph, Suzanne Hoeber, 438, 480
Russell, Robert Vane, 445

Sadasiva, Iyar, Sir. T., 434
Sangharakshita, Stavira, 465
Sanjana, J. E., 434
Santhanam, K., 439, 471
Sarana, Gopala, 441
Sarkar, R. M., 440

Sath Brahmana Ashram, 461
Sathe, Bhaurao, 472
Satyanarayana, Y., 465
Sauter, Johannes A., 434
Sayaji Rao III, Maharaja, 434
Scheduled Castes Federation, 468
Scheduled Castes Students' Federation,
   468
Schermerhorn, R. A., 460
Schur, Edwin M., 480
Seminar on Casteism — see Indian
   Conference of Social Work
Senjana, J. E. *See* Sanjana, J. E.
Sharma, Nalin Vilochan, 473
Sharma, R. S., 439
Shasmal, Kartick Chandra, 440
Shastri, Sankarananda, 465
Sherring, Matthew Atmore, 445
Sheth, Jyotsna, 465
Shinde, V. R., 451
Shrikant, L. M., 439
Shukla, S., 439
Silverberg, James, 439
Simha, Hari Mohan, 446
Singer, Milton B., 437
Singh, Hari, 439
Singh, K. K., 455
Singh, Mohinder, 434
Singh, Saint Nihal, 434
Sircar, N. C., 438
Sitaramayya, Pattabhi, 480
Sivertsen, Dagfinn, 450
Smith, Donald E., 480
Social Reform Annual, 434
Sorabji, Cornelia, 461
South India Buddhist Association, 465
Srinivas, M. N., 435, 439, 480
Srinivasan, N., 456
Stanton, H. U. Weitbrecht, 456
Starte, O. H. B., 450
Stevenson, Mrs. Sinclair (Margaret),
   442
Subramanian, N. A., 480
Subramanya Menon, K. P., 439
Sumner, William Graham, 480
Sundarananda, Swami, 461
Suryanarayana, Rao R., 434

Tagore, Rabindranath, 471, 473
Tandon (or Tondon), Laltaprasad, 434
Temple Entry Enquiry Committee, 461
Tendulkar, D. G., 471
Thakkar, A. V., 468, 471
Thakkar, K. K., 439
Thakore, Dhirajlal Keshavlal, 480
Thaliath, Joseph, 440, 449

Index

Abolition of disabilities: public enthusiasm following Independence, 26; *See also* British Disabilities, Government aid programs, Law, Politics, and Untouchability (Offences) Act

Addiss, Penelope, 17

Adi-Dravida, 37, 53, 236

Adivasis, 258

Agra, U. P., 98

Ahimsa, 7

Ahir, 233

Ahir, D. C., 139

Aiyappan, Ayinipalli, 37

Ajmer Maha Bodhi Society, 125

Aligarh, 200

Ambattan, 39

Ambedkar Bhavan, New Delhi, 127, 136

Ambedkar, Bhimrao Ramji: biographical sketch, xvi, 74-75, 79, 108, 126; basic teachings of, 99-100; Bodhisattva, 48, 98, 106; Buddhist conversion of, 91, 113; conception of caste system, 103; Congress Party relationship, 90-91; drafter of Constitution of India, 69, 90-91, 108; educator, 78; faith in modernization, 77; Hinduism reforms advocated, xvii, 76, 81, 88, 91, 231; memorials to, 94, 128, 130, 137; Nehru's eulogy of, 70, 109; organizations founded by, 78, 80, 89, 91; political parties organized by, 77; public offices held by, 69, 71, 83-85, 89, 90, 108, 198; reasons for separatist policy, 77, 83, 91; religious leadership of, 97-102, 107; Sanskritization views, 76, 78; separate electorates advocation (*See* Poona Pact), 77-81, 84, 89, 91; special names for, 102, 106, 112; view of Gandhi's policies and methods, 77, 83-87, 90, 174, 385-86, 413; views of Untouchability origins, 75, 99-100; Untouchables hero, 94, 97, 106-110, 126

Ambedkar Buddhist Mission, 124-25, 136

Ambedkar Center of Buddhist Religion and Culture, Nasik, 132

Ambedkar, S. (wife of B.R. Ambedkar) xvii, 138

Ambedkar, Yeshwant, 35, 118, 129, 135, 137

Anand, Ven., 131

Andhra Pradesh, xii, 127, 192, 196, 205, 211, 270, 306

Anglo-Indians, 220

Annadurai, C.N., xviii-xix

Anti-disabilities legislation before 1955: failure of efforts to legislate (1932-1936) at state and center levels, 238; first comprehensive penal act (Madras, 1938), 239; incidence of litigation, 264-65; Untouchables' knowledge of, 26; (*See also* Untouchability (Offences) Act)

Anti-Untouchability League, 86-87 (*See* Harijan Sevak Sangh)

Appaduraya, Pandit G., 116

Arakeri, S.S., 118, 138-40

[487]